DSM-IV Guidebook

DSM-IV Guidebook

Allen Frances, M.D.
Michael B. First, M.D.
Harold Alan Pincus, M.D.

Washington, DC
London, England

Note: The authors have worked to ensure that all information in this book concerning drug dosages, schedules, and routes of administration is accurate as of the time of publication and consistent with standards set by the U.S. Food and Drug Administration and the general medical community. As medical research and practice advance, however, therapeutic standards may change. For this reason and because human and mechanical errors sometimes occur, we recommend that readers follow the advice of a physician who is directly involved in their care or the care of a member of their family.

Books published by the American Psychiatric Press, Inc., represent the views and opinions of the individual authors and do not necessarily represent the policies and opinions of the Press or the American Psychiatric Association.

Manufactured in the United States of America on acid-free paper
98 97 96 95 4 3 2 1
First Edition

American Psychiatric Press, Inc.
1400 K Street, N.W., Washington, DC 20005

Library of Congress Cataloging-in-Publication Data
Frances, Allen, 1942–
DSM-IV guidebook / Allen Frances, Michael B. First, and Harold Alan Pincus. — 1st ed.
p. cm.
Includes bibliographical references and index.
ISBN 0-88048-415-2 (casebound : alk. paper). — ISBN 0-88048-430-6 (pbk. : alk. paper)
1. Mental illness—Diagnosis. 2. Mental illness—Classification.
3. Diagnostic and statistical manual of mental disorders.
I. First, Michael B., 1956– . II. Pincus, Harold Alan, 1951– .
III. Title.
[DNLM: 1. Mental Disorders—diagnosis. 2. Mental Disorders—classification. WM 141 F815d 1995]
RC469.F69 1995
616.89'075—dc20
DNLM/DLC
for Library of Congress 95-4140
CIP

British Library Cataloguing in Publication Data
A CIP record is available from the British Library.

To the users of DSM-IV,
to our colleagues who helped prepare it,
and, most especially, to our patients

Contents

Section I
The Foundations of Psychiatric Diagnosis

Section II
The Development and Use of DSM-IV

Section III
The DSM-IV Diagnoses

Section IV
Not Ready for Prime Time

Section V
Study Guides

Preface

The *Diagnostic and Statistical Manual of Mental Disorders, 4th Edition* (DSM-IV), is the current system of psychiatric diagnosis used in the United States and by many clinicians and researchers from around the world. Of necessity, DSM-IV is a large book and not one that invites or allows for a casual cover-to-cover read. The descriptions of each disorder contained in DSM-IV are quite extensive, but this comprehensiveness is purchased at the price of relative indigestibility. The *DSM-IV Guidebook* has several purposes:

1. To provide a road map capturing the overall landscape of DSM-IV, which is sometimes lost when attention is focused on the detailed descriptions of particular disorders
2. To annotate the DSM-IV diagnostic criteria in a way that will clarify their meaning and enhance their assessment
3. To facilitate the crucial process of differential diagnosis
4. To indicate the historical context and controversies underlying the changes introduced into DSM-IV
5. To indicate some possible future directions for psychiatric classification

This guidebook contains just about everything we know about psychiatric diagnosis. The information was derived from our collective experience with patients, supervision, consulting with colleagues, working on DSM-IV, developing the Structured Clinical Interview for DSM (SCID), and fielding interesting questions from audiences at talks and workshops. DSM-IV is the product of more than 1,000 individuals. Although we edited the final version of DSM-IV and must bear considerable responsibility for its content, we were attempting to find a voice that best captured the consensus of the entire field.

This book provides us with an opportunity to make a much more personal statement that reflects our own perspectives. The views expressed here are our own and do not necessarily reflect those of the DSM-IV Task Force or the American Psychiatric Association. Some of the material included in this guidebook is based on our previous publications, which are listed in the bibliography at the end of this book.

We apologize in advance for a repetitive statement that will appear over and over again in this guidebook—that it is crucially important to use clinical judgment in applying DSM-IV. The reader should not attribute this redundancy to careless editing. We feel compelled to combat the tendency of some individuals to regard DSM-IV as a bible or cookbook. DSM-IV is a tool to help inform clinical judgment; it is not a substitute for it.

Some people make the mistake of thinking that using DSM-IV involves just the straightforward comparison of the patient's clinical presentation with the diagnostic criteria sets. In the wonderfully complex world of real clinical situations, the evaluation of whether or not a criterion is met requires sophisticated clinical judgment. Furthermore, the clinical presentations often do not conform to the prototypical presentations defined in the criteria sets. Frequently, we are called on as consultants by clinicians who are having difficulty with the differential diagnosis for a particular patient. Although sometimes we are able to provide some clarification, more commonly we are no more successful than the referring clinician in establishing a definitive diagnosis. The reason is simple. Most patients are referred precisely because there is not a close fit between their presenting psychopathology and the diagnostic system. When mismatches occur, the system should be adapted as best it can be to the clinical situation rather than attempting to tailor the clinical presentation to fit into a diagnostic category.

It may be helpful to review the organization of this guidebook. The first two chapters ("Roots: A Brief History of Psychiatric Classification," "Conceptual Issues in Psychiatric Diagnosis") provide the reader with a perspective on the broader enterprise of psychiatric diagnosis that may be useful and interesting before we get down to the specifics of DSM-IV. Although we think these chapters provide a solid foundation for understanding DSM-IV, readers who are in a hurry may choose to skim (or even skip) them. In Chapters 3–7 ("The Preparation of DSM-IV," "The DSM-IV Road Map and Classification," "The Nuts and Bolts of Using DSM-IV," "The Yeas and Nays of the Multiaxial System," "The Joys and Perils of Differential Diagnosis"), we share what we know about how DSM-IV was developed and is meant to be used.

Next comes the heart of the guidebook. In Chapters 8–24, we discuss the specific DSM-IV disorders. Each of these chapters begins with an overview of the major diagnostic issues that were considered during the DSM-IV deliberations. This is followed by criteria sets for selected disorders, which are annotated to enhance understanding of their rationale and of how best to apply them in clinical practice.

In Chapter 25, we present a peek at the possible future of psychiatric diagnosis by examining the proposed categories in the DSM-IV appendix. In Chapter 26, we discuss our views of some of the more public controversies that surrounded the preparation and publication of DSM-IV. Chapter 27 presents a capsule summary containing what everyone should know about DSM-IV. Chapter 28 includes 100 multiple choice questions (and answers) to increase your mastery of DSM-IV. Finally, after a journey of almost 500 pages, we will take our leave from our patient reader with an Afterword, Chapter 29.

SECTION I

The Foundations of Psychiatric Diagnosis

CHAPTER 1

Roots

A Brief History of Psychiatric Classification

DSM-IV, which is simply the latest expression of the natural human predilection to categorize, emerges from the long and colorful history of psychiatric classification. Systems of taxonomy help us to simplify and organize the wide range of observable human behavior to facilitate our understanding and increase our ability to predict future outcomes. Many (if not most) of the mental disorders that afflict contemporary individuals have probably, in slightly varied forms, been part of the human condition since the origin of our species. In psychiatric classification, as in the rest of life, "the more things change, the more they stay the same."

The first recorded depiction of mental illness dates back to 3000 B.C. with a description of the syndrome of senile dementia attributed to Egyptian Prince Ptah-hotep. Sumerian and Egyptian references to melancholia and hysteria are found as early as 2600 B.C. The oldest known attempt to systematically classify presentations of mental illness is found in the 1400 B.C. system of medicine in ancient India known as the Ayur-Veda. In this system, disorders were grouped based on seven kinds of demonic possession.

Hippocrates (460–377 B.C.) was the first to place psychiatric conditions wholly within the secular and naturalistic domain of medicine. In his medical writing, he identified six conditions based on the observed phenomenology of mental disorders. These were 1) phrenitis (acute mental disturbance with fever), 2) mania (acute mental disturbance without fever), 3) melancholia (all kinds of chronic mental disturbances), 4) epilepsy (same as current meaning), 5) hysteria (paroxysmic dyspnea, pain, convulsions), and 6) Scythian disease (comparable to transvestitism). In addition, Hippocrates provided what amounted to a second diagnostic axis for noting the four temperaments (comparable to present-day personality traits) based on a presumed etiology of humoral imbalance: 1) the choleric (angry, hostile traits related to an excess of yellow bile), 2) the sanguine (optimistic, cheerful traits related to an excess of blood), 3) the melancholic (pessimistic, depressed traits related to excess of black bile), and 4) the phlegmatic (apathetic, indifferent traits related to an excess of lymph). Over the next 10 centuries, Hippocrates' list of six conditions was extended and further differentiated, culminating in a classification proposed by Paul of Aegina (624–700 A.D.) containing 23 disorders (including headaches, amnesia, and lovesickness).

The Hippocratic approach of studying the manifestations and natural history of disease in individual patients reflected the philosophical and scientific method of Aristotle and was firmly fixed on the empirical world of the senses and observed events. Plato, a near contemporary of Hippocrates, had a radically different philosophical approach to classification. He maintained that the unchangeable reality resided in universal ideas rather than in the individual objects of our senses. In the *Phaedrus,* he classified "madness" (mania) based on his conceptualizations of its ideal form or underlying nature. Plato first distinguished "madness given us by divine gift" from that which is the consequence of physical disease. He further divided divine madness into 1) prophetic madness (given by Apollo), 2) religious madness (given by Dionysus), 3) poetic madness (given by the Muses), and 4) erotic madness (given by Aphrodite and Eros).

Throughout history, these two contrasting attitudes (i.e., the Hippocratic observational and empirical approach versus the Platonic rationalist search for universal ideas or causes) have continued to exist side by side; one approach is in favor for a period of time, only to give way to the other. The observational approach led to the development of a variety of different descriptive systems that group disorders based on their similarity of presentation and make minimal assumptions about etiology. In contrast, the rationalist approach has tended to group disorders based on the then-current understanding of their underlying nature, using one explanatory model or another.

One of the first completely etiologically based classifications was proposed by the Persian physician Rhazes (864–925 A.D.). This system, foreshadowing dimensional models of classification, is based on excess or deficit in each one of the "three souls" (i.e., the classical Aristotelian division of the human psyche): the vegetative, the animal, and the rational. For example, an excess in the animal soul was considered to cause lust; a failure in the animal soul resulted in a lack of fervor, pride, and courage. Many later etiological models have been elaborated based on the belief system and technology most in favor at a particular time. Not surprisingly, none of these causal systems has had very much endurance, and each has been superseded by another belief system or, more recently, by new scientific findings.

Sydenham (1624–1663), who was the father of modern medical thinking, rejected the notion that there was a single dysfunction at the root of all ailments (e.g., disturbed humoral balance or a disturbance in the tensions of the solid tissues in the body). Instead, he postulated that each disease has an independent existence with a uniform presentation in different individuals so that the same phenomena "that you would observe in the sickness of a Socrates you would observe in the sickness of a simpleton." Sydenham proposed that the diseases should be subjected to careful observation and reduced to species in just the same way as the emerging science of botany was beginning to classify plants. Following these principles, François Boissier de Sauvages and Carl Linnaeus, who were both physicians and botanists, proposed elaborate medical nosologies with the diseases grouped into classes, orders, and genera. The system proposed by Boissier de Sauvages listed over 2,400 species of diseases in which each species was essentially a separate symptom.

In the second half of the eighteenth century, there emerged a less systematic but more clinical approach to classification that had as its goal the relief of the misery of psychiatric patients, who were beginning to be housed in the asylums. The move toward a simplified classification was spurred by clinicians who reacted against what they regarded as the overly complex and impractical nature of the systematic nosologies described previously. Instead, they adopted practical rule-of-thumb lists focusing on a relatively smaller number of especially relevant clinical types. For example, after initially proposing a complex elaboration of the Boissier de Sauvages nosology, Philippe Pinel (1745–1820) discarded his own system and proposed a simple classification consisting of only four fundamental clinical types: 1) mania (all conditions with acute excitement or fury), 2) melancholia (depressive conditions, delusions with limited topics), 3) dementia (lack of cohesion in the ideas), and 4) idiotism (including idiocy and organic dementia).

This trend toward a simplified and practical classification was continued by Jean-Dominique Esquirol, who inaugurated the scientific study of asylum statistics to elucidate the longitudinal course and prognosis of mental illness. Esquirol was also the first to introduce the words *remission* and *intermission* to describe the course of mental illness. This emphasis on course was a relatively novel idea compared with previous classifications, which tended to focus on the cross-sectional presentation of the illness manifested at the time of evaluation.

Benedict-Augustin Morel (1809–1873) was the first to describe an illness primarily on the basis of course. This illness, which he referred to as *demence precoce* and is now known as schizophrenia, was characterized by mental deterioration with an early onset that evolved rapidly (i.e., over a few months to a few years). Karl Ludwig Kahlbaum (1826–1899) continued the emphasis on course, systematically noting the characteristic age at onset of the disturbance and the characteristic development of the disturbance. His work anticipated much of Kraepelin's later classification and introduced a number of fundamental psychiatric concepts that remain important in our current systems of classification (e.g., the distinction between "temporary symptom complex" and underlying personality disturbance and the distinction between organic and nonorganic mental illness).

Discoveries of the specific organic etiologies of several disorders (e.g., the findings of Paul Broca that some forms of aphasia were attributable to lesions in certain locations of the cortex) initiated a trend toward purely organic psychiatry. William Griesinger (1817–1868) stated that "mental diseases are brain diseases," expressing the expectation that all mental disorders would ultimately be classified according to their underlying brain lesions. In cases where a brain lesion was not demonstrable under the microscope, it was assumed that vascular or nutritional disturbances were responsible. However, recognizing that incomplete knowledge of brain anatomy and pathology would render this endeavor limited for the foreseeable future, Griesinger acknowledged that clinicians would have to be content with a functional classification.

Emil Kraepelin (1856–1926) synthesized the various nosological approaches of the second half of the nineteenth century, compiling a classification system whose structure forms the basis for our current psychiatric classification systems. Kraepelin developed nine editions of his widely influential textbook of psychiatry, and his "classifications" were in fact initially no more than the table of contents of his textbooks. This system, which was not designed to be anything like an official classification, was organized instead in a way that would best communicate the information to his readers.

Kraepelin's fundamental approach was that mental disorders could be isolated by grouping together patients whose disorders had the same course and then determining the combination of clinical features these patients had in common. He carefully delineated dementia praecox (i.e., schizophrenia) from manic-depressive psychosis, and he established the association of mania and depression as components of the same illness. He viewed mental illnesses as organic disease entities that could be described and classified according to etiology, course, and outcome. He divided acute disorders into recoverable and deteriorating types, separated dementia from delirium, and noted the difference between dementia praecox and paranoia. Finally, he established a method of research adapted from the natural sciences, which investigated the course of mental illnesses in individual cases from the earliest onset of symptomatology to the illness's remission (or deterioration).

Adolf Meyer (1866–1950) was largely responsible for the introduction and dissemination of Kraepelin's classification in the United States. However, although Meyer embraced Kraepelin's emphasis on prognosis for its practical applicability in the treatment of hospitalized patients, he voiced scientific concerns about Kraepelin's approach of generalizing from large groups of cases to the individual patient, as well as about setting up arbitrary disease entities in the absence of supporting empirical data. Meyer eventually proposed his own classification system based on the concept of reaction types in which disorders were viewed as pathological reactions of the individual to environmental stresses.

Eugen Bleuler (1857–1937) combined the Kraepelinian and Meyerian approaches, analyzing the psychological reaction types associated with the various syndromes. He proposed a reconceptualization of Kraepelin's dementia praecox as a disorder in the function of mental associations. Bleuler introduced the term *schizophrenia* in place of dementia praecox to emphasize the fundamental intellectual-emotional disharmonies that he felt were the result of the disturbance in associations.

Born in the same year as Kraepelin, Freud had almost as much influence on the diagnosis of the less severe (or neurotic) conditions as did Kraepelin on diagnosis of the psychoses. Part of the difference in their respective emphases resulted from differences in their practice patterns. Kraepelin was a psychiatrist working in large inpatient psychiatric facilities with very severely disturbed individuals. Freud had little psychiatric training and was a neurologist whose practice consisted of relatively healthy outpatient presentations. Freud's classification of anxiety neurosis, depressive neurosis, hysterical neurosis, and obsessive-compulsive neurosis very much informed DSM-I and DSM-II and remain influential in DSM-III and DSM-IV.

Another more recent trend in the history of classifications has been the need to aggregate and interpret statistics for both scientific and public health purposes. By the end of the 1800s, different insane asylums were each developing their own classification systems intended primarily for the purposes of keeping statistics on their inpatients. By the turn of the century, there were almost as many statistical outlines in use in the United States as there were mental hospitals. Most of these classification systems were based on Kraepelinian principles, with some modifications.

Concerned that the lack of a uniform classification would inhibit the emerging science of psychiatry by preventing accurate comparisons among patient groups in different institutions, the Committee on Statistics of the American Medico-Psychological Association (which later became the American Psychiatric Association) introduced in 1917 a 22-item list of disorders that could be used in every hospital in the country. The list was largely Kraepelinian in concept and included separate categories for dementia praecox, manic-depressive psychosis, melancholia, paranoia, and neurosis. However, it primarily focused on the etiologies of organic psychoses (with 14 categories for psychoses due to different etiologies, such as traumatic psychosis, psychosis with pellagra, psychosis with brain tumor). This classification was used by the Army in World War I and was adopted by most mental hospitals until 1935, when a revised and expanded version was incorporated into the second edition (1935) of the American Medical Association's *Standard Classified Nomenclature of Diseases.*

This classification proved inadequate in settings other than the hospitals for chronic inpatients. In particular, the significant number of acute psychiatric problems that developed among servicemen during World War II (10% of premature discharges during the war were for psychiatric reasons) prompted the Armed Forces to develop their own classification systems. By the end of the war, the were four major competing systems: 1) the 1935 Standard Classified Nomenclature, 2) the U.S. Army classification, 3) the U.S. Navy classification, and 4) the Veterans Administration System.

Around this same time, the first attempts to develop an official international classification of mental disorders were being made. In 1948, the World Health Organization (WHO) took responsibility for the sixth revision of the *International List of Causes of Death,* renaming it the *International Classification of Diseases, Injuries, and Causes of Death* (ICD-6). WHO added for the first time a section for the classification of mental disorders, containing 10 categories of psychosis, 9 categories of psychoneurosis, and 7 categories of disorders of character, behavior, and intelligence. Unfortunately, problems with this classification rendered it unsatisfactory for use in the United States and other countries (only five countries, including the United Kingdom, made official use of it). Several important categories, such as the dementias, many personality disorders, and adjustment disorders, were not included, and many diagnostic terms used in ICD-6 had etiological implications that were at odds with the various schools of psychiatry.

In the United States, an alternative to the mental disorders section of ICD-6 was developed and was published in 1952 as the *Diagnostic and Statistical Manual: Mental Disorders* (DSM-I). For the first time in an official classification, DSM-I provided a glossary of definitions of the categories in addition to the names of the disorders. DSM-I attempted to reflect contemporary thinking as much as possible and included the concepts that were most influential in American psychiatry in the 1940s and 1950s. For example, the term *reaction* was used throughout the classification, reflecting Adolf Meyer's perspective that mental disorders represented reactions of the person to psychological, social, and biological factors. Similarly, psychoanalytic concepts were reflected in the frequent references to defense mechanisms as explanations for the neuroses and personality disorders.

In recognition of the widespread lack of acceptance of the ICD-6 classification, WHO asked Erwin Stengel, a British psychiatrist, to offer recommendations as to how the next revision of the *International Classification of Diseases* (ICD) should proceed. He made the seminal recommendation that there be operational and explicit definitions of disorders that were independent of any etiological theories. Although not adopted in time for ICD-8, these suggestions contributed to the introduction of diagnostic criteria into DSM-III. In 1959, WHO (with the assistance of psychiatrists in the United States) started work on the next revision of the ICD with the goal of creating a system that would represent a consensus about concepts and terms that would be acceptable to all of its member nations. The resulting system, ICD-8, become effective in 1968 (the mental disorder section of ICD-7, which appeared in 1955, was identical to the section in ICD-6).

In 1965, the American Psychiatric Association started to prepare a second edition of the DSM based on ICD-8, defining each disorder for use in the United States. Such definitions were necessary because ICD-8 was initially published without an accompanying glossary (a glossary was eventually published in 1974, 6 years after the introduction of DSM-II). DSM-II no longer used the term *reaction,* and, unlike DSM-I, DSM-II encouraged clinicians to make multiple diagnoses, even if one diagnosis was causally related to another (e.g., alcoholism secondary to depression).

In the early 1970s, several developments had a significant impact on future classification schemes. To compare diagnostic practices across different nations, two cross-national studies were conducted that used a structured interview to reduce any differences in diagnosis that may have been due to variability in interviewing technique. These studies provided an impetus for an emerging scientific descriptive psychiatry based on statistical methods.

The United States–United Kingdom Diagnostic Project used the Present State Examination (PSE) to determine whether differences in diagnosis were due to differences intrinsic to the patient populations or to differences in the diagnostic concepts. The study found that most of the differences were due to a very broad concept of schizophrenia being used by psychiatrists in the United States, compared with the much narrower concept used by their British counterparts. The differences were not in the patients or even in the symptoms observed by the clinicians, but rather in the way in which these symptoms were interpreted and classified. One effect of these findings is that subsequent United States classifications adopted a narrower definition of schizophrenia and a broader construct for psychotic mood disorder—much in line with what had been the British practice.

The International Pilot Study of Schizophrenia was conducted under the auspices of WHO with several goals in mind. First, several previous studies had demonstrated that psychiatric diagnosis suffered from poor reliability and called into question whether it was possible to achieve high reliability in diagnosing mental disorders. One goal of the pilot study was to determine whether the use of standardized instruments and procedures (e.g., the PSE) by clinicians in a number of different countries (both developed and nondeveloped) would result in reliable judgments about psychopathology. The results indicated a high level of reliability, demonstrating that psychiatric diagnosis is not inherently unreliable. Another goal was to examine whether similar groups of individuals with schizophrenia could be identified across the different sites, which would indicate whether the concept of schizophrenia was relatively stable across the different countries and cultures. This question was examined cross-sectionally and also longitudinally by conducting follow-up evaluations. The study found that, except in the Washington, D.C., and Moscow sites, the same concept of schizophrenia was held by virtually all of local psychiatrists. In the United States and Soviet sites, a much broader concept of schizophrenia was then being utilized. When a computer program was used to compile the diagnostic groupings, it became possible to identify features that were consistent across all centers.

The early 1970s also saw the introduction of explicit diagnostic criteria created originally for research purposes. The DSM-I innovation of including a short glossary definition of each of the disorders was an improvement over having just a list of diagnostic terms, as in previous systems; however, these brief paragraphs were too vague and inexact for use in identifying homogeneous groups of patients for research studies.

Researchers responded to this problem by developing their own more explicit diagnostic criteria for the particular disorders they were studying. A group of researchers at the Washington University School of Medicine, led by Robins and Guze, developed the first systematic and extensive set of diagnostic criteria for research. These have become known as the Feighner criteria, after the senior author of the paper that presented the criteria. Research criteria were provided for 16 diagnostic categories that listed those features required for each (known as inclusion criteria), and those features whose presence would rule out each diagnosis (i.e., exclusion criteria). Acknowledging the heterogeneity of diagnostic features within groups of patients, the authors constructed the criteria by using a polythetic structure (e.g, any combination of three criteria might be required from a list of eight possible criteria) rather than a strictly monothetic style (e.g., A plus B plus C is required in all instances). The immense utility and popularity of the research criteria are illustrated by the large number of times they have been cited in other papers (1,650 citations from 1972 to 1982 and an average of 2.1 citations per paper in the same journal).

To meet the needs of a National Institute of Mental Health (NIMH)-sponsored collaborative project on the psychobiology of depression, the Research Diagnostic Criteria (RDC) were developed by modifying the Feighner criteria and adding criteria for several additional disorders. A structured interview, known as the Schedule for Affective Disorders and Schizophrenia (SADS), was developed to help researchers elicit the symptoms necessary for determining whether criteria were met for the RDC diagnoses. Both the SADS and the RDC became popular among researchers and were heavily used, especially in research on the psychotic and mood disorders.

After reviewing early drafts of ICD-9 (scheduled to go into effect in 1979), the American Psychiatric Association in 1974 opted to develop a third edition of the *Diagnostic and Statistical Manual* (DSM-III). There were a number of reasons for this decision: 1) the international nature of the ICD-9 resulted in inconsistent definitions, 2) the subtyping of ICD-9 was inadequate for clinical and research use, and, most importantly, 3) ICD-9 did not include important new innovations that were by then technically feasible and of demonstrable utility (e.g., diagnostic criteria and the multiaxial system). Under the leadership of Robert Spitzer, successive drafts of DSM-III were prepared by 14 advisory committees composed of professionals with special expertise in each of the various diagnostic categories.

DSM-III was designed to provide comprehensive descriptions of the manifestations of disorders without regard to etiology, except for those disorders that included etiological statements as part of their definitions (e.g., the organic mental disorders, adjustment disorders, posttraumatic stress disorder, brief reactive psychosis). This approach was intended to allow DSM-III to be useful across all theoretical orientations and was largely responsible for its wide acceptance among mental health professionals from varied disciplines and backgrounds. Although a biologically oriented therapist and a cognitive therapist might have two different understandings of the etiological mechanism underlying a panic attack (i.e., the hyperactivity of neurons in the locus coeruleus versus overattentiveness to internally generated physical sensations), both can agree on the descriptive features of a panic attack.

Two methodological innovations were introduced by DSM-III: explicit diagnostic criteria for each of the disorders and a multiaxial system for classification. One of the main motivations for including diagnostic criteria in DSM-III was to improve the reliability of the diagnostic judgments. By adopting criteria sets in a diagnostic manual intended for general use, DSM-III was both a reflection of and a catalyst for the increased emphasis on empirical data in psychiatric practice and research. It also facilitated the transfer of information between the ever-growing clinical research literature and clinical practice. Because the same criteria were used for diagnosing patients in both settings, it became easier to translate findings of a research paper to the diagnosis and treatment of the next patient that one might see in an office practice.

Many of the DSM-III criteria sets were based on the RDC criteria, with additional criteria sets developed based on expert clinical consensus generated by the advisory committees. The improvement in reliability over DSM-II (which provided only brief glossary definitions) was demonstrated by a DSM-III field trial in which two or more clinicians were asked to independently evaluate patients by using drafts of the DSM-III criteria. The adoption of a multiaxial system facilitated the use of a biopsychosocial model of evaluation by separating (and thereby calling attention to) developmental and personality disorders (Axis II), physical conditions (Axis III), stressors (Axis IV), and degree of adaptive functioning (Axis V) from the usually more florid presenting diagnoses (Axis I).

In terms of utilization, DSM-III has been overwhelmingly successful. Since its introduction in 1980, DSM-III has been adopted as the official nomenclature in virtually all mental health facilities in the United States and is used as the basis for psychiatric diagnosis by mental health professionals from all disciplines. Spurred by widespread international interest, it has been translated into at least 14 different languages, and more than one million copies are in print.

Despite its important contributions, DSM-III was by no means universally popular or without its own disadvantages. Perhaps the most serious problem was not inherent to the contents of DSM-III but resulted from how the manual was viewed and used. Many users have tended to reify the criteria sets of DSM-III and use them in a mechanical or rigid manner—for example, ascribing special significance to certain threshold or duration requirements despite the fact that these were based on expert opinion rather than systematically collected empirical evidence. There has also been some concern that DSM-III encouraged excessive attention to the determination of psychiatric diagnosis at the expense of a more complex and rounded formulation of the patient's problems. DSM-III has been criticized for its length and complexity. There were also numerous specific controversies stirred by DSM-III. Some of these concerned the definition of particular diagnoses; others related more generally to professional, forensic, economic, or social consequences of the system.

Work on a revision of DSM-III began in 1983 and resulted in the publication of DSM-III-R in 1987. Originally, the revision process was intended only as fine-tuning to provide corrections of inconsistencies and problems identified after the publication of DSM-III. However, as the revision process progressed, more substantive changes were made, many reflecting new evidence not available to the developers of DSM-III. Although DSM-III-R was useful in demonstrating that the system is self-correcting, a disadvantage was that it may have been too major a change so soon after the introduction of DSM-III, with consequent disruption to clinical, research, and educational endeavors. The last link in this historical chain, the preparation of DSM-IV, is described in the next chapter.

The Last Word

Those who do not know history are doomed to repeat it. Many issues now current in psychiatric diagnosis have extensive historical precedents. It is especially worth remembering that heated controversies have flourished in the absence of a real knowledge of the underlying etiology of mental disorders. We are still very much in the same boat. Perhaps the most important lesson taught to us by the history of psychiatric classification is that it is probably best to be humble in asserting any particular position until we have acquired a much more profound understanding of the causes of mental disorders.

CHAPTER 2

Conceptual Issues in Psychiatric Diagnosis

A number of interesting conceptual issues have been raised over and over again during the long history of psychiatric classification. An exploration of the assumptions underlying the task of classification may be helpful in understanding the uses and limitations of the diagnostic system.

Epistemology of the Diagnostic Endeavor

Epistemology is the study of the nature of knowledge. The DSM-IV Task Force was aware of the long-standing debate (beginning with Aristotle and Plato and renewed in the Middle Ages) over how the human mind perceives and constructs our world. We pondered the views of the following three umpires, each of whom has a very different understanding of the way in which their baseball world is experienced and organized:

> **Epistemological Umpire I:** There are balls and there are strikes and I call them as they are.
> **Epistemological Umpire II:** There are balls and there are strikes and I call them as I see them.
> **Epistemological Umpire III:** There are no balls and there are no strikes until I call them.

Umpire I expresses the view (labeled as realism in the Middle Ages) that balls and strikes are real entities that exist independently of the mind of the observer. In contrast, Umpire III expresses the diametrically opposite view (labeled as nominalism) that balls and strikes do not have any independent reality outside the mind of the observer. Umpire II takes the middle-ground approach (favored by DSM-IV) that what are labeled as balls and strikes are mental conceptions that reflect (albeit imperfectly) an external reality.

This debate as to the nature of the reality of balls and strikes has profound implications for understanding the nature of psychiatric classification. The nominalist versus realist debate resurfaced in various ways during the development of DSM-IV, as it necessarily must in the development of any psychiatric nosology. "Do psychiatric disorders exist as entities in nature, or do they arise as mental constructs created in the minds of the classifiers?"

The three umpires quoted above represent three different answers to this question. At one extreme (Umpire I: "I call them as they are") are those who take a reductionistically realistic view of the world and its phenomena and believe that there actually is a thing or entity out there that we call schizophrenia and that it can be captured in the bottle of psychiatric diagnosis. In contrast, there are the solipsistic nominalists (Umpire III: "there are no balls and no strikes until I call them") who might contend that nothing, especially psychiatric disorders, inherently exists except as it is constructed in the minds of people. For the past 30 years this view has been espoused most clearly by Thomas Szasz.

DSM-IV represents an attempt to forge some middle ground between a naive realism and a heuristically barren solipsism. Like Umpire II, we attempted to "call them as we saw them." Most, if not all, mental disorders are better conceived as no more than (but also no less than) valuable heuristic constructs. Psychiatric constructs as we know them are not well-defined entities that describe nature exactly as it is. On the other hand, one must not follow Szasz in underestimating the clinical and research value of these constructs or in failing to recognize their consistency of presentation across observers, eras, and cultures. Certainly mental disorders are constructs, but they are constructs with considerable practical and heuristic value in predicting course, family history, treatment response, and biological test results and indeed in making what are sometimes life-and-death treatment and management decisions.

Definition of a Mental Disorder

Although DSM-IV provides a classification of what are called mental disorders, it must be admitted that no available definition adequately specifies precise boundaries for the concept *mental disorder.* Like many other concepts in medicine and science, mental disorder lacks a consistent operational definition that covers all situations. Ideally, of course, a psychiatric classification would include a precise definition of what constitutes a mental disorder. Such a definition would help to establish the border both between normality and pathology and between mental and physical illness, and it would have significant impact on clinical practice (e.g., in establishing boundaries with other specialties), reimbursement, and forensic proceedings (many legal definitions of insanity require the presence of a "mental disorder"). Unfortunately, no previous definition of illness, disease, or disorder has ever been particularly successful, and it seems unlikely that any explicit set of criteria for illness will cover all cases or settle boundary questions.

The concept of *disorder* in the context of psychiatry is like other concepts in medicine and science in failing to have a clear and consistent definition. Medical illnesses are defined on a widely varied conceptual basis, reflecting our historically evolving concept of disease. With each new wave of medical technology, new diseases are added, and, from each stage of our understanding, some diseases have been retained. Mitral stenosis and ulcerative colitis are based on gross anatomy, carcinomas on histopathology, tuberculosis on bacteriology and on Koch's concept of an etiological agent, and porphyria on biochemistry. Other disorders are defined based on statistical deviance from a norm (e.g., hypertension, hypercholesterolemia). For those illnesses whose etiologies remain unknown and whose structural pathology is not apparent, a syndromal definition is used based on symptom presentation (e.g., migraine).

Like other medical disorders, mental disorders have also been defined by a variety of concepts, for example, distress, dyscontrol, disadvantage, disability, inflexibility, irrationality, etiology, and statistical deviation. Each is a useful indicator for mental disorder but none is equivalent to the concept, and different situations call for different definitions. A practical definition of mental disorders and medical conditions that is often implicitly used is "that which clinicians treat." Of course, this is tautological and could even be used in a self-serving or turf-defending way, but other more abstract concepts consistently fail to provide greater explanatory power.

Any definition of mental disorder is most successful in classifying those conditions that are at the core of psychopathology, not those at the boundary with normality. Before the post-World War II era, when the majority of patients being classified were severely ill individuals living in asylums, there were fewer and more easily defined categories of mental disorders.

The ever-increasing number of new categories meant to describe the less impaired outpatient population raises the question of where psychopathology ends and the wear and tear of everyday life begin. DSM-IV answers this question somewhat tautologically by emphasizing the requirement that the condition cause clinically significant impairment or distress, but it does not clearly operationalize the term *clinical significance.* The evaluation of clinical significance is likely to vary in different cultures and to depend on the availability and interests of clinicians.

Despite its limitations, the definition of a mental disorder that is used in both DSM-III and DSM-III-R is as serviceable as any other and has helped guide decisions regarding which conditions on the border between normality and pathology should be included in DSM-IV. In DSM-IV, each of the mental disorders is conceptualized as a clinically significant behavioral or psychological syndrome or pattern. For every diagnosis in DSM-IV, the symptoms by which the person meets the criteria threshold must cause

> present distress (e.g., a painful symptom) or disability (i.e., impairment in one or more important areas of functioning).... In addition, this syndrome or pattern must not be merely an expected and culturally sanctioned response to a particular event, for example, the death of a loved one. Whatever its original cause, it must currently be considered a manifestation of a behavioral, psychological, or biological dysfunction in the individual. Neither deviant behavior (e.g., political, religious, or sexual) nor conflicts that are primarily between the individual and society

> are mental disorders unless the deviance or conflict is a symptom of a dysfunction in the individual, as described above. (DSM-IV, pp. xxi–xxii)

Szasz and others have argued that psychiatry has taken upon itself the unsavory task of pathologizing statistically or morally deviant individuals. Perhaps that has indeed been the case to some degree for Antisocial Personality Disorder, Conduct Disorder, Intermittent Explosive Disorder, Paraphilia, Substance Abuse, and a few other DSM-IV diagnoses. In addition to the risk of forensic misuse, an overinclusive definition of mental disorder might give the profession a wider purview of influence and social control than it can reasonably handle. On the other hand, psychiatry often does have much to say, or at least much to learn, even about these most questionable conditions. It should also be emphasized that an individual diagnosed with a mental disorder is by no means automatically relieved from legal or other responsibility.

The Term *Mental Disorder*

At least since Descartes there has been an unfortunate philosophical position that dichotomizes the mind and the body. The effects of Cartesian dualism of mind and body continue to plague psychiatric classification and are evident in the survival of other misleading derivative dichotomies (e.g., terms such as *organic* versus *nonorganic* and *mental disorders* versus *physical disorders*). Fortunately, Descartes's dialectic is yielding to a modern synthesis forged by the converging trends of philosophy (Ryle's exorcism of the "ghost in the machine") and science (the emerging understanding of the specific ways in which the brain works to produce behaviors). Research continues to inform us that there is much that is physical in the so-called mental disorders and much that is mental in the physical disorders.

The use of the term *mental disorder* in the title of DSM-IV (The *Diagnostic and Statistical Manual of Mental Disorders)* is an anachronistic preservation of the Cartesian view. This term appears increasingly silly as we learn more and more about the physical correlates of thought, emotion, and psychopathology. The term most frequently suggested as an alternative to replace *mental disorders* has been *brain disorders,* but this is equally unfortunate and reductionist in the opposite extreme. Preferable terms for the universe of conditions defined in DSM-IV would be *psychiatric disorders* or *psychological disorders,* but neither of these is feasible because of the possible professional turf conflicts they might incite among psychiatrists, psychologists, and other mental health professionals. Unfortunately, we could not come up with a better term than *mental disorders* and thus it survives in DSM-IV.

Descriptive Syndromal Diagnosis Versus Disease

No one level of abstraction characterizes all DSM disorders. Some (e.g., Dementia of the Alzheimer's Type) have a sufficiently well-established pathogenesis to be considered fairly well-established diseases. In contrast, some DSM disorders are really no more than fairly circumscribed symptom presentations (e.g., Specific Phobia). Most DSM disorders are clusters of correlated symptoms at a syndromal level of abstraction that is somewhere between diseases and symptoms. A *syndrome* is a group or pattern of symptoms, affects, thoughts, and behaviors that tend to appear together in clinical presentations. The assumption is that the symptoms cluster together because they are associated in some clinically meaningful way, which perhaps may reflect a common etiological process, course, or treatment response. Alternatively, many classifications have historically emphasized the individual symptom as the fundamental conceptual entity so that an individual presentation would be classified by enumerating all the relevant target symptoms that might serve as a guide to treatment or research.

The most important advantage of the syndromal approach is in facilitating the understanding and treatment of mental disorders. The very process of delimiting groups of patients based on patterns of co-occurring symptoms aims to define subpopulations that share intrinsic features like response to treatment, degree of impairment, course, family history, biological markers, and comorbid disorders. It is this association between descriptively defined syndromes and the aspects they help to predict that has made a syndromal classification system like the DSM useful in clinical, research, and educational settings.

The main disadvantage of syndromal classifications is the tendency for the descriptively defined syndromes to become reified and treated as if they truly represent independent disease entities. Therefore, it is important for the user of a syndromal classification to realize that the syndromal groupings reflect only the state of understanding that was obtained during the drafting of that version of the classification. Regular revisions in the classification system are needed to allow the syndromes to be redefined in order to reflect the evolving understanding of the pathophysiology of mental disorders, with the ultimate goal of arriving at definitions that correspond more fully to underlying pathogenic entities and targets of treatment.

Throughout the history of medical classification, there have been oscillations among systems that emphasize the definition of disease, syndromes, or symptoms. Confusion occurs when the level of abstraction implied by the definition of a given disorder is misunderstood, particularly when each DSM disorder is regarded as a "disease" or "separate diagnostic entity." Most DSM disorders are defined at the descriptive level. That patients who meet criteria for a given diagnosis are similar descriptively does not guarantee that their disorders will have a similar etiology, pathogenesis, or treatment response.

The DSM "mental disorders" are best understood as descriptive syndromes likely to assist in our increased understanding of the underlying disease, but only in selected cases do they, as currently defined, actually represent such diseases. The descriptive syndromal system embodied in DSM-III and its successors has been and continues to be enormously useful in facilitating clinical management and research. However, it is to be hoped fervently that the descriptive system of diagnosis will gradually yield to categorization that is based on a more fundamental understanding of the pathogenesis of mental disorders.

Nosology: Categorical Versus Dimensional Diagnosis

People construct and interpret the world differently. Some are dualists who naturally dichotomize and make distinctions that are polar or black and white. Others are more alert to shadings, focusing on the grays. Historically, there have been two different methods of classification of mental disorders reflecting these two different, but complementary, interpretations.

The dichotomizers create categorical systems based on straightforward naming.

A categorical strategy works best in situations where there are clear boundaries between the things named and all members of the class are homogeneous with regard to their defining features. Most of the classifying we do in everyday life is categorical: a table is a table and a chair is a chair. Unfortunately, life and mental disorders can be complicated, and the categorical model breaks down in situations characterized by unclear boundaries and heterogeneity within a category. In geometry, a triangle and a square are never the same; all squares have four sides and 90-degree angles; all triangles have three sides. In contrast, most mental disorders merge imperceptibly into near neighbors (e.g., for Mood Disorders, there is no absolute boundary with either Schizophrenia or Anxiety Disorders).

Most of the categories of mental disorders are defined with criteria that identify what may be remarkably heterogeneous presentations. For example, the criteria set for a Major Depressive Episode includes on one end of the spectrum very mild presentations that are barely distinguishable from normal sadness and on the other end of the spectrum some of the most severe conditions encountered in clinical practice. Two patients qualifying for a diagnosis of Major Depressive Disorder can thus in many important ways be much more different than alike.

The introduction to DSM-IV states that "there is no assumption that each category of mental disorder is a completely discrete entity with absolute boundaries dividing it from other mental disorders or from no mental disorder" (p. xxii). Nevertheless, DSM-IV follows the tradition of using the categorical method of diagnosis, which is most useful for labeling conditions with sharp boundaries. In using the categorical model, one must recognize its limitations. Kraepelin, best known for his emphasis on demarcating distinct syndromes, acknowledged that "wherever we try to mark out the frontier between mental health and disease, we find a neutral territory, in which the imperceptible change from the realm of normal mental life to that of obvious derangement takes place."

There is an accumulating recent literature that suggests ways of modifying the assumptions of the categorical approach to make it more useful in psychiatric diagnosis. There are two ways to correct the problems that arise with the rigid application of the categorical system to psychiatric classification: 1) use of a dimensional system and 2) use of a prototypal approach to categorization.

We use dimensional systems in everyday life to describe continuous variables that are more accurately depicted with numbers, not names (e.g., inches of height, moles of atoms, pounds of weight, or IQ points of intelligence). Dimensional systems have many advantages over categorical systems in reliably and precisely describing variables that are distributed on a continuum. A dimensional system is better for labeling borderline cases and can be manipulated mathematically. Many dimensional systems have been devised for use in describing psychiatric and psychological dysfunction. Dimensional systems are especially suited for classifying the personality disorders because these merge imperceptibly with each other and with normality.

The major disadvantages of dimensional systems are that they are less familiar and more cumbersome, that they have not been widely accepted, and that it remains difficult to know which dimensions are most useful and accessible to measurement. There is also concern that use of a dimensional system may obscure what could in fact be distinct and independent categories.

Of course, there is no reason to think that dimensional and categorical systems are mutually exclusive. In our descriptions of color, the names red, blue, and white help to describe in a simple and vivid way what, in a dimensional system, would be denoted as visible light with *a, b,* and *c* wavelengths. Indeed, we are lucky to have both categorical names and dimensional numbers for describing and classifying psychopathology. Because there remain less research and agreement on appropriate dimensions, DSM-IV remains basically categorical. However, it is expected that future systems will incorporate additional dimensional aspects.

For now, the prototypal approach to the use of categories serves to bridge the categorical and dimensional approaches and eases the application of the categorical approach to the "fuzzy set" problem of psychiatric diagnosis. The prototypal approach recognizes the fuzzy boundaries and heterogeneity within the DSM-IV criteria sets. Definitions are seen as the prototypal forms of the disorder, and individual class members are expected to vary greatly in the degree to which they resemble one or another prototypal category. Sorting is based on the probabilistic estimation of the resemblance of an individual member to the prototypes. If one regards the DSM-IV categories as prototypes, one is less likely to reify categories and more likely to respect boundary cases rather than trying to force them into one or another category. A research consequence of a prototypal approach is the realization that different patients approximate the prototype with different degrees of fidelity that should be assessed and studied. Some research projects should probably use criteria sets that are more narrowly defined to focus on prototypal patients. In other designs, it is important to have a wider range of pathology to increase generalizability.

In summary, psychiatric disorders are neither homogeneous nor divided by clear boundaries. The two most important issues to understand in using DSM-IV are that 1) there is considerable heterogeneity of the presentations encountered even within each disorder, and 2) the boundaries between disorders are often fuzzy; many patients have presentations that fall through the cracks and cannot be comfortably forced into any of the DSM-IV categories.

Polythetic Versus Monothetic Criteria

There was an increased use in DSM-III-R of polythetic criteria sets in which the diagnosis is made if the presentation includes only a proportion of the items that define the disorder. Polythetic criteria sets are contrasted with the more traditional monothetic criteria sets in which all of the items must be present for the diagnosis to be made.

Monothetic sets have many disadvantages. They carry the implication that diagnostic features are more pathognomonic than is usually the case, exclude items that are clinically useful but are not invariably present, and are usually less reliable because the limiting factor in the reliability of the entire criteria set becomes the reliability of its least reliable item. However, there are also disadvantages in the use of polythetic criteria sets. They may allow for more heterogeneity in the diagnosis than is desirable. For example, there are more than 100 different ways for the criteria for Borderline Personality Disorder to be met, and two patients may each have presentations that meet the criteria for Obsessive-Compulsive Disorder without sharing even a single criterion for the diagnosis.

Multiple Diagnoses and Comorbidity

A number of features built into DSM-III have resulted in many patients having presentations that meet criteria for more than one disorder. DSM-III-R further encouraged multiple diagnoses by removing many diagnostic exclusion criteria. The profusion of new categories and the division of old ones in DSM-III and DSM-III-R have also increased the trend toward multiple diagnoses. DSM-I had 106 different diagnostic categories, DSM-II had 182, DSM-III listed 265, and DSM-III-R included 292. The more diagnoses included in a system, the more clearly these are defined, and the fewer the exclusionary hierarchies, the more multiple diagnoses there will be. The use of structured interviews in clinical practice also contributes to the trend toward multiple diagnoses. DSM-IV has reversed this trend somewhat by reinstating some diagnostic hierarchies (e.g., Anorexia Nervosa excludes Bulimia Nervosa if binges occur exclusively during the course of Anorexia Nervosa).

Although multiple diagnoses can be unwieldy in clinical practice, the removal of many of the diagnostic exclusion criteria that established a hierarchical ranking of "more" versus "less" fundamental disorders also has its advantages. The allowance for multiple diagnoses means that information is saved, reliability is improved, and one avoids assumptions about priority and causality that are difficult to make in clinical practice and are unsupported by empirical evidence. Certain important differential diagnoses remain in DSM-IV and are highlighted whenever exclusionary criteria are present. Future advances in knowledge beyond the descriptive validity of diagnoses will increase the precision and importance of differential diagnosis.

Use of multiple diagnoses is in itself neither good nor bad, so long as the implications are understood. The extensive recent literature on the comorbidity of psychiatric diagnoses often assumes naively that a patient who has a presentation that meets criteria for more than one diagnosis has multiple independent conditions. This is certainly not the only possible relationship. In fact, there are six different ways in which two comorbid conditions may be related to one another:

1. Condition A may cause or predispose to condition B.
2. Condition B may cause or predispose to condition A.
3. An underlying condition C may cause or predispose to both condition A and condition B.
4. Conditions A and B may in fact be part of a more complex unified syndrome that has been artificially split in the diagnostic system.
5. The relationship between conditions A and B may be artifactually enhanced by definitional overlap.
6. The presence of conditions A and B may be a chance co-occurrence, which may be particularly likely for those conditions that have high base rates.

The nature of the relationships is often very difficult to determine. The major point to keep in mind is that having more than one DSM-IV diagnosis does not mean that an individual has more than one underlying pathophysiological process. Instead, DSM-IV diagnoses should be considered descriptive building blocks useful for communicating diagnostic information.

Clinical Versus Research Criteria

In contrast to DSM-IV, which provides just one set of diagnostic criteria to be used for both clinical and research purposes, the *International Statistical Classification of Diseases and Related Health Problems,* 10th Revision (ICD-10), has separate clinical guidelines and research criteria. The ICD-10 approach has the advantage of greater simplicity and flexibility but the disadvantage of reducing the generalizability of research findings to clinical practice. DSM-IV will continue to have one set of criteria. This approach ensures greater clarity of communication within and among areas of psychiatric practice. It provides greater generalizability of findings generated by the research setting to the clinician's office. Most importantly, this approach facilitates the necessary dialogue and mutual influence between clinicians and researchers. The translation of findings across the clinical-research interface is one of the most crucial tasks as our empirical science grows. Having one set of criteria for both purposes will facilitate the conveyance of information between research and practice.

Core Versus Discriminating Features

The DSM-IV criteria sets are used for two related, but also separable, activities: to define the mental disorders and also to diagnose them. To serve both purposes, the ideal criterion would both capture that which is core to the definition of the disorder and would also maximize its distinction from near neighbors. Often enough, both functions are well served by the same item (e.g., thought disorder is both a core component of Schizophrenia and a fairly useful way of distinguishing it from Delusional and Mood Disorders).

Unfortunately, items at the core of the definition are sometimes poor at discriminating the disorder, and items that are more discriminating may not be close to the core. Hallucinations in Schizophrenia, impulsivity in Borderline Personality Disorder, and sadness in Major Depressive Disorder are each core aspects of their disorders that are not very discriminating because they are also frequently present in near neighbors. DSM-III-R attempted to decrease the frequency of multiple diagnoses by deleting overlapping items from some of the Personality Disorders, but such attempts to increase discrimination may delete shared features essential to the definition of a particular disorder. In contrast, an emphasis on core features can result in poor discrimination and multiple diagnoses based on definitional artifact.

Given the relative lack of pathognomonic items to identify most psychiatric disorders, how do we balance attention to core features against attention to discriminating features? Generally, this is done by balancing sensitivity (which reflects the degree to which the item is typical of the disorder and useful in depicting it) against specificity (which reflects its discriminating value). One must recognize, however, the great impact on specificity that is exerted by the choice of comparison groups and the setting in a given study. Impulsivity may be very specific to Borderline Personality Disorder in an outpatient clinic, but not in a prison or a drug treatment setting. In choosing criteria based on their discriminating value, it is important to determine performance characteristics in the widest range of settings and comparison groups because that is how the criteria will be used in general practice.

Level of Clinical Inference in Criteria Sets

The explicitness of the DSM diagnostic criteria has been the major source of improved reliability. Nonetheless, increased reliability may not always result in improved validity or clinical utility. For example, the DSM-III and DSM-III-R criteria for Antisocial Personality Disorder have been criticized for compromising validity by emphasizing easily identifiable delinquent behavior at the expense of more inferential aspects of the syndrome (e.g., lack of guilt and failure to bond).

Reducing the level of clinical inference narrows the construct that the items purportedly represent and reduces the role of clinical judgment. At one extreme, items would be included into diagnostic criteria sets only if worded so that a ready clinical interview question could be fashioned to assess them. Although such a process increases reliability of items, it has the unintended effect of restricting items to those that can be gleaned by self-report. This reduces the emphasis in criteria sets on the admittedly more inferential but nonetheless crucial data obtained by clinical observation, assessment, and judgment.

Moreover, as diagnostic items become more specific, more items are needed to adequately represent the construct. This situation may result in long, impossible-to-remember criteria sets that reduce clinical utility. Criteria sets should neither be so behaviorally specific as to be cumbersome and off the point, nor so inferential as to be unreliable and subject to idiosyncratic uses.

Diagnostic Tests as Criteria

Diagnoses in the rest of medicine are often heavily influenced by laboratory tests. The increasing use of laboratory tests in psychiatric research raises the question of whether and when these tests should be included within the diagnostic criteria sets. The expanding technological capacity of numerous techniques makes possible the direct measurement of brain anatomy (e.g., computed axial tomography [CAT], magnetic resonance imaging [MRI]), brain functioning (e.g., MRI, positron-emission tomography [PET], brain electrical activity mapping [BEAM]), static and dynamic neurochemical metabolism, other neurophysiological functions (e.g., eye tracking, sleep electroencephalogram [EEG]), and increasingly sophisticated psychological testing.

There are several possible relationships between test results and psychiatric diagnoses. A laboratory test may be pathognomonic of the psychiatric diagnosis so that a positive test result is completely predictive of, and sometimes essential for, making the diagnosis. Indeed, test results may add such important information to clinical assessment (as in diabetes and pneumonia) that they are diagnostic of the condition. The only areas in psychiatry in which test results now assume such importance are Mental Retardation (IQ tests), Learning Disorders (achievement test scores), and some specific sleep disorders (polysomnography). DSM-IV does include IQ and achievement tests as part of the criteria sets for Mental Retardation and Learning Disorders. It was ultimately decided not to include sleep EEG results in the criteria sets for the Sleep Disorders but instead to include them in the text because laboratory studies are expensive and not always readily available, and most sleep disorder diagnoses can be made on clinical grounds alone.

More commonly in psychiatry, a laboratory test result is informative but is not sufficiently sensitive and specific to be considered diagnostic of the disorder. Instead of informing diagnosis, the test results may be better considered as confirming the construct of the disorder and telling us something about its pathogenesis. For example, numerous studies have confirmed that, on average, groups of individuals with Schizophrenia have an increased ventricular size observable with brain imaging studies. However, because the range of values for individuals with Schizophrenia greatly overlaps with both normal values and values seen in other conditions, brain imaging cannot be used as a diagnostic test to indicate the presence of Schizophrenia for a given patient. Nonetheless, the findings of brain imaging do support the neuropsychiatric hypothesis for the etiology of Schizophrenia. Such laboratory findings are included in the "Associated Laboratory Findings" section of the DSM-IV text for the disorder.

Why Classify Mental Disorders?

Up to this point, we have acted as if the need to classify psychiatric disorders is self-evident, and indeed to us this seems to be the case. However, some have argued that the entire enterprise of psychiatric classification is at the very least misguided; at the worst, it is more detrimental to the individual being classified than it is worth. Although some of this criticism is merely the grumbling of the "antipsychiatry movement," four reasonable concerns have been raised: 1) being assigned a psychiatric diagnosis may expose the individual to potential stigma, 2) there may be a labeling effect such that the individual who receives the diagnostic label acts in accord with it, 3) the psychiatric label stresses a reductionistic commonality at the expense of a broader and more humanistic appreciation of individual differences, and 4) the diagnostic system is inappropriately expanding its purview by labeling normal human behavior and moral failings.

We acknowledge and embrace each of these concerns and tried to be mindful of them in the preparation of DSM-IV. Nonetheless, despite their importance, none of the concerns individually or in aggregate outweighs the enormous benefits that are obtained when DSM-IV is used and understood thoughtfully and with full respect for its limitations. DSM-IV allows its users to communicate more effectively with each other by establishing an effective shorthand for describing the conditions that are being categorized (saying to a colleague that a patient has Schizophrenia quickly communicates the type of symptoms that would be expected, as well as the more or less characteristic course).

DSM-IV also facilitates the identification, treatment, and prevention of mental disorders in both clinical and research settings. Although they can sometimes cause mischief, diagnostic labels often provide considerable and important predictive power. For example, making a diagnosis of Bipolar Disorder suggests that certain treatments may be preferentially effective (e.g., lithium carbonate), that a certain course may be likely (e.g., recurrent, episodic, risk of suicide), and that there is an increased likelihood of this disorder in offspring.

By defining more or less homogeneous groups of patients for study, DSM-IV also facilitates efforts to develop a deeper understanding of the etiology of mental disorders. The DSM classifications have been both a manifestation of, and a major contributor to, the development of an empirical science of psychiatry. Furthermore, it is hoped that the best is yet to come and that the descriptive classification of mental disorders will promote a more profound understanding of their etiology, as the periodic table in chemistry helped to promote an understanding of the atomic structure of the elements and the Linnaean system of botanical and zoological classification helped to develop evolutionary theory.

DSM-IV is also an important tool for education. By organizing disorders into major classes, the classification system offers a structure for teaching phenomenology and differential diagnosis. The system is also useful in helping patients to learn that their pattern of symptoms has been identified and studied and is not unique. The development of specific diagnostic criteria has also aided in creating comprehensive, semistructured psychiatric interviews, which in modified form can be adapted for use in clinical practice.

However, it should always be remembered that assigning a DSM-IV diagnosis represents just one step in the ongoing care of an individual. Although DSM-IV diagnosis conveys pertinent information, other factors (e.g., an individual's personal and family history, previous treatment responses, psychological factors and coping styles, and the influence of the psychosocial environment) are also crucial to treatment planning and must be addressed during the evaluation process. Finally, it is essential to recognize that individuals whose symptoms meet the criteria for a particular diagnosis are not alike in every way; important differences often exist among individuals with the same diagnosis.

The Last Word

Do not be a DSM-IV idolater who allows clinical observation and common sense to be distorted by a need to shoehorn patients into the DSM-IV pigeonholes, independent of whether they fit or not. At the same time, avoid being a DSM-IV heretic who derides the whole system because it is not always successful in providing an appropriate category for each and every patient. Being mindful of the many epistemological limitations of DSM-IV will result in a more flexible and clinically practical perspective that does not put more weight on the system than it can bear. Perhaps the most important rule in applying DSM-IV is not to take the rules so seriously that one's clinical judgment is blinded.

SECTION II

The Development and Use of DSM-IV

CHAPTER 3

The Preparation of DSM-IV

Of all the questions we are asked, undoubtedly the most frequent is "what is the biggest single change in DSM-IV?" In our view, the biggest change in DSM-IV is not so much any revisions in the definitions of particular disorders, but rather in the way DSM-IV was prepared. DSM-IV is best envisioned as a modification and refinement of previous editions of DSM rather than a radical reconceptualization. As such, most of the underlying assumptions and conventions of DSM-III and DSM-III-R are retained in DSM-IV.

The DSM-IV revision process aimed to provide a systematic review of the current empirical data base so that any changes were maximally informed by clinical research findings. In contrast, the definitions included in DSM-III, DSM-III-R, and the *International Statistical Classification of Diseases and Related Health Problems,* 10th Revision (ICD-10), were for the most part the product of expert consensus. In the development of previous systems, meetings were held with an invited group of researchers and clinicians who shared their experiences and general knowledge of the literature. Afterward, the discussions were distilled into criteria sets, which were then distributed to the meeting participants for comment and review and ultimately to a wider audience via drafts of the criteria. Although the experts consulted were familiar with the then-current state of knowledge, no mechanisms were in place to ensure that all of the available data were systematically considered and presented for archival review. The criteria sets were subjected to field testing for acceptability and reliability, but these trials were conducted on extremely limited budgets that necessitated serious methodological limitations, with consequent difficulties in reporting and interpretation.

The relative lack of research in psychopathology before DSM-III created a vacuum that could only be filled by a near total reliance on expert consensus. Indeed, the expert-consensus method was a necessary and useful starting point to generate initial criteria sets that could then be used in research studies and clinical practice. In starting work on DSM-IV, we benefited from the availability of a much wider data base of research that was in part stimulated by the availability of DSM-III and DSM-III-R. This was a fortunate turn of events because the expert-consensus method has serious limitations and is subject to various kinds of bias. The most obvious bias results from the inclusion or omission of particular experts or points of view. Almost as important is the concern that decisions might be unduly influenced by the persuasiveness, persistence, or prestige of a given expert.

The debates during the preparation of DSM-III and DSM-III-R were often remarkably heated. It is surprising how passionate experts can become in their need to have the system reflect their understanding of the clinical "truth." Participants in the DSM-III and DSM-III-R process often thought that it was unclear how and why particular decisions were made, and there was little or no documentation of the supporting evidence and rationale. Another limitation of the expert-consensus method has not been widely noted but nonetheless deserves consideration. Experts, almost by definition, have considerable research and clinical experience with a given disorder, but usually this experience is acquired in the rarefied atmosphere of a university tertiary care center. The special referral-pattern characteristics of these settings lead to considerable bias in patient selection and may inspire conceptions about the conditions that may not generalize very well to state hospitals, community mental health centers, office practice, and primary care settings.

For all of these reasons, our goal from the outset has been to base the DSM-IV decisions on the widest and most systematic review of the empirical evidence and to provide documentation indicating on what rationale the decisions were made. We will briefly describe the sequential steps in the preparation of DSM-IV that led to this goal and its implementation.

Step 1: Decision to Embark on DSM-IV (Fall 1988)

The decision to start work on DSM-IV was made in 1988 and was based largely on the fact that the World Health Organization was well on its way in the preparation of ICD-10. It was deemed necessary to begin work on DSM-IV so that the two systems could be coordinated and brought into greater convergence. In some ways, this timing was unfortunate, coming so soon on the heels of the publication of DSM-III-R. Concerns that frequent changes in the diagnostic system are disruptive to clinical, research, and educational activities had to be balanced against the huge advantages that could be derived by coordinating the efforts of the separate groups working on DSM-IV and ICD-10. From the outset, it was recommended that DSM-IV not represent a radical shift in perspective and that any changes to DSM-III-R be based on a thorough review of the empirical evidence.

The simultaneous work on DSM-IV and ICD-10 allowed for much mutual influence and increased the convergence of the two systems. Throughout the years of preparation of DSM-IV and ICD-10, there were dozens of formal and informal consultations where participants discussed the rationale for differences between the systems and ways of bringing them closer together. This consultation was greatly facilitated by the efforts of the National Institute of Mental Health (NIMH) and particularly of Darrel Regier, M.D. As a result of this close collaboration, there is complete compatibility in the diagnostic codes and terms used in the two systems, ensuring ease of communication between them. The collaboration between the architects of DSM-IV and ICD-10 has resulted in improvements in both systems. Indeed, in the best of all possible worlds, it probably would have been desirable to have developed a single diagnostic manual, completely joining together the DSM-IV and ICD-10 efforts to arrive at a common product. Such a manual proved to be unrealistic at this time, given the different rates of development and needs of the two systems.

This story has a surprising and somewhat ironic ending. Although ICD-10 was published in 1993, its implementation in the United States by the U.S. government has been postponed at least until the turn of the century. It turns out that the costs of changing from the *International Classification of Diseases,* 9th Revision, Clinical Modification (ICD-9-CM) coding system to the radically different ICD-10 coding system are considerable. The ICD-9-CM diagnostic codes are used to determine reimbursements for all medical treatments (not just for psychiatry) covered under third-party insurance in the United States. Before adopting a new system, all medical record applications throughout the country would have to be reprogrammed and then field-tested to establish their effects on reimbursement patterns and policies. Although the conversion of the psychiatric section of ICD-9-CM to ICD-10 might be a more manageable endeavor, it cannot be done separately from the rest of medicine.

All things considered, the decision to publish DSM-IV in 1994 probably makes sense, even retrospectively when taking into account the delay in implementing ICD-10. The need to have the two systems be compatible remains valid despite the delay in making ICD-10 official. Moreover, the work on DSM-IV provided an opportunity to develop the first diagnostic system that is systematically based on a thorough review of the available evidence.

Step 2: Appointment of Task Force and Work Group Members (Spring 1989)

After the appointment of the Chair of the DSM-IV Task Force, the next step was the development of an organizational structure for preparing DSM-IV. A major goal was to ensure the widest possible participation in the decision-making process. A Task Force on DSM-IV was appointed consisting of 27 members. Thirteen of these individuals also chaired individual Work Groups, each focused on a particular group of disorders and consisted of 5–10 members. Each of the Work Groups selected advisory groups, which usually consisted of 50–100 people. Participants were chosen after wide canvassing of the various fields to ensure that we obtained the best people to represent the diversity of views on a particular diagnostic category.

Members of the Work Groups were usually chosen not just for their wide clinical and research experience, but also for their ability to adopt a wider consensus-scholar view. The construction of certain Work Groups also took into account previously simmering controversies in a particular field, with individuals chosen to represent different positions in an effort to reconcile these positions through the DSM-IV process of empirical data review. The advisory groups were chosen to represent the wide diversity of opinions in the field and to ensure that the widest and fairest reviews of the empirical data were conducted. People were eager to participate. Out of the more than 1,000 people asked to participate in DSM-IV, only a handful declined—usually based on the commitment of time required. Most participants (including us) found themselves working far beyond what they had bargained for but usually did this with dedication, collegiality, and good cheer.

Step 3: Establishing the Parameters for Decision Making (Spring/Summer/Fall 1989)

Before beginning the actual work on DSM-IV, there were a series of Task Force meetings to lay out the goals, methods, criteria for change, and governance structure that would be used in preparing the document.

Goals

There was surprisingly quick and unanimous agreement on what should be the major goals of DSM-IV. It was decided that by far the most important goal of DSM-IV is to promote communication in clinical practice. The second most important goal is to facilitate research and communication across the clinical-research interface. Although the first two goals are in most ways completely compatible, there were two areas in which the predominance of the clinical goal impacted on the research goal. It was decided that new diagnoses would be included not to stimulate research, but only after their utility and the implications of including them were well established by research. It was also decided to review and perhaps revise those categories that contained criteria sets resembling excessively detailed research checklists rather than a clinically useful definition of the disorder.

The third most important goal of DSM-IV is the education of clinicians, trainees, and patients. To this end, a large part of the DSM-IV effort was devoted to updating and improving the text descriptions that accompany each disorder. The fourth major goal was to facilitate record keeping and reporting of psychiatric diagnoses. In this regard, there would be a thorough review of the accuracy of the diagnostic codes included in DSM-III-R and a close collaboration with the World Health Organization and with the National Center for Health Statistics to ensure that DSM-IV would be fully compatible with both ICD-9-CM and ICD-10.

A number of other important uses of the diagnostic system that might be impacted by its revision were not considered to be central goals in the preparation of DSM-IV. These include the use of DSM-IV in forensic proceedings, disability determinations, and establishing eligibility for treatment benefits. The accuracy, utility, and credibility of DSM-IV depend on its being faithful to the clinical situation and to research evidence, and these goals were to be kept primary. However, because we were concerned about the possible misuse of DSM-IV in some of its applications, we had the drafts of DSM-IV reviewed by individuals with special expertise in these areas to identify and correct any potential problems and misunderstandings.

Methods

Once it was decided that DSM-IV would be based on the widest possible review of the empirical evidence, the next question naturally was how best to implement this decision. A series of Methods conferences were held (often cosponsored by NIMH or the MacArthur Foundation) to cover the following issues: 1) establishing a systematic method for literature reviews, 2) developing the method of data reanalysis, 3) establishing the protocols for field trials, 4) establishing guidelines for criteria writing, 5) exploring the impact of culture on psychiatric diagnosis, 6) exploring the role of developmental issues on psychiatric diagnosis, and 7) outlining a method for developing DSM-IV to make it especially suitable for use in primary care settings.

The choice of the three-stage process of empirical review was particularly important in the development of DSM-IV. The three stages consisted of 1) reviews of the published literature, 2) review and reanalysis of previously collected but unpublished data sets, and 3) collection of new data under the auspices of field trials. The actual implementation of this plan is discussed in steps 4, 5, and 7 below.

Criteria for Change

The threshold for change in DSM-IV was set at a much higher level than was the case for either DSM-III or DSM-III-R. Previously, new diagnoses were included when some group of experts thought that they would be clinically useful or were likely to promote needed research. This policy improved the coverage of the system but made it increasingly cumbersome and likely to promote artificially high rates of comorbidity. Overall, DSM-IV is a relatively conservative document that made changes from DSM-III-R only when they were necessary to respond to new findings, to increase compatibility with ICD-10, or to increase clarity and user-friendliness. A conservative DSM-IV is less likely to disrupt clinical communication and ongoing research projects.

Governance

The decision-making process was envisioned as follows. The Task Force was the main decision-making body of DSM-IV. It established the policy, methods, and thresholds for changes and ultimately approved all of the various criteria sets. The preparatory work for the Task Force decisions was done by the DSM-IV Work Groups.

The Work Groups, in collaboration with their advisers, were responsible for identifying the important diagnostic issues in their section and for choosing a Work Group member to lead the group's review process. Work Groups were given considerable autonomy in their reviews so long as they adhered to the overall review methods and criteria for change. The ultimate assignment for the Work Group was to summarize the empirical data and the advantages and disadvantages of the options they considered and to make recommendations to the Task Force, which would be responsible for the final decision making.

Early on, we decided that the decision-making process would not benefit from tallying votes. Throughout, the method was to encourage an extensive discussion and review of the data so that the explicit differences in interpretation could be highlighted and points of agreement could be found. With very few exceptions, this process worked wonderfully well and resulted in consensus agreements that all participants could regard as a reasonable representation of the conclusions that would be drawn by a consensus scholar.

Openness of Process

From the start, a major effort was initiated to air issues as widely as possible to identify potential problems and controversies and to include the widest array of data and opinions. The exchange of information took a number of different forms. The DSM-IV Task Force published a series of "DSM-IV Updates" that apprised the field as to the ongoing progress and questions that remained open. A DSM-IV column in *Hospital and Community Psychiatry* served a similar function. There were literally hundreds of presentations at national and international conferences and numerous journal articles. Beyond the inclusion of large advisory bodies to each of the Work Groups, there were a number of formal and informal liaisons with numerous professional organizations representing a wide array of mental health, medical, and governmental interests and specialties. Finally, work on DSM-IV benefited from the participation and perspective of numerous international advisers. A critical aspect of openness of process is the documentation of the rationale and evidence for the decisions that were made. This documentation is described below in step 11.

Step 4: Literature Reviews (Fall 1989–Summer 1991)

As a first step, approximately 150 questions that most deserved consideration for DSM-IV were identified. Each of these questions was then the subject of an extensive and systematic review of the literature to determine what evidence was available and what additional evidence would need to be collected to support possible changes. The instructions for conducting literature reviews included a standardized search format to ensure comprehensiveness and reduction of bias. The reviews were meant to take the perspective of the consensus scholar, who would begin the process of data aggregation and interpretation without a preconceived point of view. The reporting of the literature reviews also followed a standardized format that guided the presentation of the data and the pros and cons of each of the alternative suggestions for criteria sets that arose from searching the literature.

The first drafts of the literature reviews were distributed to the Work Group members and to the wide cohort of advisers to ensure that all relevant studies were included and that the interpretation represented a consensus of the field. Often, the final draft of the literature review was the culmination of an extensive series of revisions informed by the critiques and including the new data provided by the advisers and the field. The literature reviews formed the basis for the development of the *DSM-IV Options Book* (see step 6 below) and were published in the *DSM-IV Sourcebook* (see step 11 below).

Step 5: Data Reanalysis (Spring 1990–Spring 1993)

In some areas, a review of the literature revealed a lack of evidence, or conflicting evidence, for the resolution of a particular diagnostic issue. In many of these cases, we were able to make use of the additional resource of data reanalysis. The reanalyses of existing and relevant unpublished data sets were supported by a grant to the American Psychiatric Association by the John D. and Catherine T. MacArthur Foundation. Most of the data reanalyses involved the collaboration of several investigations at different sites (often including international sites). These investigators jointly subjected their data to questions posed by the Work Groups concerning specific criteria that were included in DSM-III-R or that might be included in DSM-IV. Data reanalyses also made it possible for the Work Groups to generate several data-based criteria sets (e.g., for Antisocial Personality Disorder and Somatization Disorder), which were studied further in the DSM-IV Focused Field Trials. This methodology had the added benefit of increasing the generalizability of the findings by pooling data collected from diverse sources.

Step 6: Options Book (September 1, 1991)

Unlike DSM-III and DSM-III-R, which were preceded by first drafts of diagnostic criteria, DSM-IV was preceded by publication of the *DSM-IV Options Book* to solicit wide opinion on which of the possible alternative criteria sets should be included in a future draft of DSM-IV. The *DSM-IV Options Book* included brief discussions of the pros and cons of each of the major suggestions for change made by the Work Groups after consideration of the literature reviews and the results of the data reanalyses. A response form was included in the back of the *DSM-IV Options Book* to facilitate reactions from the field concerning possible problems and inconsistencies, to elicit opinions about the implications of the various alternatives, and to invite the submission of additional published or unpublished data that had not yet been reviewed. These responses were forwarded to the relevant Work Groups and incorporated into their further decision-making process. The DSM-IV process had up to this point already included the opinions of a very large group of advisers. The *DSM-IV Options Book* provided an added opportunity to ensure that we were obtaining the widest input and not missing anything that might later turn out to be problematic.

Step 7: Focused Field Trials (Fall 1991–Spring 1993)

The 12 DSM-IV field trials were sponsored by NIMH in collaboration with the National Institute of Drug Abuse and the National Institute of Alcohol Abuse and Alcoholism. The field trials studied Antisocial Personality Disorder, Disruptive Behavior Disorders, Mixed Anxiety Depressive Disorder, Mood Disorders, Obsessive-Compulsive Disorder, Panic Disorder, Pervasive Developmental Disorders, Posttraumatic Stress Disorder, Schizophrenia, Sleep Disorders, Somatization Disorder, and Substance-Related Disorders. Because of the availability of external funding, the DSM-IV field trials were performed with a degree of rigor never before possible in the field testing of other diagnostic systems. These field trials gave the DSM-IV Work Groups the opportunity to study the possible impact of many of the changes mentioned in the *DSM-IV Options Book*. Each field trial compared DSM-III, DSM-III-R, ICD-10, and DSM-IV proposals in 5–10 sites with 50–100 subjects per site. Diverse sites were selected, including widely representative groups of subjects with a range of sociocultural and ethnic backgrounds, to ensure generalizability of the field trial results and to test some of the most difficult questions in differential diagnosis.

Each field trial collected information on the reliability and performance characteristics of each criteria set as a whole, as well as the specific items within the criteria set. The field trials served several purposes. They helped us select the optimum definition of the various disorders and reduced the risk that changes would result in unanticipated shifts in the definition of caseness and prevalence of the various disorders. Field trials are an important link between clinical research and clinical practice. For the most part, the empirical data derived from the literature review and data reanalyses had been collected under tightly controlled protocols in university settings under conditions emphasizing the protection of the internal validity of the study. As a result, most of the existing literature might or might not generalize to the very different clinical settings in which DSM-IV is also used. In contrast, the DSM-IV field trial protocols were sufficiently inclusive to ensure external validity and greater generalizability to everyday clinical practice.

Step 8: Near Final Decision Making (Fall 1992–Spring 1993)

The final DSM-IV Work Group recommendations on each issue were informed by the data obtained through the three-stage process of empirical documentation, the extensive written comments from the advisers, and correspondence in response to the *DSM-IV Options Book.* In evaluating each of the hundreds of Work Group recommendations, the Task Force had to find a balance between micromanaging and rubber stamping. The Task Force paid particular attention to those questions that would have the widest impact, that crossed boundaries between Work Groups, and that occasioned the widest disagreement. The general tendency was for the Task Force to be more conservative than the individual Work Groups and to enforce the discipline of a high threshold for making changes based on empirical evidence that was established at the Methods Conferences. The Task Force was consistently more concerned about false-positives than the Work Groups had been; the latter often were more concerned about false-negatives. On a number of occasions, the Work Groups made suggestions for lowered thresholds and for adding new diagnoses that ultimately were not accepted by the Task Force.

One often asked question is how much DSM-IV really is based on empirical evidence versus its being the result of the same kind of expert consensus that informed DSM-III, DSM-III-R, and ICD-10. For many issues, this is a false dichotomy. Very rarely in any science, and almost never in the clinical science of psychiatry, do empirical data stand up and say "this is the only way I can be understood!" All scientific judgments require some combination of evidence and interpretation that results in the formulation of new hypotheses that are then subject to the collection of more evidence and interpretation, and so on. Although based on empirical data, DSM-IV decisions were the result of expert consensus on how best to interpret the data. Moreover, a number of decisions were not based on data at all. These fell into two categories. Some decisions were broadly conceptual (e.g., eliminating the term *organic),* whereas others entailed no more than detailed editing of phrases to increase clarity of language.

Step 9: Final Draft of Criteria (March 1, 1993)

In March 1993, a near final draft of the criteria sets was made widely available to give the field one last opportunity to provide substantive comment and to alert us to errors we may have made in the criteria sets. It was gratifying to the Task Force that the reaction to this draft was quite positive, and few suggestions for further changes were made.

Step 10: Final Preparation of Text and Criteria (Spring 1993–Spring 1994)

Once the criteria sets were nearly finalized, we could devote our full attention to the final editing of the text for each disorder. The Work Groups had prepared first drafts of the text, which had to be edited for consistency of style and content. It was especially important to ensure the congruency across disorders of the material contained in the differential diagnoses sections. Drafts of text were reviewed by the Work Groups, as well as by individuals with special expertise in forensic psychiatry and on the impact of developmental, gender, and cultural issues on diagnosis. During this period, the appendixes were developed in collaboration with a number of different groups (especially the American Health Information Management Association and the World Health Organization).

Step 11: Approval by the American Psychiatric Association

The governance system of the American Psychiatric Association required several levels of approval for the Task Force recommendations before publication of DSM-IV. These included the Committee on Diagnosis and Assessment, the Council on Research, the Assembly, and the Board of Trustees. Some uninformed critics (fortunately, very few) have argued that DSM-IV is some sort of conspiratorial document driven by the guild goals of psychiatry. In fact, our experience of the DSM-IV process was that it was remarkably free of any political pressures. All of the Task Force recommendations were accepted in their entirety by each of the oversight bodies without any suggested revisions or changes.

Step 12: Documentation in Sourcebook and Articles

As discussed above, one of the most important goals of the DSM-IV process was to be explicit about the steps of the decision-making process. The *DSM-IV Sourcebook* is a companion publication that provides the field with the opportunity to review the details of the decision-making process. It contains all of the literature reviews, data reanalyses, and field trial results, as well as statements by the Work Groups summarizing the rationale for their recommendations. Moreover, the work on DSM-IV stimulated the publication of dozens of journal articles reporting the data that had been collected during the process.

Our Final Impression of the DSM-IV Process

One of the welcome advantages of the DSM-IV emphasis on empirical data was the impact it had on the process of decision making and on the level of discourse. Because issues were decided based on an appeal to data rather than to personal belief, there was remarkably little controversy and disagreement. People who had argued vigorously for opposing points of view during the DSM-III and DSM-III-R processes were forced jointly to interpret tables of data accumulated during the three stages of empirical review. It was pleasing for us to witness how many times they were able to change their minds when reviewing data that did not support their previously strongly held beliefs. In this regard, the review of empirical data was a learning experience for us all. People often commiserate with us, assuming that the development of DSM-IV must have been an arduous task. In fact, it was a great deal of fun, and we thank all of the people who helped us in the work and play of its preparation.

CHAPTER 4

The DSM-IV Road Map and Classification

DSM-IV is a lot easier to use when one has a good grasp of its overall structure. Some people use the book every day for years but still seem to be lost among the trees in the forest without really understanding how the manual is constructed and what it can offer. This chapter provides an overview of the entire manual that we hope will assist the reader's exploration of its individual parts.

Before getting into the specifics of the individual mental disorders, DSM-IV begins with several introductory sections that serve to provide information that applies across the entire system. The "Introduction" includes discussions of the history of psychiatric classification and the development of DSM-IV, provides a definition of mental disorder, and notes several caveats in the use of the manual. The "Use of the Manual" section provides information on coding procedures, terms, and conventions. The "DSM-IV Classification" provides a comprehensive listing of the official codes and categories. Next is a description of how to do a "Multiaxial Assessment." It has been our experience that some DSM-IV users (and many of its critics) skip over these introductory sections. Not unlike those who in their haste to get started bypass reading the instruction manual to their VCR, those who fail to master these introductory chapters are depriving themselves of a real understanding of how the system is to be used and may miss out on some of the more important features of DSM-IV.

The body of DSM-IV consists of descriptive text and accompanying criteria sets for the DSM-IV disorders. These are grouped into 16 major diagnostic classes and one additional section called "Other Conditions That May Be a Focus of Clinical Attention." Although the major innovation of DSM is to provide diagnostic criteria sets for each disorder, most of the information in DSM-IV is contained in the text sections. These sections provide additional detail, illustrative examples, and other relevant information essential to the appropriate diagnosis and management of the individual's symptoms. In fact, as is stated in the introduction to the "Mini-D" (the nickname for the *Quick Reference to the Diagnostic Criteria From DSM-IV),* the appropriate use of the criteria really requires at least some familiarity with the DSM-IV text.

To facilitate finding specific types of relevant information, the text for each disorder is organized into nine subsections. The **Diagnostic Features** section is included to expand on the terse information outlined in the diagnostic criteria sets and provides specific illustrative examples, definitions of terms, and practical assessment tips. Of course, not every interesting clinical feature can (or should) be included in the diagnostic criteria sets. The section titled **Associated Features and Disorders** is for describing additional clinical features that often are associated with the disorder (but are not essential features for making the diagnosis). For convenience, these features are subdivided into three types: **Associated Descriptive Features and Mental Disorders** (which include associated psychiatric symptoms and the most frequent comorbid psychiatric disorders), **Associated Laboratory Findings** (which include diagnostic, confirmatory, or associated laboratory findings), and **Associated Physical Examination Findings and General Medical Conditions** (which include medical conditions that are either etiological or contributory to the psychiatric symptoms or are complications of the mental disorder).

The diagnostic criteria sets were purposely designed to be generic. Variations in symptom presentation that may be attributable to the individual's developmental stage, cultural setting, or gender are included in **Specific Culture, Age, and Gender Features**. For example, in some cultures, symptoms of Major Depressive Disorder may be expressed more as somatic complaints than as feelings of sadness. The **Prevalence** section provides whatever specific information was available on the rates of the disorder in clinical and community settings. In general, most of the data on community prevalence were drawn from three large national epidemiological studies: the Epidemiological Catchment Area Study, conducted in the early 1980s; the National Comorbidity Study, conducted in the late 1980s; and the National Household Drug Survey, conducted in the early 1980s.

Course describes the typical lifetime presentation of the disorder. This section covers issues such as age at onset, type of onset, episodic versus continuous nature of the symptoms, and progression of the illness versus stability over time. Data on the frequency of the disorder among first-degree biological relatives compared with the frequency in the general population are included in the **Familial Pattern** section. It should be noted that familial loading does not necessarily imply genetic transmission of the disorder. When the data are available, the degree of genetic heritability is suggested by comparisons between rates in monozygotic and dizygotic twins and between rates in biological and adoptive relatives of adopted away probands. This section also notes other disorders that may occur more frequently in family members. The section on **Differential Diagnosis** provides guidelines on how to differentiate the disorder from others with similar symptom presentations.

DSM-IV also includes a number of appendixes that provide additional diagnostic and coding aids and information for researchers. Appendix A, "Decision Trees for

Differential Diagnosis," provides six decision trees organized by presenting symptom, which can be of assistance in differential diagnosis. Appendix B, "Criteria Sets and Axes Provided for Further Study," provides 26 research criteria sets and axes. Although the DSM-IV Task Force decided that there was insufficient empirical evidence to include these disorders as official diagnostic categories, sets of suggested research criteria are included to facilitate further study (see "Some Future Contenders," Chapter 25, p. xx). Appendix C, "Glossary of Technical Terms," provides definitions of terms used throughout the manual. Appendix D, "Annotated Listing of Changes in DSM-IV," provides a succinct summary by disorder of changes from DSM-III-R. Appendix E and Appendix F provide alphabetical and numerical lists, respectively, of DSM-IV disorders. Appendix G, "ICD-9-CM Codes for Selected General Medical Conditions and Medication-Induced Disorders," is included for the clinician's convenience in coding general medical conditions. Appendix H provides the "DSM-IV Classification with ICD-10 Codes." Appendix I, "Outline for Cultural Formulation and Glossary of Culture-Bound Syndromes," provides a glossary of cultural-bound syndromes and a guideline for cultural formulation.

Development of the DSM-IV Classification

The DSM-IV Classification is a stand-alone summary that contains all of the diagnostic codes, terms, subtypes, and specifiers that compose the DSM-IV system. It is a small triumph of condensation and as such provides a very convenient vehicle for reviewing the whole system and finding the appropriate diagnostic terminology and code. The hardest part of formatting the classification was to indicate those subtypes and specifiers that apply to many diagnoses without repeating them over and over again. This problem was solved in either of two ways: placement of subtypes and specifiers at the beginning of a given section (e.g., see "Sexual Dysfunctions") or disorder (e.g., see "Schizophrenia") or, in more complex situations, the designation of subtypes and specifiers by footnotes (e.g., see "Substance-Related Disorders" and "Mood Disorders").

The DSM-IV Classification

NOS = Not Otherwise Specified.

An χ appearing in a diagnostic code indicates that a specific code number is required.

An ellipsis (. . .) is used in the names of certain disorders to indicate that the name of a specific mental disorder or general medical condition should be inserted when recording the name (e.g., 293.0 Delirium Due to Hypothyroidism).

If criteria are currently met, one of the following severity specifiers may be noted after the diagnosis:

Mild
Moderate
Severe

If criteria are no longer met, one of the following specifiers may be noted:

In Partial Remission
In Full Remission
Prior History

Disorders Usually First Diagnosed in Infancy, Childhood, or Adolescence

MENTAL RETARDATION

Note: *These are coded on Axis II.*

317 Mild Mental Retardation
318.0 Moderate Mental Retardation
318.1 Severe Mental Retardation
318.2 Profound Mental Retardation
319 Mental Retardation, Severity Unspecified

LEARNING DISORDERS

315.00 Reading Disorder
315.1 Mathematics Disorder
315.2 Disorder of Written Expression
315.9 Learning Disorder NOS

MOTOR SKILLS DISORDER

315.4 Developmental Coordination Disorder

COMMUNICATION DISORDERS

315.31 Expressive Language Disorder
315.31 Mixed Receptive-Expressive Language Disorder
315.39 Phonological Disorder
307.0 Stuttering
307.9 Communication Disorder NOS

PERVASIVE DEVELOPMENTAL DISORDERS

299.00 Autistic Disorder
299.80 Rett's Disorder
299.10 Childhood Disintegrative Disorder
299.80 Asperger's Disorder
299.80 Pervasive Developmental Disorder NOS

ATTENTION-DEFICIT AND DISRUPTIVE BEHAVIOR DISORDERS

314.xx Attention-Deficit/Hyperactivity Disorder
.01 Combined Type
.00 Predominantly Inattentive Type
.01 Predominantly Hyperactive-ImpulsiveType
314.9 Attention-Deficit/Hyperactivity Disorder NOS
312.8 Conduct Disorder
Specify type: Childhood-Onset Type/Adolescent-Onset Type
313.81 Oppositional Defiant Disorder
312.9 Disruptive Behavior Disorder NOS

FEEDING AND EATING DISORDERS OF INFANCY OR EARLY CHILDHOOD

307.52 Pica
307.53 Rumination Disorder
307.59 Feeding Disorder of Infancy or Early Childhood

TIC DISORDERS

307.23 Tourette's Disorder
307.22 Chronic Motor or Vocal Tic Disorder
307.21 Transient Tic Disorder
Specify if: Single Episode/Recurrent
307.20 Tic Disorder NOS

ELIMINATION DISORDERS

—.– Encopresis
787.6 With Constipation and Overflow Incontinence
307.7 Without Constipation and Overflow Incontinence
307.6 Enuresis (Not Due to a General Medical Condition)
Specify type: Nocturnal Only/Diurnal Only/Nocturnal an Diurnal

OTHER DISORDERS OF INFANCY, CHILDHOOD, OR ADOLESCENCE

309.21 Separation Anxiety Disorder
Specify if: Early Onset
313.23 Selective Mutism
313.89 Reactive Attachment Disorder of Infancy or Early Childhood
Specify type: Inhibited Type/Disinhibited Type

307.3 Stereotypic Movement Disorder
Specify if: With Self-Injurious Behavior
313.9 Disorder of Infancy, Childhood, or Adolescence NOS

Delirium, Dementia, and Amnestic and Other Cognitive Disorders

DELIRIUM

293.0 Delirium Due to . . . *[Indicate the General Medical Condition]*
—.– Substance Intoxication Delirium *(refer to Substance-Related Disordersfor substance-specific codes)*
—.– Substance Withdrawal Delirium *(refer to Substance-Related Disorders for substance-specific codes)*
—.– Delirium Due to Multiple Etiologies *(code each of the specific etiologies)*
780.09 Delirium NOS

DEMENTIA

290.xx Dementia of the Alzheimer's Type, With Early Onset *(also code 331.0 Alzheimer's disease on Axis III)*
.10 Uncomplicated
.11 With Delirium
.12 With Delusions
.13 With Depressed Mood
Specify if: With Behavioral Disturbance
290.xx Dementia of the Alzheimer's Type, With Late Onset *(also code 331.0 Alzheimer's disease on Axis III)*
.0 Uncomplicated
.3 With Delirium
.20 With Delusions
.21 With Depressed Mood
Specify if: With Behavioral Disturbance
290.xx Vascular Dementia
.40 Uncomplicated
.41 With Delirium
.42 With Delusions
.43 With Depressed Mood
Specify if: With Behavioral Disturbance
294.9 Dementia Due to HIV Disease *(also code 043.1 HIV infection affecting central nervous system on Axis III)*
294.1 Dementia Due to Head Trauma *(also code 854.00 head injury on Axis III)*
294.1 Dementia Due to Parkinson's Disease *(also code 332.0 Parkinson's disease on Axis III)*
294.1 Dementia Due to Huntington's Disease *(also code 333.4 Huntington's disease on Axis III)*
290.10 Dementia Due to Pick's Disease *(also code 331.1 Pick's disease on Axis III)*
290.10 Dementia Due to Creutzfeldt-Jakob Disease *(also code 046.1 Creutzfeldt-Jakob disease on Axis III)*
294.1 Dementia Due to . . . *[Indicate the General Medical Condition not listed above] (also code the general medical condition on Axis III)*
—.– Substance-Induced Persisting Dementia *(refer to Substance-Related Disorders for substance-specific codes)*
—.– Dementia Due to Multiple Etiologies *(code each of the specific etiologies)*
294.8 Dementia NOS

AMNESTIC DISORDERS

294.0 Amnestic Disorder Due to . . . *[Indicate the General Medical Condition]*
Specify if: Transient/Chronic
—.– Substance-Induced Persisting Amnestic Disorder *(refer to Substance-Related Disorders for substance-specific codes)*
294.8 Amnestic Disorder NOS

OTHER COGNITIVE DISORDERS

294.9 Cognitive Disorder NOS

Mental Disorders Due to a General Medical Condition Not Elsewhere Classified

293.89 Catatonic Disorder Due to . . . *[Indicate the General Medical Condition]*

310.1 Personality Change Due to . . . *[Indicate the General Medical Condition]*
Specify type: Labile Type/Disinhibited Type/Aggressive Type/Apathetic Type/ Paranoid Type/Other Type/Combined Type/Unspecified Type

293.9 Mental Disorder NOS Due to . . . *[Indicate the General Medical Condition]*

Substance-Related Disorders

[a]*The following specifiers may be applied to Substance Dependence:*

With Physiological Dependence/ Without Physiological Dependence
Early Full Remission/Early Partial Remission
Sustained Full Remission/Sustained Partial Remission
On Agonist Therapy/In a Controlled Environment

The following specifiers apply to Substance-Induced Disorders as noted:

[I]With Onset During Intoxication/[W]With Onset During Withdrawal

ALCOHOL-RELATED DISORDERS

Alcohol Use Disorders

303.90 Alcohol Dependence[a]
305.00 Alcohol Abuse

Alcohol-Induced Disorders

303.00 Alcohol Intoxication
291.8 Alcohol Withdrawal
Specify if: With Perceptual Disturbances
291.0 Alcohol Intoxication Delirium
291.0 Alcohol Withdrawal Delirium
291.2 Alcohol-Induced Persisting Dementia
291.1 Alcohol-Induced Persisting Amnestic Disorder
291.x Alcohol-Induced Psychotic Disorder
.5 With Delusions[I,W]
.3 With Hallucinations[I,W]
291.8 Alcohol-Induced Mood Disorder[I,W]
291.8 Alcohol-Induced Anxiety Disorder[I,W]
291.8 Alcohol-Induced Sexual Dysfunction[I]
291.8 Alcohol-Induced Sleep Disorder[I,W]
291.9 Alcohol-Related Disorder NOS

AMPHETAMINE (OR AMPHETAMINE-LIKE)–RELATED DISORDERS

Amphetamine Use Disorders

304.40 Amphetamine Dependence[a]
305.70 Amphetamine Abuse

Amphetamine-Induced Disorders

292.89 Amphetamine Intoxication
Specify if: With Perceptual Disturbances
292.0 Amphetamine Withdrawal
292.81 Amphetamine Intoxication Delirium
292.xx Amphetamine-Induced Psychotic Disorder
.11 With Delusions[I]
.12 With Hallucinations[I]
292.84 Amphetamine-Induced Mood Disorder[I,W]
292.89 Amphetamine-Induced Anxiety Disorder[I]
292.89 Amphetamine-Induced Sexual Dysfunction[I]
292.89 Amphetamine-Induced Sleep Disorder[I,W]
292.9 Amphetamine-Related Disorder NOS

CAFFEINE-RELATED DISORDERS

Caffeine-Induced Disorders

305.90 Caffeine Intoxication
292.89 Caffeine-Induced Anxiety Disorder[I]
292.89 Caffeine-Induced Sleep Disorder[I]
292.9 Caffeine-Related Disorder NOS

CANNABIS-RELATED DISORDERS

Cannabis Use Disorders

304.30 Cannabis Dependence[a]
305.20 Cannabis Abuse

Cannabis-Induced Disorders

292.89 Cannabis Intoxication
Specify if: With Perceptual Disturbances
292.81 Cannabis Intoxication Delirium
292.xx Cannabis-Induced Psychotic Disorder
.11 With Delusions[I]
.12 With Hallucinations[I]
292.89 Cannabis-Induced Anxiety Disorder[I]
292.9 Cannabis-Related Disorder NOS

COCAINE-RELATED DISORDERS

Cocaine Use Disorders

304.20 Cocaine Dependence[a]
305.60 Cocaine Abuse

Cocaine-Induced Disorders

292.89 Cocaine Intoxication
Specify if: With Perceptual Disturbances
292.0 Cocaine Withdrawal
292.81 Cocaine Intoxication Delirium
292.xx Cocaine-Induced Psychotic Disorder
.11 With Delusions[I]
.12 With Hallucinations[I]
292.84 Cocaine-Induced Mood Disorder[I,W]
292.89 Cocaine-Induced Anxiety Disorder[I,W]
292.89 Cocaine-Induced Sexual Dysfunction[I]
292.89 Cocaine-Induced Sleep Disorder[I,W]
292.9 Cocaine-Related Disorder NOS

HALLUCINOGEN-RELATED DISORDERS

Hallucinogen Use Disorders

304.50 Hallucinogen Dependence[a]
305.30 Hallucinogen Abuse

Hallucinogen-Induced Disorders

292.89 Hallucinogen Intoxication
292.89 Hallucinogen Persisting Perception Disorder (Flashbacks)
292.81 Hallucinogen Intoxication Delirium
292.xx Hallucinogen-Induced Psychotic Disorder
.11 With Delusions[I]
.12 With Hallucinations[I]
292.84 Hallucinogen-Induced Mood Disorder[I]
292.89 Hallucinogen-Induced Anxiety Disorder[I]
292.9 Hallucinogen-Related Disorder NOS

INHALANT-RELATED DISORDERS

Inhalant Use Disorders

304.60 Inhalant Dependence[a]
305.90 Inhalant Abuse

Inhalant-Induced Disorders

292.89 Inhalant Intoxication
292.81 Inhalant Intoxication Delirium
292.82 Inhalant-Induced Persisting Dementia
292.xx Inhalant-Induced Psychotic Disorder
.11 With Delusions[I]
.12 With Hallucinations[I]
292.84 Inhalant-Induced Mood Disorder[I]
292.89 Inhalant-Induced Anxiety Disorder[I]
292.9 Inhalant-Related Disorder NOS

NICOTINE-RELATED DISORDERS

Nicotine Use Disorder
305.10 Nicotine Dependence[a]

Nicotine-Induced Disorder
292.0 Nicotine Withdrawal
292.9 Nicotine-Related Disorder NOS

OPIOID-RELATED DISORDERS

Opioid Use Disorders
304.00 Opioid Dependence[a]
305.50 Opioid Abuse

Opioid-Induced Disorders
292.89 Opioid Intoxication
Specify if: With Perceptual Disturbances
292.0 Opioid Withdrawal
292.81 Opioid Intoxication Delirium
292.xx Opioid-Induced Psychotic Disorder
.11 With Delusions[I]
.12 With Hallucinations[I]
292.84 Opioid-Induced Mood Disorder[I]
292.89 Opioid-Induced Sexual Dysfunction[I]
292.89 Opioid-Induced Sleep Disorder[I,W]
292.9 Opioid-Related Disorder NOS

PHENCYCLIDINE (OR PHENCYCLIDINE-LIKE)–RELATED DISORDERS

Phencyclidine Use Disorders
304.90 Phencyclidine Dependence[a]
305.90 Phencyclidine Abuse

Phencyclidine-Induced Disorders
292.89 Phencyclidine Intoxication
Specify if: With Perceptual Disturbances
292.81 Phencyclidine Intoxication Delirium
292.xx Phencyclidine-Induced Psychotic Disorder
.11 With Delusions[I]
.12 With Hallucinations[I]
292.84 Phencyclidine-Induced Mood Disorder[I]
292.89 Phencyclidine-Induced Anxiety Disorder[I]
292.9 Phencyclidine-Related Disorder NOS

SEDATIVE-, HYPNOTIC-, OR ANXIOLYTIC-RELATED DISORDERS

Sedative, Hypnotic, or Anxiolytic Use Disorders
304.10 Sedative, Hypnotic, or Anxiolytic Dependence[a]
305.40 Sedative, Hypnotic, or Anxiolytic Abuse

Sedative-, Hypnotic-, or Anxiolytic-Induced Disorders
292.89 Sedative, Hypnotic, or Anxiolytic Intoxication
292.0 Sedative, Hypnotic, or Anxiolytic Withdrawal
Specify if: With Perceptual Disturbances
292.81 Sedative, Hypnotic, or Anxiolytic Intoxication Delirium
292.81 Sedative, Hypnotic, or Anxiolytic Withdrawal Delirium
292.82 Sedative-, Hypnotic-, or Anxiolytic-Induced Persisting Dementia
292.83 Sedative-, Hypnotic-, or Anxiolytic-Induced Persisting Amnestic Disorder
292.xx Sedative-, Hypnotic-, or Anxiolytic-Induced Psychotic Disorder
.11 With Delusions[I,W]
.12 With Hallucinations[I,W]
292.84 Sedative-, Hypnotic-, or Anxiolytic-Induced Mood Disorder[I,W]
292.89 Sedative-, Hypnotic-, or Anxiolytic-Induced Anxiety Disorder[W]
292.89 Sedative-, Hypnotic-, or Anxiolytic-Induced Sexual Dysfunction[I]

292.89 Sedative-, Hypnotic-, or Anxiolytic-Induced Sleep Disorder[I,W]
292.9 Sedative-, Hypnotic-, or Anxiolytic-Related Disorder NOS

POLYSUBSTANCE-RELATED DISORDER
304.80 Polysubstance Dependence[a]

OTHER (OR UNKNOWN) SUBSTANCE-RELATED DISORDERS

Other (or Unknown) Substance Use Disorders
304.90 Other (or Unknown) Substance Dependence[a]
305.90 Other (or Unknown) Substance Abuse

Other (or Unknown) Substance–Induced Disorders
292.89 Other (or Unknown) Substance Intoxication
Specify if: With Perceptual Disturbances
292.0 Other (or Unknown) Substance Withdrawal
Specify if: With Perceptual Disturbances
292.81 Other (or Unknown) Substance–Induced Delirium
292.82 Other (or Unknown) Substance–Induced Persisting Dementia
292.83 Other (or Unknown) Substance–Induced Persisting Amnestic Disorder
292.xx Other (or Unknown) Substance–Induced Psychotic Disorder
.11 With Delusions[I,W]
.12 With Hallucinations[I,W]
292.84 Other (or Unknown) Substance–Induced Mood Disorder[I,W]
292.89 Other (or Unknown) Substance–Induced Anxiety Disorder[I,W]
292.89 Other (or Unknown) Substance–Induced Sexual Dysfunction[I]
292.89 Other (or Unknown) Substance–Induced Sleep Disorder[I,W]
292.9 Other (or Unknown) Substance–Related Disorder NOS

Schizophrenia and Other Psychotic Disorders

295.xx Schizophrenia

The following Classification of Longitudinal Course applies to all subtypes of Schizophrenia:

Episodic With Interepisode Residual Symptoms (*specify if:* With Prominent Negative Symptoms)/ Episodic With No Interepisode Residual Symptoms
Continuous (*specify if:* With Prominent Negative Symptoms)
Single Episode In Partial Remission (*specify if:* With Prominent Negative Symptoms)/Single Episode In Full Remission
Other or Unspecified Pattern

.30 Paranoid Type
.10 Disorganized Type
.20 Catatonic Type
.90 Undifferentiated Type
.60 Residual Type

295.40 Schizophreniform Disorder
Specify if: Without Good Prognostic Features/With Good Prognostic Features
295.70 Schizoaffective Disorder
Specify type: Bipolar Type/ Depressive Type
297.1 Delusional Disorder
Specify type: Erotomanic Type/ Grandiose Type/Jealous Type/ Persecutory Type/Somatic Type/ Mixed Type/Unspecified Type
298.8 Brief Psychotic Disorder
Specify if: With Marked Stressor(s)/Without Marked Stressor(s)/With Postpartum Onset
297.3 Shared Psychotic Disorder
293.xx Psychotic Disorder Due to . . . *[Indicate the General Medical Condition]*

.81 With Delusions
.82 With Hallucinations
——.– Substance-Induced Psychotic Disorder *(refer to Substance-Related Disorders for substance-specific codes)*
Specify if: With Onset During Intoxication/With Onset During Withdrawal
298.9 Psychotic Disorder NOS

Mood Disorders

Code current state of Major Depressive Disorder or Bipolar I Disorder in fifth digit:

1 = Mild
2 = Moderate
3 = Severe Without Psychotic Features
4 = Severe With Psychotic Features
Specify: Mood-Congruent Psychotic Features/Mood-Incongruent Psychotic Features
5 = In Partial Remission
6 = In Full Remission
0 = Unspecified

The following specifiers apply (for current or most recent episode) to Mood Disorders as noted:

[a]Severity/Psychotic/Remission Specifiers/[b]Chronic/[c]With Catatonic Features/[d]With Melancholic Features/[e]With Atypical Features/[f]With Postpartum Onset

The following specifiers apply to Mood Disorders as noted:

[g]With or Without Full Interepisode Recovery/ [h]With Seasonal Pattern/[i]With Rapid Cycling

DEPRESSIVE DISORDERS
296.xx Major Depressive Disorder,
.2x Single Episode[a,b,c,d,e,f]
.3x Recurrent[a,b,c,d,e,f,g,h]
300.4 Dysthymic Disorder
Specify if: Early Onset/Late Onset
Specify: With Atypical Features
311 Depressive Disorder NOS

BIPOLAR DISORDERS
296.xx Bipolar I Disorder,
.0x Single Manic Episode[a,c,f]
Specify if: Mixed
.40 Most Recent Episode Hypomanic[g,h,i]
.4x Most Recent Episode Manic[a,c,f,g,h,i]
.6x Most Recent Episode Mixed[a,c,f,g,h,i]
.5x Most Recent Episode Depressed[a,b,c,d,e,f,g,h,i]
.7 Most Recent Episode Unspecified[g,h,i]
296.89 Bipolar II Disorder[a,b,c,d,e,f,g,h,i]
Specify (current or most recent episode): Hypomanic/Depressed
301.13 Cyclothymic Disorder
296.80 Bipolar Disorder NOS

293.83 Mood Disorder Due to . . . *[Indicate the General Medical Condition]*
Specify type: With Depressive Features/With Major Depressive–Like Episode/With Manic Features/ With Mixed Features

——.– Substance-Induced Mood Disorder *(refer to Substance-Related Disorders for substance-specific codes)*
Specify type: With Depressive Features/With Manic Features/ With Mixed Features
Specify if: With Onset During Intoxication/With Onset During Withdrawal
296.90 Mood Disorder NOS

Anxiety Disorders

300.01 Panic Disorder Without Agoraphobia
300.21 Panic Disorder With Agoraphobia
300.22 Agoraphobia Without History of Panic Disorder
300.29 Specific Phobia
Specify type: Animal Type/Natural Environment Type/Blood-Injection-Injury Type/Situational Type/Other Type

300.23 Social Phobia
Specify if: Generalized
300.3 Obsessive-Compulsive Disorder
Specify if: With Poor Insight
309.81 Posttraumatic Stress Disorder
Specify if: Acute/Chronic
Specify if: With Delayed Onset
308.3 Acute Stress Disorder
300.02 Generalized Anxiety Disorder
293.89 Anxiety Disorder Due to . . . *[Indicate the General Medical Condition]*
Specify if: With Generalized Anxiety/ With Panic Attacks/With Obsessive-Compulsive Symptoms
—.– Substance-Induced Anxiety Disorder *(refer to Substance-Related Disorders for substance-specific codes)*
Specify if: With Generalized Anxiety/ With Panic Attacks/With Obsessive-Compulsive Symptoms/ With Phobic Symptoms
Specify if: With Onset During Intoxication/With Onset During Withdrawal
300.00 Anxiety Disorder NOS

Somatoform Disorders

300.81 Somatization Disorder
300.81 Undifferentiated Somatoform Disorder
300.11 Conversion Disorder
Specify type: With Motor Symptom or Deficit/With Sensory Symptom or Deficit/With Seizures or Convulsions/ With Mixed Presentation
307.xx Pain Disorder
.80 Associated With PsychologicalFactors
.89 Associated With Both Psychological Factors and a General Medical Condition
Specify if: Acute/Chronic
300.7 Hypochondriasis
Specify if: With Poor Insight
300.7 Body Dysmorphic Disorder
300.81 Somatoform Disorder NOS

Factitious Disorders

300.xx Factitious Disorder
.16 With Predominantly Psychological Signs and Symptoms
.19 With Predominantly Physical Signs and Symptoms
.19 With Combined Psychological and Physical Signs and Symptoms
300.19 Factitious Disorder NOS

Dissociative Disorders

300.12 Dissociative Amnesia
300.13 Dissociative Fugue
300.14 Dissociative Identity Disorder
300.6 Depersonalization Disorder
300.15 Dissociative Disorder NOS

Sexual and Gender Identity Disorders

SEXUAL DYSFUNCTIONS

The following specifiers apply to all primary Sexual Dysfunctions:

Lifelong Type/Acquired Type/ Generalized Type/Situational Type
Due to Psychological Factors/Due to Combined Factors

Sexual Desire Disorders
302.71 Hypoactive Sexual Desire Disorder
302.79 Sexual Aversion Disorder

Sexual Arousal Disorders
302.72 Female Sexual Arousal Disorder
302.72 Male Erectile Disorder

Orgasmic Disorders
302.73 Female Orgasmic Disorder
302.74 Male Orgasmic Disorder
302.75 Premature Ejaculation

Sexual Pain Disorders

302.76 Dyspareunia (Not Due to a General Medical Condition)

306.51 Vaginismus (Not Due to a General Medical Condition)

Sexual Dysfunction Due to a General Medical Condition

625.8 Female Hypoactive Sexual Desire Disorder Due to . . . *[Indicate the General Medical Condition]*

608.89 Male Hypoactive Sexual Desire Disorder Due to . . . *[Indicate the General Medical Condition]*

607.84 Male Erectile Disorder Due to . . . *[Indicate the General Medical Condition]*

625.0 Female Dyspareunia Due to . . . *[Indicate the General Medical Condition]*

608.89 Male Dyspareunia Due to . . . *[Indicate the General Medical Condition]*

625.8 Other Female Sexual Dysfunction Due to . . . *[Indicate the General Medical Condition]*

608.89 Other Male Sexual Dysfunction Due to . . . *[Indicate the General Medical Condition]*

—.– Substance-Induced Sexual Dysfunction *(refer to Substance-Related Disorders for substance-specific codes)*
Specify if: With Impaired Desire/ With Impaired Arousal/With Impaired Orgasm/With Sexual Pain
Specify if: With Onset During Intoxication

302.70 Sexual Dysfunction NOS

PARAPHILIAS

302.4 Exhibitionism

302.81 Fetishism

302.89 Frotteurism

302.2 Pedophilia
Specify if: Sexually Attracted to Males/ Sexually Attracted to Females/ Sexually Attracted to Both
Specify if: Limited to Incest
Specify type: Exclusive Type/ Nonexclusive Type

302.83 Sexual Masochism

302.84 Sexual Sadism

302.3 Transvestic Fetishism
Specify if: With Gender Dysphoria

302.82 Voyeurism

302.9 Paraphilia NOS

GENDER IDENTITY DISORDERS

302.xx Gender Identity Disorder
.6 in Children
.85 in Adolescents or Adults
Specify if: Sexually Attracted to Males/Sexually Attracted to Females/Sexually Attracted to Both/Sexually Attracted to Neither

302.6 Gender Identity Disorder NOS

302.9 Sexual Disorder NOS

Eating Disorders

307.1 Anorexia Nervosa
Specify type: Restricting Type; Binge-Eating/Purging Type

307.51 Bulimia Nervosa
Specify type: Purging Type/ Nonpurging Type

307.50 Eating Disorder NOS

Sleep Disorders

PRIMARY SLEEP DISORDERS

Dyssomnias

307.42 Primary Insomnia

307.44 Primary Hypersomnia
Specify if: Recurrent

347 Narcolepsy

780.59 Breathing-Related Sleep Disorder

307.45 Circadian Rhythm Sleep Disorder
Specify type: Delayed Sleep Phase Type/Jet Lag Type/Shift Work Type/ Unspecified Type

307.47 Dyssomnia NOS

Parasomnias

307.47 Nightmare Disorder

307.46 Sleep Terror Disorder

307.46 Sleepwalking Disorder

307.47 Parasomnia NOS

SLEEP DISORDERS RELATED TO ANOTHER MENTAL DISORDER

307.42 Insomnia Related to . . . *[Indicate the Axis I or Axis II Disorder]*
307.44 Hypersomnia Related to . . . *[Indicate the Axis I or Axis II Disorder]*

OTHER SLEEP DISORDERS

780.xx Sleep Disorder Due to . . . *[Indicate the General Medical Condition]*
.52 Insomnia Type
.54 Hypersomnia Type
.59 Parasomnia Type
.59 Mixed Type
——.– Substance-Induced Sleep Disorder *(refer to Substance-Related Disorders for substance-specific codes)*
Specify type: Insomnia Type/Hypersomnia Type/Parasomnia Type/Mixed Type
Specify if: With Onset During Intoxication/With Onset During Withdrawal

Impulse-Control Disorders Not Elsewhere Classified

312.34 Intermittent Explosive Disorder
312.32 Kleptomania
312.33 Pyromania
312.31 Pathological Gambling
312.39 Trichotillomania
312.30 Impulse-Control Disorder NOS

Adjustment Disorders

309.xx Adjustment Disorder
.0 With Depressed Mood
.24 With Anxiety
.28 With Mixed Anxiety and Depressed Mood
.3 With Disturbance of Conduct
.4 With Mixed Disturbance of Emotions and Conduct
.9 Unspecified
Specify if: Acute/Chronic

Personality Disorders

Note: *These are coded on Axis II.*
301.0 Paranoid Personality Disorder
301.20 Schizoid Personality Disorder
301.22 Schizotypal Personality Disorder
301.7 Antisocial Personality Disorder
301.83 Borderline Personality Disorder
301.50 Histrionic Personality Disorder
301.81 Narcissistic Personality Disorder
301.82 Avoidant Personality Disorder
301.6 Dependent Personality Disorder
301.4 Obsessive-Compulsive Personality Disorder
301.9 Personality Disorder NOS

Other Conditions That May Be a Focus of Clinical Attention

PSYCHOLOGICAL FACTORS AFFECTING MEDICAL CONDITION

316 *. . . [Specified Psychological Factor]Affecting . . . [Indicate the General Medical Condition]*
Choose name based on nature of factors:
Mental Disorder Affecting Medical Condition
Psychological Symptoms Affecting Medical Condition
Personality Traits or Coping Style Affecting Medical Condition
Maladaptive Health Behaviors Affecting Medical Condition
Stress-Related Physiological Response Affecting Medical Condition
Other or Unspecified Psychological Factors Affecting Medical Condition

MEDICATION-INDUCED MOVEMENT DISORDERS

332.1 Neuroleptic-Induced Parkinsonism
333.92 Neuroleptic Malignant Syndrome

333.7 Neuroleptic-Induced Acute Dystonia
333.99 Neuroleptic-Induced Acute Akathisia
333.82 Neuroleptic-Induced Tardive Dyskinesia
333.1 Medication-Induced Postural Tremor
333.90 Medication-Induced Movement Disorder NOS

OTHER MEDICATION- INDUCED DISORDER

995.2 Adverse Effects of Medication NOS

RELATIONAL PROBLEMS

V61.9 Relational Problem Related to a Mental Disorder or General Medical Condition
V61.20 Parent-Child Relational Problem
V61.1 Partner Relational Problem
V61.8 Sibling Relational Problem
V62.81 Relational Problem NOS

PROBLEMS RELATED TO ABUSE OR NEGLECT

V61.21 Physical Abuse of Child *(code 995.5 if focus of attention is on victim)*
V61.21 Sexual Abuse of Child *(code 995.5 if focus of attention is on victim)*
V61.21 Neglect of Child *(code 995.5 if focus of attention is on victim)*
V61.1 Physical Abuse of Adult *(code 995.81 if focus of attention is on victim)*
V61.1 Sexual Abuse of Adult *(code 995.81 if focus of attention is on victim)*

ADDITIONAL CONDITIONS THAT MAY BE A FOCUS OF CLINICAL ATTENTION

V15.81 Noncompliance With Treatment
V65.2 Malingering
V71.01 Adult Antisocial Behavior
V71.02 Child or Adolescent Antisocial Behavior
V62.89 Borderline Intellectual Functioning
Note: *This is coded on Axis II.*
780.9 Age-Related Cognitive Decline
V62.82 Bereavement
V62.3 Academic Problem
V62.2 Occupational Problem
313.82 Identity Problem
V62.89 Religious or Spiritual Problem
V62.4 Acculturation Problem
V62.89 Phase of Life Problem

Additional Codes

300.9 Unspecified Mental Disorder (nonpsychotic)
V71.09 No Diagnosis or Condition on Axis I
799.9 Diagnosis or Condition Deferred on Axis I
V71.09 No Diagnosis on Axis II
799.9 Diagnosis Deferred on Axis II

Multiaxial System

Axis I Clinical Disorders
Other Conditions That May Be a Focus of Clinical Attention
Axis II Personality Disorders
Mental Retardation
Axis III General Medical Conditions
Axis IV Psychosocial and Environmental Problems
Axis V Global Assessment of Functioning

The Last Word

DSM-IV is a forest with many, many, many trees. Very often, clinicians and students use it in a piecemeal fashion, referring only to the text for the particular disorder that most immediately comes to mind after seeing a given patient. The diagnostic process is generally more complicated and requires consideration of a number of different possibilities that might plausibly explain a given presentation. Therefore, it is important to grasp how the whole system is put together, not just the definitions of the individual disorders. The material provided in this chapter is meant to provide the reader with this kind of overview.

CHAPTER 5

The Nuts and Bolts of Using DSM-IV

DSM-IV is easy enough to use once clinicians get the hang of it. Unfortunately, however, getting the hang of it can take some doing. This *Guidebook,* and particularly this chapter, is meant to help. We hope to bridge the gap between the clinical evaluation of the patient and the process of making and coding a DSM-IV diagnosis. The format for this chapter follows a catechism of questions and answers.

How Do I Locate Disorder *X*?

Rarely does anyone read DSM-IV cover to cover. The more typical DSM-IV user wants to find the section of the book that most applies to the patient who has just been seen. Because DSM-IV is a big book, sometimes disorders seem to get lost within it. There are several ways of locating a disorder that seems to be trying to hide in the thicket of DSM-IV. For those familiar with the overall layout of DSM-IV, it is probably easiest to refer to the "DSM-IV Classification" to find the appropriate page number of the text and criteria for the disorder. Alternatively, the user can refer to the DSM-IV index. One advantage of the index is that the disorders are listed alphabetically both under their own name and also under the diagnostic grouping in which they appear in the manual (e.g., Social Phobia appears both under "S" and also under "A" within the listing for Anxiety Disorders).

Can I Ever Feel Comfortable With the DSM-IV Coding System?

The answer to this question is a resounding yes—in fact, it is really much easier than clinicians might think. Moreover, the accurate coding of the DSM-IV disorder is crucial. These codes are often used in determining reimbursement, in utilization review, and in aggregating statistics. Unfortunately, however, many DSM-IV users are intimidated by the apparent complexity of the system and defer to office staff or medical-record librarians. It may be refreshing to realize that you can learn the coding system with only a minimal investment of time and effort. If, however, you are one of the DSM-IV users who do not have a reason to report codes, you can skip this section.

The curious three- to five-digit codes that are in front of the names of the DSM-IV diagnoses are derived from the *International Classification of Diseases,* 9th Revision, Clinical Modification (ICD-9-CM), the official coding system for recording morbidity and mortality in the United States. Your next question (which we hear all the time) might be, What is the relationship between the DSM-IV codes and the ICD-9-CM codes? In fact, these are one and the same; there is no such thing as a separate DSM-IV code—all of the codes in DSM-IV are official ICD-9-CM codes. Your third question might be why the DSM-IV coding system starts at 290 and begins to fade out at 319 rather than achieving the decimal elegance of ranging between 1 and 100. This is because the DSM codes are only a small subset embedded within the complete ICD-9-CM coding system, which ranges all the way from 1 to 999. Finally, your fourth question might be why different DSM-IV disorders sometimes have the same code (e.g., 300.7 applies to both Body Dysmorphic Disorder and Hypochondriasis). Indeed, this overlap is unfortunate but unavoidable because the selection of diagnostic codes for DSM-IV was limited to those included in ICD-9-CM, which made fewer distinctions than now seem useful.

Despite its quirks (and there are many), the coding system works reasonably well. The best way to get an overview of coding in DSM-IV is to leaf through the DSM-IV Classification (see Chapter 4 in this book), which contains the names and codes for all of the disorders and conditions diagnosed on Axis I and Axis II. A few disorders have a three-digit code, and the rest have either four or five digits. Unfortunately, there is often no compelling rationale to explain why a given diagnostic code has a particular number of digits, nor is there a simple sequential order among the various diagnoses. That is because the numerical assignment of codes was based on the order of their listing in ICD-9, which differs from that in DSM-IV. Most often, the selection of the specific diagnostic code and term is fairly straightforward. However, some of the DSM-IV criteria sets have coding notes, and some disorders have text sections labeled "Recording Procedures"; these are included whenever more complicated coding problems are encountered.

The DSM-IV Classification has certain coding conventions. For instance, certain diagnostic codes contain an *x.* This indicates that the user must insert a specific digit in place of the *x* (usually indicating a subtype or the level of severity) when recording the diagnosis. For example, the DSM-IV Classification lists the diagnostic code for Major Depressive Disorder, Recurrent, as 296.3x. When actually recording the diagnostic code, the clinician must replace the *x* with a digit indicating the severity of the current Major Depressive Episode (296.31 for Mild, 296.32 for Moderate, 296.33 for Severe Without Psychotic Features, 296.34 for Severe With Psychotic Features, 296.35 for Partial Remission, 296.36 for Full Remission, and 296.30 for Unspecified). Furthermore, certain diagnoses are listed without any codes and instead are preceded by a "—.—" This notation indicates that the clinician must look somewhere else in the classification to find the appropriate diagnostic code. The most common use for this convention is as a placeholder for the generic substance-induced disorders, which are meant to be coded based on the specific substance that is involved. For example, the generic Substance-Induced Mood Disorder has "—.—" listed as its code. To get the diagnostic code for Cocaine-Induced Mood Disorder, however, the clinician must look in the Cocaine section for the specific code (i.e., 292.84).

Before DSM-IV, it was quite burdensome for the average clinician to provide codes for Axis III conditions. That was because these codes were available only in one or another version of the voluminous and expensive ICD-9-CM tabular list and index. To facilitate Axis III coding, DSM-IV includes in Appendix G the ICD-9-CM codes for the most frequently encountered and clinically significant general medical conditions. The list provided in Appendix G is necessarily an exercise in extreme condensation. The many thousands of ICD-9-CM diseases have been boiled down to a less specific but much more user-friendly list of several hundred conditions. Many of the listed codes are at the same level of specificity as they are in ICD-9-CM. An asterisk indicates those codes for which greater specificity is available in the complete ICD-9-CM volume.

For the real coding enthusiast, DSM-IV also includes three appendixes designed specifically to facilitate diagnostic coding. Appendix E lists the disorders alphabetically and is useful to retrieve quickly a diagnostic code without having to find its place in the classification. Appendix F lists the disorders sequentially based on the numeric code and is useful in locating the diagnostic term if only the code is known. Appendix H provides the DSM-IV classification with *International Statistical Classification of Diseases and Related Health Problems,* 10th Revision (ICD-10), codes instead of ICD-9-CM codes. When we began work on DSM-IV, we expected that it would be published with ICD-10 codes. However, this was not possible because the official implementation of the ICD-10 system by the U.S. government has been delayed by the vast retooling necessary to change systems. It is estimated that ICD-10 will not become official until at least the year 2000.

Fortunately, most DSM-IV diagnoses are easy to record and code. One just looks up the name and code from either the DSM-IV Classification or the appropriate section of the text. For some diagnoses (e.g., Schizophrenia, Mood Disorders), code selection depends on the particular subtype or specifier chosen. For example, the code listed in the classification for Schizophrenia is 295.xx. The full code depends on the particular subtype, such as 295.30 for Paranoid Type and 295.20 for Catatonic subtype. However, most of the subtypes and specifiers cannot be indicated in the coding system and can only be communicated by including them in the name of the disorder. In some cases, the name and code are considerably more complicated (e.g., Substance-Induced Disorders, Dementia of the Alzheimer's Type, Mood Disorders). Please refer to the specific coding notes placed within selected criteria sets and the "Recording Procedures" sections in DSM-IV for more information.

How Do I Indicate the Severity of a Disorder?

DSM-IV is really more useful for indicating the severity of a disorder than is commonly recognized. Many people are not aware that DSM-IV provides a generic set of severity and course specifiers (reproduced below) that are meant to be applied to all of the diagnoses in the system. This relative unawareness probably is because these specifiers are tucked away in the "Use of the Manual" section of DSM-IV and are not mentioned in conjunction with the individual disorders. The failure to note routinely the severity of a disorder is unfortunate because differences in severity account for a major portion of the heterogeneity of symptomatic presentation, prognosis, and treatment response and may also be involved in establishing eligibility for mental health benefits. It should be noted that a few diagnoses (i.e., Mental Retardation, Conduct Disorder, Major Depressive Episode, Manic Episode, Mixed Episode) have their own specially tailored severity and course definitions that take precedence over the following generic definitions:

Mild: Few, if any, symptoms in excess of those required to make the diagnosis, and symptoms result in no more than minor impairment in social or occupational functioning.

Moderate: Symptoms or functional impairment between "mild" and "severe."

Severe: Many symptoms in excess of those required to make the diagnosis, or several symptoms that are particularly severe, are present, or the symptoms result in marked impairment in social or occupational functioning.

In Partial Remission: The full criteria for the disorder were previously met, but currently only some of the symptoms or signs of the illness remain.

In Full Remission: There are no longer any symptoms or signs of the disorder, but it is still clinically relevant to note the disorder—for example, in an individual with previous episodes of Bipolar Disorder who has been symptom-free on lithium for the past 3 years. After a period of time in full remission, the clinician may judge the individual to be recovered and, therefore, would no longer code the disorder as a current diagnosis. The differentiation of In Full Remission from recovered requires consideration of many factors, including the characteristic course of the disorder, the length of time since the last period of disturbance, the total duration of the disturbance, and the need for continued evaluation or prophylactic treatment.

Prior History: For some purposes, it may be useful to note a history of the criteria having been met for a disorder even when the individual is considered to be recovered from it. Such past diagnoses of mental disorder would be indicated by using the specifier Prior History (e.g., Separation Anxiety Disorder, Prior History, for an individual with a history of Separation Anxiety Disorder who has no current disorder or who currently meets criteria for Panic Disorder).

The specifiers Mild, Moderate, and Severe should be used only when the full criteria for the disorder are currently met. Although these specifiers are meant to describe the current presentation, DSM-IV does not actually provide a precise definition of the time frame to be included within the term *current.* If the assessment of severity is limited to the moment of the examination, it may misleadingly ignore recent exacerbations that are important in planning management or treatment. The particular time frame should reflect what is most important in a given clinical situation. For example, if the individual made a suicide attempt just a few days ago, the designation Severe may apply despite the fact that the individual's clinical state during the interview does not reflect immediate suicidality. One rule of thumb is to rate what has been the most severe aspect of the presentation during the past month.

When the individual's presentation improves so that the some criteria are still present but the full criteria are no longer met, the specifier In Partial Remission can be used. Although this specifier often indicates that considerable improvement has occurred, it should be noted that technically all that is required is a decrement of one symptom below the diagnostic threshold. Not infrequently, the presentation may indicate that the disorder is In Partial Remission, but this is small consolation to the patient whose remaining symptoms may continue to be quite devastating. For example, a patient might have gone from having six of the nine symptoms of Major Depressive Disorder to having four of the symptoms, but he or she could still be so incapacitated by the remaining symptoms that continued hospitalization is necessary. In such situations, it is up to the clinician to decide whether to follow the literal definition of In Partial Remission or its spirit.

If the improvement is such that no criteria are present, several options are available: 1) use of the specifier In Full Remission, 2) use of the specifier Prior History, and 3) no longer recording anything about that diagnosis. People often wonder how to draw the line between In Full Remission and recovered. This distinction may be important in determining whether to continue maintenance treatment and may also impact on how patients feel about themselves and how they are regarded by others. The question is particularly controversial in regard to Substance Dependence; some clinicians believe that it is unwise for patients ever to consider themselves fully recovered. In fact, *recovered* is not an official DSM-IV designation but instead refers to the situation in which the diagnosis would no longer be noted.

The specifier In Full Remission can be applied for any duration (even for life) after the individual with a DSM-IV disorder has fully improved. Such a designation has the value of alerting the individual and the clinician to the possible treatment and prognostic implications of ever having had the disorder. It would not make sense to define anyone who required continued treatment or prophylactic intervention as recovered. However, use of the specifier In Full Remission must be balanced against the possible negative consequences of perpetually including the diagnosis as part of the diagnostic evaluation. That may be misleading (and stigmatizing), particularly for disorders that are less likely to recur. For example, it would be foolish to continue to record Separation Anxiety Disorder, In Full Remission, for a 50-year-old who had Separation Anxiety Disorder many years before as a child.

Even though a patient may have completely recovered from a disorder, it may sometimes be useful to note that he or she has a history of the disorder. For example, it is nice to be able to report that a patient had an episode of Major Depressive Disorder 3 years ago and there are no current symptoms and no requirement for maintenance treatment. There was no way of indicating this common clinical situation in DSM-III-R other than perpetuating the diagnosis of Major Depressive Disorder in Full Remission.

DSM-IV has introduced a new course specifier, Prior History, to describe individuals like the one just mentioned who have recovered from their disorder. Indicating the specifier Prior History may be particularly useful in predicting prognosis and in studies exploring lifetime comorbidity and risk factors for current disorders.

Something of a hole exists in this system of course specifiers. There is no available designation for someone who was in full remission and now has a return of symptoms, although not to the extent that the full criteria are again met. These partial relapses occur frequently in clinical practice. It is very important for both patients and clinicians to be alert to the early signs of a possible recurrence so that a timely intervention may be instituted. The specifier In Partial Remission does not apply to this situation because it requires that the individual is recovering after having fully met the criteria. The possible addition to the course specifiers of the term *in partial relapse* was considered and rejected because the term implied an unwarranted degree of certainty that the full clinical picture would eventually return. Instead, DSM-IV suggests that the following clinical judgment be made when the patient has a partial return of symptoms. If the clinician feels fairly confident that a new episode is in the making, it is possible to make the diagnosis even if the usual thresholds are not met. For example, the clinician should not feel compelled to wait for a full week of manic symptoms to diagnose a recurrence of Bipolar Disorder in someone with a well-established previous history who has had several days of severe grandiose mood, increased activity, and sleeplessness. Alternatively, the partial recurrence may be indicated by the specifier *provisional* (e.g., Bipolar Disorder, Most Recent Episode Manic [Provisional]) or by citing the appropriate Not Otherwise Specified category (e.g., Bipolar Disorder NOS).

One of the weaknesses of the DSM system has been its excessive emphasis on the cross-sectional symptom presentation at the expense of providing information concerning the longer term course features of the disorder. Often, the past history of the disorder is the best predictor of the future course and response to treatment. In this regard, DSM-III and DSM-III-R did not really live up to their reputation for being "Kraepelinian" because the essence of Kraepelin's classification method was the emphasis on course. There were two reasons for this relative lack of emphasis on course features in defining disorders. First, there was the assumption that the assessment of lifetime psychopathology would be inherently much less reliable than that of cross-sectional symptom presentation. Second, it was believed that current symptoms would be more relevant for treatment planning.

Although far from ideal, DSM-IV does pay more attention to course than other classification systems. The text sections describing the characteristic course of each disorder were expanded and cover the following:

1. Age at onset
2. Mode of onset (e.g., sudden, insidious)
3. Whether the disorder is typified by a single episode, recurrent episodes with symptom-free periods, or a continuous course
4. The number of episodes and their typical duration
5. Overall progression of the condition (e.g., worsening or improving with age)
6. If there is more than one condition, the temporal sequencing of those conditions

Also, for certain disorders (Schizophrenia, Major Depressive Disorder and Bipolar Disorder, Substance Dependence), special sets of course specifiers are provided. Finally, as discussed above, Prior History has been included as a course specifier.

Why Does DSM-IV Have so Many Subtypes and Specifiers?

The criteria sets for each disorder in DSM-IV are intended to identify individuals who share features that are likely to predict commonalities in course, family history, laboratory results, and treatment response. However, there is often considerable heterogeneity even among individuals who have the same disorder. For many DSM-IV disorders, subtypes and specifiers have been provided to increase the diagnostic specificity. The subtypes and specifiers are meant to identify interesting subgroups of patients based on differences in symptomatic presentation, age at onset, course, severity, or etiology. Unfortunately, however, because the coding system (i.e., ICD-9-CM) is difficult to modify, most of the subtypes and specifiers do not have separate codes. By now, the reader must be wondering what the difference is between a subtype and a specifier. In fact, although DSM-IV maintains a distinction between these terms, it is really somewhat esoteric, and, for all intents and purposes, you can consider them to be equivalent.

Although all of the subtypes and specifiers appear in the DSM-IV Classification as if they were of equal diagnostic importance, this is far from being the case. Some of the subtypes and specifiers are defined with complete criteria sets (e.g., in the Schizophrenia section, there are separate criteria sets for Paranoid Type, Catatonic Type, Disorganized Type, Undifferentiated Type, and Residual Type), whereas others are described in only a few words. Perhaps the most important specifiers in the whole system are those contained in the "Mood Disorders" section because these specifiers reduce much of the symptomatic heterogeneity of the various mood disorders and have significant treatment implications.

For an overview of all of the subtypes and specifiers included in DSM-IV, refer to the DSM-IV Classification that concludes Chapter 4 in this book. Subtypes are indicated by the instruction "specify type," whereas specifiers are indicated by the instruction "specify if."

Who Is at Fault if I Have To Use a Not Otherwise Specified Category—Me or DSM-IV?

Neither! The Not Otherwise Specified (NOS) category has been the unfairly maligned stepchild of the DSM-IV system. We must admit that we are rather fond of NOS categories and would encourage clinicians to use them with pride and understanding. Although the DSM-IV categories are successful in covering the majority of presentations seen in clinical practice, it is no great surprise that patients often fall between the cracks. Nature did not choose to craft psychiatric disorders into neat little packages with clear boundaries. The NOS categories provide a means for adapting the necessarily simplified DSM system to the richness, variety, and complexity encountered in everyday clinical practice.

DSM-IV includes 57 NOS categories in the system (see the DSM-IV Classification in Chapter 4 in this book to review the wide range of NOS categories that are a part of the system). Clinicians are often uncomfortable making a NOS diagnosis and may become frustrated with the DSM system because it does not provide a category that completely captures the particularities of each patient's presentation. However, to describe successfully every conceivable patient presentation, it would probably be necessary to include twice as many diagnoses as we have in DSM-IV, making the system impossibly cumbersome. The NOS categories that appear throughout the manual provide an appropriate solution for diagnostic quandaries at the boundaries between disorders and in other uncertain situations.

In the following instances, the clinician should make the appropriate NOS diagnosis with confidence and without shame:

Subthreshold presentations. The categorical nature of the DSM system requires the establishment of specific cut points below which the diagnosis does not apply. Although these cut points are necessary to provide a convention for clinical and research communication, they are to a great degree arbitrary. They must be taken with a grain of salt and used with clinical judgment. The thresholds established for most of the DSM-IV disorders were originally chosen as best guesses arrived at by expert consensus. The empirical review conducted for DSM-IV allowed us to determine how well most of these guesses have performed and served as a basis for making decisions concerning the thresholds to be included in DSM-IV.

Each threshold was established to provide an optimal balance between false-positive and false-negative diagnoses. To avoid excessive false-positives, the thresholds had to be set relatively high, necessarily resulting in unavoidable false-negatives. Therefore, it should not be surprising that some individuals fall shy of the DSM-IV symptom or duration thresholds but nonetheless have a clinically significant condition that warrants diagnosis. For example, an individual with three of nine depressive symptoms lasting all day, every day, for 2 weeks does not meet the criteria for Major Depressive Disorder but may have sufficient clinically significant impairment to warrant a diagnosis of Depressive Disorder NOS. Some of the research criteria sets included in Appendix B refer to subthreshold presentations that can be diagnosed in DSM-IV by using the appropriate NOS categories (e.g., Cognitive Disorder NOS for mild neurocognitive disorder, Depressive Disorder NOS for minor depressive disorder and recurrent brief depressive disorder, Anxiety Disorder NOS for mixed anxiety-depressive disorder).

"Other" presentations. As discussed above, it was not possible for DSM-IV to include every conceivably useful syndrome. In fact, the threshold for including new disorders in DSM-IV was set quite high so that very few new conditions were added. Research criteria sets for several potentially useful categories that were not added as official categories in DSM-IV appear in Appendix B (Criteria Sets and Axes Provided for Further Study). The appropriate NOS category can be used for recording these presentations when they are clinically significant.

Many of these Appendix B categories are also listed as examples under the appropriate NOS designation (e.g., caffeine withdrawal under Caffeine-Related Disorder NOS, postpsychotic depressive disorder of Schizophrenia under Depressive Disorder NOS, premenstrual dysphoric disorder under Depressive Disorder NOS). Simple deteriorative disorder (simple Schizophrenia) is the only Appendix B condition that is not mentioned as an example of a particular NOS category; instead, it is designated as an Unspecified Mental Disorder (see the "Additional Codes" section of DSM-IV, p. 687). This is because the presenting symptoms in simple deteriorative disorder (i.e., deterioration without any history of psychotic symptoms) fall between the cracks of the major categories in DSM-IV. This presentation cannot be considered a Psychotic Disorder NOS because there are no psychotic symptoms; also it cannot be considered a Personality Disorder NOS because of the ongoing deteriorating course.

Uncertainty whether the disorder is primary, substance-induced, or due to a general medical condition. DSM-IV emphasizes the need to decide whether the presenting symptomatology is due to the direct physiological effects of substance use or a general medical condition before assuming that it is a primary disorder. The use of the term *due to* is meant to establish that there is a fairly high degree of certainty that the substance use or the general medical condition is causing the psychopathology. Unfortunately, many clinical situations are not so clear-cut. Very frequently, it can be established that substance use or a general medical condition is present, but it is much more difficult to establish that it is causative (see Chapter 7 of this book for a discussion of guidelines to help make this differential diagnosis). For example, you should feel comfortable making a diagnosis of Depressive Disorder NOS when depressive symptoms co-occur with a general medical condition or medication, but it is not clear whether the symptoms are actually due to the medication or general medical condition.

Insufficient information to make a more specific diagnosis. It is part of everyday clinical life that a diagnostic statement must be made before all the relevant diagnostic information can be gathered. Initial evaluations (especially in emergency room settings) are particularly likely to result in insufficient information. It is inherently difficult to extract in one sitting all the information necessary to determine whether the criteria for a specific condition are met. Making a diagnosis is especially challenging when the patient is a poor informant, when the family and the treating clinician are unavailable, or when old charts are inaccessible. Sometimes the problem is not that there is too little information, but rather that the different sources conflict with one another and provide multiple contradictory views of the clinical situation.

Fortunately, it is almost always possible to place the patient within a particular group of disorders (e.g., Anxiety Disorder NOS) even if it is not possible to select the particular diagnosis from within that group. In some cases, the only definitive diagnostic judgment that can be made is whether or not the individual is psychotic. If so, Psychotic NOS would be indicated. Otherwise, Unspecified Mental Disorder can be used to indicate that a nonpsychotic mental disorder is present but that its nature cannot be more specifically described (see DSM-IV, p. 687). Such a designation, although not as complete or specific as one might desire, nonetheless conveys quite a bit of useful information that may impact on decision making.

DSM-IV provides additional options for indicating diagnostic uncertainty. Sometimes, there is enough information so that the clinician is on the verge of making a particular diagnosis, but the clinching piece of information is still missing. In such situations, the clinician has the option of either sticking with the appropriate NOS category (e.g., Depressive Disorder NOS) or making the diagnosis but indicating the remaining uncertainty with the specifier *provisional* (e.g., Major Depressive Disorder, Single Episode [Provisional]). Finally, in some situations it is currently impossible to make any judgment as to the presence of an Axis I or an Axis II disorder. In such cases, Diagnosis Deferred on Axis I or Diagnosis Deferred on Axis II can be indicated (with the code 799.9). This designation is more commonly used for Axis II diagnoses because of the difficulty in evaluating Personality Disorders in the presence of Axis I conditions.

How Do I Know if It Is Okay To Make Two Diagnoses at the Same Time?

Patients often have clinical presentations that meet the diagnostic criteria for more than one DSM-IV disorder. DSM-IV permits multiple diagnoses to be made unless there are specific exclusions that are indicated within the criteria sets. We indicate the interpretation of the following exclusion criteria, which might appear in a hypothetical Disorder A:

1. The disturbance is not due to the direct physiological effects of a substance (e.g., a drug of abuse, a medication) or a general medical condition. This is the most important exclusion criterion in that it alerts the clinician to this crucial differential diagnostic consideration. This issue is discussed in much more detail in Chapter 7. For a given episode of psychopathology, substance-induced or general medical etiologies take precedence over a diagnosis of a primary disorder. For example, if a patient has an episode of depression that is judged to be due to withdrawal from cocaine, the diagnosis is Cocaine-Induced Mood Disorder, and no separate diagnosis of Major Depressive Disorder need be given.

2. The disturbance has never met the criteria for disorder B. This is the most absolute exclusion criterion and is used in relatively few disorders in DSM-IV. This exclusion criterion is used to define a lifetime hierarchy between disorder A and disorder B so that once disorder B is diagnosed, the clinician can never make a diagnosis of disorder A. For example, once a diagnosis of Bipolar Disorder is made, it preempts a diagnosis of Major Depressive Disorder for the rest of the individual's life. Similarly, Substance Abuse is preempted if there has ever been a diagnosis of Substance Dependence, and Delusional Disorder is preempted if there has ever been a diagnosis of Schizophrenia.

3. The disturbance does not occur exclusively during the course of disorder B. This is the most common exclusion criterion in DSM-IV. It is used to avoid multiple diagnoses and artifactual comorbidity when the presentation is better considered as an associated feature of another more pervasive disorder. This criterion prohibits disorder A from being diagnosed when its symptom presentation occurs only during the course of disorder B. For example, Conversion Disorder is not diagnosed separately if it occurs only during Somatization Disorder because the defining pseudoneurological symptoms of Conversion Disorder are included in the criteria set for Somatization Disorder. Similarly, Dysthymic Disorder is not diagnosed separately if it occurs exclusively during the course of Schizophrenia because chronic dysphoria is so frequently an associated feature of Schizophrenia.

It should be noted that the phrase *course of another disorder* is meant to include not just periods when the full criteria are met, but also periods of partial remission. For example, it may make clinical sense to continue to exclude a separate diagnosis of Primary Insomnia in an individual who has a partial remission from Major Depressive Disorder. It should be noted that the phrase *exclusively during* implies that the clinician should diagnose disorder A if it occurs independently of disorder B (e.g., when disorder B is in full remission).

4. The disturbance is not better accounted for by disorder B. This criterion serves to alert the clinician to other disorders that may account for the presenting symptom. In contrast to the previous exclusion criteria, this criterion allows for the diagnosis of both disorder A and disorder B if the clinician judges that both are present. For example, the Sexual Dysfunctions include a criterion stating that they should not be diagnosed if they are better accounted for by another disorder (e.g., Mood Disorder). This criterion is included because sexual dysfunctions are often an associated feature of a Mood Disorder and in such cases would not warrant a separate diagnosis. However, there are situations in which it makes clinical sense to give both diagnoses (e.g., when the sexual dysfunction is the main focus of attention or when it predates the Mood Disorder). The phrase *not better accounted for* leaves the decision up to the clinician.

How Does the Situation in Which I Use DSM-IV Affect Its Use?

The strength of, but also a potential problem with, the DSM-IV criteria sets is that they are generic enough to apply to a wide range of patient populations and settings. In the remainder of this chapter, we discuss the special issues and problems that may arise when using DSM-IV in specific contexts.

Developmental Contexts

The DSM-IV Task Force considered the question of whether a single criteria set could successfully encompass the presentations of any given disorder across all stages of the life cycle. The literature reviews suggested that for the most part the presentations of psychiatric disorders are essentially equivalent whether they occur in the childhood, adulthood, or geriatric phases of development.

Certainly, for some disorders, however, differences in the symptomatic presentations and types of impairment are related to differences in cognitive and physical capacities and in role expectations at different developmental stages. For example, depressed children are less likely to state that they are experiencing depressed mood and instead are more likely to complain of somatic symptomatology. Similarly, children with Obsessive-Compulsive Disorder are less likely than adults to have insight into the fact that their repetitive thoughts or behaviors are excessive or unreasonable. Psychotic disorders with a later age at onset are more likely to be associated with sensory deficits and to include delusions and hallucinations with persecutory content (rather than disorganized and negative symptoms). Impairment in occupational functioning takes different forms in children (e.g., schoolwork), adults (e.g., job functioning), and the geriatric population (e.g., hobbies during retirement). For very good reasons, DSM-IV provides generic criteria sets that apply across the developmental spectrum. However, differences in presentation are indicated either in notes to the criteria set or in the DSM-IV text section devoted to "Culture, Age, and Gender Features."

Sex Ratio: Gender Bias or Clinical Reality?

It is of considerable interest that a number of psychiatric disorders have markedly different rates of occurrence in women and men. There are two possible contributions to these apparent gender differences. There seem to be true gender differences in the occurrence of certain conditions (e.g., Paraphilias). On the other hand, at least some gender differences are probably an artifactual result of biases in ascertainment, definition, or assessment. Gender differences in treatment-seeking or referral patterns may explain the different gender ratios that occur in community samples as opposed to more selected clinical samples. For example, there is a higher ratio of women with Major Depressive Disorder in clinical samples than in epidemiological samples, perhaps because women are more likely to recognize and admit to depression. In contrast, there is a higher ratio of men with Schizophrenia in clinical samples than in epidemiological samples, perhaps because men with Schizophrenia are more disruptive and likely to require treatment intervention.

Biases in definition may also play a role in gender differences in prevalence (e.g., the specific items selected in the criteria sets for Conduct Disorder may underdiagnose females, whereas the criteria set for Histrionic Personality Disorder may overdiagnose females). There may also be gender differences in prevalence due to biases in the evaluator that may lead to misinterpretation of the diagnostic criteria. The DSM-IV text sections describe what is known about gender differences in presentation and frequency, when this information is pertinent.

Different Cultural Contexts

Because DSM-IV is used in many countries across the world as well as with the vast number of different cultural groups who have migrated to the United States, great attention was devoted to ensuring that DSM-IV be applicable cross-culturally. Although the major syndromes in their broad definition are probably ubiquitous expressions of human nature, the specific presentations of these disorders may be very much influenced by contextual cultural influences. Any diagnostic system that emphasizes the generic aspects of human nature will miss important particularities, and any system that is too attentive to the particularities may include relatively minor distinctions and miss central generic features.

In DSM-IV, there is an attempt to strike a balance between generic and culturally specific features. The DSM criteria sets are stated in general enough terms to be cross-culturally useful. However, the specific cultural manifestations are described within a text section devoted to special aspects of cross-cultural presentation. Moreover, Appendix I in DSM-IV catalogs the best described "culture-bound" syndromes and, in some cases, indicates their possible relationships to DSM-IV disorders. Culture-bound syndromes (an admittedly unfortunate term) are clinical presentations that are found in particular societies or cultural areas. This listing may be particularly useful for the clinician trying to understand atypical presentations found in unfamiliar cultural groups. Appendix I also includes an "Outline for Cultural Formulation," which guides the clinician in assessing those issues that are most critical to understanding the impact of the cultural context: 1) the cultural identity of the individual, 2) cultural explanations of the individual's illness (e.g., common idioms through which symptoms are expressed), 3) cultural factors related to psychosocial environment and functions (e.g., role of religion and kin in providing support), 4) cultural elements of the relationship between the individual and the clinician (e.g., differences in social status or culture), and 5) overall cultural assessment for diagnosis and care. Probably the most common clinical error related to cultural factors is to diagnose inappropriately as psychotic experiences those experiences that are a recognized part of a culture that the evaluator is unfamiliar with (e.g., voice of a dead relative, feelings of being possessed by spirits).

Forensic Contexts

It is actually quite remarkable (and somewhat unsettling) how often DSM-IV makes an appearance in the courtroom. No doubt these frequent appearances partly reflect the usefulness of the diagnostic system in helping to inform discussions on issues regarding civil commitment, competence, criminal responsibility, and the establishment of damages in tort cases. Unfortunately, however, the diagnostic system is often incorrectly applied in forensic contexts. It must be noted that there is something of a mismatch between the goals and limitations of the DSM-IV and the requirements of the legal system. DSM-IV is a clinical document that is intended for collegial use in an atmosphere that is very different from the adversarial nature of the typical forensic proceeding.

Statements in DSM-IV can be read out of context to make points that may be much at odds with the thrust of its use in clinical practice. Most legal questions require a black-and-white dichotomization that is very much at odds with the shades of gray that characterize most clinical situations. Moreover, there is a tendency in legal settings to assume that the assigning of a diagnostic label implies that all of the prototypical features of the disorder apply to the particular individual who is the focus of the legal question. In fact, clinical presentations of any given diagnosis are quite heterogeneous so that two individuals with the same DSM-IV diagnosis can and do differ in many ways that are likely to be important in answering any forensic question (e.g., legal responsibility). Perhaps most fundamentally, the clinical definition of mental disorder in DSM-IV is not at all equivalent to legal definitions of *mental disorder, mental disability, mental disease,* and *mental defect.*

Although DSM-IV must often be used in forensic settings, this should always be done with caution, common sense, and the awareness that the adversarial system may result in distortions. A few particularly egregious examples of the misuse of the diagnostic system in recent years include 1) claiming that what were previously considered rare diagnoses (e.g., Dissociative Amnesia, Dissociative Identity Disorder) are very common explanations for criminal behavior that might absolve individuals of responsibility; 2) overuse of Posttraumatic Stress Disorder to increase damage awards and disability entitlement and to diminish criminal responsibility; and 3) credulous acceptance that all individuals who "recover" memories of earlier sexual and physical abuse qualify for a diagnosis of Dissociative Amnesia for events that actually occurred, rather than wondering whether at least some of these individuals are displaying "false memory" as a result of suggestion or the fallibility of memory of earlier life experiences.

Medical Benefits and Reimbursement Contexts

We are often asked whether the DSM-IV decisions were influenced by concerns about their possible impact on benefits and reimbursement. In fact, this issue did not influence DSM-IV in any way. During the preparation of DSM-IV, we received many requests from clinicians, legislators, and patient advocacy groups that the DSM-IV Task Force specify which of the disorders contained within the system should confer eligibility for medical benefits under insurance coverage. They suggested two standards as possible criteria in demarcating those disorders that would presumably deserve coverage: that the disorder be "biological" and/or that it be "severe and persistent."

The DSM-IV Task Force rejected this request to establish boundaries for reimbursement as outside its purview and fraught with internal contradictions. Particularly impossible (and foolhardy) would be any attempt to distinguish between "biological" and "nonbiological" mental disorders. All of the DSM-IV disorders have both biological and psychosocial elements that render meaningless this anachronistic distinction. In recognition of this false distinction, DSM-IV has eliminated terms such as *organic, psychogenic, functional,* and for the most part *physical* (see Chapter 7 of this book for a further discussion of these issues). It is almost equally impossible to declare that certain disorders are necessarily severe and persistent, and others are not. Although many of the DSM-IV disorders may sometimes present in milder forms, all of the disorders can and do present in a severe and persistent form with marked impairment and needs for treatment. The determination of thresholds for entitlement to medical benefits is a public policy issue that requires consideration far beyond the diagnosis alone.

How Do I Include DSM-IV in My Diagnostic Evaluation?

The diagnostic criteria included in DSM-III had a rapid and profound impact on clinical diagnosis. The DSM system has become an important source for the dissemination of information on psychopathology. Without necessarily being aware of its influence, most clinicians are now imbued not only with the content of the DSM-IV criteria sets but also with a different method of interviewing patients and eliciting psychopathology. Compared with pre-DSM-III days, clinical evaluations are now much more likely to be more semistructured and less open-ended. Clinicians are much more likely to ask specific questions to elicit the symptom and course information necessary to make a DSM diagnosis. Of course, evaluations have many purposes other than just determining a DSM-IV diagnosis, but no evaluation is complete unless the diagnostic questions are also asked.

The first step in learning how to conduct a diagnostic evaluation is to become thoroughly familiar with the diagnostic criteria sets, particularly the sets for those disorders clinicians are most likely to encounter frequently. The next step is to incorporate those criteria sets into the clinical interview. It is often useful, after the interview and before making the diagnosis, to glance at the pertinent criteria sets and evaluate which items describe the patient's presentation.

A more systematic way of learning psychiatric diagnosis makes use of standardized questions that were developed as part of semistructured interview procedures. Because many clinicians may not be familiar with these procedures, we describe them here. Semistructured interview instruments (e.g., Structured Clinical Interview for DSM [SCID], Schedule for Clinical Assessment in Neuropsychiatry [SCAN]) were developed mostly for research purposes to provide a comprehensive, systematic, and reliable method for making psychiatric diagnoses. Although not meant primarily for general clinical use, these instruments will almost undoubtedly find greater and greater clinical application in the future as the need for standardized assessment procedure is increasingly recognized.

The term *instrument* makes these procedures sound more invasive and arcane than they really are. Just as Alice in Wonderland realized that the King and Queen were just faces on a deck of cards, these instruments are no more than a series of useful questions that serve to tap the psychopathology embodied in the DSM-IV diagnostic criteria. Thus, the repeated use of these instruments will serve to expand the clinician's repertoire of interview questions as well as structure his or her evaluation procedure.

The term *semistructured* is used to indicate that clinical judgment is at the heart of these interviews and that what distinguishes them from fully structured interviews and patient self-report measures is the considerable latitude given to the clinician in following up on the diagnostic leads that emerge from the patient's initial replies to the questions. Although the interviews help to increase consistency, they are not meant to squelch creativity and the art of clinical practice. Thus, working with a given patient, no two clinicians conducting semistructured interviews will ask exactly the same questions, although it is hoped that they will arrive at the same diagnostic conclusion.

Other tools are available to assist the diagnostic process in clinical practice, and they may become increasingly important in the emerging managed care environment. Several computer programs have been developed to assist in the application of the DSM-IV criteria. Some programs can interact directly with the patient at the keyboard to collect clinical data. Other programs provide guidance in the application of the DSM-IV diagnostic algorithms after the clinical interview has been completed. Such programs can serve to educate the clinician about the diagnostic process, ensure that a comprehensive evaluation has been conducted, and document the diagnostic status of the patient.

All of these issues may sound quite imposing, but in fact DSM-IV is learned almost effortlessly by most clinicians. All clinicians need to do is to make a habit of keeping the book handy and referring to it after clinical evaluations.

How Do I Become a Good Diagnostician?

Great diagnosticians are partly born, partly trained, and partly tempered in the crucible of clinical experience. Each of these ingredients is necessary, but none is sufficient by itself. Diagnostic skill is not just the rote application of algorithms. Otherwise, we could relegate the diagnostic task to computer programs. Although computers can be helpful in data collection and algorithmic application, they lack common sense and clinical judgment. Our guess is that computers are (and for the foreseeable future will remain) sufficiently clueless about the nuances of human experience to be lousy diagnosticians if forced to operate on their own.

The natural talent for sizing people up must be educated with both book learning and clinical experience. In the optimal situation, these are done simultaneously. Patients are seen by day, and their conditions are studied by night. In a fairly linear way, the more patients you see and the more you read about them, the better a diagnostician you become. Because patients with the same diagnosis are treated in dramatically different settings, it is helpful, especially for trainees, to be exposed to the widest possible array of treatment settings. It is also important to follow patients over time to become familiar with the various aspects of the presentation that may be most characteristic during the evolution of its course. We have found DSM-IV to be an excellent framework for organizing and enriching our clinical experience. We hope the *Guidebook* will also serve this purpose.

The Last Word

Perhaps the most important rule in applying DSM-IV is not to take the rules so seriously that one's clinical judgment is blinded. The "Introduction" indicates that DSM-IV is meant to be a useful guide to psychiatric diagnosis and not a bible or cookbook. For example, if a given patient falls short by just one criterion of meeting a diagnosis but has each of the presenting items at a definite, enduring, and severe level, he or she probably deserves to be given that diagnosis every bit as much as does another patient who meets the suggested number of criteria, but each only at a minimal level.

If clinicians do not exercise clinical judgment, they will be slavishly following a system with admittedly and necessarily arbitrary boundaries. On the other hand, the excessively flexible and idiosyncratic application of the system (or ignorance of it) substantially reduces its utility as a common language for communication among clinicians and across the research-clinical interface.

CHAPTER 6

The Yeas and Nays of the Multiaxial System

A DSM-IV multiaxial evaluation involves an assessment on five different *axes,* each of which refers to a different domain of information that may be important in treatment planning and in the prediction of outcome. Axes I, II, and III are diagnostic axes. Axis I is for coding all of the psychiatric disorders (except for Personality Disorders and Mental Retardation, which are coded on Axis II). Axis III is for coding all clinically relevant general medical conditions. Axes IV and V are nondiagnostic axes. Axis IV is for noting clinically relevant psychosocial and environmental problems. Axis V is for indicating the individual's overall psychological, social, and occupational functioning.

In some circles, the multiaxial system engenders fierce loyalty and is the most revered innovation of DSM-III; in others, it engenders fierce opposition and cries for its abolition. As is usually the case, both seemingly polar points of view capture part of the truth, but each also misses an equally important perspective. If it is understood and applied correctly, the multiaxial system is a wonderfully useful way of gathering and communicating a full-bodied and systematic picture of the patient. Unfortunately, however, people can take the sorting of diagnoses into distinct axes far too seriously, leading to mistaken notions about the relationships among psychiatric disorders and between psychiatric disorders and other medical conditions.

The multiaxial system was developed to address several problems.

The first had to do with the tendency to overlook important clinical conditions when they were not a prominent part of the presenting problem. In adults, underlying personality disorders were often missed when clinical attention was drawn to the more florid presenting symptomatology (e.g., psychotic symptoms, depression). Similarly, a number of studies have demonstrated that psychiatric patients presenting in mental health settings have relatively high rates of general medical conditions that are often missed. The solution introduced by DSM-III was to cut the diagnostic pie into three pieces: Axis II for Personality and Developmental Disorders, Axis III for general medical conditions, and Axis I for the rest. This division would facilitate more systematic and comprehensive evaluation and reporting.

The multiaxial system also serves to emphasize that a complete evaluation of the patient often requires consideration of factors above and beyond the diagnostic assessment. The second contribution of the multiaxial system, therefore, is to increase the attention paid to the important role of psychosocial factors in the onset, exacerbation, and management of psychiatric disorders. Axis IV in its various (and admittedly ever-changing) manifestations provides an opportunity to describe the patient's external circumstances with a fullness of detail that would be lost if one focused exclusively on the diagnostic axes.

The third contribution of the multiaxial system is the provision of a system for rating the individual's level of functioning. Axis V may provide important information for determining the need and eligibility for treatment, choosing among treatments, predicting prognosis, and measuring change. However, it should also be noted that some have continued to criticize the inclusion of these nondiagnostic axes on the grounds that the DSM's mandate is only to diagnose mental disorders and that the system should restrict itself to the diagnostic Axes I, II, and III.

Despite these advantages (which are widely acknowledged even by most of the opponents of the multiaxial system), there are a number of serious disadvantages that have suggested to many that the multiaxial system causes more mischief than it is worth. The objections arise on both theoretical and practical grounds. It has been cogently argued that there is no fundamental difference between those psychiatric disorders that are grouped on Axis I and those grouped on Axis II and, more broadly, that there are no fundamental differences between psychiatric disorders and general medical conditions.

At the extremes, it is no problem to distinguish between Axis I and Axis II disorders. It is certainly easy enough to make the distinction between a late-onset acute Axis I disorder and an early onset, pervasive, and enduring Personality Disorder. However, in many clinical situations where the disorder has an early onset, a pervasive impact, and a chronic course, it becomes difficult or maybe even inherently impossible to distinguish what is best considered an Axis I condition and what is best considered a Personality Disorder. The clearest example of the overlap between Axis I and Axis II is the relationship between Generalized Social Phobia (on Axis I) and Avoidant Personality Disorder (on Axis II), which identify a virtually identical population of patients.

Similarly, there is no infallible indicator to distinguish between Axis I and Axis III disorders. The distinction between the disorders traditionally diagnosed as "psychiatric" (i.e., Axis I) and those considered to be "other medical conditions" (i.e., Axis III) is not based on any fundamental standard but rather on traditional boundaries among specialties (especially psychiatry and neurology). These boundaries have shifted over time, with the trend being that a condition leaves psychiatry and joins neurology when its pathogenesis becomes better understood (e.g., epilepsy, general paresis). As the underlying etiologies of at least some psychiatric disorders become better understood, their classification as psychiatric or nonpsychiatric will no longer depend on how well established the etiology is, but rather will be a function of the clinical skills best suited for their diagnosis and management. Alzheimer's disease is an example of how artificial the boundary is. This disorder obviously has aspects that are of diagnostic and treatment interest to both psychiatrists and neurologists. In fact, the *International Classification of Diseases,* 9th Revision, Clinical Modification (ICD-9-CM) coding system requires that it be indicated in two places (the dementia on Axis I and the disease on Axis III).

The multiaxial system is problematic not only on theoretical but also on practical grounds. It has been criticized for being cumbersome and time consuming to apply, as well as possibly contributing to discrimination against psychiatric disorders in decisions about what conditions should be included for eligibility within a medical benefit. It has been argued that distinguishing between psychiatric disorders on Axis I and II and general medical conditions on Axis III may result in the notion that psychiatric disorders are less deserving of treatment. Similarly, the distinction between Personality Disorders on Axis II and other clinical disorders on Axis I may lead to the disenfranchisement of personality disorders as a reimbursable indication for treatment. Finally, DSM-III-R Axes IV and V were criticized for being arbitrarily chosen out of a wide range of potentially nondiagnostic measures and for not being sufficiently useful to clinicians, particularly because they entail the use of unfamiliar rating scales.

Despite all of these problems, it was ultimately decided that the multiaxial system is sufficiently valuable to be retained in DSM-IV, albeit with some modifications. DSM-IV emphasizes that the multiaxial system is optional and includes a number of explicit caveats to underscore that there are no fundamental differences in conception between disorders coded on Axes I, II, and III. So long as these caveats are kept in mind, the multiaxial system can be enormously useful in guiding clinical assessment and in facilitating communication.

A Tour Through the Multiaxial System

Axis I: Clinical Disorders and Other Conditions That May Be a Focus of Attention

All psychiatric disorders in DSM-IV are listed in Axis I, with the exception of the Personality Disorders and Mental Retardation, which are noted on Axis II. Axis I can be used for diagnosing other clinical conditions of interest that are not considered mental disorders (e.g., relational problems, child abuse, bereavement). The name chosen for Axis I in DSM-IV is something of a misnomer because the conditions included in Axis II and Axis III are also, of course, clinical disorders. After an extensive search was conducted, the quest for a more descriptive and accurate name was abandoned.

A commonly asked question is why certain conditions listed outside the mental disorders section of ICD-9-CM are nonetheless coded on Axis I in DSM-IV. Such seemingly misplaced disorders include Medication-Induced Movement Disorders, Narcolepsy, Breathing-Related Sleep Disorder, Sleep Disorder Due to a General

Medical Condition, and Sexual Dysfunction Due to a General Medical Condition. The inclusion of these disorders on Axis I reflects their frequent occurrence in mental health settings and their importance in the differential diagnosis of mental disorders. It does not imply that these are to be considered mental disorders.

Axis II: Personality Disorders and Mental Retardation

Ever since the introduction of the multiaxial system in DSM-III, there have been flip-flops concerning which disorders should be featured on Axis II. In DSM-III, Axis II included Personality Disorders and Specific Developmental Disorders (i.e., reading, arithmetic, articulation, and language problems). DSM-III-R markedly broadened the purview of Axis II by adding Mental Retardation and Pervasive Developmental Disorders, with the rationale that all of the developmental disorders should be grouped together. In DSM-IV, the decision was made to return the Specific and Pervasive Developmental Disorders to Axis I and to retain only Mental Retardation and Personality Disorders on Axis II. There is no very compelling logic behind any of these decisions. As discussed above, the division between Axis I and Axis II is fairly arbitrary. However, listing the Personality Disorders and Mental Retardation on a separate axis does have the advantage of encouraging the clinician to consider the presence of these potentially more subtle conditions in every clinical assessment.

In addition to recording Personality Disorders, Axis II allows the clinician to note other aspects of personality functioning. Many clinicians do not realize that, ever since its introduction in DSM-III, the multiaxial system has allowed the clinician to indicate the presence of maladaptive *personality features* on Axis II. Personality features refer to those presentations that are below the threshold necessary to qualify for a diagnosis of Personality Disorder but are still worth noting. The recognition of personality features reflects the fact that problematic personality functioning occurs on a continuum so that the thresholds dividing a diagnosis of Personality Disorder from less severe personality traits are necessarily arbitrary. When the presence of personality features is noted, code numbers should not be used (e.g., Axis II: histrionic traits).

In addition, Axis II can be used to note the individual's habitual use of characteristic defense mechanisms or coping styles. The attention to defense mechanisms was introduced by DSM-III-R to facilitate the use of the manual by psychodynamic clinicians and researchers. The DSM-III-R glossary included definitions of a variety of defense mechanisms. DSM-IV includes a separate and expanded "Glossary of Specific Defense Mechanisms and Coping Styles" and a Defensive Functioning Scale in Appendix B (see below).

Axis III: General Medical Conditions

Axis III is provided for noting the presence of general medical conditions. A careful assessment for the possible role of general medical conditions is crucial in both differential diagnosis and management. If anything, this assessment has become even more important given the increasing size of the geriatric population and the availability of ever more sophisticated diagnostic tools and treatments.

A general medical condition can be related to Axis I or II conditions in one of four ways:

1. It can be the physiological cause of the Axis I or II disorder (e.g., Mood Disorder as a direct consequence of hypothyroidism).

2. It can precipitate the Axis I or II disorder by acting as a psychological stressor (Mood Disorder after an amputation).
3. It can be unrelated causally but nonetheless be important to consider in the management of the Axis I or II disorder (e.g., choice of antidepressant therapy in an individual with a cardiac arrhythmia).
4. It may be an incidental finding (e.g., acne).

Although it is easy to elucidate the universe of possible relationships, in practice the precise nature of the relationship and the presence of causality can be quite difficult to determine. For the convenience of clinicians who may not always have the massive ICD-9-CM coding volumes at their fingertips, DSM-IV provides ICD-9-CM codes for selected medical conditions in Appendix G.

Axis IV: Psychosocial and Environmental Problems

Everyone recognizes the importance of environmental and psychosocial problems in the pathogenesis, course, and treatment of many, if not all, mental disorders. The problem is that there has not yet been any wide agreement as to which aspects of the psychosocial context should be included in the diagnostic system. Axis IV in DSM-III and DSM-III-R focused on the important area of psychosocial stressors. An equally compelling case could have been made that Axis IV should have focused on the presence or absence of social supports.

The DSM-IV Multiaxial Work Group reviewed a variety of possible options for Axis IV and found no one of them to be compellingly superior. However, a change from the DSM-III-R Axis IV rating of stressors seemed necessary because clinicians did not find this rating scale to be particularly useful, and it had not captured the imagination of researchers. Therefore, instead of the DSM-III-R rating scales for stressors, DSM-IV has introduced a method for listing the psychosocial and environmental problems that may have an impact on diagnosis or management. Examples include death in the family, discrimination, problems at work, inadequate resources, and homelessness. It is hoped that the DSM-IV Axis IV will prove to be more useful to clinicians because it conforms more closely with the increasingly familiar problem-oriented approach to treatment planning.

There are two ways to use Axis IV. To encourage clinicians to comprehensively consider problems, a Psychosocial and Environmental Problem Checklist is provided (see the Multiaxial Evaluation Report Form below), which contains the full range of problem areas that should be considered. Alternatively, the specific relevant psychosocial or environmental problems can be listed under Axis IV without using the checklist format. In most cases, only those problems that occurred during the past year should be noted on Axis IV (unless a more remote problem, such as early childhood abuse or parental divorce, has had an enduring influence).

A common source of confusion is that a number of psychosocial stressors included as examples of problems on Axis IV are also in the "Other Conditions That May Be a Focus of Clinical Attention" section (e.g., death of a family member, child neglect, acculturation problems, academic problems). The DSM-IV convention is to indicate the psychosocial or environmental condition on Axis IV when it is judged to have an impact on the Axis I or Axis II condition. If the problem is also an independent focus of clinical attention, it may also be recorded on Axis I by using a code from the section "Other Conditions that May Be a Focus of Clinical Attention."

For convenience, the problems are grouped together in the following categories:

- **Problems with primary support group**—for example, death of a family member; health problems in family; disruption of family by separation, divorce, or estrangement; removal from the home; remarriage of parent; sexual or physical abuse; parental overprotection; neglect of child; inadequate discipline; discord with siblings; birth of a sibling
- **Problems related to the social environment**—for example, death or loss of friend; inadequate social support; living alone; difficulty with acculturation; discrimination; adjustment to life-cycle transition (such as retirement)
- **Educational problems**—for example, illiteracy; academic problems; discord with teachers or classmates; inadequate school environment
- **Occupational problems**—for example, unemployment; threat of job loss; stressful work schedule; difficult work conditions; job dissatisfaction; job change; discord with boss or co-workers
- **Housing problems**—for example, homelessness; inadequate housing; unsafe neighborhood; discord with neighbors or landlord
- **Economic problems**—for example, extreme poverty; inadequate finances; insufficient welfare support
- **Problems with access to health care services**—for example, inadequate health care services; transportation to health care facilities unavailable; inadequate health insurance
- **Problems related to interaction with the legal system/crime**—for example, arrest; incarceration; litigation; victim of crime
- **Other psychosocial and environmental problems**—for example, exposure to disasters, war, or other hostilities; discord with nonfamily caregivers such as counselor, social worker, or physician; unavailability of social service agencies

Axis V: Global Assessment of Functioning

The significance of Axis V has increased greatly in recent years for several reasons. First, the threshold for determining who is and who is not entitled to mental health benefits cannot generally be based strictly on the individual's psychiatric diagnosis because, for most conditions, there is a wide variability in severity of impairment and need for treatment. Increasingly, eligibility is determined by some combination of the presence of a specific diagnosis and the presence of sufficient functional impairment as indicated by a low score on Axis V. Second, decisions regarding the particular type of treatment (e.g., inpatient versus outpatient) and the frequency and duration of the treatment (e.g., length of stay) are also increasingly dependent on standardized measures of functioning. Third, it is often necessary to determine the level of functioning below which an individual is entitled to disability payments, Finally, it is becoming increasingly important to document treatment outcomes not only with symptom rating scales but also with scales measuring changes in functioning.

The clinician's assessment of the individual's level of psychological, social, and occupational functioning is recorded on Axis V. DSM-IV utilizes the 100-point Global Assessment of Functioning (GAF) Scale as a measure of overall functioning (see the box on the following page). To allow flexible adaptation of the GAF Scale to the needs of particular clinical settings, DSM-IV does not provide specific instructions on the time frame or method of rating the scale. In some settings, it may be useful to indicate

Global Assessment of Functioning (GAF) Scale

Consider psychological, social, and occupational functioning on a hypothetical continuum of mental health–illness. Do not include impairment in functioning due to physical (or environmental) limitations.

Code (**Note:** Use intermediate codes when appropriate, e.g., 45, 68, 72.)

100 **Superior functioning in a wide range of activities, life's problems never seem to**
get out of hand, is sought out by others because of his or her many positive
91 **qualities. No symptoms.**

90 **Absent or minimal symptoms** (e.g., mild anxiety before an exam), **good functioning in**
all areas, interested and involved in a wide range of activities, socially effective,
generally satisfied with life, no more than everyday problems or concerns (e.g., an
81 occasional argument with family members).

80 **If symptoms are present, they are transient and expectable reactions to psychoso-**
cial stressors (e.g., difficulty concentrating after family argument); **no more than slight**
impairment in social, occupational, or school functioning (e.g., temporarily falling
71 behind in schoolwork).

70 **Some mild symptoms** (e.g., depressed mood and mild insomnia) **OR some difficulty**
in social, occupational, or school functioning (e.g., occasional truancy or theft within
the household), **but generally functioning pretty well; has some meaningful interper-**
61 **sonal relationships.**

60 **Moderate symptoms** (e.g., flat affect and circumstantial speech, occasional panic attacks) **OR moderate difficulty in social, occupational, or school functioning** (e.g., few
51 friends, conflicts with peers or co-workers).

50 **Serious symptoms** (e.g., suicidal ideation, severe obsessional rituals, frequent shoplifting) **OR any serious impairment in social, occupational, or school functioning**
41 (e.g., no friends, unable to keep a job).

40 **Some impairment in reality testing or communication** (e.g., speech is at times illogical,
obscure, or irrelevant) **OR major impairment in several areas, such as work or school,**
family relations, judgment, thinking, or mood (e.g., depressed man avoids friends,
neglects family, and is unable to work; child frequently beats up younger children, is
31 defiant at home, and is failing at school).

30 **Behavior is considerably influenced by delusions or hallucinations OR serious**
impairment in communication or judgment (e.g., sometimes incoherent, acts grossly
inappropriately, suicidal preoccupation) **OR inability to function in almost all areas**
21 (e.g., stays in bed all day; no job, home, or friends).

20 **Some danger of hurting self or others** (e.g., suicide attempts without clear expectation
of death; frequently violent; manic excitement) **OR occasionally fails to maintain**
minimal personal hygiene (e.g., smears feces) **OR gross impairment in communica-**
11 **tion** (e.g., largely incoherent or mute).

10 **Persistent danger of severely hurting self or others** (e.g., recurrent violence) **OR**
persistent inability to maintain minimal personal hygiene OR serious suicidal act
1 **with clear expectation of death.**

0 Inadequate information.

the highest level of functioning that occurred over a period of time (which can be helpful in highlighting the individual's potential level of functioning once the disorder remits). In other situations, the lowest level of functioning may be indicated to highlight management needs or set a baseline for improvement. Often, both ratings are useful. The time frame can be for the current period or for some portion of the past (e.g., the previous year). Perhaps the most common use of the GAF Scale is to record current ratings over time (e.g., on admission, at discharge, and at each subsequent outpatient visit) to measure improvement as a function of treatment and the passage of time.

Although everyone agreed on the importance of rating functioning, there was far less consensus on how best to do it. Some advocated using several different scales to rate functioning on a variety of domains (e.g., vocational, interpersonal). Although such increased specificity would undoubtedly be desirable, it would also be cumbersome and probably unreliable in general clinical practice. DSM-IV opted instead for a unitary rating of overall functioning. The more separate ratings that any system requires of the clinician, the less likely it is that the rating system will be used at all.

Another question is whether Axis V should be restricted to the effects of psychiatric symptomatology, as in DSM-III-R, or should also include the impact of physical symptoms or environmental limitations. Like DSM-III-R, DSM-IV requires that the contribution of physical impairments related to general medical conditions be excluded from the GAF. For example, when assessing the GAF for a patient with depression and paraplegia after a stroke, the clinician is instructed not to count impairment due to the stroke. This instruction was criticized, particularly by clinicians working with geriatric populations or in consultation settings. They pointed out that it is often difficult (or inherently impossible) to tease out whether the impairment in functioning (e.g., not getting out of bed) is associated with the psychiatric symptoms (e.g., loss of interest) or the physical complaints (e.g., paralysis). Although the argument is in its own way reasonable, it was more than counterbalanced by the concern that including functional deficits related to physical problems would reduce the specificity of the GAF Scale in psychiatric settings.

A third question concerned whether to count the severity of psychiatric symptomatology in the overall rating of functioning. Each anchor point on the DSM-III-R GAF Scale included consideration of both the seriousness of the psychiatric symptoms and the level of impairment in social or occupational functioning. When there are disparities between severity of symptoms and the level at which the person functions, the rating should depend on whichever is lowest. In contrast, the anchor points in the DSM-III Axis V were restricted to the severity of social, occupational, or school functioning, and ratings were to be made independently of the severity of the psychiatric symptoms. There are advantages and disadvantages to each approach. At times it seems ridiculous not to include the impact of serious symptoms (e.g., suicidal or homicidal ideation, psychotic symptoms, disorganized behavior) on functioning because management of these problems takes precedence over most other concerns. However, including such symptoms in the scale reduces the independent information it provides about social and occupational functioning and confounds Axis V with the severity modifiers already available for use on Axis I and Axis II.

Despite the problems noted with DSM-III-R Axis V, it was decided to retain it in DSM-IV, albeit with one modification. DSM-III-R Axis V was only a 90-point scale and did not include the superior functioning indicated by scores between 91 and 100. The 100-point DSM-IV Axis V has added back the top range of functioning in recognition of the frequent use of Axis V as a change measure and of the fact that individuals with a mental disorder may often return to a superior level of functioning. To accommodate the needs of some clinicians and researchers for a scale that measures only functioning, a new scale, the Social and Occupational Functioning Assessment Scale (SOFAS), has been added to Appendix B of DSM-IV (see "Optional Axes" section in this chapter). It may be preferred as a measure of functioning for use in some settings.

In arriving at a GAF rating, clinicians should start at the top of the scale and move down until they reach the appropriate level. To ensure that the level is appropriate, clinicians should review the level below to make sure that it would not provide a better fit. In determining the specific number within each decile, clinicians should consider whether the patient is functioning within the higher or lower end of that range. In making the single GAF rating, two separate assessments are required: 1) how serious the symptoms are and 2) how serious the impairment in school, work, or social functioning is. The final rating is based on whichever of the two assessments is the worst. As the GAF Scale is usually used, the symptom rating tends to overshadow the ratings of functional impairment. That is particularly the case with the more serious symptoms (e.g., suicidal, homicidal, or grossly disorganized behavior). For example, an individual can have reasonable school and social functioning but cannot get a rating above 20 if there is suicidal behavior. Similarly, currently psychotic individuals have an upper limit of 40 no matter how well they function in social or occupational realms. In contrast, some individuals may have relatively mild symptoms (e.g., personality traits) but with a disproportionately low level of functioning that will take precedence in the rating.

Recording a Multiaxial Evaluation

One of the main obstacles to the acceptance of the multiaxial system is its complexity. To facilitate its use, DSM-IV provides a Multiaxial Evaluation Report Form (see the box on the following page), which is intended to serve as a model for recording multiaxial diagnoses. Multiple lines are provided for Axis I, Axis II, and Axis III diagnoses to remind the clinician of the common situation in which more than one diagnosis is made on each of these axes. When more than one diagnosis is present on an individual axis, the disorders should be listed in order of focus of attention or treatment.

Some settings may require the designation of one diagnosis as the *principal diagnosis.* The principal diagnosis is defined as "the condition established after study to be chiefly responsible for occasioning the admission of the individual" (DSM-IV, p. 3). The concept of principal diagnosis did not originate with the DSM system but was adopted by governmental agencies for statistical, regulatory, and reimbursement purposes. For inpatient admissions, the principal diagnosis is usually determined at the time of discharge, after consideration of the overall course of the hospitalization. The DSM-IV convention is to assume, unless indicated otherwise, that the first listed diagnosis on Axis I is the principal diagnosis. If an Axis II disorder is the principal diagnosis, the phrase "(Principal Diagnosis)" should be listed after the name of the disorder.

Although the concept of principal diagnosis has some clinical utility, it can also be misleading. Quite often, more than one diagnosis competes for clinical attention, and it makes little sense to highlight one diagnosis at the expense of the others. A principal diagnosis is particularly problematic in situations in which there is a dual

Multiaxial Evaluation Report Form

AXIS I: Clinical Disorders
Other Conditions That May Be a Focus of Clinical Attention

Diagnostic code	DSM-IV name
300.21	Panic Disorder, with Agoraphobia, Moderate
304.10	Diazepam Dependence, Mild
___ ___ ___.___ ___	____________________

AXIS II: Personality Disorders

Diagnostic code	DSM-IV name
301.82	Avoidant Personality Disorder
___ ___ ___.___ ___	Dependent Personality Features________

AXIS III: General Medical Conditions

ICD-9-CM code	ICD-9-CM name
424.0	Mitral Valve Prolapse
___ ___ ___.___ ___	____________________
___ ___ ___.___ ___	____________________

AXIS IV: Psychosocial and Environmental Problems

Check:

- X **Problems with primary support group** *Specify:* Marital Discord
- ☐ **Problems related to the social environment** *Specify:* __________
- ☐ **Educational problems** *Specify:* __________
- X **Occupational problems** *Specify:* Excessive Work Absences
- ☐ **Housing problems** *Specify:* __________
- ☐ **Economic problems** *Specify:* __________
- ☐ **Problems with access to health care services** *Specify:* __________
- ☐ **Problems related to interaction with the legal system/crime** *Specify:* __________
- ☐ **Other psychosocial and environmental problems** *Specify:* __________

AXIS V: Global Assessment of Functioning Scale *Code: 55 (current)*

diagnosis of substance use and a non-substance-induced psychiatric condition. For example, for a patient with a preexisting Mood Disorder who is treated for Alcohol Withdrawal on a psychiatric service, the focus of clinical attention during the first half of the admission might be Alcohol Withdrawal, and the focus during the latter half might be Major Depressive Disorder. Nonetheless, the clinician is forced to select arbitrarily one of these as the principal diagnosis.

For reporting Axis IV, the Multiaxial Evaluation Report Form includes a checklist of the types of psychosocial and environmental problems to be considered as part of a comprehensive evaluation. For each category checked, the specific psychosocial problem should be recorded. If the checklist is not being used, the specific problems should be listed on Axis IV. For Axis V, the GAF score and the period of evaluation should be indicated.

It should be remembered that the use of the multiaxial system is optional. DSM-IV includes a section instructing the clinician who really hates multiaxial reporting on how to record diagnoses without using the multiaxial system—that is, he or she simply lists the diagnoses with the principal diagnosis listed first.

Optional Axes

Once one accepts the notion of a multiaxial system, there is no obvious way to decide how many and which axes should be included. Adding additional axes has the advantage of increasing the information conveyed in the diagnostic statement but at the risk that the system will be crushed under its own weight. Each additional axis adds complexity and increases the likelihood that clinicians will ignore the system altogether. Furthermore, some axes that may be very useful in some settings or when used by practitioners with a particular orientation may not be applicable to the general DSM-IV user. Therefore, the DSM approach has been to limit the system to five axes but to supply additional optional axes that may be particularly useful in specific settings.

Three optional axes are included in Appendix B in DSM-IV: 1) the Defensive Functioning Scale, 2) the Global Assessment of Relational Functioning (GARF) Scale, and 3) the SOFAS.

Defensive Functioning Scale

Psychodynamic practitioners have argued that the DSM system is not a sufficiently useful guide to their clinical practice. Very often, psychodynamic treatments are focused on unconscious conflicts and maladaptive defense mechanisms rather than, or in addition to, targeting specific psychiatric disorders. A comprehensive approach may include not only the assessment of the individual on Axes I–V, but also an indication of prominent defense mechanisms and coping styles, which can also be listed on Axis II. To facilitate this approach, DSM-IV provides a much expanded glossary of defense mechanisms as well as a scale that groups together the 27 defined defense mechanisms into seven defense levels (see below).

High adaptive level. This level of defensive functioning results in optimal adaptation in the handling of stressors. These defenses usually maximize gratification and allow the conscious awareness of feelings, ideas, and their consequences. They also promote an optimum balance among conflicting motives. Examples of defenses at this level are

(continued)

- anticipation
- affiliation
- altruism
- humor
- self-assertion
- self-observation
- sublimation
- suppression

Mental inhibitions (compromise formation) level. Defensive functioning at this level keeps potentially threatening ideas, feelings, memories, wishes, or fears out of awareness. Examples are

- displacement
- dissociation
- intellectualization
- isolation of affect
- reaction formation
- repression
- undoing

Minor image-distorting level. This level is characterized by distortions in the image of the self, body, or others that may be employed to regulate self-esteem. Examples are

- devaluation
- idealization
- omnipotence

Disavowal level. This level is characterized by keeping unpleasant or unacceptable stressors, impulses, ideas, affects, or responsibility out of awareness with or without a misattribution of these to external causes. Examples are

- denial
- projection
- rationalization

Major image-distorting level. This level is characterized by gross distortion or misattribution of the image of self or others. Examples are

- autistic fantasy
- projective identification
- splitting of self-image or image of others

Action level. This level is characterized by defensive functioning that deals with internal or external stressors by action or withdrawal. Examples are

- acting out
- apathetic withdrawal
- help-rejecting complaining
- passive aggression

(continued)

Level of defensive dysregulation. This level is characterized by failure of defensive regulation to contain the individual's reaction to stressors, leading to a pronounced break with objective reality. Examples are

- delusional projection
- psychotic denial
- psychotic distortion

Global Assessment of Relational Functioning Scale

Practitioners with a primary interest in the family/systems approach to diagnosis and therapy also have felt relatively disenfranchised by the DSM approach. The DSM system is by definition a classification of mental disorders as these present in individual patients. In contrast, family/systems therapists often view the relational system (rather than any one individual involved in it) as the target of diagnosis and intervention. Therefore, they have been frustrated by the lack of utility of the DSM system for describing families seen in their practices.

Paying adequate attention to family/systems issues is an inherently difficult challenge for DSM-IV. However, three new features in DSM-IV should help, to some degree at least, to bridge the gap between these two approaches. DSM-IV has increased the emphasis on relational problems in the "Other Conditions That May Be a Focus of Clinical Attention" section by listing these conditions in a separate subsection. Chapters reviewing the literature on the classification of relational problems also appear in the *DSM-IV Sourcebook.* Finally, DSM-IV includes an optional axis named the Global Assessment of Relational Functioning Scale (GARF) Scale (see box below). The format of the GARF Scale is modeled after the format of the GAF Scale (Axis V): a 100-point scale with anchor points indicating levels of relational functioning along three dimensions: problem-solving ability, organization, and emotional climate. The GARF Scale can be used to rate family functioning during the current period or past period and may also be used as an outcome measure.

Global Assessment of Relational Functioning (GARF) Scale

Instructions: The GARF Scale can be used to indicate an overall judgment of the functioning of a family or other ongoing relationship on a hypothetical continuum ranging from competent, optimal relational functioning to a disrupted, dysfunctional relationship. It is analogous to Axis V (Global Assessment of Functioning Scale) provided for individuals in DSM-IV. The GARF Scale permits the clinician to rate the degree to

(continued)

Global Assessment of Relational Functioning (GARF) Scale *(continued)*

which a family or other ongoing relational unit meets the affective or instrumental needs of its members in the following areas:

A. *Problem solving*—skills in negotiating goals, rules, and routines; adaptability to stress; communication skills; ability to resolve conflict
B. *Organization*—maintenance of interpersonal roles and subsystem boundaries; hierarchical functioning; coalitions and distribution of power, control, and responsibility
C. *Emotional climate*—tone and range of feelings; quality of caring, empathy, involvement, and attachment/commitment; sharing of values; mutual affective responsiveness, respect, and regard; quality of sexual functioning

In most instances, the GARF Scale should be used to rate functioning during the current period (i.e., the level of relational functioning at the time of the evaluation). In some settings, the GARF Scale may also be used to rate functioning for other time periods (i.e., the highest level of relational functioning for at least a few months during the past year).

Note: Use specific, intermediate codes when possible, for example, 45, 68, 72. If detailed information is not adequate to make specific ratings, use midpoints of the five ranges, that is, 90, 70, 50, 30, or 10.

81–100 ***Overall:*** *Relational unit is functioning satisfactorily from self-report of participants and from perspectives of observers.*

Agreed-on patterns or routines exist that help meet the usual needs of each family/couple member; there is flexibility for change in response to unusual demands or events; and occasional conflicts and stressful transitions are resolved through problem-solving communication and negotiation.

There is a shared understanding and agreement about roles and appropriate tasks, decision making is established for each functional area, and there is recognition of the unique characteristics and merit of each subsystem (e.g., parents/spouses, siblings, and individuals).

There is a situationally appropriate, optimistic atmosphere in the family; a wide range of feelings is freely expressed and managed within the family; and there is a general atmosphere of warmth, caring, and sharing of values among all family members. Sexual relations of adult members are satisfactory.

61–80 ***Overall:*** *Functioning of relational unit is somewhat unsatisfactory. Over a period of time, many but not all difficulties are resolved without complaints.*

Daily routines are present but there is some pain and difficulty in responding to the unusual. Some conflicts remain unresolved, but do not disrupt family functioning.

Decision making is usually competent, but efforts at control of one another quite often are greater than necessary or are ineffective. Individuals and relationships are clearly demarcated but sometimes a specific subsystem is depreciated or scapegoated.

A range of feeling is expressed, but instances of emotional blocking or tension are evident. Warmth and caring are present but are marred by a family member's irritability and frustrations. Sexual activity of adult members may be reduced or problematic.

(continued)

Global Assessment of Relational Functioning (GARF) Scale *(continued)*

41–60 ***Overall:*** *Relational unit has occasional times of satisfying and competent functioning together, but clearly dysfunctional, unsatisfying relationships tend to predominate.*

Communication is frequently inhibited by unresolved conflicts that often interfere with daily routines; there is significant difficulty in adapting to family stress and transitional change.

Decision making is only intermittently competent and effective; either excessive rigidity or significant lack of structure is evident at these times. Individual needs are quite often submerged by a partner or coalition.

Pain or ineffective anger or emotional deadness interfere with family enjoyment. Although there is some warmth and support for members, it is usually unequally distributed. Troublesome sexual difficulties between adults are often present.

21–40 ***Overall:*** *Relational unit is obviously and seriously dysfunctional; forms and time periods of satisfactory relating are rare.*

Family/couple routines do not meet the needs of members; they are grimly adhered to or blithely ignored. Life cycle changes, such as departures or entries into the relational unit, generate painful conflict and obviously frustrating failures of problem solving.

Decision making is tyrannical or quite ineffective. The unique characteristics of individuals are unappreciated or ignored by either rigid or confusingly fluid coalitions.

There are infrequent periods of enjoyment of life together; frequent distancing or open hostility reflects significant conflicts that remain unresolved and quite painful. Sexual dysfunction among adult members is commonplace.

1–20 ***Overall:*** *Relational unit has become too dysfunctional to retain continuity of contact and attachment.*

Family/couple routines are negligible (e.g., no mealtime, sleeping, or waking schedule); family members often do not know where others are or when they will be in or out; there is a little effective communication among family members.

Family/couple members are not organized in such a way that personal or generational responsibilities are recognized. Boundaries of relational unit as a whole and subsystems cannot be identified or agreed on. Family members are physically endangered or injured or sexually attacked.

Despair and cynicism are pervasive; there is little attention to the emotional needs of others; there is almost no sense of attachment, commitment, or concern about one another's welfare.

0 Inadequate information.

Social and Occupational Functioning Assessment Scale

As mentioned in the discussion of Axis V above, an alternative approach to rating functioning is included in the appendix (the SOFAS; see box on the following page). This scale differs from the GAF Scale in that it is purely a functioning scale that attempts to isolate the individual's functioning from the severity of psychiatric symptomatology. The anchor points of the SOFAS and the GAF Scale are essentially the same except that the SOFAS includes descriptions of social, occupational, and school functioning and omits any reference to the severity of psychological symptoms. Furthermore, the rating of impairments in social and occupational functioning in the SOFAS can include problems that arise as a result of physical illnesses. The decision whether to use the GAF Scale or the SOFAS (or both) can be made based on whichever seems most appropriate to the particular setting.

Social and Occupational Functioning Assessment Scale (SOFAS)

Consider social and occupational functioning on a continuum from excellent functioning to grossly impaired functioning. Include impairments in functioning due to physical limitations, as well as those due to mental impairments. To be counted, impairment must be a direct consequence of mental and physical health problems; the effects of lack of opportunity and other environmental limitations are not to be considered.

Code **(Note:** Use intermediate codes when appropriate, e.g., 45, 68, 72.)

100–91 Superior functioning in a wide range of activities.

90–81 Good functioning in all areas; occupationally and socially effective.

80–71 No more than a slight impairment in social, occupational, or school functioning (e.g., infrequent interpersonal conflict, temporarily falling behind in schoolwork).

70–61 Some difficulty in social, occupational, or school functioning but generally functioning well; has some meaningful interpersonal relationships.

60–51 Moderate difficulty in social, occupational, or school functioning (e.g., few friends, conflicts with peers or co-workers).

50–41 Serious impairment in social, occupational, or school functioning (e.g., no friends, unable to keep a job).

40–31 Major impairment in several areas, such as work or school, family relations (e.g., depressed man avoids friends, neglects family, and is unable to work; child frequently beats up younger children, is defiant at home, and is failing at school).

30–21 Inability to function in almost all areas (e.g., stays in bed all day; no job, home, or friends).

20–11 Occasionally fails to maintain minimal personal hygiene; unable to function independently.

10–1 Persistent inability to maintain minimal personal hygiene. Unable to function without harming self or others or without considerable external support (e.g., nursing care and supervision).

0 Inadequate information.

The Last Word

The good news about the multiaxial system is that it is a very valuable way of communicating information, provides a more rounded view of the patient, and encourages a more systematic assessment. The bad news about the multiaxial system is that it can sometimes be cumbersome to use and that some people take it too literally. No implication is intended that the division of clinical disorders into the three axes represents some fundamental clinical distinction. At their boundaries, Axes I, II, and III overlap. Furthermore, there has not been universal agreement as to how many and which axes should be included in the system and how the ones that are included should be defined. Although DSM-IV recommends the use of the multiaxial system and provides definitions for each of the five axes, it makes clear its use is optional and provides several alternative axes that may also be useful in particular settings. Like most of DSM-IV, the multiaxial system is useful if tempered by clinical judgment and common sense.

CHAPTER 7

The Retirement of the Term *Organic*

In DSM-III and DSM-III-R, the organic mental disorders and syndromes were defined as being the result of a known or suspected "transient or permanent dysfunction of the brain" and were classified in a section separate from all other disorders. This category included Delirium; Dementia; Amnestic Syndrome; Organic Mood, Organic Anxiety, Organic Personality, and Organic Delusional Syndromes; and Organic Hallucinosis. The term *organic* covered two types of etiologies: those due to general medical conditions and those due to the effects of substance use.

The accumulating knowledge about the biological factors that contribute to the traditionally nonorganic mental disorders has made this "organic" versus "nonorganic" dichotomy foolish and obsolete. For example, no one would seriously argue that Schizophrenia or Bipolar Disorder are unrelated to brain dysfunction. In fact, a literal interpretation of the DSM-III-R definition of organic mental disorders and syndromes might dictate that the majority of the disorders in the manual be considered organic. Furthermore, the variety of factors (biological, psychological, and social) that contribute to the origins, onset, and presentation of virtually all of the mental disorders has made it essentially impossible to make very clear distinctions between organic and nonorganic. In a sense, all of the DSM-IV disorders are organic; all are also related to psychological factors and to the environmental context.

For all of these reasons, the term *organic* has been eliminated in DSM-IV. Instead, each of the organic disorders in DSM-III-R has been split in DSM-IV into two categories based on etiology—whether the psychopathology is due to a general medical condition or is substance induced. For example, the DSM-III-R category of Organic Mood Disorder in DSM-IV is split into Mood Disorder Due to a General Medical Condition and Substance-Induced Mood Disorder. The same is true for Delirium, Dementia, Amnestic Disorder, Organic Anxiety Disorder, and so forth.

There has also been a major reorganization in the placement of disorders previously contained in the DSM-III-R "Organic Mental Disorders" section. The traditional organic mental disorders (i.e., Delirium, Dementia, and Amnestic Disorder) are grouped together in the "Delirium, Dementia, and Amnestic and Other Cognitive Disorders" section of the manual. The remaining disorders are each listed twice in DSM-IV. To facilitate differential diagnosis, the text and criteria for these disorders have been placed within the diagnostic classes with which they share phenomenology (e.g., the "Mood Disorders" section contains the text and criteria for both Mood Disorder Due to a General Medical Condition and Substance-Induced Mood Disorder). Unfortunately, two disorders (Catatonic Disorder Due to a General Medical Condition and Personality Change Due to a General Medical Condition) could not be placed in any of the existing phenomenologically based diagnostic classes; these disorders are placed instead in the Mental Disorders Due to a General Medical Condition Not Elsewhere Classified chapter. To facilitate finding the range of psychopathological presentations caused by general medical conditions, the Mental Disorders Due to a General Medical Condition are listed together as a group. Similarly, to facilitate finding the range of presentations caused by a particular substance, these disorders are listed together in the Substance-Related Disorders section in DSM-IV.

Although DSM-IV deleted the term *organic* because of its anachronic connotations, the concept embodied in the term *organic* is even more important now than ever before. When someone asks you to "rule out organicity," what he or she is really asking is whether there is a general medical condition or substance that is responsible for the psychiatric presentation. This question is important because it prioritizes one's treatment planning. For example, one would not institute a course of antidepressant medication or long-term psychotherapy for a patient whose depression is due to Hypothyroidism before first trying out thyroid replacement therapy. It is for this reason that virtually all of the differential diagnosis sections in DSM-IV begin with the suggestion that a substance and a general medical condition be ruled out as an etiological factor. Therefore, the rest of this chapter provides some guidelines on how to make this important differential, which will come up over and over again in the rest of this book.

Ruling Out Substance Etiology

The first question that should always be considered in differential diagnosis is whether the presenting symptoms arise from an exogenous psychoactive substance that is exerting a direct effect on the central nervous system. This is particularly important both because substance use is an increasingly common (and often overlooked) cause of psychopathology and because identifying this etiology has obvious and immediate treatment implications. Unfortunately, it can be difficult to determine whether psychopathology is due to substance use because 1) substance use is fairly ubiquitous, 2) a wide range of different symptoms can be caused by substances, and 3) the fact that substance use and psychopathology occur together does not necessarily imply a cause-and-effect relationship.

Obviously, the first task in this differential diagnosis is to determine whether the person has been using a substance. This determination entails careful history taking, physical examination for signs of intoxication or withdrawal, and often laboratory analysis of body fluids for the presence of particular substances.

Once the substance use has been established, the next step is to determine whether there is an etiological relationship between it and the psychiatric symptomatology. This step requires the clinician to distinguish among three possible relationships between the substance use and the psychopathology: 1) the psychiatric symptoms result from the direct effects of the substance on the central nervous system (as is the case for the Substance-Induced Disorders), 2) the substance use is a consequence (or associated feature) of having a primary psychiatric disorder (e.g., self-medication), and 3) the psychiatric symptoms and the substance use are independent.

We begin with a discussion of the first possible relationship between substance use and psychopathology—what in DSM-IV are called the Substance-Induced Disorders. Virtually any presentation encountered in a mental health setting can be caused by substance use. DSM-IV describes 10 Substance-Induced Disorders based on the predominant presenting symptoms. These are Substance Intoxication, Substance Withdrawal, Substance-Induced Delirium, Substance-Induced Persisting Dementia, Substance-Induced Persisting Amnestic Disorder, Substance-Induced Psychotic Disorder, Substance-Induced Mood Disorder, Substance-Induced Anxiety Disorder, Substance-Induced Sexual Dysfunction, and Substance-Induced Sleep Disorder. A substance-induced presentation that does not meet the criteria for any of these specific Substance-Induced Disorders is indicated in DSM-IV as the specific Substance-Related Disorder Not Otherwise Specified. All of these specific substance-induced presentations are discussed further in the "Substance-Related Disorders" section in Chapter 10 of this book and in the specific chapters in which each of the Substance-Induced Disorders is included.

Three factors are important in determining whether there is a causal relationship between substance use and psychiatric symptomatology. First, the clinician must establish whether there is a close temporal relationship between the substance use and the psychiatric symptoms. Then, the clinician must consider the likelihood that the particular pattern of substance use could result in the observed psychiatric symptoms. Finally, the clinician should consider whether there are better alternative explanations for the clinical picture.

The temporal sequence between the substance use and the onset or maintenance of the psychopathology is probably the best (although still fallible) method for evaluating their etiological relationship. At the extremes, this relationship is clear-cut. If the onset of the psychopathology clearly precedes the onset of the substance use, then it is likely that the condition is primary and the substance use is secondary (e.g., self-medication) or unrelated. Conversely, if the onset of the substance use clearly and closely precedes the psychopathology, it lends greater credence to the likelihood of a Substance-Induced Disorder. Unfortunately, in practice, this seemingly simple determination can be quite difficult because the onsets of the substance use and the psychopathology may be more or less simultaneous or impossible to reconstruct retrospectively. In such situations, the clinician will have to rely more on what happens when the person no longer takes the substance. Psychiatric symptoms that occur in the context of intoxication, withdrawal, and medication use result from the effects of the substance on neurotransmitter systems. Once these effects have been removed (by a period of abstinence after the withdrawal phase), the symptoms should spontaneously resolve. Persistence of the psychiatric symptomatology for a significant period of time beyond periods of intoxication or withdrawal suggests that the psychopathology is primary and not due to substance use. The exceptions are Substance-Induced Persisting Dementia and Substance-Induced Persisting Amnestic Disorder in which, by definition, the cognitive symptoms are due to permanent central nervous system damage and not due to the acute effects of substance use and therefore "persist beyond the usual duration of Substance Intoxication or Withdrawal."

The DSM-IV criteria for substance-induced presentations suggest that psychiatric symptomatology be attributed to the substance use if the symptoms remit within 4 weeks of the cessation of acute intoxication, withdrawal, or medication use. During the DSM-IV deliberations, the choice of a 4-week limit was somewhat controversial, and this guideline must be applied with clinical judgment. Some clinicians, particularly those who work in substance use treatment settings, were most concerned about the possibility of misdiagnosing a substance-induced presentation as a primary mental disorder. Thus, they suggested allowing a 6- or 8-week period of abstinence before considering the diagnosis to be a primary mental disorder. On the other hand, those who work primarily in psychiatric settings were concerned that, given the wide use of substances among clinical populations, such a long waiting period is impractical and might result in an overdiagnosis of Substance-Induced Disorders and an underdiagnosis of primary mental disorders. Moreover, it must be recognized that any chosen generic time frame would have to apply to a wide variety of substances with very different properties and a wide variety of possibly consequent psychopathologies. One suggestion was to specify different waiting periods for each class of substance. This interesting proposal was ultimately rejected because there was insufficient evidence on which to base the setting of thresholds for each individual class of substance, and it would have made the system impossibly complex. On balance, it seems that the 4-week threshold included in DSM-IV is a useful suggestion for how long after drug use one should wait before making the diagnosis of a primary mental disorder, but a great deal of clinical judgment is required in applying it.

Sometimes, it simply is not possible to determine whether there was a period of time when the psychiatric symptoms occurred outside of periods of substance use. An example is the often encountered situation in which the patient is too poor a historian to allow careful determination of past temporal relationships. In addition, substance use and psychiatric symptoms can have their onset around the same time (often in adolescence), and both can be more or less chronic and continuous. In these situations, it may be necessary to assess the patient during a current period of abstinence from substance use. If the psychiatric symptoms persist in the absence of substance use, then the psychiatric disorder can be considered to be primary. If the symptoms remit, then the substance use is probably primary.

It is important to realize that this judgment can only be made after waiting for enough time to elapse so as to be confident that the psychiatric symptoms are not a consequence of substance withdrawal. Ideally, the best setting for making this determination is in the hospital, where the patient's access to substances can be controlled and the patient's psychiatric symptomatology can be serially assessed. Of course, it is often impossible in this era of brief hospitalizations to observe a patient for as long as 4 weeks or in a tightly controlled setting. Consequently, these judgments must be based on less controlled observation, and one's confidence in the accuracy of the diagnosis should be more guarded.

In determining the likelihood that the pattern of substance use can account for the symptoms, the clinician must also consider whether the nature, amount, and duration of substance use are consistent with the pattern of the observed psychiatric symptoms. Only certain substances are known to be causally related to particular psychiatric symptoms. Moreover, the amount of a substance taken and the duration of its use must be above a certain threshold for substance use to be considered the cause of the psychiatric symptomatology. For example, a severe and persisting depressed mood after the isolated use of a small amount of cocaine should probably not be attributed to the cocaine use, even though depressed mood is known to be associated with cocaine withdrawal.

The clinician should also take into account other factors in the presentation that suggest other etiologies. These include a history of many similar episodes not related to substance use, a strong family history of the particular primary disorder, and the presence of physical examination or laboratory findings suggesting that a particular general medical condition might be involved. It requires fine clinical judgment (and often waiting and seeing) to weigh the relative probabilities in these situations. For example, an individual may have heavy family loading for anxiety disorders and still have a cocaine-induced panic attack that does not necessarily presage the development of primary Panic Disorder.

In some cases, the substance use can be the consequence or associated feature (rather than the cause) of psychiatric symptomatology. Not uncommonly, the substance-taking behavior can be considered a form of self-medication for the psychiatric condition. For example, an individual with a primary Anxiety Disorder might use alcohol excessively for its sedative and antianxiety effects. One interesting implication of using a substance to self-medicate is that individuals with particular psychiatric disorders often preferentially choose certain classes of substances. For example, patients with negative symptoms of Schizophrenia often prefer stimulants, and patients with Anxiety Disorders often prefer central nervous system depressants.

The hallmark of a primary psychiatric disorder with secondary substance use is that the primary psychiatric disorder occurs first or exists at times when the individual is not using any substance. In the most classic situation, the period of comorbid psychiatric symptomatology and substance use is immediately preceded by a period of time when the person had the psychiatric symptomatology but was abstinent from the substance. For example, an individual who currently has 5 months of heavy alcohol use and depressive symptomatology might report that the alcohol use started in the midst of the depressive episode, perhaps as a way of counteracting insomnia. Clearly, the validity of this clinical judgment depends on the accuracy of the patient's retrospective reporting. Because such information is sometimes suspect, it may be useful to confer with other informants (e.g., family members) and review past records to document the presence of the past psychiatric syndrome in the absence of substance use.

Finally, both the psychiatric disorder and the substance use can be initially unrelated and independent of one another. The high prevalences of both psychiatric disorders and substance use disorders is such that, by chance, one would expect some patients to have two independent illnesses. Of course, however, even if initially independent, the two disorders may interact to exacerbate each other and complicate the overall treatment. This independent relationship is essentially a diagnosis made by exclusion. When confronted with a patient who has both psychiatric symptomatology and substance use, the clinician should first rule out that one is causing the other. A lack of a causal relationship in either direction is more likely if there are periods when the psychiatric symptoms occur in the absence of substance use and if the substance use occurs at times unrelated to the psychiatric symptomatology.

Rule Out a Disorder Due to a General Medical Condition

After ruling out a substance-induced etiology, the next step is to determine whether the psychiatric symptoms are due to a general medical condition. This is one of the most important and difficult distinctions in psychiatric diagnosis. It is important because many individuals with general medical conditions have psychiatric symptoms as a complication of the general medical condition, and many individuals with psychiatric symptoms have an underlying general medical condition. The treatment implications of this differential diagnostic step are also profound. Appropriate identification and treatment of the underlying general medical condition can be crucial in both avoiding medical complications and in the reduction of the psychiatric symptomatology.

This differential diagnosis can be difficult because

1. Symptoms of some psychiatric disorders and of many general medical conditions can be identical (e.g., symptoms of weight loss and fatigue can be attributable to a depressive or anxiety disorder or to a general medical condition).
2. Sometimes the first presenting symptoms of a general medical condition are psychiatric (e.g., depression preceding other symptoms in pancreatic cancer, brain tumor, Parkinson's disease).
3. The relationship between the general medical condition and the psychiatric symptoms may be complicated (e.g., depression or anxiety as a psychological reaction to having the medical condition versus the general medical

condition being a cause of the depression or anxiety via its direct physiological effect on the central nervous system).

4. Patients are often seen in settings primarily geared for the identification and treatment of mental disorders, and clinicians in these settings have a lower expectation for, and familiarity with, the diagnosis of general medical conditions.

Virtually any psychiatric presentation can be caused by a general medical condition. DSM-IV describes 10 Disorders Due to a General Medical Condition based on the predominant presenting symptoms. These include Catatonic Disorder, Personality Change, Delirium, Dementia, Amnestic Disorder, Psychotic Disorder, Mood Disorder, Anxiety Disorder, Sexual Dysfunction, and Sleep Disorder . . . all Due to a General Medical Condition. For presentations predominated by other symptoms (e.g., dissociation), Mental Disorder Not Otherwise Specified Due to a General Medical Condition should be indicated.

It's no great trick to suspect the possible etiological role of a general medical condition if the patient is encountered in a general hospital or primary care outpatient setting. The real diagnostic challenge occurs in mental health settings, where the base rate of general medical conditions is much lower but nonetheless consequential. It is neither feasible nor cost-effective to order every conceivable screening test on every patient. One should direct the history, physical examination, and laboratory tests toward the diagnosis of those general medical conditions that are most commonly encountered and most likely to account for the presenting psychiatric symptoms (e.g., thyroid function tests for depression, brain imaging for late-onset psychotic symptoms).

Once a general medical condition is established, the next step is to determine its etiological relationship, if any, to the psychiatric symptoms. The five possible relationships are

1. The general condition causes the psychiatric symptoms through a direct physiological effect on the brain.
2. The general medical condition causes the psychiatric symptoms through a psychological mechanism (e.g., depressive symptoms in response to being diagnosed with cancer—see Chapter 21, Adjustment Disorder).
3. Medication taken for the general medical condition causes the psychiatric symptoms.
4. The psychiatric symptoms cause or adversely affect the general medical condition (see Psychological Factors Affecting Medical Condition section in Chapter 24 of this book).
5. The psychiatric symptoms and the general medical condition are coincidental (e.g., hypertension and Schizophrenia).

In the real clinical world, however, several of these relationships may occur simultaneously with a multifactorial etiology. For example, a patient treated with an antihypertensive who has a stroke may develop depression due to the direct effects of the stroke on the brain, the psychological reaction to paralysis, and as a medication side effect.

DSM-IV provides several suggestions on how to determine whether the first type of relationship (i.e., direct physiological effect) applies to the current clinical situation. Unfortunately, each of these suggestions may be difficult to apply, and clinical judgment is always necessary. The first consideration has to do with the nature of the temporal relationship: Do the psychiatric symptoms follow the onset of the general medical condition, vary in severity with the severity of the general medical condition, and disappear when the general medical condition resolves? When all of these relationships can be demonstrated, a fairly compelling case can be made that the general medical condition has caused the psychiatric symptoms (although it does not establish that the relationship is physiological—the temporal covariation could also be due to a psychological reaction to the general medical condition).

Sometimes, however, the temporal relationships are not at all a good indicator of underlying etiology. For instance, psychiatric symptoms may be the first harbinger of the general medical condition and may precede by months or years any other manifestations. In the other direction, psychiatric symptoms may be a relatively late manifestation occurring months or years after the general medical condition has been well established (e.g., depression in patients with Parkinson's disease).

The second clue that a general medical condition should be considered in the differential diagnosis is a psychiatric presentation that is atypical in symptom pattern, age at onset, or course. For example, the presentation cries out for a medical workup when there is severe memory or weight loss accompanying a relatively mild depression or severe disorientation accompanying psychotic symptoms. Similarly, the first onset of a Manic Episode in an elderly patient or an uncharacteristically rapid onset or fluctuating course may suggest that a general medical condition is involved in the etiology. However, an atypical presentation does not in and of itself indicate a general medical etiology because the heterogeneity of primary disorders leads to many "atypical" presentations. Nonetheless, the bottom line is not to miss possibly important underlying general medical conditions. Establishing the nature of this causal relationship may be difficult and often requires careful evaluation, longitudinal evaluations, and trials of treatment.

The Last Word

By far the biggest change in DSM-IV is its emphasis on the need to always rule out substance use and general medical etiologies in the differential diagnosis of all presenting symptoms. This is missed surprisingly often in clinical practice. To highlight this issue, DSM-IV includes the text and criteria for disorders induced by substances and general medical conditions in the pertinent sections. For example, Mood Disorder Due to a General Medical Condition and Substance-Induced Mood Disorder are included in the Mood Disorders section, along with the text for Major Depressive Disorder, Bipolar Disorder, and so forth.

SECTION III

The DSM-IV Diagnoses

CHAPTER 8

Delirium, Dementia, Amnestic, and Other Cognitive Disorders

The disorders in this chapter have as their predominant presenting problem a cognitive impairment that is judged to be due to a general medical condition or to the effects of a drug of abuse, medication, or toxin. However, it must also be understood that cognitive impairment is not specific only to the disorders in this section and that there is a good deal of overlap between the presentation of cognitive symptoms and other forms of psychopathology. For example, disorders in many other parts of DSM-IV (most particularly Schizophrenia, Mood Disorders, Attention-Deficit/Hyperactivity Disorder, Mental Retardation, Learning Disorders, Pervasive Developmental Disorders) often present with marked cognitive impairments.

Moreover, the disorders in this chapter often have prominent psychotic, mood, and anxiety symptoms that occur with the cognitive impairment. To a large degree, Dementia of the Alzheimer's Type is not just a cognitive disorder but also must be considered a psychotic, mood, and personality change disorder. Similarly, Major Depressive Disorder is not just a Mood Disorder but may present with symptoms that are difficult to distinguish from a dementia (see the discussion of pseudodementia later in this chapter). Nonetheless, it does remain convenient and clinically useful to group together those disorders that are most markedly characterized by a cognitive impairment due to the direct effects of a diagnosable general medical condition or substance use.

Delirium

Deliria

293.0	Delirium Due to . . . *[Indicate the General Medical Condition]*
—.-	Substance Intoxication Delirium *[Refer to Substance-Related Disorders for substance-specific codes]*
—.-	Substance Withdrawal Delirium *[Refer to Substance-Related Disorders for substance-specific codes]*
—.-	Delirium Due to Multiple Etiologies *[Code each of the specific etiologies]*
780.09	Delirium Not Otherwise Specified

Delirium is characterized by a disturbance in consciousness and cognition. In contrast to Dementia, Delirium tends to have an acute onset, relatively brief duration, and minute-to-minute fluctuations in mental status. Unfortunately, the diagnosis of Delirium is often missed in medical settings, especially in those individuals who have a quiet (as opposed to agitated) presentation. Making a diagnosis of Delirium is particularly important because its underlying cause is often correctable, whereas untreated delirium is associated with a high mortality rate and can also result in serious medical complications, irreversible cognitive impairments (e.g., dementia), and suicidal or violent behavior.

The various types of delirium included in DSM-IV are differentiated based on their etiology: Due to a General Medical Condition, Substance-Induced (including medication side effects), and Due to Multiple Etiologies. In addition, Delirium Not Otherwise Specified is included in this chapter for presentations in which the clinician is able to diagnose that a delirium is present but is unable determine its specific etiology. We first present and discuss the A, B, and C Criteria shared by all of the various types of Delirium and then discuss the etiological criterion (Criterion D) that distinguishes them.

DSM-IV diagnostic criteria for Delirium

A. Disturbance of consciousness (i.e., reduced clarity of awareness of the environment) with reduced ability to focus, sustain, or shift attention.

B. A change in cognition (such as memory deficit, disorientation, language disturbance) or the development of a perceptual disturbance that is not better accounted for by a preexisting, established, or evolving dementia.

C. The disturbance develops over a short period of time (usually hours to days) and tends to fluctuate during the course of the day.

D. [Varies based on etiology—see specific disorders for discussion.]

Criterion A. The hallmark of delirium is a clouding of consciousness. The patient is unable to appreciate or respond appropriately to the external environment. This clouding is often best demonstrated by the way the patient interacts with the clinician during the examination. The patient's inability to "focus, sustain, or shift attention" is demonstrated by wandering attention, distractibility (e.g., inability to filter out irrelevant stimuli such as the sound of the TV or radio), an inability to follow instructions or reply to questions, and by perseveration (e.g., continuing to give the answer to a previous question over and over again).

Criterion B. Memory impairment and disorientation are usually present. The memory impairment is particularly for short-term recall of events. For example, a patient is more likely to remember what she was wearing at her wedding than what she had for breakfast. The disorientation is typically to time (e.g., not knowing the day of the week or even the season of the year). Less commonly, there may also be disorientation to place (e.g., not knowing that one is in a hospital) or to person (e.g., misidentifying oneself or others). The person's speech is very often rambling and difficult to follow. Perceptual disturbances range from misinterpretations (e.g., interpreting shadows on the wall to be a person) to frank hallucinations (e.g., seeing fully formed images of animals in the hospital room). Hallucinations are most commonly visual but may occur in any sensory modality.

Certain presentations of delirium are impossible to miss. The patient may be agitated and loud, pull out intravenous lines, refuse food or appropriate medical treatment, wander in a confused fashion, or even strike out at others. Much more likely to be missed is the quiet patient with delirium, who may have equal clouding of consciousness and confusion but who stays peacefully in bed and does not call attention to himself or herself.

Criterion C. The course of delirium is characteristically short term and helps to distinguish delirium from other disorders, especially dementia. Delirium tends to develop acutely, vary over the course of the day, and generally remits when the underlying etiological factor is corrected. The symptoms of delirium tend to worsen at night (sundowning) and in unstructured, unfamiliar, ambiguous, and overstimulating or understimulating environments. Delirium may sometimes be prevented or improved by the provision of orienting stimuli (e.g., night-light, clock, calendar, family pictures, and regular contact with familiar people).

293.0 Delirium Due to a General Medical Condition

In addition to Criteria A–C listed above, Delirium Due to a General Medical Condition contains Criterion D below. When communicating or recording the diagnosis, the actual name of the etiological general medical condition should be used on Axis I (e.g., 293.0 Delirium Due to Hepatic Encephalopathy). Note that all causes of Delirium Due to a General Medical Condition all have the same Axis I diagnostic code: 293.0. Furthermore, the general medical condition should also be coded on Axis III (e.g., 571.2 Cirrhosis, alcoholic). To help ease the coding burden, DSM-IV includes selected general medical codes in Appendix G.

DSM-IV diagnostic criteria for 293.0 Delirium Due to . . . *[Indicate the General Medical Condition]*

A. Disturbance of consciousness (i.e., reduced clarity of awareness of the environment) with reduced ability to focus, sustain, or shift attention.

B. A change in cognition (such as memory deficit, disorientation, language disturbance) or the development of a perceptual disturbance that is not better accounted for by a preexisting, established, or evolving dementia.

C. The disturbance develops over a short period of time (usually hours to days) and tends to fluctuate during the course of the day.

D. There is evidence from the history, physical examination, or laboratory findings that the disturbance is caused by the direct physiological consequences of a general medical condition.

Criterion D. The presence of delirium should set off alarms in the clinician and trigger a timely and comprehensive workup to determine whether there is a specific neurological or systemic medical condition that accounts for the cognitive impairment. Delirium Due to a General Medical Condition is often a medical emergency with the risk of serious complications or mortality if the underlying cause is not quickly determined and dealt with. The presence of focal neurological signs suggests a central nervous system etiology (e.g., stroke) rather than the effects of a systemic illness (e.g., electrolyte imbalance). In delirium (due to a general medical condition as well as substance induced), the electroencephalogram usually shows generalized slowing or fast activity. Although these findings are not particularly specific, a normal electroencephalogram is helpful in ruling out a delirium as the cause for the cognitive impairment. Many neurological or systemic medical conditions can lead to a delirium (see Table 8–1).

In someone who is already vulnerable, being in an unfamiliar, ambiguous, or understimulating environment can trigger the onset of a delirium. Perhaps the most

Table 8–1. General medical conditions associated with delirium

Systemic infections
Metabolic disorders (e.g., hypoxia, hypercarbia, hypoglycemia)
Fluid or electrolyte imbalances
Hepatic or renal disease
Thiamine deficiency
Postoperative states
Hypertensive encephalopathy
Postictal states
Head trauma

Source. Adapted from American Psychiatric Association 1994, p. 128.

common example is an individual admitted to a hospital for a general medical condition whose delirium may arise from a combination of compromised central nervous system functioning, strange surroundings, and the difficulty in getting a good night's sleep in the noisy and unfamiliar hospital environment.

29x.xx Substance Intoxication/Withdrawal Delirium

In addition to Criteria A–C above, Substance Intoxication Delirium and Substance Withdrawal Delirium also include Criterion D below. In recording this condition, the specific name of the substance and the context (i.e., intoxication or withdrawal) in which the delirium occurs should be used (e.g., Alcohol Withdrawal Delirium, Methylphenidate Intoxication Delirium). If alcohol is the etiological substance, the diagnostic code is 291.0. The code is 292.81 for all other substances.

The following classes of substance are known to have the potential to result in a Substance-Induced Delirium during intoxication: amphetamine; cannabis; cocaine; hallucinogen; inhalant; opioid; phencyclidine; and sedative, hypnotic, or anxiolytic. Only alcohol and the sedative, hypnotic, and anxiolytic substances are well-established causes of delirium during withdrawal. A number of medications can lead to delirium in the absence of intoxication or withdrawal. In such cases, the name of the medication should be specified (e.g., 292.81 Benztropine-Induced Delirium). Similarly, toxins that cause Delirium are coded 292.81.

DSM-IV diagnostic criteria for Substance Intoxication Delirium

A. Disturbance of consciousness (i.e., reduced clarity of awareness of the environment) with reduced ability to focus, sustain, or shift attention.

B. A change in cognition (such as memory deficit, disorientation, language disturbance) or the development of a perceptual disturbance that is not better accounted for by a preexisting, established, or evolving dementia.

C. The disturbance develops over a short period of time (usually hours to days) and tends to fluctuate during the course of the day.

D. There is evidence from the history, physical examination, or laboratory findings of either (1) or (2):
(1) the symptoms in Criteria A and B developed during Substance Intoxication
(2) medication use is etiologically related to the disturbance*

Note: This diagnosis should be made instead of a diagnosis of Substance Intoxication only when the cognitive symptoms are in excess of those usually associated with the intoxication syndrome and when the symptoms are sufficiently severe to warrant independent clinical attention.

***Note:** The diagnosis should be recorded as Substance-Induced Delirium if related to medication use. Refer to Appendix G for E-codes indicating specific medications.

(continued)

DSM-IV diagnostic criteria for Substance Intoxication Delirium *(continued)*

Code [Specific Substance] Intoxication Delirium:
(291.0 Alcohol; 292.81 Amphetamine [or Amphetamine-Like Substance]; 292.81 Cannabis; 292.81 Cocaine; 292.81 Hallucinogen; 292.81 Inhalant; 292.81 Opioid; 292.81 Phencyclidine [or Phencyclidine-Like Substance]; 292.81 Sedative, Hypnotic, or Anxiolytic; 292.81 Other [or Unknown] Substance [e.g., cimetidine, digitalis, benztropine])

DSM-IV diagnostic criteria for Substance Withdrawal Delirium

A. Disturbance of consciousness (i.e., reduced clarity of awareness of the environment) with reduced ability to focus, sustain, or shift attention.

B. A change in cognition (such as memory deficit, disorientation, language disturbance) or the development of a perceptual disturbance that is not better accounted for by a preexisting, established, or evolving dementia.

C. The disturbance develops over a short period of time (usually hours to days) and tends to fluctuate during the course of the day.

D. There is evidence from the history, physical examination, or laboratory findings that the symptoms in Criteria A and B developed during, or shortly after, a withdrawal syndrome.

Note: This diagnosis should be made instead of a diagnosis of Substance Withdrawal only when the cognitive symptoms are in excess of those usually associated with the withdrawal syndrome and when the symptoms are sufficiently severe to warrant independent clinical attention.

Code [Specific Substance] Withdrawal Delirium:
(291.0 Alcohol; 292.81 Sedative, Hypnotic, or Anxiolytic; 292.81 Other [or Unknown] Substance)

Criterion D. The term *delirium* generally refers to a relatively serious condition that requires immediate clinical attention. This must be distinguished from milder attentional difficulties and cognitive deficits characteristic of uncomplicated intoxication or withdrawal, which are usually self-limited processes with very different treatment and prognostic implications.

The DSM-IV convention is to require a diagnosis of delirium only when the cognitive disturbance is severe, warrants independent clinical attention, and is in excess of what is typically encountered with substance intoxication or withdrawal. The clinician, particularly in emergency settings, must be aware that substances (including medications) are frequently the source of symptoms of delirium, often in concert with a general medical condition.

The diagnosis of Substance-Induced Delirium is a marker for a possible medical emergency (e.g., delirium tremens [DTs] with significant associated morbidity and mortality). The clinician must also be sure to rule out the presence of a previously undetected or undertreated general medical condition because these render an individual much more vulnerable to the effects of substances and can also have a negative impact on treatment response and prognosis. Substance-Induced Delirium is much more likely to occur in those individuals who have a serious general medical condition—often one that has also been caused by substance use (e.g., cirrhosis).

The time course of Substance Intoxication Delirium or Substance Withdrawal Delirium depends on the dose and duration of ingestion and the characteristics of the specific substance. High doses of certain drugs (e.g., cocaine, hallucinogens) may cause a rapid onset of delirium, whereas with other substances (e.g., alcohol), delirium may develop only after days of use. The time interval between cessation or reduction of drug use and the onset of withdrawal symptoms (and delirium) varies depending on the half-life of the substance. Later starting and more protracted withdrawal delirium is associated with those substances that have a longer half-life.

Substance-Induced Delirium comes in three forms: Substance Intoxication Delirium, Substance Withdrawal Delirium, and Substance-Induced Delirium for medications that can cause delirium in the absence of an intoxication or withdrawal syndrome. This classification is in contrast to the convention for the other Substance-Induced Disorders, in which it is optional to indicate whether the psychopathology had its onset during intoxication or withdrawal (i.e., by specifying "with onset during intoxication" or "with onset during withdrawal"). The special provision of Substance Intoxication Delirium and Substance Withdrawal Delirium is meant to alert the clinician particularly to the serious morbidity of Alcohol Withdrawal Delirium (DTs) and Sedative Withdrawal Delirium.

Delirium Due to Multiple Etiologies

Delirium Due to Multiple Etiologies is included in DSM-IV to emphasize the important point that finding one putative etiology for delirium does not mean that the search is over. Instead, delirium may be (and often is) due to the simultaneous contribution of more than one general medical condition, more than one substance, or some combination of a general medical condition and a substance. Indeed, the reason why substance intoxication or substance withdrawal leads to a delirium is often precisely because there is an underlying neurological (e.g., head trauma, stroke) or systemic (e.g., infections, cirrhosis) medical problem. Moreover, individuals with general medical conditions are often on one or more medications. Sometimes, the additive effects of the general medical condition and the medication may result in a delirium even though neither alone would be sufficient to cause it. Finally, having one general medical condition is often a risk factor for developing other medical conditions that in combination may be responsible for the delirium.

It should be noted that Delirium Due to Multiple Etiologies is not a separate DSM-IV category in that there is no single diagnostic code available for it. Each cause for the delirium must be listed and coded separately. This concept has been included only for educational purposes and communication purposes.

DSM-IV text for 780.09 Delirium Not Otherwise Specified

This category should be used to diagnose a delirium that does not meet criteria for any of the specific types described in this section.

Examples include

1. A clinical presentation of delirium that is suspected to be due to a general medical condition or substance use but for which there is insufficient evidence to establish a specific etiology
2. Delirium due to causes not listed in this section (e.g., sensory deprivation)

Dementia

Dementias

—.-	Dementia of the Alzheimer's Type
—.-	Vascular Dementia
294.9	Dementia Due to HIV Disease
294.1	Dementia Due to Head Trauma
294.1	Dementia Due to Parkinson's Disease
294.1	Dementia Due to Huntington's Disease
290.10	Dementia Due to Pick's Disease *[Also code 331.1 Pick's Disease on Axis III]*
290.10	Dementia Due to Creutzfeldt-Jakob Disease *[Also code 046.1 Creutzfeldt-Jakob Disease on Axis III]*
294.1	Dementia Due to Other General Medical Conditions *[Also code the General Medical Condition on Axis III]*
—.-	Substance-Induced Persisting Dementia *[Refer to Substance-Related Disorders for substance-specific codes]*
—.-	Dementia Due to Multiple Etiologies *[Code each of the specific etiologies]*
294.8	Dementia Not Otherwise Specified

These dementias share a common symptomatic presentation (i.e., memory impairment plus at least one additional area of cognitive impairment) but are differentiated based on their etiology. It should be noted that the format for describing Dementia of the Alzheimer's Type and Vascular Dementia is somewhat different from the format for describing Dementia Due to Other General Medical Conditions (e.g., human immunodeficiency virus [HIV] disease, head trauma, Parkinson's disease). Dementia of the Alzheimer's Type and Vascular Dementia have been provided with their own separate criteria sets, a complex method of subtyping, and the choice of more specific codes. That should not be taken to mean that there is any inherent conceptual difference among the various dementias. The different handling of Dementia of the Alzheimer's Type and Vascular Dementia reflects only the special interest historically afforded to these two conditions in psychiatry and their coding in the *International*

Classification of Diseases, 9th Revision, Clinical Modification (ICD-9-CM). The symptom patterns (delirium, delusions, depressed mood, behavioral disturbances) indicated in the subtyping for Dementia of the Alzheimer's Type and Vascular Dementia are also commonly encountered in other forms of dementia; but, for arcane coding reasons, they have to be coded separately (e.g., a Major Depressive-Like Episode that is part of Dementia Due to Parkinson's Disease is coded as Mood Disorder Due to Parkinson's Disease). For each of these dementias, the clinician is by convention required to note the presence of dementia on Axis I and the nature of the underlying causal general medical condition on Axis III.

We begin with the definition of dementia and discuss Criteria A and B, which are shared by all of the various types of dementia. We then describe the specific etiologies for dementia that are listed in DSM-IV.

DSM-IV diagnostic criteria for Dementia

A. The development of multiple cognitive deficits manifested by both
   (1) memory impairment (impaired ability to learn new information or to recall previously learned information)
   (2) one (or more) of the following cognitive disturbances:
      (a) aphasia (language disturbance)
      (b) apraxia (impaired ability to carry out motor activities despite intact motor function)
      (c) agnosia (failure to recognize or identify objects despite intact sensory function)
      (d) disturbance in executive functioning (i.e., planning, organizing, sequencing, abstracting)

B. The cognitive deficits in Criteria A1 and A2 each cause significant impairment in social or occupational functioning and represent a significant decline from a previous level of functioning.

Note: Further criteria are based on etiology—see specific disorders for discussion.

CRITERION **A1.** The hallmark of dementia is memory impairment. It is often the first symptom that develops and is usually the major source of disability. The individual has difficulty in laying down new memories and in recalling previous memories, especially recent ones.

The various aspects of memory functioning may be tested separately. These include 1) registration (can the patient repeat numbers or words immediately after hearing them), 2) short-term recall (can the patient repeat the names of three unrelated objects after a period of several minutes), 3) recognition (can the patient retrieve previously forgotten names if provided with clues), and 4) remote memory (can the patient recall important personal or historical events).

Impairment in short-term memory tends to appear early in the course, whereas long-term memory is more likely to remain relatively intact in the latter stages of severe dementia. When the memory impairment is advanced, the person may forget even the most basic personal facts like previous occupation, birthplace, or birth date and may even lose the ability to recognize family members.

It is important to bring the mental status examination down to earth and evaluate how the memory impairment impacts on the patient's everyday life. Can he or she perform at work, handle household chores, manage finances, cook without forgetting to turn off the oven, or get home without getting lost? Often the individual is an unreliable informant in this regard. He or she may be unable or unwilling to acknowledge the extent or consequences of the memory deficits. For example, the individual may complain that others are stealing or deliberately misplacing lost valuables or that others are to blame when appointment times are forgotten. The individual may also fill in memory gaps with confabulations (i.e., made-up stories to hide his or her memory deficits).

Criterion A2. This criterion lists four other cognitive disturbances, one of which must be present in addition to the memory disturbance described in Criterion A1. Mild forms of these items may not have pathological significance, especially as we age. Therefore, to be counted toward a diagnosis of dementia, the aphasia, apraxia, agnosia, or disturbance in executive functioning must cause clinically significant impairment.

Criterion A2a. The patient may have difficulty in both the understanding of language (receptive aphasia) and in the production of language (expressive aphasia). Speech may be circumstantial, empty of content, irrelevant, and filled with vague references (e.g., substituting the terms *thing* and *it* for specific words or names).

This criterion is tested by determining whether the individual can name body parts or everyday objects, follow commands, or repeat phrases. Remember that to count toward a diagnosis of dementia, the language difficulty must by itself be severe and impairing. Some mild symptoms of aphasia (e.g., word finding) are not all that uncommon, particularly in older individuals, and should not be considered sufficient for this criterion.

Criterion A2b. The individual with apraxia is unable to carry out relatively complex motor behaviors (e.g., waving good-bye, brushing teeth, dressing, chopping vegetables), despite having adequate use of the specific motor and sensory systems that are involved in these tasks. This criterion describes the cognitive deficit in organizing the motor activities rather than a neuromuscular dysfunction. Although apraxia is tested for by having the patient demonstrate the ability to carry out motor tasks (e.g., asking the patient to comb hair, assemble blocks, or draw figures), the issue is not one of specific motor ability but rather the ability to organize complex movements. As with the other deficits, apraxia must cause clinically significant impairment in its own right and must represent a new onset rather than long-standing clumsiness in the performance of complex motor acts.

Criterion A2c. Agnosia is the sensory equivalent of apraxia. It is a cognitive dysfunction consisting of the inability to process and recognize perceptions despite having intact sensory functioning. Agnosia may occur in any sensory modality (e.g., inability to recognize a table after being shown one, inability to recognize a coin by feeling it). At the extreme, the loss of recognition may extend to the faces of family members or to the person's own reflection in the mirror.

Criterion A2d. The deficits in executive functioning cover a panoply of higher level (frontal lobe) functions. Because there is such great variability among normal individuals in their ability to abstract and organize, it is particularly difficult to test executive functioning without information concerning the individual's previous capacity in this area. Individuals with dementia have a decline in their ability to plan and implement everyday activities and may therefore avoid new and challenging situations. Abstraction ability can be tested by asking the patient how two objects are either similar or different (how are a bus and train alike?).

Other tests for executive dysfunction include sequentially subtracting 7s from 100 and spelling the word *world* backward. The inability to perform routine tests successfully should not by itself constitute evidence for this criterion. A number of factors apart from dementia (e.g., normal aging, another mental disorder, performance anxiety, previous low intellectual functioning, lack of cooperation, or inattentiveness) may interfere with performance.

It is also important to determine that the dysfunction is of new onset and has a clinically significant impact on everyday life. Although formal testing for executive functioning is a routine part of a mental status examination, the interpretation must include evaluation of baseline functioning. This is necessary to avoid labeling as demented those individuals who have long-term low baseline executive functioning. It is equally important to avoid missing the diagnosis of dementia in individuals who started out with very high baseline functioning and can now respond appropriately to routine testing but display significant decrements compared with their previous attainments.

Criterion B. This criterion serves notice that the cognitive impairments in dementia are much more severe than those that accompany the normal aging process and than other milder forms of neurocognitive decline. It is not uncommon for people to become concerned as they age that their emerging memory difficulties might herald the onset of a dementia. Such declines in cognitive capacity are distinguished from dementia in that the memory difficulty is in keeping with what would be expected given the person's age. Age-Related Cognitive Decline is a new category that has been added to the section "Additional Conditions That May Be a Focus of Clinical Attention" to note problems in cognition that are consistent with the aging process.

An even more difficult task is to distinguish dementia from milder but clearly abnormal cognitive impairments that sometimes accompany various general medical conditions. The basic problem is that there is no clear boundary between dementia and these milder cognitive disturbances. The only guidance provided in DSM-IV is that each of the items (i.e., memory, aphasia, apraxia, agnosia, executive functioning) that are counted toward the diagnosis must independently be a source of clinically significant impairment. If an individual has clinically significant memory loss but only occasional and inconsequential aphasia, the diagnosis would be amnestic disorder and not dementia.

A suggested new category (mild neurocognitive disorder) was proposed to describe clinical situations in which the cognitive impairment is clinically significant but below the threshold for making a diagnosis of dementia or amnestic disorder. Perhaps the major impetus for this proposal was the frequency with which HIV disease is accompanied by cognitive impairments that fall short of a diagnosis of dementia. This proposed category was not included in DSM-IV because it has been insufficiently studied and because of the difficulty in establishing appropriate boundaries with dementia and with normal age-related cognitive decline. However, text and criteria for mild neurocognitive disorder have been included in DSM-IV Appendix B, "Criteria Sets and Axes Provided for Further Study." Such presentations would be diagnosed in DSM-IV as Cognitive Disorder Not Otherwise Specified.

Finally, it may be useful to discuss the relationship between the diagnoses of dementia and Mental Retardation. By convention, the relationship between dementia and Mental Retardation depends on the age at onset of the dementia. Both diagnoses can be given when the dementia begins before age 18 and results in an IQ below 70. When dementia occurs after age 18, a diagnosis of Mental Retardation cannot be given. It can sometimes be difficult to identify clinically significant impairments in individuals at the higher end of the IQ spectrum, who start with such great cognitive abilities that they are able to preserve higher than average functioning despite significant declines in cognitive functioning. An assessment of the ability of such individuals to perform complex tasks previously within their capacity is necessary to determine whether impairment is present.

Dementia of the Alzheimer's Type

Of all of the criteria sets in DSM-IV, this is the one most likely to become quickly outdated. As of 1995, the definite diagnosis of Alzheimer's disease can be made only by autopsy or brain biopsy, and the clinical diagnosis is a presumptive one based on a characteristic course and the exclusion of other possible causes of dementia. Fortunately, research in this area is uncovering fascinating leads concerning the genetics and pathogenesis of this form of dementia. It seems likely that before DSM-V is published, diagnostic tests for Alzheimer's disease will evolve that will supersede the current clinically based criteria set. This event should be a marvelous moment in the history of psychiatry, hopefully to be followed by advances in the prevention and treatment of Alzheimer's disease and similar advances in the understanding and diagnosis of other psychiatric conditions (e.g., Schizophrenia, Bipolar Disorder).

One peculiarity of the diagnostic coding systems is that this single entity requires two diagnostic codes: a code for Dementia of the Alzheimer's Type on Axis I and code for Alzheimer's disease on Axis III. Despite our best efforts in DSM-IV to eliminate the mind-body dualism by deleting the term *organic,* the coding system unfortunately perpetuates this artificial duality by splitting this disorder into its "mental" and "neurological" elements.

DSM-IV diagnostic criteria for Dementia of the Alzheimer's Type

A. The development of multiple cognitive deficits manifested by both
   (1) memory impairment (impaired ability to learn new information or to recall previously learned information)
   (2) one (or more) of the following cognitive disturbances:

(continued)

DSM-IV diagnostic criteria for Dementia of the Alzheimer's Type *(continued)*

(a) aphasia (language disturbance)
(b) apraxia (impaired ability to carry out motor activities despite intact motor function)
(c) agnosia (failure to recognize or identify objects despite intact sensory function)
(d) disturbance in executive functioning (i.e., planning, organizing, sequencing, abstracting)

B. The cognitive deficits in Criteria A1 and A2 each cause significant impairment in social or occupational functioning and represent a significant decline from a previous level of functioning.

C. The course is characterized by gradual onset and continuing cognitive decline.

D. The cognitive deficits in Criteria A1 and A2 are not due to any of the following:

(1) other central nervous system conditions that cause progressive deficits in memory and cognition (e.g., cerebrovascular disease, Parkinson's disease, Huntington's disease, subdural hematoma, normal-pressure hydrocephalus, brain tumor)
(2) systemic conditions that are known to cause dementia (e.g., hypothyroidism, vitamin B_{12} or folic acid deficiency, niacin deficiency, hypercalcemia, neurosyphilis, HIV infection)
(3) substance-induced conditions

E. The deficits do not occur exclusively during the course of a delirium.

F. The disturbance is not better accounted for by another Axis I disorder (e.g., Major Depressive Disorder, Schizophrenia).

Code based on type of onset and predominant features:

With Early Onset: if onset is at age 65 years or below

290.11 With Delirium: if delirium is superimposed on the dementia

290.12 With Delusions: if delusions are the predominant feature

290.13 With Depressed Mood: if depressed mood (including presentations that meet full symptom criteria for a Major Depressive Episode) is the predominant feature. A separate diagnosis of Mood Disorder Due to a General Medical Condition is not given.

290.10 Uncomplicated: if none of the above predominates in the current clinical presentation

With Late Onset: if onset is after age 65 years

290.3 With Delirium: if delirium is superimposed on the dementia

290.20 With Delusions: if delusions are the predominant feature

290.21 With Depressed Mood: if depressed mood (including presentations that meet full symptom criteria for a Major Depressive Episode) is the predominant feature. A separate diagnosis of Mood Disorder Due to a General Medical Condition is not given.

290.0 Uncomplicated: if none of the above predominates in the current clinical presentation

Specify if:

With Behavioral Disturbance

Coding note: Also code 331.0 Alzheimer's disease on Axis III.

Criteria C and D. In the absence of a brain biopsy, the diagnosis of Dementia of the Alzheimer's Type must be made on clinical grounds based on a characteristic pattern of onset and the progression of the cognitive impairments, as well as the absence of other established etiologies. It is important to distinguish Dementia of the Alzheimer's Type from other potential causes of dementia because some of these may be reversible (e.g., subdural hematoma, normal-pressure hydrocephalus, vitamin deficiency, metabolic disturbances) or may have specific interventions (e.g., treatment of hypertension or vascular disease) that might prevent further progression. Typically, other causes of dementia are ruled out on the basis of history and physical examination (e.g., the characteristic family history and abnormal movements of Huntington's disease) and laboratory testing (e.g., positive HIV test, neuroimaging findings).

Obtaining detailed information from the patient, family members, and prior medical records is particularly useful in establishing the course of the disorder. Dementia of the Alzheimer's Type typically has a slowly progressive, insidious course. In contrast, Vascular Dementia commonly (but not always) has a more stepwise course and is usually associated with other neurological signs and symptoms.

Criterion E. Individuals with dementia are at risk for developing a delirium, especially when there is an active general medical condition or serious medication side effects or when the patient has been placed in an unfamiliar environment. A particularly challenging situation is to determine whether an individual who presents with a delirium also has an underlying dementia because, cross-sectionally, both disorders present with multiple cognitive impairments. In general, before a diagnosis of dementia can be considered, one must treat the delirium first and then see what the individual is like once it clears. If there is an established history of a preexisting Dementia of the Alzheimer's Type, the development of delirium is not indicated by giving a separate diagnosis. In such situations, the delirium is noted by using the With Delirium subtype.

Criterion F. The characteristic cognitive deficits of Alzheimer's disease can be difficult to distinguish from similar cognitive deficits that may accompany Major Depressive Disorder. Diagnostic errors can occur in both directions. Patients with late-onset depression and memory deficits can be mistakenly labeled as having Alzheimer's disease (pseudodementia). Patients with Alzheimer's disease, the earliest manifestation of which is often depression, may be diagnosed as having a Major Depressive Disorder and the Alzheimer's disease may be missed. This differential can be informed by careful clinical evaluation, neuropsychological testing, brain imaging, and response to treatment. Although Alzheimer's disease and Schizophrenia may share some clinical features (cognitive deficits, hallucinations, delusions, dysphoria) and a deteriorating course, the two disorders are not often confused because they have different characteristic symptoms and age at onset. Furthermore, severe memory impairment is unusual in Schizophrenia.

Subtypes. Although the most characteristic feature of Alzheimer's disease is dementia, it is a complex syndrome that is also very frequently characterized by a variety of other symptoms including delirium, delusions, depressed mood, and behavioral disturbances. In fact, these associated features may sometimes predominate in the clinical presentation and determine the management and choice of treatment and treatment setting.

Dementia of the Alzheimer's Type is subtyped and coded based on which of the accompanying features is predominant. It is also subtyped based on age at onset because of evidence suggesting that early and late-onset Alzheimer's disease may differ in genetic transmission, pathogenesis, and course. Unlike most other subtypes in DSM-IV, the use of which is optional, use of these subtypes is obligatory because the five-digit diagnostic code depends on the particular subtype. An exception is "With Behavioral Disturbance," which is optional and not coded because there is no code available in the ICD-9-CM system for indicating this subtype.

290.4x Vascular Dementia

Because cerebrovascular disease is common in the same generally elderly group of individuals who are at risk for Alzheimer's disease, it can sometimes be very difficult to differentiate Vascular Dementia from Dementia of the Alzheimer's Type. Further complicating the situation is that both causes of dementia may coexist. In fact, a mixed vascular/Alzheimer's type was proposed for DSM-IV and has been included in ICD-10. Instead, DSM-IV includes Dementia Due to Multiple Etiologies in recognition of this common clinical situation.

DSM-IV diagnostic criteria for 290.4x Vascular Dementia

A. The development of multiple cognitive deficits manifested by both
   (1) memory impairment (impaired ability to learn new information or to recall previously learned information)
   (2) one (or more) of the following cognitive disturbances:
      (a) aphasia (language disturbance)
      (b) apraxia (impaired ability to carry out motor activities despite intact motor function)
      (c) agnosia (failure to recognize or identify objects despite intact sensory function)
      (d) disturbance in executive functioning (i.e., planning, organizing, sequencing, abstracting)

B. The cognitive deficits in Criteria A1 and A2 each cause significant impairment in social or occupational functioning and represent a significant decline from a previous level of functioning.

C. Focal neurological signs and symptoms (e.g., exaggeration of deep tendon reflexes, extensor plantar response, pseudobulbar palsy, gait abnormalities, weakness of an extremity) or laboratory evidence indicative of cerebrovascular disease (e.g., multiple infarctions involving cortex and underlying white matter) that are judged to be etiologically related to the disturbance.

D. The deficits do not occur exclusively during the course of a delirium.

Code based on predominant features:
290.41 With Delirium: if delirium is superimposed on the dementia
290.42 With Delusions: if delusions are the predominant feature

(continued)

DSM-IV diagnostic criteria for 290.4x Vascular Dementia *(continued)*

290.43 With Depressed Mood: if depressed mood (including presentations that meet full symptom criteria for a Major Depressive Episode) is the predominant feature. A separate diagnosis of Mood Disorder Due to a General Medical Condition is not given.

290.40 Uncomplicated: if none of the above predominates in the current clinical presentation

Specify if:

With Behavioral Disturbance

Coding note: Also code cerebrovascular condition on Axis III.

CRITERION C. In DSM-IV, the diagnosis of Vascular Dementia requires three steps: 1) there must be evidence of cerebrovascular disease on physical examination and laboratory studies (typically brain imaging), 2) the damage must be judged sufficient to account for the deficits and, 3) there is no other more likely etiology (e.g., Parkinson's disease). DSM-III-R also included clinical course in its definition of this category ("stepwise deteriorating course with 'patchy' distribution of deficits") in an attempt to distinguish it from the characteristic course of Alzheimer's (i.e., "generally progressive deteriorating course"). Although sometimes quite helpful, this course distinction was eliminated as a required feature in DSM-IV because of evidence that many individuals with Vascular Dementia have a more gradual clinical course that is indistinguishable from the course of Alzheimer's disease.

CRITERION D. See the annotation for Criterion E for Dementia of the Alzheimer's Type. The same issues apply here.

294.9 Dementia Due to HIV Disease

Dementia Due to HIV Disease should be diagnosed only when the dementia is due to the direct central nervous systems effects of the virus. It must be remembered that individuals with HIV disease are also at elevated risk for dementia arising from many other causes (e.g., primary central nervous system lymphoma, toxoplasmosis, cytomegalovirus, cryptococcus, and tuberculosis). Therefore, it is important to rule these conditions out before assuming that the dementia is due to the HIV infection.

294.1 Dementia Due to Head Trauma

The characteristics of Dementia Due to Head Trauma and its associated features depend on the severity and location of the head injury and whether the dementia results from a single injury or repeated injuries (as in boxing). The differential diagnosis for dementia in individuals with a history of Alcohol Dependence can be challenging because such individuals are at increased risk both for dementia due to repeated head injuries and for dementia due to the effects of prolonged, heavy alcohol use and its associated nutritional deficiencies.

294.1 Dementia Due to Parkinson's Disease

Dementia occurs in 20%–60% of patients with Parkinson's disease, which is characterized by tremor, rigidity, and slowed movements. Dementia appears to be more likely in those individuals with Parkinson's disease who are older or who have more severe disease. However, it is important not to assume that cognitive dysfunction in Parkinson's disease necessarily means that the individual has dementia. Depression is also commonly associated with Parkinson's disease and may itself lead to cognitive dysfunction or may exacerbate a coexisting dementia.

294.1 Dementia Due to Huntington's Disease

Dementia Due to Huntington's Disease is an inherited dementia that is associated with characteristic abnormal movements (i.e., choreoathetosis). The disease is transmitted by a single autosomal dominant gene for which a diagnostic test is now available. Children of individuals with the disease have a 50% chance of themselves developing the disease, usually with an onset in their 30s or 40s.

290.10 Dementia Due to Pick's Disease

Dementia Due to Pick's Disease results from degenerative brain atrophy, particularly affecting the frontal and temporal lobes. Confirmation of the diagnosis and distinguishing it from other causes of frontal or temporal lobe atrophy can be done only at autopsy.

290.10 Dementia Due to Creutzfeldt-Jakob Disease

Dementia Due to Creutzfeldt-Jakob Disease is a rare form of dementia caused by a "slow virus." It is accompanied by involuntary movements (particularly myoclonus) and characteristic electroencephalogram changes. The typical course is rapidly downhill, although sometimes the decline is more gradual and resembles that of other dementias. The diagnosis can only be confirmed by biopsy or autopsy.

294.1 Dementia Due to Other General Medical Conditions

Dementia Due to Other General Medical Conditions should be used when the dementia is caused by a general medical condition other than one of those listed above (e.g., brain tumor, subdural hematoma, hydrocephalus, multiple sclerosis, hypothyroidism, hypercalcemia, hypoglycemia, vitamin deficiencies, neurosyphilis, cryptococcosis, renal or hepatic failure, intracranial radiation, and childhood and adult storage diseases). When actually recording this diagnosis, the clinician should insert the name of the specific general medical condition in place of "Other General Medical Condition" on Axis I (e.g., 294.1 Dementia Due to Cryptococcosis) and list the general medical condition again on Axis III (e.g., 117.5 Cryptococcosis).

291.2, 292.82 Substance-Induced Persisting Dementia

Substance-Induced Persisting Dementia should be distinguished from the cognitive impairment that is a common and reversible manifestation of Substance Intoxication or Withdrawal. In contrast, Substance-Induced Persisting Dementia results from neurotoxicity that persists even after the individual has stopped using the substance. The deficits are usually permanent. In general, this disorder occurs in individuals who have had a history of many years of heavy alcohol or drug use. There may also be other contributory factors (e.g., head trauma). The specific code depends upon the particular substance involved: 291.2 for Alcohol and 292.82 for inhalants, sedative, hypnotics, anxiolytics, or other substances.

Dementia Due to Multiple Etiologies

Not infrequently, more than one etiological factor may contribute to the dementia. As with delirium, this category has been included in DSM-IV only for educational and communication purposes and does not have a separate diagnostic code. Each cause for the dementia must be listed and coded separately. Alzheimer's disease and cerebrovascular disease are particularly likely to coexist.

DSM-IV text for 294.8 Dementia Not Otherwise Specified

This category should be used to diagnose a dementia that does not meet criteria for any of the specific types described in this section. An example is a clinical presentation of dementia for which there is insufficient evidence to establish a specific etiology.

Amnestic Disorders

Amnestic Disorders

294.0	Amnestic Disorder Due to . . . *[Indicate the General Medical Condition]*
---.-	Substance-Induced Persisting Amnestic Disorder *[Refer to Substance-Related Disorders for substance-specific code]*
294.8	Amnestic Disorder Not Otherwise Specified

Unlike delirium and dementia, the cognitive impairment characterizing the amnestic disorders is limited to a single function: memory. Amnestic disorders have several different etiologies: due to a general medical condition, due to the persisting effects of a substance, or due to a dissociative phenomenon. Only those situations in which the memory impairment is due to a general medical condition or a substance are included in this section. Amnesia as a dissociative symptom is included in the criteria sets for several diagnoses in the "Dissociative Disorders" section of DSM-IV (i.e., Dissociative Amnesia, Dissociative Fugue, and Dissociative Identity Disorder); it is also a feature of Posttraumatic Stress Disorder, Acute Stress Disorder, and Somatization Disorders. Amnestic disorders also do not include blackouts that are related to Substance Intoxication or Withdrawal.

We begin with the definition of amnestic disorder and discuss Criteria A–C, which are shared by Amnestic Disorder Due to a General Medical Condition and Substance-Induced Persisting Amnestic Disorder. We then describe these specific etiologies.

DSM-IV diagnostic criteria for Amnestic Disorder

A. The development of memory impairment as manifested by impairment in the ability to learn new information or the inability to recall previously learned information.

B. The memory disturbance causes significant impairment in social or occupational functioning and represents a significant decline from a previous level of functioning.

C. The memory disturbance does not occur exclusively during the course of a delirium or a dementia.

Note: Further criteria are based on etiology—see specific disorders for discussion.

Criterion A. Refer to Criterion A for Dementia listed earlier in this chapter for a discussion of memory impairment.

CRITERION B. One of the three authors of this *Guidebook* (the oldest but perhaps not the wisest) has learned from painful personal experience that his advancing age has resulted in an inevitable decline in both close vision and memory—among many other declines. Amnestic disorders are not meant to apply to these expected decrements in memory.

CRITERION C. Amnestic disorder is meant to describe a specific deficit involving memory rather than a pattern of multiple cognitive impairments that might involve attention, executive functioning, or other deficits such as aphasia, agnosia, and apraxia. Therefore, the diagnosis of amnestic disorder is not made if other such symptoms are present.

294.0 Amnestic Disorder Due to a General Medical Condition

General medical conditions that cause focal damage to diencephalic and middle temporal lobe structures (e.g., mammillary bodies, hippocampus, fornix) are most likely to lead to amnestic disorder rather than to more global disturbances like delirium or dementia. These conditions include closed head trauma, penetrating bullet wounds, surgical intervention, radiation, hypoxia, infarction of the posterior cerebral artery, and herpes simplex encephalitis.

DSM-IV diagnostic criteria for 294.0 Amnestic Disorder Due to . . . *[Indicate the General Medical Condition]*

A. The development of memory impairment as manifested by impairment in the ability to learn new information or the inability to recall previously learned information.

B. The memory disturbance causes significant impairment in social or occupational functioning and represents a significant decline from a previous level of functioning.

C. The memory disturbance does not occur exclusively during the course of a delirium or a dementia.

D. There is evidence from the history, physical examination, or laboratory findings that the disturbance is the direct physiological consequence of a general medical condition (including physical trauma).

Specify if:

Transient: if memory impairment lasts for 1 month or less
Chronic: if memory impairment lasts for more than 1 month

Coding note: Include the name of the general medical condition on Axis I, e.g., 294.0 Amnestic Disorder Due to Head Trauma; also code the general medical condition on Axis III.

291.1, 292.83 Substance-Induced Persisting Amnestic Disorder

The specific diagnostic code depends on the particular substance involved: 291.1 for Alcohol and 292.83 for sedative, hypnotics, anxiolytics, or other substances (including toxins such as lead, mercury, carbon monoxide, organophosphate insecticides, and industrial solvents and including medications such as anticonvulsants and intrathecal methotrexate). Far and away, the most common form of this disorder is Alcohol-Induced Persisting Amnestic Disorder (Korsakoff's syndrome). This amnestic disorder often follows an episode of Wernicke's encephalopathy, which is manifested by confusion, ataxia, extraocular muscle palsy, nystagmus, and other focal neurological signs. Timely treatment of Wernicke's encephalopathy with large doses of thiamine (or prophylactic doses for those individuals at risk for it) can prevent the development of a persisting amnestic disorder. However, once established, the memory impairment usually remains indefinitely. In contrast, the course of Sedative-, Hypnotic-, or Anxiolytic-Induced Persisting Amnestic Disorder is more variable, with full recovery more likely.

It should be noted that certain substances and medications frequently may result in memory impairment that is not related to permanent central nervous system damage and is therefore not "persisting." Depending on the circumstances, DSM-IV classifies such presentations in several different ways. Blackouts occur not infrequently in the context of intoxication or withdrawal, particularly involving alcohol. These blackouts are typically considered to be covered by the diagnosis of Substance Intoxication or Withdrawal. If memory loss is particularly prominent and warrants independent clinical attention, it might be noted as a Substance-Related Disorder Not Otherwise Specified. Memory impairments that accompany medication use (e.g., lithium, hypnotics) can be indicated by either 292.9 Other (or Unknown) Substance-Related Disorder NOS or 995.2 Adverse Effects of Medication NOS.

DSM-IV diagnostic criteria for Substance-Induced Persisting Amnestic Disorder

A. The development of memory impairment as manifested by impairment in the ability to learn new information or the inability to recall previously learned information.

B. The memory disturbance causes significant impairment in social or occupational functioning and represents a significant decline from a previous level of functioning.

C. The memory disturbance does not occur exclusively during the course of a delirium or a dementia and persists beyond the usual duration of Substance Intoxication or Withdrawal.

(continued)

DSM-IV diagnostic criteria for Substance-Induced Persisting Amnestic Disorder *(continued)*

D. There is evidence from the history, physical examination, or laboratory findings that the memory disturbance is etiologically related to the persisting effects of substance use (e.g., a drug of abuse, a medication).

Code [Specific Substance]–Induced Persisting Amnestic Disorder:
(291.1 Alcohol; 292.83 Sedative, Hypnotic, or Anxiolytic; 292.83 Other [or Unknown] Substance)

DSM-IV text for 294.8 Amnestic Disorder Not Otherwise Specified

This category should be used to diagnose an amnestic disorder that does not meet criteria for any of the specific types described in this section.

An example is a clinical presentation of amnesia for which there is insufficient evidence to establish a specific etiology (i.e., dissociative, substance induced, or due to a general medical condition).

DSM-IV text for 294.9 Cognitive Disorder Not Otherwise Specified

This category is for disorders characterized by cognitive dysfunction presumed to be due to the direct physiological effect of a general medical condition that do not meet criteria for any of the specific deliriums, dementias, or amnestic disorders listed in this section and that are not better classified as Delirium Not Otherwise Specified, Dementia Not Otherwise Specified, or Amnestic Disorder Not Otherwise Specified. For cognitive dysfunction due to a specific or unknown substance, the specific Substance-Related Disorder Not Otherwise Specified category should be used.

Examples include

1. Mild neurocognitive disorder: impairment in cognitive functioning as evidenced by neuropsychological testing or quantified clinical assessment, accompanied by objective evidence of a systemic general medical condition or central nervous system dysfunction

2. Postconcussional disorder: following a head trauma, impairment in memory or attention with associated symptoms

The Last Word

All of the disorders in this chapter are characterized by cognitive impairment that is the direct result of a general medical condition or substance use (including medication side effects and toxin exposure). It is important to remember that these disorders are differentiated based on phenomenology, not on factors such as course or reversibility.

Delirium is distinguished by clouding of consciousness accompanied by changes in cognition (e.g., memory loss, language disturbance, hallucinations or illusions, disorientation). Dementia is defined as multiple impairing cognitive deficits with memory loss accompanied by aphasia, agnosia, apraxia, and/or disturbances in executive functioning. Amnestic disorder is memory impairment in the absence of other clinically significant cognitive changes. Delirium and dementia often occur together. However, the clinician cannot make a definitive diagnosis of dementia until the delirium clears and it is possible to assess the individual's baseline cognitive functioning.

CHAPTER 9

Mental Disorders Due to a General Medical Condition

Mental Disorders Due to a General Medical Condition Not Elsewhere Classified

293.89	Catatonic Disorder Due to . . . *[Indicate the General Medical Condition]*
310.1	Personality Change Due to . . . *[Indicate the General Medical Condition]*
293.9	Mental Disorder Not Otherwise Specified Due to . . . *[Indicate the General Medical Condition]*

This curiously brief and somewhat tagalong chapter resulted from the decision in DSM-IV to omit the construct Organic Mental Disorder. The reader is referred to Chapter 7, which contains a detailed discussion of the DSM-IV reorganization of the DSM-III-R Organic Mental Disorders. Chapter 9 serves two purposes. It lists in one spot all of the mental disorders that are due to a general medical condition (although the text and criteria for eight of these are located in the sections with which they share phenomenology). It also provides a home for three categories that did not fit in anywhere else (Catatonic Disorder Due to a General Medical Condition, Personality Change Due to a General Medical Condition, and Mental Disorder Not Otherwise Specified Due to a General Medical Condition).

The common feature of the disorders in this section is that the presenting psychopathology is a direct physiological consequence of a general medical condition. For a further discussion of the process of differentiating a Mental Disorder Due to a General Medical Condition from a primary mental disorder, see Chapter 7. The 11 Mental Disorders Due to a General Medical Condition are as follows:

293.0	Delirium Due to . . . *[Indicate the General Medical Condition]*
—.-	Dementia Due to . . . *[Indicate the General Medical Condition]*
294.0	Amnestic Disorder Due to . . . *[Indicate the General Medical Condition]*
293.8x	Psychotic Disorder Due to . . . *[Indicate the General Medical Condition]*
293.83	Mood Disorder Due to . . . *[Indicate the General Medical Condition]*
293.89	Anxiety Disorder Due to . . . *[Indicate the General Medical Condition]*
—.-	Sexual Dysfunction Due to . . . *[Indicate the General Medical Condition]*
780.5x	Sleep Disorder Due to . . . *[Indicate the General Medical Condition]*
293.89	Catatonic Disorder Due to . . . *[Indicate the General Medical Condition]*
310.1	Personality Change Due to . . . *[Indicate the General Medical Condition]*
293.9	Mental Disorder Not Otherwise Specified Due to . . . *[Indicate the General Medical Condition]*

293.89 Catatonic Disorder Due to . . . *[Indicate the General Medical Condition]*

An important change in DSM-IV is its much more comprehensive presentation of the differential diagnosis of catatonia. Previously, many clinicians incorrectly assumed that catatonia has a special relationship with Schizophrenia because it is included as a subtype of Schizophrenia. In fact, statistically speaking, most catatonic symptoms are not associated with Schizophrenia but occur instead in conjunction with Mood Disorders, general medical conditions, or the use of psychoactive substances or neuroleptic medications. The likelihood that the catatonia is due to a particular condition varies with setting. The association with Schizophrenia is probably strongest in facilities that treat chronically mentally ill persons. The association with Mood Disorders is probably strongest in general psychiatric settings. The association with neurological or other general medical conditions is probably strongest in a general hospital or nursing home setting.

DSM-IV clarified the differential diagnosis of catatonic symptoms in several ways: 1) the inclusion of this category (Catatonic Disorder Due to a General Medical Condition), 2) the inclusion of a new subtype for Mood Disorders (With Catatonic Features), and 3) the provision of a new section for Medication-Induced Movement Disorders.

DSM-IV diagnostic criteria for 293.89 Catatonic Disorder Due to . . . *[Indicate the General Medical Condition]*

A. The presence of catatonia as manifested by motoric immobility, excessive motor activity (that is apparently purposeless and not influenced by external stimuli), extreme negativism or mutism, peculiarities of voluntary movement, or echolalia or echopraxia.

B. There is evidence from the history, physical examination, or laboratory findings that the disturbance is the direct physiological consequence of a general medical condition.

C. The disturbance is not better accounted for by another mental disorder (e.g., a Manic Episode).

D. The disturbance does not occur exclusively during the course of a delirium.

Coding note: Include the name of the general medical condition on Axis I, e.g., 293.89 Catatonic Disorder Due to Hepatic Encephalopathy; also code the general medical condition on Axis III.

Criterion A. Compared with the presentation of catatonia when it is caused by other etiologies (e.g., Schizophrenia, Mood Disorders), Catatonic Disorder Due to a General Medical Condition is more likely to be characterized by motoric immobility and excessive motoric excitement rather than the more classic catatonic symptoms such as waxy flexibility and bizarre posturing. (See Chapter 12 for a description of catatonic symptoms.)

Criterion B. General medical conditions that can cause catatonia include certain neurological conditions (e.g., tumors, trauma, stroke, infections) and metabolic conditions (e.g., diabetic ketoacidosis, liver disease).

310.1 Personality Change Due to . . . *[Indicate the General Medical Condition]*

Personality Change Due to a General Medical Condition was called Organic Personality Disorder in DSM-III-R. The term *organic* was dropped for reasons described in Chapter 7. The term *personality change* replaces *personality disorder* because it more clearly states that there must be a definable change in personality caused by the direct physiological effects of a medical condition. Moreover, it is important not to confuse personality change with an Axis II Personality Disorder. Personality Disorder has an early onset and a relatively stable course and represents a pervasive pattern of characteristic behaviors. In contrast, personality change can arise at any point in the life cycle as a result of the direct effects of a general medical condition and may wax and wane depending on the status of the medical condition. Furthermore, the change in personality is typically manifested by the new onset (or exacerbation) of a specific trait (e.g., aggressiveness, paranoia), not a complex cluster of cognitions and behaviors. Personality change is coded on Axis I and is included in this section of DSM-IV rather than being grouped with the Personality Disorders, which are coded on Axis II.

DSM-IV diagnostic criteria for 310.1 Personality Change Due to . . . *[Indicate the General Medical Condition]*

A. A persistent personality disturbance that represents a change from the individual's previous characteristic personality pattern. (In children, the disturbance involves a marked deviation from normal development or a significant change in the child's usual behavior patterns lasting at least 1 year).

B. There is evidence from the history, physical examination, or laboratory findings that the disturbance is the direct physiological consequence of a general medical condition.

C. The disturbance is not better accounted for by another mental disorder (including other Mental Disorders Due to a General Medical Condition).

D. The disturbance does not occur exclusively during the course of a delirium and does not meet criteria for a dementia.

E. The disturbance causes clinically significant distress or impairment in social, occupational, or other important areas of functioning.

Specify type:

Labile Type: if the predominant feature is affective lability
Disinhibited Type: if the predominant feature is poor impulse control as evidenced by sexual indiscretions, etc.
Aggressive Type: if the predominant feature is aggressive behavior
Apathetic Type: if the predominant feature is marked apathy and indifference
Paranoid Type: if the predominant feature is suspiciousness or paranoid ideation
Other Type: if the predominant feature is not one of the above, e.g., personality change associated with a seizure disorder
Combined Type: if more than one feature predominates in the clinical picture
Unspecified Type

Coding note: Include the name of the general medical condition on Axis I, e.g., 310.1 Personality Change Due to Temporal Lobe Epilepsy; also code the general medical condition on Axis III.

CRITERION A. The personality change can take many different forms depending on the person's premorbid personality characteristics, the region of brain involvement, and the characteristics of the general medical condition. Five specific types of personality change are described and can be indicated by using the subtyping scheme. Very often, no one behavioral manifestation is predominant, and the Combined Type must be indicated. Making the diagnosis of Personality Change Due to a General Medical Condition in childhood is complicated by the fact that it is much less clear what the child's baseline personality is. For example, if a child develops disinhibited behavior sometime after a concussion at age 3, it may be difficult to judge whether the behavior is a direct result of the head trauma or might have emerged anyway.

Criterion B. Many neurological and general medical conditions may cause this condition through a direct physiological mechanism. Personality Change Due to a General Medical Condition must be differentiated from the even more frequent situation in which personality changes develop in response to the psychosocial effects of having a general medical condition. Very often, individuals with a severe and/or chronic general medical condition undergo a personality change in the direction of becoming increasingly dependent and avoidant. This change (unlike Personality Change Due to a General Medical Condition) does not constitute a direct physiological effect and instead would be diagnosed as an Adjustment Disorder. Please refer to Chapter 7 for guidelines on how to establish this etiological connection.

Criterion C. This category must also be distinguished from the personality changes that are a common associated feature, and consequence, of most chronic mental disorders. It is impossible to have Schizophrenia, chronic depression, or long-standing Agoraphobia without also having concomitant changes in personality.

Criterion D. Because personality change is such a common associated feature of dementia (and, less frequently, delirium), an additional diagnosis of Personality Change Due to a General Medical Condition is not made. In some such circumstances (e.g., disinhibited behavior) the dementia subtype "With Behavioral Disturbance" may be appropriate.

Criterion E. Personality Changes Due to a General Medical Condition do not always cause distress or impairment. Occasionally, the change may even seem to be an improvement (e.g., a previously anxious and hypervigilant individual may welcome the symptoms of relative calm that may occur after brain surgery). Such positive personality changes do not, of course, constitute a mental disorder. More often, the personality change may be undesirable but not of sufficient severity or duration to cause clinically significant distress of impairment or warrant a diagnosis.

Subtypes. In the Labile Type, the individual may have rapid and exaggerated emotional responses (e.g., crying suddenly with only minimal provocation but then quickly recovering when distracted). In the Disinhibited Type, the individual may say and do all sorts of inappropriate and impulsive things that are out of character with his or her previous behavior (e.g., making lewd remarks, exposing self, criticizing others, stealing impulsively). In the Aggressive Type, the individual may strike out without warning or consideration of the consequences. In the Apathetic Type, the individual may have a blank face, loss of interest, and unwillingness to participate in previous work activities, hobbies, or social relationships. In the Paranoid Type, the individual may develop the notion that others are acting malevolently. (*Note.* If the individual is delusional, Psychotic Disorder Due to a General Medical Condition is diagnosed instead.)

DSM-IV text for 293.9 Mental Disorder Not Otherwise Specified Due to a General Medical Condition

This residual category should be used for situations in which it has been established that the disturbance is caused by the direct physiological effects of a general medical condition, but the criteria are not met for a specific Mental Disorder Due to a General Medical Condition (e.g., dissociative symptoms due to complex partial seizures).

Coding note: Include the name of general medical condition on Axis I, e.g., 293.9 Mental Disorder Not Otherwise Specified Due to HIV Disease; also code the general medical condition on Axis III.

The Last Word

This chapter is so short because most of the other Mental Disorders Due to a General Medical Condition are contained in other sections of DSM-IV to facilitate differential diagnosis. Despite this chapter's brevity, the concept it embodies is one of the fundamental aspects of differential diagnosis in psychiatry. Many general medical conditions are manifest by psychiatric symptoms. In some cases, the psychiatric symptoms are the first to develop. Therefore, you should always keep the possibility that a psychiatric presentation is due to an underlying general medical condition at the top of your differential diagnostic list and carry out the appropriate physical examination and laboratory testing.

CHAPTER 10

Substance-Related Disorders

Taking exogenous substances to alter mood and behavior has been an integral part of human history and prehistory. Many individuals can partake of substances without having any clinically significant problems that would warrant DSM-IV diagnosis. However, Substance-Related Disorders are among the most common and impairing of the mental disorders. Because substance-related presentations are so frequently encountered in mental health, substance treatment, and primary care settings, a Substance-Related Disorder must be considered in every differential diagnosis.

There are two types of substance-related diagnoses in DSM-IV: the Substance Use Disorders, which describe a pattern of problematic substance use (i.e., Substance Dependence and Substance Abuse); and the Substance-Induced Disorders, which describe behavioral syndromes that are caused by a direct effect of the substance on the central nervous system (CNS) (i.e., intoxication, withdrawal and substance-induced delirium, dementia, amnestic syndrome, psychotic disorder, mood disorder, anxiety disorder, sleep disorder, and sexual dysfunction). Although DSM-IV distinguishes between Substance Use and Substance-Induced Disorders, it should be noted that more often than not Substance-Induced Disorders occur in the context of an accompanying Substance Use Disorder. When this occurs, both should be diagnosed (e.g., Alcohol Withdrawal and Alcohol Dependence).

Twelve classes of substances are recognized in DSM-IV: alcohol; amphetamine and related substances; caffeine; cannabis; cocaine; hallucinogens; inhalants; nicotine; opioids; phencyclidine (PCP) and related substances; sedatives, hypnotics, or anxiolytics; and other substances. One controversy that arose in the organization of the "Substance-Related Disorders" section was how best to classify the problems that sometimes arise as side effects from prescribed or over-the-counter medications normally not considered to be drugs of abuse. In DSM-IV, the term *substance* is intended to refer not only to drugs of abuse, but also to medications and exposure to toxins. Medications that are especially liable to lead to dependence or abuse are included in the drug classes listed above (e.g., opioids, sedatives, amphetamines). However, other medications with psychoactive effects (e.g., steroids, anticholinergics) may occasionally become drugs of abuse. In DSM-IV, these are included under Other (or Unknown) Substance Dependence and Other (or Unknown) Substance Abuse; the comparable categories in DSM-III-R were Psychoactive Substance Dependence Not Otherwise Specified and Psychoactive Substance Abuse Not Otherwise Specified.

The much more commonly encountered problem is that many medications have side effects that are occasionally severe enough to be considered a clinically significant behavioral syndrome (e.g., hallucinations, severe depression, panic attacks). In DSM-III-R, this issue was mentioned only obliquely by including medications among the examples of Other or Unspecified Psychoactive Substance-Induced Organic Mental Disorder. DSM-IV also classifies such presentations as Other (or Unknown) Substance-Related Disorders but is much more explicit in suggesting that medications and toxins be considered in evaluating the cause of psychopathology. Although this decision was certainly the most practical way of dealing with medication-induced psychopathology, it was nonetheless appropriately criticized for lumping together in one category presentations that are caused by drugs of abuse and those that result from the much more innocent use of medication.

It should be noted that not every class of substance causes each and every type of substance-related disorder. A table (Table 10–1) has been provided in DSM-IV to indicate which substances causes which types of problems. For simplicity, DSM-IV has adopted a mix-and-match approach to be used in the generation of the substance-related diagnoses. You begin by indicating the name of the specific substance, followed by the particular substance-related syndrome (e.g., Alcohol Dependence, Inhalant Intoxication, Cocaine-Induced Mood Disorder). Then, you can indicate any appropriate specifiers that may apply. For Substance Dependence, these include With and Without Physiological Dependence and course specifiers. For Substance-Induced Disorders, these include With Onset During Intoxication or With Onset During Withdrawal.

The format for this section differs from the rest of DSM-IV. Rather than having separate criteria sets for each class of substance (e.g., criteria sets for Alcohol Dependence, Cannabis Dependence, Cocaine Dependence, and so forth), DSM-IV provides one generic criteria set for Dependence that is meant to apply to all of the classes of substances that cause Dependence. Similarly, there is a generic criteria set for Substance Abuse, Substance Intoxication, Substance Withdrawal, and for each of the Substance-Induced Disorders (e.g., Substance-Induced Psychotic Disorder). The generic criteria are convenient and also provide a unified construct for defining the Substance-Related Disorders. The disadvantage of this generic approach is that it may obscure differences between drug classes in the presentation of Substance-Related Disorders. For example, although the dependence criteria for opioids and cannabis are the same, Opioid Dependence almost invariably involves physical addiction, whereas Cannabis Dependence almost never does.

Table 10–1. Diagnoses associated with class of substance

	Dependence	Abuse	Intoxication	Withdrawal	Intoxication Delirium	Withdrawal Delirium	Dementia	Amnestic Disorder	Psychotic Disorders	Mood Disorders	Anxiety Disorders	Sexual Dysfunctions	Sleep Disorders
Alcohol	X	X	X	X	I	W	P	P	I/W	I/W	I/W	I	I/W
Amphetamines	X	X	X	X	I				I	I/W	I	I	I/W
Caffeine			X								I		I
Cannabis	X	X	X		I				I		I		
Cocaine	X	X	X	X	I				I	I/W	I/W	I	I/W
Hallucinogens	X	X	X		I				I*	I	I		
Inhalants	X	X	X		I		P		I	I	I		
Nicotine	X			X									
Opioids	X	X	X	X	I				I	I		I	I/W
Phencyclidine	X	X	X		I				I	I	I		
Sedatives, hypnotics, or anxiolytics	X	X	X	X	I	W	P	P	I/W	I/W	W	I	I/W
Polysubstance	X												
Other	X	X	X	X	I	W	P	P	I/W	I/W	I/W	I	I/W

*Also Hallucinogen Persisting Perception Disorder (Flashbacks).

Note: X, I, W, I/W, or P indicates that the category is recognized in DSM-IV. In addition, *I* indicates that the specifier With Onset During Intoxication may be noted for the category (except for Intoxication Delirium); *W* indicates that the specifier With Onset During Withdrawal may be noted for the category (except for Withdrawal Delirium); and *I/W* indicates that either With Onset During Intoxication or With Onset During Withdrawal may be noted for the category. *P* indicates that the disorder is Persisting.

This problem is handled in several ways:

1. The text descriptions for the different classes of substances indicate the specific ways in which each disorder most characteristically presents.
2. Separate criteria sets are provided for the specific intoxication and withdrawal syndromes characteristic of each substance.
3. For Substance Dependence, subtypes are available to indicate the presence of tolerance or withdrawal.

Furthermore, it should be noted that even within a given class of substance, there may be marked variations in the likelihood of a particular Substance-Related Disorder depending on route of administration (e.g., intravenous use, smoking, oral), speed of action (e.g., immediate versus delayed), and duration of effects (e.g, short versus long acting). These variations are also described in some detail in the DSM-IV text for each class of substance.

In some settings (e.g., the emergency room, dual-diagnosis treatment units), substance-induced presentations may be the most commonly encountered diagnoses. Although there were relatively few changes between DSM-III-R and DSM-IV in the specific definitions of the disorders in this section, DSM-IV goes to some length to highlight the increasingly important role of substances in the etiology of psychopathology. This is done in a number of different ways:

1. The criteria sets for the many DSM-IV disorders in which a Substance-Induced Disorder is important in the differential diagnosis include an item requiring that substance use be considered as an etiology to be ruled out.
2. Specific Substance-Induced Disorders are placed in those sections in which substance-induced etiologies are relevant (e.g., Substance-Induced Mood Disorder in the Mood Disorders section, alongside Major Depressive Disorder and Bipolar Disorder).
3. DSM-IV includes additional substance-induced presentations (e.g., Alcohol-Induced Mood Disorder, Alcohol-Induced Sexual Dysfunction) that were not in DSM-III-R.

It is important to recognize that cultural differences in what is considered acceptable and expectable substance use may complicate the diagnosis of a Substance Use Disorder. There are extreme examples on both ends of the spectrum. Within a culture or a religion that requires absolute abstinence, an individual may experience legal, social, or interpersonal consequences that qualify for a diagnosis of Substance Abuse after using relatively minimal amounts and without any impairment except that related to the strict social sanctions. In contrast, individuals in other cultures where considerable substance use is part of the daily norm (e.g., Mediterranean wine drinking) may develop physiological dependence without having a pattern of compulsive use that would warrant a diagnosis of Substance Dependence. Whether giving a Substance Use Disorder diagnosis is warranted in these circumstances is not always clear-cut and depends on the severity of the consequences and the degree of impairment (e.g., has the individual developed cirrhosis?).

The assessment of Substance-Related Disorders is also made difficult by the fact that most individuals underestimate the amount of substances they use, the problems and impairments that result, and their inability to exert control over use. Collateral sources of information are often necessary to supplement what can be learned from careful (and sometimes skeptical) history taking. The clinical interview should be supplemented by laboratory measures reflecting both recent (e.g., blood and urine levels) and longer term use (e.g., liver enzymes); speaking to family members, friends, and the patient's primary care physician and other caretakers; and review of previous medical and legal records. Many individuals use multiple substances simultaneously. If a person admits to using one drug, it is always important to be systematic in inquiring about the use of other classes of substances. The DSM-IV convention is to allow as many Substance-Related Disorders to be diagnosed as are applicable.

We begin with a discussion of Substance Dependence and Substance Abuse that applies across all of the drug classes. We then discuss the Substance-Induced Disorders. Because Substance-Induced Disorders can mimic the presentation of virtually any disorder described in the rest of the manual, they should always be considered in the differential diagnosis of every clinical presentation. Finally, we focus on some of the specific features of each of the 12 substance classes included in DSM-IV.

Substance Use Disorders

Substance Dependence

Substance Dependence

303.90	Alcohol Dependence
304.40	Amphetamine Dependence
304.30	Cannabis Dependence
304.20	Cocaine Dependence
304.50	Hallucinogen Dependence
304.60	Inhalant Dependence
305.10	Nicotine Dependence
304.00	Opioid Dependence
304.90	Phencyclidine Dependence
304.10	Sedative, Hypnotic, or Anxiolytic Dependence
304.80	Polysubstance Dependence
304.90	Other (or Unknown) Substance Dependence

DSM-III had a fairly narrow definition of Substance Dependence that required evidence of physiological dependence (i.e., development of tolerance to the effects of the substance or the development of withdrawal symptoms when substance use is reduced). Although this definition applied well to substances like alcohol, opioids, or sedatives, whose dependence syndrome routinely included tolerance or withdrawal, it was not nearly as relevant to other substances like cannabis, hallucinogens, inhalants, or PCP, which lead to a pattern of compulsive use in the absence of signs of physiological addiction.

In response to this limitation, DSM-III-R incorporated a much broader definition of Dependence that no longer required the presence of tolerance and withdrawal and placed much greater emphasis on aspects of compulsive use. The DSM-III-R reformulation resulted in a higher prevalence of the diagnosis of Substance Dependence (at the expense of Substance Abuse) and much more heterogeneous presentations within the diagnosis of Dependence. To reduce this heterogeneity, DSM-IV includes a subtyping scheme for indicating the presence of Physiological Dependence and provides a more precisely delineated definition of Abuse (see below).

The DSM-IV criteria for Substance Dependence define a cluster of symptoms that indicate that the individual has a pattern of impaired control over substance use. The seven criteria for Dependence can be separated into two types: those pertaining to physiological dependence (Criterion 1 for tolerance and Criterion 2 for withdrawal) and those pertaining to compulsive use (Criteria 3, 4, 5, 6, and 7).

DSM-IV criteria for Substance Dependence

A maladaptive pattern of substance use, leading to clinically significant impairment or distress, as manifested by three (or more) of the following, occurring at any time in the same 12-month period:

(1) tolerance, as defined by either of the following:
- (a) a need for markedly increased amounts of the substance to achieve intoxication or desired effect
- (b) markedly diminished effect with continued use of the same amount of the substance

(2) withdrawal, as manifested by either of the following:
- (a) the characteristic withdrawal syndrome for the substance (refer to Criteria A and B of the criteria sets for Withdrawal from the specific substances)
- (b) the same (or a closely related) substance is taken to relieve or avoid withdrawal symptoms

(3) the substance is often taken in larger amounts or over a longer period than was intended

(4) there is a persistent desire or unsuccessful efforts to cut down or control substance use

(5) a great deal of time is spent in activities necessary to obtain the substance (e.g., visiting multiple doctors or driving long distances), use the substance (e.g., chain-smoking), or recover from its effects

(6) important social, occupational, or recreational activities are given up or reduced because of substance use

(7) the substance use is continued despite knowledge of having a persistent or recurrent physical or psychological problem that is likely to have been caused or exacerbated by the substance (e.g., current cocaine use despite recognition of cocaine-induced depression, or continued drinking despite recognition that an ulcer was made worse by alcohol consumption)

Specify if:

With Physiological Dependence: evidence of tolerance or withdrawal (i.e., either Item 1 or 2 is present)

(continued)

DSM-IV criteria for Substance Dependence *(continued)*

Without Physiological Dependence: no evidence of tolerance or withdrawal (i.e., neither Item 1 nor 2 is present)

Course specifiers:

Early Full Remission
Early Partial Remission
Sustained Full Remission
Sustained Partial Remission
On Agonist Therapy
In a Controlled Environment

Criterion 1. The development of tolerance occurs most frequently with alcohol, amphetamine, cocaine, nicotine, opioids, and sedatives (especially barbiturates). Tolerance refers to the body's acclimation to the effects of the substance. The person must take larger and larger amounts of the substance to achieve the desired effect. If the dose is not increased (usually because of the limited availability or expense of the drug), the effects of having taken the drug are diminished.

Comparing the measured blood levels with the observed mental status is often helpful in determining whether tolerance is present. For example, the presence of tolerance is suggested when there is a high blood level of the substance that does not result in a change in mental and neurological status. However, because there is wide variability in inborn tolerance (i.e., tolerance independent of drug-taking experience), it is also important to document that there has been a change over time in the amount of substance required to produce a given effect. Some people cannot drink more than a small amount of alcohol without developing a headache, upset stomach, or dizziness. Others appear to have an inborn capacity to drink large quantities of alcohol without displaying signs of intoxication.

Criterion 2. Withdrawal is indicated by the development of the characteristic substance-specific withdrawal syndrome shortly after stopping or decreasing the amount of the substance. In some cases, the individual never allows the withdrawal syndrome to develop because he or she starts taking more of the substance in anticipation of the onset of withdrawal symptoms. The severity and clinical significance of the withdrawal syndrome vary by the class of substance. Characteristic withdrawal syndromes are most apparent with alcohol, sedatives, opioids, and nicotine. Criteria sets are also provided for withdrawal from amphetamine and cocaine. Although withdrawal symptoms sometimes occur, no specific criteria sets are provided for withdrawal from cannabis, hallucinogens, inhalants, and PCP. Caffeine withdrawal is a special case and is discussed below.

Criteria 3 and 4. There is something of a paradox inherent in the evaluation of whether the individual is taking more substance than he or she intends or has a persistent desire to cut down substance use. To qualify for these items, the individual must have developed enough insight about having a substance use problem to want to control its use. These items are therefore impossible to evaluate in someone who has a very heavy pattern of use but denies any need to control or cut down use. For example, heavy users of cannabis are often unlikely to attempt to cut down or control their use of the substance because of their perception that cannabis is harmless and congruent with their lifestyle.

Criterion 5. This item (a great deal of time spent obtaining, taking, or recovering from effects of the substance) is especially variable across the classes of drugs because of differences in cost, availability, legality, and the typical pattern of use of the particular substance. For example, the high cost, daily need, and relative unavailability of opioids are much more likely to result in an individual's becoming totally preoccupied with the daily task of procuring them. In contrast, this item is less likely to apply to inhalants because of their low cost, wide availability, and the typical pattern of intermittent use.

Criterion 6. This item (important activities given up) is a reflection of the extent to which the substance has become the focal point of the person's life. Activities surrounding substance use crowd out other aspects of the person's repertoire of interests and activities. This item is often a consequence of Criterion 5 in that the time spent obtaining the substance, using it, and recovering from its effects prevents the person from doing anything else. Moreover, the desire to achieve the drug high may take precedence over pleasure derived from other activities and hobbies.

Criterion 7. The evaluation of this item (continued use despite problems) is a source of considerable confusion. It is meant to tap the pattern of compulsive use of the substance and does not refer merely to the adverse physical or psychological consequences of using the substance. This item applies only when the person is aware that the substance is causing or exacerbating a physical or psychological problem. If the individual has not yet been informed about the problem or does not know that the problem is a consequence of using the substance, the pattern of previous use would not constitute evidence of the kind of loss of control that is defined by this item. For example, this criterion would not apply to an individual merely because he or she has cirrhosis of the liver. It would apply only if he or she continued to drink after the diagnosis was made, despite urgent recommendations to stop. During the DSM-IV deliberations, it was considered whether the presence of a characteristic physical (e.g., cirrhosis) or psychological (e.g., paranoia) sequela in and of itself should count toward a diagnosis of Dependence. Such an item was not included in the criteria set because these types of complications may be due to other etiologies, have relatively low sensitivity, and often appear only late in the course.

Course Modifiers for Substance Dependence

Substance Dependence is hard to overcome. People often have numerous setbacks before gaining control of this problem. The definition of Remission that applies across most of the other disorders in DSM-IV might be misleading and is insufficiently informative in regard to the heterogeneous patterns of Remission that characterize Substance Dependence. Much more detailed and specific course modifiers have been provided to describe the different patterns of Remission from Substance

Dependence that may occur. The price of this increased specificity is the complexity and potential cumbersomeness of the system.

Remission Specifier for Substance Dependence

The following Remission specifiers can be applied only after no criteria for Dependence or Abuse have been met for at least 1 month. Note that these specifiers do not apply if the individual is on agonist therapy or in a controlled environment (see below).

Early Full Remission. This specifier is used if, for at least 1 month, but for less than 12 months, no criteria for Dependence or Abuse have been met.

⇤ Dependence ⇥⇤ 1 month ⇥⇤ 0–11 months ⇥

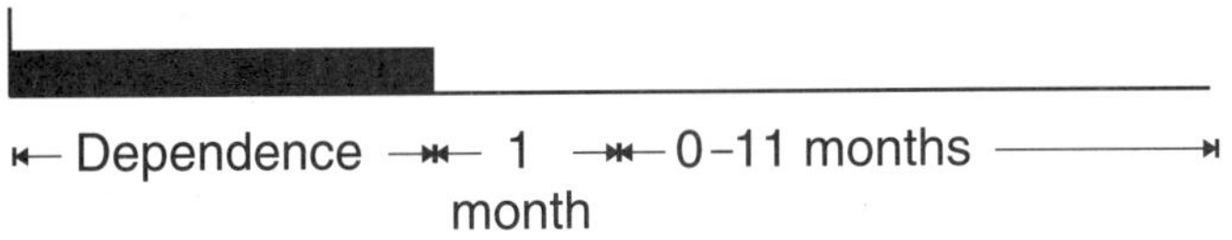

Early Partial Remission. This specifier is used if, for at least 1 month, but less than 12 months, one or more criteria for Dependence or Abuse have been met (but the full criteria for Dependence have not been met).

⇤ Dependence ⇥⇤ 1 month ⇥⇤ 0–11 months ⇥

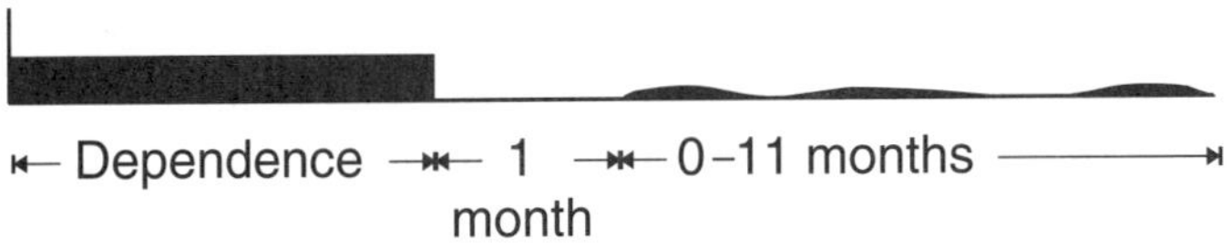

Sustained Full Remission. This specifier is used if none of the criteria for Dependence or Abuse have been met at any time during a period of 12 months or longer.

⇤ Dependence ⇥⇤ 1 month ⇥⇤ 11+ months ⇥

Sustained Partial Remission. This specifier is used if full criteria for Dependence have not been met for a period of 12 months or longer; however, one or more criteria for Dependence or Abuse have been met.

⇤ Dependence ⇥⇤ 1 month ⇥⇤ 11+ months ⇥

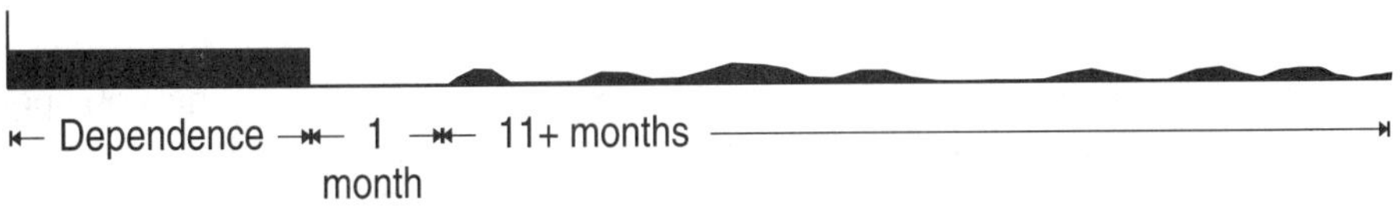

(continued)

> The following specifiers apply if the individual is on agonist therapy or in a controlled environment:
>
> **On Agonist Therapy.** This specifier is used if the individual is on a prescribed agonist medication, and no criteria for Dependence or Abuse have been met for that class of medication for at least the past month (except tolerance to, or withdrawal from, the agonist). This category also applies to those being treated for Dependence using a partial agonist or an agonist/antagonist.
>
> **In a Controlled Environment.** This specifier is used if the individual is in an environment where access to alcohol and controlled substances is restricted, and no criteria for Dependence or Abuse have been met for at least the past month. Examples of these environments are closely supervised and substance-free jails, therapeutic communities, or locked hospital units.

The first course distinction concerns the duration of time that has elapsed since the individual's pattern of substance use last met criteria for Dependence. In DSM-IV, individuals in Early Remission "graduate" to Sustained Remission only after being able to maintain the remission for at least 12 continuous months. The failure to make this distinction in DSM-III-R was problematic because it implied that individuals who have been abstinent for a relatively short period of time (6 months) had the same likelihood to relapse as individuals who have been clean for many years.

The second distinction between Full Remission and Partial Remission is much more controversial. The DSM-IV definitions are fairly liberal in allowing use of the term *remission.* An individual is considered to be in Partial Remission even in the face of continued problematic substance use so long as the full criteria for Dependence or Abuse have not been met. Moreover, these Remission specifiers apply independently to each class of substance for which Dependence criteria have previously been met. Therefore, an individual can be in Sustained Full Remission from alcohol despite continuing to use substances from another class (e.g., diazepam or cocaine). Some clinicians would argue for a much higher standard for the use of the term *remission,* requiring that there be complete abstinence from all substances. Although potentially misleading in its use of the word *remission,* the DSM-IV approach has the advantages of providing a more specific picture of the patient's patterns of drug use on a drug-by-drug basis.

There are certain circumstances in which the use of Early and Sustained Remission does not make any clinical sense. In particular, these specifiers do not apply when individuals are on agonist therapy (e.g., methadone treatment for heroin addiction) or are in an environment where their access to substances is severely restricted (e.g., jail or therapeutic community). The specifiers On Agonist Therapy and In a Controlled Environment have been provided in DSM-IV to correct two paradoxes resulting from the straight application of the DSM-III-R Remission specifiers. In DSM-III-R, those who were successfully treated with agonist therapy were still considered to be fully dependent, whereas those who were drug-free by virtue of incarceration nonetheless would qualify for Full Remission. In contrast, the DSM-IV specifier On Agonist Therapy differentiates between pathological dependence on a street drug and physiological dependence on a prescribed agonist. Furthermore, In A Controlled Environment recognizes that abstinence occurring in the context of limited access has a different prognosis for relapse than abstinence occurring in the face of ready access to substances.

Substance Abuse

Substance Abuse

305.00	Alcohol Abuse
305.70	Amphetamine Abuse
305.20	Cannabis Abuse
305.60	Cocaine Abuse
305.30	Hallucinogen Abuse
305.90	Inhalant Abuse
305.50	Opioid Abuse
305.90	Phencyclidine Abuse
305.40	Sedative, Hypnotic, or Anxiolytic Abuse
305.90	Other (or Unknown) Substance Abuse

At the same time it was greatly expanding the inclusiveness of the concept of Substance Dependence, DSM-III-R was narrowing the concept of Abuse into a mere afterthought. In fact, the early drafts of DSM-III-R deleted Abuse from the system altogether because it was felt that most individuals with clinically significant substance use would qualify for Dependence. In the final drafts of DSM-III-R, Substance Abuse was restored as a residual category, with two criteria that were taken verbatim from items in the DSM-III-R Substance Dependence criteria set.

The DSM-IV literature review, data reanalyses, and field trials suggest that many individuals maintain a stable pattern of Substance Abuse that is characterized by harmful consequences but without evidence of tolerance, withdrawal, or compulsive use. DSM-IV provides a more clear-cut differentiation between Dependence and Abuse, which now have no overlapping items. Dependence is defined by tolerance, withdrawal, or compulsive use, whereas Abuse is defined by adverse consequences in the absence of Dependence.

DSM-IV criteria for Substance Abuse

A. A maladaptive pattern of substance use leading to clinically significant impairment or distress, as manifested by one (or more) of the following, occurring within a 12-month period:

(continued)

DSM-IV criteria for Substance Abuse *(continued)*

(1) recurrent substance use resulting in a failure to fulfill major role obligations at work, school, or home (e.g., repeated absences or poor work performance related to substance use; substance-related absences, suspensions, or expulsions from school; neglect of children or household)
(2) recurrent substance use in situations in which it is physically hazardous (e.g., driving an automobile or operating a machine when impaired by substance use)
(3) recurrent substance-related legal problems (e.g., arrests for substance-related disorderly conduct)
(4) continued substance use despite having persistent or recurrent social or interpersonal problems caused or exacerbated by the effects of the substance (e.g., arguments with spouse about consequences of intoxication, physical fights)

B. The symptoms have never met the criteria for Substance Dependence for this class of substance.

Criterion A. One of the challenges in defining Substance Abuse is how to set its boundary with recreational substance use. Just how adverse must the consequences be before substance use is considered to be Substance Abuse? This criterion uses the words *maladaptive pattern* and *recurrent* to help distinguish between Substance Abuse and nonproblematic use. It should also be noted that an individual with an isolated substance-related incident is not considered to have Substance Abuse no matter how severe the consequences of that one episode.

Criterion A1. In DSM-III-R, impaired role functioning was included as part of the criteria set for Substance Dependence, not Substance Abuse. Indeed, such problems are a fairly ubiquitous feature of Substance Dependence and a consequence of a pattern of compulsive use. In DSM-IV, this item is included in the criteria set for Abuse because problems in role functioning are also an important adverse consequence of substance use that may occur without other evidence of Dependence. This is especially the case when the problem in role functioning is intermittent rather than continuous (e.g., missing a final examination or leaving a child unattended because of intoxication or a hangover).

Criterion A2. A common error in applying this item (use when dangerous) is to be overinclusive and assume that any level of substance use in a situation that requires alertness would qualify. The item applies only when the substance use causes sufficient impairment to create a physically hazardous condition (e.g., driving or hunting while intoxicated). Although certainly undesirable, substance use at a level that does not cause physical or cognitive impairment when alertness is required does not constitute Substance Abuse.

Criterion A3. DSM-IV does not address the question of whether this item should include legal problems resulting from procurement or possession of illicit substances, as well as legal problems that are a direct consequence of the effects of the substance (e.g., violent behavior resulting from intoxication). The item is also particularly hard to evaluate because the occurrence of legal problems is so much a function of local laws, attitudes, and enforcement policies.

CRITERION **A4.** Occasionally this item is difficult to evaluate when the interpersonal conflict is possibly attributable to a relational problem rather than to a problem with the individual's substance use. For example, we would not count toward this item fights about occasional nonproblematic substance use that are initiated by a spouse who is a rabid teetotaler.

CRITERION **B.** For any given class of substance, Abuse is considered to be residual to Dependence. The vast majority of individuals with Substance Dependence suffer adverse consequences and therefore have a pattern that also meets criteria for Substance Abuse. However, to avoid uninformative comorbidity, Substance Abuse is not diagnosed separately in those individuals with current (a or history of) Substance Dependence. Once an individual is diagnosed with Dependence, a diagnosis of Abuse can never be made for that same class of substance. Individuals with a past history of Dependence who develop symptoms of Abuse are therefore considered to be relapsing rather than developing Abuse.

Substance-Induced Disorders

The Substance-Induced Disorders result from the direct physiological effects of acute or chronic substance use on the CNS. These disorders include

Intoxication
Withdrawal
Substance-Induced Delirium
Substance-Induced Persisting Dementia
Substance-Induced Persisting Amnestic Disorder
Substance-Induced Psychotic Disorder
Substance-Induced Mood Disorder
Substance-Induced Anxiety Disorder
Substance-Induced Sexual Dysfunction
Substance-Induced Sleep Disorder

Substance Intoxication/Withdrawal

By far, the most commonly encountered Substance-Induced Disorders are Substance Intoxication and Substance Withdrawal. Criteria sets are provided on pages 184 and 195 in DSM-IV to define the generic concepts of Substance Intoxication and Substance Withdrawal. However, in practice these criteria sets are rarely used and instead are superseded by the substance-specific criteria sets provided in DSM-IV indicating the particular nature of Intoxication and Withdrawal as they apply to each class of substance. In this *Guidebook,* we present the substance-specific Intoxication and Withdrawal syndromes when we discuss each of the classes of substances (discussion follows).

DSM-IV defines Substance Intoxication as "a reversible substance-specific syndrome due to the recent ingestion of (or exposure to) a substance." The DSM-IV concept of Substance Intoxication also requires that this syndrome be maladaptive and result in clinically significant impairment. This definition differs from the more general use of the term *intoxication,* which also covers responses to substance use (e.g., mild euphoria, diminished social anxiety at a party) for which a diagnosis of mental disorder would not be appropriate.

DSM-IV defines Substance Withdrawal as "a substance-specific syndrome due to the cessation of (or reduction in) substance use that has been heavy and prolonged." Very often the symptoms associated with Withdrawal from a substance are opposite from those that characterize Intoxication with it (e.g., drowsiness occurs in Opioid Intoxication, and insomnia occurs in Opioid Withdrawal). When an individual is taking more than one substance (e.g., opioids and cocaine), it may be difficult to determine whether a particular symptom (e.g., insomnia or psychomotor agitation) is due to Intoxication with one substance or Withdrawal from the other.

A number of substances (e.g., alcohol, amphetamines, cannabis, cocaine, opioids, PCP, sedatives) can produce severe perceptual disturbances in association with Intoxication or Withdrawal. In DSM-III-R, these would have been diagnosed as Organic Hallucinosis, a term that was dropped in DSM-IV. In its place, DSM-IV includes three categories that cover such presentations: Substance Intoxication With Perceptual Disturbances, Substance Withdrawal With Perceptual Disturbances, and Substance-Induced Psychotic Disorder With Hallucinations. The specifier With Perceptual Disturbances is provided to describe those presentations in which the Intoxication or Withdrawal is accompanied by clinically significant auditory, visual, or tactile illusions; altered perceptions; or hallucinations with intact reality testing. It should be used only when the perceptual disturbances are beyond what might be expected for the particular substance and are clinically significant in their own right. The decision to use the specifier With Perceptual Disturbances versus Substance-Induced Psychotic Disorder With Hallucinations depends on whether the person maintains reality testing as to the nature of the altered perceptions. For example, if an individual has pleasant hallucinations during the use of PCP, the diagnosis would be Phencyclidine Intoxication. However, if the hallucinations are particularly disturbing and a focus of clinical attention, the diagnosis should be Phencyclidine Intoxication With Perceptual Disturbance. Finally, if the individual is responding to the hallucinations under the belief that they are real (e.g., responding to a command auditory hallucination to hurt someone), the diagnosis is Phencyclidine-Induced Psychotic Disorder, With Hallucinations.

Other Substance-Induced Disorders

Not infrequently, Substance Intoxication and Substance Withdrawal are characterized by psychopathology that mimics the other disorders contained in the rest of DSM-IV. The other Substance-Induced Disorders (e.g., Substance-Induced Mood

Disorder, Substance-Induced Persisting Dementia) have been included in DSM-IV to diagnose such presentations and emphasize that they must be considered in the differential diagnosis of all psychiatric presentations (see Chapter 7 for a discussion of how to make this differential).

It should be noted, however, that not every dysphoria need be diagnosed as Substance-Induced Mood Disorder and not every confusion as Substance-Induced Delirium. Frequently, a diagnosis of Substance Intoxication or Substance Withdrawal will suffice. A more specific Substance-Induced Disorder (e.g., Substance-Induced Anxiety Disorder) should be diagnosed only when the symptom is in excess of that usually encountered with the Intoxication or Withdrawal syndrome characteristic of that substance and warrants independent clinical attention. In such cases, it is not necessary to give an additional diagnosis of Substance Intoxication or Substance Withdrawal. Instead, the specifier With Onset During Intoxication or With Onset During Withdrawal can be indicated.

The psychiatric sequelae to substance use can occur in any of the following four contexts:

1. As an acute effect of Substance Intoxication
2. As an acute effect of Substance Withdrawal
3. As a medication side effect not necessarily related to Intoxication or Withdrawal
4. As an effect that endures even after the substance is no longer present

Diagnosis of a Substance-Induced Disorder that occurs in the first three contexts is discussed in some detail in the next part of this chapter. The fourth context is known in DSM-IV as Substance-Induced Persisting Disorder. The presumption here is that the psychopathology results not from the acute effects of the substance (including toxins) but rather from the structural damage it has caused to the CNS. DSM-IV recognizes only three such disorders: Substance-Induced Persisting Dementia, Substance-Induced Persisting Amnestic Disorder, and Hallucinogen Persisting Perception Disorder. Other substance-induced persisting syndromes (e.g., psychotic disorder, personality change) have been described in the literature but were thought to be not well enough established to be officially recognized as separate categories in DSM-IV. These presentations would be diagnosed by using the substance-specific Not Otherwise Specified (NOS) category (e.g., Cannabis-Related Disorder NOS for personality changes related to long-term use of cannabis; Hallucinogen-Related Disorder NOS for persisting delusions lasting after the acute effects of lysergic acid diethylamide [LSD] have worn off).

To facilitate differential diagnosis, the text and criteria for the Substance-Induced Disorders (other than Substance Intoxication and Substance Withdrawal) are included in the sections of DSM-IV with which they share phenomenology. In a parallel fashion, we have distributed these criteria sets in the appropriate sections of the *Guidebook* (e.g., the text and criteria sets for Substance-Induced Mood Disorder are included in Chapter 12, "Mood Disorders"). Most of the DSM-IV Substance-Induced Disorders share the following criteria, which are included as a guide to the clinical judgment of whether substance use is causing the presenting symptom picture.

Summary of DSM-IV diagnostic criteria for Substance-Induced Disorders (Substance-Induced Delirium, Psychotic Disorder, Mood Disorder, Anxiety Disorder, Sexual Dysfunction, Sleep Disorder)

A. Presence of the particular psychiatric symptom.

B. There is evidence from the history, physical examination, or laboratory findings that either (1) or (2)

   (1) the symptoms in A developed during, or within a month of, Substance Intoxication or Withdrawal

   (2) medication use is etiologically related to the disturbance

C. The disturbance is not better accounted for by a mental disorder that is not substance-induced. Evidence that the symptoms are better accounted for by a mental disorder that is not substance-induced might include: the symptoms precede the onset of the substance abuse or dependence (or medication use or toxin exposure); symptoms persist for a substantial period of time (e.g., about a month) after the cessation of acute withdrawal or severe intoxication, or are substantially in excess of what would be expected given the character, duration, or amount of the substance used; or there is other evidence suggesting the existence of an independent non-substance-induced mental disorder (e.g., a history of recurrent non-substance-related episodes).

   Note: This diagnosis should be made instead of a diagnosis of Substance Intoxication or Substance Withdrawal only when the symptoms are in excess of those usually associated with the intoxication or withdrawal syndrome and when the symptoms are sufficiently severe to warrant independent clinical attention.

Specify if:

With Onset During Intoxication: if the criteria are met for Intoxication with the substance

With Onset During Withdrawal: if criteria are met for Withdrawal from the substance and the symptoms develop during, or within 4 weeks of, the withdrawal syndrome

---

Note: This is a summary of six criteria sets.

CRITERION A. In each of the Substance-Induced Disorders, Criterion A describes the characteristic psychiatric symptomatology. Substances can produce most of the psychopathology known to humankind. The specific substance-induced presentations covered in DSM-IV include delirium, memory impairment, delusions, hallucinations, mood disturbances, anxiety, obsessions, compulsions, phobias, sexual dysfunctions, and sleep disturbances.

Other substance-induced presentations are not covered by any of the Substance-Induced Disorders listed specifically in DSM-IV. Perhaps the most common of these are dissociative symptoms of depersonalization and derealization associated with substance use. If the dissociative symptoms are not in excess of what is usually encountered with Intoxication or Withdrawal, the diagnosis of Substance Intoxication or Substance Withdrawal should be given. In cases where the dissociation is particularly problematic, this can be indicated by a diagnosis of the specific Substance-Related Disorder Not Otherwise Specified (e.g., Cannabis-Related Disorder NOS for depersonalization due to cannabis use).

It should be noted that in order to qualify for a diagnosis of a Substance-Induced Disorder, the psychiatric symptoms need only be clinically significant. They do not have to conform to the specific symptom patterns or thresholds that define the disorders in that section (e.g., depressed mood need not last for at least 2 weeks for a diagnosis of Substance-Induced Mood Disorder).

Not infrequently, substances produce presentations that are characterized by a mix of psychopathology that cuts across a number of different diagnostic groups (e.g., a presentation with psychotic, mood, and anxiety symptoms). Generally in such cases, only the most prominent Substance-Induced Disorder is diagnosed. In mixed pictures, delirium always takes priority (as indicated by an exclusion criterion for substance-induced delirium that is part of the criteria set for each of the other substance-specific disorders). Next on the list would be Substance-Induced Psychotic Disorder, which is generally given preference over other presentations. For the rest, it is a matter of clinical judgment which of the presenting symptoms is most prominent or in need of clinical attention. Necessarily, this decision is sometimes arbitrary, especially in the not-uncommon mix of equally prominent mood and anxiety symptoms.

CRITERION B. It should be recalled that when DSM-IV uses the generic term *substance,* it is meant to include drugs of abuse, medication side effects, and the effects of toxin exposure. As a result, this criterion has been split into two parts. The first part pertains to psychopathology caused by those drugs of abuse (and some medications) that produce Intoxication or Withdrawal syndromes. The second part is for psychopathology caused by medication side effects or toxin exposure not occurring in the context of an Intoxication or Withdrawal syndrome.

The first part of this criterion serves to establish a temporal relationship between substance use and the onset of psychopathology by requiring that the onset of the psychiatric symptoms must be within a month of Intoxication or Withdrawal. Psychiatric symptoms due to Intoxication develop during the period in which the person is experiencing the acute effects of having taken the substance. In Withdrawal, the symptoms develop after the acute effects of having taken the substance have subsided and the blood level of the substance is falling. The actual time frame depends on the particular pharmacokinetics of the substance: For substances with a short half-life (e.g., cocaine), symptoms of Withdrawal develop shortly after the person stopped using the substance; for substances with a protracted half-life (e.g., long-acting benzodiazepines), a relatively long period of time (sometimes up to several weeks) might elapse before the emergence of Withdrawal symptoms.

The second part of Criterion B suggests that clinical judgment must be used in determining whether medication use or toxin exposure is etiologically related to the psychopathology. In our experience, this is a crucial and often underrecognized problem. Not infrequently, the role of medication side effects in causing psychopathology is missed, and patients may receive even more medication to treat a problem that was created by medication in the first place. For example, the misattribution of insomnia to depression rather than to a medication side effect may result in the inappropriate raising rather than lowering of an antidepressant dosage. In many situations, the only way to clarify the etiology of the psychopathology is to reduce or discontinue the medication and do systematic follow-up evaluations.

Criterion C. This is the criterion that provides guidelines for distinguishing between a primary psychopathology and one that is substance induced. Despite many attempts at wordsmithing, it is not easy to read because of a confusing double negative. Criterion C winds up defining guidelines for NOT attributing the psychopathology to the substance, rather than the other way around. For a detailed discussion that may help the clinician wade through this quagmire, refer to Chapter 7, "Ruling Out Substance Etiology," in this book.

Annotation for Note. This note was added to clarify the circumstances when the clinician should diagnose Intoxication or Withdrawal instead of one of the Substance-Induced Disorders listed above. It is meant to prevent an overdiagnosis of Substance-Induced Disorders. Obviously, mood, anxiety, sleep, sexual, cognitive, and even psychotic symptoms are part of the criteria sets (or are associated features) of various types of Substance Intoxication or Withdrawal. In most cases, however, it does not make sense to pull out individual symptoms and make a separate diagnosis of a specific Substance-Induced Disorder. These diagnoses of Substance-Induced Disorders are reserved for those special situations that cry out for special attention.

Annotation for Specifiers. DSM-IV provides specifiers to indicate whether the Substance-Induced Disorder has its onset during Intoxication or during Withdrawal. These specifiers were included because of their possible importance for management and prognosis. Because of the availability of these specifiers, it is generally not necessary to give a separate diagnosis of Substance Intoxication or Withdrawal when the individual has a specific Substance-Induced Disorder. However, if it is important to call attention to both (e.g., an individual who has physical symptoms of Alcohol Withdrawal and severe enough mood symptoms to be suicidal), then each can be diagnosed.

It must be recognized that the determination of whether the symptoms have their onset during Intoxication or Withdrawal is often difficult or impossible. Even if the individual has taken only one substance, it may be difficult to say with any degree of certainty whether the symptoms are due to the intoxicating effects of the drug or to withdrawal effects related to falling drug levels. This is even more of a problem in the not infrequently encountered clinical situation of multiple substance use in which the individual may be intoxicated with one substance and withdrawing from another.

Specific Substances

The "Depressants": Alcohol-Related Disorders and Sedative-, Hypnotic-, or Anxiolytic-Related Disorders

Depressants

Alcohol-Related Disorders

Alcohol Use Disorders

303.90 Alcohol Dependence

305.00 Alcohol Abuse

(continued)

Alcohol-Induced Disorders	
303.00	Alcohol Intoxication
291.8	Alcohol Withdrawal
291.0	Alcohol Intoxication Delirium
291.0	Alcohol Withdrawal Delirium
291.2	Alcohol-Induced Persisting Dementia
291.1	Alcohol-Induced Persisting Amnestic Disorder
291.5	Alcohol-Induced Psychotic Disorder, With Delusions
291.3	Alcohol-Induced Psychotic Disorder, With Hallucinations
291.8	Alcohol-Induced Mood Disorder
291.8	Alcohol-Induced Anxiety Disorder
291.8	Alcohol-Induced Sexual Dysfunction
291.8	Alcohol-Induced Sleep Disorder
291.9	Alcohol-Related Disorder Not Otherwise Specified
Sedative-, Hypnotic-, or Anxiolytic-Related Disorders	
Sedative, Hypnotic, or Anxiolytic Use Disorders	
304.10	Sedative, Hypnotic, or Anxiolytic Dependence
305.40	Sedative, Hypnotic, or Anxiolytic Abuse
Sedative-, Hypnotic-, or Anxiolytic-Induced Disorders	
292.89	Sedative, Hypnotic, or Anxiolytic Intoxication
292.0	Sedative, Hypnotic, or Anxiolytic Withdrawal
292.81	Sedative, Hypnotic, or Anxiolytic Intoxication Delirium
292.81	Sedative, Hypnotic, or Anxiolytic Withdrawal Delirium
292.82	Sedative-, Hypnotic-, or Anxiolytic-Induced Persisting Dementia
292.83	Sedative-, Hypnotic-, or Anxiolytic-Induced Persisting Amnestic Disorder
292.11	Sedative-, Hypnotic-, or Anxiolytic-Induced Psychotic Disorder, With Delusions
292.12	Sedative-, Hypnotic-, or Anxiolytic-Induced Psychotic Disorder, With Hallucinations
292.84	Sedative-, Hypnotic-, or Anxiolytic-Induced Mood Disorder
292.89	Sedative-, Hypnotic-, or Anxiolytic-Induced Anxiety Disorder
292.89	Sedative-, Hypnotic-, or Anxiolytic-Induced Sexual Dysfunction
292.89	Sedative-, Hypnotic-, or Anxiolytic-Induced Sleep Disorder
292.89	Sedative-, Hypnotic-, or Anxiolytic-Related Disorder Not Otherwise Specified

In DSM-IV, the CNS depressants are divided into one section for alcohol and another section for the sedatives, hypnotics, and anxiolytics. This division is somewhat artificial because all the CNS depressants have similar Intoxication and Withdrawal syndromes and induce cross-tolerance with one another (e.g., an individual with tolerance to alcohol will be able to ingest relatively high doses of sedatives with less than their usual effect). In fact, the criteria sets for Intoxication and Withdrawal are identical for the two classes. Nonetheless, the division between alcohol and the sedatives, hypnotics, and anxiolytics does have some utility because of differences in demographics, patterns of use, and complications.

Alcohol is the most commonly abused substance in most parts of the world and is responsible for a great deal of morbidity and mortality. More than most other substances, the use of alcohol directly leads to a number of potentially very serious medical complications (e.g., cirrhosis, pancreatitis, gastrointestinal bleeding, peripheral neuropathy). The sedatives, hypnotics, and anxiolytics include all prescription sleeping medications and almost all prescription antianxiety medications (except nonbenzodiazepine agents) and are available both by prescription and from illicit sources. The use of medications with a short to intermediate duration of effect is especially likely to result in a pattern of Dependence or Abuse. Sedatives, hypnotics, and anxiolytics can be lethal at high doses, particularly when mixed with alcohol. Intoxication with the CNS depressants is a frequent contributing factor in accidents, suicides, and violence. Especially in high doses, these substances may cause blackouts—loss of memory for events that occurred during Intoxication.

The timely recognition of Alcohol and Sedative, Hypnotic, or Anxiolytic Withdrawal is of particular importance. DSM-IV handles delirium occurring during withdrawal from CNS depressants (delirium tremens [DTs]) in a special way because it is particularly dangerous and has such different implications from those of delirium occurring in the context of Intoxication. DSM-IV provides two separate criteria sets for delirium associated with CNS depressants: one for Intoxication Delirium and one for Withdrawal Delirium. In contrast, for other substances, only a single criteria set is provided for Substance-Induced Delirium, with the onset indicated by using the specifiers With Onset During Intoxication or With Onset During Withdrawal. The criteria for Withdrawal Delirium are located in Chapter 8, and we discuss there the boundary between delirium and Withdrawal. The clinician should be aware that the onset of Withdrawal symptoms from CNS depressants can be delayed hours to days after the last dose, especially for the longer acting substances.

Summary of DSM-IV diagnostic criteria for 303.00 Alcohol Intoxication and 292.89 Sedative, Hypnotic, or Anxiolytic Intoxication

A. Recent ingestion of alcohol or use of a sedative, hypnotic, or anxiolytic.

B. Clinically significant maladaptive behavioral or psychological changes (e.g., inappropriate sexual or aggressive behavior, mood lability, impaired judgment, impaired social or occupational functioning) developing during, or shortly after, use.

C. At least one of the following signs, developing during or shortly after use:
(1) slurred speech
(2) incoordination
(3) unsteady gait
(4) nystagmus
(5) impairment in attention or memory
(6) stupor or coma

D. Not due to a general medical condition and not better accounted for by another mental disorder.

Note: This is a summary of two criteria sets.

Summary of DSM-IV diagnostic criteria for 291.8 Alcohol Withdrawal and 292.0 Sedative, Hypnotic, or Anxiolytic Withdrawal

A. Cessation (or reduction) of alcohol (or sedative, hypnotic, or anxiolytic) use that has been heavy and prolonged.

B. At least two of the following, developing within several hours to a few days after A:
   (1) autonomic hyperactivity (e.g., sweating or pulse rate greater than 100)
   (2) increased hand tremor
   (3) insomnia
   (4) nausea or vomiting
   (5) transient visual, tactile, or auditory hallucinations or illusions
   (6) psychomotor agitation
   (7) anxiety
   (8) grand mal seizures

C. The symptoms in B cause clinically significant distress or impairment in social, occupational, or other important areas of functioning.

D. Not due to a general medical condition and not better accounted for by another mental disorder.

Specify if:
With Perceptual Disturbances

Note: This is a summary of two criteria sets.

The "Stimulants": Amphetamine (or Amphetamine-Like)–Related Disorders and Cocaine-Related Disorders

Stimulants

Amphetamine (or Amphetamine-Like)–Related Disorders

Amphetamine Use Disorders

304.40	Amphetamine Dependence
305.70	Amphetamine Abuse

Amphetamine-Induced Disorders

292.89	Amphetamine Intoxication
292.0	Amphetamine Withdrawal
292.81	Amphetamine Intoxication Delirium
292.11	Amphetamine-Induced Psychotic Disorder, With Delusions
292.12	Amphetamine-Induced Psychotic Disorder, With Hallucinations
292.84	Amphetamine-Induced Mood Disorder
292.89	Amphetamine-Induced Anxiety Disorder
292.89	Amphetamine-Induced Sexual Dysfunction
292.89	Amphetamine-Induced Sleep Disorder
292.9	Amphetamine-Related Disorder Not Otherwise Specified

Cocaine-Related Disorders

Cocaine Use Disorders

304.20	Cocaine Dependence
305.60	Cocaine Abuse

Cocaine-Induced Disorders

292.89	Cocaine Intoxication
292.0	Cocaine Withdrawal
292.81	Cocaine Intoxication Delirium
292.11	Cocaine-Induced Psychotic Disorder, With Delusions
292.12	Cocaine-Induced Psychotic Disorder, With Hallucinations
292.84	Cocaine-Induced Mood Disorder
292.89	Cocaine-Induced Anxiety Disorder
292.89	Cocaine-Induced Sexual Dysfunction
292.89	Cocaine-Induced Sleep Disorder
292.9	Cocaine-Related Disorder Not Otherwise Specified

DSM-IV divides the stimulants into three drug classes: amphetamines and other similarly acting stimulants (e.g., methylphenidate and some appetite suppressants), cocaine, and caffeine. Because caffeine has such a different pattern of use and implications, it is discussed separately below.

Amphetamine and cocaine have similar psychoactive effects and have identical criteria sets to describe Intoxication and Withdrawal. However, unlike cocaine, amphetamines do not have local anesthetic properties, have less risk for inducing certain general medical conditions (e.g., cardiac arrhythmias and seizures), and can be obtained through legal channels because amphetamines are indicated in the treatment of several disorders (e.g., Attention-Deficit/Hyperactivity Disorder, Narcolepsy). The most common route for amphetamine administration is oral, although they can also be taken intravenously, and methamphetamine (speed) can be snorted.

Cocaine is available in several different forms (and called by different names), but the active substance is the same. Cocaine in powder form is usually snorted and less often is taken intravenously. Because "crack" (a cocaine alkaloid extracted from its powdered hydrochloride salt) is smoked, its effects have an extremely rapid onset. This preparation of cocaine is particularly nefarious because of its wide availability, relatively low cost, high risk of addiction, and tendency to cause severe psychiatric and medical complications.

The symptomatic nature of the Intoxication syndrome depends on the specific drug and dosage pattern, the route of administration, the environmental context, and characteristics of the user (e.g., tolerance, rate of absorption, chronicity of use). Two patterns of use characterize these classes of substances: episodic use (binges) and chronic daily use. The most characteristic symptoms of Intoxication are euphoria and increased psychomotor and autonomic activity (e.g., increased pulse rate and elevated blood pressure). However, some chronic users instead develop the opposite effects (e.g., sadness, decreased blood pressure). Intoxication, particularly with cocaine, can sometimes lead to serious medical complications (e.g., myocardial infarction, stroke, seizures) or sudden death from respiratory or cardiac arrest. What goes up ultimately also comes down. Withdrawal from stimulants is characterized by symptoms that are in the opposite direction from those typical of Intoxication (e.g., dysphoria, low energy, hypersomnia, suicidal thoughts).

Summary of DSM-IV diagnostic criteria for 292.89 Amphetamine Intoxication and 292.89 Cocaine Intoxication

A. Recent use of amphetamine or a related substance (e.g., methylphenidate)/cocaine.

B. Clinically significant maladaptive behavioral or psychological changes (e.g., euphoria or affective blunting; changes in sociability; hypervigilance; interpersonal sensitivity; anxiety, tension, or anger; stereotyped behaviors; impaired judgment; or impaired social or occupational functioning) developing during, or shortly after, use of amphetamine or a related substance.

C. At least two of the following, developing during, or shortly after, use:
(1) tachycardia or bradycardia
(2) pupillary dilation
(3) elevated or lowered blood pressure
(4) perspiration or chills
(5) nausea or vomiting
(6) evidence of weight loss
(7) psychomotor agitation or retardation
(8) muscular weakness, respiratory depression, chest pain, or cardiac arrhythmias
(9) confusion, seizures, dyskinesias, dystonias, or coma

D. Not due to a general medical condition and not better accounted for by another mental disorder.

Specify if:
With Perceptual Disturbances: auditory, visual, or tactile illusions; altered perceptions or hallucinations with intact reality testing

Note: This is a summary of two criteria sets.

Summary of DSM-IV diagnostic criteria for 292.0 Amphetamine Withdrawal and 292.0 Cocaine Withdrawal

A. Cessation (or reduction) of amphetamine (or related substance) use that has been heavy and prolonged.

B. Dysphoric mood and at least two of the following physiological changes, developing within a few hours to several days after A:
(1) fatigue
(2) vivid, unpleasant dreams
(3) insomnia or hypersomnia
(4) increased appetite
(5) psychomotor retardation or agitation

C. The symptoms in B cause clinically significant distress or impairment in social, occupational, or other important areas of functioning.

D. Not due to a general medical condition and not better accounted for by another mental disorder.

Note: This is a summary of two criteria sets.

Caffeine-Related Disorders

Caffeine

Caffeine-Related Disorders

Caffeine-Induced Disorders

305.90	Caffeine Intoxication
292.89	Caffeine-Induced Anxiety Disorder
292.89	Caffeine-Induced Sleep Disorder
292.9	Caffeine-Related Disorder Not Otherwise Specified

Caffeine is available from many different sources and is by far the most commonly used psychoactive substance in the world. The most potent source of caffeine is coffee, with amounts ranging from 50 to 125 mg per 6 ounces depending on the type, strength, and method of preparation. Tea and caffeinated soft drinks provide smaller amounts (40–50 mg per serving). Caffeine is also available at the drug store in a wide variety of nonprescription products (as a component of analgesics, cold preparations, and appetite suppressants and in pure tablet form as a stimulant to counteract sleep). Caffeine is even available at the candy counter, although in much lower doses (e.g., 5 mg per chocolate bar).

There was much discussion (and a literature review) concerning whether caffeine dependence and caffeine withdrawal should be included in DSM-IV. It is certainly well established that heavy caffeine users can develop physiological dependence on caffeine that includes tolerance and withdrawal. The issue was not whether these syndromes exist, but rather whether they cause sufficient clinically significant distress and impairment to warrant being included as separate categories in DSM-IV, with the implication that these are to be considered mental disorders.

Caffeine Intoxication is included in DSM-IV because it is an important differential diagnostic consideration for a number of psychiatric disorders (e.g., anxiety, mood, substance) and general medical conditions (e.g., cardiovascular, gastrointestinal). Certainly symptoms of caffeine withdrawal (e.g., headache, drowsiness, dysphoria, gastrointestinal complaints) are common enough among heavy caffeine users. Nonetheless, the decision was made not to include caffeine withdrawal as an official category precisely because it is so ubiquitous and so rarely associated with clinically significant distress or impairment and because it had received relatively little research attention. This should not lead the clinician to overlook caffeine withdrawal as part of the differential diagnosis of Mood and Anxiety Disorders and general medical conditions. Caffeine withdrawal may also sometimes be an important target of clinical intervention when it promotes caffeine dependence in an individual for whom this dependence is problematic (e.g., when caffeine exacerbates an arrhythmia or peptic ulcer). A research criteria set for caffeine withdrawal is included in DSM-IV Appendix B. Within the DSM-IV classification, clinically significant caffeine withdrawal is diagnosed as Caffeine-Related Disorder Not Otherwise Specified.

DSM-IV diagnostic criteria for 305.90 Caffeine Intoxication

A. Recent consumption of caffeine, usually in excess of 250 mg (e.g., more than 2–3 cups of brewed coffee).

B. Five (or more) of the following signs, developing during, or shortly after, caffeine use:
   (1) restlessness
   (2) nervousness
   (3) excitement
   (4) insomnia
   (5) flushed face
   (6) diuresis
   (7) gastrointestinal disturbance
   (8) muscle twitching
   (9) rambling flow of thought and speech
   (10) tachycardia or cardiac arrhythmia
   (11) periods of inexhaustibility
   (12) psychomotor agitation

C. The symptoms in Criterion B cause clinically significant distress or impairment in social, occupational, or other important areas of functioning.

D. The symptoms are not due to a general medical condition and are not better accounted for by another mental disorder (e.g., an Anxiety Disorder).

Cannabis-Related Disorders

Cannabis

Cannabis-Related Disorders

Cannabis Use Disorders

304.30	Cannabis Dependence
305.20	Cannabis Abuse

Cannabis-Induced Disorders

292.89	Cannabis Intoxication
292.81	Cannabis Intoxication Delirium
292.11	Cannabis-Induced Psychotic Disorder, With Delusions
292.12	Cannabis-Induced Psychotic Disorder, With Hallucinations
292.89	Cannabis-Induced Anxiety Disorder
292.9	Cannabis-Related Disorder Not Otherwise Specified

Cannabis is the most frequently used illicit drug. Cannabis is usually smoked in the form of marijuana leaves or hashish (the dried resin from marijuana plants) but may also be ingested orally. The most active ingredient in the various preparations of cannabis is delta-9-tetrahydrocannabinol (known as THC). When cannabis is smoked, Cannabis Intoxication occurs within minutes and usually lasts for several hours. When it is ingested, intoxication may take several hours to begin and will persist for a comparably longer period of time. The nature of the intoxication usually depends on the dose, method of administration, environmental context, and individual features of the user. Although symptoms of cannabis withdrawal (dysphoric mood, tremor, perspiration, nausea, and sleep disturbances) may occasionally occur after episodes of heavy use, this is not included in DSM-IV as a separate diagnosis because such symptoms rarely occasion clinical attention.

In high doses and in susceptible individuals, cannabis can produce effects that resemble hallucinogen-induced "bad trips" (e.g., illusions, depersonalization, derealization, paranoid ideation, delusions, or hallucinations). If reality testing as to the source of these symptoms is preserved, the diagnosis would be Cannabis Intoxication With Perceptual Disturbances. Cannabis-Induced Psychotic Disorder is the appropriate diagnosis when reality testing has been lost and the patient is delusional or hallucinating.

DSM-IV diagnostic criteria for 292.89 Cannabis Intoxication

A. Recent use of cannabis.

B. Clinically significant maladaptive behavioral or psychological changes (e.g., impaired motor coordination, euphoria, anxiety, sensation of slowed time, impaired judgment, social withdrawal) that developed during, or shortly after, cannabis use.

C. Two (or more) of the following signs, developing within 2 hours of cannabis use:
   (1) conjunctival injection
   (2) increased appetite
   (3) dry mouth
   (4) tachycardia

D. The symptoms are not due to a general medical condition and are not better accounted for by another mental disorder.

Specify if:
With Perceptual Disturbances

Hallucinogen-Related Disorders

Hallucinogens

Hallucinogen-Related Disorders

Hallucinogen Use Disorders

304.50 Hallucinogen Dependence

305.30 Hallucinogen Abuse

(continued)

Hallucinogen-Induced Disorders

292.89	Hallucinogen Intoxication
292.89	Hallucinogen Persisting Perception Disorder (Flashbacks)
292.81	Hallucinogen Intoxication Delirium
292.11	Hallucinogen-Induced Psychotic Disorder, With Delusions
292.12	Hallucinogen-Induced Psychotic Disorder, With Hallucinations
292.84	Hallucinogen-Induced Mood Disorder
292.89	Hallucinogen-Induced Anxiety Disorder
292.9	Hallucinogen-Related Disorder Not Otherwise Specified

In their various forms, hallucinogens have been used for thousands of years and in a wide variety of cultures around the world. The hallucinogens include such compounds as LSD, morning glory seeds, mescaline, MDMA (3,4-methylenedioxymethamphetamine or Ecstasy), psilocybin, certain types of mushrooms, and miscellaneous other compounds. Despite the fact that PCP and cannabis can also cause perceptual disturbances, by convention DSM-IV considers these to be separate classes of substances. Most of the hallucinogens are taken orally. Although physiological tolerance to hallucinogens can develop with persistent and repeated heavy use, a withdrawal syndrome has not been described. Because physiological dependence on hallucinogens is relatively rare, it is the compulsive use of the substance that marks Hallucinogen Dependence.

Perceptual changes are the hallmark of Hallucinogen Intoxication. At low doses, these changes usually take the form of illusions (misperception of a real stimulus, e.g., interpreting a flame as a flower). Hallucinogens also cause the interesting phenomenon of synesthesia (a transformation of sensory experience from one modality to another, e.g., sounds appearing as colors). At higher doses, there may be hallucinations. These are usually visual but more rarely may also be auditory or tactile.

Intoxication with hallucinogens usually results in perceptual distortions with intact reality testing. Rather than responding to the perceptions as if they were real, the user realizes that the perceptual changes stem from having taken the drug. Occasionally, however, the perceptual changes after hallucinogen use may evolve into frank psychosis with hallucinations and delusions—especially when the dose is high and the individual is susceptible. Intoxication with hallucinogens can sometimes be deadly due to the dangerous behavioral reactions that occur (e.g., jumping off a roof because of the fear of being pursued or the conviction that one can fly).

The psychotic symptoms are usually short-lived. On occasion, however, the use of hallucinogens appears to provoke a persistent psychotic state that lasts long after the effect of the hallucinogens should have have worn off. Often, it is not clear in these situations whether the psychotic symptoms would have occurred anyway, independently of hallucinogen use, or whether they represent a persistent complication of hallucinogen use. This evaluation is complicated by the fact that psychotic reactions to hallucinogens appear to be more common in individuals with preexisting mental disorders. The DSM-IV Substance Use Work Group reviewed the suggestion to include a Hallucinogen-Induced Persisting Psychotic Disorder but decided that there was as yet insufficient evidence to warrant its inclusion. In any given case, however, when the clinician believes that a persistent psychotic state is the direct physiological consequence of hallucinogen use, the diagnosis would be Hallucinogen-Related Disorder Not Otherwise Specified.

Much more common than persisting psychotic reactions are flashbacks, which recall aspects of past episodes of Hallucinogen Intoxication. In DSM-IV, these can be diagnosed as Hallucinogen Persisting Perception Disorder when they lead to clinically significant distress or impairment. By definition, reality testing for the misperceptions must remain intact in a flashback.

DSM-IV diagnostic criteria for 292.89 Hallucinogen Intoxication

A. Recent use of a hallucinogen.

B. Clinically significant maladaptive behavioral or psychological changes (e.g., marked anxiety or depression, ideas of reference, fear of losing one's mind, paranoid ideation, impaired judgment, or impaired social or occupational functioning) that developed during, or shortly after, hallucinogen use.

C. Perceptual changes occurring in a state of full wakefulness and alertness (e.g., subjective intensification of perceptions, depersonalization, derealization, illusions, hallucinations, synesthesias) that developed during, or shortly after, hallucinogen use.

D. Two (or more) of the following signs, developing during, or shortly after, hallucinogen use:

(1) pupillary dilation
(2) tachycardia
(3) sweating
(4) palpitations
(5) blurring of vision
(6) tremors
(7) incoordination

E. The symptoms are not due to a general medical condition and are not better accounted for by another mental disorder.

DSM-IV diagnostic criteria for 292.89 Hallucinogen Persisting Perception Disorder (Flashbacks)

A. The reexperiencing, following cessation of use of a hallucinogen, of one or more of the perceptual symptoms that were experienced while intoxicated with the hallucinogen (e.g., geometric hallucinations, false perceptions of movement in the peripheral visual fields, flashes of color, intensified colors, trails of images of moving objects, positive afterimages, halos around objects, macropsia, and micropsia).

B. The symptoms in Criterion A cause clinically significant distress or impairment in social, occupational, or other important areas of functioning.

C. The symptoms are not due to a general medical condition (e.g., anatomical lesions and infections of the brain, visual epilepsies) and are not better accounted for by another mental disorder (e.g., delirium, dementia, Schizophrenia) or hypnopompic hallucinations.

Inhalant-Related Disorders

Inhalants

Inhalant-Related Disorders

Inhalant Use Disorders

304.60	Inhalant Dependence
305.90	Inhalant Abuse

Inhalant-Induced Disorders

292.89	Inhalant Intoxication
292.81	Inhalant Intoxication Delirium
292.82	Inhalant-Induced Persisting Dementia
292.11	Inhalant-Induced Psychotic Disorder, With Delusions
292.12	Inhalant-Induced Psychotic Disorder, With Hallucinations
292.84	Inhalant-Induced Mood Disorder
292.89	Inhalant-Induced Anxiety Disorder
292.9	Inhalant-Related Disorder Not Otherwise Specified

Of all the substances of abuse, the inhalants are by far the cheapest and most readily available. Among other easily accessible sources, inhalants can be found in the hardware store (e.g., paint thinners), toy store (e.g., airplane glue), stationery store (e.g., typewriter correction fluid), and auto garage (e.g., gasoline). Unfortunately, inhalants are also among the most dangerous of substances, causing damage to the nervous system, liver, kidneys, and bone marrow and causing sudden death due to arrhythmias and hypoxia. Chemically, all of these substances are aliphatic or aromatic hydrocarbons with esters, ketones, or glycols. Because they are inhaled, they reach the bloodstream very quickly and have a rapid onset of action. Although tolerance and withdrawal related to inhalants have not been well documented, there is a common enough Dependence syndrome based on their tendency to lead to compulsive use.

The term *inhalants* is in some ways unfortunate. Although it accurately describes the means by which these aromatic or aliphatic hydrocarbons are used (i.e., absorption through the lungs), this drug class is not meant to include other substances of abuse that are also inhaled. For example, in DSM-IV the inhaling of nitrous oxide and amyl nitrite is classified as being in the miscellaneous category Other (or Unknown) Substance-Related Disorders (see below). Moreover, the term *inhalant* does not refer to substances that are absorbed through the lungs through smoking (e.g., crack) or through the nasal passages by snorting (e.g., cocaine).

DSM-IV diagnostic criteria for 292.89 Inhalant Intoxication

A. Recent intentional use or short-term, high-dose exposure to volatile inhalants (excluding anesthetic gases and short-acting vasodilators).

B. Clinically significant maladaptive behavioral or psychological changes (e.g., belligerence, assaultiveness, apathy, impaired judgment, impaired social or occupational functioning) that developed during, or shortly after, use of or exposure to volatile inhalants.

(continued)

DSM-IV diagnostic criteria for 292.89 Inhalant Intoxication *(continued)*

C. Two (or more) of the following signs, developing during, or shortly after, inhalant use or exposure:
   (1) dizziness
   (2) nystagmus
   (3) incoordination
   (4) slurred speech
   (5) unsteady gait
   (6) lethargy
   (7) depressed reflexes
   (8) psychomotor retardation
   (9) tremor
   (10) generalized muscle weakness
   (11) blurred vision or diplopia
   (12) stupor or coma
   (13) euphoria

D. The symptoms are not due to a general medical condition and are not better accounted for by another mental disorder.

Nicotine-Related Disorders

Nicotine

Nicotine-Related Disorders

Nicotine Use Disorder

305.10 Nicotine Dependence

Nicotine-Induced Disorder

292.0 Nicotine Withdrawal

292.9 Nicotine-Related Disorder Not Otherwise Specified

Despite the fact that nicotine does not produce a dramatic high, it is among the most addicting of substances. It is quite remarkable that more than 95% of smokers eventually become regular, daily users—a higher proportion of use to dependence than for any other substance. Reflecting upon this sad state of affairs, Mark Twain noted that giving up tobacco was so easy that he had done it hundreds of times.

Nicotine Dependence and Nicotine Withdrawal were included for the first time in DSM-III. This was a controversial decision at the time because the high prevalence of nicotine use (particularly smoking) suggested to some that it should not be considered a mental disorder. The countervailing argument, which appears even more compelling now with the passage of time, is that tobacco use has such devastating medical consequences that its diagnosis, treatment, and prevention should be a high public health priority. Moreover, having another mental disorder is a particularly strong risk factor for nicotine use.

The relative ability of tobacco products to produce Dependence correlates with nicotine content, the rapidity of absorption (e.g., smoking results in faster absorption than chewing), and associated conditioned features (e.g., oral gratification from smoking or chewing). Craving can be intense during Nicotine Withdrawal and may account for the hard time individuals have in stopping smoking. During Nicotine Withdrawal, there may also be a craving for sweets that results in weight gain. Factors predicting greater difficulty in stopping nicotine use include level of current and previous consumption, having a first cigarette immediately after waking, smoking when ill, and smoking more in the morning than in the afternoon. Smoking may also be used as a form of weight control, particularly among young women.

Nicotine intoxication is not included in DSM-IV because it rarely occurs. Nicotine abuse is not included because it almost invariably is associated with Nicotine Dependence.

DSM-IV diagnostic criteria for 292.0 Nicotine Withdrawal

A. Daily use of nicotine for at least several weeks.

B. Abrupt cessation of nicotine use, or reduction in the amount of nicotine used, followed within 24 hours by four (or more) of the following signs:
   (1) dysphoric or depressed mood
   (2) insomnia
   (3) irritability, frustration, or anger
   (4) anxiety
   (5) difficulty concentrating
   (6) restlessness
   (7) decreased heart rate
   (8) increased appetite or weight gain

C. The symptoms in Criterion B cause clinically significant distress or impairment in social, occupational, or other important areas of functioning.

D. The symptoms are not due to a general medical condition and are not better accounted for by another mental disorder.

Opioid-Related Disorders

Opioids

Opioid-Related Disorders

Opioid Use Disorders

304.00 Opioid Dependence

305.50 Opioid Abuse

(continued)

Opioid-Induced Disorders

292.89	Opioid Intoxication
292.0	Opioid Withdrawal
292.81	Opioid Intoxication Delirium
292.11	Opioid-Induced Psychotic Disorder, With Delusions
292.12	Opioid-Induced Psychotic Disorder, With Hallucinations
292.84	Opioid-Induced Mood Disorder
292.89	Opioid-Induced Sexual Dysfunction
292.89	Opioid-Induced Sleep Disorder
292.9	Opioid-Related Disorder Not Otherwise Specified

The opioids are used as pain relievers (e.g., morphine, Demerol, Dilaudid), anesthetics (e.g., fentanyl), cough suppressants (e.g., codeine), and antidiarrheal agents (e.g., diphenoxylate hydrochloride [Lomotil]). Heroin, which is particularly potent and without medical application, is one of the most often abused opioids. Methadone, which is commonly prescribed for the treatment of Opioid Dependence and Withdrawal, is itself an opioid that has its own appeal on the street among opioid addicts.

Depending on the specific drug, opioids can be injected (e.g., morphine, heroin), taken orally (codeine), or snorted (e.g., purer forms of heroin). Although the main source of opioids is illicit purchase on the street, some are obtained by prescription from physicians, usually by feigning pain symptoms of one sort or another. Individuals whose occupations provide access to these drugs (e.g., physicians, nurses, other hospital employees) may be more likely to develop Opioid Dependence.

Tolerance to opioids tends to develop rapidly and differentially, with the euphoric effect disappearing relatively quickly in a way that may encourage escalating dosages that can lead to respiratory depression. High doses of opioid can also result in coma or accidental death even among experienced users because of the difficulty of determining exact dosages with these often illicitly obtained drugs. Although generally not life threatening, Opioid Withdrawal (as opposed to withdrawal from alcohol and anxiolytics) tends to be extremely unpleasant. As a result, a pattern of Opioid Abuse is likely to evolve into Opioid Dependence, which in turn is especially likely to be related to criminal behavior (driven by the need to ensure a daily supply of the drug).

Although the use of opioid medications presents serious risks, it is often indispensable in the treatment of severe pain syndromes. If anything, opioids are probably underutilized because of concerns about inducing Opioid Dependence in patients, even in those situations in which this risk is more than counterbalanced by their advantages (e.g., pain relief in terminally ill cancer patients).

DSM-IV diagnostic criteria for 292.89 Opioid Intoxication

A. Recent use of an opioid.

B. Clinically significant maladaptive behavioral or psychological changes (e.g., initial euphoria followed by apathy, dysphoria, psychomotor agitation or retardation,

(continued)

DSM-IV diagnostic criteria for 292.89 Opioid Intoxication *(continued)*

impaired judgment, or impaired social or occupational functioning) that developed during, or shortly after, opioid use.

C. Pupillary constriction (or pupillary dilation due to anoxia from severe overdose) and one (or more) of the following signs, developing during, or shortly after, opioid use:

(1) drowsiness or coma
(2) slurred speech
(3) impairment in attention or memory

D. The symptoms are not due to a general medical condition and are not better accounted for by another mental disorder.

Specify if:
With Perceptual Disturbances

DSM-IV diagnostic criteria for 292.0 Opioid Withdrawal

A. Either of the following:

(1) cessation of (or reduction in) opioid use that has been heavy and prolonged (several weeks or longer)
(2) administration of an opioid antagonist after a period of opioid use

B. Three (or more) of the following, developing within minutes to several days after Criterion A:

(1) dysphoric mood
(2) nausea or vomiting
(3) muscle aches
(4) lacrimation or rhinorrhea
(5) pupillary dilation, piloerection, or sweating
(6) diarrhea
(7) yawning
(8) fever
(9) insomnia

C. The symptoms in Criterion B cause clinically significant distress or impairment in social, occupational, or other important areas of functioning.

D. The symptoms are not due to a general medical condition and are not better accounted for by another mental disorder.

Phencyclidine (or Phencyclidine-Like)–Related Disorders

Phencyclidine

Phencyclidine (or Phencyclidine-Like)–Related Disorders

Phencyclidine Use Disorders

304.90	Phencyclidine Dependence
305.90	Phencyclidine Abuse

Phencyclidine-Induced Disorders

292.89	Phencyclidine Intoxication
292.81	Phencyclidine Intoxication Delirium
292.11	Phencyclidine-Induced Psychotic Disorder, With Delusions
292.12	Phencyclidine-Induced Psychotic Disorder, With Hallucinations
292.84	Phencyclidine-Induced Mood Disorder
292.89	Phencyclidine-Induced Anxiety Disorder
292.9	Phencyclidine-Related Disorder Not Otherwise Specified

This class of substances includes PCP (angel dust) and similarly acting compounds such as ketamine, which is used as an anesthetic. The routes of administration include oral ingestion, intravenous injection, and smoking. Although assigned its own drug class in DSM-IV, PCP shares many features with drugs from the hallucinogen class. As with the other hallucinogens, whether PCP causes physiological dependence is uncertain, and it is the compulsive use of the substance that characterizes the Dependence syndrome. Phencyclidine Intoxication is particularly notable because it has been associated with suicidal and aggressive behavior.

DSM-IV diagnostic criteria for 292.89 Phencyclidine Intoxication

A. Recent use of phencyclidine (or a related substance).

B. Clinically significant maladaptive behavioral changes (e.g., belligerence, assaultiveness, impulsiveness, unpredictability, psychomotor agitation, impaired judgment, or impaired social or occupational functioning) that developed during, or shortly after, phencyclidine use.

C. Within an hour (less when smoked, "snorted," or used intravenously), two (or more) of the following signs:

(1) vertical or horizontal nystagmus
(2) hypertension or tachycardia
(3) numbness or diminished responsiveness to pain
(4) ataxia
(5) dysarthria
(6) muscle rigidity

(continued)

DSM-IV diagnostic criteria for 292.89 Phencyclidine Intoxication *(contiued)*

(7) seizures or coma
(8) hyperacusis

D. The symptoms are not due to a general medical condition and are not better accounted for by another mental disorder.

Specify if:
With Perceptual Disturbances

Polysubstance-Related Disorder

304.80 Polysubstance Dependence

This category is often confused with the frequently encountered situation in which the individual is dependent on several different substances at the same time. This category does not apply in such situations. Instead, each type of Substance Dependence should be coded separately. Polysubstance Dependence describes an individual who is using a number of substances more or less indiscriminately and does not care which particular substance is used so long as a high results. Because the person does not consistently use any one substance, the pattern of drug use does not meet criteria for Dependence for any one class.

The category of Polysubstance Dependence applies when the individual has a pattern of maladaptive substance use involving three or more different classes of substances. This pattern meets criteria for Substance Dependence only when the substances are considered as a group. The use of nicotine or caffeine should not count toward this diagnosis. It should be noted that DSM-IV does not include a category for Polysubstance Abuse; in such situations, Substance Abuse for each particular type of substance should be noted.

Other (or Unknown) Substance–Related Disorders

Other (or Unknown) Substances
Other (or Unknown) Substance-Related Disorders
Other (or Unknown) Substance Use Disorders
304.90 Other (or Unknown) Substance Dependence
305.90 Other (or Unknown) Substance Abuse
Other (or Unknown) Substance-Induced Disorders
292.89 Other (or Unknown) Substance Intoxication

(continued)

292.0	Other (or Unknown) Substance Withdrawal
292.81	Other (or Unknown) Substance-Induced Delirium
292.82	Other (or Unknown) Substance-Induced Persisting Dementia
292.83	Other (or Unknown) Substance-Induced Persisting Amnestic Disorder
292.11	Other (or Unknown) Substance-Induced Psychotic Disorder, With Delusions
292.12	Other (or Unknown) Substance-Induced Psychotic Disorder, With Hallucinations
292.84	Other (or Unknown) Substance-Induced Mood Disorder
292.89	Other (or Unknown) Substance-Induced Anxiety Disorder
292.89	Other (or Unknown) Substance-Induced Sexual Dysfunction
292.89	Other (or Unknown) Substance-Induced Sleep Disorder
292.9	Other (or Unknown) Substance-Related Disorder Not Otherwise Specified

The residual class of Other (or Unknown) Substance–Related Disorders applies to the following situations not covered by one of the specific drug classes: 1) other drugs of abuse, 2) other medications, 3) other toxin exposure, and 4) unknown substances (i.e., when a substance clearly is involved in the etiology of the presenting symptoms, but it cannot yet be identified).

There are a number of other drugs of abuse that are not included in any of the above classes but can nonetheless cause psychopathology. These include

- **Anabolic steroids:** may produce mild euphoria with episodic use, but repeated use often leads to fatigue, irritability, depression, and medical complications (e.g., liver disease).
- **Nitrite inhalants (poppers):** produce mild euphoria, perceptual disturbances, and medical complications (e.g., immune system impairment, toxic reactions, respiratory problems). Note that nitrite inhalants are not included in the inhalant class.
- **Nitrous oxide (laughing gas):** produces light-headedness, a floating sensation, confusion, and reversible paranoid states. Note that nitrous oxide is also not included in the inhalant class.
- Other substances capable of producing mild intoxications include **catnip, betel nut,** and **kava.**

Psychopathology may also be caused by medications and exposure to toxins. The wide variety of medications that may, at times, cause Dependence, Abuse, and Substance-Induced Disorders include anesthetics and analgesics, anticholinergic agents, anticonvulsants, antihistamines, antihypertensive and cardiovascular medications, antimicrobials, antiparkinsonian medications, chemotherapeutic agents, corticosteroids, gastrointestinal medications, muscle relaxants, nonsteroidal antiinflammatory medications, other over-the-counter medications, antidepressant medications, and disulfiram.

Toxins that may cause psychopathology include heavy metals (e.g., lead or aluminum), rat poisons containing strychnine, pesticides containing acetylcholinesterase inhibitors, nerve gases, ethylene glycol (antifreeze), carbon monoxide, and carbon dioxide. The volatile substances (e.g., fuel, paint) are classified as inhalants if they are used for the purpose of becoming intoxicated; they are considered to be toxins when exposure is accidental or part of intentional poisoning.

The Last Word

Substance use can mimic virtually every psychiatric presentation known to humankind. Therefore, a substance etiology should always be at the top of your list of possible suspects in tracking down a differential diagnosis. In younger individuals, the most likely culprits are drugs of abuse. In older individuals, medication side effects are frequent offenders, particularly because these patients may have a reduced ability to clear the drugs.

CHAPTER 11

Schizophrenia and Other Psychotic Disorders

Schizophrenia and Other Psychotic Disorders

295.30	Schizophrenia, Paranoid Type
295.10	Schizophrenia, Disorganized Type
295.20	Schizophrenia, Catatonic Type
295.90	Schizophrenia, Undifferentiated Type
295.60	Schizophrenia, Residual Type
295.40	Schizophreniform Disorder
295.70	Schizoaffective Disorder
297.1	Delusional Disorder
298.8	Brief Psychotic Disorder
297.3	Shared Psychotic Disorder
293.xx	Psychotic Disorder Due to . . . *[Indicate the General Medical Condition]*
293.81	With Delusions
293.82	With Hallucinations
—.—	Substance-Induced Psychotic Disorder *[Refer to Substance-Related Disorders for substance-specific codes]*
298.9	Psychotic Disorder Not Otherwise Specified

This section joins together what were organized as three separate sections in DSM-III-R: Schizophrenia, Delusional Disorder, and Psychotic Disorders Not Elsewhere Classified. It includes all of the psychotic disorders in the manual except those disorders that are related to Mood Disorder, dementia, delirium, and Catatonic Disorder Due to a General Medical Condition. This reorganization simplifies and facilitates the differential diagnosis of psychotic disorders.

Although all disorders in this section share in common the presence of prominent psychotic symptoms, it is worthy of note that the term *psychotic* has been used in different ways historically and is also not used in any uniform way in DSM-IV. The most restrictive definition of psychosis requires a break in reality testing that is manifested by delusions or hallucinations about which the individual has no insight. A somewhat less restrictive definition of psychosis would also describe hallucinations as psychotic even if the person has insight as to their origin. Under this definition, a person who is hallucinating and is fully aware that the hallucinations result from Schizophrenia or having taken lysergic acid diethylamide (LSD) would still be considered psychotic. A much broader definition goes beyond delusions and hallucinations and also considers grossly disorganized speech and catatonic or grossly disorganized behavior as evidence of psychosis. Finally, the term *psychosis* was in the past used quite broadly to refer to any condition causing serious functional impairment. This nonphenomenological definition is not used at all in DSM-IV.

The universe of symptoms covered by the word *psychotic* varies from disorder to disorder in this section. In Delusional Disorder and Shared Psychotic Disorder the psychotic symptoms are restricted to prominent delusions. Psychotic Disorder Due to a General Medical Condition and Substance-Induced Psychotic Disorder are characterized by prominent delusions and only those hallucinations about which the person lacks insight. Finally, the remaining disorders (Schizophrenia, Schizophreniform Disorder, Schizoaffective Disorder, Brief Psychotic Disorder) are based on the broader definition of psychosis, which includes delusions, hallucinations, disorganized speech, and catatonic or disorganized behavior.

Schizophrenia

Schizophrenia is a clinical syndrome of unknown etiology and pathophysiology. No symptoms are pathognomonic to Schizophrenia, and there are no clinically useful laboratory or imaging markers. The characteristic features of Schizophrenia are heterogeneous, and the boundaries with other disorders can be difficult to delineate. All of this makes for quite a diagnostic challenge, as well as creating problems for research. The clinical diagnosis of Schizophrenia is currently based on the pattern of characteristic signs, symptoms, and course of illness.

The DSM-IV definition is best understood by placing it in the context of its historical precedents. What we now call Schizophrenia has been recognized and described throughout much of recorded history. Although there were many earlier literary and medical descriptions, Emil Kraepelin is typically credited with developing the first comprehensive definition of Schizophrenia. His term *dementia praecox* gained wide acceptance and emphasized the early onset of the illness and the chronic, deteriorating course. Kraepelin's differentiation of dementia praecox from manic-depressive illness and late-onset dementia had important prognostic utility and remains a fundamental distinction in psychiatry. Kraepelin's emphasis on the presence of psychotic symptoms and deteriorating course defined a narrow group of severely ill patients with chronic symptoms and a poor prognosis.

Eugen Bleuler suggested the term *schizophrenia* in an effort to emphasize the fragmentation of thought or splitting of the mind that he believed to be the fundamental aspect of the disorder. Bleuler described a group of symptoms (the 4As—associations, affect, autism, and ambivalence) that he considered to be fundamental to the disorder. Bleuler's definition was different from Kraepelin's. He de-emphasized the importance of the course of illness and considered delusions and hallucinations to be accessory symptoms because they also occurred in other illnesses. Bleuler's ideas were widely accepted and guided the diagnostic practice of European and American psychiatrists for several decades. His description of Schizophrenia emphasized deficit symptoms and defined a much broader and more heterogeneous group of patients, many of whom were less ill (and certainly less psychotic) than those who had been described by Kraepelin.

A third contribution to the definition of Schizophrenia was provided by the German psychiatrist Kurt Schneider. Partly in response to diagnostic uncertainties inherent in Bleuler's broadly defined concepts, Schneider emphasized the discrimination of symptoms that he hoped would be reliably assessed and relatively specific to Schizophrenia. Schneider identified a particular group of delusions and hallucinations that he considered to be of "first rank" significance in defining the disorder. These included thought insertion, thought withdrawal, thought broadcasting, voices communicating with or about the person, and delusions of being externally controlled. Schneider's description of Schizophrenia emphasized the presence of one or more of these psychotic symptoms and was cross-sectional in its definition of the illness. His concepts defined an acutely ill group of patients significantly different from either Kraepelin's (who were more chronic) or Bleuler's (who were less psychotic). Although later research suggested that Schneiderian symptoms are not particularly specific to schizophrenia, his ideas gained prominence in the 1970s and were incorporated into many interview instruments and the diagnostic criteria for Schizophrenia in DSM-III.

Recent work on Schizophrenia has focused on sorting out the heterogeneous symptom presentations into more homogeneous groupings. The goal is to define subgroups that might share similar prognosis, treatment response, family loading, and pathogenesis. Because they have been less than satisfactory in this regard, there has been considerable interest in refining, replacing, or complementing the traditional subtypes of Schizophrenia with a more dimensional approach. The most popular alternative suggestion has been the positive/negative dichotomy. Under this conceptualization, positive symptoms are additions to or distortions of normal functioning (e.g., delusions, hallucinations), whereas negative symptoms are deficits in normal functioning (e.g., a decrement in affective or verbal expression and motivation). This dichotomy has proven to be unwieldy, particularly because a number of symptoms (disorganized speech and disorganized behavior) are not clearly positive or clearly negative. It is, therefore, not surprising that more recent studies support a three-factor model of Schizophrenia: a psychotic factor, a disorganized factor, and a negative factor.

Even though one of the aims in the development of DSM-IV was concordance with *International Statistical Classification of Diseases and Related Health Problems,* 10th Revision (ICD-10), there are still several important differences between the systems. In ICD-10, Schneiderian symptoms continue to have greater significance in the definitions of both Schizophrenia and Schizoaffective Disorder. ICD-10 does not include Kraepelin's notion of deterioration in its definition and has no criterion corresponding to the DSM-IV requirement for a decline in social or occupational functioning. The ICD-10 definition requires just 1 month of active symptoms for the diagnosis of Schizophrenia and therefore encompasses both Schizophrenia and Schizophreniform Disorder (see annotation to Criterion C below).

DSM-IV diagnostic criteria for Schizophrenia

A. *Characteristic symptoms:* Two (or more) of the following, each present for a significant portion of time during a 1-month period (or less if successfully treated):
   (1) delusions
   (2) hallucinations
   (3) disorganized speech (e.g., frequent derailment or incoherence)
   (4) grossly disorganized or catatonic behavior
   (5) negative symptoms, i.e., affective flattening, alogia, or avolition

   Note: Only one Criterion A symptom is required if delusions are bizarre or hallucinations consist of a voice keeping up a running commentary on the person's behavior or thoughts, or two or more voices conversing with each other.

B. *Social/occupational dysfunction:* For a significant portion of the time since the onset of the disturbance, one or more major areas of functioning such as work, interpersonal relations, or self-care are markedly below the level achieved prior to the onset (or when the onset is in childhood or adolescence, failure to achieve expected level of interpersonal, academic, or occupational achievement).

C. *Duration:* Continuous signs of the disturbance persist for at least 6 months. This 6-month period must include at least 1 month of symptoms (or less if successfully treated) that meet Criterion A (i.e., active-phase symptoms) and may include periods of prodromal or residual symptoms. During these prodromal or residual periods, the signs of the disturbance may be manifested by only negative symptoms or two or more symptoms listed in Criterion A present in an attenuated form (e.g., odd beliefs, unusual perceptual experiences).

D. *Schizoaffective and Mood Disorder exclusion:* Schizoaffective Disorder and Mood Disorder With Psychotic Features have been ruled out because either (1) no Major Depressive, Manic, or Mixed Episodes have occurred concurrently with the active-phase symptoms; or (2) if mood episodes have occurred during active-phase symptoms, their total duration has been brief relative to the duration of the active and residual periods.

E. *Substance/general medical condition exclusion:* The disturbance is not due to the direct physiological effects of a substance (e.g., a drug of abuse, a medication) or a general medical condition.

F. *Relationship to a Pervasive Developmental Disorder:* If there is a history of Autistic Disorder or another Pervasive Developmental Disorder, the additional diagnosis of Schizophrenia is made only if prominent delusions or hallucinations are also present for at least a month (or less if successfully treated).

Classification of longitudinal course (can be applied only after at least 1 year has elapsed since the initial onset of active-phase symptoms):

(continued)

DSM-IV diagnostic criteria for Schizophrenia *(continued)*

Episodic With Interepisode Residual Symptoms (episodes are defined by the reemergence of prominent psychotic symptoms); *also specify if:* **With Prominent Negative Symptoms**
Episodic With No Interepisode Residual Symptoms
Continuous (prominent psychotic symptoms are present throughout the period of observation); *also specify if:* **With Prominent Negative Symptoms**
Single Episode In Partial Remission; *also specify if:* **With Prominent Negative Symptoms**
Single Episode In Full Remission
Other or Unspecified Pattern

CRITERION A. This criterion defines a very heterogeneous group of schizophrenic symptom presentations. Those patients who qualify by virtue of having delusions and hallucinations manifest the most typically Kraepelinian form of the disorder. Those who qualify by virtue of disorganized speech, disorganized behavior, and negative symptoms have a more Bleulerian form of Schizophrenia. Those who qualify under the note, which allows for the diagnosis when a single characteristic psychotic symptom is present, are included because of a (probably misplaced) deference to Schneider.

The individual is said to be in the *active phase* during those periods when the symptoms are particularly severe. The diagnosis of Schizophrenia requires that there be an active phase lasting at least 1 month. The parenthetical "or less if successfully treated" has been added to emphasize that clinical judgment is required when applying this threshold. If the other aspects of the illness are unequivocally present, it may not make sense to withhold the diagnosis for an individual who has been promptly and aggressively treated with antipsychotic medication. In clinical practice, however, it is very unusual for the treatment of active-phase symptoms to be so effective as to cause a full remission in so short a period as 1 month, even in those patients who do show a substantial clinical response.

CRITERION A1. Delusions are fixed, false beliefs that are not widely held within the context of the individual's cultural or religious group. The convictions are impervious to compelling evidence of their implausibility, and the person remains totally convinced of their veracity, rejecting alternative explanations out of hand. A delusion involves impairment in the ability to make logical inferences—the way conclusions are drawn from observation of the person's environment or self (e.g., phone hang-ups indicate that the person is being spied on). There is often no clear boundary between delusional conviction and strongly held overvalued ideas.

In deciding whether a belief is fixed and false enough to be considered a delusion, the interviewer must first determine that a serious error in inference and reality testing has occurred and then determine the strength of the conviction. It may be helpful to ask the patient to talk at length about his or her conviction because it is often only in the specific details that the errors of inference become apparent. In evaluating the strength of the delusional conviction, the interviewer should present alternative explanations (e.g., is it possible that the phone hang-ups are due to people dialing a wrong number). The patient who cannot even acknowledge the possibility of these explanations is most likely to be delusional. When the interviewer is unfamiliar with the beliefs characteristic of the individual's cultural or religious background, consultation with another individual who is familiar with the patient's culture may be required to avoid the overdiagnosis of delusions.

Delusions that are judged to be bizarre meet the Criterion A even if other Criterion A symptoms are not present. Bizarre delusions are those whose content is totally implausible. Unfortunately, the reliability is modest for the judgment of whether a delusion is bizarre. In DSM-III-R, bizarre delusions were given much more prominence in formatting the diagnosis of Schizophrenia than is the case in DSM-IV. This prominence placed too much emphasis on this problematic concept and made the criteria set impossibly cumbersome. This criterion was retained in DSM-IV to avoid disrupting ongoing research, but it has been reduced to a footnote.

Criterion A2. To count toward a diagnosis of Schizophrenia, the hallucinations have to be prominent. The determination that hallucinations are prominent is particularly important because it sometimes sets the boundary between Schizophrenia and Delusional Disorder. Hallucinations are generally not present in Delusional Disorder, but, if they occur at all, they must only be fleeting and not be an important part of the clinical picture. Whether a hallucination is prominent is a matter of clinical judgment informed by the amount of distress or impairment caused by the hallucination and the amount of time during the day the person experiences the hallucination. Certainly, the patient does not have to be hearing voices all day every day for them to be considered prominent. However, hearing one's name being called once or twice a day probably shouldn't count as prominent.

When an individual with Schizophrenia has hallucinations, they are usually auditory and consist of one or more voices talking. Although patients with Schizophrenia sometimes have visual, olfactory, gustatory, or tactile hallucinations, these should always arouse suspicion of an etiological general medical condition or substance use.

As already mentioned above, certain types of hallucination have historically been given special emphasis in the diagnosis of Schizophrenia. These so-called Schneiderian hallucinations include a voice keeping a running commentary about the person's action (e.g., "now he's walking across the room, now he's sitting down") and two or more voices talking about the person. DSM-III introduced the Schneiderian approach by allowing individuals to be diagnosed as having Schizophrenia so long as these characteristic hallucinations were present even in the absence of other psychotic symptoms. This decision has been extremely controversial because of the accumulating literature indicating that these hallucinations also occur in other psychotic conditions, most particularly Mood Disorders. Because of its conservative nature, DSM-IV has continued to give special dispensation for Schneiderian hallucinations in the diagnosis of Schizophrenia. However, the clinician should be cautious in making a diagnosis of Schizophrenia or Schizophreniform Disorder just on this basis, particularly if the patient has had a relatively good premorbid course and recovers from these hallucinations without sequelae. In such cases, another diagnosis (e.g., Mood Disorder, a general medical condition, substance use) should be considered carefully.

Not infrequently, patients with a long history of Schizophrenia develop the realization that their voices are symptoms of their illness rather then real perceptions.

Some clinicians would, at this point, no longer regard such hallucinations as evidence of psychosis. Others would disagree and believe that any hallucination, regardless of reality testing, is evidence of psychosis, particularly if it occurs in the context of Schizophrenia (rather than substance use). Hallucinations (in which the perception occurs in the absence of a stimulus) also have to be distinguished from illusions (in which the perception is a distortion of an actual stimulus—e.g., a shadow that is perceived as a bat).

Some clinicians also make a distinction between hallucinations (in which the perceptions seem to arise from outside the head) and pseudohallucinations (in which the perceptions arise from inside the head and may be no more than thoughts), but this distinction has not been validated. Nonpsychotic hallucinations also occur in some patients with Conversion Disorder in the absence of other symptoms of Schizophrenia. Such "hallucinations" often occur in many modalities and have a childlike storybook quality (e.g., having a conversation with an imaginary human-sized rabbit). Finally, it should be noted that culturally syntonic hallucinations also do not count toward a diagnosis of Schizophrenia (e.g., hearing the voice of a dead relative in a person from a culture where this is a ubiquitous experience).

Command hallucinations deserve special mention. These involve auditory instructions ordering the person to do things, often of a dangerous nature ("pick up the knife, bring it close to your wrist, cut, cut, cut"). For obvious reasons, such hallucinations tend to terrify clinicians and often lead to hospitalization. It is important to evaluate how the individual has coped with command hallucinations in the past. Such hallucinations are particularly worrisome in individuals with a recent onset, no insight, and the inability to resist the peremptory nature of the commands. On the other hand, command hallucinations are less dangerous in an individual who has a long track record of ignoring or not responding to them.

Criterion A3. This criterion refers to the aspect of Schizophrenia—loosening of associations—that Bleuler thought was most fundamental to the disorder. He saw Schizophrenia as first and foremost a deficit in the integrative capacities of the human mind, most obviously displayed in the inability to weave logical and coherent threads of thought. The umbrella term *formal thought disorder* has been used to refer to this symptom, emphasizing that the deficit is in the form of the person's thoughts rather than in the content (as in delusions).

The thought processes of the individual with Schizophrenia are characterized by internal inconsistencies, an inability to stay on track (derailment), circumstantiality (talking around the point because of an inability to select pertinent details and suppress irrelevant ones), and tangentiality (digression onto irrelevant topics). In more extreme forms, the individual speaks in an incoherent "word salad," which is virtually unintelligible. The term *disorganized speech* is used in DSM-IV rather than *loosening of associations* (as in DSM-III-R) because this symptom is most often detected by considering the person's spoken speech. However, it may also be useful to get writing samples, which have the advantage of being available for more detailed perusal and can serve as a baseline.

The problem with the assessment of this criterion is that it requires a subjective judgment by the clinician as to the "understandability" of the patient's speech. The most common error of beginning trainees is to have too low a threshold for disorganization, leading to an overdiagnosis of Schizophrenia. It must be remembered that none of us is totally organized in every utterance. It is unwise to assume that every subtle illogical shift from one topic to another necessarily has pathological significance. Latitude should be given to account for variations in style, particularly in the stressful situation of a psychiatric interview. Only speech that is severely disorganized and very difficult to interpret should be considered a psychotic symptom indicative of the active phase of Schizophrenia. Furthermore, there are a number of other situations in which the individual may have disorganized speech that is not indicative of Schizophrenia. The most important conditions that must be considered and ruled out include Substance Intoxication, Delirium, Dementia, aphasia, a Manic Episode (flight of ideas), and Schizotypal Personality Disorder. A final caution is that the patient's unfamiliarity with language should not be misdiagnosed as disorganized speech.

Unlike most of the other characteristic symptoms of Schizophrenia, which may sometimes be feigned (particularly to gain hospitalization or to avoid responsibility), it is virtually impossible to produce a convincing version of disorganized speech. This is an interesting testimony to the powerful inborn tendency toward a logical and grammatical speech.

Criterion A4. To count as an active-phase symptom of Schizophrenia, behavior must be disorganized in a major way. This evaluation of whether behavior is grossly disorganized is extremely difficult and probably not very reliable. The first problem has to do with judging severity. Lots of people are disorganized in their behavior and some are even characterologically odd or eccentric. Such mild or moderate disorganization should not be counted as one of the active-phase symptoms that qualifies the individual for a diagnosis of Schizophrenia. Instead, the disorganization must be severely impairing and obvious even to the most casual observer. Disorganized behavior must also be distinguished from other unusual or bizarre behaviors (e.g., a compulsion, a tic, a stereotypy).

Finally, DSM-IV cautions against a broad application of this criterion and recommends not counting "organized behavior that is motivated by delusional beliefs." This line between disorganized behavior and organized bizarre behavior can be hard to draw and occasions disagreement even among experts. Examples of unusual behavior that is organized (therefore not counting toward this criterion) include not using the telephone because of a conviction that it is tapped, stalking a movie star as a consequence of an erotomanic delusion, and trying to contact the president to share one's plans for world harmony. Examples of disorganized behavior include wandering around disheveled and accosting strangers about the end of the world, standing on a street corner staring directly at the sun, and collecting hordes of worthless items from trash dumpsters. It should be noted that, like disorganized speech, disorganized behavior is certainly not specific to Schizophrenia, and other disorders characterized by disorganized behavior (e.g., Pervasive Developmental Disorder, Delirium, Dementia, Substance Intoxication) must be considered and ruled out.

The fact that both catatonic and disorganized behaviors are listed as part of the same item does not imply that these behaviors are diagnostically interchangeable or have a close pathogenetic relationship. In fact, in the subtyping of Schizophrenia, these symptoms are distributed across two different subtypes (Catatonic and Disorganized). The differential diagnosis of catatonia also includes Mood Disorder, Catatonic Disorder Due to a General Medical Condition, and Neuroleptic-Induced Movement Disorder.

Criterion A5. The inclusion of a separate item for negative symptoms in DSM-IV reflects a somewhat increased emphasis on the thinking of Bleuler. Literature reviews have shown negative symptoms to be reliable, internally consistent, stable over time, and correlated with cognitive impairment, differential treatment response, poor outcome, motor abnormalities, and magnetic resonance imaging findings. Although a number of negative symptoms have been described in the literature, DSM-IV includes only three such symptoms (affective flattening, alogia, and avolition) in the criteria set. Alogia and avolition are new terms for old concepts. Alogia is equivalent to poverty of speech, and avolition is equivalent to lack of motivation for goal-directed behavior. Other less specific negative symptoms (e.g., anhedonia, lack of insight, concrete thinking) are considered to be associated features of Schizophrenia.

Negative symptoms are particularly difficult to evaluate for two reasons. Like disorganized speech and grossly disorganized behavior, each of the negative symptoms has a continuum of severity, and only the most severe, pervasive, persistent, and impairing forms are meant to count toward this criterion. The range of affective expression varies widely in the population and among different cultural groups. Many people are laconic without having Schizophrenia. The lack of goal direction meant to be conveyed by the term *avolition* is at the extreme end of a spectrum and should not be confused with lesser and more common difficulties in getting started.

The second issue is perhaps even more problematic. The behaviors that are described as negative symptoms are by no means specific to Schizophrenia. Before assuming that affective flattening, avolition, and alogia are best considered negative symptoms, other possible explanations for the same behaviors must be ruled out. The most common confusion in this regard is probably due to the fact that the very medications used to treat Schizophrenia can produce side effects that appear to be negative symptoms. For example, many patients on antipsychotic medication experience loss of facial expressiveness, reduced speech and movements, dysphoria, and loss of energy. This confound between negative symptoms and medication side effects is especially difficult to tease apart because patients often require long-term maintenance medication to prevent a return of positive symptoms. It is useful to inquire whether negative symptoms were present before the onset of the neuroleptic treatment. A reduction or change in medication or the addition of an anticholinergic agent may sometimes be informative. It is also difficult to distinguish between negative symptoms (affective flattening, alogia, and avolition) and the depressive symptoms (constricted affect, psychomotor retardation, indecisiveness, loss of energy, and loss of pleasure) that not infrequently accompany psychotic disorders.

A third issue is distinguishing negative symptoms from behaviors that are secondary to positive symptoms. For example, a patient experiencing a command hallucination to remain perfectly quiet would not also be considered to have the negative symptom alogia. Similarly, a patient who is unable to maintain a job because of persecutory delusions would not also be counted as having avolition. Finally, chronic institutionalization can result in environmental-stimulus deprivation or demoralization that should not be confused with negative symptoms.

Criterion B. This criterion reflects Kraepelin's view that Schizophrenia is accompanied by marked impairment in functioning. There is, however, a lively controversy concerning the degree to which Schizophrenia should be typecast as a poor-prognosis condition. Recent longitudinal studies suggest that there is a much more favorable long-term outcome for a substantial minority of individuals with Schizophrenia than would have been anticipated by Kraepelin. As written in DSM-IV, this criterion establishes a definition of Schizophrenia that requires a major impairment in functioning during at least a significant portion of the current episode. This criterion is a milder version of the DSM-III requirement that there be "deterioration in functioning" with its misleading implication of invariably poor prognosis.

Although it is not spelled out clearly in the wording of the criterion, the nature of the dysfunction in Schizophrenia may help distinguish it from Delusional Disorder. The dysfunction in Schizophrenia often arises from the disorganized speech, disorganized behavior, or negative symptoms. In Delusional Disorder, the dysfunction is attributable to the consequences of the delusions, and the individual may function quite well in areas of life that do not impinge on the delusional beliefs.

Criterion C. Although the 6-month duration required for diagnosis of Schizophrenia in DSM-IV differs from the 1-month requirement in ICD-10, there is less to this difference than meets the eye. Essentially DSM-IV has divided ICD-10 Schizophrenia into two types: 1) Schizophreniform Disorder, with a better prognosis and a duration of 1–6 months; and 2) Schizophrenia, a more chronic illness with a 6-month minimum duration that predicts worse future prognosis. It should be noted that the requirement for a 6-month duration refers to the duration of the total disturbance. Some symptoms need to be present for the entire 6 months, but these need not be at the relatively high threshold established in the Criterion A above. Less severe symptoms are referred to as *prodromal* or *residual,* depending on whether they precede or follow the full active-phase period in which the symptoms are present at the threshold established in Criterion A. To determine the total duration of the disturbance, you add up the duration of a continuous period of prodromal, active, and residual symptoms.

DSM-III and DSM-III-R contained cumbersome and unproven lists of specific prodromal and residual symptoms. DSM-IV replaced these with a much simpler (but equally unproven) definition of residual and prodromal symptoms. A patient is considered to have prodromal or residual symptoms when there are considerable negative symptoms equivalent to those present during the active phase (see Criterion A5). Alternatively, the patient can be considered to have prodromal or residual symptoms when he or she has milder versions of the symptoms listed in Criteria A1–A4 above. For example, before becoming frankly delusional or after recovering from delusions, the patient may have overvalued ideas, ideas of reference, or magical thinking with content similar to what, in the active phase, is a delusional conviction. Less commonly, the patient who experiences hallucinations during the active phase may have unusual perceptual experiences in the prodromal or residual phases (e.g., recurrent illusions, perceptions of auras, sensing a force). Disorganized speech that may be incoherent during the active phase may be digressive, vague, or overelaborate in the prodromal or residual phase. The person may continue to act in a peculiar fashion but no longer may exhibit grossly disorganized behavior.

Criterion D. This criterion delineates the boundary between Schizophrenia and its two near neighbors: Schizoaffective Disorder and Mood Disorder With Psychotic Features. Perhaps the most crucial change in diagnostic practice introduced by DSM-III was in the boundary between Schizophrenia and Mood Disorders. Studies done in the early 1970s suggested that U.S. psychiatrists used a much broader definition of Schizophrenia than did their counterparts in Great Britain. Patients who were diagnosed as having Schizophrenia by U.S. psychiatrists very often received a Mood Disorder diagnosis by the British psychiatrists. DSM-III responded to this discrepancy between U.S. and British diagnostic habits by opting for the British viewpoint. If the psychotic symptoms are confined to mood episodes, the DSM-III diagnosis was Mood Disorder With Psychotic Features instead of Schizophrenia. The

DSM-III definition of Schizophrenia became the narrowest definition ever offered up until that time. It should be noted that the reason why this definition was the most narrow had more to do with the priority given to the temporal relationship of the mood and psychotic symptoms and was not much influenced by the choice of symptoms used to define Schizophrenia.

Criterion E. Evaluating the possible etiological role of a substance or general medical condition is usually not much of a problem in individuals who have a chronic and established pattern of Schizophrenia. The issue can be very important, however, in individuals early in their course, perhaps having their first psychotic episode. Particularly given the high use rates of substances that can cause delusions, hallucinations, disorganized speech, and disorganized behavior, it is crucial not to reach premature closure on a diagnosis of Schizophrenia before this etiology is considered and carefully ruled out. Similarly, an atypically late onset of psychotic symptoms should suggest a general medical condition or a medication side effect before the clinician makes a diagnosis of Schizophrenia.

Criterion F. In an adolescent or an adult, Residual Schizophrenia and Pervasive Developmental Disorder can look alike. The differential diagnosis between these is made by history and often requires the assistance of informants. Schizophrenia and the Pervasive Developmental Disorders have very different typical ages at onset. By definition, Pervasive Developmental Disorders have their onset in infancy or very early childhood. Although Schizophrenia can sometimes have a childhood onset, it is more common in adolescence and adulthood. Moreover, Pervasive Development Disorder is not characterized by prominent delusions and hallucinations. If these occur in someone with an already established diagnosis of Pervasive Developmental Disorder, an additional diagnosis of Schizophrenia may be warranted.

Annotation for Longitudinal Course Specifiers. The DSM-IV course modifiers for Schizophrenia were derived from ICD-10 and are considerably different from those included in DSM-III and DSM-III-R (Subchronic, Chronic, and In Remission). Instead of rating a given episode, the DSM-IV course specifiers indicate whether the lifetime longitudinal pattern of the Schizophrenia is episodic or continuous. An episode of Schizophrenia ends when the patient goes from the active phase (meeting Criterion A) to the residual phase or to remission. Episodic presentations are subdivided depending on whether there are interepisodic residual symptoms. Presentations in which there has been only one single episode currently in partial or full remission can also be indicated. The Continuous specifier applies to those individuals who never get out of their first episode or who may have had a brief flurry of episodes early in their course but whose symptoms have evolved into a continuous course.

Schizophrenia Subtypes

What are now considered the subtypes of Schizophrenia were originally described as separate disorders until Kraepelin brought them together under the rubric *dementia praecox*. The need for subtypes reflects the fact that the term *schizophrenia* includes a wide array of quite different appearing presentations—so different in fact that Bleuler referred to them as the "group of Schizophrenias." The subtypes have been criticized because of their relatively poor reliability, stability over time, and prognostic value. During the DSM-IV deliberations, there was some sentiment in favor of abandoning these classical subtypes and replacing them with a dimensional approach that was based on factor analytic studies suggesting that the symptoms could be grouped into three factors (psychotic, disorganized, negative). Although this suggestion had considerable appeal, it was too radical a shift given the supporting evidence. Moreover, the literature review suggested that the classical subtypes probably have sufficient prognostic value to be retained. The Paranoid and Catatonic Types have the best prognosis, the Undifferentiated Type an intermediate prognosis, and the Disorganized Type the worst prognosis.

The Schizophrenia subtypes describe the clinical state of the patient during the time of the most recent examination. Because at any particular point in time a patient may present with symptoms that cut across several subtypes, these are set up in a hierarchical fashion so that only one subtype can be diagnosed at any time. Thus, the Catatonic Type is at the top of the hierarchy and is diagnosed even if prominent paranoid or disorganized symptoms are also present. Next in the hierarchy is the Disorganized Type, which is diagnosed even if prominent delusions or hallucinations are also present. This definition of the Disorganized Type (first introduced into DSM-III-R and slightly modified in DSM-IV) is much wider than the definition for Disorganized Type included in DSM-III. Many patients who in DSM-III would have been considered to have the Undifferentiated Type would be classified as having Disorganized Type in DSM-III-R and DSM-IV. The Paranoid Type is diagnosed only when the individual has prominent delusions or hallucinations without symptoms characteristic of the Disorganized and Catatonic Types. The Paranoid Type of Schizophrenia differs from Delusional Disorder in that there must be deterioration and either bizarre delusions or prominent hallucinations. The patients left behind to qualify for the Undifferentiated Type of Schizophrenia are often those who have some disorganized symptoms in combination with delusions and/or hallucinations. The Residual Type is equivalent to "In Partial Remission." This subtype applies when the patient no longer has any prominent delusions or hallucinations, disorganized speech, or disorganized or catatonic behavior, and it is characterized by the residual symptoms covered in Criterion C.

DSM-IV diagnostic criteria for 295.30 Paranoid Type

A type of Schizophrenia in which the following criteria are met:

A. Preoccupation with one or more delusions or frequent auditory hallucinations.

B. None of the following is prominent: disorganized speech, disorganized or catatonic behavior, or flat or inappropriate affect.

DSM-IV diagnostic criteria for 295.10 Disorganized Type

A type of Schizophrenia in which the following criteria are met:

A. All of the following are prominent:
  (1) disorganized speech
  (2) disorganized behavior
  (3) flat or inappropriate affect

B. The criteria are not met for Catatonic Type.

DSM-IV diagnostic criteria for 295.20 Catatonic Type

A type of Schizophrenia in which the clinical picture is dominated by at least two of the following:

(1) motoric immobility as evidenced by catalepsy (including waxy flexibility) or stupor
(2) excessive motor activity (that is apparently purposeless and not influenced by external stimuli)
(3) extreme negativism (an apparently motiveless resistance to all instructions or maintenance of a rigid posture against attempts to be moved) or mutism
(4) peculiarities of voluntary movement as evidenced by posturing (voluntary assumption of inappropriate or bizarre postures), stereotyped movements, prominent mannerisms, or prominent grimacing
(5) echolalia or echopraxia

DSM-IV diagnostic criteria for 295.90 Undifferentiated Type

A type of Schizophrenia in which symptoms that meet Criterion A are present, but the criteria are not met for the Paranoid, Disorganized, or Catatonic Type.

DSM-IV diagnostic criteria for 295.60 Residual Type

A type of Schizophrenia in which the following criteria are met:

A. Absence of prominent delusions, hallucinations, disorganized speech, and grossly disorganized or catatonic behavior.

(continued)

DSM-IV diagnostic criteria for 295.60 Residual Type *(continued)*

B. There is continuing evidence of the disturbance, as indicated by the presence of negative symptoms or two or more symptoms listed in Criterion A for Schizophrenia, present in an attenuated form (e.g., odd beliefs, unusual perceptual experiences).

295.40 Schizophreniform Disorder

Ever since Kraepelin, Schizophrenia has generally been considered a chronic condition with a relatively poor prognosis. However, some patients present with a clinical picture that looks exactly like Schizophrenia on cross-sectional examination but does not have a course characterized by deterioration or chronicity. Schizophreniform Disorder was introduced in DSM-III (and continues in DSM-III-R and DSM-IV) to describe such patients and differentiate them from those with Schizophrenia. Its definition is equivalent to that of Schizophrenia in symptomatic presentation, except that there is no requirement for a decline in functioning and the duration is set between 1 and 6 months. It should be recognized that the distinction between Schizophreniform Disorder and Schizophrenia is based exclusively on course and presumed prognosis and that these disorders are on a continuum and probably share a common pathogenesis.

This diagnosis applies in two different circumstances. In one, the patient has already recovered within the 6-month time frame, and the episode is clearly diagnosed as Schizophreniform Disorder. Often, however, the clinician must assign a diagnosis to a patient who meets the symptomatic criteria for Schizophrenia but who has not yet reached the 6-month minimum duration requirement. Such a patient would be diagnosed as having Schizophreniform Disorder (Provisional). The final diagnosis depends on whether the patient recovers before 6 months (Schizophreniform Disorder) or has a persistence of symptoms beyond 6 months (Schizophrenia). The specifier With Good Prognostic Features includes a number of characteristics that have been correlated with a lower likelihood of later progression to Schizophrenia.

DSM-IV diagnostic criteria for 295.40 Schizophreniform Disorder

A. Criteria A, D, and E of Schizophrenia are met.

B. An episode of the disorder (including prodromal, active, and residual phases) lasts at least 1 month but less than 6 months. (When the diagnosis must be made without waiting for recovery, it should be qualified as "Provisional.")

(continued)

DSM-IV diagnostic criteria for 295.40 Schizophreniform Disorder *(continued)*

Specify if:

Without Good Prognostic Features

With Good Prognostic Features: as evidenced by two (or more) of the following:

(1) onset of prominent psychotic symptoms within 4 weeks of the first noticeable change in usual behavior or functioning
(2) confusion or perplexity at the height of the psychotic episode
(3) good premorbid social and occupational functioning
(4) absence of blunted or flat affect

295.70 Schizoaffective Disorder

This category fills a necessary and important hole in the diagnostic system, but unfortunately it does not do its job very well. As its name suggests, Schizoaffective Disorder is intended to identify the illness of those patients who straddle the boundary between Schizophrenia and Mood Disorder With Psychotic Features.

The broadened definition of Psychotic Mood Disorder in DSM-III markedly narrowed the way the field thought of Schizoaffective Disorder. Before DSM-III, many patients with mood episodes and psychotic features that were not thematically related to the mood were considered to have Schizoaffective Disorder. DSM-III changed the diagnostic emphasis away from a consideration of the content of the psychotic symptoms and instead focused on an evaluation of the temporal relationship between the mood and the psychotic symptoms. Whenever psychotic symptoms occurred only during a mood episode, they were deemed to be part of a Mood Disorder, regardless of the particular content of the psychotic symptoms. This narrowing of Schizoaffective Disorder and broadening of Psychotic Mood Disorders was supported by studies suggesting that individuals at the boundary were more akin to those with Mood Disorder in their course, family histories, and treatment response.

Because of the lack of agreement on how best to define the condition and the very limited research that had been done on it, Schizoaffective Disorder was the only diagnosis in DSM-III that was presented without a criteria set. A diagnostic criteria set for Schizoaffective Disorder was introduced into DSM-III-R, but it proved to be problematic. It required information about the relationship between mood symptoms and psychotic symptoms that was difficult to obtain from patients and was subject to widely different interpretations among clinicians. Moreover, the criteria set did not make it clear whether Schizoaffective Disorder was meant to describe just the most recent episode of illness or the individual's entire lifetime course.

Although these problems were recognized during the DSM-IV deliberations, it was decided not to attempt to radically change the definition of Schizoaffective Disorder in the absence of any alternative definition with clear advantages. The one problem that has been addressed in DSM-IV was the confusion regarding whether the DSM-III-R criteria set for Schizoaffective Disorder is intended to apply to an episode of illness or to the overall lifetime course. Take, for example, a patient who has two episodes combining mood and psychotic symptoms: one episode characterized by psychotic symptoms that persist after the mood symptoms have resolved and the second episode characterized by psychotic symptoms confined to the mood episode. If the diagnostic criteria are applied separately to each episode, the diagnosis would be Schizoaffective Disorder for the first episode and Mood Disorder With Psychotic Features for the second episode. If the criteria are applied to the entire course of illness, both episodes would be considered part of an overall lifetime diagnosis of Schizoaffective Disorder.

The decision in DSM-IV is to restrict the diagnosis of Schizoaffective Disorder to a given episode. This was meant to increase the reliability of the diagnosis, but can result in the somewhat strange situation of an individual's sequentially presenting with fairly similar symptom patterns that nonetheless are labeled as episodes of Schizoaffective Disorder, episode of Schizophreniform Disorder or as psychotic mood episodes. It should be understood that any such changes in diagnosis over the course of the person's lifetime reflect the recognized limitations of this diagnostic convention more than an implication that the condition has changed fundamentally with time. Finally, one last caution: The "episode" of Schizoaffective Disorder may last for most of a lifetime. Some patients never get over the active psychotic symptoms. Many others have residual symptoms that persist in between the active episodes.

That the DSM-IV definition of Schizoaffective Disorder constitutes no great leap forward should probably not be surprising or disappointing. The descriptive boundary between Schizophrenia and Mood Disorder will necessarily remain arbitrary until we have a more profound understanding of the pathogenesis of these conditions. As we learn more, it may turn out that some patients who would now receive this diagnosis would be better classified as having Schizophrenia or Mood Disorder; others would perhaps be classified in ways that are not currently known. This situation reflects the ongoing debate about the degree to which Schizophrenia and Psychotic Mood Disorders are qualitatively distinct conditions versus being different aspects of the same dimension. In the meantime, it is expected that despite its poor reliability, this category will continue to engender great interest, particularly in regard to treatment decisions and genetic studies.

Because the criteria for Schizoaffective Disorder can be difficult to understand and interpret, it may be useful to summarize the separate contributions to the diagnosis made by Criteria A, B, and C. Keep in mind that Criterion A ensures that there is a period of overlap between the mood and psychotic symptoms, Criterion B ensures that there is a significant period of psychotic symptoms occurring in the absence of prominent mood symptoms, and Criterion C ensures that the mood is a significant part of the total clinical picture.

DSM-IV diagnostic criteria for 295.70 Schizoaffective Disorder

A. An uninterrupted period of illness during which, at some time, there is either a Major Depressive Episode, a Manic Episode, or a Mixed Episode concurrent with symptoms that meet Criterion A for Schizophrenia.

Note: The Major Depressive Episode must include Criterion A1: depressed mood.

(continued)

DSM-IV diagnostic criteria for 295.70 Schizoaffective Disorder *(continued)*

B. During the same period of illness, there have been delusions or hallucinations for at least 2 weeks in the absence of prominent mood symptoms.

C. Symptoms that meet criteria for a mood episode are present for a substantial portion of the total duration of the active and residual periods of the illness.

D. The disturbance is not due to the direct physiological effects of a substance (e.g., a drug of abuse, a medication) or a general medical condition.

Specify type:

Bipolar Type: if the disturbance includes a Manic or a Mixed Episode (or a Manic or a Mixed Episode and Major Depressive Episodes)

Depressive Type: if the disturbance only includes Major Depressive Episodes

CRITERION A. This criterion reflects the fact that Schizoaffective Disorder combines elements of Schizophrenia and Mood Disorder. Although no actual number of days is given explicitly in this criterion, it is implied that the minimum duration of a Major Depressive Episode, Manic Episode, or Mixed Episode applies. Therefore the minimum duration for the overlap of mood and psychotic symptoms that constitutes Criterion A would be 2 weeks when the patient is depressed and 1 week when the patient is manic. In clinical practice, however, the actual durations of overlap are usually much longer, comprising months or even years.

It can be a difficult clinical challenge to sort out the degree to which particular behaviors reflect a mood episode, Criterion A of Schizophrenia, medication side effects, or some combination of the three. For example, it is sometimes inherently impossible to distinguish depressive symptoms from negative symptoms or from medication side effects. It is sometimes equally difficult to determine whether to attribute disorganized, excited behavior to Criterion A of Schizophrenia or to a Manic Episode. This difficulty is one factor accounting for the lack of reliability in the diagnosis. The note to Criterion A is an attempt, in some small way, to sharpen the distinction between the definition of a Major Depressive Episode and Criterion A of Schizophrenia. In the next chapter, the reader will learn that loss of interest can substitute for depressed mood in the definition of a Major Depressive Episode. The note makes clear that this substitution should not be allowed when diagnosing a Major Depressive Episode in the context of Schizoaffective Disorder. That is because it is virtually impossible to determine whether the loss of interest is part of a depressive episode or is better accounted for as avolition or anhedonia of Schizophrenia.

CRITERION B. This criterion is what distinguishes Schizoaffective Disorder from Mood Disorder With Psychotic Features. In prototypical psychotic Mood Disorder, the psychotic features are confined to the episodes of Mood Disorder. In contrast, in an episode of Schizoaffective Disorder, the psychotic symptoms either precede the mood symptoms or persist after the mood symptoms significantly improve. In Schizoaffective Disorder, the delusions and/or hallucinations usually persist in the absence of mood symptoms for much longer than the required 2 weeks. One frequent question is "does this mean that the patient whose mood symptoms respond to medication faster than the psychotic symptoms must be given the diagnosis of Schizoaffective Disorder, even if the psychotic symptoms resolve soon after the 2-week requirement?" This is a tough call and another reason why this disorder is often unreliably diagnosed. Some cases that may meet the letter of this criterion seem in spirit to be better diagnosed as Mood Disorder With Psychotic Features.

Adding up the required durations in Criteria A and B results in a minimum duration for an episode of Schizoaffective Disorder of at least 3 weeks if the mood episode is manic and 4 weeks if the mood episode is depressive. More often, however, the duration is much longer.

Criterion C. This criterion is what distinguishes Schizoaffective Disorder from Schizophrenia. Relatively brief periods of mood symptoms are a common associated feature of Schizophrenia and do not warrant a change of diagnosis from Schizophrenia to Schizoaffective Disorder. This criterion indicates that the diagnosis of Schizoaffective Disorder should be made only when the mood symptoms constitute a "substantial portion of the total duration" of the episode. This criterion provides the greatest source of unreliability in making the diagnosis of Schizoaffective Disorder because of varying interpretations of what constitutes a substantial portion. One very rough rule of thumb is that the mood symptoms should constitute at least 10% of the total duration to be considered substantial. For example, a couple of weeks of mood symptoms in a 5-year disorder would not be considered a substantial portion, whereas mood symptoms present for a third of the time would be.

Annotation of Subtypes. Of the two subtypes, the Bipolar Type seems to be closer to Mood Disorder and the Depressive Type to be closer to Schizophrenia in regard to course, family loading, and treatment response.

297.1 Delusional Disorder

Even since Kraepelin distinguished Schizophrenia as a chronic and deteriorating form of psychotic illness, the relationship between Delusional Disorder and Schizophrenia has been the subject of considerable debate but very little study. The DSM-IV definition of Schizophrenia includes Kraepelin's emphasis on deterioration, Schneider's emphasis on the presence of certain characteristic bizarre delusions, and Bleuler's emphasis on disorganized speech and behavior and negative symptoms. In contrast, the central feature of Delusional Disorder is the presence of nonbizarre delusions with the preservation of functioning apart from the results of the delusions. It is unclear to what degree Delusional Disorder shares a common pathogenesis with Schizophrenia, or whether it is caused by a distinctly different process.

The DSM-IV definition of Delusional Disorder is essentially unchanged from DSM-III-R. A revolutionary change was suggested and rejected for DSM-IV because it was ahead of its time (and the available evidence). As is discussed later, there are presentations that appear similar to Obsessive-Compulsive Disorder, Hypochondriasis, and Body Dysmorphic Disorder but differ in that the obsessions, health fears, or concerns about appearance reach a delusional level of conviction. It was argued that each of these disorders should include a subtype "With Delusions" to indicate such presentations. This suggestion would have had the advantage of emphasizing the similarities between the nonpsychotic and psychotic forms of each of these conditions but had the disadvantage of fragmenting the concept of Delusional Disorder.

Until more compelling data are available, it seems wise to take a conservative approach in DSM-IV that saves information without prejudging the nature of possible relationships. Delusional Disorder can be diagnosed in addition to Obsessive-Compulsive Disorder and Body Dysmorphic Disorder when the strength of the belief in these disorders takes on the character of a delusional conviction. When the beliefs about having a serious disease in Hypochondriasis become of delusional proportions, the diagnosis changes from Hypochondriasis to Delusional Disorder, Somatic Type.

DSM-IV diagnostic criteria for 297.1 Delusional Disorder

A. Nonbizarre delusions (i.e., involving situations that occur in real life, such as being followed, poisoned, infected, loved at a distance, or deceived by spouse or lover, or having a disease) of at least 1 month's duration.

B. Criterion A for Schizophrenia has never been met. **Note:** Tactile and olfactory hallucinations may be present in Delusional Disorder if they are related to the delusional theme.

C. Apart from the impact of the delusion(s) or its ramifications, functioning is not markedly impaired and behavior is not obviously odd or bizarre.

D. If mood episodes have occurred concurrently with delusions, their total duration has been brief relative to the duration of the delusional periods.

E. The disturbance is not due to the direct physiological effects of a substance (e.g., a drug of abuse, a medication) or a general medical condition.

Specify type (the following types are assigned based on the predominant delusional theme):

Erotomanic Type: delusions that another person, usually of higher status, is in love with the individual

Grandiose Type: delusions of inflated worth, power, knowledge, identity, or special relationship to a deity or famous person

Jealous Type: delusions that the individual's sexual partner is unfaithful

Persecutory Type: delusions that the person (or someone to whom the person is close) is being malevolently treated in some way

Somatic Type: delusions that the person has some physical defect or general medical condition

Mixed Type: delusions characteristic of more than one of the above types but no one theme predominates

Unspecified Type

Criterion A. Delusional Disorder is characterized by nonbizarre delusions occurring in the absence of other psychotic symptoms. Although patients with Schizophrenia can and often do have nonbizarre delusions (as long as they are accompanied by other psychotic symptoms), by definition, patients with Delusional Disorder do not have bizarre delusions. Unfortunately, it must be admitted that the judgment whether a delusion is bizarre can be quite subjective. One person's *bizarre* is another person's *strange but plausible.*

Clinicians who primarily treat patients with Schizophrenia often think that they have seen it all and tend to develop a relatively high threshold for labeling any delusion as bizarre. In contrast, clinicians with relatively little exposure to psychotic patients may consider virtually any delusion to be bizarre. The examples given in Criterion A, especially the conviction that one is being deceived or has a disease, are clearly possible and plausible events that can and sometimes do happen in real life. In contrast, the clearly bizarre delusion involves mechanisms or situations that are, on the face of it, completely implausible (e.g., someone who believes with absolute conviction that his or her brain has been transplanted from someone else). Thought broadcasting, thought insertion, and thought withdrawal are all considered to be examples of bizarre delusions. One might make the judgment that a delusion is bizarre because it involves a mechanism that is technologically impossible (e.g., radar that "reads" thoughts).

Criterion B. This criterion clarifies that Schizophrenia and Delusional Disorder are mutually exclusive and indicates how to draw the line between them. Schizophrenia is the more pervasive disorder. In addition to delusions, Schizophrenia may include hallucinations, disorganized speech, disorganized or catatonic behavior, and negative symptoms. Delusional Disorder can be diagnosed instead of Schizophrenia only for the restricted presentation of nonbizarre delusions occurring alone, without the other characteristic symptoms of Schizophrenia.

The note to Criterion B does allow tactile and olfactory hallucinations to accompany thematically related delusions. For example, the patient may have the hallucination of emitting a bad odor accompanying the delusion that people on the street are laughing at him or her. However, the presence of tactile or olfactory hallucination is also suggestive of a neurological or substance etiology. It should be noted that the wording of Criterion B (i.e., Criterion A for Schizophrenia has never been met) allows for the presence of some of the symptoms characteristic of Schizophrenia as long as these fall below the duration and significance thresholds established in Criterion A for Schizophrenia. For example, it is possible for individuals with Delusional Disorder to have transient auditory hallucinations. However, if these persist and are prominent for most of a month, then the diagnosis would be Schizophrenia.

Criterion C. One of the historical distinctions between Schizophrenia and Delusional Disorder concerned the level of functioning presumed to be associated with each. The deterioration considered to be an inherent part of Schizophrenia is exhibited in many spheres of functioning. In contrast, the prototypical individual with Delusional Disorder may appear perfectly normal as long as the delusional material is not touched on.

In fact, clinical presentations of these disorders are not so straightforward. There are some individuals with Schizophrenia, particularly those in treatment, who do quite well and may not show continuing signs of deterioration. On the other hand, some individuals with Delusional Disorder may be quite impaired because their delusional concerns impact on many areas of functioning. For instance, if a woman feels that she is emitting a horrible odor that other people cannot stand and that they are plotting against her because of it, she may quit her job, cut off relationships with friends, and become completely housebound, bathing herself day and night. In this case, the deterioration in behavior is a direct result of the delusion rather than (as in Schizophrenia) a direct manifestation of the disorganized thinking, disorganized behavior, or negative symptoms.

Criterion D. Because patients with delusions often have significant mood symptoms, the differential diagnosis between Mood Disorder and Delusional Disorder can sometimes be difficult. The first thing to determine is whether the delusional symptoms occur exclusively during a mood episode, in which case the diagnosis is Mood Disorder With Psychotic Features rather than Delusional Disorder. In contrast, if the person has persistent and prominent delusions for many years with only occasional and relatively brief mood episodes, the diagnosis would clearly be Delusional Disorder. In that case, if the clinician felt the need to indicate the presence of the mood episodes (for instance, if the patient becomes suicidal), an additional diagnosis of Depressive Disorder Not Otherwise Specified or Bipolar Disorder Not Otherwise Specified should be indicated.

The middle ground, analogous to Schizoaffective Disorder, in which persistent delusions are accompanied by significant mood symptoms, is not covered by any specific category in DSM-IV. Such presentations of persistent delusions accompanied by substantial periods of mood symptoms are not all that uncommon and are diagnosed in DSM-IV as Psychotic Disorder Not Otherwise Specified with either Depressive Disorder Not Otherwise Specified or Bipolar Disorder Not Otherwise Specified—an admittedly awkward solution.

Criterion E. Because delusions are so often due to substance use or general medical conditions, these possibilities should be first on your mind before assuming that the diagnosis is a primary Delusional Disorder. In younger individuals with delusions, the most likely etiology is a drug of abuse (e.g., amphetamines). In older individuals, one should consider alcohol, medication side effects, or a general medical condition. It should be noted that this criterion also covers delusions occurring in the context of delirium or dementia because, by definition, all cases of delirium and dementia are due either to a general medical condition or to substance use. Dementia of the Alzheimer's Type and Vascular Dementia both also have a subtype to indicate delusional presentations.

298.8 Brief Psychotic Disorder

The diagnosis of Brief Psychotic Disorder is only infrequently made and has received little systematic study. Brief Psychotic Disorder applies to psychotic presentations that last at least 1 day but less than 1 month and are not better accounted for by the other disorders listed in Criterion C (especially Mood Disorders). Commonly, the episode is characterized by florid symptomatology accompanied by confusion and emotional turmoil.

The definition differs from the DSM-III-R diagnosis of Brief Reactive Psychosis in that an etiological stressor is no longer required. Most often, however, this condition does occur in association with marked stressors, and the clinician can indicate this fact with the subtype With Marked Stressors. The most typical stressors occur in military settings, prison environments, the freshman year of college, and starting a new job. The episodes usually last for only a few days, and the individual quickly returns to premorbid levels of functioning.

The extremely transient psychotic episodes lasting minutes to hours that sometimes occur in individuals with Borderline or Schizotypal Personality Disorder would not qualify for the diagnosis of Brief Psychotic Disorder. Instead, these episodes would either get no separate diagnosis at all or would receive a diagnosis of Psychotic Disorder Not Otherwise Specified. Unlike Schizophreniform Disorder, in which the diagnosis can be made provisionally without waiting for the individual to recover, Brief Psychotic Disorder can be diagnosed only after the patient has recovered within the 1-month time frame. For patients who are in the first weeks of an episode but who have yet to recover, the diagnosis is Psychotic Disorder Not Otherwise Specified.

DSM-IV diagnostic criteria for 298.8 Brief Psychotic Disorder

A. Presence of one (or more) of the following symptoms:
   (1) delusions
   (2) hallucinations
   (3) disorganized speech (e.g., frequent derailment or incoherence)
   (4) grossly disorganized or catatonic behavior

   Note: Do not include a symptom if it is a culturally sanctioned response pattern.

B. Duration of an episode of the disturbance is at least 1 day but less than 1 month, with eventual full return to premorbid level of functioning.

C. The disturbance is not better accounted for by a Mood Disorder With Psychotic Features, Schizoaffective Disorder, or Schizophrenia and is not due to the direct physiological effects of a substance (e.g., a drug of abuse, a medication) or a general medical condition.

Specify if:

With Marked Stressor(s) (brief reactive psychosis): if symptoms occur shortly after and apparently in response to events that, singly or together, would be markedly stressful to almost anyone in similar circumstances in the person's culture

Without Marked Stressor(s): if psychotic symptoms do *not* occur shortly after, or are not apparently in response to events that, singly or together, would be markedly stressful to almost anyone in similar circumstances in the person's culture

With Postpartum Onset: if onset within 4 weeks postpartum

293.7 Shared Psychotic Disorder (Folie à Deux)

Shared Psychotic Disorder is an intriguing but very uncommon disorder. It is distinguished from the other disorders in this section by virtue of the interpersonal etiology of the psychotic symptoms. The psychotic symptoms develop in a suggestible individual under the influence of another person who is psychotic and is usually suffering from one of the other disorders in this section. Typically, the individual with the Shared Psychotic Disorder has had a long-standing enmeshed and submissive relationship with the more dominant psychotic person and has limited exposure to the outside influences that might bring reality to bear.

The psychotic symptoms in Shared Psychotic Disorder usually have the theme of persecution or the need to respond to a shared threat from the outside world. These symptoms can lead the pair to become even more cut off and enmeshed. Most commonly, the pair consists either of a parent and child of the same sex or a husband and wife. In some instances, entire families can share the delusion promulgated by a dominant psychotic parent, and there have also been some notorious instances of Shared Psychotic Disorder among groups of cult followers. The best way to differentiate this disorder from a primary Psychotic Disorder is to remove the person from the influence of the psychotic family member, although the attempt to extract the person is often vigorously resisted. In Shared Psychotic Disorder, the delusion will usually remit spontaneously over time.

DSM-IV diagnostic criteria for 297.3 Shared Psychotic Disorder

A. A delusion develops in an individual in the context of a close relationship with another person(s), who has an already-established delusion.

B. The delusion is similar in content to that of the person who already has the established delusion.

C. The disturbance is not better accounted for by another Psychotic Disorder (e.g., Schizophrenia) or a Mood Disorder With Psychotic Features and is not due to the direct physiological effects of a substance (e.g., a drug of abuse, a medication) or a general medical condition.

Psychotic Disorder Due to . . . *[Indicate the General Medical Condition]*

The first step in the differential diagnosis of psychotic symptoms is to rule out general medical conditions and substance use as etiologies. If a general medical condition is present and determined to be the direct physiological cause of the psychotic

Table 11–1. General medical conditions that cause psychotic symptoms

Neurological conditions (e.g., neoplasms, cerebrovascular disease, Huntington's disease, epilepsy, auditory nerve injury, deafness, migraine, central nervous system infections)
Endocrine conditions (e.g., hyper- and hypothyroidism, hyper- and hypoparathyroidism, hypocortisolism)
Metabolic conditions (e.g., hypoxia, hypercarbia, hypoglycemia)
Fluid or electrolyte imbalances
Hepatic or renal diseases
Autoimmune disorders with central nervous system involvement (e.g., systemic lupus erythematosus)

Source. Adapted from American Psychiatric Association 1994, p. 308.

symptoms, Psychotic Disorder Due to a General Medical Condition is diagnosed. Table 11–1 lists some of the general medical conditions that have been reported to cause delusions or hallucinations.

When communicating or recording the diagnosis, the actual name of the etiological general medical condition should be used on Axis I (e.g., 293.81 Psychotic Disorder Due to Hyperthyroidism, With Delusions). Note that delusions due to a general medical condition are coded as 293.81 and hallucinations due to a general medical condition are coded as 293.82, regardless of the type of general medical condition. Furthermore, the general medical condition should also be coded on Axis III (e.g., 571.2 Cirrhosis, alcoholic). To help ease the coding burden, DSM-IV includes selected general medical codes in Appendix G.

Not uncommonly, the psychiatric presentation due to a general medical condition is characterized by a mixture of symptoms from more than one section of DSM-IV (e.g., psychotic, mood, and sleep symptoms). In most cases, the clinician should indicate only the psychotic symptoms unless the other symptoms are particularly clinically relevant, in which case these additional disorders due to a general medical condition can also be included.

DSM-IV diagnostic criteria for 293.xx Psychotic Disorder Due to . . . *[Indicate the General Medical Condition]*

A. Prominent hallucinations or delusions.

B. There is evidence from the history, physical examination, or laboratory findings that the disturbance is the direct physiological consequence of a general medical condition.

C. The disturbance is not better accounted for by another mental disorder.

(continued)

DSM-IV diagnostic criteria for 293.xx Psychotic Disorder Due to . . .
[Indicate the General Medical Condition] (continued)

D. The disturbance does not occur exclusively during the course of a delirium.

Code based on predominant symptom:
.81 With Delusions: if delusions are the predominant symptom
.82 With Hallucinations: if hallucinations are the predominant symptom

Coding note: Include the name of the general medical condition on Axis I, e.g., 293.81 Psychotic Disorder Due to Malignant Lung Neoplasm, With Delusions; also code the general medical condition on Axis III.

Coding note: If delusions are part of a preexisting dementia, indicate the delusions by coding the appropriate subtype of the dementia if one is available, e.g., 290.20 Dementia of the Alzheimer's Type, With Late Onset, With Delusions.

Substance-Induced Psychotic Disorder

It is critical to consider whether psychotic symptoms are due to the direct effects of a substance. If it is determined that the etiology of the delusions or hallucinations is a substance, then the appropriate diagnosis is either Substance Intoxication, Substance Withdrawal, or a Substance-Induced Psychotic Disorder. Table 11–2 lists those drugs of abuse, medications, and toxins that DSM-IV indicates can cause a Substance-Induced Psychotic Disorder. It should be noted that this list is not exhaustive. For a detailed explanation of these criteria, refer to the discussion about Other Substance-Induced Disorders in Chapter 10.

When the diagnosis is recorded, the diagnostic code depends on the class of substance and whether the predominant symptoms are delusions or hallucinations. For alcohol, the code is 291.5 if the clinical presentation is predominated by delusions and 291.3 if the presentation is predominated by hallucinations. For all other substances (including medications and toxins), the code is 292.11 if predominated by delusions and 292.12 if predominated by hallucinations. When communicating the name of the disorder, clinicians should insert the specific etiological substance in place of the word *substance* (e.g., Alcohol-Induced Psychotic Disorder, Methylphenidate-Induced Psychotic Disorder, Carbon Monoxide-Induced Psychotic Disorder). The predominant type of psychotic symptom is indicated by adding With Delusions or With Hallucinations. Moreover, the context of the onset of the symptoms can be indicated by adding With Onset During Intoxication or With Onset During Withdrawal.

Table 11–2. Substances that can induce clinically significant Psychotic Disorders

Intoxication with—
Alcohol
Amphetamines and related substances
Cannabis
Cocaine
Hallucinogens
Inhalants
Opioids (meperidine)
Phencyclidine and related substances
Sedatives, hypnotics, and anxiolytics

Withdrawal from—
Alcohol
Sedatives, hypnotics, and anxiolytics

Medications
Analgesics
Anesthetics
Anticholinergic agents
Anticonvulsants
Antidepressant medications
Antihistamines
Antihypertensive and cardiovascular medications
Antimicrobial medications
Antiparkinsonian medications
Chemotherapeutic agents cyclosporine and procarbazine)
Corticosteroids
Disulfiram
Gastrointestinal medications
Muscle relaxants
Nonsteroidal antiinflammatory medications
Over-the-counter medications (phenylephrine, pseudoephedrine)

Toxins
Heavy metals
Anticholinesterase
Organophosphate insecticides
Nerve gases
Carbon monoxide
Carbon dioxide
Volatile substances such as fuel and paint

Source. Adapted from American Psychiatric Association 1994, pp. 312–313.

DSM-IV diagnostic criteria for Substance-Induced Psychotic Disorder

A. Prominent hallucinations or delusions. **Note:** Do not include hallucinations if the person has insight that they are substance induced.

B. There is evidence from the history, physical examination, or laboratory findings of either (1) or (2):

(1) the symptoms in Criterion A developed during, or within a month of, Substance Intoxication or Withdrawal
(2) medication use is etiologically related to the disturbance

C. The disturbance is not better accounted for by a Psychotic Disorder that is not substance induced. Evidence that the symptoms are better accounted for by a Psychotic Disorder that is not substance induced might include the following: the

(continued)

DSM-IV diagnostic criteria for Substance-Induced Psychotic Disorder *(continued)*

symptoms precede the onset of the substance use (or medication use); the symptoms persist for a substantial period of time (e.g., about a month) after the cessation of acute withdrawal or severe intoxication, or are substantially in excess of what would be expected given the type or amount of the substance used or the duration of use; or there is other evidence that suggests the existence of an independent non-substance-induced Psychotic Disorder (e.g., a history of recurrent non-substance-related episodes).

D. The disturbance does not occur exclusively during the course of a delirium.

Note: This diagnosis should be made instead of a diagnosis of Substance Intoxication or Substance Withdrawal only when the symptoms are in excess of those usually associated with the intoxication or withdrawal syndrome and when the symptoms are sufficiently severe to warrant independent clinical attention.

Code [Specific Substance]–Induced Psychotic Disorder:

(291.5 Alcohol, With Delusions; 291.3 Alcohol, With Hallucinations; 292.11 Amphetamine [or Amphetamine-Like Substance], With Delusions; 292.12 Amphetamine [or Amphetamine-Like Substance], With Hallucinations; 292.11 Cannabis, With Delusions; 292.12 Cannabis, With Hallucinations; 292.11 Cocaine, With Delusions; 292.12 Cocaine, With Hallucinations; 292.11 Hallucinogen, With Delusions; 292.12 Hallucinogen, With Hallucinations; 292.11 Inhalant, With Delusions; 292.12 Inhalant, With Hallucinations; 292.11 Opioid, With Delusions; 292.12 Opioid, With Hallucinations; 292.11 Phencyclidine [or Phencyclidine-Like Substance], With Delusions; 292.12 Phencyclidine [or Phencyclidine-Like Substance], With Hallucinations; 292.11 Sedative, Hypnotic, or Anxiolytic, With Delusions; 292.12 Sedative, Hypnotic, or Anxiolytic, With Hallucinations; 292.11 Other [or Unknown] Substance, With Delusions; 292.12 Other [or Unknown] Substance, With Hallucinations)

Specify if:

With Onset During Intoxication: if criteria are met for Intoxication with the substance and the symptoms develop during the intoxication syndrome

With Onset During Withdrawal: if criteria are met for Withdrawal from the substance and the symptoms develop during, or shortly after, a withdrawal syndrome

DSM-IV text for 298.9 Psychotic Disorder Not Otherwise Specified

This category includes psychotic symptomatology (i.e., delusions, hallucinations, disorganized speech, grossly disorganized or catatonic behavior) about which there is inadequate information to make a specific diagnosis or about which there is contradictory information, or disorders with psychotic symptoms that do not meet the criteria for any specific Psychotic Disorder.

(continued)

DSM-IV text for 298.9 Psychotic Disorder Not Otherwise Specified *(continued)*

Examples include

1. Postpartum psychosis that does not meet criteria for Mood Disorder With Psychotic Features, Brief Psychotic Disorder, Psychotic Disorder Due to a General Medical Condition, or Substance-Induced Psychotic Disorder
2. Psychotic symptoms that have lasted for less than 1 month but that have not yet remitted, so that the criteria for Brief Psychotic Disorder are not met
3. Persistent auditory hallucinations in the absence of any other features
4. Persistent nonbizarre delusions with periods of overlapping mood episodes that have been present for a substantial portion of the delusional disturbance
5. Situations in which the clinician has concluded that a Psychotic Disorder is present, but is unable to determine whether it is primary, due to a general medical condition, or substance induced

The Last Word

This section groups together all of the disorders with psychotic presentations except those due to dementia, delirium, or Mood Disorder. The disorders in this section differ based on duration (Schizophrenia versus Schizophreniform Disorder versus Brief Psychotic Disorder), the nature of the psychotic symptoms (Schizophrenia versus Delusional Disorder), the relationship between mood and psychotic symptoms (Schizophrenia versus Schizoaffective Disorder versus Mood Disorder With Psychotic Features), and etiology (Psychotic Disorder Due to a General Medical Condition versus Substance-Induced Psychotic Disorder versus Shared Psychotic Disorder versus Primary Psychotic Disorder).

CHAPTER 12

Mood Disorders

This section describes disorders in which the predominant disturbance is in the patient's mood. The DSM-IV glossary defines mood as "a pervasive and sustained emotion that colors the person's perception of the world. Common examples of mood include depression, elation, anger, and anxiety." Although this definition of mood lists anxiety and anger as examples, traditionally the term *mood disorder* is restricted to individuals with prominently depressed, elevated, or irritable mood. Despite its rather impressive length in DSM-IV, the Mood Disorders section actually contains only seven specific disorders: Major Depressive Disorder, Dysthymic Disorder, Bipolar I Disorder, Bipolar II Disorder, Cyclothymic Disorder, Mood Disorder Due to a General Medical Condition, and Substance-Induced Mood Disorder.

One of the difficulties in diagnosing Mood Disorders is that mood symptoms are by no means confined to disorders in this section of DSM-IV and commonly occur as presenting features of a wide variety of disorders classified elsewhere in the manual. For example, mood symptoms also occur in Adjustment Disorder, Substance-Related Disorders, Dementias, Schizophrenia and other psychotic disorders, Bereavement, Anxiety Disorders, Somatoform Disorders, and a number of Childhood Disorders.

There has been some confusion regarding the terms *mood* and *affect*. The term *affective* has also been used to refer to this class of disorders, and DSM-III labeled this section of the diagnostic manual as "Affective Disorders." Remnants of this designation still are found in the name *Schizoaffective Disorder* rather than *Schizomood Disorder*. Although mood and affect are often used interchangeably, medical dictionaries and the DSMs have attempted to differentiate between these two related concepts. The DSM-IV glossary defines affect as " . . . the subjective experience or expression of a feeling state (emotion) . . . in contrast to mood, which refers to a more pervasive and sustained emotional 'climate,' affect refers to more fluctuating changes in emotional 'weather.'"

Mood Episodes

Many of the Mood Disorders occur in an episodic pattern, with periods of disturbed mood alternating with often extended periods of normal functioning. For purposes of convenience, this section begins with the definitions of the mood episodes used later in the section as the building blocks for defining Major Depressive Disorder, Bipolar I Disorder, and Bipolar II Disorder. Four types of mood episode are defined in DSM-IV:

- **Major Depressive Episode:** at least 2 weeks of depressed mood accompanied by a characteristic pattern of depressive symptoms
- **Manic Episode:** at least 1 week of elevated, euphoric, or irritable mood accompanied by a characteristic pattern of manic symptoms
- **Mixed Episode:** at least 1 week of a mixture of manic and depressive symptoms
- **Hypomanic Episode:** at least 4 days of elevated, euphoric, or irritable mood that is less severe than a manic episode

Users of DSM-IV are sometimes confused about the relationship between these four types of mood episode and the seven types of codable DSM-IV Mood Disorder. It must be remembered that these mood episodes are not themselves codable as separate diagnoses. For example, a patient's presentation cannot legitimately be diagnosed as a Manic Episode but rather must be placed in the overall context of the disorder (e.g., Bipolar I Disorder, Most Recent Episode Manic). Text and criteria are provided for each of these episodes only for convenience.

Major Depressive Episode

This is one of the oldest and best studied criteria sets in DSM-IV and has undergone relatively few changes since it was first formulated in the early 1970s. Although clearly serviceable and enduring, this criteria set has a number of limitations: 1) it selects for a remarkably heterogeneous group of patients, ranging from the mildest to the most severe cases of depression encountered in clinical practice; 2) the severity and duration thresholds are set too high to capture some clinically significant problems and too low to avoid false-positive diagnoses; and 3) the items are particularly hard to apply in medically ill populations.

DSM-IV criteria for Major Depressive Episode

A. Five (or more) of the following symptoms have been present during the same 2-week period and represent a change from previous functioning; at least one of the symptoms is either (1) depressed mood or (2) loss of interest or pleasure.

Note: Do not include symptoms that are clearly due to a general medical condition, or mood-incongruent delusions or hallucinations.

(1) depressed mood most of the day, nearly every day, as indicated by either subjective report (e.g., feels sad or empty) or observation made by others (e.g., appears tearful). **Note:** In children and adolescents, can be irritable mood.
(2) markedly diminished interest or pleasure in all, or almost all, activities most of the day, nearly every day (as indicated by either subjective account or observation made by others)
(3) significant weight loss when not dieting or weight gain (e.g., a change of more than 5% of body weight in a month), or decrease or increase in appetite nearly every day. **Note:** In children, consider failure to make expected weight gains.
(4) insomnia or hypersomnia nearly every day
(5) psychomotor agitation or retardation nearly every day (observable by others, not merely subjective feelings of restlessness or being slowed down)
(6) fatigue or loss of energy nearly every day
(7) feelings of worthlessness or excessive or inappropriate guilt (which may be delusional) nearly every day (not merely self-reproach or guilt about being sick)
(8) diminished ability to think or concentrate, or indecisiveness, nearly every day (either by subjective account or as observed by others)
(9) recurrent thoughts of death (not just fear of dying), recurrent suicidal ideation without a specific plan, or a suicide attempt or a specific plan for committing suicide

B. The symptoms do not meet criteria for a Mixed Episode.

C. The symptoms cause clinically significant distress or impairment in social, occupational, or other important areas of functioning.

D. The symptoms are not due to the direct physiological effects of a substance (e.g., a drug of abuse, a medication) or a general medical condition (e.g., hypothyroidism).

E. The symptoms are not better accounted for by Bereavement, i.e., after the loss of a loved one, the symptoms persist for longer than 2 months or are characterized by marked functional impairment, morbid preoccupation with worthlessness, suicidal ideation, psychotic symptoms, or psychomotor retardation.

CRITERION A. The individual symptoms described in Criterion A are not uncommon, especially in their milder forms. What distinguishes a Major Depressive Episode is the severity of the symptoms and the fact that they cluster together nearly every day for at least 2 weeks (although often the duration is much longer and may become chronic). One common misunderstanding that results in overdiagnosis is the assumption that if the depressed mood has lasted nearly every day, so have the other depressive symptoms. Therefore, it is important to ensure that each individual symptom has also persisted nearly every day for at least 2 weeks before counting the symptoms as present. Another issue is whether to consider as part of the depressive episode the individual symptoms that were present before the onset of the episode (e.g., chronic insomnia). Such symptoms count toward the diagnosis only if they have gotten appreciably worse during the depressive episode.

The cardinal symptom of this cluster is depressed mood. However, in some cases a Major Depressive Episode occurs in the absence of the subjective feeling of depression. Some patients, particularly those with severe presentations, have lost the capacity to feel sadness. Others may have a cognitive style or come from a cultural setting in which feelings of sadness are downplayed. Therefore, an alternative anchor symptom that is considered to be a "depressive-equivalent" has been provided (*loss of interest or pleasure*). In every psychiatric evaluation, the clinician should screen for the presence of a Major Depressive Episode by asking whether depressed mood or loss of interest has been present for at least 2 weeks, either currently or at any time in the past. When considering the diagnostic significance of a specific behavior, it is important to determine its underlying cause. For example, you should evaluate whether inability to get out of bed represents item 2 (loss of pleasure in all activities, i.e., loss of desire to get up and face the day), item 6 (fatigue, i.e., not enough energy to get up), item 4 (hypersomnia), or item 8 (paralysis at the decision of whether to get out of bed). Careful questioning is therefore critical in translating behaviors into diagnostic items.

One of the greatest difficulties in assessment results from the fact that many of these so-called depressive symptoms (e.g., weight loss, sleeplessness, fatigue) are not particularly specific to depression and also occur in a wide variety of general medical conditions. For example, in an individual with human immunodeficiency virus (HIV) infection and depressed mood, it may be inherently impossible to tell whether symptoms such as weight loss, sleep disturbance, and fatigue result from the HIV infection, are part of a Major Depressive Episode, or arise from both causes acting together.

Several different proposals were considered for dealing with this issue in DSM-IV. One *(inclusive)* alternative was always to count such questionable symptoms toward the diagnosis of a Major Depressive Episode regardless of whether or not the clinician could determine definitively whether their cause was the general medical condition or the depression. This convention would serve to reduce the current underrecognition of depression in medically ill patients but would result in false-positive diagnoses. A second *(exclusive)* alternative was never to count such symptoms toward a depressive episode and instead to assume that they arise from the general medical condition. This convention would avoid false-positive diagnoses but would avoid them at the expense of false-negatives—that is, cases of depression would sometimes be missed. A third *(substitutive)* alternative was to provide a different criteria set (emphasizing cognitive symptoms and omitting somatic symptoms) for use specifically with individuals who have a general medical condition. This interesting suggestion was not accepted because of insufficient research evidence to indicate which depressive symptoms should be substituted. Ultimately, the Task Force decided to continue the DSM-III-R approach, which encourages the symptoms to be counted toward a Major Depressive Episode except when they seem to be clearly due to the general medical condition (e.g., a 50-pound weight loss in an individual with lung cancer and a sad mood probably should not count toward a diagnosis of a

Major Depressive Episode). This approach allows the question to be decided on the basis of the clinician's admittedly often difficult judgment.

Similarly, symptoms should not count toward a diagnosis of a Major Depressive Episode if they are better accounted for by another disorder. For example, if weight loss is clearly due to a delusion of the food being poisoned, it should not count as a depressive symptom. For some symptoms (e.g., anhedonia, psychomotor agitation or retardation), the attribution to a mood episode or to another disorder may be impossible.

Criterion A1. Irritable mood is common in a Major Depressive Episode and in DSM-III was even included as a depressive-equivalent (i.e., the presence of irritability could be used as a substitute for the requirement of a depressed mood). In DSM-III-R, the diagnosis of a Major Depressive Episode required either depressed mood or loss of interest and no longer could be made with only irritable mood in the absence of these other symptoms. This change was intended to create a more homogeneous definition of a Major Depressive Episode and to sharpen the boundary between depressive and manic episodes (which often include irritable mood). DSM-IV allows irritability to substitute for depressed mood only in children and adolescents because they may be less likely to report their depressed feelings and cognitions. However, caution must be exercised to avoid the overdiagnosis of depression in surly or oppositional adolescents.

Criterion A2. The commonly employed term *anhedonia* (absence of capacity for pleasure) was not used in this item because most individuals retain at least some capacity for pleasure even when they are depressed.

Criterion A3. Early in the course of a Major Depressive Episode, the diagnosis of this item usually depends on the change in appetite rather than the resulting loss or gain in weight because these usually take much longer than 2 weeks to develop. If weight loss occurs with normal or increased appetite, a General Medical Condition (especially malignancy) should be considered. Weight gain may suggest the presence of a Major Depressive Episode With Atypical Features.

Criterion A4. Insomnia is often present. The most common types are middle-of-the-night awakening or early morning awakening, but some patients report having trouble falling asleep. Less commonly, hypersomnia is present and should also suggest the presence of Atypical Features.

Criterion A5. Psychomotor agitation and psychomotor retardation refer to changes in motor activity and rate of thinking. Many patients with depression describe a subjective feeling of being restless or slowed down, but this item should not be counted unless these symptoms are visibly apparent to an outside observer. Psychomotor agitation is manifested by feelings of restlessness, pacing, and an inability to sit still. In psychomotor retardation, the person may seem to move and think as if in slow motion, taking a long time to get dressed in the morning, talking more slowly and softly, and responding to questions only after long pauses. Feelings of impatience on the part of the interviewer may suggest the presence of psychomotor retardation. It is important for the clinician to adjust to the rate of the patient's activity both as a matter of courtesy and to get more information.

Criterion A6. Some patients report feeling tired all the time, as if they are operating on low power or are totally drained even after undertaking what previously would have been relatively simple activities. This item is sometimes confused with psychomotor retardation—not an easy distinction, especially because both symptoms frequently occur together. However, patients with fatigue experience a distinct lack of energy; whereas, with psychomotor retardation, patients feel as if they are in a tank of water, moving against resistance.

Criterion A7. This item is often overdiagnosed in clinical practice. An unrealistically negative self-evaluation is fairly ubiquitous and does not necessarily count toward a diagnosis of Major Depressive Episode unless the individual has the more extreme distortion of feeling worthless or inappropriately guilty about the consequences of behaviors, feelings, or thoughts. At the extreme, the person may have a distorted false conviction of guilty responsibility at a level of intensity and persistence that is delusional (e.g., the conviction of being personally responsible for the world's poverty).

Criterion A8. Many individuals report mild to severe cognitive impairment—occasionally severe enough to resemble dementia. Sometimes the person is unable to concentrate on any activity (e.g., watching TV, reading the newspaper) due to an inability to filter out brooding thoughts of worthlessness, guilt, or hopelessness. The person may report feeling paralyzed by even the simplest decisions.

Criterion A9. Suicidal behavior is the most serious and sometimes irrevocable complication of Major Depressive Episode and should be the subject of extensive evaluation and efforts to intervene. It is important to determine the urgency of current suicidal thoughts, the degree to which definite plans have been formulated and acted on, the availability of a means of suicide, the lethality of the method, the urgency of the impulse, the presence of psychotic symptoms, the history of previous suicidal thoughts and attempts, a family history of suicidal behavior, and current and past substance use. The degree of suicidality is on a continuum ranging from recurrent wishes to be dead, to feelings that others would be better off if one were dead (passive suicidal thoughts), to formulating suicidal plans, to overt suicidal behaviors. This is the only item that need not be present every day for the 2-week period. Although suicidal ideation would have to be recurrent, a single suicide attempt would suffice to meet this item.

Criterion B. Without this criterion, all Mixed Episodes lasting 2 weeks or longer would also meet criteria for a Major Depressive Episode. This exclusion helps avoid such meaningless comorbidity.

Criterion C. The cluster of depressive symptoms must cause clinically significant impairment or distress. This item is necessary to avoid a false-positive diagnosis in an individual who meets five criteria but meets them at a very mild level that clinically does not warrant the diagnosis of a Major Depressive Episode.

The thresholds for severity and duration established in DSM-III and DSM-III-R were necessarily somewhat arbitrary, were not based on very strong evidence, and were criticized in two ways: 1) the thresholds may have been set too low, creating too much heterogeneity in severity (which may explain some of the variability in treatment response); and 2) the thresholds may have been set too high, resulting in missed cases of clinically significant depression (as measured by functional disability and health care utilization), particularly in primary care and community settings.

Two very different types of subthreshold depression were proposed for inclusion in DSM-IV: one that is subthreshold in symptom severity *(minor depression)* and another that is subthreshold in duration *(brief recurrent depression).* (Brief recurrent depression consists of at least 12 episodes a year, each meeting the full symptom-severity criteria of major depression but only lasting from 2 days to less than 2 weeks.)

Although of considerable interest, the suggested diagnoses of minor depression and brief recurrent depression were not included as official categories in DSM-IV for four reasons:

1. Studies of these disorders have had serious methodological limitations, particularly that patients diagnosed with these conditions may have received inadequate assessments (at least some of those patients' presentations might indeed have met criteria for a Major Depressive Episode if they had been diagnosed more carefully.
2. Inclusion of these disorders as official categories might lead to overdiagnosis and an artificially inflated prevalence of Mood Disorders.
3. Because these disorders have not been studied sufficiently in regard to the treatment response, the risk-benefit ratio of initiating treatment is unknown.
4. The inclusion of these milder categories might trivialize the construct of mental disorder and artificially inflate prevalence rates.

On the other hand, not including these categories may deprive patients of effective treatment. In DSM-IV, Minor Depressive Disorder and Brief Recurrent Depressive Disorder are included as specific examples in the Depressive Disorder Not Otherwise Specified section, and text and research criteria are included in Appendix B, "Criteria Sets and Axes Provided for Further Study." These diagnoses are discussed further in Chapter 25 of this book.

Criterion D. Determining the possible etiological role of a general medical condition or substance use in a depressive presentation is one of the most important and difficult distinctions in psychiatric diagnosis. It is important because many individuals with general medical conditions or substance use experience depression as a complication and because many individuals with depression have an underlying general medical condition or substance use as a cause. Obviously, this distinction has important treatment implications.

Criterion E. Many of the symptoms of a Major Depressive Episode occur as a normal phenomenon after the death of a loved one. In most of these instances, the symptoms should not be considered a mental disorder and instead are an understandable aspect of Bereavement (included in the "Other Conditions That May Be a Focus of Clinical Attention" section in DSM-IV). However, this consideration must be balanced against the fact that such episodes may not get better with time and grieving, and they may have a severity, persistence, and treatment response that are indistinguishable from those of a Major Depressive Episode.

The DSM-IV literature review indicated that if symptoms of depression persist for at least 2 months after the loss of a loved one, it is very likely that they will still be present at 1 year. This evidence led to changes in this criterion, encouraging the clinician to diagnose Major Depressive Disorder when the criteria for a Major Depressive Episode continue to be met fully at the 2-month point after the loss. Moreover, the presence of certain particularly severe symptoms (e.g., suicidal ideation, psychomotor retardation) regardless of duration also suggests that the presentation is best conceptualized as a Major Depressive Episode. The DSM-IV approach should help to reduce what has been an underdiagnosis of Major Depressive Episode in the context of the loss of a loved one.

Manic Episode

The symptoms listed below are important to remember and hard to miss. Because patients with manic episodes generally have tons of energy, terrible judgment, and minimal insight, they often get into a great deal of trouble and are impossible to treat in an outpatient setting. Once out of the office, the patient is likely never to return.

DSM-IV criteria for Manic Episode

A. A distinct period of abnormally and persistently elevated, expansive, or irritable mood, lasting at least 1 week (or any duration if hospitalization is necessary).

B. During the period of mood disturbance, three (or more) of the following symptoms have persisted (four if the mood is only irritable) and have been present to a significant degree:

(1) inflated self-esteem or grandiosity
(2) decreased need for sleep (e.g., feels rested after only 3 hours of sleep)
(3) more talkative than usual or pressure to keep talking
(4) flight of ideas or subjective experience that thoughts are racing
(5) distractibility (i.e., attention too easily drawn to unimportant or irrelevant external stimuli)
(6) increase in goal-directed activity (either socially, at work or school, or sexually) or psychomotor agitation
(7) excessive involvement in pleasurable activities that have a high potential for painful consequences (e.g., engaging in unrestrained buying sprees, sexual indiscretions, or foolish business investments)

C. The symptoms do not meet criteria for a Mixed Episode.

D. The mood disturbance is sufficiently severe to cause marked impairment in occupational functioning or in usual social activities or relationships with others, or to necessitate hospitalization to prevent harm to self or others, or there are psychotic features.

E. The symptoms are not due to the direct physiological effects of a substance (e.g., a drug of abuse, a medication, or other treatment) or a general medical condition (e.g., hyperthyroidism).

Note: Manic-like episodes that are clearly caused by somatic antidepressant treatment (e.g., medication, electroconvulsive therapy, light therapy) should not count toward a diagnosis of Bipolar I Disorder.

Criterion A. It is sometimes difficult to distinguish an abnormally elevated mood from just feeling good. This is especially true for chronically depressed patients, for whom a period of uncharacteristically normal mood might be misinterpreted as a "high." This distinction is made on the basis of severity and duration. Although 1 or even 2 days of feeling on top of the world might follow a celebratory event, it would be unusual for the elevated or irritable mood to last, night and day, for an entire week. If hospitalization is required, a shorter duration is allowable because in such cases the pathological nature of the mood is usually not in question. Even though a euphoric and expansive mood is considered to be the classic manic symptom, some patients have a Manic Episode characterized by a more irritable mood. Usually the irritable mood is most evident when the individual is thwarted, but there may be a general sense of extreme impatience or of having a very short fuse. To be indicative of a Manic Episode, the irritability must be generalized and not just confined to one situation or relationship.

Criterion B. Manic Episodes with irritable mood require four additional symptoms (rather than the three required for euphoric mania) because an irritable Manic Episode is particularly easy to confuse with agitated depression and with the irritability characteristic of many psychotic disorders.

Criterion B1. Many manic individuals feel that they are especially talented or knowledgeable and insightful. This belief should be counted only if it represents a change from their usual self-concept. When extreme, the grandiosity may be delusional, with the person becoming convinced that he or she has a special relationship with God or with a famous person.

Criterion B2. One of the most characteristic features of a Manic Episode is a significantly decreased need for sleep. In a person with a history of recurrent Manic Episodes, reduced sleep is often the first symptom of relapse and can be used as a warning sign for the development of a full-blown Manic Episode. Unlike Primary Insomnia, in which the individual usually feels tired the next day, the manic patient does not feel the need for sleep and is full of energy despite sleeping only a couple of hours. This item should be counted only if there is a significant change in the number of hours of sleep and does not apply to individuals who habitually need only a few hours.

Criterion B3. There is an increase in both the rate and amount of speech. The individual may experience an inner pressure to keep talking, as if there is so much to say and not nearly enough time to say it. The interviewer may not be able to get a word in edgewise. Typical manic speech also includes a barrage of jokes and puns.

Criterion B4. This criterion is closely related to the previous item in that the pressured speech may be an attempt by the individual to relate racing thoughts. Most patients will be able to acknowledge the presence of this symptom (i.e., "my thoughts are racing through my head"). Sometimes flight of ideas must be inferred from the content of the person's speech. The person may jump from one topic to another very quickly, with only the slightest thread of thematic connection between topics. In some cases, the connection may be based on sound rather than meaning (clang associations). Flight of ideas supposedly differs from loosening of associations (which refers to the speech pattern most characteristic of Schizophrenia) in that the listener is able to understand the connection between one thought and another. This judgment is inherently unreliable because it is based not only on the nature of the patient's thoughts, but also on the interviewer's ability to glean meaningful connections. In practice, if disorganized speech occurs in the context of other manic symptoms, there is a tendency to use the label *flight of ideas;* if it occurs in the context of other symptoms characteristic of Schizophrenia, the tendency is to use the term *loosening of associations.*

Criterion B5. Distractibility refers to an inability to filter out extraneous stimuli when attempting to concentrate on a particular task or activity. This symptom becomes evident when the patient keeps getting distracted by things such as extraneous sounds (e.g., after hearing an ambulance siren, the patient recounts a tale of being arrested by the police), physical attributes of the interview room, or the examiner's clothing or physical appearance. Other causes of distractibility (e.g., delirium, substance intoxication, attention-deficit/hyperactivity disorder) must also be considered.

Criterion B6. As a consequence of the elevated mood, increased energy, or increased self-esteem, the person feels driven to be involved in more activities than usual. In some cases, the increase in activity is much less goal directed and may take the form of motor restlessness or pacing.

Criterion B7. This item taps the hedonistic pleasure-seeking quality of mania. In the pursuit of excitement or thrills, the person may engage in activities that are not characteristic of usual functioning, without regard for the possible negative consequences. For example, the person may buy an expensive luxury item on credit or take an expensive vacation without any possibility of being able to afford it. Other reckless behavior may include driving at high speeds for the thrill of it, drug-taking behavior (usually amphetamines or cocaine), and unsafe sexual behavior. Sometimes this item is erroneously applied to any behavior that gets the person into trouble (e.g., being arrested by the police for accosting strangers with the news that doomsday is approaching). Behavior should be considered to meet this criterion only when the motivation is pleasure seeking rather than in response to delusional thinking or hallucinations.

Criterion C. Without this criterion, all Mixed Episodes would also meet criteria for a Manic Episode. This exclusion helps avoid such meaningless comorbidity.

Criterion D. Typically, this criterion serves to set the boundary between having a mental disorder and not having a mental disorder. However, if the patient's clinical presentation is below the severity threshold for a Manic Episode, then a Hypomanic Episode should be considered. Manic and hypomanic episodes occur on a continuum, with the term *Manic Episode* intended to apply only to those episodes in which there is a severe degree of impairment.

The boundary between Manic and Hypomanic Episodes can be inherently difficult to draw. Energized argumentativeness bordering on insubordination at work is more on the hypomanic side, whereas quitting the job because the boss does not acknowledge one's greatness is more on the manic side. Similarly, calling up all of one's friends during the day is more on the hypomanic side, but calling them between midnight and dawn is more on the manic side. Unusual for DSM-IV, a treatment decision (e.g., necessitating hospitalization) is included in this criterion on the assumption that requiring hospitalization is a marker for extreme severity. However, the problem with using hospitalization as a criterion is that the factors that determine hospitalization are variable across settings, geographical locations, and time.

CRITERION E. Manic behavior caused by substance use may be indistinguishable on presentation from a primary Manic Episode. The diagnosis often requires urine testing and establishing the temporal relationship between drug use and the development of manic symptoms. It should be noted that a positive drug screen does not by itself prove an etiological connection because manic individuals may also often use drugs as part of their hedonistic pattern. A family history or past history of Manic or Hypomanic Episodes while not using substances increases the likelihood that the presentation is primary and not substance induced.

Especially noteworthy is the fact that some individuals treated for depression with medication, light therapy, or electroconvulsive therapy go on to develop manic-like episodes. There has been considerable controversy about how to diagnose such individuals. DSM-III-R counted these treatment-induced episodes toward the diagnosis of Bipolar I Disorder. This would result in a change in diagnosis from Recurrent Major Depressive Disorder to Bipolar I Disorder after only a single antidepressant-induced manic episode. The concern about the DSM-III-R convention is that, without adequate data, it assumed that treatment-induced Manic Episodes are equivalent to Manic Episodes arising de novo. Researchers in this field have coined the term *Bipolar III Disorder* to describe such presentations to indicate the disorder's distinctness from Bipolar I and Bipolar II Disorders. Based on the available evidence, it is not yet clear whether (or which) patients whose Manic Episodes occur only in the context of treatment are best considered unipolar, bipolar, or something in-between. Therefore, in contrast to DSM-III-R, DSM-IV does not count treatment-induced episodes toward the diagnosis of either Bipolar Disorder or the rapid-cycling type. Instead, DSM-IV suggests assigning two diagnoses: Substance-Induced Mood Disorder With Manic Features (for the treatment-induced manic symptom) and Major Depressive Disorder (for the Major Depressive Episode requiring antidepressant treatment). This decision was meant to suspend judgment and save information. However, clinical judgment is required. If treatment-induced episodes occur in the context of a previously well-established Bipolar Disorder or in an individual with a strong family history of Bipolar Disorder, it probably makes more sense to consider them as evidence of Manic Episodes.

More rarely, a general medical condition (e.g., hyperthyroidism, Cushing's disease) can be the direct cause of the manic symptoms. This possibility should be come to mind especially when a first Manic Episode occurs late in life. Establishing this etiology can be critical because medical intervention alone can sometimes alleviate the disturbance.

Mixed Episode

Mixed Episodes can occur in two different contexts. For some patients with Bipolar Disorder, these are no more than transitional states during the switch between a Manic Episode and a Major Depressive Episode (or, less commonly, vice versa). In other patients, Mixed Episodes represent the most characteristic form of an episode of elevated or irritable mood. Patients in a Mixed Episode often present special management problems, may be treatment resistant, and are at particularly high risk for suicidal or aggressive behavior.

DSM-IV criteria for Mixed Episode

A. The criteria are met both for a Manic Episode and for a Major Depressive Episode (except for duration) nearly every day during at least a 1-week period.

B. The mood disturbance is sufficiently severe to cause marked impairment in occupational functioning or in usual social activities or relationships with others, or to necessitate hospitalization to prevent harm to self or others, or there are psychotic features.

C. The symptoms are not due to the direct physiological effects of a substance (e.g., a drug of abuse, a medication, or other treatment) or a general medical condition (e.g., hyperthyroidism).

Note: Mixed-like episodes that are clearly caused by somatic antidepressant treatment (e.g., medication, electroconvulsive therapy, light therapy) should not count toward a diagnosis of Bipolar I Disorder.

Hypomanic Episode

A separate criteria set for Hypomanic Episode was introduced into DSM-IV to clarify issues in its assessment and avoid overdiagnosis of Bipolar II Disorder.

DSM-IV criteria for Hypomanic Episode

A. A distinct period of persistently elevated, expansive, or irritable mood, lasting throughout at least 4 days, that is clearly different from the usual nondepressed mood.

B. During the period of mood disturbance, three (or more) of the following symptoms have persisted (four if the mood is only irritable) and have been present to a significant degree:

(1) inflated self-esteem or grandiosity
(2) decreased need for sleep (e.g., feels rested after only 3 hours of sleep)
(3) more talkative than usual or pressure to keep talking
(4) flight of ideas or subjective experience that thoughts are racing
(5) distractibility (i.e., attention too easily drawn to unimportant or irrelevant external stimuli)

(continued)

DSM-IV criteria for Hypomanic Episode *(continued)*

(6) increase in goal-directed activity (either socially, at work or school, or sexually) or psychomotor agitation

(7) excessive involvement in pleasurable activities that have a high potential for painful consequences (e.g., the person engages in unrestrained buying sprees, sexual indiscretions, or foolish business investments)

C. The episode is associated with an unequivocal change in functioning that is uncharacteristic of the person when not symptomatic.

D. The disturbance in mood and the change in functioning are observable by others.

E. The episode is not severe enough to cause marked impairment in social or occupational functioning, or to necessitate hospitalization, and there are no psychotic features.

F. The symptoms are not due to the direct physiological effects of a substance (e.g., a drug of abuse, a medication, or other treatment) or a general medical condition (e.g., hyperthyroidism).

Note: Hypomanic-like episodes that are clearly caused by somatic antidepressant treatment (e.g., medication, electroconvulsive therapy, light therapy) should not count toward a diagnosis of Bipolar II Disorder.

CRITERION A. Hypomanic Episodes are essentially milder forms of Manic Episodes and are difficult to distinguish from periods of normal good mood. The addition of Bipolar II Disorder in DSM-IV makes this determination even more important because the presence of even one Hypomanic Episode in a patient with recurrent Major Depressive Disorder is sufficient to change the diagnosis to Bipolar II for life, with all of the possible consequent treatment and prognostic implications. Careful questioning is therefore required to determine that this period of elevated mood is clearly different from the person's usual mood (Criteria C and D also help with this distinction).

CRITERION B. The items and thresholds defining a Hypomanic Episode are the same as those in Criterion B for a Manic Episode. By definition, however, a Hypomanic Episode does not cause marked impairment, and the individual presents a milder version of these symptoms than would be characteristic of a Manic Episode. Individuals with Hypomanic Episodes often feel more creative and productive and thus are often reluctant to initiate treatment at the first signs of elevated mood, even though prompt initiation of treatment might help prevent the development of a full-blown Manic Episode.

Four associated symptoms must accompany irritable mood (while only three are required for elevated or expansive mood) because it is particularly difficult to diagnose a Hypomanic Episode in the presence of irritability. This difficult differentiation most often comes up with adolescents, whose irritability might also be accounted for by depression, attention-deficit/hyperactivity disorder, substance use, personality features, the developmental aspects of being an adolescent, or interpersonal problems.

Criteria C and D. These two criteria serve to define the boundary between normality and a Hypomanic Episode. A diagnosis of Hypomanic Episode is unique in DSM-IV in that it does not require the presence of clinically significant distress or impairment. In fact, many individuals with Hypomanic Episodes report that they are more productive and function better during these episodes. Having Hypomanic Episodes per se does not indicate that the individual has a mental disorder unless these are associated with impairment (e.g., job loss) or Major Depressive Episodes (as in Bipolar II Disorder). However, the level of functioning that results from the hypomanic mood must be demonstrated to be different from the level of functioning associated with the person's normal mood when not symptomatic. Because individuals (particularly those with mood disorder) often have a poor ability to self-monitor mood changes, other informants are often helpful to document the change in both mood and level of functioning. Note that this item does not necessarily require that other informants be contacted—instead, the individual may relate that other people have commented that he or she has been acting differently.

Criterion E. Although Criteria C and D serve to establish the boundary between normality and a Hypomanic Episode, this criterion sets the boundary between a Hypomanic Episode and a Manic Episode.

Criterion F. See Criterion D for Manic Episode.

Mood Disorders

There are only seven specific Mood Disorders in this section. These are grouped based on two distinctions. The *primary* Mood Disorders are listed first, followed by those in which the etiology has been established (e.g., Mood Disorder Due to a General Medical Condition and Substance-Induced Mood Disorder). The primary Mood Disorders are divided into the unipolar (*depressive*) and the *bipolar*—a distinction that has very important treatment implications (i.e., whether a mood stabilizer is needed in the management).

Depressive Disorders

Depressive Disorders

296.xx	Major Depressive Disorder
296.2x	Single Episode
296.3x	Recurrent
300.4	Dysthymic Disorder
311	Depressive Disorder Not Otherwise Specified

The Depressive Disorders are divided into Major Depressive Disorder and Dysthymic Disorder, based on severity and whether or not the depressed mood occurs in episodes. Major Depressive Disorder consists of one or more Major Depressive Episodes, whereas Dysthymic Disorder is characterized by chronic depressed mood that is below the severity threshold of a Major Depressive Episode. Although descriptively useful and helpful in treatment planning, this division is artificial. Major Depressive Disorder and Dysthymic Disorder are often no more than two aspects of the overall course of a depressive disorder. Many individuals who start out with Dysthymic Disorder go on to develop Major Depressive Disorder. Moreover, an appreciable minority of individuals with either Major Depressive Disorder or Dysthymic Disorder go on to develop Manic or Hypomanic Episodes, warranting a switch in diagnosis to Bipolar I Disorder, Bipolar II Disorder, or Cyclothymic Disorder.

Major Depressive Disorder

Major Depressive Disorder is the codable disorder for individuals with one or more Major Depressive Episodes and no Manic or Hypomanic Episodes. As indicated below in Criterion A, Major Depressive Disorders are coded based on whether there has only been a single Major Depressive Episode or whether the episodes are recurrent.

DSM-IV diagnostic criteria for Major Depressive Disorder

A. Presence of a single Major Depressive Episode (296.2x Major Depressive Disorder, Single Episode) or two or more Major Depressive Episodes (296.3x Major Depressive Disorder, Recurrent).

 Note: To be considered separate episodes, there must be an interval of at least 2 consecutive months in which criteria are not met for a Major Depressive Episode.

B. The Major Depressive Episodes are not better accounted for by Schizoaffective Disorder, and are not superimposed on Schizophrenia, Schizophreniform Disorder, Delusional Disorder, or Psychotic Disorder Not Otherwise Specified.

C. There has never been a Manic Episode or Hypomanic Episode.

 Note: This exclusion does not apply if all of the manic-like, mixed-like, or hypomanic-like episodes are substance or treatment induced or are due to the direct physiological effects of a general medical condition.

 Code in fifth digit: 1 = Mild; 2 = Moderate; 3 = Severe Without Psychotic Features; 4 = Severe With Psychotic Features (Specify Mood-Congruent/Mood-Incongruent); 5 = In Partial Remission; 6 = In Full Remission; 0 = Unspecified

Specify (for current or most recent episode):
Severity/Psychotic/Remission Specifiers

(continued)

DSM-IV diagnostic criteria for Major Depressive Disorder *(continued)*

Chronic
With Catatonic Features
With Melancholic Features
With Atypical Features
With Postpartum Onset

Specify:
Longitudinal Course Modifiers
With Seasonal Pattern

Note. This is a summary of two criteria sets.

CRITERION A. Unlike Bipolar Disorder, which is almost always characterized by a lifetime of recurring episodes, Major Depressive Disorder is more likely to have a variable course. An individual who has a single Major Depressive Episode has about a 50% chance of developing another episode at some later point. Once an individual has two episodes, the odds of having a third increase to about 70%. A third episode increases the chances of a fourth to 90%. Approximately 10%–20% of individuals develop the chronic form in which the criteria are met for a Major Depressive Episode for at least 2 years.

If there has only been one Major Depressive Episode, the DSM-IV disorder Major Depressive Disorder, Single Episode, should be diagnosed (code 296.2x should be noted); if there are two or more major depressive episodes, the DSM-IV disorder Major Depressive Disorder, Recurrent, should be diagnosed (code 296.3x should be noted).

Because depressive episodes can wax and wane, it is not always obvious when one episode ends and another begins, and there has been a great deal of debate in the literature concerning how best to define remission, relapse, and recurrence for Major Depressive Episodes. As a rough guide, DSM-IV suggests that it be considered a new episode only if there has been a period of at least 2 months in which the full criteria for a Major Depressive Episode have not been met. Other proposed alternatives included requiring a longer duration of remission (6 months) or a stricter definition of remission (no significant symptoms of depression) before symptoms would count toward a new episode. The final DSM-IV wording was chosen to reflect the fact that many patients begin with Dysthymic Disorder and go on to develop Major Depressive Episodes, and, when they recover between episodes, they return to their dysthymic baseline. The requirement that interepisode remission last for at least 2 months was continued from DSM-III-R and must be applied with clinical judgment. For example, the clinician may decide to consider as one episode (rather than two separate episodes) the situation in which a patient on medication has a slight improvement for 2 months (so that the presentation just barely falls short of a Major Depressive Episode) and then has a slight relapse (so that the presentation again is above the threshold for an episode).

Like Bipolar I Disorder, Major Depressive Disorder requires a fifth digit to indicate current severity. If a Major Depressive Episode is currently present, the code indicates the severity of the disorder (1 = mild, 2 = moderate, 3 = severe without psychotic features, and 4 = severe with psychotic features). If a Major Depressive Episode is not currently present, a fifth digit of 5 indicates that the symptoms are in partial remission (i.e., full criteria are not currently met but some symptoms persist, or there have been no significant symptoms for less than 2 months), and a 6 indicates that the symptoms are in full remission (i.e., there have been no significant symptoms for at least 2 months).

Criterion B. When psychotic symptoms occur exclusively during a mood episode, the diagnosis is Major Depressive Disorder and not another psychotic disorder. If, however, psychotic symptoms are present in the absence of prominent mood symptoms, a psychotic disorder diagnosis (Schizophrenia, Schizoaffective Disorder, Delusional Disorder) should be considered. See Chapter 11 for a more detailed discussion of this differential diagnosis.

Major Depressive Episodes not infrequently occur in the context of Schizophrenia (or another psychotic disorder like Schizophreniform or Delusional Disorder), particularly in the postpsychotic phase when the delusions or hallucinations are no longer prominent. In fact, much of the suicidal behavior associated with Schizophrenia may occur as part of these episodes. By convention, a diagnosis of Major Depressive Disorder is not compatible with a simultaneous diagnosis of Schizophrenia. When a Major Depressive Episode does occur during Schizophrenia, it is diagnosed as Depressive Disorder Not Otherwise Specified. A new category (Postpsychotic Depressive Disorder of Schizophrenia) was proposed for DSM-IV to deal more specifically with this situation. This category was not included in DSM-IV (although it is included in Appendix B) because 1) it can be extremely difficult to differentiate symptoms of a Major Depressive Episode from medication side effects (e.g., akinesia) and the negative symptoms of Schizophrenia (e.g., lack of motivation, loss of capacity to experience pleasure), and 2) it has not been sufficiently studied whether encouraging antidepressant use in this population may lead to detrimental effects (e.g., worsening of psychotic symptoms). This category is discussed further in Chapter 25.

Criterion C. The distinction between Unipolar and Bipolar Disorder is of considerable importance because of its potential impact on management (e.g., choice of medication, duration of maintenance treatment) and prognosis. It is, therefore, very important to inquire about the presence of Manic or Hypomanic Episodes in every patient with a current or past Major Depressive Episode. A family history of Bipolar Disorder is also very informative. Among individuals previously diagnosed as having Major Depressive Disorder, approximately 5%–10% will have a later Manic Episode necessitating a change in diagnosis to Bipolar I Disorder. It is less clear what percentage of individuals with Major Depressive Disorder will have at least one Hypomanic Episode requiring a change in diagnosis to Bipolar II Disorder.

300.4 Dysthymic Disorder

Dysthymic Disorder was introduced into DSM-III to describe a nonepisodic chronic depression with a symptom severity below that for Major Depressive Disorder. At least in clinical samples, most individuals who qualify for this diagnosis also will eventually have periods of depression that meet the symptom and duration thresholds for Major

Depressive Disorder. Although the combination of Dysthymic Disorder and Major Depressive Disorder has been called *double depression* (and DSM-IV assigns two separate diagnoses), it is probably better to consider this combination as a waxing and waning course of a single depressive condition.

DSM-IV diagnostic criteria for 300.4 Dysthymic Disorder

A. Depressed mood for most of the day, for more days than not, as indicated either by subjective account or observation by others, for at least 2 years. **Note:** In children and adolescents, mood can be irritable and duration must be at least 1 year.

B. Presence, while depressed, of two (or more) of the following:

(1) poor appetite or overeating
(2) insomnia or hypersomnia
(3) low energy or fatigue
(4) low self-esteem
(5) poor concentration or difficulty making decisions
(6) feelings of hopelessness

C. During the 2-year period (1 year for children or adolescents) of the disturbance, the person has never been without the symptoms in Criteria A and B for more than 2 months at a time.

D. No Major Depressive Episode has been present during the first 2 years of the disturbance (1 year for children and adolescents); i.e., the disturbance is not better accounted for by chronic Major Depressive Disorder, or Major Depressive Disorder, In Partial Remission.

Note: There may have been a previous Major Depressive Episode provided there was a full remission (no significant signs or symptoms for 2 months) before development of the Dysthymic Disorder. In addition, after the initial 2 years (1 year in children or adolescents) of Dysthymic Disorder, there may be superimposed episodes of Major Depressive Disorder, in which case both diagnoses may be given when the criteria are met for a Major Depressive Episode.

E. There has never been a Manic Episode, a Mixed Episode, or a Hypomanic Episode, and criteria have never been met for Cyclothymic Disorder.

F. The disturbance does not occur exclusively during the course of a chronic Psychotic Disorder, such as Schizophrenia or Delusional Disorder.

G. The symptoms are not due to the direct physiological effects of a substance (e.g., a drug of abuse, a medication) or a general medical condition (e.g., hypothyroidism).

H. The symptoms cause clinically significant distress or impairment in social, occupational, or other important areas of functioning.

Specify if:

Early Onset: if onset is before age 21 years
Late Onset: if onset is age 21 years or older

Specify (for most recent 2 years of Dysthymic Disorder):

With Atypical Features

Criterion A. Depressed mood in Dysthymic Disorder is defined as it is in a Major Depressive Episode; there is nothing different about the quality or even the intensity of the depressed mood itself. As the criterion notes, patients with Dysthymic Disorder can still have occasional good days, so long as the bad days outnumber the good ones and there are not more than 2 months of good days in a row (see Criterion C).

Criterion B. There is considerable controversy concerning how best to define the list of characteristic symptoms that accompany the depressed mood in Dysthymic Disorder. Two issues have been raised in this regard. The first has to do with the nature of the symptoms chosen. The symptom list in DSM-IV (which has been carried over from DSM-III-R) places relatively great emphasis on somatic symptoms (e.g., eating, sleep, energy level). A number of studies (including the DSM-IV field trial) suggest that Dysthymic Disorder may be better characterized by a wider array of cognitive and interpersonal symptoms, especially the following: generalized loss of interest or pleasure; social withdrawal; feelings of guilt; brooding about the past; subjective feelings of irritability or excessive anger; and decreased activity, effectiveness, or productivity. The DSM-IV Mood Disorders Work Group was especially conservative and decided that there was insufficient evidence to justify a change in the symptoms of Dysthymic Disorder. Instead these items are included in Appendix B.

The second issue concerns the severity of Dysthymic Disorder and its relationship to Major Depressive Disorder. The symptom threshold for Dysthymic Disorder (three of a possible seven symptoms) is set almost as high as that required for a Major Depressive Episode (five of nine symptoms). A patient with Dysthymic Disorder who develops one or two additional depressive symptoms (even if these are at a fairly mild level and exist for a relatively short duration) would then qualify for a diagnosis of a Major Depressive Episode.

It is unclear when and to what degree so-called double depression is no more than an artifact resulting from the lack of a clear definitional boundary between Dysthymic Disorder and Major Depressive Disorder and when double depression really represents two more distinct disorders—an intermittent episodic disorder superimposed on (and perhaps predisposed by) the chronic depression. To create a clearer boundary between Dysthymic Disorder and Major Depressive Disorder, it would have been necessary either to lower the severity threshold for Dysthymic Disorder, revise upward the severity or duration requirement for Major Depressive Disorder, or to do both. It seemed unlikely that the number of items required for Dysthymic Disorder could be lowered much more without making the diagnosis ubiquitous in clinical (and perhaps even in nonclinical) samples. The other alternative (raising of the severity and/or the duration threshold for Major Depressive Disorder) was considered to be too radical a change.

Criterion C. Some caution should be exercised when evaluating this criterion because patients who are currently depressed have a tendency to distort retrospectively their reports of past experience in a negative direction. This pessimism about the past may be analogous to hopelessness about the future. It may be helpful to consult with other informants to clarify the patient's prior course and to use daily mood diaries to chart the future course. Although the diagnosis of Dysthymic Disorder is intended to describe a relatively chronic nonepisodic mood disturbance, some periods of euthymic mood are allowed so long as they do not last more than 2 months at a time. Less persistent mood symptoms are diagnosed as the residual Depressive Disorder Not Otherwise Specified.

Criterion D. This criterion was introduced into DSM-III-R to provide a definitional distinction between Dysthymic Disorder and the nonremitting forms of Major Depressive Disorder (i.e., Major Depressive Disorder, Chronic, and Major Depressive Disorder, In Partial Remission). The distinction is based on the mode of onset. Some individuals begin with Dysthymic Disorder and then go on to have recurrent superimposed Major Depressive Episodes (double depression). Other individuals begin with a Major Depressive Episode that never completely remits. Retrospectively, it can be quite difficult to determine the nature of the onset, especially because the difference between severe Dysthymic Disorder and mild Major Depressive Disorder is vanishingly thin. This cumbersome criterion attempts to operationalize an algorithmic distinction. The presence of Major Depressive Episodes is compatible with a diagnosis of Dysthymic Disorder so long as there is at least a 2-year period of Dysthymic Disorder before there is a first Major Depressive Episode. The second half of the criterion was added to cover the relatively uncommon situation in which Dysthymic Disorder follows a Major Depressive Episode after a period of remission. Such a period of remission is required to ensure that what appears to be Dysthymic Disorder is not simply a partially treated chronic Major Depressive Disorder.

Criterion E. This criterion firmly places Dysthymic Disorder in the unipolar spectrum. It should be noted that in actual practice it is not all that uncommon to have Dysthymic Disorder as an antecedent to Bipolar I or Bipolar II Disorder. Unfortunately, DSM-IV does not provide any way to indicate this.

Criterion F. Chronic dysphoric mood is so commonly encountered in chronic psychotic disorders that its occurrence should be considered as no more than an associated feature secondary to these disorders, rather than warranting a separate diagnosis of Dysthymic Disorder.

Criterion G. General medical and substance etiologies should be particularly considered when Dysthymic Disorder has a late onset. Many individuals with Substance Dependence are chronically dysphoric. Furthermore, some medical conditions (e.g., hypothyroidism, anemia) can masquerade as depression and go undiagnosed for years. As is always the case, the diagnosis of Dysthymic Disorder would remain appropriate if the chronic depressive symptoms are a psychological reaction to (not a direct physiological consequence of) a general medical condition. For example, an individual who becomes chronically depressed after becoming disabled from an amputation would qualify for Dysthymic Disorder.

Criterion H. The boundary with normality is particularly important to draw for this disorder. Not all people who are "downers" with a chronically gloomy perspective on life qualify for a diagnosis of Dysthymic Disorder. On the other hand, because Dysthymic Disorder is defined as subthreshold in severity to Major Depressive Disorder, there is a tendency for some clinicians to underestimate the degree of impairment or distress that may be associated with it. Chronic depression takes a huge toll not only on the individual, but also on family members and friends.

Specifier for Early Onset/Late Onset. The fact that Dysthymic Disorder is so frequently encountered in clinical samples of children validates a statement made by many adult patients that they have been depressed as long as they can remember. Early onset Dysthymic Disorder has been associated with especially high rates of depressive illness among biological relatives. Some feel that early onset Dysthymic Disorder is better considered a personality disorder related to Major Depressive Disorder in the same way that Schizotypal Personality Disorder is related to Schizophrenia. In fact, a proposal for a Depressive Personality Disorder is included in Appendix B of DSM-IV. Later onset Dysthymic Disorder, in some cases at least, may represent demoralization consequent to having to deal with severe psychosocial stressors, physical illness, or having another mental disorder.

DSM-IV text for 311 Depressive Disorder Not Otherwise Specified

The Depressive Disorder Not Otherwise Specified category includes disorders with depressive features that do not meet the criteria for Major Depressive Disorder, Dysthymic Disorder, Adjustment Disorder With Depressed Mood, or Adjustment Disorder With Mixed Anxiety and Depressed Mood. Sometimes depressive symptoms can present as part of an Anxiety Disorder Not Otherwise Specified. Examples of Depressive Disorder Not Otherwise Specified include

1. Premenstrual dysphoric disorder: in most menstrual cycles during the past year, symptoms (e.g., markedly depressed mood, marked anxiety, marked affective lability, decreased interest in activities) regularly occurred during the last week of the luteal phase (and remitted within a few days of the onset of menses). These symptoms must be severe enough to markedly interfere with work, school, or usual activities and be entirely absent for at least 1 week postmenses
2. Minor depressive disorder: episodes of at least 2 weeks of depressive symptoms but with fewer than the five items required for Major Depressive Disorder
3. Recurrent brief depressive disorder: depressive episodes lasting from 2 days up to 2 weeks, occurring at least once a month for 12 months (not associated with the menstrual cycle)
4. Postpsychotic depressive disorder of Schizophrenia: a Major Depressive Episode that occurs during the residual phase of Schizophrenia
5. A Major Depressive Episode superimposed on Delusional Disorder, Psychotic Disorder Not Otherwise Specified, or the active phase of Schizophrenia
6. Situations in which the clinician has concluded that a depressive disorder is present but is unable to determine whether it is primary, due to a general medical condition, or substance induced

Bipolar Disorders

Bipolar Disorders

296.xx	Bipolar I Disorder
296.0x	Single Manic Episode
296.40	Most Recent Episode Hypomanic
296.4x	Most Recent Episode Manic

(continued)

296.6x	Most Recent Episode Mixed
296.5x	Most Recent Episode Depressed
296.7	Most Recent Episode Unspecified
296.89	Bipolar II Disorder
301.13	Cyclothymic Disorder
296.80	Bipolar Disorder Not Otherwise Specified

Bipolar I Disorder

Bipolar I Disorder is the codable disorder for individuals with a Mood Disorder that includes one or more Manic Episodes. There are several important ways in which Bipolar I Disorder differs from Major Depressive Disorder. Unlike Major Depressive Disorder, in which there is a predominance of females and a fairly even distribution of age at onset throughout the life span, Bipolar I Disorder is equally distributed in both sexes and usually has an onset during adolescence or early adulthood. Bipolar I Disorder is also less common than Major Depressive Disorder, with a prevalence of about 1%. Finally, individuals tend to have many more episodes of Bipolar I Disorder during their lives. It is almost always recurrent, and the episodes tend to become more frequent as the course progresses.

Because of coding constraints that are more complicated than you would want to hear about, the Bipolar I Disorders are divided into Single Manic Episode and various types of recurrent episodes. The distinction between Single Episode and Recurrent Bipolar Disorder is really fairly meaningless because 90%–95% of individuals with a Single Manic Episode go on to have additional Manic or Major Depressive Episodes. Therefore, once a Single Manic Episode has occurred, it is crucial that the patient and family be cautioned that additional episodes are inevitable. The onset of Bipolar I Disorder is an indication for a thorough psychoeducation program, teaching the patient ways of preventing recurrence (e.g., avoiding stimulants and excessive stress and maintaining circadian regularity) and of identifying early warning signs (e.g., insomnia). It should be noted that DSM-IV does not use the term *recurrent* but instead indicates the type of the most recent episode. Although DSM-IV provides separate criteria sets for each type, for convenience we have condensed these into a single generic criteria set.

DSM-IV diagnostic criteria for 296.0x Bipolar I Disorder, Single Manic Episode

A. Presence of only one Manic Episode and no past Major Depressive Episodes.

Note: Recurrence is defined as either a change in polarity from depression or an interval of at least 2 months without manic symptoms.

(continued)

DSM-IV diagnostic criteria for 296.0x Bipolar I Disorder, Single Manic Episode *(continued)*

B. The Manic Episode is not better accounted for by Schizoaffective Disorder and is not superimposed on Schizophrenia, Schizophreniform Disorder, Delusional Disorder, or Psychotic Disorder Not Otherwise Specified.

Specify if:
Mixed: if symptoms meet criteria for a Mixed Episode

Specify (for current or most recent episode):
Severity/Psychotic/Remission Specifiers
With Catatonic Features
With Postpartum Onset

DSM-IV diagnostic criteria for Bipolar I Disorder, Most Recent Episode [*Indicate* Hypomanic, Manic, Mixed, Depressed, or Unspecified]

A. Currently (or most recently) in a Hypomanic (296.40), Manic (296.4x), Mixed (296.6x), or Major Depressive Episode (296.5x). If the criteria are met for one of these episodes except for duration, the episode is considered unspecified (296.7).

Note: An *x* in the diagnostic code indicates that a fifth digit indicating severity is required.

B. There has previously been at least one Manic or Major Depressive Episode.
C. The mood episodes in A and B are not better accounted for by Schizoaffective Disorder and are not superimposed on Schizophrenia, Schizophreniform Disorder, Delusional Disorder, or Psychotic Disorder Not Otherwise Specified.

Specify (for current or most recent episode):
Severity/Psychotic/Remission Specifiers
Chronic
With Catatonic Features
With Melancholic Features
With Atypical Features
With Postpartum Onset

Specify:
With Seasonal Pattern (applies only to the pattern of Major Depressive Episodes)
With Rapid Cycling

Note. This a summary of five criteria sets.

Criteria A and B. Because mood episodes can wax and wane, it is not always obvious when one episode ends and another begins. This judgment influences the coding choice between Single Episode (fourth digit is 0) and the recurrent types (fourth digit is 4, 5, 6, or 7). A Manic Episode is deemed to be in full remission when there are no manic symptoms for at least 2 months, whether or not the patient is being treated. If symptoms sufficient to meet criteria for a Manic or Hypomanic Episode return after this 2-month period of remission, the episode is considered to be new and the disorder is considered to be recurrent. The episode is also considered to be a different type of recurrent mood episode when there is a switch in polarity from a Major Depressive Episode to a Manic or Mixed Episode, or vice versa.

Five types of recurrent Bipolar I Disorder are described: Most Recent Episode Hypomanic (code 296.40), Most Recent Episode Manic (code 296.4x), Most Recent Episode Mixed (code 296.6x), Most Recent Episode Depressed (code 296.5x), and Most Recent Episode Unspecified (code 296.7). Note that most of these codes have an *x* to mark the spot where the clinician must also provide a fifth digit. If the criteria are currently met for a Hypomanic, Manic, Mixed, or Major Depressive Episode, the fifth digit code indicates the severity of the disorder (1 = mild, 2 = moderate, 3 = severe without psychotic features, and 4 = severe with psychotic features). If a Hypomanic, Manic, Mixed, or Major Depressive Episode is not currently present, a fifth digit of 5 indicates that the symptoms are in partial remission; a fifth digit of 6 indicates full remission (i.e., no significant symptoms for at least 2 months).

It should be noted that Bipolar I Disorder often begins with one or more Major Depressive Episodes before the first Manic or Mixed Episode. Males are more likely to have a manic first episode, whereas females are more likely to have a depressive first episode. About 10%–15% of individuals with recurrent Major Depressive Episodes will at some later point in their lives develop a Mixed or Manic Episode and thereby convert to having Bipolar I Disorder. In evaluating the individual's level of risk for having a later Manic Episode, it is useful to determine whether there is a family history of Bipolar Disorder.

CRITERION C (CRITERION B FOR SINGLE MANIC EPISODE). When psychotic symptoms occur exclusively during a mood episode, the diagnosis is Bipolar I Disorder. When psychotic symptoms are present in the absence of prominent mood symptoms, a psychotic disorder diagnosis (Schizophrenia, Schizoaffective Disorder, Delusional Disorder) should be considered. See Chapter 11 for a more detailed discussion of this differential. It should be noted that this criterion prevents a comorbid diagnosis of a chronic psychotic disorder (like Schizophrenia) and Bipolar I Disorder. Manic Episodes occurring during a chronic psychotic disorder are part of Schizoaffective Disorder, Bipolar Type (if mood episodes are a substantial portion of the total duration), or are diagnosed as Bipolar Disorder Not Otherwise Specified (if they are brief compared with the duration of the psychotic symptoms).

Bipolar II Disorder

Bipolar II Disorder is perhaps the most important of the few "new" diagnoses introduced into DSM-IV. In fact, however, Bipolar II Disorder is not particularly new. For more than 20 years, it has been observed that some patients present with descriptive features and a course intermediary between the unipolar and the bipolar Mood Disorders. Such individuals have recurrent Major Depressive Episodes (as in Major Depressive Disorder) and also have Hypomanic Episodes. The existing evidence suggests that, as a group, these so-called Bipolar II patients are more similar to bipolar than to unipolar patients in course, family loading, and treatment response. This category may have an important impact on practice habits. In such patients, one should be cautious in the use of antidepressant treatment (for fear of triggering a substance-induced Manic Episode or rapid cycling), should consider adding a prophylactic mood stabilizer (such as lithium), and should provide psychoeducation concerning ways of avoiding and identifying Manic or Hypomanic Episodes.

DSM-IV diagnostic criteria for 296.89 Bipolar II Disorder

A. Presence (or history) of one or more Major Depressive Episodes.

B. Presence (or history) of at least one Hypomanic Episode.

C. There has never been a Manic Episode or a Mixed Episode.

D. The mood symptoms in Criteria A and B are not better accounted for by Schizoaffective Disorder and are not superimposed on Schizophrenia, Schizophreniform Disorder, Delusional Disorder, or Psychotic Disorder Not Otherwise Specified.

E. The symptoms cause clinically significant distress or impairment in social, occupational, or other important areas of functioning.

Specify current or most recent episode:
Hypomanic: if currently (or most recently) in a Hypomanic Episode
Depressed: if currently (or most recently) in a Major Depressive Episode

Specify (for current or most recent Major Depressive Episode only if it is the most recent type of mood episode):
Severity/Psychotic/Remission Specifiers
Chronic
With Catatonic Features
With Melancholic Features
With Atypical Features
With Postpartum Onset

Specify:
Longitudinal Course Specifiers (With and Without Interepisode Recovery)
With Seasonal Pattern (applies only to the pattern of Major Depressive Episodes)
With Rapid Cycling

CRITERION A. The Major Depressive Episodes in Bipolar II Disorder are more likely to have atypical features and to occur in a seasonal pattern than are those in Major Depressive Disorder.

CRITERION B. There are potential problems with both the underdiagnosis and overdiagnosis of Hypomanic Episodes in patients with Major Depressive Episodes. Let's start with underdiagnosis. Patients with Bipolar II Disorder generally come for treatment when in the midst of a Major Depressive Episode. Clinicians should be aware of the fact that patients rarely volunteer information about the presence of past Hypomanic Episodes. Hypomanic Episodes are the only condition in DSM-IV that does not require impairment, and very often individuals will have experienced them as desirable rather than pathological. Because of the possible treatment implications discussed above, it is therefore especially important to thoroughly ask patients and families members about such periods.

Overdiagnosis can also be a problem. It can be very difficult to assess the presence of hypomania, especially retrospectively in individuals with relatively long-standing depression for whom any temporary lifting of the depressive cloud may be experienced incorrectly as a relative high (rather than as a rare moment of euthymia). As noted in the annotation for a Hypomanic Episode, several criteria (i.e., an "unequivocal change" that is "observable by others") have been added as safeguards. This is a particular concern because, as written, Bipolar II Disorder requires only one Hypomanic Episode lasting only 4 days for a patient's lifetime diagnosis to be switched from Major Depressive Episode, Recurrent, to Bipolar II Disorder. Clinical judgment is required. In fact, the authors would be quite hesitant to follow the letter of the DSM-IV law if the patient had only one episode of just 4 days of hypomanic symptoms. Usually patients will have had many such Hypomanic Episodes.

Criterion C. The distinction between Bipolar I Disorder and Bipolar II Disorder rests completely on differentiating between a Manic Episode and a Hypomanic Episode. This is not always the easiest thing in the world to do. Remember that the symptom lists and item thresholds for a Manic Episode and a Hypomanic Episode are identical so that the difference between them hinges solely on the clinical judgment of whether marked impairment is present and on the duration (7 days versus 4 days). The development of a Manic or Mixed Episode in a patient with Bipolar II Disorder would warrant a switch to a diagnosis of Bipolar I Disorder.

Criteria D and E. Some people mistakenly consider Bipolar II Disorder to be a less severe mood disorder than either Bipolar I Disorder or Major Depressive Disorder because Hypomanic Episodes need not even cause impairment. Be mindful, however, that the Major Depressive Episodes in Bipolar II Disorder can be extremely severe and include psychotic features.

301.13 Cyclothymic Disorder

Cyclothymic Disorder is a potentially intriguing and important condition that has received virtually no systematic study. The degree to which Cyclothymic Disorder constitutes a temperamental predisposition to the eventual development of a Bipolar Disorder remains to be seen. Moreover, some clinicians believe that Borderline Personality Disorder is really Cyclothymic Disorder in disguise. The whole issue of the relationship between Personality Disorder and Mood Disorder is discussed in Chapter 22.

DSM-IV diagnostic criteria for 301.13 Cyclothymic Disorder

A. For at least 2 years, the presence of numerous periods with hypomanic symptoms and numerous periods with depressive symptoms that do not meet criteria for a Major Depressive Episode. **Note:** In children and adolescents, the duration must be at least 1 year.

B. During the above 2-year period (1 year in children and adolescents), the person has not been without the symptoms in Criterion A for more than 2 months at a time.

C. No Major Depressive Episode (p. 327), Manic Episode (p. 332), or Mixed Episode has been present during the first 2 years of the disturbance.

Note: After the initial 2 years (1 year in children and adolescents) of Cyclothymic Disorder, there may be superimposed Manic or Mixed Episodes (in which case both Bipolar I Disorder and Cyclothymic Disorder may be diagnosed) or Major Depressive Episodes (in which case both Bipolar II Disorder and Cyclothymic Disorder may be diagnosed).

D. The symptoms in Criterion A are not better accounted for by Schizoaffective Disorder and are not superimposed on Schizophrenia, Schizophreniform Disorder, Delusional Disorder, or Psychotic Disorder Not Otherwise Specified.

E. The symptoms are not due to the direct physiological effects of a substance (e.g., a drug of abuse, a medication) or a general medical condition (e.g., hyperthyroidism).

F. The symptoms cause clinically significant distress or impairment in social, occupational, or other important areas of functioning.

Criterion A. Cyclothymic Disorder is defined as relatively mild ups and downs, neither of which are severe enough to be diagnosed as full-fledged Manic or Major Depressive Episodes. Note that a diagnosis of Cyclothymic Disorder does require that there be periods of *both* hypomania and depression. A disorder in which there are only recurrent episodes of hypomania (a condition that is not all that uncommon among psychiatric nosologists) is diagnosed as the residual category Bipolar Disorder Not Otherwise Specified.

Criterion B. The diagnosis of Cyclothymic Disorder is intended to describe a relatively chronic mood disturbance. It does allow for some periods of normal mood, but they cannot last for more than 2 months at a time. Disturbances with hypomania and depressed mood but with intervening periods of normal mood lasting longer than 2 months must be diagnosed as the residual category Bipolar Disorder Not Otherwise Specified.

Criterion C. The reason for this criterion is to establish the course relationship between Cyclothymic Disorder and Bipolar I and Bipolar II Disorders. An individual is considered to have Cyclothymic Disorder when he or she has an insidious onset of alternating hypomanic and mild depressive symptoms for at least 2 years before the onset of a Major Depressive or Manic Episode. If the same symptoms occur as an immediate prodrome to or following Bipolar Disorder, a separate diagnosis of Cyclothymic Disorder is not given. Instead, the symptoms are considered to constitute periods of poor interepisode recovery. The risk for developing Bipolar I or Bipolar II Disorder in individuals with Cyclothymic Disorder has been variously reported to be as low as 15% or as high as 50%.

CRITERION D. A cyclothymic-like pattern of fluctuating mood symptoms can sometimes be an associated feature of a psychotic disorder. In such cases, an additional diagnosis of Cyclothymic Disorder is not given.

CRITERION E. Recurrent Substance Intoxication and Substance Withdrawal can perfectly mimic Cyclothymic Disorder, and these need to be ruled out before the diagnosis of Cyclothymic Disorder can be made. A number of general medical conditions are also characterized by mood lability.

CRITERION F. The impairment can occur either because of the depressed or hypomanic periods or because of the individual's discomfort in being unable to predict or control his or her emotional states. Others may regard these individuals as erratic or unreliable.

DSM-IV text for 296.80 Bipolar Disorder Not Otherwise Specified

The Bipolar Disorder Not Otherwise Specified category includes disorders with bipolar features that do not meet criteria for any specific bipolar disorder. Examples include

1. Very rapid alteration (over days) between manic symptoms and depressive symptoms that do not meet minimal duration criteria for a Manic Episode or a Major Depressive Episode
2. Recurrent Hypomanic Episodes without intercurrent depressive symptoms
3. A Manic or Mixed Episode superimposed on Delusional Disorder, residual Schizophrenia, or Psychotic Disorder Not Otherwise Specified
4. Situations in which the clinician has concluded that a bipolar disorder is present but is unable to determine whether it is primary, due to a general medical condition, or substance-induced

Other Mood Disorders

293.83 Mood Disorder Due to a General Medical Condition

The first step in the differential diagnosis of mood symptoms is to rule out general medical conditions and substance use as etiologies. When a general medical condi-

Table 12–1. General medical conditions that cause mood symptoms

Degenerative neurological illnesses (e.g., Parkinson's disease, Huntington's disease)
Cerebrovascular disease (e.g., depressive features after strokes)
Metabolic conditions (e.g., B_{12} deficiency)
Endocrine conditions (e.g., hyper- and hypothyroidism, hyper- and hypoparathyroidism, hyper- and hypoadrenocorticism)
Autoimmune conditions (e.g., systemic lupus erythematosus)
Viral or other infections (e.g., hepatitis, mononucleosis, human immunodeficiency virus [HIV])
Certain cancers (e.g., carcinoma of the pancreas)

Source. Adapted from American Psychiatric Association 1994, p. 368.

tion is present and determined to be the direct physiological cause of the mood symptoms, Mood Disorder Due to a General Medical Condition is diagnosed. In contrast, when the mood symptoms are a psychological reaction to having a general medical condition, the diagnosis would be Major Depressive Disorder if the full criteria for a Major Depressive Episode are met or Adjustment Disorder With Depressed Mood if these criteria are not met. Table 12–1 lists some of the general medical conditions that have been reported to cause clinically significant mood symptoms. For a more detailed discussion on how to make the often difficult differential diagnosis, see Chapter 7, "Ruling Out a Disorder Due to a General Medical Condition").

When communicating or recording the diagnosis, the clincian should use the actual name of the etiological general medical condition on Axis I (e.g., 293.83 Mood Disorder Due to Hyperthyroidism, With Manic Features). Note that all causes of mood due to a general medical condition have the same Axis I diagnostic code: 293.83. Furthermore, the general medical condition should also be coded on Axis III (e.g., Hypothyroidism). To help ease the coding burden, Appendix G of DSM-IV includes selected general medical codes. Not uncommonly, the psychiatric presentation due to a general medical condition is characterized by a mixture of symptoms (e.g., mood, anxiety, and sleep). In most cases, the clinician should choose the diagnosis that reflects the most prominent aspect of the symptom presentation.

DSM-IV diagnostic criteria for 293.83 Mood Disorder Due to . . . *[Indicate the General Medical Condition]*

A. A prominent and persistent disturbance in mood predominates in the clinical picture and is characterized by either (or both) of the following:
   (1) depressed mood or markedly diminished interest or pleasure in all, or almost all, activities
   (2) elevated, expansive, or irritable mood

(continued)

DSM-IV diagnostic criteria for 293.83 Mood Disorder Due to . . . *[Indicate the General Medical Condition] (continued)*

B. There is evidence from the history, physical examination, or laboratory findings that the disturbance is the direct physiological consequence of a general medical condition.

C. The disturbance is not better accounted for by another mental disorder (e.g., Adjustment Disorder With Depressed Mood in response to the stress of having a general medical condition).

D. The disturbance does not occur exclusively during the course of a delirium.

E. The symptoms cause clinically significant distress or impairment in social, occupational, or other important areas of functioning.

Specify type:

With Depressive Features: if the predominant mood is depressed but the full criteria are not met for a Major Depressive Episode

With Major Depressive-Like Episode: if the full criteria are met (except Criterion D) for a Major Depressive Episode

With Manic Features: if the predominant mood is elevated, euphoric, or irritable

With Mixed Features: if the symptoms of both mania and depression are present but neither predominates

Substance-Induced Mood Disorders

It is critical to consider whether mood symptoms are due to the direct effects of a substance; if so, the diagnosis would be Substance Intoxication, Substance Withdrawal, or a Substance-Induced Mood Disorder. Because mood symptoms are so frequently encountered as part of Substance Intoxication or Substance Withdrawal, in most instances one of these diagnoses would suffice. A diagnosis of Substance-Induced Mood Disorder should be reserved for those situations in which the mood symptoms are especially noteworthy; in other words, they are in excess of the symptoms expected and warrant independent clinical attention. Table 12–2 lists those drugs of abuse, medications, and toxins that according to DSM-IV can cause a Substance-Induced Mood Disorder. It should be noted that this is not an exhaustive list.

When the diagnosis is recorded, the diagnostic code depends on the class of substance. For alcohol, the code is 291.8; for all other substances (including medications and toxins), the code is 292.84. When communicating the name of the disorder, the specific etiological substance should be inserted in place of the word *substance* (e.g., Alcohol-Induced Mood Disorder, Methylphenidate-Induced Mood Disorder, Carbon Monoxide-Induced Mood Disorder). The clinician can indicate the context of the onset of the symptoms by adding With Onset During Intoxication or With Onset During Withdrawal. Moreover, the specific type of mood symptoms can be indicated by adding one of the following specifiers: With Depressive Features, With Manic Features, or With Mixed Features.

Table 12–2. Substances that can induce clinically significant mood disorders

Substance intoxication
- Alcohol
- Amphetamines and related substances
- Cocaine
- Hallucinogens
- Inhalants
- Opioids
- Phencyclidine and related substances
- Sedatives, hypnotics, and anxiolytics

Substance withdrawal
- Alcohol
- Amphetamines and related substances
- Cocaine
- Sedatives, hypnotics, and anxiolytics

Medications
- Analgesics
- Anesthetics
- Anticholinergics
- Anticonvulsants
- Antihypertensives
- Antiparkinsonian medications
- Antiulcer medications
- Cardiac medications
- Muscle relaxants
- Oral contraceptives
- Psychotropic medications (e.g., antidepressants, benzodiazepines, antipsychotics, disulfiram)
- Steroids
- Sulfonamides

Heavy metals and toxins
- Volatile substances such as gasoline and paint
- Organophosphate insecticides
- Nerve gases
- Carbon monoxide
- Carbon dioxide

Source. Adapted from American Psychiatric Association 1994, pp. 372–373.

DSM-IV diagnostic criteria for Substance-Induced Mood Disorder

A. A prominent and persistent disturbance in mood predominates in the clinical picture and is characterized by either (or both) of the following:
   (1) depressed mood or markedly diminished interest or pleasure in all, or almost all, activities
   (2) elevated, expansive, or irritable mood

B. There is evidence from the history, physical examination, or laboratory findings of either (1) or (2):
   (1) the symptoms in Criterion A developed during, or within a month of, Substance Intoxication or Withdrawal
   (2) medication use is etiologically related to the disturbance

C. The disturbance is not better accounted for by a Mood Disorder that is not substance induced. Evidence that the symptoms are better accounted for by a Mood Disorder that is not substance induced might include the following: the symptoms precede the onset of the substance use (or medication use); the symptoms persist for a substantial period of time (e.g., about a month) after the cessation of acute withdrawal or severe intoxication or are substantially in excess

(continued)

DSM-IV diagnostic criteria for Substance-Induced Mood Disorder *(continued)*

of what would be expected given the type or amount of the substance used or the duration of use; or there is other evidence that suggests the existence of an independent non-substance-induced Mood Disorder (e.g., a history of recurrent Major Depressive Episodes).

D. The disturbance does not occur exclusively during the course of a delirium.

E. The symptoms cause clinically significant distress or impairment in social, occupational, or other important areas of functioning.

Note: This diagnosis should be made instead of a diagnosis of Substance Intoxication or Substance Withdrawal only when the mood symptoms are in excess of those usually associated with the intoxication or withdrawal syndrome and when the symptoms are sufficiently severe to warrant independent clinical attention.

Code [Specific Substance]–Induced Mood Disorder:
(291.8 Alcohol; 292.84 Amphetamine [or Amphetamine-Like Substance]; 292.84 Cocaine; 292.84 Hallucinogen; 292.84 Inhalant; 292.84 Opioid; 292.84 Phencyclidine [or Phencyclidine-Like Substance]; 292.84 Sedative, Hypnotic, or Anxiolytic; 292.84 Other [or Unknown] Substance)

Specify type:
With Depressive Features: if the predominant mood is depressed
With Manic Features: if the predominant mood is elevated, euphoric, or irritable
With Mixed Features: if symptoms of both mania and depression are present and neither predominates

Specify if:
With Onset During Intoxication: if the criteria are met for Intoxication with the substance and the symptoms develop during the intoxication syndrome
With Onset During Withdrawal: if criteria are met for Withdrawal from the substance and the symptoms develop during, or shortly after, a withdrawal syndrome

Mood Specifiers

Mood specifiers that apply to episodes:

Mild, Moderate, Severe, With Psychotic Features, In Partial Remission, In Full Remission
With Melancholic Features
With Atypical Features
With Catatonic Features
With Postpartum Onset

Mood specifiers that apply to the longitudinal course of the disorders:

With Seasonal Pattern
With Rapid Cycling
With and Without Full Interepisode Recovery

The mood specifiers listed above provide the clinician with an opportunity to be much more specific in describing the Mood Disorders. This is important both because Mood Disorders have enormously varied presentations and because many of the specifiers are associated with particular treatment options. The specifiers in the first list describe some aspect of the most recent episode. For example, the specifier With Atypical Features refers to the symptom pattern of the most recent Major Depressive Episode, whether it is in the context of Major Depressive Disorder, Bipolar I Disorder, or Bipolar II Disorder. When the diagnosis is recorded, the specifier follows the name of the disorder (e.g., Major Depressive Disorder, Recurrent, With Atypical Features).

The specifiers in the second list describe the overall course of the disorder (not just the presentation of the most recent episode). For example, With Seasonal Onset refers to the fact that the Major Depressive Episodes as a group occur during the same time of the year, rather than conveying information about any one episode. For recording purposes, these course specifiers are noted after any episode specifiers that may apply (e.g., Bipolar I Disorder, Most Recent Episode Depressed, With Atypical Features, With Seasonal Onset).

Episode Specifiers

Severity/Psychotic/Remission Specifiers

The severity and remission specifiers for Major Depressive Disorder and Bipolar I Disorder differ from the generic DSM-IV severity specifiers in three ways: 1) they are required to arrive at the diagnostic code, 2) operationalized criteria to define these specifiers are provided, and 3) the "severe" specifier has been further subdivided to indicate the presence or absence of psychotic features. Indicating the presence of psychotic features is especially important because patients who have had psychotic features during a mood episode are more likely to be severely impaired, require hospitalization, develop a chronic course, become psychotic during recurrences, maintain the particular content of their delusions across episodes, commit suicide, and require different treatment (i.e., such patients respond poorly to antidepressants or neuroleptics when these are given alone but do respond to combinations of such medications or to electroconvulsive therapy).

For patients with psychotic features, the clinician also has the option of indicating whether the content of the psychotic features is congruent with the nature of the mood symptoms. For Major Depressive Episodes, features are defined as Mood-Congruent when their content is "entirely consistent with the typical depressive themes of personal inadequacy, guilt, disease, death, nihilism, or deserved punishment." For Manic Episodes, Mood-Congruent Psychotic Features include delusions or hallucinations with themes of "inflated worth, power, knowledge, identity, or special relationship to a deity or famous person." In contrast, Mood-Incongruent Psychotic Features include persecutory delusions (not directly related to depressive themes or manic themes), thought insertion, thought broadcasting, and delusional control. As discussed in Chapter 11, this distinction was included first in DSM-III and had the effect of greatly broadening the construct of Mood Disorder. The presence of mood-incongruent, compared with mood congruent, psychotic symptoms may predict somewhat greater severity, worse outcome, and more likely family history of Schizophrenia.

DSM-IV criteria for Severity/Psychotic/Remission Specifiers for current (or most recent) Major Depressive Episode

Note: Code in fifth digit. Can be applied to the most recent Major Depressive Episode in Major Depressive Disorder and to a Major Depressive Episode in Bipolar I or II Disorder only if it is the most recent type of mood episode.

.x1—Mild: Few, if any, symptoms in excess of those required to make the diagnosis and symptoms result in only minor impairment in occupational functioning or in usual social activities or relationships with others.
.x2—Moderate: Symptoms or functional impairment between "mild" and "severe."
.x3—Severe Without Psychotic Features: Several symptoms in excess of those required to make the diagnosis, **and** symptoms markedly interfere with occupational functioning or with usual social activities or relationships with others.
.x4—Severe With Psychotic Features: Delusions or hallucinations. If possible, specify whether the psychotic features are mood-congruent or mood-incongruent:

Mood-Congruent Psychotic Features: Delusions or hallucinations whose content is entirely consistent with the typical depressive themes of personal inadequacy, guilt, disease, death, nihilism, or deserved punishment.

Mood-Incongruent Psychotic Features: Delusions or hallucinations whose content does not involve typical depressive themes of personal inadequacy, guilt, disease, death, nihilism, or deserved punishment. Included are such symptoms as persecutory delusions (not directly related to depressive themes), thought insertion, thought broadcasting, and delusions of control.

.x5—In Partial Remission: Symptoms of a Major Depressive Episode are present but full criteria are not met, or there is a period without any significant symptoms of a Major Depressive Episode lasting less than 2 months following the end of the Major Depressive Episode. (If the Major Depressive Episode was superimposed on Dysthymic Disorder, the diagnosis of Dysthymic Disorder alone is given once the full criteria for a Major Depressive Episode are no longer met.)
.x6—In Full Remission: During the past 2 months, no significant signs or symptoms of the disturbance were present.
.x0—Unspecified.

Criteria for Severity/Psychotic/Remission Specifiers for current (or most recent) Manic Episode

Note: Code in fifth digit. Can be applied to a Manic Episode in Bipolar I Disorder only if it is the most recent type of mood episode.

.x1—Mild: Minimum symptom criteria are met for a Manic Episode.
.x2—Moderate: Extreme increase in activity or impairment in judgment.
.x3—Severe Without Psychotic Features: Almost continual supervision required to prevent physical harm to self or others.

(continued)

Criteria for Severity/Psychotic/Remission Specifiers for current (or most recent) Manic Episode *(continued)*

.x4—Severe With Psychotic Features: Delusions or hallucinations. If possible, specify whether the psychotic features are mood-congruent or mood-incongruent:

Mood-Congruent Psychotic Features: Delusions or hallucinations whose content is entirely consistent with the typical manic themes of inflated worth, power, knowledge, identity, or special relationship to a deity or famous person.

Mood-Incongruent Psychotic Features: Delusions or hallucinations whose content does not involve typical manic themes of inflated worth, power, knowledge, identity, or special relationship to a deity or famous person. Included are such symptoms as persecutory delusions (not directly related to grandiose ideas or themes), thought insertion, and delusions of being controlled.

.x5—In Partial Remission: Symptoms of a Manic Episode are present but full criteria are not met, or there is a period without any significant symptoms of a Manic Episode lasting less than 2 months following the end of the Manic Episode.
.x6—In Full Remission: During the past 2 months no significant signs or symptoms of the disturbance were present.
.x0—Unspecified.

Criteria for Severity/Psychotic/Remission Specifiers for current (or most recent) Mixed Episode

Note: Code in fifth digit. Can be applied to a Mixed Episode in Bipolar I Disorder only if it is the most recent type of mood episode.

.x1—Mild: No more than minimum symptom criteria are met for both a Manic Episode and a Major Depressive Episode.
.x2—Moderate: Symptoms or functional impairment between "mild" and "severe."
.x3—Severe Without Psychotic Features: Almost continual supervision required to prevent physical harm to self or others.
.x4—Severe With Psychotic Features: Delusions or hallucinations. If possible, specify whether the psychotic features are mood-congruent or mood-incongruent:

Mood-Congruent Psychotic Features: Delusions or hallucinations whose content is entirely consistent with the typical manic or depressive themes.

Mood-Incongruent Psychotic Features: Delusions or hallucinations whose content does not involve typical manic or depressive themes. Included are such symptoms as persecutory delusions (not directly related to grandiose or depressive themes), thought insertion, and delusions of being controlled.

.x5—In Partial Remission: Symptoms of a Mixed Episode are present but full criteria are not met, or there is a period without any significant symptoms of a Mixed Episode lasting less than 2 months following the end of the Mixed Episode.
.x6—In Full Remission: During the past 2 months, no significant signs or symptoms of the disturbance were present.
.x0—Unspecified.

Catatonic Features Specifier

DSM-IV introduced this specifier With Catatonic Features into the Mood Disorders section because catatonic symptoms are most often associated with mood episodes as compared to other possible causes (i.e., medication side effects, general medical conditions, Schizophrenia; see p. xx for a discussion of this differential). Catatonic symptoms take three forms: 1) severe reductions in spontaneous movement or in responsiveness to the environment, 2) extreme excitement and overactivity, and/or 3) bizarre behavior.

Although there has been considerable discussion in the literature suggesting ways of differentiating between extreme psychomotor retardation and catatonic immobility and between extreme psychomotor agitation and catatonic excitement, such distinctions are often too subtle to have much utility. The diagnostic question is whether the severity of the retardation or excitement is extreme enough to be in the catatonic range. For example, slowing down of movements that causes a person to spend 2 hours getting dressed would not by itself constitute catatonia, but complete immobility for several days would. Similarly, frenetic but goal-directed efforts to accomplish nine tasks at one time would be characteristic of manic behavior but not be considered catatonic. Individuals with catatonic excitement appear to be in a world of their own, with seemingly purposeless excited behavior that is not influenced by external stimuli except when they are in restraints.

To reduce false-positive diagnoses, DSM-IV requires that at least two manifestations of catatonic behavior be present. Also be mindful that retardation and agitation are both common manifestations of substance use (especially intoxication) and general medical conditions (especially those leading to delirium), and these should be ruled out before attributing the behavior to the mood episode.

Some of the bizarre behaviors associated with catatonia are hard to miss and unforgettable. The patient may place body parts in unusual positions and hold these for hours or even days on end. Patients may assume bizarre postures spontaneously or maintain them in response to placement made by the clinician (waxy flexibility, i.e., molding the body as if it were made of hot wax). Two other unusual behaviors refer to the patient's parrotlike imitation of others' speech (echolalia) and the seemingly involuntary mimicking of other's movements (echopraxia).

DSM-IV criteria for Catatonic Features Specifier

Specify if:

With Catatonic Features (can be applied to the current or most recent Major Depressive Episode, Manic Episode, or Mixed Episode in Major Depressive Disorder, Bipolar I Disorder, or Bipolar II Disorder)

The clinical picture is dominated by at least two of the following:

(continued)

DSM-IV criteria for Catatonic Features Specifier *(continued)*

(1) motoric immobility as evidenced by catalepsy (including waxy flexibility) or stupor
(2) excessive motor activity (that is apparently purposeless and not influenced by external stimuli)
(3) extreme negativism (an apparently motiveless resistance to all instructions or maintenance of a rigid posture against attempts to be moved) or mutism
(4) peculiarities of voluntary movement as evidenced by posturing (voluntary assumption of inappropriate or bizarre postures), stereotyped movements, prominent mannerisms, or prominent grimacing
(5) echolalia or echopraxia

Melancholic Features Specifier

The presence of melancholic features in a Major Depressive Episode predicts that the patient is likely to have a poor response to placebo and a good response to electroconvulsive therapy and antidepressant therapy, and may also indicate an increased likelihood of positive results on a number of biological tests. It is not yet clear whether the melancholic subtype denotes a qualitatively distinct type of depression that applies across the different levels of severity mentioned above or whether it is just another way of indicating severe depression (and thus does not convey much additional information).

The DSM-IV literature review for melancholia compared nine different systems for defining it and found great heterogeneity in the way the term has been used. At least 15 different symptom features and nine different course features are included in at least one of the available systems for defining melancholia, and most of these symptom and course features are included in fewer than one-half of the systems. Certain items recur as most characteristic of melancholia across many systems and studies. These include psychomotor retardation, anhedonia, early morning worsening, unreactive mood, and distinct quality to the mood.

Perhaps the least useful definition of melancholia was the one included in DSM-III-R. Its liabilities included extreme complexity and the idiosyncratic inclusion of items covering treatment response and absence of premorbid personality features. The need for change had to be balanced against the considerable concern that the definition of melancholia has been changed so frequently and disruptively across rating instruments, across the years, and across diagnostic systems. The conservative solution adopted by DSM-IV was to return to a slightly modified version of the DSM-III definition.

DSM-IV criteria for Melancholic Features Specifier

Specify if:

With Melancholic Features (can be applied to the current or most recent Major Depressive Episode in Major Depressive Disorder and to a Major Depressive Episode in Bipolar I or Bipolar II Disorder only if it is the most recent type of of mood episode)

A. Either of the following, occurring during the most severe period of the current episode:

(1) loss of pleasure in all, or almost all, activities
(2) lack of reactivity to usually pleasurable stimuli (does not feel much better, even temporarily, when something good happens)

B. Three (or more) of the following:

(1) distinct quality of depressed mood (i.e., the depressed mood is experienced as distinctly different from the kind of feeling experienced after the death of a loved one)
(2) depression regularly worse in the morning
(3) early morning awakening (at least 2 hours before usual time of awakening)
(4) marked psychomotor retardation or agitation
(5) significant anorexia or weight loss
(6) excessive or inappropriate guilt

Atypical Features Specifier

In many ways, the specifiers With Atypical Features and With Melancholic Features describe opposite presentations. Whereas the depressed mood in patients with the Melancholic subtype is relatively impervious to joyful external events, in patients with the Atypical Features subtype the mood symptoms are often exquisitely sensitive to good or bad news. Frequently, the episode may be triggered by an interpersonal loss (e.g., breakup of a romantic relationship) and may be much improved or even cured when the loss is made good (e.g., by getting back together again or meeting someone new). The characteristic vegetative symptoms are also in the opposite direction. Whereas in melancholia there is a tendency toward insomnia and anorexia, in the atypical features subtype there is hypersomnia and overeating (particularly of sweets).

This specifier was introduced into DSM-IV because of evidence suggesting a differential somatic treatment response (i.e., the Atypical Features specifier predicted nonresponsiveness to tricyclic antidepressants). The label *atypical* is unfortunate because this presentation is quite frequently encountered, especially in outpatient practice. The term was derived from the fact that most early studies of depression were conducted in inpatient settings, where such presentations are in fact less typical. The term *atypical* survives only in the absence of any more recognizable or more descriptive alternatives.

DSM-IV criteria for Atypical Features Specifier

Specify if:

With Atypical Features (can be applied when these features predominate during the most recent 2 weeks of a Major Depressive Episode in Major Depressive Disorder or in Bipolar I or Bipolar II Disorder when the Major Depressive Episode is the most recent type of mood episode, or when these features predominate during the most recent 2 years of Dysthymic Disorder)

A. Mood reactivity (i.e., mood brightens in response to actual or potential positive events)

B. Two (or more) of the following features:
   (1) significant weight gain or increase in appetite
   (2) hypersomnia
   (3) leaden paralysis (i.e., heavy, leaden feelings in arms or legs)
   (4) long-standing pattern of interpersonal rejection sensitivity (not limited to episodes of mood disturbance) that results in significant social or occupational impairment

C. Criteria are not met for With Melancholic Features or With Catatonic Features during the same episode.

Postpartum Onset Specifier

This is a new specifier that has been introduced into DSM-IV. Many women have a relatively mild period of postpartum "blues" after delivery. This is not what is meant by the specifier With Postpartum Onset, which applies only when the full criteria are met for a mood episode. This specifier was included precisely to alert clinicians that occasionally a mother has a much more severe episode that requires immediate attention both for her sake and for the baby's. This subtype may also have prognostic value in predicting those at risk for future postpartum episodes. The most frightening of such episodes are accompanied by psychotic symptoms, sometimes including delusions or hallucinations threatening the welfare of the baby. It should be noted that this specifier can also be applied for psychotic presentations in which the full criteria are not met for a mood disorder, in which case the diagnosis is Brief Psychotic Disorder, With Postpartum Onset.

DSM-IV criteria for Postpartum Onset Specifier

Specify if:

With Postpartum Onset (can be applied to the current or most recent Major Depressive, Manic, or Mixed Episode in Major Depressive Disorder, Bipolar I Disorder, or Bipolar II Disorder; or to Brief Psychotic Disorder)

Onset of episode within 4 weeks postpartum

Longitudinal Course Specifiers (With and Without Full Interepisode Recovery)

DSM-IV tends to overemphasize cross-sectional symptom presentations at the expense of the course features of the illness. This has resulted in part because symptoms are easier to rate reliably than are course descriptors and because of a lack of any widely accepted method for classifying course. DSM-IV has added a specifier to indicate whether or not there was full recovery from mood symptoms prior to the current (or most recent) episode.

DSM-IV criteria for Longitudinal Course Specifiers

Specify if (can be applied to Recurrent Major Depressive Disorder or Bipolar I or II Disorder):

With Full Interepisode Recovery: if full remission is attained between two most recent Mood Episodes

Without Full Interepisode Recovery: if full remission is not attained between the two most recent Mood Episodes

A longitudinal picture of the patient's course can be gained when these specifiers are used in conjunction with the indication of whether Dysthymic Disorder preceded episodes of Major Depressive Disorder. DSM-IV provides four prototypical depictions of the course of Major Depressive Disorder (see Figure 12–1). Some individuals (picture A) have episodes of Major Depressive Disorder punctuating otherwise normal mood functioning. Some patients (picture B) develop an episodic course of Major Depressive illness without ever fully recovering between the episodes. Another common course that has been called double depression (picture D) begins with Dysthymic Disorder and is punctuated by Major Depressive Episodes with returns to the Dysthymic baseline. The course patterns in pictures B and D suggest that more aggressive treatment for the depression should be considered. Finally, picture C depicts a clinical situation of long-standing Dysthymic Disorder, punctuated by Major Depressive Episodes, in which there is later in the course a treatment response resulting in full remission between episodes. Previously this course pattern has been relatively uncommon, but it may be encountered more often as effective treatments for depression are more widely implemented. When applied to Bipolar I or Bipolar II Disorder, the lack of interepisode recovery refers to any mix of subthreshold mood symptoms.

A. Recurrent, with full interepisode recovery, with no Dysthymic Disorder
B. Recurrent, without full interepisode recovery, with no Dysthymic Disorder
C. Recurrent, with full interepisode recovery, superimposed on Dysthymic Disorder (also code 300.4)
D. Recurrent, without full interepisode recovery, superimposed on Dysthymic Disorder (also code 300.4)

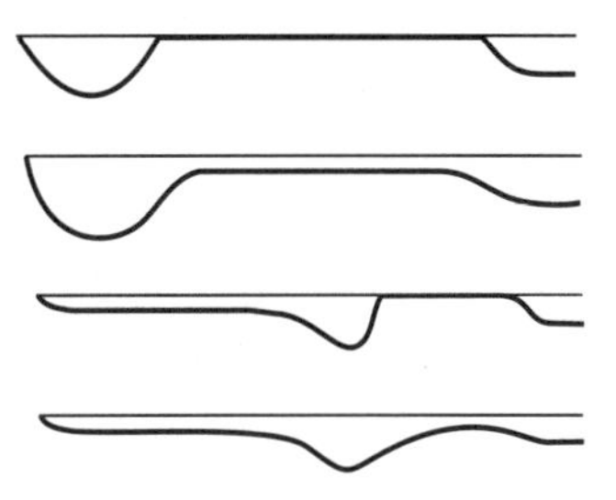

Figure 12–1. Four prototypical depictions of the course of Major Depressive Disorder.

Seasonal Pattern Specifier

DSM-III-R introduced a seasonal modifier for mood disorder. This was done mostly because of treatment studies suggesting that patients with winter depression may be responsive to the use of bright light therapy. The major problem in this literature has been that there have been very few studies on the psychometric properties of the various possible definitions for seasonal mood disorder. Researchers in the field had generally not adopted the strict DSM-III-R criteria, finding them too narrow. DSM-IV is somewhat less restrictive in defining the temporal parameters of seasonality (e.g., it requires 2 instead of 3 years of seasonally timed episodes). However, the DSM-IV definition does restrict the application of this specifier to Major Depressive Episodes occurring during the same time of the year. Most commonly, such episodes occur in the fall or early winter in conjunction with the shortening day length.

DSM-IV criteria for Seasonal Pattern Specifier

Specify if:

With Seasonal Pattern (can be applied to the pattern of Major Depressive Episodes in
Bipolar I Disorder, Bipolar II Disorder, or Major Depressive Disorder, Recurrent)

A. There has been a regular temporal relationship between the onset of Major Depressive Episodes in Bipolar I or Bipolar II Disorder or Major Depressive Disorder, Recurrent, and a particular time of the year (e.g., regular appearance of the Major Depressive Episode in the fall or winter).

Note: Do not include cases in which there is an obvious effect of seasonal-related psychosocial stressors (e.g., regularly being unemployed every winter).

B. Full remissions (or a change from depression to mania or hypomania) also occur at a characteristic time of the year (e.g., depression disappears in the spring).

(continued)

DSM-IV criteria for Seasonal Pattern Specifier *(continued)*

C. In the last 2 years, two Major Depressive Episodes have occurred that demonstrate the temporal seasonal relationships defined in Criteria A and B, and no nonseasonal Major Depressive Episodes have occurred during that same period.

D. Seasonal Major Depressive Episodes (as described above) substantially outnumber the nonseasonal Major Depressive Episodes that may have occurred over the individual's lifetime.

Rapid-Cycling Specifier

DSM-IV has introduced this specifier to describe a particularly problematic course of Bipolar Disorder. This pattern of frequent episodes is associated with considerable morbidity and suicide risk, difficulties in management, and a poor response to lithium (with the frequent need to consider the use of alternative mood stabilizers and high-dose thyroid replacement). Risk factors for the development of a rapid cycling pattern include female gender, previous exposure to antidepressants, hypothyroidism, and positive family history. It appears that Rapid Cycling is equally prevalent in Bipolar I Disorder and Bipolar II Disorder. DSM-IV provides a relatively narrow definition of Rapid Cycling in which each episode must meet the full symptom and duration criteria. In practice, some patients are encountered who have a large number of episodes, each of which has a brief duration of only a few days. Although such patients would not be diagnosed as Bipolar Disorder, With Rapid Cycling in the conservative world of DSM-IV, they may present with similar course, management, and treatment response problems. The clinician may want to override this strict interpretation and consider such patients as Rapid Cycling. A more faithful application of the DSM-IV algorithm would apply a diagnosis of Bipolar Disorder Not Otherwise Specified (if they have never had full manic episode) or Bipolar Disorder Currently Unspecified (if there has been a prior manic episode).

DSM-IV criteria for Rapid-Cycling Specifier

Specify if:

With Rapid Cycling (can be applied to Bipolar I Disorder or Bipolar II Disorder)

At least four episodes of a mood disturbance in the previous 12 months that meet criteria for a Major Depressive, Manic, Mixed, or Hypomanic Episode.

Note: Episodes are demarcated either by partial or full remission for at least 2 months or a switch to an episode of opposite polarity (e.g., Major Depressive Episode to Manic Episode).

The Last Word

The two organizing principles for this section are etiology (primary versus due to a general medical condition versus substance-induced) and whether the symptom pattern is unipolar (Major Depressive Disorder/Dysthymic Disorder) versus bipolar (Bipolar I/Bipolar II/Cyclothymic Disorders). To guide treatment planning, DSM-IV provides a number of specifiers that describe the nature of the episodes and course patterns. For example, Melancholic Features suggest the need for somatic treatment, Atypical Features suggest not using tricyclic antidepressants, Catatonic Features suggest the need for electroconvulsive therapy, Psychotic Features suggest the need for ECT or a combination of neuroleptic and antidepressant medication, Seasonal Pattern suggests the need for light therapy, and Rapid Cycling suggests caution in using antidepressants and the need for mood stabilizers other than lithium.

medications
Relaxation

CHAPTER 13

Anxiety Disorders

Freud's work laid the foundation for the classification of anxiety disorders in a fashion that parallels Kraepelin's seminal role in the classification of Schizophrenia and Mood Disorders. In an attempt to differentiate the disorders that until then were collectively known as neurasthenia, Freud described a distinct syndrome that he called anxiety-neurosis and later went on to describe phobic neurosis, obsessive-compulsive neurosis, and posttraumatic stress disorder.

Although DSM-I and DSM-II both used the concept of *neurosis* as a major organizing principle, these manuals employed vague, unexplicit definitions for the Anxiety Disorders and lost the rich descriptions set forth by Freud. DSM-III gave much greater prominence to Anxiety Disorders by providing a separate section for them and by splitting the DSM-II neuroses into more specific, descriptive categories that were each accompanied by explicit diagnostic criteria. Anxiety Neurosis was split into Panic Disorder and Generalized Anxiety Disorder. Phobic Neurosis was split into Agoraphobia, Social Phobia, and Specific Phobia. This division into smaller units of description resulted in increased reliability and clarity but led to its own set of possible misunderstandings. The splitting apart of what may be a single more complex anxiety syndrome does not imply that the newly created, more narrowly defined disorders are necessarily caused by different underlying pathogenic processes.

The organization of this section resembles the organization of the Mood Disorders section. It begins with separate criteria sets for Panic Attack and for Agoraphobia because these can occur as features of a number of the disorders in this section. Although the only disorder that requires their presence is Panic Disorder, Panic Attacks can also form part of the clinical presentation of Social Phobia, Specific Phobia, Posttraumatic Stress Disorder, Acute Stress Disorder, and Obsessive-Compulsive Disorder. Agoraphobia is part of the definition of Panic Disorder With Agoraphobia and Agoraphobia Without History of Panic Disorder. Because Panic Attacks and Agoraphobia are not separate diagnoses in and of themselves, they do not have their own diagnostic codes.

Definitions of Panic Attack and Agoraphobia

Panic Attack

A major innovation of DSM-III and DSM-III-R was to highlight the importance of Panic Attacks as a presenting complaint and to indicate their role in the pathogenesis of other Anxiety Disorders, especially Agoraphobia. The clinician should pay great attention to the symptoms that characterize a Panic Attack because this frequent and important syndrome is often missed (or misattributed) by the patient and the attending clinicians. Very often, the patient presents to the emergency room with concerns that the physical symptoms (e.g., palpitations, shortness of breath, chest pain) indicate the presence of a severe cardiovascular condition or that the psychological symptoms (e.g., derealization, depersonalization, fear of losing control) are evidence of "going crazy." Clinicians make two types of mistakes: 1) dismissing the patient's complaints as not warranting clinical attention and 2) overreacting by ordering extensive and unnecessary cardiovascular tests or by misdiagnosing panic attacks as evidence of a psychotic episode.

DSM-IV criteria for Panic Attack

Note: A Panic Attack is not a codable disorder. Code the specific diagnosis in which the Panic Attack occurs (e.g., 300.21 Panic Disorder With Agoraphobia [p. 402]).

A discrete period of intense fear or discomfort, in which four (or more) of the following symptoms developed abruptly and reached a peak within 10 minutes:

(1) palpitations, pounding heart, or accelerated heart rate
(2) sweating
(3) trembling or shaking
(4) sensations of shortness of breath or smothering
(5) feeling of choking
(6) chest pain or discomfort
(7) nausea or abdominal distress
(8) feeling dizzy, unsteady, lightheaded, or faint
(9) derealization (feelings of unreality) or depersonalization (being detached from oneself)

(continued)

DSM-IV criteria for Panic Attack *(continued)*

(10) fear of losing control or going crazy
(11) fear of dying
(12) paresthesias (numbness or tingling sensations)
(13) chills or hot flushes

It is of interest that Freud's original description of Panic Attack included 10 of the above 13 characteristic symptoms. What differentiates a Panic Attack from other forms of anxiety is its discrete and crescendo quality. The symptoms are intense, begin abruptly, reach a peak quickly, and generally subside within approximately an hour or so. Many of the symptoms (shortness of breath, palpitations, choking, light-headedness, paresthesias) probably result from the effects of hyperventilation, which usually has an important role in the pathogenesis of panic attacks. Often, there is a vicious cycle in which anxiety results in hyperventilation, which causes frightening somatic symptoms, which leads to catastrophized fears of serious physical or mental illness, which causes more hyperventilation—and so on.

Freud also noted that anxious expectation, irritability, hypersensitivity to bodily stimuli, and an increased concern over one's health were all common consequences of having had panic attacks. More recent work, based on cognitive-behavioral methods, has confirmed that individuals prone to Panic Attacks are hypervigilant and catastrophic about their bodily sensations.

We find it useful to have the patient review the DSM-IV criteria to demonstrate that the physical symptoms can be explained as part of a panic attack. We also explain that most of the symptoms result from the effects of hyperventilation and its lowering of blood carbon dioxide levels. This message may be vividly demonstrated by asking the patient to take rapid deep breaths and to report the resulting bodily sensations, which often resemble the prodrome to a panic attack (e.g., light-headedness, paresthesias, tetany, tachycardia).

Patients and clinicians often make the error of assuming that hyperventilation requires obvious heavy breathing. In fact, a lowered blood carbon dioxide level can result from hyperventilation that is more chronic and subtle—taking an extra breath per minute for an hour, a slight increase in depth of breathing, or a shift from diaphragmatic to chest breathing. A simple method of breathing retraining can be initiated by having the patient place one hand on the chest wall and the other hand on the abdomen to increase awareness of his or her current mode of breathing (chest or diaphragmatic) and to increase diaphragmatic activity. The cognitive-behavioral treatment of Panic Disorder also includes desensitization to the interoceptive bodily symptoms of panic attacks and the cognitive reframing of their significance.

Although the DSM-IV data reanalysis and field trial confirmed that the four-symptom threshold is optimal for defining a Panic Attack, some individuals have *limited-symptom attacks* with a similar onset and quality but fewer than the four symptoms. Research suggests that individuals who present with limited-symptom attacks and those who present with full Panic Attacks may have similar biological vulnerability, morbidity, family history, course, and treatment response. Limited-symptom attacks are also common as the condition improves with treatment.

Agoraphobia

The literal Greek meaning of the term *agoraphobia* is "fear of the marketplace." Although the concept of Agoraphobia has a long and hallowed tradition, its relationship to Panic Disorder has been the subject of some controversy. It should be noted that the criteria set for Agoraphobia does not stand alone. Agoraphobia cannot be coded separately but instead must be diagnosed as part of Panic Disorder With Agoraphobia (coded as 300.21) or Agoraphobia Without History of Panic Disorder (coded as 300.22).

DSM-IV criteria for Agoraphobia

Note: Agoraphobia is not a codable disorder. Code the specific disorder in which the Agoraphobia occurs (e.g., 300.21 Panic Disorder With Agoraphobia [p. 402] or 300.22 Agoraphobia Without History of Panic Disorder [p. 404]).

A. Anxiety about being in places or situations from which escape might be difficult (or embarrassing) or in which help may not be available in the event of having an unexpected or situationally predisposed Panic Attack or panic-like symptoms. Agoraphobic fears typically involve characteristic clusters of situations that include being outside the home alone; being in a crowd or standing in a line; being on a bridge; and traveling in a bus, train, or automobile.

   Note: Consider the diagnosis of Specific Phobia if the avoidance is limited to one or only a few specific situations, or Social Phobia if the avoidance is limited to social situations.

B. The situations are avoided (e.g., travel is restricted) or else are endured with marked distress or with anxiety about having a Panic Attack or panic-like symptoms, or require the presence of a companion.

C. The anxiety or phobic avoidance is not better accounted for by another mental disorder, such as Social Phobia (e.g., avoidance limited to social situations because of fear of embarrassment), Specific Phobia (e.g., avoidance limited to a single situation like elevators), Obsessive-Compulsive Disorder (e.g., avoidance of dirt in someone with an obsession about contamination), Posttraumatic Stress Disorder (e.g., avoidance of stimuli associated with a severe stressor), or Separation Anxiety Disorder (e.g., avoidance of leaving home or relatives).

Criterion A. This central criterion in the DSM-IV definition of Agoraphobia is something of a hybrid that represents a melding of the DSM-III-R and *International Statistical Classification of Diseases and Related Health Problems,* 10th Revision (ICD-10), definitions of Agoraphobia. The first sentence comes from DSM-III-R and expresses a conception of Agoraphobia that emphasizes the motivation for the avoidance (i.e., fears of being unable to escape or of being left helpless by a Panic Attack or by panic-like symptoms). This statement reflects a view that Agoraphobia is best conceptualized as a complication of having Panic Attacks—an observation that was first elaborated by Freud. The second sentence is adapted from ICD-10 and DSM-III, which define Agoraphobia based on the number and/or types of situations that are avoided rather than on the motivation for avoiding them. Agoraphobia would thus be defined by the requirement that there be a cluster of many phobias, rather than considering that the reason for the patient's avoidance of these situations is a fear of having a panic attack.

The marriage of these two approaches usually works quite well because most individuals with Agoraphobia have a presentation that qualifies based on both their reason for the avoidance and the wide range of situations avoided. On occasion, however, each definition would result in a different diagnostic recommendation. Let's take the example of an individual who develops Panic Attacks while driving a car and then goes on to avoid driving (but no other situations) because of the fear of having additional Panic Attacks in the car. According to the DSM-III-R approach, this individual would have Panic Disorder With Agoraphobia. In contrast, according to the ICD-10 approach, this individual would have Specific Phobia because the ICD-10 definition of Agoraphobia would require avoidance of a number of different situations.

We have spent more time than we would like to admit debating all the nuances of this fine point and have never come to total agreement on it. Fortunately, the difference of opinion usually turns out to be moot in clinical practice. Because of the unexpected nature of Panic Attacks in Panic Disorder and the tendency for individuals to generalize avoidance behavior across a number of different situations, it is quite unusual for there to be avoidance of just one single situation in the context of Panic Disorder.

Criterion B. The degree of impairment associated with Agoraphobia can be remarkably varied. In its most severe form, individuals become both totally housebound and unable to be alone. Up a notch are those individuals who are housebound but can stay home alone. Next are those who can venture forth beyond their front door if they have the perceived safety embodied in a trusted "phobic companion." Others can venture outside alone but only within a very circumscribed perimeter that is considered a safe zone. Then there are patients whose travel is not restricted by distance but who have all sorts of situations that they must avoid (e.g., airplane travel, busy highways, bridges), resulting in intricate travel arrangements. Other individuals' travel options are not restricted, but they will avoid particular situations (e.g., crowded stores, elevators, center seats in movie theaters). Finally, there are those brave souls who are able to plow through; they do not avoid their feared situations but experience them with considerable and unremitting dread and are rarely comfortable except at home or with a trusted companion.

Criterion C. The core feature of Agoraphobia is the avoidance of situations. The problem in defining Agoraphobia is that so many other forms of psychopathology are also characterized by avoidance behavior that is either a diagnostic or an associated feature of the particular condition. The clinical question is when a pattern of avoidance constitutes Agoraphobia rather than one of the other disorders characterized by a more specific avoidance pattern. One method involves asking the patient why he or she is avoiding the situation. Agoraphobia is the diagnosis if the fear is of having an unexpected or situationally predisposed Panic Attack or some other incapacitating or embarrassing symptom (e.g., dizziness, incontinence). In contrast, if the focus of the fear is on some aspect of the situation (e.g., seeing a spider in Specific Phobia, giving a talk in Social Phobia, shaking hands in Obsessive-Compulsive Disorder), the diagnosis is one of the other disorders. Because this decision ultimately rests on clinical judgment, the criterion uses the phrase *not better accounted for.*

The Codable Anxiety Disorders

Codable Anxiety Disorders

300.01	Panic Disorder Without Agoraphobia
300.21	Panic Disorder With Agoraphobia
300.22	Agoraphobia Without History of Panic Disorder
300.29	Specific Phobia
300.23	Social Phobia
300.3	Obsessive-Compulsive Disorder
309.81	Posttraumatic Stress Disorder
308.3	Acute Stress Disorder
300.02	Generalized Anxiety Disorder
293.89	Anxiety Disorder Due to . . . *[Indicate the General Medical Condition]*
—.—	Substance-Induced Anxiety Disorder *[Refer to Substance-Related Disorders for substance-specific codes]*
300.00	Anxiety Disorder Not Otherwise Specified

Panic Disorder With (300.21) and Without (300.01) Agoraphobia

The relationship between Panic Disorder and Agoraphobia has been controversial. Freud emphasized the precedence of the anxiety attack in the development of Agoraphobia; in other words, the person would usually first have a Panic Attack and then, through conditioning, become fearful and avoidant of the situations in which the attacks were most likely to occur. In contrast, DSM-III gave Agoraphobia precedence over Panic Disorder by including categories for Agoraphobia (with and without Panic Attacks) and Panic Disorder (which could be diagnosed only in the absence of Agoraphobia). DSM-III-R reversed the DSM-III convention and created a combined category of Panic Disorder With Agoraphobia. That was in recognition of the fact that these two syndromes occur frequently together, with the phobic avoidance often resulting from fears of having a Panic Attack.

DSM-IV continues the DSM-III-R approach of largely relegating Agoraphobia to a subtype of Panic Disorder. The DSM-IV literature review confirmed that agoraphobic avoidance is usually secondary to Panic Attacks or the associated symptoms of panic. In subjects reporting both panic and Agoraphobia, Panic Attacks usually precede phobic avoidance, and the more the individual is afraid of having a Panic Attack, the more likely it is that there will be agoraphobic avoidance.

Panic Attacks are the focus of treatment in both the cognitive-behavioral and pharmacological approaches to Agoraphobia. The most effective cognitive-behavioral treatments are not those that target only the avoidance aspect of the syndrome but rather those that also focus on exposure and desensitization to the patient's subjective somatic experiences during the Panic Attack (e.g., dizziness, palpitations, paresthesias) and the consequent catastrophizing that is related to them ("I am going to die," "I am going crazy").

Unfortunately, ICD-10 has come down on the opposite side of this question and gives its priority to Agoraphobia in individuals who have both avoidance and Panic Attacks. This decision was apparently made because of the belief still held by some that Panic Attacks are an associated (rather than essential) feature of Agoraphobia. Others have argued that these diagnoses should have remained separate without prejudging the presumed etiological relationship between them—in keeping with the general tendency in DSM-IV to avoid combined categories and etiological judgments. The best bet on this controversy is to keep an open mind and to take a careful history to determine for each patient what the temporal and psychological relationship has been between the Panic Attacks and the agoraphobic avoidance.

Summary of DSM-IV diagnostic criteria for 300.01 Panic Disorder Without Agoraphobia and 300.21 Panic Disorder With Agoraphobia

A. Both (1) and (2):
   (1) recurrent unexpected Panic Attacks
   (2) at least one of the attacks has been followed by at least a month of the following:
      (a) persistent concern about having additional attacks
      (b) worry about the implications of the attack or its consequences (e.g., losing control, having a heart attack, "going crazy")
      (c) a significant change in behavior related to the attacks

B. This criterion differs for Panic Disorder With and Without Agoraphobia as follows:
   For 300.21 Panic Disorder With Agoraphobia: the presence of Agoraphobia
   For 300.01 Panic Disorder Without Agoraphobia: absence of Agoraphobia

C. The Panic Attacks are not due to the direct physiological effects of a substance (e.g., a drug of abuse, medication) or a general medical condition (e.g., hyperthyroidism).

D. The Panic Attacks are not better accounted for by another mental disorder, such as Social Phobia (e.g., occurring on exposure to feared social situations), Specific Phobia (e.g., on exposure to the phobic situation), Obsessive-Compulsive Disorder (e.g., on exposure to dirt in someone with an obsession about contamination), Posttraumatic Stress Disorder (e.g., in response to stimuli associated with a severe stressor), or Separation Anxiety Disorder (e.g., in response to being away from home or close relatives).

Note: This is a summary of two criteria sets.

CRITERION A. After determining that the individual suffers from Panic Attacks, the next step is to determine the context in which the attacks occur, especially the presence or absence of predictable triggers. The unexpected Panic Attacks that define Panic Disorder are characterized by the absence of predictable triggers for the attacks. Individuals with unexpected attacks often say that the attacks seem to come with no warning or out of the blue. In contrast, Panic Attacks that occur only in response to particular triggering events or situations (situationally bound) are much more characteristic of the other Anxiety Disorders (e.g., Social Phobia, Specific Phobia).

A third type of Panic Attack (situationally predisposed) is characterized by a less predictable relationship between the Panic Attacks and the triggers: The Panic Attacks usually, but not invariably, occur after exposure to a particular trigger. Furthermore, in contrast to situationally bound attacks—which occur in anticipation of or immediately on exposure to the trigger—situationally predisposed attacks may occur after some period of time has elapsed (e.g., half an hour after being confronted with a feared trigger). Although situationally predisposed Panic Attacks occur more frequently in Panic Disorder (particularly later in the course), they also can occur in other Anxiety Disorders as well.

The frequency, severity, and duration thresholds for Panic Disorder included in DSM-III and DSM-III-R were based on very limited evidence and were controversial. Studies have indicated that a significant number of individuals have Panic Attacks at a frequency lower than that required by DSM-III (three attacks in 3 weeks) or the more restrictive criteria of DSM-III-R (four attacks in 4 weeks). Individuals with less frequent attacks are equivalent to individuals whose Panic Attacks meet the full criteria for DSM-III and DSM-III-R Panic Disorder in terms of their clinical picture, level of subjective distress and disability, demographic factors, family history, and response to biological challenge tests. Therefore, DSM-IV dropped the requirement that there be a specific number of panic attacks over a particular period of time. DSM-IV instead requires only that the Panic Attacks be recurrent and associated with evidence of clinical significance. This evidence most often takes the form of persistent worry about having another attack or that the attacks mean that something terrible is happening (usually cardiac disease or mental illness). Alternatively, a change in behavior in response to the Panic Attacks (e.g., avoidance) can also count as evidence of clinical significance.

CRITERION B. In clinical samples, Panic Disorder Without Agoraphobia is much less common than Panic Disorder With Agoraphobia, although the reverse may be true in community samples. Panic Disorder Without Agoraphobia is often an early stage that eventually evolves into Panic Disorder With Agoraphobia because it may take many unexpected Panic Attacks in a variety of different situations to promote the development of Agoraphobia. For this reason, timely treatment of Panic Attacks may prevent the future development of Agoraphobia. Preexisting personality features may also influence the vulnerability of individuals to develop severe avoidance in response to Panic Attacks. Those with a prior history of Separation Anxiety or Avoidant Personality Disorder are especially prone to develop Agoraphobia in response to unexpected Panic Attacks.

CRITERION C. Many substances and medications can induce Panic Attacks in susceptible individuals (particularly stimulants, caffeine, decongestants, weight loss aids, alcohol, cannabis, and hallucinogens). A variety of general medical conditions that can cause Panic Attacks should be ruled out, especially in late-onset cases. The contribution of mitral valve prolapse (floppiness in the mitral valve) to the development of Panic Attacks has been controversial. Although individuals with mitral valve prolapse may have some increased risk of developing Panic Attacks, the etiological relationship is unclear, and DSM-IV does not recognize mitral valve prolapse as a cause of Anxiety Disorder Due to a General Medical Condition.

CRITERION D. As discussed before, Panic Attacks are not specific to Panic Disorder and can occur in a wide variety of other Anxiety Disorders. What distinguishes Panic Disorder from these other Anxiety Disorders is the presence of unexpected Panic Attacks.

300.22 Agoraphobia Without History of Panic Disorder

Agoraphobia Without History of Panic Disorder is a controversial category. Some clinicians claim never to see such patients; others claim to see them relatively frequently.

DSM-IV diagnostic criteria for 300.22 Agoraphobia Without History of Panic Disorder

A. The presence of Agoraphobia related to fear of developing panic-like symptoms (e.g., dizziness or diarrhea).

B. Criteria have never been met for Panic Disorder.

C. The disturbance is not due to the direct physiological effects of a substance (e.g., a drug of abuse, a medication) or a general medical condition.

D. If an associated general medical condition is present, the fear described in Criterion A is clearly in excess of that usually associated with the condition.

CRITERIA A AND B. As discussed above, most cases of Agoraphobia develop in individuals who fear having full-blown Panic Attacks. However, agoraphobic avoidance sometimes develops because of a fear of developing incapacitating or embarrassing symptoms in other contexts having actually experienced the symptom in public (e.g., vomiting, fainting, loss of bladder control), knowing someone who experienced the symptom in public, having a medical condition that might predispose the individual to developing a symptom (see Criterion D, below), and having limited symptom attacks.

CRITERION C. See the annotation for Criterion C in Panic Disorder.

CRITERION D. Some individuals, particularly elderly persons, have a physical condition (e.g., vertigo, post heart attack, Crohn's disease) that makes their fears of embarrassment to some degree realistic. This criterion indicates that clinical judgment must be applied in deciding whether the avoidance associated with such a general medical condition warrants separate notation as Agoraphobia or should be considered a reasonable response to the risks entailed. For example, a patient who for years refuses to walk away from arm's reach of a wall after having had one fainting episode secondary to a cardiac arrhythmia would probably warrant this diagnosis. In contrast, wanting to stay close to home immediately after being discharged after a heart attack would not warrant this diagnosis.

300.23 Social Phobia

For most people, some degree of social anxiety is more the rule than the exception. Very few people are completely free of anxiety when giving a speech or having to mingle with strangers at a party. This social anxiety does not mean that an individual has the clinical diagnosis of Social Phobia. Instead, the diagnosis is reserved for those individuals whose social anxiety is so severe as to be significantly impairing.

Social Phobia comes in two varieties that can have very different presentations and responses to treatment. Some individuals have the circumscribed type of Social Phobia in which the focus of worry is on the embarrassment that might arise when performing a particular activity in public (e.g., giving a talk, playing a musical instrument, using a public rest room, eating in a restaurant). At the other extreme are those individuals who are anxious in virtually any situation that involves social interaction. These globally shy individuals usually have an early onset and pattern of pervasive avoidance that is virtually indistinguishable from Avoidant Personality Disorder. During the DSM-IV deliberations, there was a proposal to divide this condition into two separate disorders: one for performance anxiety and the other for social anxiety. This was not done mainly because there are so many individuals who have both or are somewhere in the middle.

In contrast to the unitary criteria set for most disorders in DSM-III-R, there were separate childhood and adult versions of Social Phobia. The childhood version was known as Avoidant Disorder of Childhood. In DSM-IV, this distinction has been eliminated, and the criteria set has been modified to accommodate childhood presentations. In the "Specific Culture, Age, and Gender Features" section of the DSM-IV text for Social Phobia, such children are described as excessively timid, shrinking from contact with others, refusing to participate in group play, and staying on the periphery of social activities.

DSM-IV diagnostic criteria for 300.23 Social Phobia

A. A marked and persistent fear of one or more social or performance situations in which the person is exposed to unfamiliar people or to possible scrutiny by others. The individual fears that he or she will act in a way (or show anxiety symptoms) that will be humiliating or embarrassing. **Note:** In children, there must be

(continued)

DSM-IV diagnostic criteria for 300.23 Social Phobia *(continued)*

evidence of the capacity for age-appropriate social relationships with familiar people and the anxiety must occur in peer settings, not just in interactions with adults.

B. Exposure to the feared social situation almost invariably provokes anxiety, which may take the form of a situationally bound or situationally predisposed Panic Attack.
Note: In children, the anxiety may be expressed by crying, tantrums, freezing, or shrinking from social situations with unfamiliar people.

C. The person recognizes that the fear is excessive or unreasonable.
Note: In children, this feature may be absent.

D. The feared social or performance situations are avoided or else are endured with intense anxiety or distress.

E. The avoidance, anxious anticipation, or distress in the feared social or performance situation(s) interferes significantly with the person's normal routine, occupational (academic) functioning, or social activities or relationships, or there is marked distress about having the phobia.

F. In individuals under age 18 years, the duration is at least 6 months.

G. The fear or avoidance is not due to the direct physiological effects of a substance (e.g., a drug of abuse, a medication) or a general medical condition and is not better accounted for by another mental disorder (e.g., Panic Disorder With or Without Agoraphobia, Separation Anxiety Disorder, Body Dysmorphic Disorder, a Pervasive Developmental Disorder, or Schizoid Personality Disorder).

H. If a general medical condition or another mental disorder is present, the fear in Criterion A is unrelated to it, e.g., the fear is not of Stuttering, trembling in Parkinson's disease, or exhibiting abnormal eating behavior in Anorexia Nervosa or Bulimia Nervosa.

Specify if:
Generalized: if the fears include most social situations (also consider the additional diagnosis of Avoidant Personality Disorder)

CRITERION A. This wording of this criterion covers the two different arenas in which Social Phobias most commonly occur: those in which the person must perform some activity in front of others (performance anxiety) and those involving interpersonal interactions (e.g., dating, parties). The key focus of the fear in cases of performance anxiety is embodied by the word *scrutiny.* The person generally has no problem performing the activity in the privacy of his or her own home. For example, the person can comfortably give a speech in front of a mirror or flawlessly perform a piano concerto as long as there is no audience. The fear in social settings is that the person will appear foolish and unsure or develop visible anxiety symptoms (e.g., sweating, trembling, a Panic Attack).

The note in Criterion A that applies to children serves two purposes: 1) to clarify the differential diagnosis between the social avoidance in Social Phobia and the lack of capacity for social relationships in a Pervasive Developmental Disorder and 2) to avoid the overdiagnosis of Social Phobia in children who are shy only with adults because such shyness is common and not, in and of itself, pathological.

Criterion B. This criterion emphasizes the almost invariable, conditioned, stimulus-response quality of the Social Phobia. The diagnosis of Social Phobia should be called into question if the anxiety symptoms develop only intermittently in response to a particular social situation. This criterion also clarifies the wide range of anxiety responses that can characterize Social Phobia. At its most extreme, the onset of the anxiety may be so abrupt and the intensity so severe as to meet the criteria for a full-blown Panic Attack. However, in contrast to the unexpected Panic Attacks characteristic of Panic Disorder, Panic Attacks in Social Phobia are closely connected to the social phobic stimulus and are either situationally bound or situationally predisposed.

Criterion C. This criterion sets the boundary between Social Phobia and the social avoidance in disorders such as Schizophrenia and Schizotypal Personality Disorder. In these other conditions, the socially anxious person is typically not aware that the anxiety is excessive or unreasonable and, instead, believes that it is justified by paranoid concerns.

Criterion D. There are some unusually stoic individuals with Social Phobia who have little or no social avoidance. Although they give their talks or concerts, go to parties, date, and go on job interviews, the activities are performed only with great distress. In contrast, there are other people with Social Phobia who may avoid more and more situations so that they may ultimately become globally avoidant or even housebound.

Criterion E. Virtually everybody has some social anxiety. In fact, anxiety about performance situations is adaptive to the degree that it motivates people to practice and improve their performance. This criterion serves to remind the clinician that Social Phobia should be diagnosed only when the symptoms cause considerable impairment or distress. This judgment is not always easy to make. Some individuals rationalize their markedly constricted lifestyle, claiming that it is a matter of taste and that they in fact prefer to be alone. There may also be cultural and gender differences in the degree to which social avoidance is sanctioned or even encouraged.

Criterion F. This criterion was added to prevent a false-positive diagnosis for the relatively brief periods of social avoidance that may commonly occur as a developmentally appropriate stage in children that is ultimately outgrown.

Criterion G. Although prototypical patients with Panic Disorder With Agoraphobia are clearly distinguishable from prototypical patients with Social Phobia, there are patients in the middle who have caused us nosological nitpickers many a sleepless night. For example, there is the medical intern without a prior history of social avoidance who has a couple of unexpected Panic Attacks while making presentations during rounds. He or she then becomes worried about having additional Panic Attacks in that situation and begins dreading and avoiding daily rounds.

There is disagreement among the authors about how best to diagnose such an individual. One of us (a Panic Disorder booster) would diagnose such a patient as having Panic Disorder With Agoraphobia because the focus of the person's fear is on having another Panic Attack, and the condition began with unexpected Panic Attacks. Another of us (the Social Phobia-philiac) would be much more impressed by the fact that the current pattern of social avoidance is entirely characteristic of Social Phobia than by the fact that the original onset consisted of unexpected Panic Attacks. We do agree that the best way of handling these boundary situations is to consider the course of the presentation. The best diagnosis is Social Phobia if the intern goes on to become a resident and then an attending physician and for many years continues to dread and avoid only making presentations but does not have additional unexpected Panic Attacks. If, on the other hand, he or she continues to have unexpected Panic Attacks in other situations and the avoidance behavior starts to spread, the diagnosis would be Panic Disorder With Agoraphobia.

Many other mental disorders have social avoidance as an essential or associated feature, and a sampling of these disorders is provided in Criterion G. In most of these cases, an additional diagnosis of Social Phobia is not warranted. However, a separate diagnosis of Social Phobia may sometimes be justified when there is social avoidance above and beyond that typically associated with the condition or when the avoidance involves a situation unrelated to the condition. For example, a person who is socially avoidant because of a fear of being embarrassed by a facial defect (as in Body Dysmorphic Disorder) may also have a circumscribed fear of eating in public; if that fear independently causes impairment, it might justify an additional diagnosis of Social Phobia.

Criterion H. If we could do it all over again, we would love to have a chance to fix this criterion. We suggest that the clinician use it, as we do, with a great deal of flexibility and common sense. The issue is that many people are embarrassed about having a general medical condition or mental disorder and may avoid social situations as a consequence. This criterion, which was introduced in DSM-III-R, is meant to prevent the additional diagnosis of Social Phobia in individuals whose avoidance might be considered understandable given the potentially embarrassing nature of their symptoms.

The problem with this criterion is that some individuals clearly overreact to the possible embarrassment occasioned by their psychiatric or medical symptoms and may respond to the same treatments as do those whose Social Phobia is not in the context of a general medical condition or another mental disorder. For example, an individual with a slight stutter who refuses all opportunities to have job interviews because of the fear that the interviewer will make disparaging comments may warrant a separate diagnosis of Social Phobia.

Two suggestions for dealing with this problem were considered and rejected in the DSM-IV deliberations. One proposal (the most inclusive) would have placed no restrictions on giving a diagnosis of Social Phobia to individuals who avoid situations as a result of a general medical condition. Another position (the middle ground) would allow Social Phobia to be diagnosed in individuals whose avoidance is judged to be in excess of what might be expected given the nature of their psychiatric or medical symptoms. In fact, a similarly worded criterion is included in the criteria set for Agoraphobia Without History of Panic Disorder to deal with a similar problem. This explicit allowance for clinical judgment was not included in the criteria for Social Phobia because the impact of such a change had not yet been studied systematically, and there was a concern about whether such a judgment could be made reliably.

Our own practice is to apply the diagnosis of Social Phobia in those situations in which the avoidance is prominent, far out of proportion to the psychiatric or medical symptom, and warrants independent clinical attention.

Annotation for Subtype. Individuals with the Generalized Type of Social Phobia tend to have an early onset and a chronic and stable course that in every way resembles Avoidant Personality Disorder. This subtype is a particularly clear example of the artificiality of Axis I/Axis II distinctions in dealing with personality disorders that are on a spectrum of Axis I conditions. Those who do not meet criteria for the Generalized Type fall into two groups. Some patients have circumscribed performance anxiety and are perfectly fine in social situations that do not require performance of the specific act (e.g., playing an instrument). Other patients have a more limited form of the Generalized Type, being afraid of only one or two social situations.

300.29 Specific Phobia

Virtually everyone has at least one thing or situation that is a source of fear and subsequent avoidance. It is only when the fear is excessive or unreasonable and is clinically significant that a diagnosis of a phobic disorder is warranted. Because Social Phobia can in a way be considered a special case of Specific Phobia, the two criteria sets were developed so as to be identically worded wherever this was appropriate (i.e., in Criteria B, C, D, E, and F).

DSM-IV diagnostic criteria for 300.29 Specific Phobia

A. Marked and persistent fear that is excessive or unreasonable, cued by the presence or anticipation of a specific object or situation (e.g., flying, heights, animals, receiving an injection, seeing blood).

B. Exposure to the phobic stimulus almost invariably provokes an immediate anxiety response, which may take the form of a situationally bound or situationally predisposed Panic Attack. **Note:** In children, the anxiety may be expressed by crying, tantrums, freezing, or clinging.

C. The person recognizes that the fear is excessive or unreasonable. **Note:** In children, this feature may be absent.

D. The phobic situation(s) is avoided or else is endured with intense anxiety or distress.

E. The avoidance, anxious anticipation, or distress in the feared situation(s) interferes significantly with the person's normal routine, occupational (or academic) functioning, or social activities or relationships, or there is marked distress about having the phobia.

(continued)

DSM-IV diagnostic criteria for 300.29 Specific Phobia *(continued)*

F. In individuals under age 18 years, the duration is at least 6 months.

G. The anxiety, Panic Attacks, or phobic avoidance associated with the specific object or situation are not better accounted for by another mental disorder, such as Obsessive-Compulsive Disorder (e.g., fear of dirt in someone with an obsession about contamination), Posttraumatic Stress Disorder (e.g., avoidance of stimuli associated with a severe stressor), Separation Anxiety Disorder (e.g., avoidance of school), Social Phobia (e.g., avoidance of social situations because of fear of embarrassment), Panic Disorder With Agoraphobia, or Agoraphobia Without History of Panic Disorder.

Specify type:

Animal Type
Natural Environment Type (e.g., heights, storms, water)
Blood-Injection-Injury Type
Situational Type (e.g., airplanes, elevators, enclosed places)
Other Type (e.g., phobic avoidance of situations that may lead to choking, vomiting, or contracting an illness; in children, avoidance of loud sounds or costumed characters)

CRITERION A. This criterion provides the two basic components of this disorder: that there is fear triggered by exposure to a specific stimulus and that the fear is out of proportion to what would be reasonable. Although phobias can develop by aversive conditioning to virtually any stimulus, the fear of a number of evolutionarily dangerous situations seems to have been "hardwired" into us. Many specific phobias represent an inborn preparedness to be afraid of, and to avoid, those things that were inherently dangerous to our predecessors. This helps to explain why we are naturally more afraid of lightning, snakes, and heights than of the more modern (and deadly) hazards of cars, electric sockets, and guns.

CRITERION B. This criterion is identical to Criterion B in Social Phobia (see annotation on p. 248).

CRITERION C. This criterion sets the boundary between Specific Phobia and avoidance of situations based on delusional concerns. For example, the patient with a Specific Phobia of cats acknowledges that the magnitude of his or her fear is out of proportion to the real danger. In contrast, someone who avoids cats because of the conviction that they are servants of Satan believes that the avoidance is justified.

CRITERION D. This criterion is identical to Criterion D in Social Phobia. It describes two ways of coping with the fear. Some individuals avoid any situation they think might result in exposure to the feared stimulus (e.g., an individual who has a phobia of thunderstorms avoids going outside when clouds look threatening). Other individuals (usually out of necessity) are willing to expose themselves to the their personal sources of terror but do so at great emotional cost.

Criterion E. Because phobias are a ubiquitous human experience, this criterion attempts to set the threshold between normal phobic avoidance and the clinical entity of Specific Phobia. The likelihood that there will be marked impairment or distress is directly related to the ease or difficulty with which the person can avoid the situation. The national sportscaster is more impaired by a fear of flying than someone who may be equally afraid but never has the need to take an airplane. Similarly, a physician with a blood-injection-injury phobia is more impaired by it than his of her patient, unless the patient has a medical condition that requires regular injections or blood drawing (e.g., diabetes).

Some people "treat" their phobias by environmental manipulation so that there is no longer enough impairment to qualify for the diagnosis, despite the fact that the strength of the phobic avoidance is unchanged. For example, a person who develops an elevator phobia after being stuck for hours in an elevator sells his or her high-rise apartment and moves to a ranch house.

Criterion F. The development of transient phobias (of animals, storms, water, loud sounds, clowns) is so much a part of childhood that it makes no sense to consider transient phobias as aspects of a mental disorder unless they are both persistent and clinically significant. This criterion sets a 6-month duration requirement to help screen out transient presentations.

Criterion G. Many disorders in DSM-IV are characterized by avoidance behavior. Some representative examples are listed in this criterion. Specific Phobia should be diagnosed only when the avoidance is related to a situation not covered in another disorder. Perhaps the most difficult differential diagnosis is between Specific Phobia, Situational Type, and Panic Disorder With Agoraphobia, particularly in individuals who avoid more than one situation.

The prototypical patient with Panic Disorder and Agoraphobia begins with unexpected Panic Attacks and starts to avoid numerous situations that he or she believes are likely to trigger additional Panic Attacks. In contrast, the prototypical patient with a Specific Phobia and Panic Attacks has the Panic Attacks only in anticipation of, or when confronted with, a specific phobic stimulus. The patient in the middle is someone who starts out by having an unexpected Panic Attack in a specific situation (e.g., elevators) and then has anxiety or Panic Attacks only in those situations. One of us calls this Panic Disorder, and the other calls it Specific Phobia. This is the clinician's call and is probably best determined by the subsequent course.

Annotation for Subtypes. DSM-IV provides specifiers reflecting the type of phobic stimulus. The Animal and Natural Environment Types typically have their onset in childhood and involve stimuli that were dangerous to our evolutionary ancestors. The most common Animal phobias involve insects, snakes, dogs, and cats. Natural Environment phobias include heights, lightning, darkness, and drowning. In contrast, the Situational Type may be the consequence of exposure to a traumatic event (e.g., fear of closed spaces developing after being trapped in an elevator or locked in a closet), and its age at onset tends to be later in life. Blood-Injection-Injury Type involves fear of seeing blood, having blood drawn, getting an injection or another invasive medical procedure, or witnessing a bloody injury. In contrast to the other types, in which there is generally an increase in pulse, this type is characterized by a vasovagal reflex that causes a decrease in pulse and blood pressure that results in fainting.

300.3 Obsessive-Compulsive Disorder

The distinction between obsessions and compulsions has been clarified in DSM-IV and differs from how most people think these are defined. Many of us were trained to believe that obsessions and compulsions differ depending on whether the repetitive phenomena consist of thoughts or actions: Obsessions were restricted to repetitive thoughts, and compulsions were restricted to repetitive actions. In DSM-IV, obsessions and compulsions are defined along functional lines that are much more relevant to treatment. An obsession is a repetitive and intrusive thought, impulse, or image that causes marked anxiety or distress, whereas a compulsion is a repetitive and ritualistic behavior or mental act that aims to reduce anxiety.

A consequence of this definition is that thoughts can be considered to be either obsessions or cognitive compulsions depending on whether they lead to, or reduce, anxiety. An example of a cognitive compulsion is counting from 1 to 100 ten times forward and then ten times backward to reduce the anxiety caused by having an obsessive blasphemous thought.

It should be noted that the DSM-IV definition of Obsessive-Compulsive Disorder is not actually a change from DSM-III-R—just a more explicit statement of what was already implied. The treatment relevance of this definition resides in the fact that the obsessions and compulsions require different interventions and are differentially responsive to behavioral treatment. Compulsions (including cognitive compulsions) can be treated by having the patient resist the urge to perform the mental or physical act, which allows exposure and desensitization to the underlying anxiety. Obsessions are much less responsive to treatment.

The placement of Obsessive-Compulsive Disorder among the Anxiety Disorders has been the subject of considerable debate. Although there was no perfect fit, the disorder was first included here because anxiety is a prominent feature always accompanying obsessions and is also associated with compulsions if the urge to perform them is resisted. However, this decision has been criticized because Obsessive-Compulsive Disorder also differs from the other Anxiety Disorders and may be related to its own spectrum of conditions with respect to phenomenology, course, family history, treatment response, and perhaps etiology (e.g., Tic Disorders, Body Dysmorphic Disorder, Hypochondriasis, Trichotillomania). An alternative suggestion was to create a new diagnostic class for Obsessive-Compulsive Disorders including that the proposed spectrum of disorders, but this was not done because of the embryonic status of the research support and the conservative nature of the DSM-IV approach.

DSM-IV diagnostic criteria for 300.3 Obsessive-Compulsive Disorder

A. Either obsessions or compulsions:

Obsessions as defined by (1), (2), (3), and (4):

(1) recurrent and persistent thoughts, impulses, or images that are experienced, at some time during the disturbance, as intrusive and inappropriate and that cause marked anxiety or distress

(continued)

DSM-IV diagnostic criteria for 300.3 Obsessive-Compulsive Disorder *(continued)*

(2) the thoughts, impulses, or images are not simply excessive worries about real-life problems
(3) the person attempts to ignore or suppress such thoughts, impulses, or images, or to neutralize them with some other thought or action
(4) the person recognizes that the obsessional thoughts, impulses, or images are a product of his or her own mind (not imposed from without as in thought insertion)

Compulsions as defined by (1) and (2):

(1) repetitive behaviors (e.g., hand washing, ordering, checking) or mental acts (e.g., praying, counting, repeating words silently) that the person feels driven to perform in response to an obsession, or according to rules that must be applied rigidly
(2) the behaviors or mental acts are aimed at preventing or reducing distress or preventing some dreaded event or situation; however, these behaviors or mental acts either are not connected in a realistic way with what they are designed to neutralize or prevent or are clearly excessive

B. At some point during the course of the disorder, the person has recognized that the obsessions or compulsions are excessive or unreasonable. **Note:** This does not apply to children.

C. The obsessions or compulsions cause marked distress, are time consuming (take more than 1 hour a day), or significantly interfere with the person's normal routine, occupational (or academic) functioning, or usual social activities or relationships.

D. If another Axis I disorder is present, the content of the obsessions or compulsions is not restricted to it (e.g., preoccupation with food in the presence of an Eating Disorder; hair pulling in the presence of Trichotillomania; concern with appearance in the presence of Body Dysmorphic Disorder; preoccupation with drugs in the presence of a Substance Use Disorder; preoccupation with having a serious illness in the presence of Hypochondriasis; preoccupation with sexual urges or fantasies in the presence of a Paraphilia; or guilty ruminations in the presence of Major Depressive Disorder).

E. The disturbance is not due to the direct physiological effects of a substance (e.g., a drug of abuse, a medication) or a general medical condition.

Specify if:

With Poor Insight: if, for most of the time during the current episode, the person does not recognize that the obsessions and compulsions are excessive or unreasonable

Tx: Luvox Cognitive Behavior

CRITERION A. To paraphrase what a Supreme Court justice once remarked about pornography, it is hard to come up with a satisfyingly descriptive definition of obsessions and compulsions, but you can usually recognize them when you see them. This relative ease of recognition is indeed fortunate because many other disorders in DSM-IV are characterized by repetitive thoughts or behaviors that must be distinguished from obsessions and compulsions. For example, although the definitions in Criterion A struggle with only limited success to distinguish between obsessions and the repetitive worries in Generalized Anxiety Disorder and between compulsions and tics, these distinctions are actually fairly easy to make in actual clinical practice.

In those occasional situations where the differential is more challenging, it may be useful to consider the fact that obsessions and compulsions usually go together (90% of the time according to the DSM-IV Obsessive-Compulsive Disorder field trial). Therefore, in trying to distinguish between an Obsessive-Compulsive Disorder obsession and a Generalized Anxiety Disorder worry, the clinching point may be whether compulsions are also present. Similarly, in trying to decide whether a repetitive behavior is an Obsessive-Compulsive Disorder compulsion or a complex motor tic, it is useful to inquire about the possible presence of accompanying obsessions.

Obsessions A1 and A2. The rather plain and not very descriptive wording of these two criteria probably does not convey to the reader the enormous number of hours spent trying to wordsmith them. These criteria attempt to communicate that the essence of an obsession is something different and stranger than the worries or preoccupations that characterize Generalized Anxiety Disorder or a normal reaction to life's unpredictability. At the extreme, the distinction is clear when stated in examples rather than words. For example, the recurrent, intrusive, and anxiety-provoking thought that "God is dog spelled backward" (an endless litany of God/dog/God/dog/God/dog/God/dog/God/dog) is an obsession. Spending an equivalent amount of time worrying about one's retirement is more likely to be an aspect of Generalized Anxiety Disorder.

At the boundaries, however, the distinction between an Obsessive-Compulsive Disorder obsession and a Generalized Anxiety Disorder worry can seem arbitrary and difficult to make. Perhaps the most common obsessions have to do with contamination. Because germs are in fact ubiquitous, it may sometimes be difficult to determine whether ruminations about them are "inappropriate" (as in Obsessive-Compulsive Disorder) or "excessive" (as in Generalized Anxiety Disorder).

Trying to put this distinction into words has not been easy. DSM-III used the term *ego-dystonic* to convey the idea that obsessive thoughts are "not experienced as voluntarily produced but rather as thoughts that invade consciousness and are experienced as senseless or repugnant." DSM-III-R dropped the term *ego-dystonic,* presumably because of difficulty operationalizing it, and instead substituted the term *senseless.* The word *senseless* was confusing in its own way because it could also misleadingly imply a loss of reality testing, which is more characteristic of delusions than obsessions. Although we might have preferred a revival of the term *ego-dystonic,* the final wording of the criterion captures the same idea with the notion that the thoughts are "intrusive and inappropriate."

Obsession A3. This criterion provides the functional link between obsessions and compulsions. The DSM-IV field trial determined that the vast majority of individuals have both obsessions and compulsions, supporting the hypothesis that they may be functionally related. It was even suggested that the presence of both obsessions and compulsions be required for the diagnosis of Obsessive-Compulsive Disorder, but this suggestion was rejected because a small but still significant minority of individuals (fewer than 10%) have one without the other (typically, compulsions without obsessions). As indicated above, this frequent co-occurrence may be important to keep in mind when trying to differentiate obsessions from other repetitive thoughts and compulsions from other repetitive behaviors.

Obsession A4. We mentioned above that obsessions have an intrusive, inappropriate, and "ego-alien" quality. So do delusions, particularly those of thought insertion (i.e., the unshakable conviction that the thoughts are being inserted by an outside force). This criterion was included to make clear that the presence of delusions of thought insertion warrants the diagnosis of a psychotic disorder rather than Obsessive-Compulsive Disorder.

Compulsion A1. Compulsions are repetitive behaviors that the person feels driven to perform. In DSM-III-R, compulsive behaviors were also characterized as being "purposeful and intentional" to help distinguish these from other repetitive behaviors that feel less purposeful (e.g., tics, stereotypies). However, in attempting to clear up this one problem, DSM-III-R created a much worse confusion. One of the most characteristic aspects of having to perform a compulsion is the individual's sense that the behavior is *not* willed, purposeful, or intentional. Because these behaviors are experienced as outside the person's control, these terms have been eliminated.

Compulsion A2. In DSM-IV, compulsions are distinguished from other forms of repetitive behavior by the underlying motivation for the behavior—to reduce or prevent the anxiety associated with an obsession. For example, hand washing alleviates the anxiety triggered by the obsession that one is contaminated, and repeating a prayer exactly 36 times is meant to counteract the distress caused by having an obsessive obscene image. Determining that the compulsive behavior is meant to reduce the anxiety accompanying an obsession is very helpful in differentiating a compulsion from other repetitive behaviors like tics and stereotypies.

This criterion is also helpful in distinguishing between compulsive acts and impulsive acts, both of which are repetitive and hard to resist. What differentiates the two (at least in theory and at the extremes) is the underlying motivation for the behavior. In the prototypical impulsive act, the behavior results in "pleasure, gratification, or relief." In the prototypical compulsive act, the behavior is "aimed at preventing or reducing distress or preventing some dreaded event or situation."

The DSM-IV definition of a compulsion is much narrower than its increasingly broad use in the colloquial world (compulsive overeating, shopping, sex, gambling). The primary goal of colloquially defined compulsive behavior is to attain pleasure rather than to reduce or prevent anxiety. However, reviewing the definitions of *compulsive* and *impulsive* acts back-to-back and considering boundary cases reveal just how artificial the distinction between them can sometimes be. It is not always obvious whether a given tension-reducing act like hair pulling constitutes "pleasurable relief" (as in Impulse-Control Disorder) or "reduction in distress" (as in Obsessive-Compulsive Disorder). This issue is taken up again in the section on Impulse-Control Disorders.

This criterion distinguishes realistic prudence from a true compulsion. Checking the oven once (or even twice), washing one's hands, and other preventative or checking behaviors should only be considered compulsive when they go beyond what is reasonable. This boundary is not always easy to draw, especially because individuals can be very determined to portray the behavior as absolutely necessary and adaptable, and different clinicians are themselves differentially compulsive.

Criterion B. This criterion relates to the boundary between Obsessive-Compulsive Disorder and Delusional Disorder, both of which may be characterized by strongly held unusual beliefs. At the extremes, this distinction is easy. The prototypical patient with Obsessive-Compulsive Disorder is fully aware that it is ridiculous to be concerned about contamination from germs that would result from touching newspapers, but nonetheless this patient avoids newspapers like the plague. The prototypical delusional patient cannot even entertain the possibility that the conviction is unfounded and is likely to elaborate much more implausible explanations. At the boundary are patients who have what have been called overvalued ideas, which are held with less than delusional intensity but are not fully renounced as "excessive or unreasonable."

This criterion is not completely successful but is meant to assist in the distinction between Obsessive-Compulsive Disorder and Delusional Disorder. The notion is that patients with Delusional Disorder usually do not have a period in which they have insight into the unreasonable nature of their beliefs or actions. The relationship of insight to Obsessive-Compulsive Disorder is much more complicated. Early in the course of Obsessive-Compulsive Disorder, the patient generally realizes that the concerns expressed in the obsessions or compulsions are unjustified. The application of this criterion is made difficult by the fact that children with Obsessive-Compulsive Disorder often do not have insight, and patients with the disorder sometimes become less insightful as the years pass.

Criterion C. Obsessions and compulsions (e.g., superstitious rituals) are a common part of everyday life. This criterion is intended to help set the boundary with such normal phenomena. For Obsessive-Compulsive Disorder, this standard clinical-significance criterion also includes a phrase indicating that the obsessions or compulsions are "time consuming (take more than 1 hour a day)." This phrase allows the clinician to conclude that impairment is present even in the face of the patient's apparent lack of concern about the behavior or the rationalization that it is useful. Many individuals with this disorder come to lack insight about its devastating impact on their lives. They may deny having any distress or impairment despite the fact that it is apparent to all of those around them that they have become slavishly adherent to their highly ritualized behaviors. By the way, like all of the DSM-IV time thresholds, there is nothing magical about the 1-hour time limit—so don't be compulsive about applying it!

Obsessive-Compulsive Disorder should not be confused with rituals that are culturally or religiously prescribed and sanctioned. Certainly not everyone who spends an hour or more a day engaged in religious rituals deserves a diagnosis of Obsessive-Compulsive Disorder. However, an Obsessive-Compulsive Disorder diagnosis may be suitable for someone who suddenly stops work and cannot resist spending 12 hours a day in ritualized praying, thereby raising the concerns of both family members and clergy. The distinction between rituals within the cultural norm and those that reflect Obsessive-Compulsive Disorder may be challenging, especially when the clinician and the patient have different cultural or religious backgrounds.

Criterion D. Many DSM-IV disorders are characterized by recurrent, intrusive upsetting thoughts or behaviors. This criterion clarifies that an additional diagnosis of Obsessive-Compulsive Disorder need not be applied in such cases to describe these thoughts or behaviors. However, the disorders listed in this criterion may occasionally co-occur with Obsessive-Compulsive Disorder. As long as the repetitive thoughts or behaviors are not better accounted for by another Axis I disorder, an additional diagnosis of Obsessive-Compulsive Disorder can be given. For example, a patient with Anorexia Nervosa may also have contamination fears and perform repetitive hand washing at a level that might warrant an additional diagnosis of Obsessive-Compulsive Disorder.

Criterion E. This criterion is meant to remind the clinician not to confuse Obsessive-Compulsive Disorder with stereotypies or compulsive behaviors that sometimes occur in relation to substance use or neurological conditions.

Annotation for Subtypes. The specifier With Poor Insight refers to those individuals with Obsessive-Compulsive Disorder who do not have good insight into the unreasonableness of the obsessions or compulsions. Insight may fluctuate over the course of the disorder. The designation With Poor Insight is meant to apply to the current state of affairs. The individuals with Obsessive-Compulsive Disorder who are most likely to lack insight are children and adults who are more advanced in their course and have a more severe presentation. See the annotation for Criterion B for a further discussion.

Some consideration was given to having a psychotic subtype of Obsessive-Compulsive Disorder (see "Delusional Disorder" in Chapter 11 of this book). This subtype was considered because of the clinical impression that patients' levels of insight as to the unreasonableness of their obsessions or compulsions exist on a continuum. Similar suggestions were made for including psychotic types of Body Dysmorphic Disorder and Hypochondriasis in the "Somatoform Disorders" section of DSM-IV.

The psychotic subtype of Obsessive-Compulsive Disorder was not adopted because it would have been a marked change, radically reducing the scope of Delusional Disorder. Research also had not yet demonstrated that patients with psychotic and nonpsychotic types of Obsessive-Compulsive Disorder respond to treatment in the same way. The DSM-IV method for identifying those individuals with Obsessive-Compulsive Disorder who are currently delusional about their Obsessive-Compulsive Disorder concerns is far from elegant, but it will have to serve until more data about such patients are available. To save information, DSM-IV allows the clinician to give both the diagnosis of Obsessive-Compulsive Disorder and the diagnosis of Delusional Disorder. This admittedly clumsy solution is descriptively accurate and useful, however, it should not be taken to mean that the patient has two different pathogenetic processes.

309.81 Posttraumatic Stress Disorder

Although people have very different abilities to endure stress, it seems likely that everyone has a breaking point if exposed long enough to an extreme enough stressor. It is noteworthy that once Posttraumatic Stress Disorder occurs, its symptom pattern is remarkably uniform regardless of the individual's previous psychological history or cultural background. However different people are before developing Posttraumatic Stress Disorder, there is a very characteristic human pattern of response to an extreme stressor that includes avoidance of stimuli that remind the person of the stressor, reexperiencing the stressor in a number of ways, and increased physiological arousal, particularly on exposure to memory-jogging triggers.

There were two types of controversy in relation to Posttraumatic Stress Disorder, each with a potentially profound impact on how widely or narrowly the disorder would be defined. The first question had to do with how broadly to define the types of allowable stressors that can qualify an individual for a diagnosis of Posttraumatic Stress Disorder. The second question had to do with how broadly to define the symptom pattern that can qualify an individual for a diagnosis of Posttraumatic Stress Disorder.

Posttraumatic Stress Disorder had its roots on the battlefield. The diagnosis was derived originally from the *combat neurosis* observed in soldiers exposed to the ravages of war. In adapting this category to civilian life, the problem has been how to translate combat stressors to those encountered in everyday life. Certainly, life-threatening automobile accidents, exposure to natural disasters, and being a victim of a violent crime are comparable to military experiences in their capacity to cause Posttraumatic Stress Disorder. The major question in defining Posttraumatic Stress Disorder is whether or not to include reactions to the numerous stressors that are upsetting but not life threatening. This question has important implications because Posttraumatic Stress Disorder is frequently used (and misused) in disability determinations, in determining awards for damages in litigation cases, and in assessment of criminal responsibility. This issue is discussed in detail in the annotation for Criterion A.

Another issue that was the focus of considerable controversy concerned the degree to which extreme stressors could be held accountable for different types of psychopathology that are commonly encountered in clinical practice. One increasingly vocal school of thought espouses the notion that extreme stress can, and often does, lead to diverse symptom presentations that go far beyond the Posttraumatic Stress Disorder symptom pattern and include features from many other parts of DSM-IV (personality changes, depression, dissociation, generalized anxiety). This notion led to three different suggestions: 1) that Borderline Personality Disorder be considered a form of Posttraumatic Stress Disorder, 2) that a victimization disorder be included for individuals who have been exposed to chronic extreme stressors, and 3) that a subtype (complicated Posttraumatic Stress Disorder) be added to cover long-term sequelae of extreme stress not included in the Posttraumatic Stress Disorder criteria set.

The serious methodological problem in evaluating these suggestions is that most studies and all clinical experiences relating stress to psychopathology are subject to considerable bias because of their retrospective and uncontrolled nature. It is very difficult to establish a cause-and-effect relationship between current psychopathology and the previous exposure to a stressor. Life-threatening events are relatively common and may be incidental and not responsible for later symptoms. In this regard, it should be noted that many victims of extreme stress do not develop subsequent psychopathology. This question of cause and effect is fundamentally important in understanding psychopathology and will require a great deal more study.

DSM-IV took its usual conservative stance. The symptom criteria for Posttraumatic Stress Disorder remain relatively narrowly defined, as they were in DSM-III-R, but the "Associated Features and Disorders" section of the text includes some of the additional symptoms that were described as part of the broader Posttraumatic Stress Disorder construct.

DSM-IV diagnostic criteria for 309.81 Posttraumatic Stress Disorder

A. The person has been exposed to a traumatic event in which both of the following were present:
   (1) the person experienced, witnessed, or was confronted with an event or events that involved actual or threatened death or serious injury, or a threat to the physical integrity of self or others
   (2) the person's response involved intense fear, helplessness, or horror. **Note:** In children, this may be expressed instead by disorganized or agitated behavior

B. The traumatic event is persistently reexperienced in one (or more) of the following ways:
   (1) recurrent and intrusive distressing recollections of the event, including images, thoughts, or perceptions. **Note:** In young children, repetitive play may occur in which themes or aspects of the trauma are expressed.
   (2) recurrent distressing dreams of the event. **Note:** In children, there may be frightening dreams without recognizable content.
   (3) acting or feeling as if the traumatic event were recurring (includes a sense of reliving the experience, illusions, hallucinations, and dissociative flashback episodes, including those that occur on awakening or when intoxicated). **Note:** In young children, trauma-specific reenactment may occur.
   (4) intense psychological distress at exposure to internal or external cues that symbolize or resemble an aspect of the traumatic event
   (5) physiological reactivity on exposure to internal or external cues that symbolize or resemble an aspect of the traumatic event

C. Persistent avoidance of stimuli associated with the trauma and numbing of general responsiveness (not present before the trauma), as indicated by three (or more) of the following:
   (1) efforts to avoid thoughts, feelings, or conversations associated with the trauma
   (2) efforts to avoid activities, places, or people that arouse recollections of the trauma
   (3) inability to recall an important aspect of the trauma
   (4) markedly diminished interest or participation in significant activities
   (5) feeling of detachment or estrangement from others
   (6) restricted range of affect (e.g., unable to have loving feelings)
   (7) sense of a foreshortened future (e.g., does not expect to have a career, marriage, children, or a normal life span)

D. Persistent symptoms of increased arousal (not present before the trauma), as indicated by two (or more) of the following:
   (1) difficulty falling or staying asleep
   (2) irritability or outbursts of anger
   (3) difficulty concentrating
   (4) hypervigilance
   (5) exaggerated startle response

(continued)

TY EMDR - Bilaterial eye movement

DSM-IV diagnostic criteria for
309.81 Posttraumatic Stress Disorder *(continued)*

E. Duration of the disturbance (symptoms in Criteria B, C, and D) is more than 1 month.

F. The disturbance causes clinically significant distress or impairment in social, occupational, or other important areas of functioning.

Specify if:
Acute: if duration of symptoms is less than 3 months
Chronic: if duration of symptoms is 3 months or more

Specify if:
With Delayed Onset: if onset of symptoms is at least 6 months after the stressor

Criterion A. This criterion acts as a gatekeeper for the diagnosis. Regardless of what the symptom pattern is, the diagnosis is not considered to be Posttraumatic Stress Disorder unless the stressor is of a certain nature and severity. There has been considerable controversy about how high to set the stressor threshold. The DSM-III-R criterion describing the nature of the stressor was criticized as being vague, inaccurate, and unreliable. It required that the event be "outside the range of usual human experience." It is an unfortunate testimony to the current (and probably past and future) state of the human condition that life-threatening events are well within the range of usual human experience. Indeed, the DSM-IV field trial revealed that the majority of people, at some point, had had at least one threat to their lives resulting from crimes, automobile accidents, domestic abuse, combat experience, and/or natural disasters. Clearly, the DSM-III-R wording had to be changed.

The wording of the DSM-IV stressor criterion is dense enough to require a bit of explication and a lot of clinical judgment. This criterion is meant to describe fairly serious and horrible events, not merely unpleasant ones. First, the criterion has been split into two parts: one to describe the nature of stressor and the other to describe the person's subjective response to it. Two aspects of the nature of the stressor need to be evaluated: the context of exposure ("experienced, witnessed, or was confronted with") and the type of stressor ("actual or threatened death or serious injury or a threat to the physical integrity of self or others").

The context of the exposure includes having one's life threatened; having the direct personal experience of seeing someone else being threatened, injured, or killed; or hearing the news of a loved one being hurt. It is not meant to include more indirect and impersonal experiences such as watching from the safety of one's living room a news report of a catastrophe occurring to strangers. "Threatened death or serious injury" refers to immediate and serious threats, not the existential concern about life and death or even the realistic fear that one may someday be a crime victim or have a car accident. Although learning that one has a life-threatening illness would count, in clinical practice this knowledge rarely results in the characteristic symptoms of Posttraumatic Stress Disorder. One would generally not count toward Posttraumatic Stress Disorder the expected death of a loved one of natural causes at an advanced age. The phrase "physical integrity" was included to ensure that all experiences of sexual assault would be covered, not just those in which the person perceives a threat to life or limb.

These defining components combine in complex ways that require clinical judgment. The literature clearly indicates that the risk of developing Posttraumatic Stress Disorder increases according to the proximity, severity, and duration of the stressor and whether it occurs at the hands of another person. In evaluating whether the stressor criterion should apply, it is important to take into account the context of the experience and the nature of the threat. Directly experiencing a gun pointed toward one's head is more stressful than watching someone else being robbed, which is in turn more stressful than hearing about a robbery. Moreover, the criterion requires that the person be profoundly affected by the stressor and react to it with extreme feelings of "fear, helplessness, or horror." Children are less likely to articulate their feelings, and this item may be inferred by a change in their behavior.

One function of this criterion is to screen out stressors that are distressing but not life threatening. This was a controversial decision and one that was studied in the DSM-IV field trial. Some clinicians describe seeing a pattern of Posttraumatic Stress Disorder-like symptoms emerging after less severe stressors and would have preferred to increase the coverage of this category and reduce false-negatives by toning down Criterion A or eliminating it altogether. The field trial compared various thresholds of severity of stressors and found that these had no impact on the prevalence of Posttraumatic Stress Disorder in the settings studied. This finding might argue for allowing a considerably less stringent definition of the gateway stressor. However, there were compelling arguments for requiring that the stressor be life threatening to avoid the overdiagnosis of Posttraumatic Stress Disorder. This diagnosis, especially, lends itself to misuse because it may result in beneficial consequences to the claimant and has a symptom pattern that is well known and easy to feign. Providing a relatively tight definition for the range of allowable stressors is an important way to protect against false-positives and to increase the validity of the diagnostic assignment of Posttraumatic Stress Disorder.

Criterion B. The symptoms listed in this criterion are fairly ubiquitous after exposure to an extreme stressor. Reexperiencing the event can be terrifying in itself and can also lead individuals to become concerned that they are losing control or losing their minds. Reassurance that this reexperience is a common sequela can reduce the possibility that the full Posttraumatic Stress Disorder syndrome will develop.

Individuals can reexperience the event spontaneously during both the waking and sleeping states, or the reexperience can be triggered by a wide variety of stimuli that recall the event to the individual. For example, for a woman who has been raped, the trigger may be as broad as the presence of any man or may be restricted to individuals with the same physical characteristics as the assailant. Flashbacks to wartime may be triggered by loud noises, seeing war movies, and tropical rainstorms. In some cases, the trigger may be a symbolic representation of the actual stimulus (e.g., a policeman may be a trigger for a concentration camp survivor). Occasionally, a person experiencing a flashback may mistakenly be thought of as psychotic. In contrast to psychotic symptoms, the relived experiences in Posttraumatic Stress Disorder are transient, self-limited, and understandable in the context of reexperiencing a prior stressor. This criterion has been controversial because some individuals have used flashbacks as a criminal defense. Although only one Criterion B item is required, typically most or all are present.

CRITERION C. This criterion embodies three concepts. The first concept is related to the individual's desire to avoid the triggers that would lead to reexperiencing the trauma. The emotional numbing covered in items C4–C6 can be considered a broader form of avoidance unrelated to any specific triggers. Item C7 covers the common experience of living on borrowed time and in some individuals may reflect a feeling of guilt about having survived. This sense of a foreshortened future should raise a red flag in the clinician's mind that clinically significant depression and suicidal feelings may also be present.

CRITERION D. The presence of these characteristic symptoms forms the basis for including Posttraumatic Stress Disorder with the other Anxiety Disorders. One of the challenges in evaluating this criterion is that many individuals who develop Posttraumatic Stress Disorder may have had some preexisting symptoms. The question is the degree to which exposure to the extreme stressor has resulted in a clinically significant change.

CRITERION E. DSM-IV maintains the DSM-III-R minimum duration of 1 month. A diagnosis of Acute Stress Disorder may apply for Posttraumatic Stress Disorder-type symptom patterns that occur in the immediate aftermath of an extreme stressor but resolve before 1 month.

CRITERION F. This criterion was added to the Posttraumatic Stress Disorder criteria set in DSM-IV to emphasize the fact that some individuals may have persisting symptoms after exposure to an extreme stressor that are not sufficiently disturbing or maladaptive to require a mental disorder diagnosis.

308.3 Acute Stress Disorder

Acute Stress Disorder is one of the few "new" categories in DSM-IV. A little-known fact is that a similar category (Gross Stress Reaction) was included in DSM-I and that such presentations were also covered under the DSM-III definition of Posttraumatic Stress Disorder, which had no minimum duration. In the immediate aftermath of an extreme stressor, it is not uncommon for an individual to have a brief episode of symptoms that resemble those that occur in Posttraumatic Stress Disorder. Whether these should be considered sufficiently outside the norm to meet the definition of mental disorder is an interesting question. One view is that, similar to bereavement, such symptoms are an expectable response to extreme stressors and therefore do not warrant a diagnosis of a mental disorder. However, some individuals exposed to extreme stressors display severe impairment that requires immediate diagnosis and treatment, and the early development of such symptoms is the best predictor of whether the individual will ultimately develop Posttraumatic Stress Disorder.

The diagnosis of Acute Stress Disorder was included in DSM-IV because an ounce of prevention is worth a pound of cure. Once Posttraumatic Stress Disorder is established, it is difficult to treat and often becomes chronic. It can be immensely useful to identify those individuals who are having difficulty after exposure to the stressor in order to provide them with psychoeducation about the nature of their symptoms and to predict their likely course. This education helps the individual to get a sense of control over the symptoms, which is especially important in the aftermath of having experienced a terrifying stressor that rendered him or her helpless and out of control. The inclusion of this disorder may also assist in triage efforts after disasters and help clinical and research efforts to predict which individuals are likely to develop Posttraumatic Stress Disorder. No apparent false-positive problems were caused by including the diagnosis beyond the possible unfortunate consequences that might accrue from labeling a large proportion of disaster victims with a mental disorder diagnosis.

Plans to introduce this category into DSM-IV raised questions about where it should be placed in the classification. Because of its similarities to Posttraumatic Stress Disorder, it seemed advisable to place Acute Stress Disorder next to Posttraumatic Stress Disorder in the "Anxiety Disorders" section of DSM-IV. There were, however, two other suggestions for placement. The most interesting alternative would have been to create a new section in DSM-IV based on a stress-related etiology that would have contained Acute Stress Disorder, Posttraumatic Stress Disorder, and Adjustment Disorder. Another suggestion, reflecting the dissociative aspects of Acute Stress Disorder, proposed that it be included among the Dissociative Disorders. These were not accepted because they were considered too radical a departure from the conservative spirit of DSM-IV.

DSM-IV diagnostic criteria for 308.3 Acute Stress Disorder

A. The person has been exposed to a traumatic event in which both of the following were present:
   (1) the person experienced, witnessed, or was confronted with an event or events that involved actual or threatened death or serious injury, or a threat to the physical integrity of self or others
   (2) the person's response involved intense fear, helplessness, or horror

B. Either while experiencing or after experiencing the distressing event, the individual has three (or more) of the following dissociative symptoms:
   (1) a subjective sense of numbing, detachment, or absence of emotional responsiveness
   (2) a reduction in awareness of his or her surroundings (e.g., "being in a daze")
   (3) derealization
   (4) depersonalization
   (5) dissociative amnesia (i.e., inability to recall an important aspect of the trauma)

C. The traumatic event is persistently reexperienced in at least one of the following ways: recurrent images, thoughts, dreams, illusions, flashback episodes, or a sense of reliving the experience; or distress on exposure to reminders of the traumatic event.

D. Marked avoidance of stimuli that arouse recollections of the trauma (e.g., thoughts, feelings, conversations, activities, places, people).

(continued)

DSM-IV diagnostic criteria for 308.3 Acute Stress Disorder *(continued)*

E. Marked symptoms of anxiety or increased arousal (e.g., difficulty sleeping, irritability, poor concentration, hypervigilance, exaggerated startle response, motor restlessness).

F. The disturbance causes clinically significant distress or impairment in social, occupational, or other important areas of functioning or impairs the individual's ability to pursue some necessary task, such as obtaining necessary assistance or mobilizing personal resources by telling family members about the traumatic experience.

G. The disturbance lasts for a minimum of 2 days and a maximum of 4 weeks and occurs within 4 weeks of the traumatic event.

H. The disturbance is not due to the direct physiological effects of a substance (e.g., a drug of abuse, a medication) or a general medical condition, is not better accounted for by Brief Psychotic Disorder, and is not merely an exacerbation of a preexisting Axis I or Axis II disorder.

Criterion A. This range of allowable stressors is identical to that in Posttraumatic Stress Disorder.

Criterion B. The main difference in the criteria sets for Acute Stress Disorder and Posttraumatic Stress Disorder is the inclusion of this criterion, which requires the presence of dissociative symptoms. The literature review and data analysis found that such symptoms are particularly common during the immediate aftermath of an extreme stressor and contribute to much of the impairment.

Criteria C, D, and E. These are "collapsed" versions of Criteria B, C, and D for Posttraumatic Stress Disorder.

Criterion F. Like bereavement, the development of symptoms in response to an extreme stressor is often expectable and without clinical significance. This criterion serves to set the boundary with no mental disorder by requiring that the symptoms cause significant impairment or distress.

Criterion G. Acute Stress Disorder fills a diagnostic gap between Posttraumatic Stress Disorder and Adjustment Disorder that was created by DSM-III-R when it set a 1-month minimum duration for Posttraumatic Stress Disorder. This gap could have been filled in DSM-IV in one of two ways: 1) going back to the DSM-III convention and eliminating the minimum duration for Posttraumatic Stress Disorder or 2) introducing this new disorder. Although there was no compelling reason to favor one of these alternatives over the other, on balance it seemed wise to maintain a fairly narrow and homogeneous Posttraumatic Stress Disorder construct. It should be recognized, however, that the duration boundary between Acute Stress Disorder and Posttraumatic Stress Disorder is artificial and that these are two aspects of one phenomenon.

Criterion H. Not infrequently, people exposed to extreme stressors sustain physical as well as psychological injuries that may be responsible for the symptoms. For example, head trauma can cause dissociative and other symptoms that may resemble Acute Stress Disorder. Therefore, it is imperative to rule out medical causes of the symptoms before attributing them to Acute Stress Disorder. Similarly, individuals may attempt to drown out the experience of the trauma with alcohol or the use of other substances. Symptoms of Intoxication or Withdrawal must, therefore, also be ruled out. Brief Psychotic Disorder is specifically mentioned in this criterion because it may sometimes be difficult to distinguish between dissociative symptoms and psychotic symptoms in the aftermath of an extreme stressor. When well-documented psychotic symptoms are present, the diagnosis should be Brief Psychotic Disorder With Marked Stressor(s).

300.02 Generalized Anxiety Disorder

Generalized Anxiety Disorder has been one of the most maligned, unsatisfactory, and radically revised categories in DSM-IV. It was created when DSM-III split the DSM-II construct of Anxiety Neurosis into two new diagnoses: Panic Disorder (characterized by Panic Attacks) and Generalized Anxiety Disorder (characterized by generalized and persistent anxiety with motor tension, autonomic hyperactivity, apprehensive expectation, and vigilance).

Because of the lack of specificity of this definition and the heterogeneity of the patients it identified, DSM-III-R tightened the definition of Generalized Anxiety Disorder by increasing the duration from 1 to 6 months and emphasizing the cognitive component of the anxiety. The DSM-III-R definition continued to be criticized because 1) its boundaries with normality and with a number of other disorders (especially Obsessive-Compulsive Disorder and Hypochondriasis) were unclear, 2) its 18-symptom list was cumbersome and user-unfriendly, 3) its threshold was set so high as to result in poor coverage, 4) it placed excessive emphasis on the cognitive component of Generalized Anxiety Disorder at the expense of the somatic component, and 5) it failed to identify a group of patients with clinically significant correlates, including treatment responsiveness.

A proposal to eliminate the category of Generalized Anxiety Disorder entirely in DSM-IV was rejected because it would have created such a sizable hole in the classification of Anxiety Disorders. Instead, as a result of the literature review, data reanalysis, and field trial, the criteria were revised yet again in an effort to improve the category rather than abandon it. During the DSM-IV discussions, there was something of a tug of war between those who believed that the cognitive symptoms are the most essential features of Generalized Anxiety Disorder and those who place more weight on the somatic symptoms. Those with a cognitive bent tend to target the worry as the primary symptom for cognitively based treatments. Those with a somatic bent are concerned that the relative lack of medication responsiveness in Generalized Anxiety Disorder may be an artifact of the definition, which they believe overemphasizes the importance of worry and underemphasizes somatic symptoms. It remains to be seen whether the balance struck in DSM-IV will result in a more useful definition of this disorder.

In contrast to the unitary criteria set for most disorders in DSM-III-R, there were separate childhood and adult versions of Generalized Anxiety Disorder. The childhood version was known as Overanxious Disorder of Childhood. In DSM-IV, this distinction has been eliminated, and the criteria set has been modified to accommodate childhood presentations. The "Specific Culture, Age, and Gender Features" section of the DSM-IV text for Generalized Anxiety Disorder suggests that children and adolescents with this disorder are likely to be particularly worried about catastrophic events (e.g., nuclear war), school and athletic performance, and punctuality.

DSM-IV diagnostic criteria for 300.02 Generalized Anxiety Disorder

A. Excessive anxiety and worry (apprehensive expectation), occurring more days than not for at least 6 months, about a number of events or activities (such as work or school performance).

B. The person finds it difficult to control the worry.

C. The anxiety and worry are associated with three (or more) of the following six symptoms (with at least some symptoms present for more days than not for the past 6 months). **Note:** Only one item is required in children.
   (1) restlessness or feeling keyed up or on edge
   (2) being easily fatigued
   (3) difficulty concentrating or mind going blank
   (4) irritability
   (5) muscle tension
   (6) sleep disturbance (difficulty falling or staying asleep, or restless unsatisfying sleep)

D. The focus of the anxiety and worry is not confined to features of an Axis I disorder, e.g., the anxiety or worry is not about having a Panic Attack (as in Panic Disorder), being embarrassed in public (as in Social Phobia), being contaminated (as in Obsessive-Compulsive Disorder), being away from home or close relatives (as in Separation Anxiety Disorder), gaining weight (as in Anorexia Nervosa), having multiple physical complaints (as in Somatization Disorder), or having a serious illness (as in Hypochondriasis), and the anxiety and worry do not occur exclusively during Posttraumatic Stress Disorder.

E. The anxiety, worry, or physical symptoms cause clinically significant distress or impairment in social, occupational, or other important areas of functioning.

F. The disturbance is not due to the direct physiological effects of a substance (e.g., a drug of abuse, a medication) or a general medical condition (e.g., hyperthyroidism) and does not occur exclusively during a Mood Disorder, a Psychotic Disorder, or a Pervasive Developmental Disorder.

Criterion A. This criterion is meant to establish the boundary between Generalized Anxiety Disorder and "normal" worries. In contrast to everyday worries, the worries in Generalized Anxiety Disorder must be excessive, persistent, and pervasive. The duration requirement is set purposely high (more days than not for 6 months) to distinguish Generalized Anxiety Disorder from more transient and often stress-related worries. An inherent problem in defining this boundary is the lack of any standard for what constitutes reasonable as opposed to excessive worry. This is probably the single most salient cause for the unreliability of this diagnosis.

The evaluation should include an assessment of the range of different situations on which the worry is focused, the amount of time spent worrying, and the severity of the worry compared with the reality of the risks being faced. For example, worrying about one's child from the moment he or she walks out the front door to go to school in the morning until he or she comes back in the afternoon would clearly be excessive. On the other hand, worrying for several days about a child going to camp for the first time would certainly not qualify as excessive. It should be noted that the judgment about the excessiveness of the worry must be informed by the fact that different cultures sanction (and even expect) different degrees of worry. In evaluating the reasonableness of the patient's proclivity to worry, the clinician should also be aware of (and not unduly influenced by) his or her own tendencies in this regard.

Criterion B. This criterion has been added to further clarify the boundary between the worry in Generalized Anxiety Disorder and normal worry. Individuals with Generalized Anxiety Disorder are more than just worrywarts. In addition to being excessive (as required in Criterion A), the worry must also be difficult to control. In contrast to normal worries, which are often adaptive and serve to focus attention and motivate behavior, the worries in Generalized Anxiety Disorder are more likely to be counterproductive and tend to interfere with the person's ability to handle the problem effectively. For example, the inability to control the worries about passing a course may interfere with the ability to prepare effectively for a final examination.

Criterion C. DSM-III-R listed 18 symptoms that were meant to represent the somatic manifestations of anxiety. This particular criterion was among the most unpopular in DSM-III-R. It was cumbersome, unsupported by empirical evidence, and included many items that overlapped with those that defined a Panic Attack. This overlap may have been responsible for creating artificial comorbidity between Generalized Anxiety Disorder and Panic Disorder. As a result of the DSM-IV literature review and data reanalysis, DSM-IV has a shortened item list consisting of those symptoms that are most specific for Generalized Anxiety Disorder.

Criteria D and F. Perhaps the most fundamental problem in defining Generalized Anxiety Disorder is that worry is one of the most nonspecific symptoms in psychiatry. In fact, anxiety or worry is a defining or associated feature encountered in most disorders in the manual. Criterion D serves to limit the range of worries under consideration to those that are not covered by other more specific DSM-IV diagnoses. For example, worries about contamination or of being humiliated in social situations would not be included as evidence of the pervasiveness of the worry when considering a comorbid diagnosis of Generalized Anxiety Disorder in individuals with Obsessive-Compulsive Disorder or Social Phobia, respectively. However, an additional diagnosis of Generalized Anxiety Disorder may be appropriate when the worries extend far beyond the more narrow focus of concern characteristic of the other Axis I disorder. For example, it is not uncommon for individuals with Social Phobia to have a whole panoply of additional worries unrelated to their fears in social situations.

Criterion F serves to exclude a diagnosis of Generalized Anxiety Disorder if the worries occur exclusively during a number of other disorders for which worry is an associated feature. If this criterion were not included, Generalized Anxiety Disorder would be given as a constant and meaningless comorbid diagnosis with Major Depressive Disorder, Schizophrenia, and so forth.

Anxiety is a common consequence of substance use (including medication side effects) and general medical conditions. Because Generalized Anxiety Disorder often has its onset early in life, the clinician should be particularly alert to substance use or a general medical condition in individuals who have a late onset of generalized anxiety.

CRITERION E. The boilerplate clinical-significance criterion that appears throughout DSM-IV is especially necessary here precisely because it is so difficult to draw the boundary between Generalized Anxiety Disorder and normality.

293.89 Anxiety Disorder Due to a General Medical Condition

The first step in the differential diagnosis of anxiety symptoms is to rule out general medical conditions and substance use as etiologies. If a general medical condition is present and determined to be the direct physiological cause of the anxiety symptoms, Anxiety Disorder Due to a General Medical Condition is diagnosed. Table 13–1 lists some of the general medical conditions that have been reported to cause clinically significant anxiety symptoms. For a more detailed discussion on how to make the often difficult differential diagnosis, see the section "Differential Diagnosis One Step at a Time" in Chapter 7.

When communicating or recording the diagnosis, the clinician should use the actual name of the etiological general medical condition on Axis I (e.g., 293.89 Anxiety Disorder Due to Hyperthyroidism, With Panic Attacks). Note that all causes of Anxiety Disorder Due to a General Medical Condition have the same Axis I diagnostic code: 293.89. Furthermore, the general medical condition should also be coded on Axis III (e.g., 292.9 Hyperthyroidism). To help ease the coding burden, DSM-IV includes selected general medical codes in Appendix G. Not uncommonly, the psychiatric presentation due to a general medical condition is characterized by a mixture of symptoms (e.g., mood, anxiety, and sleep). In most cases, the clinician should choose the diagnosis that reflects the most prominent aspect of the symptom presentation.

Table 13–1. General medical conditions that cause anxiety symptoms

Endocrine conditions (e.g., hyper- and hypothyroidism, pheochromocytoma, hypoglycemia, hyperadrenocorticism)
Cardiovascular conditions (e.g., congestive heart failure, pulmonary embolism, arrhythmia)
Respiratory conditions (e.g., chronic obstructive pulmonary disease, pneumonia, hyperventilation)
Metabolic conditions (e.g., vitamin B_{12} deficiency, porphyria)
Neurological conditions (e.g., neoplasms, vestibular dysfunction, encephalitis)

Source. Adapted from American Psychiatric Association, p. 438.

DSM-IV diagnostic criteria for 293.89 Anxiety Disorder Due to . . . *[Indicate the General Medical Condition]*

A. Prominent anxiety, Panic Attacks, or obsessions or compulsions predominate in the clinical picture.

B. There is evidence from the history, physical examination, or laboratory findings that the disturbance is the direct physiological consequence of a general medical condition.

C. The disturbance is not better accounted for by another mental disorder (e.g., Adjustment Disorder With Anxiety in which the stressor is a serious general medical condition).

D. The disturbance does not occur exclusively during the course of a delirium.

E. The disturbance causes clinically significant distress or impairment in social, occupational, or other important areas of functioning.

Specify if:

With Generalized Anxiety: if excessive anxiety or worry about a number of events or activities predominates in the clinical presentation

With Panic Attacks: if Panic Attacks predominate in the clinical presentation

With Obsessive-Compulsive Symptoms: if obsessions or compulsions predominate in the clinical presentation

Coding note: Include the name of the general medical condition on Axis I, e.g., 293.89 Anxiety Disorder Due to Pheochromocytoma, With Generalized Anxiety; also code the general medical condition on Axis III.

Substance-Induced Anxiety Disorder

It is also important to consider whether anxiety symptoms are due to the direct effects of a substance, in which case the appropriate diagnosis is Substance Intoxication, Substance Withdrawal, or a Substance-Induced Anxiety Disorder. Because anxiety symptoms are so frequent encountered as part of Substance Intoxication or Substance Withdrawal, in most instances these diagnoses would suffice. A diagnosis of Substance-Induced Anxiety Disorder should be reserved for those situations in which the anxiety symptoms are especially noteworthy: in other words, when they are in excess of what is expected and warrant independent clinical attention. Table 13–2 lists those drugs of abuse, medications, and toxins that DSM-IV indicates can cause a Substance-Induced Anxiety Disorder. It should be noted that this list is not exhaustive.

When recording the diagnosis, the diagnostic code depends on the class of substance. For alcohol, the code is 291.8, and for all other substances (including medications and toxins) the code is 292.89. When communicating the name of the disorder, the specific etiological substance should be inserted in place of the word *substance* (e.g., Alcohol-Induced Anxiety Disorder, Methylphenidate-Induced Anxiety Disorder, Carbon Monoxide-Induced Anxiety Disorder). The context of the onset of the symptoms can be indicated by adding With Onset During Intoxication or With Onset During Withdrawal. Moreover, the specific type of anxiety symptoms can be indicated by adding one of the following specifiers: With Generalized Anxiety, With Panic Attacks, With Obsessive-Compulsive Symptoms, or With Phobic Symptoms.

Table 13–2. Substances that can induce clinically significant anxiety disorders

Substance intoxication
Alcohol
Amphetamines and related substances
Caffeine
Cannabis
Cocaine
Hallucinogens
Inhalants
Phencyclidine and related substances

Substance withdrawal
Alcohol
Cocaine
Sedatives, hypnotics, and anxiolytics

Medications
Analgesics
Anesthetics
Anticholinergics
Anticonvulsants
Antidepressant medications
Antihistamines
Antihypertensive and cardiovascular medications
Antiparkinsonian medications
Antipsychotic medications
Corticosteroids
Insulin
Lithium carbonate
Oral contraceptives
Sympathomimetics or other bronchodilators
Thyroid preparations

Toxins
Carbon dioxide
Carbon monoxide
Gasoline and paint
Heavy metals
Nerve gases
Organophosphate insecticides

Source. Adapted from American Psychiatric Association, p. 441.

DSM-IV diagnostic criteria for Substance-Induced Anxiety Disorder

A. Prominent anxiety, Panic Attacks, or obsessions or compulsions predominate in the clinical picture.

B. There is evidence from the history, physical examination, or laboratory findings of either (1) or (2):

(1) the symptoms in Criterion A developed during, or within 1 month of, Substance Intoxication or Withdrawal

(2) medication use is etiologically related to the disturbance

C. The disturbance is not better accounted for by an Anxiety Disorder that is not substance induced. Evidence that the symptoms are better accounted for by an Anxiety Disorder that is not substance induced might include the following: the symptoms precede the onset of the substance use (or medication use); the symptoms persist for a substantial period of time (e.g., about a month) after the cessation of acute withdrawal or severe intoxication or are substantially in excess of what would be expected given the type or amount of the substance used or the duration of use; or there is other evidence suggesting the existence of an independent non-substance-induced Anxiety Disorder (e.g., a history of recurrent non-substance-related episodes).

D. The disturbance does not occur exclusively during the course of a delirium.

(continued)

DSM-IV diagnostic criteria for Substance-Induced Anxiety Disorder *(continued)*

E. The disturbance causes clinically significant distress or impairment in social, occupational, or other important areas of functioning.

Note: This diagnosis should be made instead of a diagnosis of Substance Intoxication or Substance Withdrawal only when the anxiety symptoms are in excess of those usually associated with the intoxication or withdrawal syndrome and when the anxiety symptoms are sufficiently severe to warrant independent clinical attention.

Code [Specific Substance]–Induced Anxiety Disorder
(291.8 Alcohol; 292.89 Amphetamine (or Amphetamine-Like Substance); 292.89 Caffeine; 292.89 Cannabis; 292.89 Cocaine; 292.89 Hallucinogen; 292.89 Inhalant; 292.89 Phencyclidine (or Phencyclidine-Like Substance); 292.89 Sedative, Hypnotic, or Anxiolytic; 292.89 Other [or Unknown] Substance)

Specify if:
With Generalized Anxiety: if excessive anxiety or worry about a number of events or activities predominates in the clinical presentation
With Panic Attacks: if Panic Attacks predominate in the clinical presentation
With Obsessive-Compulsive Symptoms: if obsessions or compulsions predominate in the clinical presentation
With Phobic Symptoms: if phobic symptoms predominate in the clinical presentation

Specify if:
With Onset During Intoxication: if the criteria are met for Intoxication with the substance and the symptoms develop during the intoxication syndrome
With Onset During Withdrawal: if criteria are met for Withdrawal from the substance and the symptoms develop during, or shortly after, a withdrawal syndrome

DSM-IV text for 300.00 Anxiety Disorder Not Otherwise Specified

This category includes disorders with prominent anxiety or phobic avoidance that do not meet criteria for any specific Anxiety Disorder, Adjustment Disorder With Anxiety, or Adjustment Disorder With Mixed Anxiety and Depressed Mood. Examples include

1. Mixed anxiety-depressive disorder: clinically significant symptoms of anxiety and depression, but the criteria are not met for either a specific Mood Disorder or a specific Anxiety Disorder
2. Clinically significant social phobic symptoms that are related to the social impact of having a general medical condition or mental disorder (e.g., Parkinson's disease, dermatological conditions, Stuttering, Anorexia Nervosa, Body Dysmorphic Disorder)
3. Situations in which the clinician has concluded that an Anxiety Disorder is present but is unable to determine whether it is primary, due to a general medical condition, or substance induced

The Last Word

Although many of the disorders in this section may include Panic Attacks in their presentation, the diagnosis of Panic Disorder is distinguished by the fact that, at least at some point in the course, the Panic Attacks were unexpected and occurred out of the blue. Agoraphobia usually occurs as a consequence of a conditioned fear of having additional Panic Attacks. The Panic Attacks that occur in Specific Phobia, Social Phobia, Posttraumatic Stress Disorder, and Obsessive-Compulsive Disorder are triggered by exposure to a particular feared stimulus. Panic Attacks differ from Generalized Anxiety Disorder in the time course of the panic episode—a crescendo that usually lasts less than an hour.

CHAPTER 14

Somatoform Disorders

The "somatoform disorders" section in DSM-IV includes disorders in which the defining feature is a physical complaint or bodily concern that is not better accounted for by a general medical condition or other mental disorder. The Somatoform Disorders are divided into three groups based on the focus of the individual's concerns:

1. In Somatization Disorder, Undifferentiated Somatoform Disorder, Pain Disorder, and Conversion Disorder, the focus of concern is on the physical symptoms.
2. In Hypochondriasis, the focus is on the belief that one has a serious physical illness.
3. In Body Dysmorphic Disorder, the focus is on the belief that one has a defect in physical appearance.

Somatoform Disorders

300.81	Somatization Disorder
300.81	Undifferentiated Somatoform Disorder
300.11	Conversion Disorder
307.xx	Pain Disorder
307.80	Associated With Psychological Factors
307.89	Associated With Both Psychological Factors and a General Medical Condition

(continued)

300.7	Hypochondriasis
300.7	Body Dysmorphic Disorder
300.81	Somatoform Disorder Not Otherwise Specified

Because the problems discussed in this section are on the boundary between general medical conditions and mental disorders, they have received insufficient attention from both fields. Individuals presenting with these problems tend to be shuttled back and forth between medical and psychiatric settings. This may lead to misdiagnosis on both sides (sometimes with potentially tragic consequences); for example, an individual with Somatization Disorder may have several unnecessary surgical procedures, and a patient with multiple sclerosis may be diagnosed as having Conversion Disorder. Therefore, clinicians must become increasingly alert to the fact that many individuals present to primary care and psychiatric settings with physical symptoms that cannot be explained by the accompanying physical findings. There are four ways of understanding such unexplained physical symptoms:

1. The subjective symptoms can be accounted for by an underlying general medical condition that has not yet manifested itself with clearly discernible objective findings (e.g., multiple sclerosis).
2. The physical symptoms are best accounted for by a DSM-IV disorder outside the "Somatoform Disorders" section (e.g., Panic Disorder, Major Depressive Disorder, Cocaine Withdrawal).
3. The physical symptoms are intentionally produced by the individual (i.e., Factitious Disorder, Malingering).
4. The physical symptoms are accounted for by a Somatoform Disorder (e.g., Conversion Disorder).

Somatoform Disorders Versus General Medical Conditions

In determining whether an unexplained physical symptom is attributable to a Somatoform Disorder, the presence of a general medical condition must first be considered and ruled out. The evaluation must include a consideration of the patient's past history of general medical conditions, review of systems, mental status examination, and a careful review of the development of the patient's symptoms in the context of his or her current life situation. Clearly, contact with the patient's general medical provider is essential, as is a review of the patient's medical records. A physical examination should be performed either by the examining psychiatrist or by the patient's general medical physician.

Ultimately, the determination of whether a general medical condition *fully* accounts for the patient's condition is an inherently imperfect judgment. The clinician must keep an open mind and continue to observe and assess the patient over time. Even if the clinician determines that the general medical condition accounts for the patient's symptoms, psychological factors could play a major role in the initiation and course of the illness and in the patient's response to treatment. The category of Psychological Factors Affecting Medical Condition is used to characterize these latter situations.

Somatoform Disorders Versus Other Mental Disorders

Clinicians often forget that individuals with a variety of other psychiatric disorders may, and very often do, present with physical complaints. In fact, the appropriate DSM-IV diagnosis is often missed either because the individual is so focused on the physical symptoms or because the clinician overlooks the less obvious psychiatric symptoms that make up the full syndrome. Many cases of Major Depressive, Panic, Generalized Anxiety, and Substance Use Disorders in which the patient presents with physical symptoms are missed in this way—especially in primary care settings but also in mental health care settings. When an individual presents with atypical or unexplained physical symptoms, the clinician must be particularly thorough in reviewing for the presence of pertinent DSM-IV mental disorders. For example, if an individual presents with unexplained shortness of breath, dizziness, and palpitations, it is crucial to ask whether the symptoms occur during discrete episodes of panic.

Somatoform Disorders Versus Factitious Disorder and Malingering

The differential diagnosis between Somatoform Disorders versus Factitious Disorder and Malingering can be difficult because of the presentation of similar patterns of unconfirmed symptoms and similar motivations (i.e., to seek care and/or attention in the sick role). The main difference is in the intentionality of the behavior. For example, an individual presents in the emergency room with a lower limb paralysis and stocking anesthesia that follow no known anatomical distribution. If this were Factitious Disorder or Malingering, the individual would be conscious of feigning the symptomatology (and, by the way, would probably feign a more convincing clinical picture based on reading medical textbooks). The diagnosis is more appropriately Conversion Disorder when the individual truly believes that the neurological symptoms are present and thinks that he or she cannot move the leg. This distinction is often difficult to make in practice because of problems in evaluating these motivations and because there may be a continuum between intentional feigning and unconscious symptom production.

Cultural factors must often be considered when evaluating individuals for a Somatoform Disorder. Culture influences the type, frequency, and mode of expression of the somatic symptoms that accompany mental disorders and psychosocial stress. It must be remembered that mood, anxiety, and somatic symptoms very frequently coexist. In fact, somatic symptoms are the most common presentation of major Mood and Anxiety Disorders in many cultures and in primary care settings. The narrow focus on the somatic symptoms may contribute to the underdetection of Anxiety and Mood Disorders.

The diagnosis of Somatoform Disorders should be made with caution in cultural settings where 1) the only available avenue for medical or psychiatric care or attention is the presentation of somatic symptoms; 2) somatic symptoms are part of common cultural idioms of distress or reflect other prevalent cultural concerns; 3) parasitic or infectious diseases, poor nutrition, and recurrent medical conditions with multiple systemic effects are endemic; or 4) dissociative experiences, including loss of consciousness or seizure-like behavior, are expected aspects of religious or healing rituals.

300.81 Somatization Disorder

The DSM-IV definition of Somatization Disorder sets a high threshold for making this diagnosis. It requires the presence of numerous symptoms occurring over an extended course. Patients whose presentations are subthreshold to the full symptom picture required by this diagnosis may nonetheless meet the criteria for one of the other Somatoform Disorders (e.g., Undifferentiated Somatoform Disorder, Conversion Disorder, Pain Disorder).

Although many DSM-IV disorders from outside the "Somatoform Disorders" section are associated with somatic symptoms, they are rarely confused with the characteristic picture of Somatization Disorder. There are, however, two difficult differentials that must be noted: Generalized Anxiety Disorder and the chronic forms of Mood Disorder (i.e., Dysthymic Disorder, chronic Major Depressive Disorder). These can present with multiple somatic complaints, early onset, and a persistent course. Further confusing the picture, patients with Somatization Disorder often have symptoms of depression and anxiety, and multiple diagnoses may sometimes be warranted, including both Somatization Disorder and the other mental disorder.

Usualy indivrduuls who have difficulty expressing feelings.

DSM-IV diagnostic criteria for 300.81 Somatization Disorder

A. A history of many physical complaints beginning before age 30 years that occur over a period of several years and result in treatment being sought or significant impairment in social, occupational, or other important areas of functioning.

B. Each of the following criteria must have been met, with individual symptoms occurring at any time during the course of the disturbance:

(1) *four pain symptoms:* a history of pain related to at least four different sites or functions (e.g., head, abdomen, back, joints, extremities, chest, rectum, during menstruation, during sexual intercourse, or during urination)

(2) *two gastrointestinal symptoms:* a history of at least two gastrointestinal symptoms other than pain (e.g., nausea, bloating, vomiting other than during pregnancy, diarrhea, or intolerance of several different foods)

(3) *one sexual symptom:* a history of at least one sexual or reproductive symptom other than pain (e.g., sexual indifference, erectile or ejaculatory dysfunction, irregular menses, excessive menstrual bleeding, vomiting throughout pregnancy)

(continued)

DSM-IV diagnostic criteria for 300.81 Somatization Disorder *(continued)*

(4) *one pseudoneurological symptom:* a history of at least one symptom or deficit suggesting a neurological condition not limited to pain (conversion symptoms such as impaired coordination or balance, paralysis or localized weakness, difficulty swallowing or lump in throat, aphonia, urinary retention, hallucinations, loss of touch or pain sensation, double vision, blindness, deafness, seizures; dissociative symptoms such as amnesia; or loss of consciousness other than fainting)

C. Either (1) or (2):

(1) after appropriate investigation, each of the symptoms in Criterion B cannot be fully explained by a known general medical condition or the direct effects of a substance (e.g., a drug of abuse, a medication)

(2) when there is a related general medical condition, the physical complaints or resulting social or occupational impairment are in excess of what would be expected from the history, physical examination, or laboratory findings

D. The symptoms are not intentionally produced or feigned (as in Factitious Disorder or Malingering).

Criterion A. The course of this disorder in many ways resembles that of a Personality Disorder, with its early onset, chronicity, and marked impairment. Somatization Disorder is not meant to describe mild, brief, or late-onset presentations of unexplained physical symptoms. The diagnosis of Somatization Disorder is justified only when the physical complaints result in seeking treatment or cause clinically significant impairment or distress.

Criterion B. The DSM-III-R criteria set for Somatization Disorder was impossibly complex to remember and to use in clinical practice. It included 35 separate symptoms of which 13 had to be present to make the diagnosis. The DSM-IV criteria set for Somatization Disorder is a much simplified version that was generated from the literature review and data reanalysis. The 35 DSM-III-R symptoms were regrouped into four thematic areas (i.e., pain, gastrointestinal, sexual, and pseudoneurological symptoms) to facilitate their being remembered and used in practice. This criteria set was tested in a multisite field trial that demonstrated good reliability and that the criteria set identified the same group of patients as did the DSM-III and DSM-III-R criteria sets and the original definition of Briquet's syndrome.

Criterion C. The differential diagnosis between Somatization Disorder and general medical conditions is a particularly difficult one that often leads to mistakes in both directions. Before a correct diagnosis of Somatization Disorder is made, many patients endure a barrage of unnecessary and potentially dangerous medical or surgical procedures in the effort to identify and treat their physical complaints. In contrast, once Somatization Disorder is identified, legitimate physical complaints may be inappropriately dismissed on the assumption that the patient is crying wolf.

It must be recognized that patients with Somatization Disorder do also get medical illnesses and that patients with general medical conditions can also qualify for the diagnosis of Somatization Disorder if their complaints are unrelated to, or far in excess of, their condition. Moreover, some general medical conditions can mimic Somatization Disorder by affecting multiple systems before objective findings can be established. Multiple sclerosis, porphyria, systemic lupus erythematosus, and hyperparathyroidism are particularly likely to have an atypical presentation and course with numerous medical symptoms and an easily missed etiology. Be on the alert for them. In diagnosing Somatization Disorder, the art is in knowing how extensive a physical workup to do at various points along the way.

300.81 Undifferentiated Somatoform Disorder

The diagnosis of Undifferentiated Somatoform Disorder was introduced into DSM-III-R based on the concern that the high symptom count then required for Somatization Disorder would result in inadequate coverage for many individuals who present with clinically significant somatoform complaints. The decision to create this category was unusual for DSM-III-R, which usually depended on the Not Otherwise Specified category for cases that did not meet criteria for more narrowly defined disorders. Because of this inconsistency and the disorder's lack of definitional specificity (other than 6-month duration), Undifferentiated Somatoform Disorder was considered a candidate for possible deletion from DSM-IV. It was retained only because of its familiarity and possible utility in primary care settings.

DSM-IV diagnostic criteria for 300.81 Undifferentiated Somatoform Disorder

A. One or more physical complaints (e.g., fatigue, loss of appetite, gastrointestinal or urinary complaints).

B. Either (1) or (2):
   (1) after appropriate investigation, the symptoms cannot be fully explained by a known general medical condition or the direct effects of a substance (e.g., a drug of abuse, a medication)
   (2) when there is a related general medical condition, the physical complaints or resulting social or occupational impairment is in excess of what would be expected from the history, physical examination, or laboratory findings

C. The symptoms cause clinically significant distress or impairment in social, occupational, or other important areas of functioning.

D. The duration of the disturbance is at least 6 months.

E. The disturbance is not better accounted for by another mental disorder (e.g., another Somatoform Disorder, Sexual Dysfunction, Mood Disorder, Anxiety Disorder, Sleep Disorder, or Psychotic Disorder).

F. The symptom is not intentionally produced or feigned (as in Factitious Disorder or Malingering).

Criterion A. There was some controversy about how to construct this criterion. As it now stands, Criterion A defines a rather nonspecific disorder characterized by a single physical complaint that cannot be accounted for by a general medical condition. Concerns that this threshold was set too low led to suggestions that more than one symptom be required or that there be symptoms from more than one organ system. Ultimately, because of a paucity of data about this condition, the admittedly weak DSM-III-R definition was retained in DSM-IV.

It is of interest that this DSM-IV category might pertain to individuals who present with a chief complaint of severe fatigue lasting at least 6 months. Two popular terms (not included in DSM-IV) have been used to describe similar presentations: neurasthenia and chronic fatigue syndrome. These were not included as DSM-IV diagnoses because they describe nonspecific and heterogeneous presentations and because fatigue occurs in a wide variety of medical conditions and mental disorders. Before labeling chronic fatigue as Undifferentiated Somatoform Disorder, a careful general medical and psychiatric evaluation must be performed to avoid missing more specific medical or psychiatric diagnoses.

Criterion B. See discussion for Criterion C in Somatization Disorder (which is identical).

Criteria C and D. These criteria provide minimum severity and duration thresholds to distinguish this disorder from the mild or transient physical complaints that commonly occur as part of everyday life and constitute a substantial part of primary care practice.

Criterion E. Somatic symptoms are also commonly encountered as part of the presentation of a number of other mental disorders. One potential drawback of including the diagnosis of Undifferentiated Somatoform Disorder in DSM-IV is that it might lead to an incomplete evaluation of the presence of another more specific and useful diagnosis that might account for the somatic symptom. This criterion is included to alert clinicians to consider these other potential diagnoses.

300.11 Conversion Disorder

The concept of Conversion Disorder was introduced by Freud as an explanation for what was then called *hysteria* (i.e., somatic presentations that he suggested were due to unconscious psychological conflicts). Freud's theory was that the conversion symptom served to reduce anxiety and bind mental energy by resolving an internal conflict between forbidden wishes and superego injunctions (e.g., paralysis of the arm to avoid striking one's father). In Freud's model, the symptom was a symbolic compromise formation that would express both the wish and the punishment and would keep the conflict out of consciousness (primary gain). The term *conversion* reflected this channeling of psychological energy into physical manifestations. Freud also noted that the conversion symptom might afford secondary gain (i.e., obtaining external benefits or avoiding responsibilities).

Because the DSM system is designed for general use (i.e., not just by psychodynamically oriented clinicians), the definition of Conversion Disorder does not require an evaluation of unconscious motivations. Instead, it substitutes a more general requirement that psychological factors be associated with the onset or exacerbation of the symptoms.

There was a debate during the DSM-IV deliberations concerning the best placement for this disorder. Some argued that Conversion Disorder should be included in the "Dissociative Disorders" section because 1) it is included among the Dissociative Disorders in the *International Statistical Classification of Diseases and Related Health Problems,* 10th Revision (ICD-10), which has dropped the term *conversion* in favor of Dissociative Sensory Loss, Dissociative Motor Loss, and Dissociative Seizures; and 2) the disorder conforms to the concept of dissociation (i.e., a breakdown in the usually integrated functions of consciousness, memory, perception of self or the environment, or sensory/motor behavior).

Despite these arguments, DSM-IV continues to include Conversion Disorder among the Somatoform Disorders primarily because this organization is most useful for the differential diagnosis of somatic symptoms. People with Conversion Disorder most often present in emergency room or primary care settings.

DSM-IV diagnostic criteria for 300.11 Conversion Disorder

A. One or more symptoms or deficits affecting voluntary motor or sensory function that suggest a neurological or other general medical condition.

B. Psychological factors are judged to be associated with the symptom or deficit because the initiation or exacerbation of the symptom or deficit is preceded by conflicts or other stressors.

C. The symptom or deficit is not intentionally produced or feigned (as in Factitious Disorder or Malingering).

D. The symptom or deficit cannot, after appropriate investigation, be fully explained by a general medical condition, or by the direct effects of a substance, or as a culturally sanctioned behavior or experience.

E. The symptom or deficit causes clinically significant distress or impairment in social, occupational, or other important areas of functioning or warrants medical evaluation.

F. The symptom or deficit is not limited to pain or sexual dysfunction, does not occur exclusively during the course of Somatization Disorder, and is not better accounted for by another mental disorder.

Specify type of symptom or deficit:

With Motor Symptom or Deficit
With Sensory Symptom or Deficit
With Seizures or Convulsions
With Mixed Presentation

Criterion A. A major issue in defining Conversion Disorder in DSM-IV was whether to return to the narrow definition that has historically focused exclusively on neurological symptoms or, as in DSM-III-R, to have a widened definition that allows any alteration in physical functioning suggestive of a general medical condition to be included within this diagnosis. As with DSM-II, DSM-IV uses a precise definition of Conversion Disorder that is limited to neurological symptoms involving the voluntary motor or special sensory functions. Therefore, Conversion Disorder now excludes other neurologically related symptoms (e.g., fainting spells included in Dissociative Disorder Not Otherwise Specified and Somatoform Disorder Not Otherwise Specified), symptoms mediated by the autonomic nervous system (e.g., vomiting, which is included in Undifferentiated Somatoform Disorder), and nonneurological symptoms (e.g., pseudocyesis, which is included in Somatoform Disorder Not Otherwise Specified).

Criterion B. Whereas a psychological pathogenesis plays an important role in the onset or exacerbation of many DSM-IV disorders, Conversion Disorder is one of the few in which psychological factors are included as a required criterion. This requirement serves the important function of narrowing the definition of the disorder so that it will not include all of the many patients who present with unexplained neurological symptoms. Conversion Disorder requires both that the symptoms not be explainable in physical terms and that there be a presumptive psychological explanation. It must be admitted that this evaluation often is problematic because psychological causality is inherently difficult to establish. Moreover, psychological factors are fairly ubiquitous aspects of human experience and not particularly specific to Conversion Disorder. For example, a patient with a variety of psychological conflicts can still have multiple sclerosis.

In clinical practice, there are many ways of attempting to establish psychological causality. Criterion B focuses on the importance of the temporal relationship between the psychological factors and the onset of the symptoms. For example, paralysis would be much more convincingly related to an individual's unacceptable aggressive feelings if it followed shortly after a serious fight with his or her father. However, because the presence of possible stressors is so common, it is hard to know with any degree of certainty after the fact whether a given stressor played a causal role or whether it was an incidental or a secondary finding. Other interpretative ways to attempt to establish causality could not be included in the criteria set because they require a higher level of inference. For example, the clinician may attempt to understand the role of the individual's past fights with his or her father, his or her history of aggressive behavior, his or her defenses against aggression, whether other family members have conversion symptoms, and so forth. Although such information may be helpful in the evaluation of Criterion B, it must be admitted that establishing the causal role of psychological factors requires an inherently difficult, and probably not very reliable, judgment.

Criterion C. This criterion reminds the clinician that in Conversion Disorder, the symptoms are not intentionally produced by the individual, as would be the case in Factitious Disorder or Malingering. This differential diagnosis is very difficult because there is something of a continuum between a conscious production of symptoms (as in Factitious Disorder and Malingering) and the unconscious processes producing the symptoms that characterize Conversion Disorder.

Criterion D. Many clinicians have had the unhappy experience of following a patient with the diagnosis of Conversion Disorder only to discover later in the course that there was an underlying brain tumor or a diagnosis of multiple sclerosis. Fortunately, missed diagnoses are becoming less common because of the wider availability of more powerful diagnostic tools. Nonetheless, one should not jump to a diagnosis of Conversion Disorder without careful and repeated evaluations of possible general medical etiologies.

The differential diagnosis with neurological conditions is sometimes made doubly difficult by the fact that individuals with certain neurological disorders (e.g., epilepsy) may be precisely the ones who are also likely to have conversion symptoms (e.g., pseudoseizures) in addition to their neurological symptoms (e.g., electroencephalogram-documented seizures). This criterion notes that after appropriate investigation, the symptoms are not fully explained by a medical diagnosis. The term *fully* allows the clinician the freedom to make a diagnosis of both Conversion Disorder and a neurological condition when both are present.

Typically, the neurological symptoms occur in a nonphysiological pattern that represents the individual's uninformed understanding (e.g., hand-glove distributions of anesthesia that do not follow the distribution of nerves in the arms). The pattern and nature of the symptoms can be inconsistent from one examination to another and may change depending on the environmental context (e.g., a "paralysis" may disappear when the individual is distracted or concentrating on other activities). It should not be forgotten, however, that some patients with Conversion Disorder (e.g., doctors and nurses) do know their anatomy and may present with a more convincing clinical picture.

Traditionally, the observation of *la belle indifference* and *secondary gain* were thought to be helpful in the differential diagnosis between Conversion Disorder and a neurological condition. Unfortunately, neither of these is particularly specific or helpful. La belle indifference (i.e., inappropriate nonchalance in the face of what would appear to be a disabling condition) and secondary gain (i.e., concrete benefits obtained as a result of having the symptom) both can occur frequently in the presentation of severe general medical illness and are not at all specific to Conversion Disorder. Similarly, temporary improvement or removal of the symptom by suggestion or hypnosis is also nonspecific and may occur with neurological conditions.

Criterion E. Conversion symptoms may, in some situations, be considered within the normal range and not warrant a diagnosis of Conversion Disorder (e.g., a temporarily impaired coordination or balance after the death of a loved one). This criterion indicates that the deficits must be severe enough to require clinical attention. In some cultural settings, even fairly severe but transient neurological deficits that occur in response to serious stressors and are part of a fully culturally sanctioned response pattern would not warrant a Conversion Disorder diagnosis.

Criterion F. It is redundant and therefore unnecessary to diagnose Conversion Disorder when criteria are met for Somatization Disorder. This is because conversion symptoms, which are nested within the definition of Somatization Disorder, represent one manifestation of that multisymptom disorder. Likewise, although certain pain and sexual symptoms do involve neurological presentations (e.g., impotence, sciatica), Criterion F establishes that the more specific Pain Disorder or Sexual Dysfunction should be diagnosed instead of Conversion Disorder. Both Conversion Disorder and Hypochondriasis are characterized by unexplained physical symptoms but differ in that conversion symptoms are restricted to the nervous system and individuals with Hypochondriasis have anything but la belle indifference.

Pain Disorder

The diagnosis and management of pain syndromes have become an increasingly important focus of attention among mental health practitioners. In the past, their work was made more difficult by the serious problems in the way in which these disorders were defined and named in DSM-III and DSM-III-R. DSM-III introduced the category Psychogenic Pain Disorder and defined it to require the presence of etiological psychological factors. DSM-III-R changed the name of this disorder to Somatoform Pain Disorder. It also broadened the construct by eliminating the requirement for etiological psychological factors and substituted the criterion that the pain be grossly in excess of what would be expected from the physical findings. Although this change was an improvement over the excessively stringent DSM-III definition, three serious problems remained:

1. Because pain is inherently a subjective experience, it is impossible to judge whether the level of pain is in fact in excess of what would be expected given the underlying general medical condition.
2. The underlying general medical condition may not have yet reached the threshold of clinical detection.
3. Even if the pain is totally commensurate with the general medical condition (and therefore does not meet the DSM-III-R or ICD-10 definitions for a Pain Disorder), it may still respond to treatment with either psychotropic drugs or psychological techniques.

Several changes were made in DSM-IV to deal with these problems. The name has been changed (from Somatoform Pain Disorder to Pain Disorder), and the definition has been broadened to cover circumstances in which a general medical condition contributes to the etiology of the pain. DSM-IV no longer excludes cases in which the pain is not in excess of what would be expected given the presence of an associated general medical condition, as long as psychological factors are judged to have an important role in the onset, maintenance, or exacerbation of the pain.

DSM-IV, therefore, includes two types of Pain Disorder: Pain Disorder Associated With Psychological Factors and Pain Disorder Associated With Both Psychological Factors and a General Medical Condition. The associated general medical condition (or anatomical site of the pain, if no specific underlying general medical condition has yet been established) is coded on Axis III. A third variety of pain presentation, Pain Disorder Associated With a General Medical Condition, does not require the presence of psychological factors at all. It is not considered to be a mental disorder and in fact is coded on Axis III. This condition is listed alongside the other types of Pain Disorder in DSM-IV only for completeness of differential diagnosis and because individuals with this condition may benefit from treatments delivered by mental health professionals. For Pain Disorder Associated With a General Medical Condition, the diagnostic code for the pain is selected based on the underlying general medical condition (e.g., 714.0 Arthritis, Rheumatoid) or the anatomical location of the pain if the etiology is unknown (e.g., 719.4 Joint Pain).

DSM-IV diagnostic criteria for Pain Disorder

A. Pain in one or more anatomical sites is the predominant focus of the clinical presentation and is of sufficient severity to warrant clinical attention.

B. The pain causes clinically significant distress or impairment in social, occupational, or other important areas of functioning.

C. Psychological factors are judged to have an important role in the onset, severity, exacerbation, or maintenance of the pain.

D. The symptom or deficit is not intentionally produced or feigned (as in Factitious Disorder or Malingering).

E. The pain is not better accounted for by a Mood, Anxiety, or Psychotic Disorder and does not meet criteria for Dyspareunia.

Code as follows:

307.80 Pain Disorder Associated With Psychological Factors: psychological factors are judged to have the major role in the onset, severity, exacerbation, or maintenance of the pain. (If a general medical condition is present, it does not have a major role in the onset, severity, exacerbation, or maintenance of the pain.) This type of Pain Disorder is not diagnosed if criteria are also met for Somatization Disorder.

Specify if:

Acute: duration of less than 6 months
Chronic: duration of 6 months or longer

307.89 Pain Disorder Associated With Both Psychological Factors and a General Medical Condition: both psychological factors and a general medical condition are judged to have important roles in the onset, severity, exacerbation, or maintenance of the pain. The associated general medical condition or anatomical site of the pain (see below) is coded on Axis III.

Specify if:

Acute: duration of less than 6 months
Chronic: duration of 6 months or longer

Note: The following is not considered to be a mental disorder and is included here to facilitate differential diagnosis.

Pain Disorder Associated With a General Medical Condition: a general medical condition has a major role in the onset, severity, exacerbation, or maintenance of the pain. (If psychological factors are present, they are not judged to have a major role in the onset, severity, exacerbation, or maintenance of the pain.) The diagnostic code for the pain is selected based on the associated general medical condition if one has been established or on the anatomical location of the pain if the underlying general medical condition is not yet clearly established—for example, low back (724.2), sciatic (724.3), pelvic (625.9), headache (784.0), facial (784.0), chest (786.50), joint (719.4), bone (733.90), abdominal (789.0), breast (611.71), renal (788.0), ear (388.70), eye (379.91), throat (784.1), tooth (525.9), and urinary (788.0).

Criteria A and B. Pain is a ubiquitous phenomenon in human life and disease but does not usually reach a sufficient level of severity or duration to warrant a separate diagnosis of Pain Disorder. This category should be used only when the pain is a major focus of clinical attention and management (and not when, as is so often the case, the pain is an important but not central focus of clinical diagnosis and care).

Criterion C. At any given moment, many patients in medical and surgical settings may be experiencing pain, and many are receiving medication for it. The diagnosis of Pain Disorder should be reserved only for those patients for whom psychological factors play an important role in the pathogenesis of the pain.

Criterion D. Very often, individuals with Factitious Disorder or Malingering present with pain symptoms. The differential diagnosis between Pain Disorder and Factitious Disorder or Malingering follows the principles described above in the "Somatoform Disorders Versus Factitious Disorder and Malingering" section but may be especially difficult because it is often necessary to rely entirely on the patient's reporting of symptoms.

Criterion E. Because pain is a common associated feature of other DSM-IV disorders (e.g., Major Depressive Disorder), Pain Disorder is not given as a separate diagnosis unless it is unusually severe, persistent, and becomes a main focus of clinical attention. Very often, individuals with pain syndromes develop ideas that might be construed as hypochondriacal, for example, that a serious disease is responsible for the pain and has been missed despite negative testing and reassurances. To avoid meaningless comorbidity in such cases, a diagnosis of Pain Disorder usually takes priority and the additional diagnosis of Hypochondriasis is generally not necessary. On the other hand, the presence of Dyspareunia takes precedence over the diagnosis of Pain Disorder.

Subtypes. The two subtypes of Pain Disorder are included to allow the clinician to indicate the relative contribution of physical and psychological factors to the etiology of the Pain Disorder. Pain Disorder Associated With Psychological Factors describes those situations in which either there are no medical findings or no concurrent medical condition plays a major role in its onset, severity, exacerbation, or maintenance. Pain Disorder Associated With Both Psychological Factors and a General Medical Condition is for those many cases encountered in mental health practice in which some combination of both physical and psychological factors are present and contribute to the etiology of the pain.

It is redundant and therefore unnecessary to diagnose Pain Disorder Associated With Psychological Factors if criteria are met for Somatization Disorder. This is because pain symptoms with a psychological etiology are nested within the definition of Somatization Disorder and represent a special case of that multisymptom disorder.

300.7 Hypochondriasis

As with patients who have other Somatoform Disorders, people with hypochondriasis all too often have real but as yet undetected general medical conditions or mental disorders (e.g., Panic Disorder). It is important that pertinent findings from physical and mental status examinations and laboratory tests be thoroughly evaluated to rule out an underlying medical etiology or another mental disorder. However, it also must be noted that such individuals receive excessive, and sometimes dangerous, medical evaluations and treatment and that some balance must be found between dismissing them as "crocks" and undertaking excessive diagnostic testing and interventions.

DSM-IV diagnostic criteria for 300.7 Hypochondriasis

A. Preoccupation with fears of having, or the idea that one has, a serious disease based on the person's misinterpretation of bodily symptoms.

B. The preoccupation persists despite appropriate medical evaluation and reassurance.

C. The belief in Criterion A is not of delusional intensity (as in Delusional Disorder, Somatic Type) and is not restricted to a circumscribed concern about appearance (as in Body Dysmorphic Disorder).

D. The preoccupation causes clinically significant distress or impairment in social, occupational, or other important areas of functioning.

E. The duration of the disturbance is at least 6 months.

F. The preoccupation is not better accounted for by Generalized Anxiety Disorder, Obsessive-Compulsive Disorder, Panic Disorder, a Major Depressive Episode, Separation Anxiety, or another Somatoform Disorder.

Specify if:

With Poor Insight: if, for most of the time during the current episode, the person does not recognize that the concern about having a serious illness is excessive or unreasonable

CRITERION A. Criterion A has two parts: 1) that the patient is preoccupied with having a serious disease and 2) that this preoccupation arises from misinterpretation of actual physical signs and symptoms. There was considerable discussion during the preparation of DSM-IV about eliminating the second part of this criterion. It was argued that some individuals do develop the belief that they have a serious disease in the absence of having any physical symptoms (e.g., an individual who becomes convinced that he or she is positive for the human immunodeficiency virus because of presumed exposure to the virus rather than development of symptoms). Eventually, it was decided to maintain a narrow definition of Hypochondriasis that requires some physical symptoms so that individuals without physical symptoms are diagnosed with Somatoform Disorder Not Otherwise Specified (admittedly, not a very satisfying solution).

Another fine distinction, but one worth noting, is between the fear of already having a disease, which is the defining feature of Hypochondriasis, and the fear of getting a disease, which is a feature of Specific Phobia and Obsessive-Compulsive

Disorder (when the patient has contamination fears). Individuals with Hypochondriasis embark on a constant quest of doctor visits to elicit confirmation of their worst fears. In contrast, individuals with illness phobias or Obsessive-Compulsive Disorder exhibit excessive and maladaptive avoidance behaviors designed to avoid getting the feared disease.

CRITERIA B, D, AND E. Concerns about physical health and fears of having disease are common (and sometimes adaptive) behaviors that should not be routinely considered evidence of a mental disorder. It is only when the concerns become persisting preoccupations that endure despite appropriate medical reassurance that this diagnosis should be considered.

CRITERION C. One of the most difficult differentials is between the more serious and impairing forms of Hypochondriasis and certain Psychotic Disorders with somatic delusions. Because Schizophrenia and Mood Disorder have other characteristic symptoms, it is usually relatively easy to distinguish these from Hypochondriasis. In contrast, the boundary between severe Hypochondriasis and Delusional Disorder, Somatic Type, rests solely on the judgment of whether the conviction about having a disease has reached delusional proportions.

Unfortunately, there is no clear boundary between a compelling but nondelusional idea that one has a medical condition (referred to as an overvalued idea) and the unshakable conviction of disease that characterizes a somatic delusion. Moreover, during the course of the disorder, the individual's conviction may vary in its intensity and susceptibility to challenge. At certain times, the patient may accept reassurances and evidence that his or her concerns are excessive; at other times, he or she may be completely fixed on the notion that a serious disease is present despite compelling evidence to the contrary. As in many of the tough boundary calls, the clinician has to rely on a judgment about the severity, duration, degree of conviction, and presence of other characteristic symptoms (e.g., accompanying paranoid delusions) in choosing between the diagnoses of Hypochondriasis and Delusional Disorder, Somatic Type. The specifier With Poor Insight is provided to describe individuals with Hypochondriasis who have overvalued hypochondriacal ideas but who are not considered to have somatic delusions.

CRITERION F. Concern about having a serious illness characterizes a number of other disorders. If such concerns are considered associated features of any one of these disorders, no separate diagnosis of Hypochondriasis is necessary. There can be a great deal of overlap between other Somatoform Disorders (e.g., Somatization Disorder) and Hypochondriasis. All are characterized by unexplained physical symptoms and may have a similar course. The difference is based on the patient's focus of concern. For example, in the most typical case of Somatization Disorder, the patient is preoccupied with the discomfort resulting from physical complaints and does not have a clearly defined conception of what is causing the problem. In the most typical case of Hypochondriasis, the physical complaints are overshadowed by a persistent fear or idea that a serious illness is responsible. In practice, of course, the presentation of symptoms and concerns about their implications often overlap. In such cases, the diagnosis of Somatization Disorder would take priority over the diagnosis of Hypochondriasis. (Note: In DSM-III-R, both diagnoses would have been given, but that was changed in DSM-IV to avoid artificial comorbidity.)

300.7 Body Dysmorphic Disorder

Although Body Dysmorphic Disorder has a long clinical tradition, it did not enter the official diagnostic nomenclature until DSM-III-R. Since then, the availability of a criteria set has stimulated research efforts suggesting that the condition may be underdiagnosed, particularly in dermatological and plastic surgery settings. Body Dysmorphic Disorder is included in the "Somatoform Disorders" section because, like the other Somatoform Disorders, it is most frequently encountered in general or specialty medical clinics. However, there may be closer links (in phenomenology and treatment response) to Social Phobia and Obsessive-Compulsive Disorder.

Perhaps the biggest controversy in relation to this disorder is how to determine when a preoccupation with an imagined physical deformity should be considered delusional. *Delusion* is defined in the DSM-IV glossary as "a false belief based on incorrect inference about external reality that is firmly sustained despite what almost everyone else believes and despite what constitutes incontrovertible and obvious proof or evidence to the contrary. . . . Delusional conviction occurs on a continuum and can sometimes be inferred from an individual's behavior. It is often difficult to distinguish between a delusion and an overvalued idea (in which case the individual has an unreasonable belief or idea but does not hold it as firmly as is the case with a delusion)."

This definition is especially difficult to apply to concerns about physical appearance because the external reality in this instance is particularly personal and subjective and lacks consensus standards. In this regard, it is of considerable interest that some clinical researchers report remarkably high rates of delusional beliefs among individuals with Body Dysmorphic Disorder. These researchers have a low threshold for diagnosing psychosis and would include those patients who hold firmly to their evaluation of physical defects despite reassurance that the concerns are greatly exaggerated. We would recommend a much higher threshold for considering preoccupations about physical appearance as evidence of somatic delusions and would require that the beliefs be particularly unusual or that the consequent behavior be self-destructive or bizarre (e.g., self-mutilation to correct the defect).

DSM-IV diagnostic criteria for 300.7 Body Dysmorphic Disorder

A. Preoccupation with an imagined defect in appearance. If a slight physical anomaly is present, the person's concern is markedly excessive.

B. The preoccupation causes clinically significant distress or impairment in social, occupational, or other important areas of functioning.

C. The preoccupation is not better accounted for by another mental disorder (e.g., dissatisfaction with body shape and size in Anorexia Nervosa).

Criterion A. The most common concerns about physical appearance are centered on the shape, size, or some other aspect of the face or head (e.g., hair thinning, acne, wrinkles, scars, vascular markings, paleness or redness of the complexion, swelling, facial asymmetry or disproportion, excessive facial hair). However, any other part of the body may be the focus of attention and dissatisfaction (e.g., the genitals, breasts, buttocks, abdomen, arms, hands, feet, legs, hips, shoulders, spine, larger body regions, overall body size).

CRITERION B. The boundary between this disorder and "normal" concerns or dissatisfactions about appearance can be difficult to draw. The diagnosis should be reserved for those who become preoccupied by their supposed deformity and are tormented by it. In many cases, these individuals' worries about appearance become a dominant focus of their life. They may spend hours a day thinking about the "defect" and be unable to concentrate on other activities. They may frequently check their appearance using mirrors (or any other reflective surface) or try completely to avoid seeing their reflection. They may fear or believe that other people are paying special attention to the supposed defect and perhaps laughing about it, and they may go to great lengths to hide the defect (e.g., spending hours applying makeup, wearing elaborate wigs, hiding behind sunglasses or floppy hats).

The intense feelings of self-consciousness often lead to avoidance of work or public situations. In extreme cases, persons with Body Dysmorphic Disorder may become completely housebound. They may insistently seek surgical correction or other forms of medical treatment for the imagined defect. Usually, they are disappointed about the outcome and sometimes become litigious.

CRITERION C. Several other mental disorders include concerns about appearance as associated features. For example, concerns about body shape are ubiquitous in Eating Disorders, and discomfort with one's sexual characteristics is part of the definition of Gender Identity Disorder. Body Dysmorphic Disorder should be diagnosed only when the concerns about appearance are not accounted for by the other condition (e.g., an excessive preoccupation with having a big nose in an individual with Anorexia Nervosa may warrant an additional diagnosis).

DSM-IV text for 300.89 Somatoform Disorder Not Otherwise Specified

This category includes disorders with somatoform symptoms that do not meet the criteria for any specific Somatoform Disorder. Examples include

1. Pseudocyesis: a false belief of being pregnant that is associated with objective signs of pregnancy, which may include abdominal enlargement (although the umbilicus does not become everted), reduced menstrual flow, amenorrhea, subjective sensation of fetal movement, nausea, breast engorgement and secretions, and labor pains at the expected date of delivery. Endocrine changes may be present, but the syndrome cannot be explained by a general medical condition that causes endocrine changes (e.g., a hormone-secreting tumor).
2. A disorder involving nonpsychotic hypochondriacal symptoms of less than 6 months' duration.
3. A disorder involving unexplained physical complaints (e.g., fatigue or body weakness) of less than 6 months' duration that are not due to another mental disorder.

The Last Word

In diagnosing a Somatoform Disorder, the clinician must achieve a balance between the need for a careful medical workup to explore the possibility of an underlying general medical condition versus the need to avoid unnecessary and potentially harmful tests and treatments in an individual with a true Somatoform Disorder. Certain individuals and certain cultures favor physical complaints as a primary outlet for expressing psychiatric distress. Because unexplained physical complaints are common associated features of other mental disorders (especially Mood and Anxiety Disorders), the clinician should conduct a careful psychiatric evaluation to determine whether another more specific (and perhaps more treatable) mental disorder may account for the unexplained physical symptoms.

CHAPTER 15

Factitious Disorder and Malingering

Factitious Disorder

300.16	With Predominantly Psychological Signs and Symptoms
300.19	With Predominantly Physical Signs and Symptoms
300.19	With Combined Psychological and Physical Signs and Symptoms
300.19	Factitious Disorder Not Otherwise Specified
V65.2	Malingering

In this chapter, we discuss those situations in which the patient feigns or intentionally produces symptoms to deceive the clinician. One of the most difficult determinations to make in clinical practice is whether physical or psychological symptoms have been intentionally produced. Most of our work depends on a collaborative effort between caregiver and patient to uncover the nature and cause of the presenting symptomatology. At times, however, the patient may choose to deceive the caregiver by producing or feigning physical or psychological symptoms. Clinicians are not usually on the alert for detecting deception and have generally not received training in how to do so.

Certain situations should trigger suspicion and further investigation. In determining whether the symptoms are being faked, the clinician should look for atypical presentations (e.g., an unusually early or late age at onset, an unusual cluster of symptoms), reporting of symptoms in a way that reflects popular conception of psychiatric symptomatology ("I'm schizophrenic, Doc. I have multiple personalities"), frequent hospitalizations with lack of outpatient follow-up, noncompliance with medical advice, and competition with the physician about who knows more about the condition. It is important that clinicians retain a basic faith in the truthfulness of their patients, but it is equally important that they not be gullible.

Once it has been determined that the symptoms have been feigned, the next diagnostic distinction is based on the presumed motivation for the behavior. DSM-IV includes two categories that are characterized by the feigning of symptoms: Malingering and Factitious Disorder. In Malingering, the motivation for the behavior is to achieve some kind of concrete and readily understandable gain. These gains include financial advantage (e.g., disability, workmen's compensation), avoiding legal responsibility, getting out of the army, obtaining drugs, or even getting out of the cold. In contrast, the motivation for Factitious Disorder resides in the individual's need to assume the sick role.

It should be noted that Malingering is not considered to be a mental disorder and instead is included in the section titled "Other Conditions That May Be a Focus of Clinical Attention." On the other hand, Factitious Disorder is included in its own section in the manual. A variant of Factitious Disorder, factitious disorder by proxy, is also included in DSM-IV Appendix B, "Criteria Sets and Axes Provided for Further Study." It describes situations in which an individual produces symptoms in another person for the purpose of indirectly assuming the sick role (e.g., a mother injecting a child with heparin to simulate a clotting disorder) (see Chapter 25 for the research criteria set for this disorder).

Factitious Disorder

Historically, Factitious Disorder was called Munchausen syndrome. The definition of the term *factitious* in *Merriam-Webster's Collegiate Dictionary,* 10th Edition, includes "produced by humans rather than by natural forces," "sham," and "produced by special effort." The DSM-IV concept of Factitious Disorder goes beyond this definition by focusing on the underlying motivation for the feigning. Factitious Disorder was introduced by DSM-III into the official nomenclature. The diagnosis of Factitious Disorder requires difficult clinical judgments and may be subject to errors in either of two directions:

1. Prematurely assuming that presenting symptoms are factitious and missing true mental disorders or general medical conditions
2. Missing the diagnosis of Factitious Disorder and inappropriately prescribing tests or treatments that may be both expensive and dangerous and may further promote the pattern of factitious behavior

DSM-IV diagnostic criteria for Factitious Disorder

A. Intentional production or feigning of physical or psychological signs or symptoms.

B. The motivation for the behavior is to assume the sick role.

C. External incentives for the behavior (such as economic gain, avoiding legal responsibility, or improving physical well-being, as in Malingering) are absent.

Code based on type:

300.16 With Predominantly Psychological Signs and Symptoms: if psychological signs and symptoms predominate in the clinical presentation

300.19 With Predominantly Physical Signs and Symptoms: if physical signs and symptoms predominate in the clinical presentation

300.19 With Combined Psychological and Physical Signs and Symptoms: if both psychological and physical signs and symptoms are present but neither predominates in the clinical presentation

Criterion A. The major misunderstanding in the interpretation of Criterion A has to do with the concept of "intentional production or feigning." *Intentional* is included in the definition to make clear that individuals with Factitious Disorder are invariably aware that they are faking the symptoms. Although the feigning is intentional, it should not be inferred that such individuals are in complete control of their behavior. In fact, most individuals with Factitious Disorder experience what feels like an irresistible need to achieve the sick role. The variety of presentations seen in Factitious Disorder reflects the ingenuity and often the professional experiences of such individuals, who may themselves be health care providers. Individuals with Factitious Disorder may feign physical symptoms (e.g., injecting pus to form abscesses, complaining of abdominal pains to get surgical intervention, creating fevers of unknown origin, putting blood or sugar in urine) or psychological symptoms (e.g., psychosis, suicidal ideation), or they may do both.

Awareness of the Factitious Disorder subtype With Predominantly Physical Signs and Symptoms is widespread both because there is a considerable literature on this form of the disorder and because it tends to trigger great fascination among medical care providers. The Factitious Disorder subtype With Predominantly Psychological Signs and Symptoms is probably much more common, but it is often missed because it tends to blend into the day-to-day work of mental health settings. The clinical picture most consistent with the possibility of Factitious Disorder is the individual who has had repeated psychiatric hospitalizations with a wide variety of different symptom patterns and diagnoses over time.

Criterion B. Patients rarely admit (and may not even be aware of) the motivation for their behavior. The motivation for Factitious Disorder usually must be inferred from their behavior. Such individuals are heavy users of medical and psychiatric services, spend a good part of their lives in hospital settings, and become experts on the details of the disorders they are attempting to replicate.

CRITERION C. To distinguish Factitious Disorder from Malingering, the clinician must investigate in detail the underlying motivation, the past history, and the current context of the presentation. For example, a malingerer with Opioid Dependence presenting with abdominal pain would likely be arguing strongly for analgesic medication rather than surgery, whereas the patient with Factitious Disorder might well volunteer that he or she has abdominal adhesions that respond only to surgery.

SUBTYPES. DSM-III-R had separate criteria sets for Factitious Disorder With Physical Symptoms and Factitious Disorder With Psychological Symptoms and required the use of the Not Otherwise Specified category for individuals who present with mixed pictures. Because mixed cases are frequently encountered, DSM-IV merged the disorders into a single criteria set, with three subtypes: With Predominantly Psychological Signs and Symptoms, With Predominantly Physical Signs and Symptoms, and with Combined Psychological and Physical Signs and Symptoms when neither predominates.

V65.2 Malingering

DSM-IV text for V65.2 Malingering

The essential feature of Malingering is the intentional production of false or grossly exaggerated physical or psychological symptoms, motivated by external incentives such as avoiding military duty, avoiding work, obtaining financial compensation, evading criminal prosecution, or obtaining drugs. Under some circumstances, Malingering may represent adaptive behavior—for example, feigning illness while a captive of the enemy during wartime.

Malingering should be strongly suspected if any combination of the following is noted:

1. Medicolegal context of presentation (e.g., the person is referred by an attorney to the clinician for examination)
2. Marked discrepancy between the person's claimed stress or disability and the objective findings
3. Lack of cooperation during the diagnostic evaluation and in complying with the prescribed treatment regimen
4. The presence of Antisocial Personality Disorder

Malingering differs from Factitious Disorder in that the motivation for the symptom production in Malingering is an external incentive, whereas in Factitious Disorder external incentives are absent. Evidence of an intrapsychic need to maintain the sick role suggests Factitious Disorder. Malingering is differentiated from Conversion Disorder and other Somatoform Disorders by the intentional production of symptoms and by the obvious, external incentives associated with it. In Malingering (in contrast to Conversion Disorder), symptom relief is not often obtained by suggestion or hypnosis.

Individuals who are malingering are much less likely to present their symptoms in the context of emotional conflict. Conversion Disorder may also have a secondary gain (external incentives), but the primary cause of the symptom production relates to psychological stress and the symptom production is not consciously intentional.

The Last Word

Clinicians should be neither excessively skeptical nor excessively gullible in their assessment of the veracity of their patient's presentation of symptoms. We are probably not very good at making this distinction and must try to be more mindful of it, especially as treatment resources become increasingly scarce. A particularly high index of suspicion should be held in those settings (e.g., prisons, emergency rooms) in which the base rate of feigned symptoms is especially high.

CHAPTER 16

Dissociative Disorders

Dissociative Disorders

300.12	Dissociative Amnesia
300.13	Dissociative Fugue
300.14	Dissociative Identity Disorder
300.6	Depersonalization Disorder
300.15	Dissociative Disorder Not Otherwise Specified

Dissociation is defined as a disruption in the usually integrated functions of consciousness, memory, identity, and perception. This intriguing aspect of human mental functioning has served as the foundation of many religious rituals and trance states, and became a focus of attention in medicine with the discovery of hypnosis by Mesmer in the eighteenth century. It was the effort to understand dissociation that led Janet and Freud to discover the role of unconscious forces in causing certain psychiatric symptoms.

DSM-I included one Dissociative Disorder (Dissociative Psychoneurotic Reaction). DSM-II included two Dissociative Disorders: Hysterical Neurosis, Dissociative Type, and Depersonalization Neurosis. DSM-III and DSM-III-R included four Dissociative Disorders (Psychogenic Amnesia, Psychogenic Fugue, Multiple Personality Disorder, and

Depersonalization Disorder). DSM-IV continues to have four Dissociative Disorders but with the names changed to reflect the central role of dissociation in these conditions (Dissociative Amnesia, Dissociative Fugue, Dissociative Identity Disorder, and Depersonalization Disorder). DSM-IV also includes dissociative symptoms as part of the definition of several disorders in other sections of the manual (e.g., Acute Stress Disorder, Posttraumatic Stress Disorder, Somatization Disorder), and it provides research criteria for a proposed dissociative trance disorder.

The four disorders in this section have a hierarchical relationship, so that only one of them can be diagnosed at any particular time. When it is present, Dissociative Identity Disorder takes precedence over all the other Dissociative Disorders. Fugue, amnesia, and depersonalization are all characteristic features of Dissociative Identity Disorder and are not diagnosed separately if they occur exclusively during the course of Dissociative Identity Disorder. Similarly, the presence of Dissociative Fugue preempts a diagnosis of Dissociative Amnesia and Depersonalization Disorder, and the presence of Dissociative Amnesia takes precedence over Depersonalization Disorder.

During the DSM-IV deliberations, two additional diagnoses were considered for inclusion in this section: dissociative disorder due to a general medical condition (e.g., dissociation related to complex partial seizures) and substance-induced dissociative disorder (e.g., severe depersonalization associated with cannabis use). Although such dissociation in relation to central nervous system conditions and substance use is encountered in clinical practice and certainly must be considered in the differential diagnosis, the DSM-IV Task Force decided that these conditions had not been sufficiently studied to warrant inclusion as separate diagnoses at this time. Instead, such presentations would be diagnosed in DSM-IV as Mental Disorder Not Otherwise Specified Due to Complex Partial Seizures and Cannabis-Related Disorder Not Otherwise Specified.

The evaluation of Dissociative Disorders must take into account the fact that dissociative phenomena occur frequently and are not inherently pathological. In many societies, dissociative states are common and sought-after experiences incorporated as part of widely accepted religious and cultural rituals. It is only when dissociative states lead to significant distress, impairment, or help-seeking behavior that a Dissociative Disorder should be considered.

300.12 Dissociative Amnesia

Dissociative Amnesia involves a reversible inability to retrieve memories that is not due to a general medical condition or substance use. The memories that cannot be retrieved are usually of a personal nature, involve retrograde episodic information, and are associated with a psychologically stressful event.

An issue related to the diagnosis of Dissociative Amnesia that confronted Freud 100 years ago has recently resurfaced and has occasioned a passionate debate with unusually serious and troubling consequences. Freud noted that, as part of the repression revealed by psychoanalysis, a surprisingly large percentage of his patients with hysteria reported having been sexually abused in their early childhood. These clinical observations initially led Freud to develop a model based on the assumption that sexually traumatic childhood experiences play an important and common causal role in the development of neuroses. Soon, however, Freud came to doubt that sexual abuse could be so ubiquitous in bourgeois Vienna and questioned the validity of his own observations and theory. Instead, he developed an alternative model to account for his patients' reported memories. Rather than accepting at face value the accuracy of recently recovered memories of childhood sexual abuse, Freud suggested that these "memories" are usually better understood as childhood fantasies and distortions arising at least in part from unconscious wishes. This second model postulated that neurosis was more the result of the vicissitudes of repressed and fixated infantile sexuality than the result of childhood sexual abuse. Freud never denied that child abuse occurred and was detrimental, but the emphasis of his etiological model of neurosis shifted from external abuse to internal drive and conflict.

More recently, a number of clinicians have asserted that Freud had it right the first time and that childhood sexual abuse is far more prevalent and far more important in the pathogenesis of childhood and adult psychopathology than has been realized. Recently in the United States, there has been a dramatic increase in the number of adults remembering previously forgotten childhood sexual abuse, often while they are in psychotherapy with a therapist who has a special interest in this area and uses techniques such as amobarbital sodium (Amytal) interviews, hypnosis, or suggestion to assist in the recovering of the memory. In some instances, the recovered "memories" have led to lawsuits against parents, criminal prosecution of caretakers, and even charges of Satanism.

This increase in retrospective reports of child abuse has been subject to very different interpretations. Some clinicians believe that such events previously had been profoundly underreported, especially because the victims are often children and the perpetrators are inclined to deny or distort their actions. They welcome the greater awareness of this problem among health professionals, claiming that it has resulted in the appropriate identification and treatment of previously neglected and invalidated victims of abuse and a reduction in misdiagnosis.

Other clinicians disagree strongly and instead believe that Dissociative Amnesia is now being greatly overdiagnosed. They express caution about interpreting the validity of the retrospective recall from early childhood, which can be subject to extensive distortion based on the inherent fallibility of memory, the young child's limited cognitive capacities and tendency to confabulate, the role of unconscious conflicts, the high level of suggestibility that characterizes many of the involved individuals, the search for a rationale for presenting symptoms, and the influence exerted by powerful others (including possibly overly zealous therapists). For all of these reasons, these clinicians suggest that great care must be exercised in evaluating the accuracy of retrieved memories.

In clinical practice, the diagnosis of Dissociative Amnesia is usually not made in relation to the loss of childhood memories but rather in relation to gaps in more recent memories, often after a psychologically traumatic event.

DSM-IV diagnostic criteria for 300.12 Dissociative Amnesia

A. The predominant disturbance is one or more episodes of inability to recall important personal information, usually of a traumatic or stressful nature, that is too extensive to be explained by ordinary forgetfulness.

(continued)

DSM-IV diagnostic criteria for 300.12 Dissociative Amnesia *(continued)*

B. The disturbance does not occur exclusively during the course of Dissociative Identity Disorder, Dissociative Fugue, Posttraumatic Stress Disorder, Acute Stress Disorder, or Somatization Disorder and is not due to the direct physiological effects of a substance (e.g., a drug of abuse, a medication) or a neurological or other general medical condition (e.g., Amnestic Disorder Due to Head Trauma).

C. The symptoms cause clinically significant distress or impairment in social, occupational, or other important areas of functioning.

Criterion A. The gaps in memory in Dissociative Amnesia may take a variety of forms. Most commonly, the memory loss is limited to events that occur in a circumscribed period of time (usually hours) surrounding a particularly stressful event (e.g., sexual abuse, automobile accident, episodes of self-mutilation, violent outbursts, suicidal attempts, life-threatening combat experience). Less commonly, the inability to remember is more generalized. Some individuals are unable to remember certain types of information, such as all memories relating to one's father. Rarely, some individuals may present to the police or to emergency rooms not knowing where they live.

As mentioned above, gaps in childhood memories are particularly difficult to evaluate. In the absence of corroborating evidence, there is currently no method for establishing with any degree of certainty the accuracy of previously "forgotten" childhood memories, particularly when these are brought out in the context of psychotherapy or hypnosis. In such situations, it is important that the clinician adopt a balanced view that is supportive and not invalidating of the patient but that avoids influencing the patient by suggestion.

Criterion B. Dissociative Amnesia is diagnosed by exclusion and should be considered only after other causes of the memory disturbance have been ruled out. The most important differential diagnosis is between Dissociative Amnesia and amnesia caused by a general medical condition or substance use. It is possible to miss an underlying neurological condition (e.g., concussion, epilepsy), especially because many psychologically traumatic events that sometimes trigger Dissociative Amnesia (e.g., rape) are also the occasion for physical injury. In Amnestic Disorder Due to a Brain Injury, there is usually a history of a clear-cut physical trauma, a period of unconsciousness, or clinical evidence of brain injury, and the memory disturbance includes both retrograde and anterograde amnesia. Seizure disorders can result in sudden onset of memory impairment with motor abnormalities and electroencephalographic changes. The memory loss in delirium and dementia is associated with a wider set of cognitive impairments. In Dissociative Amnesia, the memory loss is primarily for autobiographical information, whereas other cognitive abilities are generally preserved. Dissociative Amnesia should also be distinguished from blackouts due to Substance Intoxication and from the persisting memory loss associated with central nervous system damage after chronic extensive use of certain substances (e.g., alcohol).

Because dissociative amnesia is a characteristic symptom of a number of other mental disorders, it is unnecessary to give an additional diagnosis of Dissociative Amnesia if the memory loss only occurs during the course of one of these disorders.

CRITERION C. By its very nature, memory is fallible. This is especially the case in regard to the recall of early childhood memories and of recent events in elderly persons. Gaps in memory do not necessarily suggest the presence of Dissociative Amnesia unless they result in significant distress or impairment.

300.13 Dissociative Fugue

Dissociative Fugue is encountered much more often in case reports and in the movies than in actual clinical practice. Most mental health professionals have been exposed to fugue only in their readings and not through any personal experience. Therefore, in the evaluation of any apparent case of Dissociative Fugue, the clinician should first carefully consider the possibility of delirium, dementia, or Substance Intoxication (all of which may also be characterized by confusion about personal identity and wandering behavior) and of Malingering (particularly if the individual stands to gain something or to avoid responsibility by having a psychiatric diagnosis).

DSM-IV diagnostic criteria for 300.13 Dissociative Fugue

A. The predominant disturbance is sudden, unexpected travel away from home or one's customary place of work, with inability to recall one's past.

B. Confusion about personal identity or assumption of a new identity (partial or complete).

C. The disturbance does not occur exclusively during the course of Dissociative Identity Disorder and is not due to the direct physiological effects of a substance (e.g., a drug of abuse, a medication) or a general medical condition (e.g., temporal lobe epilepsy).

D. The symptoms cause clinically significant distress or impairment in social, occupational, or other important areas of functioning.

CRITERION A. The extent of the unexpected travel can be quite variable, ranging from brief trips to complex wandering (individuals have reportedly traveled thousands of miles). To the casual observer, the person in a fugue might appear to be acting perfectly normally. What usually brings the person to clinical attention is the profound Dissociative Amnesia for recent or past events. Once the fugue state ends, some individuals have amnesia for the events that occurred during the fugue.

Criterion B. Most individuals in a fugue have a confused sense about who they are rather than actually taking on a new identity (e.g., assuming a new name, taking up a new residence). Any new identity is likely to be more gregarious and uninhibited than the person's usual personality.

Criterion C. Because the features of Dissociative Fugue (e.g., Dissociative Amnesia, assumption of a new identity) are also characteristic of the more pervasive Dissociative Identity Disorder, an additional diagnosis of Dissociative Fugue in an individual with Dissociative Identity Disorder is not necessary. If it is determined that the behavior is the direct physiological consequence of a specific general medical condition (e.g., complex partial seizures, Alzheimer's disease, encephalopathy), the diagnosis is Mental Disorder Not Otherwise Specified Due to a General Medical Condition and not Dissociative Fugue. Similarly, if the behavior is a direct result of substance use (e.g., alcoholic blackouts and wandering), the diagnosis would be Substance Intoxication.

Before making a diagnosis of Dissociative Fugue, the clinician should consider Malingering, Factitious Disorder, fugue states due to a general medical condition, Substance Intoxication or Withdrawal, Dissociative Identity Disorder, Manic Episode, and Schizophrenia.

300.14 Dissociative Identity Disorder

Multiple Personality Disorder was included in the official nomenclature for the first time in DSM-III (1980). Previously, it had a long and interesting history and had been the subject of many striking case reports that captured the imagination not only of clinicians but also of the public. Perhaps as a result of the appearance of Multiple Personality Disorder in DSM-III, there has recently been a sharp increase in the diagnosis and treatment of this disorder in the United States.

This increase has been subject to very different interpretations. Some clinicians believe that Dissociative Identity Disorder had heretofore been misdiagnosed (e.g., mistaking the presence of a dissociated personality state for a delusion, mistaking the communication from one identity to another for an auditory hallucination, mistaking shifts between identity states as mood changes in Bipolar Disorder). These clinicians believe that the current greater awareness of the diagnosis and of the etiological role of childhood sexual abuse, among mental health professionals, has resulted in the earlier and more appropriate identification of cases. In contrast, many other clinicians are convinced that the syndrome is now being vastly overdiagnosed (or even iatrogenically induced) in highly suggestible individuals who are vulnerable to the suggestions of overzealous therapists. There is particular concern that efforts to communicate with previously unrecognized "alters" may, if anything, promote the tendency toward dissociation rather than cure it.

This diagnosis of Multiple Personality Disorder is now known as Dissociative Identity Disorder. The name was changed for several reasons: 1) to emphasize the role of dissociation and problems in establishing an integrated identity, 2) to dereify the notion that multiple personalities "exist" within the individual, and 3) to eliminate confusion between Dissociative Identity Disorder and the Personality Disorders.

DSM-IV diagnostic criteria for 300.14 Dissociative Identity Disorder

A. The presence of two or more distinct identities or personality states (each with its own relatively enduring pattern of perceiving, relating to, and thinking about the environment and self).

B. At least two of these identities or personality states recurrently take control of the person's behavior.

C. Inability to recall important personal information that is too extensive to be explained by ordinary forgetfulness.

D. The disturbance is not due to the direct physiological effects of a substance (e.g., blackouts or chaotic behavior during Alcohol Intoxication) or a general medical condition (e.g., complex partial seizures). **Note:** In children, the symptoms are not attributable to imaginary playmates or other fantasy play.

Criterion A. The DSM-III-R wording for this item required the "existence within the person of two or more distinct personalities or personality states." There was considerable controversy about how this criterion should be worded in DSM-IV. Those who believe that this disorder is underdiagnosed suggested that the presence of different "ego states" should also be counted. That would have resulted in a remarkably inclusive definition, capturing most individuals with Borderline Personality Disorder and probably a number of mentally healthy adolescents and young adults. Those who believe that this disorder has been reified and overdiagnosed suggested that the criterion be reworded as "the experience of two or more distinct identity or personality states" to indicate that the "multiple personalities" do not in fact exist as entities but rather are part of the individual's subjective experience. The disadvantage of this suggestion was that it relied on conscious experiencing of the identity states, which does not always occur. The substitution of "presence of" for the DSM-III-R wording "existence within" was intended, in some small way, to reduce reification.

Criterion C. There may be frequent gaps in recent or remote memory for personal history. It is sometimes difficult to evaluate amnesia precisely because the individual may not be aware of some of the alters' experiences. Often, this evaluation requires information provided by other informants who have witnessed behavior later denied by the individual, or amnesia can be confirmed when the individual discovers evidence of forgotten behaviors (e.g., finding items at home that he or she cannot remember having bought).

Criterion D. Before making the diagnosis of Dissociative Identity Disorder, it is important to ensure that ego-dystonic behavior and memory loss are not the result of a neurological condition or substance use.

300.6 Depersonalization Disorder

Depersonalization is a very common experience, particularly in younger males. Approximately 30% of individuals have had one or more episodes of depersonalization in their lifetimes, and occasional or mild episodes are not necessarily indicative of the presence of a mental disorder. Episodes of depersonalization usually become less frequent or disappear altogether as the individual gets older. Although depersonalization is common, the disorder as defined below is very rarely diagnosed because the presence of depersonalization is more often considered to be either nonpathological or part of another diagnosis.

DSM-IV diagnostic criteria for 300.6 Depersonalization Disorder

A. Persistent or recurrent experiences of feeling detached from, and as if one is an outside observer of, one's mental processes or body (e.g., feeling like one is in a dream).

B. During the depersonalization experience, reality testing remains intact.

C. The depersonalization causes clinically significant distress or impairment in social, occupational, or other important areas of functioning.

D. The depersonalization experience does not occur exclusively during the course of another mental disorder, such as Schizophrenia, Panic Disorder, Acute Stress Disorder, or another Dissociative Disorder, and is not due to the direct physiological effects of a substance (e.g., a drug of abuse, a medication) or a general medical condition (e.g., temporal lobe epilepsy).

Criterion A. The individual feels like he or she is watching his life go by as if in a dream or a movie. Episodes of depersonalization may be triggered by experiences that call the individuals' attention to themselves (e.g., looking in the mirror, hearing one's name called).

Criterion B. Some of the depersonalization experiences, especially when severe, may be confused with delusions seen in Schizophrenia and other Psychotic Disorders. It is important to note that individuals with Depersonalization Disorder maintain intact reality testing (i.e., awareness that it is only a feeling and that one is not really an automaton).

Criterion C. The individual may present for treatment because of concerns about going crazy, preoccupations with concerns about identity, and social isolation.

Criterion D. Depersonalization is a nonspecific symptom that occurs as an essential or associated feature of a large number of disorders. In fact, although depersonalization as a symptom is encountered fairly frequently in clinical practice, the diagnosis of Depersonalization Disorder is rarely made. Before making the diagnosis of Depersonalization Disorder, the clinician should consider dissociative symptoms due to a general medical condition (e.g., postictal states), Substance Intoxication or Withdrawal, and symptoms characteristic of or associated with Panic Disorder, Social Phobia, Specific Phobia, Posttraumatic Stress Disorder, Acute Stress Disorder, Schizophrenia, Major Depressive Disorder, and Borderline Personality Disorder.

DSM-IV text for 300.15 Dissociative Disorder Not Otherwise Specified

This category is included for disorders in which the predominant feature is a dissociative symptom (i.e., a disruption in the usually integrated functions of consciousness, memory, identity, or perception of the environment) that does not meet the criteria for any specific Dissociative Disorder. Examples include

1. Clinical presentations similar to Dissociative Identity Disorder that fail to meet full criteria for this disorder. Examples include presentations in which a) there are not two or more distinct personality states, or b) amnesia for important personal information does not occur.
2. Derealization unaccompanied by depersonalization in adults.
3. States of dissociation that occur in individuals who have been subjected to periods of prolonged and intense coercive persuasion (e.g., brainwashing, thought reform, or indoctrination while captive).
4. Dissociative trance disorder: single or episodic disturbances in the state of consciousness, identity, or memory that are indigenous to particular locations and cultures. Dissociative trance involves narrowing of awareness of immediate surroundings or stereotyped behaviors or movements that are experienced as being beyond one's control. Possession trance involves replacement of the customary sense of personal identity by a new identity, attributed to the influence of a spirit, power, deity, or other person, and associated with stereotyped "involuntary" movements or amnesia. Examples include *amok* (Indonesia), *bebainan* (Indonesia), *latah* (Malaysia), *pibloktoq* (Arctic), *ataque de nervios* (Latin America), and possession (India). The dissociative or trance disorder is not a normal part of a broadly accepted collective cultural or religious practice.
5. Loss of consciousness, stupor, or coma not attributable to a general medical condition.
6. Ganser syndrome: the giving of approximate answers to questions (e.g., "2 plus 2 equals 5") when not associated with Dissociative Amnesia or Dissociative Fugue.

The Last Word

Currently, Dissociative Disorders are probably overdiagnosed because of wide media coverage, iatrogenic suggestions, and the assumption that all cases of childhood sexual abuse result in these disorders. The symptoms listed in this section (e.g., depersonalization, amnesia) are common associated features of other disorders (e.g., Panic Disorder, Major Depressive Disorder, Dementia), and these should be carefully considered and ruled out before a diagnosis of Dissociative Disorder is made.

CHAPTER 17

Sexual and Gender Identity Disorders

DSM-IV includes in one section the sexual dysfunctions, the paraphilias, and the gender Identity Disorders. The Sexual Dysfunctions refer to disturbances in sexual desire or functioning, Paraphilias refer to unusual sexual preferences, and Gender Identity Disorder refers to problems in one's sense of maleness or femaleness.

Sexual Dysfunctions

Sexual Dysfunctions

Sexual Desire Disorders

302.71	Hypoactive Sexual Desire Disorder
302.79	Sexual Aversion Disorder

Sexual Arousal Disorders

302.72	Female Sexual Arousal Disorder
302.72	Male Erectile Disorder

Orgasmic Disorders

302.73	Female Orgasmic Disorder
302.74	Male Orgasmic Disorder

(continued)

302.75	Premature Ejaculation
Sexual Pain Disorders	
302.76	Dyspareunia (Not Due to a General Medical Condition)
306.51	Vaginismus (Not Due to a General Medical Condition)
Sexual Dysfunction Due to a General Medical Condition	
—.—	Substance-Induced Sexual Dysfunction *[Refer to Substance-Related Disorders for substance-specific codes]*
302.70	Sexual Dysfunction Not Otherwise Specified

It may be useful to summarize briefly the different phases of "normal" sexual response and the sexual dysfunctions that are associated with each phase.

1. **Sexual Desire.** This phase consists of fantasies about sexual activity and a desire to have sexual activity. The DSM-IV disorders related to this phase are Hypoactive Sexual Desire Disorder and Sexual Aversion Disorder.
2. **Sexual Excitement.** This phase consists of a subjective sense of sexual arousal and pleasure and accompanying physiological changes. The major changes in the female consist of vasocongestion in the pelvis, vaginal lubrication and expansion, and swelling of the external genitalia. The major changes in the male consist of penile tumescence and erection. The related DSM-IV disorders are Female Arousal Disorder and Male Erectile Disorder.
3. **Orgasm.** This phase consists of a climax of sexual pleasure with accompanying rhythmic contractions and the release of sexual tension. In the female, there are vaginal contractions. In the male, there is the sensation of ejaculatory inevitability, followed by the ejaculation of semen. The related DSM-IV disorders are Female and Male Orgasmic Disorder and Premature Ejaculation.
4. **Resolution.** This phase consists of a sense of general relaxation, well-being, and muscular relaxation. During this phase, males are physiologically refractory to further erection and orgasm for a variable period of time. In contrast, females may be able to respond to additional stimulation almost immediately. There are no disorders related to this phase.

DSM-IV also includes two disorders covering physical discomfort related to sexual intercourse: Dyspareunia (pain occurring during intercourse) and Vaginismus (vaginal spasms that interfere with sexual intercourse).

Not infrequently, problems occur in more than one phase of the sexual response cycle. Because the phases of the sexual response cycle occur in sequence, successful functioning in one phase generally requires successful functioning in the previous phases (e.g., orgasm requires some level of arousal, which requires some level of desire). However, anticipation of the recurrence of problems in a later phase (e.g., a man having difficulty ejaculating) often leads to problems in an earlier phase (e.g., consequent erectile dysfunction or low sexual desire).

The organization of this section brings up the usual "splitter" versus "lumper" debate. DSM-IV continues the DSM-III and DSM-III-R splitter approach of providing separate criteria sets and diagnostic codes for each condition, with the misleading implication that these often occur in isolation from one another. An alternative lumper approach that may have been preferable would have included only a single criteria set and code for sexual dysfunctions with the different presentations noted as subtypes. The fact that a given individual often receives more than one DSM-IV Sexual Dysfunction diagnosis should not obscure the fact that these diagnoses are often different facets of a single problem.

Perhaps the major difficulty in evaluating Sexual Dysfunctions is that there are no widely accepted guidelines for determining just what normal sexual functioning is. This is further complicated by the fact that the threshold for normal sexual functioning varies with age and with the individual's prior sexual experience, the availability and novelty of partners, and expectations and standards characteristic of the individual's cultural, ethnic, or religious group.

Successful arousal and orgasm require a level of sexual stimulation that is adequate in focus, intensity, and duration. A diagnosis of a Sexual Arousal Disorder or an Orgasmic Disorder requires a clinical judgment that the person has experienced adequate stimulation. Moreover, it must be remembered that occasional sexual dysfunction is an inherent part of human sexuality and is not indicative of a disorder unless it is persistent or recurrent and results in marked distress or interpersonal difficulty.

Once the clinical judgment has been made that the sexual dysfunction is clinically significant, the next task is to determine its underlying etiology. The possible etiologies include psychological factors (within the individual or as a consequence of a relational problem), general medical conditions, the side effects of many prescribed medications, and the consequence of drug abuse. This evaluation is made especially difficult because very often more than one etiology contributes to the sexual dysfunction. For example, it is not uncommon for someone who develops mild erectile dysfunction as a result of a general medical condition (e.g., vascular problems) to develop other sexual dysfunctions (e.g., low desire) as a psychological consequence.

Before deciding that any Sexual Dysfunction is mediated strictly by psychological factors, it is important to consider the possible contribution of a medical condition or substance (including medication side effects)—especially because these etiologies often have specific treatment implications (e.g., discontinuation of the offending medication). On the other hand, it is also important to remember that the identification of a specific etiological general medical condition, medication, or drug of abuse does not negate the important contribution of psychological factors to the etiology of the dysfunction.

The etiological contributions of each of these factors are indicated in DSM-IV as follows: If the Sexual Dysfunction is completely accounted for by a general medical condition (e.g., neurological damage), Sexual Dysfunction Due to a General Medical Condition is diagnosed. If the dysfunction is exclusively a medication side effect or a consequence of drug abuse, a diagnosis of Substance-Induced Sexual Dysfunction applies. If psychological factors (e.g., individual inhibitions, relational conflicts) play an important role, the appropriate Sexual Dysfunction is diagnosed depending on the presenting problem. Furthermore, the subtype Due to Psychological Factors or Due to Combined Factors can be noted. Due to Psychological Factors applies when psychological factors are judged to be primarily responsible for the onset, severity, exacerbation, or maintenance of the Sexual Dysfunction, and general medical conditions and substances play no role in the etiology of the sexual dysfunction. Due to Combined Factors applies when psychological factors are judged to have a role in the onset, severity, exacerbation, or maintenance of the Sexual Dysfunction, and a general medical condition or substance use is judged to be contributory but is not sufficient to account for the Sexual Dysfunction. If the causes are uncertain or unknown, the diagnosis of Sexual Dysfunction Not Otherwise Specified can be indicated.

DSM-IV provides two specifiers for indicating the onset of sexual dysfunction: Lifelong Type and Acquired Type. This distinction is useful because of the possible differences in etiology, course, and treatment planning. The specifier Lifelong Type refers to the failure to develop normal sexual function at puberty, which then persists thereafter (e.g., always had little or no sexual desire, always had difficulty maintaining an erection, has never had an orgasm). The specifier Acquired Type refers to situations in which the individual had developed the particular sexual function and then lost it at a later time. All of the etiologies listed above apply to both types. In the Acquired Type, it is especially important to determine which etiological factors (psychological, general medical condition, substance use) may have caused the loss of previous functioning. Particularly if the etiology is reversible, the prognosis is likely to be better for the Acquired Type.

DSM-IV also provides two specifiers for indicating the context in which the Sexual Dysfunction occurs: Generalized Type and Situational Type. This distinction is useful because it has implications about etiology, course, and treatment planning. The Generalized Type applies when the Sexual Dysfunction occurs across the board, irrespective of the type of stimulation, the situation, or the partner. In contrast, in the Situational Type, sexual functioning is impaired only in certain situations, with certain types of sexual stimulation, or with particular partners. When a dysfunction is situational, it is much less likely to be a consequence of a general medical condition or a medication side effect. For example, a man with a Situational Type of Orgasmic Disorder who is able to have orgasms during masturbation but not during intercourse is unlikely to have a general medical condition or medication side effect as the cause of the orgasmic difficulty. Similarly, it is always important to ask a man if a full erection occurs during masturbation or on awakening. If so, it is unlikely that any erectile disturbance occurring in other situations is due to a general medical condition or a medication side effect.

Sexual Dysfunction often occurs in the context of a relational problem. The direction of causality in these situations may be complex and difficult to determine. In some instances, the Sexual Dysfunction may be a symptom of an unsatisfactory relationship (e.g., warring spouses, unattractive or disinterested partner). In other instances, a relational problem can develop as a consequence of a Sexual Dysfunction in one or both of the partners (e.g., the conflict begins because of the sexual dysfunction rather than being the cause of the sexual dysfunction). Often the Sexual Dysfunction and the relationship dysfunction are interactive and exacerbate one another.

The definition of mental disorder in DSM-IV requires that "whatever its original cause, it must currently be considered a manifestation of a behavioral, psychological, or biological dysfunction in the individual," and that it "must not be merely an expectable and culturally sanctioned response to a particular event." Therefore, the diagnosis of a Sexual Dysfunction should be given only when it is judged that factors in the individual in some way contribute to the dysfunction and that the problem is not exclusively related to external situations (e.g., a particular partner). This distinction may be particularly difficult to make when the dysfunction is of the Situational Type and is confined to a partner with whom there is a relational problem.

Because the criteria sets for the individual Sexual Dysfunctions are so similar, we do not provide them separately in this *Guidebook*. Rather, we discuss each criterion as it applies to all of the disorders.

Criterion A

Criterion A for each of the Sexual Dysfunctions contains the following wording: **"Persistent or recurrent" . . .** ***[description of the nature of the sexual problem].***

This criterion describes the particular sexual disorder in terms of the phase in which it occurs. It requires that the dysfunction be persistent or recurrent to emphasize that occasional instances of problematic functioning do not qualify as a Sexual Dysfunction. Each of the sexual disorders is briefly described below.

302.71 Hypoactive Sexual Desire Disorder. Hypoactive Sexual Desire Disorder applies when a person has diminished desire for sexual activity and a paucity of sexual fantasies. The low sexual desire may be generalized and encompass all forms of sexual expression, or it may be limited to one particular partner or one specific sexual activity (e.g., intercourse but not masturbation). The individual usually does not initiate sexual activity at all and participates reluctantly when it is initiated by the sexual partner. It is often helpful to assess both partners when there is an apparent mismatch in sexual desire. What might appear to be "low desire" in the identified patient may instead reflect an excessive sexual need by the partner or just a mismatch in levels of desire.

302.79 Sexual Aversion Disorder. Sexual Aversion Disorder applies when a person has an extreme aversion to, and avoids, genital sexual contact with a partner. When a sexual opportunity with a partner arises, the person experiences anxiety, fear, or disgust. Although the aversion is often focused on a particular aspect of sexual experience (e.g., genital secretions, vaginal penetration), some individuals experience generalized revulsion to all sexual stimuli (including kissing and touching).

302.72 Female Sexual Arousal Disorder. Female Sexual Arousal Disorder applies when a woman is unable to attain or maintain an adequate arousal response (i.e., vasocongestion in the pelvis, vaginal lubrication and expansion, and swelling of the external genitalia) during sexual activity.

302.72 Male Erectile Disorder. Male Erectile Disorder applies when a man is unable to attain or maintain an adequate erection. This can happen at different points during a sexual encounter: from the outset, while attempting to penetrate, or during thrusting. Some men are able to have an erection only during self-masturbation. If the individual fails to have erections during masturbation or on awakening, a general medical condition, medication side effect, or drug abuse is more likely to be the cause.

302.73 Female Orgasmic Disorder. Female Orgasmic Disorder applies when a woman has recurrent difficulties having orgasm after a normal sexual arousal. This diagnosis has been controversial because of misconceptions concerning the optimal type or frequency of orgasm. Women vary widely in their orgasmic capacity (which tends to increase with age and sexual experience) and in the type or intensity of stimulation that triggers orgasm. This diagnosis should be made only when the orgasmic functioning is less than would be expected for the individual given all of these factors (i.e., age, experience, adequacy of stimulation).

302.74 Male Orgasmic Disorder. Male Orgasmic Disorder applies when a man has a delay in, or absence of, orgasm after a normal sexual arousal. This disorder can take different forms. Some men can ejaculate in response to a partner's manual or oral stimulation, but not during intercourse. Others ejaculate only during self-masturbation. In others, orgasm occurs during intercourse but only after very prolonged and intense noncoital activity. As with Female Orgasmic Disorder, this diagnosis should be made only when the orgasmic functioning is less than would be expected given the adequacy of the stimulation and the individual's age (in men, capacity tends to decline with age).

302.75 Premature Ejaculation. Premature Ejaculation applies when a man ejaculates too quickly and with minimal sexual stimulation before, on, or shortly after penetration and before he wishes it. This occurs most commonly in young and sexually inexperienced men. It is also affected by the duration of the excitement phase, the novelty of the sexual partner or situation, and the interval since the man's last orgasm. Most men with this disorder have greater control over ejaculation during self-masturbation than during intercourse.

302.76 Dyspareunia (Not Due to a General Medical Condition). Dyspareunia applies when a person experiences genital pain before, during, or after sexual intercourse. This can occur in both men and women.

306.51 Vaginismus (Not Due to a General Medical Condition). Vaginismus applies when a woman experiences involuntary spasm of the vaginal muscles that interferes with sexual intercourse or gynecological examination or causes physical discomfort when these occur. In most cases, sexual intercourse is possible but painful. The woman is usually not aware of experiencing vaginal spasms and complains of physical discomfort during sexual intercourse rather than a complete inability to engage in it.

Criterion B

Criterion B for each of the Sexual Dysfunctions contains the following wording: **"The disturbance causes marked distress or interpersonal difficulty."**

This criterion helps establish the boundary between the Sexual Dysfunctions and the occasional difficulties with sexual functioning that are part of everyday experience. The distress and impairment can take various forms. Men and women with Sexual Dysfunctions often have difficulties developing stable sexual relationships and may have marital dissatisfaction and disruption. Because of fears of embarrassment arising from poor performance, they may hesitate to date new partners and may become socially isolated. Sexual encounters with available partners may be avoided by covert strategies such as going to sleep early, traveling, neglecting personal appearance, using substances, and being overinvolved in work, social, or family activities. Some Sexual Dysfunctions (e.g., Female Sexual Arousal Disorder) may result in painful intercourse, and others (e.g., Male Orgasmic Disorder) may be the cause of unconsummated marriages and infertility.

Criterion C

Criterion C for each of the various Sexual Dysfunctions contains the following wording (with slight variations): **"The dysfunction is not better accounted for by another**

Axis I disorder (except another Sexual Dysfunction) and is not due exclusively to the direct physiological effects of a substance (e.g., a drug of abuse, medication) or a general medical condition."

Sexual problems are commonly associated with a number of mental disorders (e.g., Mood Disorders, Anxiety Disorders, Somatoform Disorders, Psychotic Disorders). An additional diagnosis of a Sexual Dysfunction is not necessary when the sexual problems are best attributed to an Axis I disorder. For example, low sexual desire occurring only during a Major Depressive Episode should not receive a separate diagnosis of Hypoactive Sexual Desire Disorder. Both diagnoses can be given only when the low sexual desire is judged to be independent of the Depressive Disorder (i.e., it precedes the onset of the depressive episode or persists long after the depression has remitted). In contrast, an additional Sexual Dysfunction diagnosis can be given in conjunction with a diagnosis of Personality Disorder. Sexual Dysfunctions commonly occur together, and as many different Sexual Dysfunction diagnoses can be given as apply. As discussed already, these multiple diagnoses should not be interpreted to mean that the disorders are unrelated in their pathogenesis or treatment response.

This exclusion criterion also distinguishes the primary Sexual Dysfunctions from Sexual Dysfunctions Due to a General Medical Condition and Substance-Induced Sexual Dysfunctions.

Sexual Dysfunction Due to a General Medical Condition

Many general medical conditions can cause sexual dysfunction, including neurological conditions (e.g., multiple sclerosis, spinal cord lesions, neuropathy, temporal lobe lesions), endocrine conditions (e.g., diabetes mellitus, hypothyroidism, hyper- and hypoadrenocorticism, hyperprolactinemia, hypogonadal states, pituitary dysfunction), vascular conditions, and genitourinary conditions (e.g., testicular disease, Peyronie's disease, urethral infections, postprostatectomy complications, genital injury or infection, atrophic vaginitis, infections of the vagina and external genitalia, postsurgical complications such as episiotomy scars, shortened vagina, cystitis, endometriosis, uterine prolapse, pelvic infections, neoplasms).

This diagnosis of Sexual Dysfunction Due to a General Medical Condition applies when the Sexual Dysfunction is judged to be exclusively due to the direct physiological effects of a general medical condition. This determination is based on history (e.g., impaired erectile functioning during masturbation), physical examination (e.g., evidence of neuropathy), and laboratory findings (e.g., nocturnal penile tumescence, penile blood pressure, pulse wave assessments, ultrasound studies, intracorporeal pharmacological testing or angiography, cavernosography). If both primary Sexual Dysfunction and a general medical condition are present, but it is judged that the dysfunction is not due exclusively to the direct physiological consequences of the general medical condition, then Sexual Dysfunction Due to Combined Factors is diagnosed. The specific diagnostic code and term for Sexual Dysfunction Due to a General Medical Condition are selected based on the nature of the dysfunction (see Table 17–1).

Table 17–1. Specific terms and codes for Sexual Dysfunction Due to a General Medical Condition

Code	Term
625.8	Female Hypoactive Sexual Desire Disorder Due to . . . *[Indicate the General Medical Condition]*
608.89	Male Hypoactive Sexual Desire Disorder Due to . . . *[Indicate the General Medical Condition]*
607.84	Male Erectile Disorder Due to . . . *[Indicate the General Medical Condition]*
625.0	Female Dyspareunia Due to . . . *[Indicate the General Medical Condition]*
608.89	Male Dyspareunia Due to . . . *[Indicate the General Medical Condition]*
625.8	Other Female Sexual Dysfunction Due to . . . *[Indicate the General Medical Condition]*
608.89	Other Male Sexual Dysfunction Due to . . . *[Indicate the General Medical Condition]*

Substance-Induced Sexual Dysfunction

Criterion C also distinguishes the primary Sexual Dysfunctions from Substance-Induced Sexual Dysfunctions. The diagnosis of Substance-Induced Sexual Dysfunction applies when a clinically significant Sexual Dysfunction is judged to be exclusively due to the direct physiological effects of a medication or drug of abuse. Sexual Dysfunctions can occur in association with intoxication with the following classes of substances: alcohol, amphetamines and related substances, cocaine, opioids, sedatives, hypnotics, and anxiolytics. Acute intoxication with or chronic abuse of substances of abuse has been reported to decrease sexual interest and cause arousal problems in both sexes. A decrease in sexual interest (both sexes), arousal disorders (both sexes), and orgasmic disorders (more common in men) may also be caused by prescribed medications, including antihypertensives, histamine H_2 receptor antagonists, antidepressants, neuroleptics, anxiolytics, anabolic steroids, and antiepileptics. Painful orgasm has been reported with the use of fluphenazine, thioridazine, and amoxapine. Priapism has been reported with use of chlorpromazine, trazodone, clozapine, and following penile injections of papaverine or prostaglandin. Serotonin reuptake blockers may cause decreased sexual desire, arousal, or orgasmic disorders.

If both primary Sexual Dysfunction and substance use are present, but it is judged that the dysfunction is not due exclusively to the direct physiological consequences of the substance use, then Sexual Dysfunction Due to Combined Factors is diagnosed. If the Sexual Dysfunction is judged to be due exclusively to the physiological consequences of both a general medical condition and substance use, Sexual Dysfunction Due to a General Medical Condition and Substance-Induced Sexual Dysfunction are both diagnosed. The specific diagnostic codes for Substance-Induced Sexual Dysfunction are 291.8 for Alcohol and 292.89 for all other substances (including medications). See page 520 of DSM-IV for recording procedures for substance-induced conditions.

DSM-IV text for 302.70 Sexual Dysfunction Not Otherwise Specified

This category includes sexual dysfunctions that do not meet criteria for any specific Sexual Dysfunction. Examples include

1. No (or substantially diminished) subjective erotic feelings despite otherwise-normal arousal and orgasm
2. Situations in which the clinician has concluded that a sexual dysfunction is present but is unable to determine whether it is primary, due to a general medical condition, or substance induced

The Last Word

The range of what is considered normal sexual functioning is broad and not very well defined. Moreover, an individual's sexual functioning may vary over time and in different contexts. The difficult judgment about whether a diagnosis of Sexual Dysfunction applies depends on a clinical evaluation that takes into account both internal factors (e.g., age) and external factors (e.g., partner) and the individual's level of distress and impairment. Even though DSM-IV presents Sexual Dysfunctions separately, they often occur together. Whenever one Sexual Dysfunction is present, the clinician should inquire about the possible presence of others.

Paraphilias

Paraphilias

302.4	Exhibitionism
302.81	Fetishism
302.89	Frotteurism
302.2	Pedophilia
302.83	Sexual Masochism
302.84	Sexual Sadism
302.3	Transvestic Fetishism
302.82	Voyeurism
302.9	Paraphilia Not Otherwise Specified

Paraphilia is the DSM-IV term for "sexual deviation" or "sexual perversion." The hallmark of a Paraphilia is recurrent, intense sexually arousing fantasies, sexual urges, or behaviors generally involving 1) nonhuman objects, 2) the suffering or humiliation of oneself or one's partner, or 3) children or other nonconsenting persons. For some individuals, paraphilic fantasies or stimuli are obligatory for erotic arousal and are always included in sexual activity. In other cases, the paraphilic preferences occur only episodically (e.g., perhaps during periods of stress), whereas at other times the person is able to function sexually without paraphilic fantasies or stimuli. Except for Sexual Masochism, the Paraphilias have been reported to occur almost exclusively in males.

The division of the Paraphilias into distinct disorders is a carryover from DSM-II. An alternative (and probably superior) approach would have been to include just one diagnostic category for Paraphilia with subtypes. Because the criteria sets for each of the Paraphilias are similar, we discuss each criterion as it applies across the separate disorders.

Criterion A

Criterion A for each of the Paraphilias contains the following wording: **"Over a period of at least 6 months, recurrent, intense sexually arousing fantasies, sexual urges, or behaviors involving . . . *[the specific paraphilic focus]*."**

The following specific paraphilias are included in DSM-IV (each with its own diagnostic code):

302.4 Exhibitionism. Exhibitionism involves the exposure of one's genitals to a stranger. Sometimes the individual masturbates while exposing himself (or while fantasizing about exposing himself). Often, the exhibitionist is aware of a desire to surprise or shock the observer, but sometimes he has the sexually arousing fantasy that the observer will become sexually aroused.

302.81 Fetishism. Fetishism involves the use of nonliving objects (the fetish). Among the more common fetish objects are women's underpants, bras, stockings, shoes, boots, or other wearing apparel. The person with Fetishism frequently masturbates while holding, rubbing, or smelling the fetish object or may ask the sexual partner to wear the object during their sexual encounters. Usually the fetish is required or strongly preferred for sexual excitement, and there may be erectile dysfunction in its absence. This Paraphilia also includes a Criterion C (i.e., that the fetish is not limited to articles of female clothing used in cross-dressing) to distinguish it from Transvestic Fetishism.

302.89 Frotteurism. Frotteurism involves touching and rubbing against a nonconsenting person. The individual usually chooses crowded places so that he can more easily escape arrest (e.g., busy sidewalks or public transportation). Typically, he rubs his genitals against the victim's thighs and buttocks or fondles her genitalia or breasts.

302.2 Pedophilia. Pedophilia involves sexual activity with a prepubescent child. Pedophilia involving girls is reported more often than Pedophilia involving boys. Some individuals prefer boys, others prefer girls, and some are aroused by both boys and girls. Some individuals with Pedophilia are sexually attracted only to children (Exclusive Type), whereas others are sometimes attracted to adults (Nonexclusive Type). This Paraphilia also includes a Criterion C (the person must be at least 16 years of age and at least 5 years older than the child).

302.83 Sexual Masochism. Sexual Masochism involves the act of being humiliated, beaten, bound, or otherwise made to suffer. Individuals may act on the masochistic sexual urges by themselves (e.g., binding themselves, sticking themselves with pins, shocking themselves electrically, or self-mutilation) or with a partner (e.g., physical bondage, blindfolding, spanking, electrical shocks, "pinning and piercing," and humiliation).

302.84 Sexual Sadism. Sexual Sadism involves acts in which the individual derives sexual excitement from the psychological or physical suffering (including humiliation) of the victim. Some individuals act on the sadistic sexual urges with a consenting partner (who may have Sexual Masochism) who willingly suffers pain or humiliation. Others act on their sadistic sexual urges with nonconsenting victims.

302.3 Transvestic Fetishism. Transvestic Fetishism involves cross-dressing. Usually the male with Transvestic Fetishism keeps a collection of female clothes that he intermittently uses to cross-dress. While cross-dressed, he usually masturbates, imagining himself to be both the male subject and the female object of his sexual fantasy. This disorder has been described only in heterosexual males. Transvestic Fetishism has a Criterion C (the cross-dressing does not occur exclusively during the course of Gender Identity Disorder). A subtype (With Gender Dysphoria) is provided to allow the clinician to note the presence of gender dysphoria as part of Transvestic Fetishism.

302.82 Voyeurism. Voyeurism involves the act of observing (peeping) unsuspecting individuals, usually strangers, who are naked, in the process of disrobing, or engaging in sexual activity. Orgasm, usually produced by masturbation, may occur during the voyeuristic activity or later in response to the memory of what the person has witnessed.

Criterion B

Criterion B for each of the Paraphilias contains the following wording: **"The fantasies, sexual urges, or behaviors cause clinically significant distress or impairment in social, occupational, or other important areas of functioning."**

Many of the fantasies and behaviors described in each of the Paraphilias may in much attenuated form be a component of "normal" lovemaking and warrant a diagnosis of a Paraphilia only when they cause clinically significant difficulties. However, some of these behaviors are inherently problematic because they involve a nonconsenting person (Exhibitionism, Voyeurism, Frotteurism) or a child (Pedophilia) and may lead to arrest and incarceration. Other behaviors may lead to physical injuries (Sexual Sadism, Sexual Masochism). The impairment from other Paraphilias (Fetishism, Transvestic Fetishism) may result from adverse effects on social or sexual relationships if the partner finds the unusual sexual behavior shameful or repugnant or refuses to cooperate in the unusual sexual preferences. In some instances, the paraphilic behavior may become the major sexual activity in the individual's life. Although often associated with considerable distress, these problems rarely cause individuals to seek treatment unless their behavior creates conflict with sexual partners or society.

The Last Word

There is wide variability in individual and cultural standards for what is considered to be appropriate sexual behavior. A diagnosis of a Paraphilia applies only when the behavior is judged to cause clinically significant distress or impairment or involves children or nonconsenting adults. The inclusion of Paraphilias in a classification of mental disorders should not be taken to imply that individuals with Paraphilias are absolved of criminal responsibility for the consequences of their behavior.

Gender Identity Disorders

Gender Identity Disorder

Gender Identity Disorder concerns severe and persisting problems in one's sense of gender identification as a male or female. The concept of gender identity must not be confused with the concept of sexual orientation, which refers to whether the individual is sexually attracted to persons of the same sex, of the opposite sex, or of both sexes. In formulating the definitional boundaries for this condition, concerns were raised that problems with gender identity may sometimes be more a function of society's intolerance for differences rather than an inherent problem within the individual.

To reduce the risk of possible overdiagnosis, a relatively high threshold was set for the definition of Gender Identity Disorder, requiring persistent cross-gender identification, persistent discomfort with one's assigned sex, and clinically significant distress or impairment. One must be cautious in making the diagnosis of Gender Identity Disorder because of the wide variability of gender traits among individuals as well as the wide variability of societal acceptance of cross-gender behavior in different settings and cultures and over time.

Making the diagnosis of Gender Identity Disorder may be particularly problematic in children for several reasons: 1) they are often unable to verbalize distress, and in some cases such distress may be unjustifiable inferred; 2) manifestations of their gender identification may be transient or developmentally related; and 3) distress about gender-related behaviors may more express parental expectations or disappointments rather than factors in the child.

DSM-III-R and the *International Statistical Classification of Diseases and Related Health Problems,* 10th Revision (ICD-10), include three Gender Identity Disorders: Gender Identity Disorder of Childhood, Gender Identity of Adolescence or Adulthood, Nontranssexual Type (GIDAANT), and Transsexualism. The DSM-IV literature review suggested that this classification was unnecessarily cumbersome and that these disorders were better conceived of as one disorder that applies across the developmental and severity spectrum.

DSM-IV diagnostic criteria for Gender Identity Disorder

A. A strong and persistent cross-gender identification (not merely a desire for any perceived cultural advantages of being the other sex).

In children, the disturbance is manifested by four (or more) of the following:

(1) repeatedly stated desire to be, or insistence that he or she is, the other sex
(2) in boys, preference for cross-dressing or simulating female attire; in girls, insistence on wearing only stereotypical masculine clothing
(3) strong and persistent preferences for cross-sex roles in make-believe play or persistent fantasies of being the other sex
(4) intense desire to participate in the stereotypical games and pastimes of the other sex
(5) strong preference for playmates of the other sex

In adolescents and adults, the disturbance is manifested by symptoms such as a stated desire to be the other sex, frequent passing as the other sex, desire to live or be treated as the other sex, or the conviction that he or she has the typical feelings and reactions of the other sex.

B. Persistent discomfort with his or her sex or sense of inappropriateness in the gender role of that sex.

In children, the disturbance is manifested by any of the following: in boys, assertion that his penis or testes are disgusting or will disappear or assertion that it would be better not to have a penis, or aversion toward rough-and-tumble play and rejection of male stereotypical toys, games, and activities; in girls, rejection of urinating in a sitting position, assertion that she has or will grow a penis, or assertion that she does not want to grow breasts or menstruate, or marked aversion toward normative feminine clothing.

In adolescents and adults, the disturbance is manifested by symptoms such as preoccupation with getting rid of primary and secondary sex characteristics (e.g., request for hormones, surgery, or other procedures to physically alter sexual characteristics to simulate the other sex) or belief that he or she was born the wrong sex.

C. The disturbance is not concurrent with a physical intersex condition.

D. The disturbance causes clinically significant distress or impairment in social, occupational, or other important areas of functioning.

Code based on current age:
302.6 Gender Identity Disorder in Children
302.85 Gender Identity Disorder in Adolescents or Adults

Specify if (for sexually mature individuals):
Sexually Attracted to Males
Sexually Attracted to Females
Sexually Attracted to Both
Sexually Attracted to Neither

CRITERION A. The wording for this criterion was carefully crafted to address the considerable concern that a degree of cross-gender identification is not necessarily pathological and to avoid an overinclusive definition of Gender Identity Disorder. For example, it is important to avoid labeling as a mental disorder a girl's normal tomboy behavior or the interest of young children in the games, pastimes, and clothing of the opposite sex. To avoid overdiagnosis, Criterion A requires the presence of a strong and persistent cross-gender identification (i.e., the desire to be, or the insistence that one is, of the other sex) and sets a high threshold (i.e., four out of five items). Age-specific and gender-specific examples are presented.

CRITERION B. The requirement that the individual experience persistent discomfort in his or her gender role further helps to reduce the possible overinclusiveness of this disorder. Some experts in the field wanted to suspend this requirement for younger children on the grounds that they might not have the cognitive capacity to express distress and that, in such cases, Gender Identity Disorder should be determined by inference on the basis of the behaviors listed in Criterion A. This suggestion was not accepted because of the previously mentioned concerns about overinclusiveness.

CRITERION C. To keep this category relatively homogeneous, individuals with physical intersex conditions (e.g., hermaphrodism) who also have gender dysphoria are not included here and rather are diagnosed as having Gender Identity Disorder Not Otherwise Specified.

CRITERION D. This criterion was added in DSM-IV to further reduce the risk of false-positives. In addition to distress, children may fail to develop age-appropriate same-sex friends, may refuse to go to school because of teasing, and may become socially isolated. In adolescents and adults, preoccupation with cross-gender wishes often interferes with ordinary activities, causes difficulties in relationships, and may impair functioning at school or at work.

DSM-IV text for 302.6 Gender Identity Disorder Not Otherwise Specified

This category is included for coding disorders in gender identity that are not classifiable as a specific Gender Identity Disorder. Examples include

1. Intersex conditions (e.g., androgen insensitivity syndrome or congenital adrenal hyperplasia) and accompanying gender dysphoria
2. Transient, stress-related cross-dressing behavior
3. Persistent preoccupation with castration or penectomy without a desire to acquire the sex characteristics of the other sex

DSM-IV text for 302.9 Sexual Disorder Not Otherwise Specified

This category is included for coding a sexual disturbance that does not meet the criteria for any specific Sexual Disorder and is neither a Sexual Dysfunction nor a

Paraphilia. Examples include

1. Marked feelings of inadequacy concerning sexual performance or other traits related to self-imposed standards of masculinity or femininity
2. Distress about a pattern of repeated sexual relationships involving a succession of lovers who are experienced by the individual only as things to be used
3. Persistent and marked distress about sexual orientation.

The Last Word

There is wide variability in individual and cultural acceptance of nonadherence to stereotypical gender roles. Caution must be exercised in applying this diagnosis, especially when it is others who are distressed by the problems in gender identity rather than the individual.

CHAPTER 18

Eating Disorders

Tx: Cognitive Behavior Therapy
Psychotherapy & medications.

population: Individuals who's employment that requires maintain weight.

Eating Disorders

307.1	Anorexia Nervosa
307.51	Bulimia Nervosa
307.50	Eating Disorder Not Otherwise Specified

Anorexia Nervosa and Bulimia Nervosa are both characterized by the individual's overemphasis on body image. In addition, Anorexia Nervosa requires an abnormally low body weight and, in women, amenorrhea. In contrast, most individuals with Bulimia Nervosa have normal or above-normal weight and all display a pattern of sequential binge eating and inappropriate compensatory behaviors to avoid gaining weight. Many individuals with Anorexia Nervosa binge eat or purge to a level that would also meet criteria for Bulimia Nervosa. A separate diagnosis of Bulimia Nervosa is not given if the binge eating or purging is restricted to episodes of Anorexia Nervosa (i.e., when the weight is below the minimally normal threshold).

The utility of the distinction between Anorexia Nervosa and Bulimia Nervosa has been challenged. The fact that many individuals move from one diagnosis to the other depending on fluctuations in weight and the presence or absence of menses suggests that Anorexia Nervosa and Bulimia Nervosa should be no more than subtypes describing the course of a more inclusively defined Eating Disorder. Nonetheless, DSM-IV maintains Anorexia Nervosa and Bulimia Nervosa as separate categories because each has different treatment implications. Moreover, there are many pure cases of Anorexia Nervosa (individuals who never binge or purge) and pure cases of Bulimia Nervosa (individuals who never fall below their normal weight).

It has also been suggested that these disorders are a kind of culture-specific diagnosis that is indigenous to the United States and other industrialized countries where there is a national preoccupation (especially among women) with dieting and thinness in the midst of what is, for most people, a too-plentiful supply of food. This hypothesis may explain why the incidence of these disorders has increased in recent years and why there is a marked predominance of females with these disorders.

307.1 Anorexia Nervosa

The hallmark of Anorexia Nervosa is the refusal to maintain normal body weight, which is related to an extreme fear of becoming fat. Anorexia Nervosa is to be contrasted with other causes of excessively low weight, which include general medical conditions (e.g., cancer), other mental disorders (e.g., Major Depressive Disorder, Substance Dependence), and poor nutrition (e.g., from poverty or poor eating habits). The term *anorexia* (which means loss of appetite) is actually a misnomer. Although these individuals deny themselves food, they generally maintain their appetite and, like most starving people, often become preoccupied with food.

DSM-IV diagnostic criteria for 307.1 Anorexia Nervosa

A. Refusal to maintain body weight at or above a minimally normal weight for age and height (e.g., weight loss leading to maintenance of body weight less than 85% of that expected; or failure to make expected weight gain during period of growth, leading to body weight less than 85% of that expected).

B. Intense fear of gaining weight or becoming fat, even though underweight.

C. Disturbance in the way in which one's body weight or shape is experienced, undue influence of body weight or shape on self-evaluation, or denial of the seriousness of the current low body weight.

D. In postmenarcheal females, amenorrhea, i.e., the absence of at least three consecutive menstrual cycles. (A woman is considered to have amenorrhea if her periods occur only following hormone, e.g., estrogen, administration.)

Specify type:

Restricting Type: during the current episode of Anorexia Nervosa, the person has not regularly engaged in binge-eating or purging behavior (i.e., self-induced vomiting or the misuse of laxatives, diuretics, or enemas)

Binge-Eating/Purging Type: during the current episode of Anorexia Nervosa, the person has regularly engaged in binge-eating or purging behavior (i.e., self-induced vomiting or the misuse of laxatives, diuretics, or enemas)

Criteria B and C. We discuss these criteria first because they capture the essence of Anorexia Nervosa. The most striking feature of this disorder is the marked distortion in the way these individuals experience their body size and shape. The cognition that drives the efforts to lose weight is the belief that one is fat or might easily become fat unless extraordinary measures are taken to prevent it. In extreme cases, the individual may be so emaciated as to resemble a concentration camp victim but may still point to a body part (e.g., hips, thighs, belly) that seems "flabby" and needs further reduction.

Criterion A. What differentiates Anorexia Nervosa from other causes of weight loss is that there is a refusal to maintain body weight based on the fears and distortions indicated in Criteria B and C. It may not always be easy to determine at what point the person's weight is below the "minimally normal body weight" noted in the criterion. There is no absolute boundary between Anorexia Nervosa and being slender. Many individuals are naturally thin, some individuals work in professions where low body weight is a requirement (e.g., ballet dancers, models), and many others diet chronically in an effort to achieve a level of thinness that does not meet the low-weight criterion for this disorder.

In distinguishing Anorexia Nervosa from normal thinness, DSM-IV relies on clinical judgment rather than providing a specific cutoff, although it offers a general guideline that the individual's weight be below 85% of that expected given her age and height. Expected weight ranges can be determined by referring to one of several published versions of the Metropolitan Life Insurance Tables or to pediatric growth charts or by calculating whether the body mass index (i.e., weight in kilograms/[height in meters]^2) is less than 17.5 kg/m^2. In extreme cases, the weight loss can be life threatening, and the individual may starve in the midst of plenty.

Criterion D. The requirement for amenorrhea in females with this disorder is an additional way to set the boundary with normality. The amenorrhea indicates physiological dysfunction and is due to abnormally low levels of estrogen. Although amenorrhea is usually a consequence of the weight loss, in a minority of individuals it may actually precede the weight loss. It should be noted that there is no corresponding criterion for males, in whom Anorexia Nervosa is much less common.

Subtypes. Individuals with Anorexia Nervosa can be divided into two more homogeneous subgroups depending on the ways in which weight loss is achieved and the presence or absence of binge eating. Those who control their weight through rigid adherence to diet or exercise (the restricting type) tend to have compulsive personalities characterized by inflexibility, strict adherence to rules, and moral scrupulosity. Those who binge eat or control their weight by purging (the binge-eating/purging type) are more likely to have impulsive behavior and engage in substance use.

307.51 Bulimia Nervosa

The hallmark of Bulimia Nervosa is frequent binge eating accompanied by inappropriate compensatory behaviors to avoid gaining weight. Bulimia Nervosa differs from Anorexia Nervosa in that the individuals are not significantly underweight and are typically of normal weight or slightly overweight.

DSM-IV diagnostic criteria for 307.51 Bulimia Nervosa

A. Recurrent episodes of binge eating. An episode of binge eating is characterized by both of the following:
   (1) eating, in a discrete period of time (e.g., within any 2-hour period), an amount of food that is definitely larger than most people would eat during a similar period of time and under similar circumstances
   (2) a sense of lack of control over eating during the episode (e.g., a feeling that one cannot stop eating or control what or how much one is eating)

B. Recurrent inappropriate compensatory behavior in order to prevent weight gain, such as self-induced vomiting; misuse of laxatives, diuretics, enemas, or other medications; fasting; or excessive exercise.

C. The binge eating and inappropriate compensatory behaviors both occur, on average, at least twice a week for 3 months.

D. Self-evaluation is unduly influenced by body shape and weight.

E. The disturbance does not occur exclusively during episodes of Anorexia Nervosa.

Specify type:

Purging Type: during the current episode of Bulimia Nervosa, the person has regularly engaged in self-induced vomiting or the misuse of laxatives, diuretics, or enemas

Nonpurging Type: during the current episode of Bulimia Nervosa, the person has used other inappropriate compensatory behaviors, such as fasting or excessive exercise, but has not regularly engaged in self-induced vomiting or the misuse of laxatives, diuretics, or enemas

Criterion A. Episodic bursts of binge eating must be distinguished from a pattern of generalized overeating (grazing) and from isolated episodes of overeating that are context specific (e.g., at an all-you-can-eat restaurant or a celebration in which there is unlimited food). Binge eating occurs during a discrete period of time, involves consuming a huge number of calories, and is characterized by the sense of having lost control. Although the person may have a feeling of gratification or a reduction in anxiety during the binge, afterward she typically feels uncomfortable, guilty, disgusted, or ashamed. The type of food consumed during binges varies but usually includes sweet, high-calorie treats such as ice cream and cake. Because some especially abstemious individuals may report having had "binges" after eating relatively small amounts of food (e.g., three cookies), it is important to inquire specifically about the quantity and type of food consumed.

Criterion B. Binge eating by itself is not sufficient to make the diagnosis of Bulimia Nervosa. It must be accompanied by inappropriate compensatory mechanisms intended to counteract the effects of the binge. The most common of these compensatory behaviors involve some form of purging (self-induced vomiting or laxative abuse). Less common compensatory behaviors include fasting, excessive exercise, and manipulation of insulin doses by diabetic persons. The distinction between purging and nonpurging compensatory mechanisms forms the basis for subtyping this disorder.

A common misconception is that purging behavior is a required feature of this disorder. It is important to inquire about other nonpurging compensatory mechanisms that are used. Individuals are often very embarrassed about both their binge eating and their compensatory mechanisms (particularly those related to purging). Therefore, such information is often not volunteered and emerges only with direct questioning. Some research suggests that binge eating in the absence of inappropriate compensatory mechanisms may also be clinically important. In DSM-IV, such individuals are diagnosed with Eating Disorder Not Otherwise Specified, and a research criteria set for binge eating disorder is included in DSM-IV Appendix B, "Criteria Sets and Axes Provided for Further Study."

CRITERION C. The minimum frequency of twice a week applies both to the binges and to the compensatory mechanisms, with the presumption that these generally occur together. As with all frequency and duration thresholds included in DSM-IV, this frequency threshold is no more than a guideline for establishing the boundary for this disorder and should not be applied rigidly without exercising clinical judgment.

CRITERION D. Individuals with Bulimia Nervosa, like those with Anorexia Nervosa, are overly focused on their body shape or size, which is often manifested by intense fear of gaining weight, desire to lose weight, and dissatisfaction with their bodies.

CRITERION E. A diagnosis of Bulimia Nervosa should not be given when the binge-eating and purging behaviors occur only during episodes of Anorexia Nervosa (in which case the diagnosis is Anorexia Nervosa, Binge-Eating/Purging Type). An unavoidable awkwardness of the DSM-IV algorithm concerning the relationship between Anorexia Nervosa and Bulimia Nervosa is that a patient may move from one diagnosis to the other by virtue of fluctuations in weight or in menstruation. For example, a patient with binge-eating and purging behavior, low weight, and amenorrhea would have a diagnosis of Anorexia Nervosa, Binge-Eating/Purging Type, until her weight rose above 85% of normal weight (or she resumed menstruation), in which case she would be reclassified as having Bulimia Nervosa, Purging Type. Subsequent loss of weight or periods would result in an oscillation back to Anorexia Nervosa, and so forth. The alternation between diagnostic terms should not be taken to mean that the patient has two distinct conditions.

SUBTYPES. Many of the medical complications occurring with this disorder are associated with the compensatory behaviors. In Bulimia Nervosa, Purging Type, self-induced vomiting or the misuse of laxatives, diuretics, or enemas can result in tooth erosion, electrolyte imbalances, laxative dependence, and, more rarely, esophageal tears. In the Nonpurging Type, use of stimulants or excessive exercise can result in Amphetamine Dependence or exercise injuries. Many researchers have considered purging to be the essential feature of Bulimia Nervosa, and most of the available literature includes only individuals who both binge and purge. In fact, early in the DSM-IV deliberations, it was proposed that purging behavior be a requirement for the diagnosis of Bulimia Nervosa. This suggestion was not adopted because individuals who use other compensatory mechanisms (e.g., fasting, excessive exercise) are encountered.

DSM-IV text for 307.50 Eating Disorder Not Otherwise Specified

The Eating Disorder Not Otherwise Specified category is for disorders of eating that do not meet the criteria for any specific Eating Disorder. Examples include

1. For females, all of the criteria for Anorexia Nervosa are met except that the individual has regular menses.
2. All of the criteria for Anorexia Nervosa are met except that, despite significant weight loss, the individual's current weight is in the normal range.
3. All of the criteria for Bulimia Nervosa are met except that the binge eating and inappropriate compensatory mechanisms occur at a frequency of less than twice a week or for a duration of less than 3 months.
4. The regular use of inappropriate compensatory behavior by an individual of normal body weight after eating small amounts of food (e.g., self-induced vomiting after the consumption of two cookies).
5. Repeatedly chewing and spitting out, but not swallowing, large amounts of food.
6. Binge-eating disorder: recurrent episodes of binge eating in the absence of the regular use of inappropriate compensatory behaviors characteristic of Bulimia Nervosa.

The Last Word

The hallmark of these disorders is that the individual's self-evaluation is unduly influenced by her body shape and weight. This characteristic helps differentiate these causes of weight loss or abnormal eating behaviors from other etiologies (e.g., a general medical condition, depression). The starvation, binge eating, and compensatory mechanisms (especially self-induced vomiting) associated with these disorders can lead to potentially serious medical complications.

CHAPTER 19

Sleep Disorders

Sleep disorders were first included as part of the official nomenclature in DSM-III-R in recognition of their importance in the presentation and differential diagnosis of mental disorders and the frequency with which they are diagnosed and treated by mental health professionals. Another sleep classification (the International Classification of Sleep Disorders [ICSD]) developed in 1991 by sleep specialists is much more detailed and includes over 100 different diagnoses. DSM-IV chose not to adopt the ICSD system because the reliability and validity of its many diagnoses have not yet been established and because it would certainly be too cumbersome for use in general clinical settings. Instead, DSM-IV includes a total of 12 disorders, which are fully compatible with the much finer grained ICSD categories. For example, the DSM-IV category of Primary Insomnia includes in one diagnosis the ICSD categories of Psychophysiological Insomnia, Sleep State Misperception, Idiopathic Insomnia, and Inadequate Sleep Hygiene. See Table 19–1 for a list of the DSM-IV Sleep Disorders.

The best way to remember the various sleep disorders is to recall that they are organized based on presumed etiology:

1. Primary Sleep Disorders
2. Sleep Disorders Related to Another Mental Disorder
3. Sleep Disorder Due to a General Medical Condition
4. Substance-Induced Sleep Disorder

Although Primary Sleep Disorders are listed first, in practice the diagnosis of a Primary Sleep Disorder can only be made after the more specific etiologies have been ruled out. The Primary Sleep Disorders are themselves divided into two groups: Dyssomnias and Parasomnias. The Dyssomnias are those disorders in which there is a disturbance in the amount, timing, or quality of sleep. They include Primary Insomnia, Primary Hypersomnia, Narcolepsy, Breathing-Related Sleep Disorder, and Circadian Rhythm Sleep Disorder. The Parasomnias are those disorders in which an abnormal or distressing event (severe nightmares, sleep terrors, and sleepwalking) occurs during sleep or at the threshold between sleep and wakefulness. They include Nightmare Disorder, Sleep Terror Disorder, and Sleepwalking Disorder.

The most important and controversial question regarding the criteria sets in this section was the degree to which they should include the findings from sleep polysomnography (e.g., monitoring of brain-wave activity, eye movements, muscle movements, and breathing). More than in most areas of psychiatry, the sleep laboratory provides sensitive and specific information that can be useful in the confirmation of sleep disorder diagnoses. For this reason, the ICSD classification includes polysomnographic findings in its definitions of sleep disorders. In contrast, the DSM-IV Work Group decided not to include these laboratory findings in the criteria sets but rather to describe them in considerable detail in the texts for each disorder. This decision reflected the fact that most sleep disorder diagnoses can be made on clinical grounds without the sleep laboratory and the fact that sleep laboratory studies are expensive and not always readily available.

Table 19–1. The sleep disorders

Primary Sleep Disorders	
Dyssomnias	
307.42	Primary Insomnia
307.44	Primary Hypersomnia
347	Narcolepsy
780.59	Breathing-Related Sleep Disorder
307.45	Circadian Rhythm Sleep Disorder
307.47	Dyssomnia Not Otherwise Specified
Parasomnias	
307.47	Nightmare Disorder
307.46	Sleep Terror Disorder
307.46	Sleepwalking Disorder
307.47	Parasomnia Not Otherwise Specified
Sleep Disorders Related to Another Mental Disorder	
307.42	Insomnia Related to . . . *[Indicate the Axis I or Axis II Disorder]*
307.44	Hypersomnia Related to . . . *[Indicate the Axis I or Axis II Disorder]*
Other Sleep Disorders	
780.xx	Sleep Disorder Due to . . . *[Indicate the General Medical Condition]*
780.52	Insomnia Type
780.54	Hypersomnia Type
780.59	Parasomnia Type
780.59	Mixed Type
—.—	Substance-Induced Sleep Disorder *[Refer to Substance-Related Disorders for substance-specific codes]*

Before we discuss the various sleep disorders, it may be useful to briefly summarizes the five stages of sleep: rapid eye movement (REM) sleep and four stages of non-rapid eye movement (NREM) sleep. Normal sleep starts with the transition from wakefulness to sleep (NREM stage 1). NREM stage 2 is characterized by specific electroencephalogram (EEG) waveforms and makes up about half of the total sleep period. Stages 3 and 4 are the deepest stages of sleep and are characterized by slow waves on EEG. REM sleep consists of periods of rapid eye movements, sleep paralysis, erections in men, and dreaming.

There is a characteristic architecture of the sleep stages throughout the night with periods of REM sleep alternating with periods of NREM sleep about every 90 minutes. The deeper stages of sleep predominate during the first half of the sleep episode, whereas the REM sleep periods increase in duration as the night wears on. As part of the aging process, sleep tends to become less efficient and more problematic with increased wakefulness and less time spent in the deeper stages of sleep.

Primary Sleep Disorders

Dyssomnias

307.42 Primary Insomnia

Insomnia can take several forms: difficulty falling asleep (initial insomnia), waking up intermittently with difficulty falling back to sleep (middle insomnia), early morning awakening with inability to fall back asleep, and nonrestorative sleep (i.e., the person has what might be considered a normal amount of sleep but does not feel rested). Primary Insomnia must be distinguished from normal difficulty in falling and staying asleep. However, several issues make it difficult to establish a clear standard for what constitutes normal sleep:

1. There is wide variability in the amount of sleep different individuals need to feel rested.
2. Sleep efficiency decreases with age.
3. Women tend to require more sleep than men.
4. Individuals with complaints of insomnia often underestimate the actual amount of time spent sleeping (as measured by polysomnography), and it is not clear how to balance their subjective complaints with the objective findings.

Although the following criteria set attempts to provide some guidelines, it is especially important that clinical judgment be exercised in the diagnosis of Primary Insomnia.

By definition, a diagnosis of Primary Insomnia means that other, more specific etiologies have been considered and ruled out (i.e., the insomnia is not a feature of another sleep disorder or due to another mental disorder, a general medical condition, or substance use). Primary Insomnia is a heterogeneous grouping likely to include a number of different etiologies as well as those frequently encountered situations in which no etiology can be found.

Primary Insomnia commonly arises from poor sleep hygiene (i.e., behaviors that disrupt sleep organization such as working late into the night, taking excessive daytime naps, and keeping irregular sleep hours). Negative conditioning can also play an important role both in the etiology and exacerbation of sleep problems. Individuals may become preoccupied with their fears of being unable to fall asleep or of being awakened, and this worrying may become a self-fulfilling prophecy. A vicious cycle develops in which worries about being unable to fall asleep lead to increased arousal before sleep, which makes it impossible to sleep, which in turn further increases the worries that one will not be able to fall asleep, and so on. Very often, the bedroom of the person with insomnia becomes a focus for this negative conditioning, and it may be easier to fall asleep when in another setting. These people's sleep improves when they are at a movie, in front of the TV, or in a hotel room.

DSM-IV diagnostic criteria for 307.42 Primary Insomnia

A. The predominant complaint is difficulty initiating or maintaining sleep, or nonrestorative sleep, for at least 1 month.

B. The sleep disturbance (or associated daytime fatigue) causes clinically significant distress or impairment in social, occupational, or other important areas of functioning.

C. The sleep disturbance does not occur exclusively during the course of Narcolepsy, Breathing-Related Sleep Disorder, Circadian Rhythm Sleep Disorder, or a Parasomnia.

D. The disturbance does not occur exclusively during the course of another mental disorder (e.g., Major Depressive Disorder, Generalized Anxiety Disorder, a delirium).

E. The disturbance is not due to the direct physiological effects of a substance (e.g., a drug of abuse, a medication) or a general medical condition.

Criteria A and B. Many people are dissatisfied with the quality or amount of their sleep, and it is difficult to set the boundary between pathological insomnia and the more or less normal and expectable problems people have sleeping. These criteria require that the sleep complaint be predominant, persist for at least 1 month, and be clinically significant, thus preventing the classification of short-lived or situational sleep disturbances as insomnia. The impairment associated with chronic insomnia includes daytime tiredness, dysphoria, and difficulty concentrating. Insomnia often leads to decreased feelings of well-being during the day.

Criterion C. Many patients with other sleep disorders present with complaints of insomnia. These more specific causes of insomnia must be considered and ruled out before a diagnosis of Primary Insomnia is made. Note that Primary Hypersomnia is not included in the list of sleep disorders that take precedence over insomnia. Individuals with insomnia often present with daytime fatigue that is best considered to be an associated feature of the insomnia.

CRITERION D. Insomnia is commonly associated with many other mental disorders. A separate diagnosis of Primary Insomnia should be given only when it is judged that the insomnia occurs independently of the other mental disorder. When prominent and persisting symptoms of insomnia precede the onset of the mental disorder, this determination is relatively clear-cut. When the prominent insomnia starts during the mental disorder (especially Major Depressive Disorder) but persists after the other symptoms of the mental disorder have remitted, it can be difficult to determine whether the insomnia is best considered primary or represents a partial remission of the mental disorder.

CRITERION E. Insomnia, more than most conditions, is associated with the use of medications and drugs of abuse. Therefore, a diagnosis of Substance-Induced Sleep Disorder rather than a diagnosis of Primary Insomnia might be warranted. When evaluating insomnia, it is extremely important to query the person about the use of prescribed medication, over-the-counter medication (e.g., diet pills, decongestants), substances of abuse (cocaine), and other readily available stimulants (caffeine-containing substances).

307.44 Primary Hypersomnia

Excessive daytime sleepiness is an extremely common problem that in most cases is due to inadequate nocturnal sleep. Before giving the diagnosis of Primary Hypersomnia, the clinician first must determine whether the individual is getting an adequate amount of sleep. Fewer than 7 hours per night suggests that the person is getting inadequate sleep, and more than 9 hours per night is more suggestive of Primary Hypersomnia. However, this guideline is complicated by the wide individual variability in the amount of sleep needed to feel refreshed the next morning. Some individuals are naturally long sleepers who develop daytime sleepiness when job, school, or social requirements result in inadequate sleep relative to their needs. Long sleeping, which is more common in women, does not qualify for a diagnosis of Primary Hypersomnia.

By definition, a diagnosis of Primary Hypersomnia means that other, more specific etiologies have been considered and ruled out (i.e., the hypersomnia is not a feature of another sleep disorder or due to another mental disorder, a general medical condition, or substance use).

DSM-IV diagnostic criteria for 307.44 Primary Hypersomnia

A. The predominant complaint is excessive sleepiness for at least 1 month (or less if recurrent) as evidenced by either prolonged sleep episodes or daytime sleep episodes that occur almost daily.

(continued)

DSM-IV diagnostic criteria for 307.44 Primary Hypersomnia *(continued)*

B. The excessive sleepiness causes clinically significant distress or impairment in social, occupational, or other important areas of functioning.

C. The excessive sleepiness is not better accounted for by insomnia and does not occur exclusively during the course of another Sleep Disorder (e.g., Narcolepsy, Breathing-Related Sleep Disorder, Circadian Rhythm Sleep Disorder, or a Parasomnia) and cannot be accounted for by an inadequate amount of sleep.

D. The disturbance does not occur exclusively during the course of another mental disorder.

E. The disturbance is not due to the direct physiological effects of a substance (e.g., a drug of abuse, a medication) or a general medical condition.

Specify if:

Recurrent: if there are periods of excessive sleepiness that last at least 3 days occurring several times a year for at least 2 years

CRITERION A. The diagnosis of Primary Hypersomnia is not meant to be given to individuals who have only occasional episodes of excessive sleepiness or to those who choose to burn the candle at both ends. Individuals with Primary Hypersomnia have a persistent condition with episodes of nighttime sleep that may last as long as 12 hours or a frequent need to take daytime naps that do not relieve the sleepiness, or both.

CRITERION B. There may also be inadvertent episodes of falling asleep, which are especially likely to occur in situations that provide very little stimulation. This condition can be life threatening if the sleep episodes occur when the person drives long distances.

CRITERION C. Patients with other sleep disorders may present with excessive sleepiness, and these disorders must be considered and ruled out before the diagnosis of Primary Hypersomnia is made. In contrast to Primary Insomnia (which is often accompanied by daytime sleepiness), the actual quality of nighttime sleep in Primary Hypersomnia is normal. In contrast to Narcolepsy, Primary Hypersomnia causes the individual to experience a gradual onset of daytime sleepiness rather a sudden sleep attack.

CRITERIA D AND E. These two criteria are identical to Criteria D and E in Primary Insomnia, and the annotations to those criteria apply here as well.

347 Narcolepsy

Although not considered a mental disorder, Narcolepsy is included in DSM-IV because it is important in the differential diagnosis of hypersomnia. Narcolepsy is characterized by repeated sleep attacks in which the person has an irresistible need to take a nap and then wakes up refreshed. Episodes of cataplexy also occur in many individuals with Narcolepsy. There are brief, sudden losses of muscle tone, often triggered by strong emotions such as anger or surprise. In addition, there may be intrusions of elements of REM sleep on falling asleep or on awakening. These include hypnogogic hallucinations (i.e., intense dream-like imagery when falling asleep), hypnopompic hallucinations (i.e., imagery on awakening), and sleep paralysis (i.e., awakening and finding oneself unable to move or speak).

780.59 Breathing-Related Sleep Disorder

Although not considered a mental disorder, Breathing-Related Sleep Disorder is included in DSM-IV because of its importance in the differential diagnosis of insomnia and hypersomnia and its clinical significance (both prognostically and for its treatment implications). Breathing-Related Sleep Disorder is characterized by sleep disruption due to abnormalities of ventilation. The most common presenting complaint is excessive daytime sleepiness, but there may also be complaints about frequent nighttime awakening.

The most common cause of Breathing-Related Sleep Disorder is obstructive sleep apnea, which usually occurs in overweight individuals and consists of repeated episodes of upper-airway obstruction. This apnea is often manifested by prominent snoring or periods of stopped breathing with loud "resuscitative" snores, gasps, moans or mumbling, or whole body movements. Because the individual is typically unaware of these events, it is important to gather information from bedpartners. This diagnosis may also require sleep laboratory evaluation to document the presence and type of the Sleep-Related Breathing Disorder.

307.45 Circadian Rhythm Sleep Disorder

As with the other dyssomnias, the chief complaint in Circadian Rhythm Sleep Disorder is excessive sleepiness or insomnia. However, in contrast to other Primary Sleep Disorders, there is nothing wrong with the individual's inherent ability to initiate and maintain a normal sleep episode. Instead, the problem arises because there is a mismatch between the individual's endogenous circadian sleep-wake cycle and the demands of the external environment. This mismatch most commonly occurs in three situations, each of which can be indicated by a subtype:

1. Delayed Sleep Phase Type (i.e., night owls whose preferred sleep pattern is delayed relative to job or school demands for what seems to them to be early rising)
2. Jet Lag Type (i.e., a mismatch between the individual's endogenous sleep cycle and the schedule required by a new time zone)

3. Shift Work Type (i.e., a mismatch between the individual's endogenous cycle and the schedule requirements of night shift work or frequently changing shifts)

An Unspecified Type is included, particularly for early birds with advanced sleep phase problems that prevent them from staying awake in the evening. It should be noted that individuals vary widely in their ability to accommodate external scheduling demands. Most mismatches are insufficiently severe or persisting to require a diagnosis.

Parasomnias

The Parasomnias are the second type of Primary Sleep Disorders in DSM-IV. A Parasomnia is defined as an abnormal behavior or physiological event that occurs during sleep or a sleep-wake transition. They include Nightmare Disorder, Sleep Terror Disorder, and Sleepwalking Disorder. These Primary Sleep Disorders can be diagnosed only after other causes of the abnormal sleep behavior have been ruled out (e.g., Sleep Disorder Due to a General Medical Condition, Parasomnia Type; Substance-Induced Sleep Disorder, Parasomnia Type). Occasional episodes of nightmares, sleep terrors, or sleepwalking are not infrequent, especially in children. Only when these are recurrent and cause clinically significant distress or impairment should a diagnosis be made. A frequent reason for presentation is the individual's avoidance of situations that would reveal the behavior to others. In children, the problem might be revealed at summer camp. In adults, the problem might become apparent when acquiring a college roommate, joining the military, or sleeping with a bedpartner.

307.47 Nightmare Disorder

Nightmare Disorder is characterized by frightening dreams leading to awakenings. In contrast to a person with Sleep Terror Disorder, a person with Nightmare Disorder quickly becomes fully alert on awakening and generally recalls the content of the dream. Of course, from time to time, nightmares are a feature of everyone's sleep. This diagnosis should be considered only in cases when the nightmares are recurrent and particularly distressing. The individual may do everything possible to avoid going to sleep because of the fear of awakening in a nightmare. Nightmares arise almost exclusively during REM sleep. They are more likely to occur toward morning because REM sleep periods typically become longer and dreaming becomes more intense in the second half of the night.

307.46 Sleep Terror Disorder

Sleep Terror Disorder is characterized by abrupt awakenings from sleep that begin with a panicky scream or cry accompanied by autonomic arousal and intense fear typically lasting 1–10 minutes. In contrast to a person with Nightmare Disorder, a person with Sleep Terror Disorder is difficult to awaken or comfort, the dream is not remembered, and there is amnesia for the event on awakening. Sleep terrors usually begin during stage 3 or 4 of NREM sleep and are more likely to occur early in the sleep episode because these stages are concentrated in the first third of the night.

307.46 Sleepwalking Disorder

Sleepwalking Disorder is characterized by episodes of complex behavior occurring during sleep. These may include sitting up in bed; eating; talking; and walking into closets, up and down stairs, and even out of buildings. The episodes may last from several minutes up to a half hour. While sleepwalking, the person usually has reduced alertness and a blank stare, is relatively unresponsive to communication with others, and can be awakened only with great difficulty. If awakened during the episode, the person may be briefly confused or disoriented, and typically there is amnesia for the event. Like Sleep Terrors, episodes of Sleepwalking usually begin during stage 3 or 4 of NREM sleep and are more likely to occur early in the sleep episode.

Sleep Disorders Related to Another Mental Disorder

307.42 Insomnia Related to Another Mental Disorder, 307.44 Hypersomnia Related to Another Mental Disorder

In contrast to the Primary Sleep Disorders, Sleep Disorder Due to a General Medical Condition, and Substance-Induced Sleep Disorder, the sleep disturbances in this section are judged to be related to another mental disorder. Two disorders are included: Insomnia Related to Another Mental Disorder and Hypersomnia Related to Another Mental Disorder.

It is interesting to note that the provision of these diagnoses in DSM-IV violates a general principle followed in the rest of the manual. DSM-IV defines syndromal presentations (clusters of symptoms occurring together) rather than allowing the separate diagnosis of individual target symptoms. In contrast, Sleep Disorders Related to Another Mental Disorder elevates a single symptom (insomnia or hypersomnia) that is an essential or associated feature of another mental disorder to the level of a separate diagnosis. Suggestions for parallel elevations for other single symptoms (e.g., suicidal behavior, pain) were rejected on the grounds that such splitting of syndromes results in unneeded complexity and might give the misleading impression that the individual has two separate disorders. An exception was made for Sleep Disorders to maintain consistency with DSM-III-R and compatibility with ICSD, as well as to provide a convenient approach to the comprehensive differential diagnosis of insomnia and hypersomnia.

One of the problems in applying these diagnoses is that insomnia and hypersomnia are common features of many mental disorders (especially Mood Disorder, Anxiety Disorder, and Schizophrenia). DSM-IV does not mean to suggest that a separate diagnosis of insomnia or hypersomnia be given every time these sleep disorders appear in the context of other mental disorders. These diagnoses are reserved only for those relatively infrequent situations in which the sleep disturbance is the predominant complaint and is sufficiently severe to warrant independent clinical attention. For example, the diagnosis might be appropriate for individuals who focus almost exclusively on insomnia or hypersomnia as their chief complaint or when the sleep disturbance is out of proportion to the severity of the other symptoms characteristic of the related mental disorder.

It is sometimes difficult to determine whether a mental disorder is causing a sleep problem, a sleep problem is causing a mental disorder, or they are independent conditions. Indeed, the DSM-IV Sleep Disorders Field Trial demonstrated that this determination is made with poor reliability. There are no hard-and-fast rules, but the evaluation may be informed by considering the temporal relationships of the onsets and offsets of sleep problems relative to the other psychopathology and the longitudinal evolution of the course.

A diagnosis of Insomnia or Hypersomnia Related to Another Mental Disorder is given only when the sleep disturbance occurs exclusively during the course of the other mental disorder. In other words, the onset of the sleep problem occurs after the onset of the other mental disorder and it remits more or less as the mental disorder does. In contrast, the diagnosis might be Primary Insomnia for an individual with Major Depressive Disorder and severe insomnia if the insomnia were present long before the onset of the other symptoms of depression or persisted very long after the other symptoms remitted.

Other Sleep Disorders

780.xx Sleep Disorder Due to a General Medical Condition

Sleep Disorder Due to a General Medical Condition is diagnosed when sleep problems (i.e., insomnia, hypersomnia, parasomnia, or some combination) are caused by a general medical condition. The condition may interfere with sleep through a direct effect on the central nervous system (as in Parkinson's disease) or by causing a physical symptom that interferes with sleep (e.g., pain, coughing, itching). This category is not meant to apply to sleep disturbances that result from the psychological response to having a general medical condition. For example, an individual who cannot sleep due to worry about cancer might instead receive a diagnosis of Adjustment Disorder. (See Chapter 7 for a further discussion of differentiating primary disorders from those due to the direct effects of a general medical condition.) This diagnosis is reserved for those disturbances that are severe enough to warrant independent attention (e.g., those requiring prolonged hypnotic medication). It is not intended to be applied to every person with a general medical condition who has some difficulty sleeping.

Substance-Induced Sleep Disorder

Substance-Induced Sleep Disorder is diagnosed when sleep problems (i.e., insomnia, hypersomnia, parasomnia, or some combination) are caused by the effects of a drug of abuse, a medication, or toxin exposure. DSM-IV notes that the following classes of substances can be etiologically associated with sleep disturbance: alcohol; amphetamine and related stimulants; caffeine; cocaine; opioids; sedatives, hypnotics, and anxiolytics; and a variety of other substances.

The diagnosis of Substance-Induced Sleep Disorder is reserved for those disturbances that are severe enough to warrant independent attention and are in excess of those usually associated with intoxication with, or withdrawal from, a given substance. This diagnosis is not intended to be given to every drug user who has some trouble sleeping. Perhaps the most difficult aspect of making this diagnosis is determining whether the sleep disorder is primary or due to a substance or medication. Sometimes, there are chicken-and-egg problems. An individual may have had a Primary Insomnia for which medications were prescribed. After a time, the hypnotics are no longer effective and may in fact cause a more severe insomnia than they were originally meant to treat. For a discussion of this issue, see Chapter 7.

The Last Word

There is wide variability in what might be considered normal sleep requirements and patterns. The sleep disorders apply only when there is a judgment that they cause clinically significant distress or impairment. Furthermore, sleep problems commonly occur as associated features of other mental disorders, substance use, or a general medical condition. A separate sleep diagnosis is given only when independent clinical attention for the sleep problem is warranted. Once it is decided that a separate sleep diagnosis is warranted, the next step is to determine whether the disorder is primary or due to another mental disorder, a general medical condition, or substance use.

CHAPTER 20

Impulse-Control Disorders Not Elsewhere Classified

Impulse-Control Disorders Not Elsewhere Classified

312.34	Intermittent Explosive Disorder
312.32	Kleptomania
312.33	Pyromania
312.31	Pathological Gambling
312.39	Trichotillomania
312.30	Impulse-Control Disorder Not Otherwise Specified

As is suggested by the title of this chapter, no one section in DSM-IV systematically and comprehensively provides a nosology for all disorders of impulse control. A number of disorders characterized by impulse-control problems are classified elsewhere (e.g., Conduct Disorder, Attention-Deficit/Hyperactivity Disorder, Oppositional Defiant Disorder, Delirium, Dementia, Substance-Related Disorders, Schizophrenia and Other Psychotic Disorders, Mood Disorders, Antisocial and Borderline Personality Disorders). Indeed, there is no one organizing principle that guided the inclusion of the various disorders in this section. For the most part, they are here only because each is characterized by clinically significant impulsive behavior that is not better accounted for by the mental disorders listed in other parts of the manual.

Three of the Impulse-Control Disorders (Kleptomania, Pyromania, Trichotillomania) do have a unifying construct that describes the pattern of the impulsive behavior and its consequences. Their definitions all require that the particular impulsive act be preceded by a sense of tension and be followed by a feeling of pleasure or relief of tension. Thus, impulsive behavior (in which the motive is pleasure or tension release) is distinguished from compulsive behavior (in which the motive is reduction of distress or anxiety). In practice, however, it is often difficult to distinguish between tension release and anxiety reduction, and the boundary between the constructs of *impulsive* and *compulsive* behavior is far from clear. This confusion is reflected in the incorrect colloquial use of the word *compulsive* to describe behaviors that are better considered to be impulsive, such as "compulsive" gambling, eating, drug taking, spending, and sexual behavior.

Compulsive and impulsive behaviors have many features in common. Both are repetitious and difficult to resist despite knowledge of potential adverse consequences. The differences between compulsive and impulsive behavior are the underlying motivations and the degree to which the behavior is ego-syntonic. Initially, the goal of impulsive behavior is to experience pleasure, whereas the goal of compulsive behavior is to prevent anxiety and subjective discomfort. However, as the impulsive or compulsive behavior escalates in frequency, this boundary becomes blurred. As impulsive behavior occurs more frequently, the individual feels less in control of it and derives less pleasure from it, and the behavior may become ego-dystonic. On the other hand, compulsive behavior initially driven by the need to reduce anxiety may eventually become more ego-syntonic and acceptable to the individual.

312.34 Intermittent Explosive Disorder

Intermittent Explosive Disorder is one of the most problematic categories in DSM-IV. Unfortunately, it has been the subject of very little systematic study, has very unclear boundaries, and may be the source of serious misunderstandings, particularly when applied in forensic settings. These problems partly result from the fact that psychiatry does not have a well-established nosology of aggressive behavior and the fact that the research on this crucially important aspect of human behavior has been quite limited. Indeed, DSM-IV includes a variety of disorders that have aggression as a diagnostic or associated feature.

DSM-III introduced the categories Intermittent Explosive Disorder and Isolated Explosive Disorder, adapting what in DSM-II had been called Explosive Personality Disorder. These categories were intended to apply to discrete outbursts or attacks of aggressive behavior that were out of proportion to any precipitating stressors, were strikingly different from the individual's usual behavior, and were the cause of regret or repentance. DSM-III-R eliminated the category of Isolated Explosive Disorder and retained Intermittent Explosive Disorder, despite stated doubts concerning its existence as a separate entity distinct from other mental disorders characterized by aggressive behavior (e.g., Personality Change Due to a General Medical Condition, Antisocial or Borderline Personality Disorder, Conduct Disorder, Substance Intoxication). With some reluctance, the DSM-IV Task Force decided to retain the category of Intermittent Explosive Disorder because it has some utility in clinical settings and may serve as a stimulus to research.

DSM-IV diagnostic criteria for 312.34 Intermittent Explosive Disorder

A. Several discrete episodes of failure to resist aggressive impulses that result in serious assaultive acts or destruction of property.

B. The degree of aggressiveness expressed during the episodes is grossly out of proportion to any precipitating psychosocial stressors.

C. The aggressive episodes are not better accounted for by another mental disorder (e.g., Antisocial Personality Disorder, Borderline Personality Disorder, a Psychotic Disorder, a Manic Episode, Conduct Disorder, or Attention-Deficit/Hyperactivity Disorder) and are not due to the direct physiological effects of a substance (e.g., a drug of abuse, a medication) or a general medical condition (e.g., head trauma, Alzheimer's disease).

Criterion C. Unfortunately, it is easier to say what Intermittent Explosive Disorder is not than to define what it is. Aggressive behavior can occur in the context of many other mental disorders. By and large, Intermittent Explosive Disorder is a diagnosis of exclusion, to be made only after other possible causes for the aggressive behavior have been considered. The DSM-III and DSM-III-R definition, which was even narrower than that in DSM-IV, was so restrictive as to almost never be used.

DSM-III prohibited the Intermittent Explosive Disorder diagnosis when there was generalized impulsiveness or aggressiveness between episodes and when the episodes occurred during the course of other disorders. In contrast, DSM-IV allows the clinician to give an additional diagnosis of Intermittent Explosive Disorder in the presence of another disorder when the episodes are not better accounted for by the other disorder. This was deemed necessary because the clinical reality is that most individuals who have intermittent episodes of aggressive behavior also have some level of impulsivity between episodes.

The exclusion of Intermittent Explosive Disorder in the presence of a general medical etiology presents an interesting problem. Intermittent Explosive Disorder is not diagnosed when the aggressive episodes are a direct physiological consequence of a general medical condition. Instead, such cases would be diagnosed as Personality Change Due to a General Medical Condition, Delirium, or Dementia. However, it should be noted that individuals with Intermittent Explosive Disorder often have nonspecific findings on neurological examination (e.g., reflex asymmetries), nonspecific electroencephalographic changes, or childhood histories of head trauma. Such isolated findings are by themselves compatible with a diagnosis of Intermittent Explosive Disorder and lead to another diagnosis only when they are associated with signs and symptoms indicative of a definitely diagnosable general medical condition.

Criteria A and B. Aggressive behavior occurs for many reasons and is common in individuals without mental disorders. One of the most difficult challenges, both clinically and forensically, is to determine when aggressive behavior is attributable to a mental disorder. The central (and as yet unsolved) problem in defining Intermittent Explosive Disorder is determining on what grounds aggressive episodes by themselves constitute a diagnosable mental disorder. Criteria A and B represent a not very satisfying attempt to solve this thorny problem by establishing the clinical significance of the aggressive episodes with the requirement that the episodes be recurrent, discrete, result in serious consequences, and represent a "gross" overreaction to external circumstances.

Although not explicitly stated in DSM-IV (perhaps it should have been), many motivations for aggressive behavior are not meant to be included within this diagnosis. Intermittent Explosive Disorder does not apply when the purpose of the aggression is monetary gain, vengeance, self-defense, to make a political statement, or part of a gang behavior. Typically, the aggressive behavior in Intermittent Explosive Disorder is ego-dystonic to the individual, who feels upset, remorseful, bewildered, or embarrassed about the acts.

312.32 Kleptomania

Stealing occurs for many reasons that have nothing to do with Kleptomania. Usually, people steal for the monetary or the use value of the item stolen. This is the motivation, for example, of professional burglars and those stealing to buy drugs. Much less commonly, the stealing occurs as an act of anger or vengeance, on a dare, or as a rite of passage. All of the above reasons for stealing must be distinguished from Kleptomania, which is a much more rarely encountered and narrowly defined pattern of stealing for the pleasure or tension relief derived from the act itself. Because some individuals claim Kleptomania as grounds for evading criminal responsibility or else for mitigating punishment, it is important to distinguish it from Malingering.

Common in women in mid-life. Usualy women's life is in chaoes. Sense of power & control

DSM-IV diagnostic criteria for 312.32 Kleptomania

A. Recurrent failure to resist impulses to steal objects that are not needed for personal use or for their monetary value.

B. Increasing sense of tension immediately before committing the theft.

C. Pleasure, gratification, or relief at the time of committing the theft.

D. The stealing is not committed to express anger or vengeance and is not in response to a delusion or a hallucination.

E. The stealing is not better accounted for by Conduct Disorder, a Manic Episode, or Antisocial Personality Disorder.

Criterion A. In contrast to the motivation of a professional thief, the individual with Kleptomania is relatively indifferent to the items stolen once the act of stealing is complete and may even discard or return them. In contrast to adolescent group delinquency, the stealing is a solitary behavior that is usually kept secret.

CRITERIA B AND C. These criteria describe the specific features that distinguish the motivation for stealing in Kleptomania from the motivation for other types of stealing. They account for its being included in the "Impulse-Control Disorders" section.

CRITERIA D AND E. As indicated above, theft can occur for many other reasons and in the context of many other mental disorders. These should be considered and ruled out before attributing the behavior to Kleptomania.

312.33 Pyromania

Many motivations for fire setting have nothing to do with Pyromania. Fire setting may be motivated by monetary gain (e.g., arson of a building to collect insurance), the desire to make a political statement (e.g., a terrorist act), the need to conceal criminal activity (e.g., to cover up a murder), a need for attention or recognition (e.g., setting a fire in order to discover it and be a hero), a desire to exact revenge, or a delusional belief or a command hallucination. All of these reasons must be distinguished from Pyromania, which is recurrent fire setting for the pleasure or tension relief derived from the act itself. A potentially difficult distinction is between Pyromania and experimentation in childhood (e.g., playing with matches, lighters, or fire) because both involve pleasure derived from the fire itself.

Adolescent boys or young men. Excitement seeking & possible sexual arousal.

DSM-IV diagnostic criteria for 312.33 Pyromania

A. Deliberate and purposeful fire setting on more than one occasion.

B. Tension or affective arousal before the act.

C. Fascination with, interest in, curiosity about, or attraction to fire and its situational contexts (e.g., paraphernalia, uses, consequences).

D. Pleasure, gratification, or relief when setting fires, or when witnessing or participating in their aftermath.

E. The fire setting is not done for monetary gain, as an expression of sociopolitical ideology, to conceal criminal activity, to express anger or vengeance, to improve one's living circumstances, in response to a delusion or hallucination, or as a result of impaired judgment (e.g., in dementia, Mental Retardation, Substance Intoxication).

F. The fire setting is not better accounted for by Conduct Disorder, a Manic Episode, or Antisocial Personality Disorder.

CRITERION A. The requirement that the fire setting in Pyromania be recurrent helps to distinguish it from other motivations for fire setting.

Criteria B, C, and D. In the introductory remarks, we indicated what types of fire setting are not Pyromania. These criteria describe the features that distinguish the specific motivation for fire setting in Pyromania and account for its being included in the "Impulse-Control Disorders" section. The person with Pyromania may have a long history of being a firebug. Typically, individuals with this disorder love fires and being around fire-fighting personnel and equipment. They may set off false alarms and monitor police radios to find locations of actual fires.

Criteria E and F. Fire setting can occur for other reasons and in the context of a number of other mental disorders. These should be considered and ruled out before attributing the behavior to Pyromania.

312.31 Pathological Gambling

Gambling is a ubiquitous human activity encountered in virtually all cultures and represented by a quite remarkably inventive array of options. Social and professional gambling must be distinguished from Pathological Gambling. Social gambling is a culturally sanctioned form of recreation that does not become a preoccupation and does not result in serious consequences. Professional gambling is engaged in as a source of income by individuals who are highly schooled and disciplined in the techniques of play. In contrast, Pathological Gambling monopolizes the person's life and results in severe consequences.

Pathological Gambling has been conceptualized in a number of different ways: as an Impulse-Control Disorder, as a compulsion, and as an analogue to Substance Dependence. Pathological Gambling is akin to an Impulse-Control Disorder in that it involves an increasing sense of tension before gambling and results in pleasure, gratification, or relief while gambling. The term *compulsive gambling* reflects some of the similarities between Pathological Gambling and compulsions—the gambling is repetitive, often has ritualized aspects, and is meant to prevent or reduce distress. Pathological Gambling is akin to Substance Dependence in that it is characterized by aspects of tolerance, withdrawal, compulsive use, and adverse consequences. Although included with the Impulse-Control Disorders, the definition of Pathological Gambling provided below also conforms closely to the definition of Substance Dependence.

DSM-IV diagnostic criteria for 312.31 Pathological Gambling

A. Persistent and recurrent maladaptive gambling behavior as indicated by five (or more) of the following:

(1) is preoccupied with gambling (e.g., preoccupied with reliving past gambling experiences, handicapping or planning the next venture, or thinking of ways to get money with which to gamble)

(continued)

DSM-IV diagnostic criteria for 312.31 Pathological Gambling *(continued)*

(2) needs to gamble with increasing amounts of money in order to achieve the desired excitement
(3) has repeated unsuccessful efforts to control, cut back, or stop gambling
(4) is restless or irritable when attempting to cut down or stop gambling
(5) gambles as a way of escaping from problems or of relieving a dysphoric mood (e.g., feelings of helplessness, guilt, anxiety, depression)
(6) after losing money gambling, often returns another day to get even ("chasing" one's losses)
(7) lies to family members, therapist, or others to conceal the extent of involvement with gambling
(8) has committed illegal acts such as forgery, fraud, theft, or embezzlement to finance gambling
(9) has jeopardized or lost a significant relationship, job, or educational or career opportunity because of gambling
(10) relies on others to provide money to relieve a desperate financial situation caused by gambling

B. The gambling behavior is not better accounted for by a Manic Episode.

Escape Gambler: Systematic
Action Gambler systematic

Criterion A. This criteria set is in many ways modeled on the criteria for Substance Dependence and Abuse. Tolerance (i.e., increased amount of the substance needed to achieve the same effect) is paralleled by the need to gamble with increasing amounts of money (Criterion A2). Withdrawal (i.e., symptoms develop when substance use is cut down) is paralleled by restlessness or irritability developing when the gambling is cut down (Criterion A4). Compulsive use of a substance is paralleled by preoccupation with gambling (Criterion A1), repeated efforts to cut down (Criterion A3), gambling to escape from problems (Criterion A5), and chasing losses (Criterion A6). The adverse consequences characteristic of Substance Abuse are paralleled by lying (Criterion A7), committing illegal acts (Criterion A8), having interpersonal difficulties (Criterion A9), and having financial difficulties (Criterion A10).

The item threshold used to differentiate pathological from nonpathological forms of social or professional gambling is not well established. A survey study that compared pathological gamblers and social gamblers suggested a cut point of 5 items out of 10. However, clinical judgment should be exercised, particularly when the threshold number of items is met in the absence of significant impairment.

Criterion B. Gambling can be part of the uninhibited pleasure-seeking behavior characteristic of a Manic Episode and should not be given a separate diagnosis unless the maladaptive gambling behavior occurs at times other than during the Manic Episode. Concerns about this exclusion criterion were raised because some individuals with Pathological Gambling appear "manic" (e.g., rapid speech, not needing to sleep) during a gambling binge without having a true Manic Episode. Typically, once the individual is away from the gambling, these manic-like features dissipate. Clinical judgment is necessary to determine whether the gambling is an associated feature of a Manic Episode or whether the manic-like symptoms are an associated feature of Pathological Gambling. Rarely, both diagnoses may be appropriate if an individual has Pathological Gambling before or between episodes of Bipolar Disorder.

312.39 Trichotillomania

In the DSM-IV deliberations, there was considerable discussion concerning the appropriate placement and conceptualization for Trichotillomania. As discussed above, Trichotillomania straddles the interesting but difficult boundary between impulsive and compulsive disorders. Some preliminary evidence suggests that patients with Trichotillomania and patients with Obsessive-Compulsive Disorder have similar biological markers and treatment responses. However, this evidence was not sufficiently compelling to change the placement of the disorder in DSM-IV.

DSM-IV diagnostic criteria for 312.39 Trichotillomania

A. Recurrent pulling out of one's hair resulting in noticeable hair loss.

B. An increasing sense of tension immediately before pulling out the hair or when attempting to resist the behavior.

C. Pleasure, gratification, or relief when pulling out the hair.

D. The disturbance is not better accounted for by another mental disorder and is not due to a general medical condition (e.g., a dermatological condition).

E. The disturbance causes clinically significant distress or impairment in social, occupational, or other important areas of functioning.

Criterion A. The episodes of hair pulling may be brief and scattered throughout the day or may last for hours. The hair loss may be concentrated on a particular part of the body (e.g., scalp, eyebrows, eyelashes, nose, armpit, pubic or perirectal area). There may be circumscribed areas of complete hair loss (alopecia) or more widespread areas of thinned hair. In some individuals, hair pulling is exacerbated at times of stress (e.g., work pressure, acute interpersonal stress); in others, it increases during periods of relative relaxation (e.g., reading, watching TV, talking on the telephone). Some individuals may eat the hair they pull (trichophagia), and this can result in medical complications from the accompanying bezoars (e.g., anemia, bowel obstruction). Many people are fascinated with the root of the hair and have a particular sense of satisfaction when they pull out the complete shaft (hunting for the perfect hair).

Criteria B and C. Some individuals experience an itch-like sensation rather than a conscious feeling of tension or urge to pull the hair. When the hair pulling occurs in a state of distraction, there may not be a conscious experience of tension beforehand, and the individual may instead discover a pile of hairs. In this context, tension occurs only when the individual attempts to prevent additional hair pulling. The feeling of gratification is often described as sensual in nature and is sometimes compared with sexual gratification.

Criterion D. This diagnosis of Trichotillomania is not given when the hair loss results from a dermatological condition (e.g., alopecia areata, male-pattern baldness, chronic discoid lupus erythematosus, lichen planopilaris, folliculitis decalvans, pseudopelade, and alopecia mucinosa). Similarly, Trichotillomania is not diagnosed when the hair pulling is a feature of another mental disorder. For example, a patient with Schizophrenia may hear a voice commanding him or her to pluck out all body hair to become "pure."

Criterion E. The person is usually embarrassed by both the behavior and its consequences. Most individuals will not pull out their hair in front of other people (except immediate family members) and may avoid situations or interpersonal relationships in which the behavior might be revealed. The person usually attempts to conceal or camouflage the bald spots or hair thinning by wearing a toupee, wig, or scarf. Situations or activities where this camouflage is not possible may be avoided (e.g., sexual intercourse, swimming).

The Last Word

Most of the Impulse-Control Disorders covered in this section are relatively rare and certainly much rarer than other explanations for violent behavior, stealing, setting fires, and gambling. Impulsive behaviors more frequently occur as associated features of other mental disorders or for reasons not connected with any mental disorder (e.g., for gain or revenge). Therefore, these categories should be considered as *residual* and diagnosed only after a process of exclusion.

CHAPTER 21

Adjustment Disorders

Adjustment Disorders

309.0	With Depressed Mood
309.24	With Anxiety
309.28	With Mixed Anxiety and Depressed Mood
309.3	With Disturbance of Conduct
309.4	With Mixed Disturbance of Emotions and Conduct
309.9	Unspecified

There has been considerable misunderstanding concerning the concept of Adjustment Disorder and how this diagnosis is meant to be used. An *Adjustment Disorder* is defined as a clinically significant reaction to a psychosocial stressor with a level of psychopathology that is below the criterion thresholds established by the criteria sets for the various DSM-IV disorders. Adjustment Disorder is therefore a residual category that includes a heterogeneous array of symptom presentations and degrees of impairment. It must be remembered that the diagnosis of Adjustment Disorder does not apply when a presentation meets criteria for a more specific disorder even if stress is involved in the etiology.

To facilitate differential diagnosis, most of the sections in DSM-IV are organized based on common presenting features rather than a shared etiology (e.g., the "Mood Disorders" section includes primary mood presentations as well as those due to substance use or to a general medical condition). In keeping with the goal of facilitating differential diagnosis, it was proposed that the subtypes of Adjustment Disorder be distributed throughout the classification (e.g., Adjustment Disorder With Depressed Mood listed in the "Mood Disorders" section). Although this proposal was in many ways appealing, it was not adopted. The Adjustment Disorders continue to be grouped together in a single section to emphasize their common stress-related etiology and to reflect the common clinical situation of mixed symptom presentations (e.g., an Adjustment Disorder with a mixture of anxiety and mood symptoms).

DSM-IV diagnostic criteria for Adjustment Disorders

A. The development of emotional or behavioral symptoms in response to an identifiable stressor(s) occurring within 3 months of the onset of the stressor(s).

B. These symptoms or behaviors are clinically significant as evidenced by either of the following:
   (1) marked distress that is in excess of what would be expected from exposure to the stressor
   (2) significant impairment in social or occupational (academic) functioning

C. The stress-related disturbance does not meet the criteria for another specific Axis I disorder and is not merely an exacerbation of a preexisting Axis I or Axis II disorder.

D. The symptoms do not represent Bereavement.

E. Once the stressor (or its consequences) has terminated, the symptoms do not persist for more than an additional 6 months.

Specify if:
Acute: if the disturbance lasts less than 6 months
Chronic: if the disturbance lasts for 6 months or longer

Adjustment Disorders are coded based on the subtype, which is selected according to the predominant symptoms. The specific stressor(s) can be specified on Axis IV.
309.0 With Depressed Mood
309.24 With Anxiety
309.28 With Mixed Anxiety and Depressed Mood
309.3 With Disturbance of Conduct
309.4 With Mixed Disturbance of Emotions and Conduct
309.9 Unspecified

CRITERION A. This is one of the few disorders in DSM-IV that is defined on the basis of its presumed etiology (an identifiable stressor) rather than on the basis of its descriptive features (which can include many different emotional or behavioral symptoms). Determining that stress plays a causal role in the development of symptoms can be challenging. Stress is a fairly ubiquitous part of everyday life and may just as often be independent of, or result from, rather than cause the accompanying psychopathology. Although there is no specific guideline for establishing the etiological role of stress, this criterion requires that there be a temporal relationship between the stressor and the onset of symptoms with an interval between them that is no more than 3 months.

Criterion B. Adjustment Disorder must be distinguished from the normal reactions to psychosocial stressors that are not of sufficient clinical significance to warrant a diagnosis of a mental disorder. Adjustment Disorders must be severe enough to cause clinically significant impairment or distress, while not meeting criteria for any of the specific DSM-IV disorders. In contrast to most disorders in DSM-IV, which set a minimum symptom threshold to qualify for a diagnosis, Adjustment Disorder can be considered to have a diagnostic ceiling. However, this fact should not lead to the common misconception that because the symptom pattern of Adjustment Disorder does not meet criteria for any specific DSM-IV disorder, the symptoms of Adjustment Disorder are necessarily mild. Although generally less impairing than other DSM-IV diagnoses, Adjustment Disorders may be characterized by a wide range of impairments. At one extreme are those that are just beyond normal, expectable reactions to stress; at the other is suicide.

Criterion C. Another common error is to assume that any psychiatric symptoms occurring after a psychosocial stressor constitute an Adjustment Disorder. In fact, many (perhaps most) DSM-IV diagnoses may be triggered or exacerbated by a stressor. When a more specific mental disorder (e.g., Major Depressive Disorder) occurs apparently in response to a psychosocial stressor, this disorder is diagnosed instead of Adjustment Disorder. Similarly, when a stressor exacerbates a preexisting mental disorder (e.g., Major Depressive Disorder becomes worse after a job loss), no new diagnosis is made (although the stressor can be indicated on Axis IV).

Criterion D. Adjustment Disorder must also be distinguished from Bereavement after the death of a loved one, which is considered to be an expectable and culturally sanctioned response to the loss and therefore is not a mental disorder. However, if the reaction is judged to be in excess of what would be expected, a diagnosis of Adjustment Disorder is made. In more severe cases, the condition may meet criteria for Major Depressive Disorder.

Criterion E. Setting an upper limit on symptom duration was the most controversial aspect of the definition of Adjustment Disorder. Adjustment Disorder has been conceptualized as a time-limited reaction that occurs in response to a stressor. DSM-III and DSM-III-R operationalized this concept by establishing a maximum duration of 6 months. This time limit was problematic because many stressors have a prolonged duration (e.g., chronic illness, spouse abuse) or prolonged ongoing consequences (e.g., financial difficulty after loss of spouse). In DSM-III-R, a diagnosis of Adjustment Disorder could not be made after 6 months, even when the stressor or its consequences were present for many years. DSM-IV accommodates this situation by having the 6-month time limit apply only after the stressor or its consequences have ended. To distinguish between short-term and long-term Adjustment Disorders, DSM-IV has introduced a specifier for describing acute versus chronic presentations.

Subtypes. It should be recognized that Adjustment Disorder is a very heterogeneous category in its symptom presentations and degrees of impairment. Several types of Adjustment Disorder are included in DSM-IV, which may give the mistaken impression that Adjustment Disorder most commonly occurs as a pure type. The reader should be aware that mixed presentations are frequently encountered as are other forms of Adjustment Disorder not specifically listed (e.g., somatic complaints, work or academic problems). The subtype should be assigned based on the most predominant features.

During the revision process, an Adjustment Disorder subtype was proposed: "with suicidal behavior." This proposal was in recognition of the fact that suicidal behavior in adolescents and young adults may frequently occur in response to a stressor and in the absence of any other mental disorder. This proposed subtype was ultimately not included because of concerns that it might encourage clinicians to apply a diagnosis of Adjustment Disorder without a comprehensive assessment to determine whether a more severe and specific disorder is present.

The Last Word

The presentation of Adjustment Disorder includes heterogeneous symptoms and degrees of impairment. The diagnosis of Adjustment Disorder applies only when a presentation does not meet criteria for a more specific disorder and constitutes a maladaptive response to an identifiable psychosocial stressor. The major change in DSM-IV has been to allow for diagnosis of chronic Adjustment Disorders in response to prolonged or ongoing stressors.

Personality Disorders

All of us have personalities—that is, our own personal and particular pattern of experiencing and interacting with our environment and with other people. The DSM-IV construct of Personality Disorder is an attempt to delineate the inherently very unclear boundary separating normal personality traits from Personality Disorder. The Personality Disorders are defined as enduring patterns of inflexible and maladaptive thinking, feeling, and acting that cause significant subjective distress and/or impairment in social or occupational functioning. Individuals with a Personality Disorder have difficulty responding flexibly and adaptively to the changes and demands that are an inevitable part of everyday life. Instead, they often make things tougher for themselves by provoking negative reactions in others, by making poor decisions, and by instigating vicious interpersonal cycles that ironically fulfill their own worst expectations and fantasies.

Personality functioning has been of interest throughout the history of medicine and philosophy. Hippocrates described four personality styles and related each of these to a kind of neuroendocrine imbalance among the four "humors": the overly optimistic and extroverted or sanguine type was related to blood, the pessimistic or melancholic type was related to black bile, the irritable and hostile or choleric type was related to yellow bile, and the apathetic or phlegmatic type was related to lymph. Personality types have also been associated with differences in facial and bodily appearance (Aristotle), skull contours (Gall's phrenology), body habitus (Kretschmer's and Sheldon's endomorph, mesomorph, and ectomorph), stages of psychosexual development (Freud's libido theory), and stages of ego development (Erikson's life cycle). In the past century, there have also been numerous dimensional systems, most of them developed by psychologists, that have attempted to measure the most fundamental aspects of human nature.

Within psychiatry, the most popular method of classification has been a categorical description based on clinical experience. DSM-III much advanced the study of Personality Disorders by providing a set of explicit and specific criteria for each Personality Disorder and by placing the disorders on a separate axis. Before DSM-III, there was a tendency to overlook Personality Disorders when attention was drawn to the more florid presenting psychopathology. The provision of criteria sets for the Personality Disorders and their placement on Axis II improved their diagnostic reliability and highlighted their coexistence with, and contribution to, other psychiatric disorders. Since DSM-III, considerable empirical and clinical attention has been given to the Personality Disorders.

The major change in the DSM-IV "Personality Disorders" section is the provision of a separate criteria set defining the general attributes of a Personality Disorder. This criteria set provides guidelines for answering the question "does the patient have a personality disorder at all?" Once this question is answered, the next step is to determine which (and how many) of the specific DSM-IV Personality Disorders are present. In some cases, the general criteria for a Personality Disorder are met, but the criteria are not fully met for any of the specific Personality Disorders. This circumstance can occur because the personality pattern conforms to a disorder not included in DSM-IV (e.g., passive aggressive, self-defeating, inadequate) or because features of several disorders are present, but there are not enough items to meet the criteria for any particular one. In such circumstances, the diagnosis should be Personality Disorder Not Otherwise Specified.

DSM-IV general diagnostic criteria for a Personality Disorder

A. An enduring pattern of inner experience and behavior that deviates markedly from the expectations of the individual's culture. This pattern is manifested in two (or more) of the following areas:
   (1) cognition (i.e., ways of perceiving and interpreting self, other people, and events)
   (2) affectivity (i.e., the range, intensity, lability, and appropriateness of emotional response)
   (3) interpersonal functioning
   (4) impulse control

B. The enduring pattern is inflexible and pervasive across a broad range of personal and social situations.

C. The enduring pattern leads to clinically significant distress or impairment in social, occupational, or other important areas of functioning.

(continued)

DSM-IV general diagnostic criteria for a Personality Disorder *(continued)*

D. The pattern is stable and of long duration and its onset can be traced back at least to adolescence or early adulthood.

E. The enduring pattern is not better accounted for as a manifestation or consequence of another mental disorder.

F. The enduring pattern is not due to the direct physiological effects of a substance (e.g., a drug of abuse, a medication) or a general medical condition (e.g., head trauma).

CRITERION A. One of the reasons why Personality Disorders are more difficult to diagnose reliably than Axis I conditions is that the Personality Disorder item sets require a much wider domain of assessment that includes inner experience as well as overt behavior. An ongoing debate in constructing Personality Disorder items is the degree to which these should allow for inference. Should the items describe only the explicit and observable behaviors that are likely to be diagnosed reliably, even if central features of the personality construct may sometimes be missed? Or should the criteria sets also include items (e.g., identity disturbance) that are central to the construct of a particular Personality Disorder but may be inherently inferential and difficult to assess reliably?

Reliability is always better when specific behavioral descriptions are used to define an item. However, the use of narrowly defined behavioral criteria can be taken only so far before sacrificing diagnostic validity. A personality trait describes an overall pattern of behavior, and any particular behavior is limited and fallible in representing that pattern. Moreover, any single behavior can reflect a number of similar and even dissimilar traits. For example, the criteria set for Antisocial Personality Disorder achieves relatively high reliability by emphasizing very specific behaviors, but in the process it may have lost the central construct of psychopathy by excluding more inferential but crucial features (e.g., absence of guilt, loyalty, empathy, and responsibility). The result is a definition that may select too many criminals who are not psychopathic while missing psychopathic individuals who are not criminals. There is an attempt in DSM-IV to balance the sometimes competing goals of diagnostic reliability and diagnostic validity.

Of all of the disorders in DSM-IV, the Personality Disorders are perhaps the ones most tied to cultural expectations. By and large, the DSM-IV Personality Disorders have been found in diverse cultures across the world. On the other hand, it seems equally clear that cultural expectations differ a great deal. What may seem histrionic in a culture that values restraint may fall well within the cultural norm in a culture that values spontaneity. In contrast, what would be considered compulsive in a culture that places a high value on emotional expressiveness may be normal in a culture of self-disciplined, highly controlled stoics.

Criterion A of the general diagnostic criteria for a Personality Disorder explicitly states that the evaluation of Personality Disorder must start with the clinician's awareness of what is expected by the individual's particular culture. Unfortunately, there is no arbiter to determine the gold standard for each culture. Problems are most likely to arise when the clinician is not familiar with the ins and outs of the culture of the patient being evaluated and comes from a culture that has a different conception of normal personality functioning. In such instances, it is important to correct for one's own biases. It may be helpful (or even necessary) to consult with others who share the patient's cultural reference points before making assumptions about the presence of a Personality Disorder.

Criterion B. By definition, Personality Disorders have a pervasive impact on all (or most) areas of personality functioning and are not restricted to a single interpersonal relationship, situation, or role. If the behavior occurs with only one person (e.g., with a particular boss but not with all supervisors), it is more likely to represent a relational problem or an Adjustment Disorder than a Personality Disorder.

Furthermore, it is important to evaluate the degree to which the behaviors in question are inherent in the individual versus being the individual's reaction to the demands of a particular role expectation. For example, working "compulsively" on tax forms is part of the role of an accountant, and the diagnosis of Obsessive-Compulsive Personality Disorder should be considered only if the inflexible behavior intrudes on all aspects of the person's life. The attribution of a particular behavior to an individual's personality versus the individual's role expectation is complicated further by the fact that people often choose particular roles, positions, and jobs precisely because these complement and support their Personality Disorder or style (compulsive individuals may gravitate to accounting).

The inflexible nature of a personality trait is often the reason that it is maladaptive and enduring. Having a Personality Disorder inhibits one's ability to profit from experience. These individuals tend to experience the world through a particular and unfortunately unvarying set of glasses that filter out any input that does not conform to their preconceived expectations. For example, individuals with Paranoid Personality Disorder habitually find confirmation for their worst fears that others are taking advantage of them; such individuals do not appreciate or will rationalize away those situations in which they are in fact being treated well. This inflexibility usually leads to vicious cycles in interpersonal relationships. Patients with Paranoid Personality Disorder are so globally mistrustful and critical of other people that the other people frequently withdraw and withhold information in a way that is then misinterpreted by the patients as proof of the original assumption. Similarly, individuals who are avoidant because of feared humiliation tend to act in a halting and socially awkward way that invites the rejection they are fearful of and trying to avoid.

Criterion C. Impairment in personality functioning occurs on a continuum. Only when the personality traits are inflexible and maladaptive and cause significant functional impairment or subjective distress do they constitute Personality Disorders. Unfortunately, DSM-IV does not and cannot provide a clear-cut and satisfying way of judging the extent to which a behavior must be maladaptive, impairing, or distressing before it crosses the line from personality trait to Personality Disorder. It should also be noted that DSM-IV does allow the clinician to record on Axis II when the patient has clinically relevant personality traits that do not meet the threshold for a Personality Disorder. In such situations, no diagnostic code is indicated (e.g., Axis II: histrionic personality traits).

There are several reasons why it is particularly difficult to assess the clinical significance of an individual's personality functioning. Perhaps the most important is that personality features are typically ego-syntonic and involve characteristics that the person has come to accept as an integral part of the self. Patients with Antisocial Personality Disorder may recognize that they have had trouble with the law or with maintaining relationships, but they are less likely to recognize that the cause of this trouble is their irresponsibility, disloyalty, and lack of guilt. They may even rationalize that people who experience guilt are the ones who have a problem. Similarly, individuals with Obsessive-Compulsive Personality Disorder may consider their perfectionism and incessant devotion to work to be a cherished quality and an indication of scrupulousness, moral superiority, and dedication.

Impaired self-awareness particularly complicates the assessment of the more unflattering types of behavior. Many patients are not especially good at reporting accurately that they are self-centered (histrionic), exploitative (narcissistic), or manipulative (borderline). Even if they are aware of these unpleasant characteristics, they may deny their presence to an evaluator or others to achieve social acceptance. Further complicating the issue is the fact that the denial or exaggeration of psychopathology is itself a specific trait of some of the Personality Disorders. Patients with Histrionic or Borderline Personality Disorder are likely to exaggerate their symptomatology, whereas individuals with Narcissistic, Antisocial, Obsessive-Compulsive, and Paranoid Personality Disorder are likely to deny or minimize.

Problems in assessment also arise because clinicians have their own enduring styles of personality functioning that may color their perceptions and judgments of the personality functioning of others. For example, a clinician who has obsessive-compulsive traits may have difficulty appreciating the pathological nature of such traits when these are present in others but may be excessively harsh in judging patients with histrionic features. Indeed, one of the most important aspects of the basic training of clinicians is that they become increasingly aware of their own personality biases because these are likely to impact on patient behavior in the interview and on their clinical judgments of personality pathology in others.

Social, cultural, and gender biases can further complicate the assessment. For example, clinicians from cultures that place a high value on controlled and compulsive behavior are more likely to see as pathologically histrionic the more spontaneous behavior sanctioned by other cultures, and vice versa. Furthermore, both male and female clinicians may at times be influenced by their stereotypes about "normal" masculine and feminine behavior.

Criterion D. The term *personality disorder* is not meant to refer to time-limited and discrete episodes of illness. Rather, Personality Disorders are by definition chronic patterns with an early and insidious onset evident by late adolescence or early adulthood. Clinicians often wonder whether it makes sense to diagnose Personality Disorders in children. The desire to do so is based on the fact that, even in children and adolescents, one sometimes encounters patterns of behavior that appear to be relatively stable and that conform to the presentations described in this section. The important caution in this regard is that childhood psychopathology is often unstable, self-limited, and best conceptualized as characteristic of a particular developmental stage.

For the most part, personality features tend to mellow with age. Most adolescents with conduct problems, avoidance, or identity issues tend not to go on to have Antisocial, Avoidant, or Borderline Personality Disorder. To balance these concerns, DSM-IV allows Personality Disorders to be diagnosed in children but only in "those relatively unusual instances in which the individual's particular maladaptive personality traits appear to be pervasive, persistent, and unlikely to be limited to a particular developmental stage or an episode of an Axis I disorder" (DSM-IV, p. 631).

CRITERION E. The wording of this criterion appears simple enough to understand, but it leads to both practical and theoretical conundrums that have been a great problem in clinical practice and in research. Personality Disorders often occur in conjunction with Axis I disorders and may predispose to some of them. In fact, it is precisely because of the clinical importance of noting this common comorbidity that the Axis I-Axis II distinction was established by the multiaxial system.

However, the evaluation of Personality Disorders in the presence of Axis I conditions is often difficult or even impossible. A patient's current behavior may result more from the presence of an episodic Mood or Anxiety Disorder than from a stable personality disposition. To tease out Axis I versus Axis II relationships, the clinician must confirm that there has been a long-standing duration of the personality symptomatology before and independent of the Axis I condition. In this regard, it is important, whenever possible, to observe the patient over time to determine the degree to which the features persist even as the Axis I symptoms remit.

Assessment is further complicated by the fact that patients' ability to report accurately their past behavior may be retrospectively colored by the cognitive distortions resulting from their current condition. For example, a depressed person tends to present an overly bleak and critical description of the past. In such circumstances, it is often helpful to obtain reports from a relative or friend because these informants have observed the patient over time and without the distorting lens of an Axis I disorder. It must be recognized, however, that informants may not be entirely objective because they will often have their own emotional investment in seeing the patient a particular way.

Errors can and often are made in both directions. In the pre-DSM-III era, the most common mistake was the underrecognition of Personality Disorders and of their impact on the course, management, and treatment response of Axis I conditions. Despite the increased recent attention afforded Personality Disorders, this underrecognition remains a major problem.

There is, however, also a tendency to overdiagnose Personality Disorders in individuals whose compulsiveness, instability, avoidance, dependence, and so forth are much more the result of the Axis I condition or the interaction between the Axis I condition and preexisting personality traits (not severe enough to be disorders) than they are the result of a freestanding Personality Disorder. For example, many an individual has been called "borderline" (in a pejorative way) for irritable and irritating behaviors that may reflect their having a Mood Disorder. To the clinician's surprise, the patient's "characterological" impulsivity and lability may miraculously remit when the mood episode is successfully treated. Furthermore, baseline personality traits (e.g., especially a tendency toward dependency) are often exacerbated by the ramifications of an Axis I condition and may return to their usual level once the Axis I condition is successfully treated.

On theoretical grounds as well, it is wise not to reify the distinction between the Axis I disorders and the Axis II Personality Disorders. The boundary between Axis I and Axis II is sometimes so inherently impossible to draw that the distinction becomes meaningless. A number of Axis I conditions (Dysthymic Disorder, Agoraphobia, Generalized Anxiety Disorder, Schizophrenia, Somatization Disorder, Paraphilias) have an early onset and chronic course that is indistinguishable from Personality Disorder. Moreover, these conditions can have a pervasive impact on the way the individual thinks, feels, and behaves that is also indistinguishable from (or at least greatly influences) the individual's personality.

Some clinicians try to differentiate Personality Disorders on the basis of whether the psychopathology responds to medication. However, it would be reductionistic and contrary to the evidence to assume that Personality Disorders are without a biological substrate. In fact, recent evidence suggests that some Personality Disorders may be responsive to medication.

The distinction between Axis I and Axis II is for the most part quite useful, particularly in describing clinical presentations that are not at the boundary between them. However, it is also important to realize the limitations of this distinction and not get caught up in endless and fruitless debates about whether a particular manifestation of behavior represents an Axis I state condition or an Axis II Personality Disorder.

Criterion F. The relationship between Personality Disorders and substance use is complicated and difficult to evaluate. Clearly, there is a high degree of comorbidity, particularly between substance use and both the Antisocial and Borderline Personality Disorders. The nature of this relationship is much less clear and is probably quite heterogeneous. In some individuals, the use of substances may reflect the impulsivity characteristic of these Personality Disorders or may be a form of self-medication to regulate the dysphoric mood states that may be associated with them. In others, the behaviors that characterize the "personality disorders" may in fact be secondary to the drug taking either by direct physiological effect (e.g., the substance causes affective lability) or by the fact that obtaining the funds for illegal substances often entails antisocial behavior.

There was considerable debate in the drafting of the criteria sets for Antisocial Personality Disorder and Borderline Personality Disorder whether to exclude behaviors that were consequent to drug taking. These were not excluded because substance use is so intrinsic to these disorders that restricting the diagnosis to individuals without significant substance use would have resulted in an unnecessarily and unrealistically narrow definition of them.

The second part of Criterion F refers to the differential diagnosis between a Personality Disorder and Personality Change Due to a General Medical Condition. A number of general medical conditions can result in personality changes (see p. 172 in DSM-IV). In practice, this differential is rarely a problem because of the difference in characteristic age and mode of onset between Personality Disorder and Personality Change Due to a General Medical Condition. In Personality Disorders, there must be an early and usually gradual onset unrelated to a general medical condition. In Personality Change Due to a General Medical Condition, the onset can be at any age and must be a direct result of the effects of a general medical condition on the central nervous system. Moreover, the manifestations of personality change need not (and rarely do) conform to the specific clinical presentations characteristic of the 10 Personality Disorders.

The subtypes of Personality Change Due to a General Medical Condition describing the characteristic presentations are listed in Chapter 9 of this book. The situation in which this differential may be most difficult is when the change occurs in childhood and is not conclusively related to the general medical condition. For example, it may be difficult to evaluate whether symptoms of Conduct Disorder occurring in a child with preexisting head trauma are due to the head injury or whether the injury is incidental.

Defining the Specific DSM-IV Personality Disorders

Personality Disorders

301.0	Paranoid Personality Disorder
301.20	Schizoid Personality Disorder
301.22	Schizotypal Personality Disorder
301.7	Antisocial Personality Disorder
301.83	Borderline Personality Disorder
301.50	Histrionic Personality Disorder
301.81	Narcissistic Personality Disorder
301.82	Avoidant Personality Disorder
301.6	Dependent Personality Disorder
301.4	Obsessive-Compulsive Personality Disorder
301.9	Personality Disorder Not Otherwise Specified

The optimal number of Personality Disorders, which ones to include, and whether to use a categorical or a dimensional approach to definition were all questions that had to be decided during the DSM-IV deliberations. However, these questions will undoubtedly also be the subject of much additional research and discussion. Historically, the number of Personality Disorders has ranged from Hippocrates' four temperaments to Fourier's 810 character types to Alport's 1600 dictionary words characterizing personality attributes. Those systems with fewer Personality Disorders may fail to represent clinically important personality descriptions, but increasing the number of Personality Disorders described invariably results in overlapping categories.

The 10 specific Personality Disorders described in DSM-IV are certainly not the final word. They arise from historical tradition rather than any comprehensive, empirically derived, or theoretically driven method of dividing the domain of Personality Disorders. There have been numerous debates about adding or subtracting particular Personality Disorders. Two additional Personality Disorders of potential research and clinical interest—passive-aggressive personality disorder, which was included in DSM-III-R, and depressive personality disorder—are included in Appendix B of DSM-IV and are discussed in Chapter 25. Self-defeating personality disorder was included in Appendix A of DSM-III-R but was dropped from DSM-IV for reasons discussed in Chapter 26.

The debate over a categorical versus a dimensional model of classification is a familiar one in psychiatry, and it is particularly relevant to the Personality Disorders. (See Chapter 2 for a fuller discussion.) The medical tradition has been to use a categorical (present/absent) model for diagnosing Personality Disorders despite the fact that this model loses information by forcing a black/white choice to describe shades of gray. The Personality Disorder categories in DSM-IV cause diagnostic dilemmas, especially when patients fall, as they often do, at the boundary between normal and abnormal personality traits or between one particular Personality Disorder and another. In contrast, a dimensional approach would rate numerically the degree to which various personality styles are inflexible and maladaptive rather than demarcating qualitative distinctions.

Unfortunately, the choice of optimal dimensions on which to rate patients is far from clear. Many competing models are available to choose from, each with its own proponents and detractors. It seems very likely that future classification systems for diagnosing personality will ultimately be dimensional, but the development of dimensional systems was insufficiently advanced for their inclusion in DSM-IV.

Therefore, the categorical system lives on in DSM-IV despite its limitations for diagnosing the continuously distributed personality traits. However, one can use this model with greater comfort and flexibility by realizing that the disorders described are no more than prototypes with fuzzy boundaries, heterogeneous membership, and the absence of specific features that are required in all cases. For example, patients with Obsessive-Compulsive Personality Disorder do not all express their obsessive-compulsive style in exactly the same way. They possess enough similarities to be classified within the same prototypical category, but they are not homogeneous with respect to the defining features of that prototype. This probabilistic, prototypical, and polythetic model of classification has been accepted in DSM-IV, and each category is defined by a set of optional and at times overlapping features, only a subset of which is necessary for diagnosis.

One method for dealing with the abundance of available Personality Disorders in DSM-IV has been to group them together in three clusters based on phenomenological similarities. Cluster A (also known as the odd-eccentric cluster) includes the Paranoid, Schizoid, and Schizotypal Personality Disorders. Cluster B (also known as the dramatic-emotional cluster) includes the Antisocial, Borderline, Histrionic, and Narcissistic Personality Disorders. Cluster C (also known as the anxious-fearful cluster) includes the Avoidant, Dependent, and Obsessive-Compulsive Personality Disorders.

Although these clusters are useful as guides in remembering and teaching about Personality Disorders, they do have their limitations. The clustering has not been consistently supported by factor analysis, and many patients have disorders from more than one cluster. Indeed, one unfortunate result of using a categorical system is that the diagnosis of more than one Personality Disorder tends to be the rule rather than the exception in individuals who have any Personality Disorder—especially in clinical settings. This situation in no way implies that separate and unrelated pathogenetic processes underlie each of the diagnosed disorders. Multiple diagnoses are more likely to reflect the awkwardness of the categorical system rather than the presence of different etiologies.

One of the problems in the DSM-III and DSM-III-R definitions of the various Personality Disorders was the possibly artifactual overlap caused by the appearance of identical or nearly identical items in the definition of more than one Personality Disorder. A MacArthur data reanalysis aggregated all of the available studies pertinent to the question of how well the item sets for each Personality Disorder correlated with that Personality Disorder and with each of the others. This reanalysis allowed us to identify those items with low sensitivity or low specificity, or both. Many of these items were revised to clarify their meaning, and a few that were particularly nonspecific were deleted. Finally, the items in each criteria set were reordered based on the diagnostic efficiency of each item, listing most efficient items first.

Cluster A Personality Disorders

301.0 Paranoid Personality Disorder

Paranoid Personality Disorder describes the tendency to be suspicious, mistrustful, hypervigilant, and preoccupied with being exploited or betrayed by others. Hostility, irritability, avoidance, and anxiety may occur secondary to the paranoid beliefs. Patients with Paranoid Personality Disorder tend to make self-fulfilling suspicious prophecies because their mistrustful behavior causes others to act in an overly cautious and even deceptive way.

Adolf Meyer is often credited with introducing the concept of Paranoid Personality Disorder. However, Kraepelin, Bleuler, Schneider, and Freud all contributed early descriptions, and it has been included in all prior editions of the DSM. Studies suggest the possibility that Paranoid Personality Disorder (along with Schizotypal and Schizoid Personality Disorders) is in the Schizophrenia spectrum, providing a characterological manifestation that results from a common genetic predisposition.

The assessment of Paranoid Personality Disorder at a single meeting can be difficult and subject to overdiagnosis. It is important to realize that individuals are not always at their best or most trusting during a clinical interview, particularly if it is one that they did not initiate of their own accord and it occurs at a time when they also have an Axis I condition. In such situations, a degree of suspicion toward the clinician and withholding of information may be expected and should not in and of themselves imply the presence of a Personality Disorder. Consultations with others who are familiar with the person's longer term functioning are helpful in this regard, as are follow-up interviews once better rapport has been established.

Moreover, individuals from a different cultural group may be more likely to display guarded behaviors due to their lack of familiarity or comfort with the clinician or with the process of receiving a clinical interview. Finally, some situations are realistically threatening so that being a bit paranoid can be an adaptive response rather than a clinically significant personality feature.

DSM-IV diagnostic criteria for 301.0 Paranoid Personality Disorder

A. A pervasive distrust and suspiciousness of others such that their motives are interpreted as malevolent, beginning by early adulthood and present in a variety of contexts, as indicated by four (or more) of the following:

(1) suspects, without sufficient basis, that others are exploiting, harming, or deceiving him or her

(2) is preoccupied with unjustified doubts about the loyalty or trustworthiness of friends or associates

(3) is reluctant to confide in others because of unwarranted fear that the information will be used maliciously against him or her

(4) reads hidden demeaning or threatening meanings into benign remarks or events

(continued)

DSM-IV diagnostic criteria for 301.0 Paranoid Personality Disorder *(continued)*

(5) persistently bears grudges, i.e., is unforgiving of insults, injuries, or slights
(6) perceives attacks on his or her character or reputation that are not apparent to others and is quick to react angrily or to counterattack
(7) has recurrent suspicions, without justification, regarding fidelity of spouse or sexual partner

B. Does not occur exclusively during the course of Schizophrenia, a Mood Disorder With Psychotic Features, or another Psychotic Disorder and is not due to the direct physiological effects of a general medical condition.

Note: If criteria are met prior to the onset of Schizophrenia, add "Premorbid," e.g., "Paranoid Personality Disorder (Premorbid)."

301.20 Schizoid Personality Disorder

Schizoid Personality Disorder is characterized by a profound defect in the individual's ability to form personal relationships or to respond to others in an emotionally meaningful way. Patients with Schizoid Personality Disorder appear to be indifferent, aloof, detached, and unresponsive to praise, criticism, or any other feelings expressed by others. They often appear affectively bland, constricted, and apathetic. Despite the similarity in name, Schizoid Personality Disorder has been less clearly related to the Schizophrenia spectrum than have Schizotypal and Paranoid Personality Disorders.

Introverted schizoid styles have been prominently recognized in many personality theories developed in psychology and also in psychoanalytic object relations theory. Schizoid Personality Disorder was in all three versions of the DSM, although in DSM-I and DSM-II the descriptions included autistic magical thinking, which is now included under Schizotypal Personality Disorder. Since DSM-III, Schizoid Personality Disorder rarely has been diagnosed, partly because of the introduction of two new personality disorders that cover much of the same territory: Avoidant Personality Disorder and Schizotypal Personality Disorder.

DSM-III distinguished between Schizoid Personality Disorder and Avoidant Personality Disorder based on the individual's motivation for avoiding interpersonal contact. In Avoidant Personality Disorder, the person desires close relationships but avoids them out of fear of rejection. In contrast, the person with Schizoid Personality Disorder is presumed to have little or no such desire for interpersonal connectedness. In practice, this distinction can be very difficult. It is rare to find patients who have a complete absence of warm, tender feelings and are totally indifferent to praise, criticism, and the feelings of others. Moreover, as one gets to know the patient better, the introverted behavior that seemed to result from apathetic indifference is often better explained by anxiety and ambivalence.

Although Schizoid and Schizotypal Personality Disorders are both characterized by social detachment, DSM-III distinguished between them based on whether additional features (i.e., eccentricities of speech, thought, and/or behavior) were also present. In effect, Schizoid Personality Disorder has been squeezed out by its neighbors because most socially isolated individuals are much more likely to qualify for the diagnoses of Avoidant and Schizotypal Personality Disorders. Although no specific exclusion prevents the simultaneous diagnosis of Schizoid Personality Disorder in those patients with Schizotypal or Avoidant Personality Disorder, this diagnosis rarely adds information or makes much clinical sense.

DSM-IV diagnostic criteria for 301.20 Schizoid Personality Disorder

A. A pervasive pattern of detachment from social relationships and a restricted range of expression of emotions in interpersonal settings, beginning by early adulthood and present in a variety of contexts, as indicated by four (or more) of the following:
   (1) neither desires nor enjoys close relationships, including being part of a family
   (2) almost always chooses solitary activities
   (3) has little, if any, interest in having sexual experiences with another person
   (4) takes pleasure in few, if any, activities
   (5) lacks close friends or confidants other than first-degree relatives
   (6) appears indifferent to the praise or criticism of others
   (7) shows emotional coldness, detachment, or flattened affectivity

B. Does not occur exclusively during the course of Schizophrenia, a Mood Disorder With Psychotic Features, another Psychotic Disorder, or a Pervasive Developmental Disorder and is not due to the direct physiological effects of a general medical condition.

Note: If criteria are met prior to the onset of Schizophrenia, add "Premorbid," e.g., "Schizoid Personality Disorder (Premorbid)."

301.22 Schizotypal Personality Disorder

Schizotypal Personality Disorder encompasses a combination of odd or peculiar behavior, speech, thought, and perception. Patients with this disorder are usually withdrawn and display idiosyncratic speech patterns, eccentric beliefs, paranoid tendencies, perceptual illusion, unusual appearance, inappropriate affect, and social anxiety. Although patients with Schizotypal Personality Disorder experience subtle distortions of their perception of reality, and may even have brief psychotic breaks when stressed, they do not have the fully developed syndrome of Schizophrenia (e.g., prominent hallucinations, or delusions).

It should be noted that some patients with Schizotypal Personality Disorder will go on to develop Schizophrenia. In such cases, the apparent Schizotypal features are better considered to be part of the prodrome of the Schizophrenia and are indicated by adding the phrase *premorbid* (see the note below in the criteria set).

Schizotypal Personality Disorder was a new addition to DSM-III. The history of the diagnosis overlaps with the history of the Schizoid and Borderline Personality Disorders. Its major early precedent is Bleuler's concept of *latent schizophrenia*, which was applied to persons who displayed mild or attenuated symptoms of schizophrenia but who did not deteriorate in the classic manner suggested by Kraepelin. The term *schizotype* was coined by Rado as an abbreviation of *schizophrenic phenotype* to describe individuals who had the genotypic disposition to develop Schizophrenia but who displayed only a mild, attenuated form. The DSM-III definition of Schizotypal Personality Disorder (which is essentially unchanged in DSM-IV) was based on studies by Kety, who observed mild, subschizophrenic symptomatology in the biological relatives of patients with chronic Schizophrenia.

During the DSM-IV deliberations, the major question regarding this disorder was whether to move it to Axis I and include it in the "Schizophrenia and Other Psychotic Disorders" section. The major reasons favoring such a move were

1. To recognize the spectrum relationship described above
2. To treat the Schizophrenia spectrum and the Mood Disorders spectrum consistently (Dysthymic Disorder and Cyclothymic Disorder are in the "Mood Disorders" section, rather than in the "Personality Disorders" section)
3. To make DSM-IV compatible with *International Statistical Classification of Diseases and Related Health Problems,* 10th Revision (ICD-10)

For no very compelling reason, The Task Force decided to keep Schizotypal Personality Disorder in the "Personality Disorders" section of DSM-IV. This decision partly reflected the conservative nature of DSM-IV but also reflected the belief that spectrum conditions should fall within the province of the Personality Disorders.

DSM-IV diagnostic criteria for 301.22 Schizotypal Personality Disorder

A. A pervasive pattern of social and interpersonal deficits marked by acute discomfort with, and reduced capacity for, close relationships as well as by cognitive or perceptual distortions and eccentricities of behavior, beginning by early adulthood and present in a variety of contexts, as indicated by five (or more) of the following:
  (1) ideas of reference (excluding delusions of reference)
  (2) odd beliefs or magical thinking that influences behavior and is inconsistent with subcultural norms (e.g., superstitiousness, belief in clairvoyance, telepathy, or "sixth sense"; in children and adolescents, bizarre fantasies or preoccupations)
  (3) unusual perceptual experiences, including bodily illusions
  (4) odd thinking and speech (e.g., vague, circumstantial, metaphorical, overelaborate, or stereotyped)
  (5) suspiciousness or paranoid ideation
  (6) inappropriate or constricted affect
  (7) behavior or appearance that is odd, eccentric, or peculiar
  (8) lack of close friends or confidants other than first-degree relatives
  (9) excessive social anxiety that does not diminish with familiarity and tends to be associated with paranoid fears rather than negative judgments about self

B. Does not occur exclusively during the course of Schizophrenia, a Mood Disorder With Psychotic Features, another Psychotic Disorder, or a Pervasive Developmental Disorder.

Note: If criteria are met prior to the onset of Schizophrenia, add "Premorbid," e.g., "Schizotypal Personality Disorder (Premorbid)."

Cluster B Personality Disorders

301.7 Antisocial Personality Disorder

Antisocial Personality Disorder describes a pattern of socially irresponsible, exploitative, and guiltless behavior. The person engages in the deception and manipulation of others for personal gain and fails to abide by the law, sustain consistent employment, and develop stable relationships. Antisocial Personality Disorder is one of the oldest and best researched of the Personality Disorders. The first modern descriptions were made in the late eighteenth century by Pinel and Rush. The next contribution was by Prichard, who coined the term *moral insanity* to describe a pattern of immoral behavior that was unaccompanied by impairment in reasoning. Cleckley provided an influential formulation that emphasized the psychological traits of superficial charm; egocentricity and incapacity for love; lack of remorse, guilt, or shame; lack of insight; and failure to learn from past experience. Many of these traits were not included in DSM-III on the grounds that they were inferential and difficult to evaluate reliably. Instead, the DSM-III and DSM-III-R criteria sets were based in large part on the systematic research of Robins, which emphasized an explicit pattern of irresponsible behavior and antisocial acts.

The DSM-IV literature review, data reanalysis, and field trial dealt with an interesting paradox. Antisocial Personality Disorder, as defined in DSM-III-R, was the only Personality Disorder to consistently obtain adequate to good levels of interrater reliability. In addition, the diagnosis had substantial empirical support from epidemiological, longitudinal, psychophysiological, childhood antecedent, family history, and treatment response studies. However, the definition of Antisocial Personality Disorder had also received more criticism than any other Personality Disorder diagnosis.

Much of this criticism centered on the emphasis in the criteria set on overt criminal acts and irresponsible behaviors, to the exclusion of the traditional psychopathic traits as described by Cleckley (e.g., callous lack of empathy, manipulativeness, failure to learn from experience). It was suggested that this focus on behaviorally explicit indicators contributed to a variety of problems:

1. Failure to adequately represent traditional concepts of psychopathy
2. Overdiagnosis of Antisocial Personality Disorder in criminal and forensic settings
3. Underdiagnosis of the disorder in various noncriminal settings (e.g., on Wall Street)
4. An overly complex and cumbersome criteria set
5. Difficulties in the differentiation of Antisocial Personality Disorder from Substance Use Disorders
6. Significant overlap of Antisocial Personality Disorder with the Borderline, Narcissistic, and Histrionic Personality Disorders

The Antisocial Personality Disorder field trial compared four criteria sets: the original DSM-III-R criteria set, a simplified version of the DSM-III-R criteria set derived from data reanalysis, a 10-item criteria set also developed from data reanalysis that placed greater emphasis on *psychopathy* (glib and superficial, inflated and arrogant self-appraisal, deceitful and manipulative, lack of empathy and remorse), and the ICD-10 diagnostic criteria for research. Perhaps the most interesting result of the field trial was the somewhat surprising finding that the psychopathy items could indeed be evaluated reliably. However, there was no appreciable difference among the criteria sets with respect to their association with a variety of external validators measured in the field trial.

Because DSM-IV is a conservative document with a high threshold for incorporating changes, it was decided that the benefits that might be derived from making the criteria set more trait oriented did not outweigh the potential risk of destroying the established reliability of the behaviorally oriented DSM-III-R criteria set and disrupting ongoing research and clinical practice. The field trial did suggest that two of the DSM-III-R items could be deleted without a significant effect on the diagnosis. These items (parental irresponsibility and a failure to sustain a monogamous relationship) might be considered the residue of a more innocent age and are no longer at all specific to Antisocial Personality Disorder. The final DSM-IV criteria set has also been significantly streamlined by eliminating specific examples and the listing of the separate items required for the diagnosis of Conduct Disorder.

DSM-IV diagnostic criteria for 301.7 Antisocial Personality Disorder

A. There is a pervasive pattern of disregard for and violation of the rights of others occurring since age 15 years, as indicated by three (or more) of the following:
   (1) failure to conform to social norms with respect to lawful behaviors as indicated by repeatedly performing acts that are grounds for arrest
   (2) deceitfulness, as indicated by repeated lying, use of aliases, or conning others for personal profit or pleasure
   (3) impulsivity or failure to plan ahead
   (4) irritability and aggressiveness, as indicated by repeated physical fights or assaults
   (5) reckless disregard for safety of self or others
   (6) consistent irresponsibility, as indicated by repeated failure to sustain consistent work behavior or honor financial obligations
   (7) lack of remorse, as indicated by being indifferent to or rationalizing having hurt, mistreated, or stolen from another

B. The individual is at least age 18 years.

C. There is evidence of Conduct Disorder (see p. 90) with onset before age 15 years.

D. The occurrence of antisocial behavior is not exclusively during the course of Schizophrenia or a Manic Episode.

301.83 Borderline Personality Disorder

Borderline Personality Disorder describes a behavioral pattern of intense and chaotic relationships with fluctuating and extreme attitudes toward others. In the extreme form, patients with this disorder engage in self-destructive behaviors, are affectively unstable and impulsive, and lack a clear sense of identity. Suicide attempts or self-mutilation may be a response to rejections or disappointments in interpersonal relationships. The patients often alternate between viewing themselves—and others—as all good (idealizing) or all bad (devaluing). Their personal lives tend to be chaotic, unstable, and marked by frequent disappointments and rejections. An underlying mood of chronic anger and depression is common. During times of crisis or rejection or under the influence of alcohol or substance abuse, these patients may experience transient psychotic breaks lasting from hours to days. They may show poor control of emotions and impulses, which may result in aggressive and destructive behavior toward themselves and others.

Borderline Personality Disorder was a new addition to DSM-III. Throughout the history of the classification of psychiatric conditions, clinicians have referred to patients who fall literally on the boundary between existing diagnoses. Early precedents for a formal diagnosis are Alexander's *neurotic* and Reich's *impulsive* character disorders. The analyst Stern is credited with giving the term *borderline* formal status as a diagnosis, and Schmideberg emphasized the stable course of the unstable behavior. Kernberg used the term *borderline personality organization* far more inclusively to refer to a level of severe character pathology cutting across a number of the existing categories.

The term *borderline personality disorder* is often used indiscriminately and inappropriately in everyday practice to describe any individual who is difficult, demanding, angry, or self-destructive. One of the values of the DSM definition is that it does provide a relatively narrow version of the disorder, although even this definition captures a quite heterogeneous variety of presentations.

Perhaps the major controversy has been whether Borderline Personality Disorder is best conceived as a mood spectrum disorder or a Personality Disorder. The fact that Borderline Personality Disorder appears to have similarities to the Mood Disorders—evident in family history, follow-up, and pharmacological research—suggests to some that it is a form of chronic Mood Disorder. Others emphasize the impulsive quality of Borderline Personality Disorder and suggest that it is on a spectrum that would also include Impulse Control Disorders, Substance Use Disorders, and Antisocial Personality Disorder.

Criterion 9, a new addition to DSM-IV, was added to reflect the fact that individuals with Borderline Personality Disorder, especially those who are more severely impaired, may have transient, stress-related paranoid ideation or severe dissociative symptoms. These episodes can be quite unnerving to the individuals involved and to those around them (including the therapist). Sometimes self-mutilating behavior occurs as a means of "treating" the dissociative symptoms—the patient can feel alive only by experiencing pain. In others, self-mutilation is a means of "treating" intense dysphoria or counteracting intense anger.

DSM-IV diagnostic criteria for 301.83 Borderline Personality Disorder

A pervasive pattern of instability of interpersonal relationships, self-image, and affects, and marked impulsivity beginning by early adulthood and present in a variety of contexts, as indicated by five (or more) of the following:

(continued)

DSM-IV diagnostic criteria for 301.83 Borderline Personality Disorder *(continued)*

(1) frantic efforts to avoid real or imagined abandonment. **Note:** Do not include suicidal or self-mutilating behavior covered in Criterion 5.
(2) a pattern of unstable and intense interpersonal relationships characterized by alternating between extremes of idealization and devaluation
(3) identity disturbance: markedly and persistently unstable self-image or sense of self
(4) impulsivity in at least two areas that are potentially self-damaging (e.g., spending, sex, substance abuse, reckless driving, binge eating). **Note:** Do not include suicidal or self-mutilating behavior covered in Criterion 5.
(5) recurrent suicidal behavior, gestures, or threats, or self-mutilating behavior
(6) affective instability due to a marked reactivity of mood (e.g., intense episodic dysphoria, irritability, or anxiety usually lasting a few hours and only rarely more than a few days)
(7) chronic feelings of emptiness
(8) inappropriate, intense anger or difficulty controlling anger (e.g., frequent displays of temper, constant anger, recurrent physical fights)
(9) transient, stress-related paranoid ideation or severe dissociative symptoms

301.50 Histrionic Personality Disorder

The patient with Histrionic Personality Disorder tends to be attention seeking, self-dramatizing, excessively gregarious, seductive, manipulative, exhibitionistic, shallow, labile, vain, and demanding. Such presentations may overlap with and be difficult to distinguish from the Borderline or Narcissistic Personality Disorders. Family history and adoption studies also suggest the possibility of a genetic association between Somatization Disorder and the Histrionic and Antisocial Personality Disorders. The Histrionic and Antisocial Personality Disorders may be gender-specific phenotypic variants of the same underlying genotypic disposition. Disinhibition in women may be expressed through affective lability, manipulation of others, and numerous brief relationships that are shallow but intense. In men, it may be expressed through impulsivity, aggressive behavior, drug abuse, exploitation of others, and numerous shallow sexual relationships.

Histrionic Personality Disorder is a revision of the DSM-II *hysterical personality.* The term *hysterical* was replaced in part because of its historical baggage and sexist connotations, but a diagnosis by any other name may still be sexist. The problem is that Histrionic Personality Disorder as defined in DSM-IV may continue to represent an exaggerated version of stereotypical feminine traits and may place too little emphasis on items and examples that would tap the parallel "macho" male version expressing exaggerated masculine traits. In his own way, Stanley Kowalski in *A Streetcar Named Desire* is just as histrionic as Blanche Du Bois.

The changes in the DSM-IV criteria set for this disorder were intended to reduce overlap with Borderline, Antisocial, and Narcissistic Personality Disorders. Two DSM-III-R criteria, "constantly seeks or demands reassurance, approval, or praise" and "has no tolerance for the frustration of delayed gratification," have been omitted due to their low specificity. Two new criteria have been added: "suggestibility, i.e., easily influenced by others or circumstances" and "considers relationships to be more intimate than they actually are." The number of criteria required to diagnose Histrionic Personality Disorder has been raised from four to five out of eight.

DSM-IV diagnostic criteria for 301.50 Histrionic Personality Disorder

A pervasive pattern of excessive emotionality and attention seeking, beginning by early adulthood and present in a variety of contexts, as indicated by five (or more) of the following:

(1) is uncomfortable in situations in which he or she is not the center of attention
(2) interaction with others is often characterized by inappropriate sexually seductive or provocative behavior
(3) displays rapidly shifting and shallow expression of emotions
(4) consistently uses physical appearance to draw attention to self
(5) has a style of speech that is excessively impressionistic and lacking in detail
(6) shows self-dramatization, theatricality, and exaggerated expression of emotion
(7) is suggestible, i.e., easily influenced by others or circumstances
(8) considers relationships to be more intimate than they actually are

301.81 Narcissistic Personality Disorder

Individuals with Narcissistic Personality Disorder are egocentric, grandiose, entitled, shallow, exploitative, arrogant, and preoccupied with fame, wealth, and achievement, and they generally lack empathy and consideration for the feelings of others. Such people may be exquisitely hypersensitive to evaluation or criticism. Narcissistic individuals crave admiring attention and praise and place excessive emphasis on displaying the accoutrements of beauty, power, fame, and wealth. They typically use relationships to meet their own selfish needs with little consideration for the needs of the other person and feel that they are entitled to special rights, attention, privileges, and consideration.

Narcissistic Personality Disorder was a new addition to DSM-III that reflected a growing interest in the theoretical and clinical concept of narcissism. The term *narcissism* was originally used by in a clinical context by Havelock Ellis to describe male autoeroticism. The concept was extended to homosexuality by Sadger and developed further by many analysts, including Freud, Rank, Reich, Horney, Waelder, and others. The concept received renewed attention during the past 15 years, notably in the work of Kohut and Kernberg.

The inclusion of Narcissistic Personality Disorder has received mixed reviews. Some have suggested that using narcissism as a foundation for a distinct Personality Disorder diagnosis is misleading because it is a conflict or trait that is present to varying degrees in most individuals. The criteria set also has been criticized because it fails to recognize that narcissism sometimes appears in a variety of forms other than overt grandiosity, exhibitionism, and feelings of entitlement. It is argued that the criteria rely too heavily on the overt, superficial features of narcissism, ignoring the more subtle and indirect manifestations, such as an inability to remain in love, perverse fantasies, dependency conflicts, and the grandiose sense that one is especially inadequate. Kohut argued that the diagnosis could only be made on the basis of the emerging transferential relationship in psychoanalytic psychotherapy. However, this method of diagnosis is not possible in DSM-IV because it uses highly inferential judgments about the response to a specialized form of treatment in a way that would reduce reliability and limit the utility of the diagnosis.

A few changes were made in DSM-IV to improve specificity and help reduce overlap between Narcissistic Personality Disorder and the other Personality Disorders, particularly Antisocial and Histrionic Personality Disorders. The DSM-III-R phrase "hypersensitivity to the evaluation of others" in the preamble has been replaced with the more characteristic "need for admiration." The DSM-III-R criterion "reacts to criticism with feelings of rage, shame, or humiliation" has been deleted due to low specificity, and a new criterion, "arrogant, haughty behaviors or attitudes," has been added.

DSM-IV diagnostic criteria for 301.81 Narcissistic Personality Disorder

A pervasive pattern of grandiosity (in fantasy or behavior), need for admiration, and lack of empathy, beginning by early adulthood and present in a variety of contexts, as indicated by five (or more) of the following:

(1) has a grandiose sense of self-importance (e.g., exaggerates achievements and talents, expects to be recognized as superior without commensurate achievements)
(2) is preoccupied with fantasies of unlimited success, power, brilliance, beauty, or ideal love
(3) believes that he or she is "special" and unique and can only be understood by, or should associate with, other special or high-status people (or institutions)
(4) requires excessive admiration
(5) has a sense of entitlement, i.e., unreasonable expectations of especially favorable treatment or automatic compliance with his or her expectations
(6) is interpersonally exploitative, i.e., takes advantage of others to achieve his or her own ends
(7) lacks empathy: is unwilling to recognize or identify with the feelings and needs of others
(8) is often envious of others or believes that others are envious of him or her
(9) shows arrogant, haughty behaviors or attitudes

Cluster C Personality Disorders

301.82 Avoidant Personality Disorder

Avoidant Personality Disorder is a pattern of inhibited, introverted, and anxious behavior, with low self-esteem, hypersensitivity to rejection, social awkwardness, timidity, social discomfort, and self-conscious fears of being embarrassed or acting foolish. Although the inclusion of Avoidant Personality Disorder in DSM-III was criticized because of its lack of an extensive clinical tradition, it had precedents in Schneider's *aesthetic psychopath,* Fenichel's *phobic character,* and Millon's *active-detached personality syndrome.*

The social avoidance in Avoidant Personality Disorder may be difficult to distinguish from the social isolation in Schizoid Personality Disorder. The patient with Schizoid Personality Disorder tends to be indifferent to others, whereas the patient with Avoidant Personality Disorder greatly desires relationships but is too shy and insecure to seek them out. The prevalence rates in clinical settings for Avoidant Personality Disorder are much higher than those for the rarely diagnosed Schizoid Personality Disorder. Many more persons appear to be socially withdrawn because of an anxious insecurity than because of an apathetic indifference.

There is also considerable overlap of Avoidant Personality Disorder with Dependent Personality Disorder. Avoidant and dependent persons share interpersonal insecurity, a strong desire for interpersonal relationships, and low self-esteem. Avoidant persons have difficulty initiating relationships, whereas dependent persons have difficulty separating; however, avoidant persons are also likely to be very clinging and fearful of losing a relationship once it has begun. Avoidant Personality Disorder and Generalized Social Phobia are probably two different formulations of the same condition. (See Chapter 13, "Social Phobia," for a more detailed discussion.)

Several changes in the DSM-IV criteria were intended to clarify the construct of Avoidant Personality Disorder and distinguish it from its near neighbors, Dependent Personality Disorder and Social Phobia. The criteria set now makes clear that the low self-esteem results from the "belief that one is socially inept, personally unappealing, or inferior to others."

DSM-IV diagnostic criteria for 301.82 Avoidant Personality Disorder

A pervasive pattern of social inhibition, feelings of inadequacy, and hypersensitivity to negative evaluation, beginning by early adulthood and present in a variety of contexts, as indicated by four (or more) of the following:

(1) avoids occupational activities that involve significant interpersonal contact, because of fears of criticism, disapproval, or rejection

(2) is unwilling to get involved with people unless certain of being liked

(continued)

DSM-IV diagnostic criteria for 301.82 Avoidant Personality Disorder *(continued)*

(3) shows restraint within intimate relationships because of the fear of being shamed or ridiculed
(4) is preoccupied with being criticized or rejected in social situations
(5) is inhibited in new interpersonal situations because of feelings of inadequacy
(6) views self as socially inept, personally unappealing, or inferior to others
(7) is unusually reluctant to take personal risks or to engage in any new activities because they may prove embarrassing

301.6 Dependent Personality Disorder

Dependent Personality Disorder describes a pattern of excessive reliance on others that is reflected in the person's tendency to permit others to make important decisions, to feel helpless when alone, to subjugate his or her own needs to those of others, to tolerate mistreatment, and fail to be appropriately self-assertive. It is not uncommon for such a patient to be living with a controlling, domineering, overprotective, and infantilizing person.

Dependent Personality Disorder was included in DSM-I as a subtype of the passive-aggressive personality disorder, but it was not included in DSM-II. Historical precedents include the psychoanalytic and psychological concepts of the oral and submissive characters. DSM-III Dependent Personality Disorder was criticized for providing an excessively narrow definition (only three items) and for including a possible gender bias.

Dependent Personality Disorder is diagnosed more frequently in women. It has been suggested that this reflects masculine biases regarding what is healthy behavior and the failure to recognize masculine forms of dependent behavior. Therefore, clinicians should be aware of a possible sex bias in their diagnoses and treatment so as not to miss stereotypically masculine forms of dependency expressed through domineering behavior, ordering others to help rather than demanding or pleading.

DSM-IV diagnostic criteria for 301.6 Dependent Personality Disorder

A pervasive and excessive need to be taken care of that leads to submissive and clinging behavior and fears of separation, beginning by early adulthood and present in a variety of contexts, as indicated by five (or more) of the following:

(1) has difficulty making everyday decisions without an excessive amount of advice and reassurance from others
(2) needs others to assume responsibility for most major areas of his or her life
(3) has difficulty expressing disagreement with others because of fear of loss of support or approval. **Note:** Do not include realistic fears of retribution.

(continued)

DSM-IV diagnostic criteria for 301.6 Dependent Personality Disorder *(continued)*

(4) has difficulty initiating projects or doing things on his or her own (because of a lack of self-confidence in judgment or abilities rather than a lack of motivation or energy)
(5) goes to excessive lengths to obtain nurturance and support from others, to the point of volunteering to do things that are unpleasant
(6) feels uncomfortable or helpless when alone because of exaggerated fears of being unable to care for himself or herself
(7) urgently seeks another relationship as a source of care and support when a close relationship ends
(8) is unrealistically preoccupied with fears of being left to take care of himself or herself

301.4 Obsessive-Compulsive Personality Disorder

Persons with Obsessive-Compulsive Personality Disorder tend to be perfectionist, constricted, and excessively disciplined. Behavior is rigid, formal, emotionally cool, distant, intellectualizing, and detailed. These patients may be driven, aggressive, competitive, and impatient, with a chronic sense of time pressure and an inability to relax. They have an excessive tendency to be in control of themselves, others, and life situations. They are often tormented with anxiety over matters of uncertainty and ambiguity. Because of their need for perfection, they often have difficulty making decisions and are prone to procrastinate or obsess. On the other hand, other types of obsessional patients have a hard-driving urge to do everything now and expect the same level of efficiency from others. An undercurrent of anger is often visible in their general demeanor, although open expression of anger—or any other emotion—is difficult for them.

Superficially, these patients may appear to have drab and monotonous personalities and to drone on in excruciating detail. They are often hoarders of both money and other items. These individuals are also likely to be overly concerned with productivity and achievement. They usually have rigid moralistic attitudes toward life and are prone to criticism and moralistic judgment of others because of their rigid superego. They may also be preoccupied with orderliness, neatness, and cleanliness and expect others to meet their expectations. Inflexibility, stubbornness, rigidity, and a need for control dominate their interpersonal relationships.

Obsessive-Compulsive Personality Disorder was included in all previous versions of the DSM and has historical precedents in psychoanalysis (e.g., anal character), psychiatry (e.g., *anankast* character), and psychology (e.g., autocratic and conforming personality). Obsessive-Compulsive Personality Disorder patients were observed by Kraepelin and by Schneider, who described the anankast subtype of the "insecure psychopath." Freud, however, provided the most influential formulation, describing the covariation of the traits of orderliness, parsimony, and obstinacy. Various extensions and refinements were provided by Sadger, Brill, Jones, Abraham, Reich, Fromm, Horney, and others.

Obsessive-Compulsive Personality Disorder patients may be prone to Axis I Obsessive-Compulsive Disorder. However, many individuals with Obsessive-Compulsive Personality Disorder do not have Obsessive-Compulsive Disorder, and many persons with Obsessive-Compulsive Disorder fail to display obsessive-compulsive personality traits. Obsessive-Compulsive Personality Disorder patients are prone to depression, particularly as they get older and find that their overvalued careers are not as rewarding or successful as they had hoped and as the sacrifices they have made with respect to relationships become apparent. Obsessive-compulsive personality style may be correlated with the so-called Type A personality (e.g, intense ambition, competitiveness, time urgency, and easily aroused hostility), which may be a risk factor for cardiovascular disease.

DSM-IV diagnostic criteria for 301.4 Obsessive-Compulsive Personality Disorder

A pervasive pattern of preoccupation with orderliness, perfectionism, and mental and interpersonal control, at the expense of flexibility, openness, and efficiency, beginning by early adulthood and present in a variety of contexts, as indicated by four (or more) of the following:

(1) is preoccupied with details, rules, lists, order, organization, or schedules to the extent that the major point of the activity is lost

(2) shows perfectionism that interferes with task completion (e.g., is unable to complete a project because his or her own overly strict standards are not met)

(3) is excessively devoted to work and productivity to the exclusion of leisure activities and friendships (not accounted for by obvious economic necessity)

(4) is overconscientious, scrupulous, and inflexible about matters of morality, ethics, or values (not accounted for by cultural or religious identification)

(5) is unable to discard worn-out or worthless objects even when they have no sentimental value

(6) is reluctant to delegate tasks or to work with others unless they submit to exactly his or her way of doing things

(7) adopts a miserly spending style toward both self and others; money is viewed as something to be hoarded for future catastrophes

(8) shows rigidity and stubbornness

DSM-IV text for 301.9 Personality Disorder Not Otherwise Specified

This category is for disorders of personality functioning that do not meet criteria for any specific Personality Disorder. An example is the presence of features of more than one specific Personality Disorder that do not meet the full criteria for any one Personality Disorder ("mixed personality"), but that together cause clinically significant distress or impairment in one or more important areas of functioning (e.g., social or occupational). This category can also be used when the clinician judges that a specific Personality Disorder that is not included in the Classification is appropriate. Examples include depressive personality disorder and passive-aggressive personality disorder.

The Last Word

The evaluation of Personality Disorder is important but can be difficult, especially when an Axis I condition is also present. It is often advisable to follow a patient over time and into remission and to gather data from informants before assuming that features of the presentation are due to Personality Disorder rather than the Axis I condition. On the other hand, the presence of a Personality Disorder may have a dramatic impact on treatment planning and treatment response for Axis I conditions.

CHAPTER 23

Disorders of Infancy, Childhood, and Adolescence

The provision of a separate section for disorders that are usually first diagnosed in infancy, childhood, or adolescence is for convenience only. Although most individuals with these disorders present for clinical attention during childhood or adolescence, it is not uncommon for some of these conditions to be diagnosed for the first time in adulthood. Moreover, many disorders included in other sections of the manual often have an onset during childhood or adolescence. In evaluating an infant, child, or adolescent, the clinician should consider the diagnoses included in this section but must also consider the disorders described elsewhere in DSM-IV. Adults also may be diagnosed with disorders in this section when their clinical presentation meets relevant diagnostic criteria (e.g., Stuttering, Pica). Moreover, if an adult had symptoms as a child that met all criteria for a disorder in this section but now presents with an attenuated or residual form, the In Partial Remission modifier may be indicated (e.g., Attention-Deficit/Hyperactivity Disorder, Combined Type, In Partial Remission).

For most (but not all) DSM-IV disorders, a single criteria set is provided that applies to children, adolescents, and adults (e.g., if a child or adolescent has symptoms that meet the criteria for Major Depressive Disorder, this diagnosis should be given, regardless of the individual's age). The characteristics of any given disorder that may vary with age are described in a section in the text entitled "Specific Culture, Age, and

Gender Features." Specific issues related to the diagnosis of Personality Disorders in children or adolescents are discussed in Chapter 22.

A number of disorders included in this section are probably not best conceived of as mental disorders (e.g., Learning Disorders, Motor Skills Disorder, Communication Disorders). They are included in DSM-IV for their educational value (particularly in facilitating differential diagnosis) and because they commonly occur in children who present in mental health settings.

Mental Retardation

Mental Retardation

317	Mild Mental Retardation
318.0	Moderate Mental Retardation
318.1	Severe Mental Retardation
318.2	Profound Mental Retardation
319	Mental Retardation, Severity Unspecified

Mental Retardation is defined by the presence of low intelligence and impaired adaptive functioning that has an onset before the age of 18 years. It is the final common pathway for a wide variety of psychosocial and biological etiologies, which may often interact with one another. Not infrequently (30%–40%), an extensive evaluation fails to demonstrate any definitive etiology for the Mental Retardation. The most common specific etiologies include chromosomal changes (trisomy 21), prenatal exposure to substances or toxins, perinatal problems (e.g., hypoxia during delivery), environmental influences (e.g., deprivation of stimulation), inherited conditions (e.g., Tay-Sachs disease), and general medical conditions occurring in infancy or early childhood (e.g., trauma).

It should be emphasized that Mental Retardation often coexists with other mental disorders (e.g., in association with Pervasive Developmental Disorder) and is usually not by itself the presenting problem in mental health settings. When a diagnosis of Mental Retardation is made, the clinician should conduct a thorough psychiatric evaluation to determine whether another coexisting condition is present. Mental Retardation is coded on Axis II to ensure that an assessment of intelligence and adaptive functioning is not ignored in the presence of more florid symptomatology.

DSM-IV diagnostic criteria for Mental Retardation

A. Significantly subaverage intellectual functioning: an IQ of approximately 70 or below on an individually administered IQ test (for infants, a clinical judgment of significantly subaverage intellectual functioning).

(continued)

DSM-IV diagnostic criteria for Mental Retardation *(continued)*

B. Concurrent deficits or impairments in present adaptive functioning (i.e., the person's effectiveness in meeting the standards expected for his or her age by his or her cultural group) in at least two of the following areas: communication, self-care, home living, social/interpersonal skills, use of community resources, self-direction, functional academic skills, work, leisure, health, and safety.

C. The onset is before age 18 years.

Code based on degree of severity reflecting level of intellectual impairment:

317 Mild Mental Retardation: IQ level 50–55 to approximately 70
318.0 Moderate Mental Retardation: IQ level 35–40 to 50–55
318.1 Severe Mental Retardation: IQ level 20–25 to 35–40
318.2 Profound Mental Retardation: IQ level below 20 or 25
319 Mental Retardation, Severity Unspecified: when there is stron presumption of Mental Retardation but the person's intelligence is untestable by standard tests

Criterion A. Although the IQ cutoff point for a diagnosis of Mental Retardation is set at 70 (about 2 standard deviations below the mean), it must be recognized that the measurement error associated with standard IQ tests is plus or minus 5 points. Therefore, in some cases a measured IQ of up to 75 could be compatible with a diagnosis of Mental Retardation when the clinical picture is also accompanied by significant impairment in adaptive functioning (see Criterion B). IQ testing must be conducted individually and must be interpreted in light of possible mediating factors that could affect test results (e.g., impaired attention, visual impairment, language barriers).

Criterion B. The diagnosis of Mental Retardation is not based just on the level of the IQ but also requires impairment in adaptive functioning. Because IQ tends to be relatively stable over time, it is often assumed that Mental Retardation is lifelong. However, improvement in adaptive functioning (e.g., as a result of maturation, education, or rehabilitative experiences) can result in sufficient improvement in functioning so that a diagnosis of Mental Retardation is no longer appropriate.

Criterion C. By convention, development after the age of 18 years of a lowered IQ and impairment in adaptive functioning as a result of a general medical condition or toxin exposure does not warrant a separate diagnosis of Mental Retardation and is usually diagnosed as Dementia. However, Dementia and Mental Retardation can both be diagnosed when the onset of deficits occurs before age 18 (e.g., severe head trauma in a child leading to lowered IQ).

Learning Disorders

Learning Disorders

315.00	Reading Disorder
315.1	Mathematics Disorder
315.2	Disorder of Written Expression
315.9	Learning Disorder Not Otherwise Specified

Reading Disorder (dyslexia) is for problems with reading accuracy, speed, or comprehension. Mathematics Disorder includes problems with calculations, copying numbers correctly, and understanding or recognizing mathematical terms, symbols, and signs. In Disorder of Written Expression, there are grammatical errors, punctuation errors, and poor paragraph organization.

Although also commonly associated with Learning Disorders, spelling errors and poor handwriting do not by themselves qualify an individual for the diagnosis. DSM-IV provides three separate codable disorders; however, they often occur together and as many can be diagnosed as apply. Reading Disorder is by far the most common. Learning Disorders and Mental Retardation are different from most other disorders in DSM-IV in that they require test results to establish the diagnosis. Because the criteria sets for each of the three Learning Disorders are so similar, we include a single generic set that captures the essential features of each.

Summary of DSM-IV diagnostic criteria for Learning Disorders

A. Academic achievement (i.e., reading, mathematics, or written expression), as measured by individually administered standardized tests, is substantially below that expected given the person's chronological age, measured intelligence, and age-appropriate education.

B. The disturbance in Criterion A significantly interferes with academic achievement or activities of daily living.

C. If a sensory deficit is present, the difficulties are in excess of those usually associated with it.

Coding note: If a general medical (e.g., neurological) condition or sensory deficit is present, code the condition on Axis III.

Note: This is a summary of three criteria sets.

CRITERION A. Learning Disorders are distinguished by a marked discrepancy between achievement in one specific academic area and the person's overall intelligence. Therefore, it is possible to diagnose a Learning Disorder in an individual with Mental Retardation when the deficit in a particular area is substantially worse than one would expect given the individual's IQ. This criterion does not provide a precise cutoff point, and clinical judgment is required in interpreting the test results.

Although group-administered standardized tests may be helpful for screening purposes, confirmation of the diagnosis requires the use of an individually administered and interpreted test. There are a number of reasons why a score on a group-administered standardized test may not be a true reflection of the person's actual academic abilities: 1) language barriers, 2) cultural differences, and 3) the presence of other disorders that may compromise performance (e.g., Attention-Deficit/Hyperactivity Disorder).

CRITERION B. The required impairment usually first becomes apparent in the early grades when the child has difficulty in developing these academic skills as they are taught in school. However, in children with high IQs, Learning Disorders may not become apparent until the later grades because their intelligence provides them with a buffer that allows for adequate performance of academic tasks in earlier grades. Such children begin to have difficulty only when required to master more advanced tasks in the later grades.

CRITERION C. DSM-III-R excluded this diagnosis when the learning disability was attributable to a sensory deficit. DSM-IV allows clinical judgment in applying this exclusion because some children with sensory deficits have learning problems that are out of proportion to the extent of the sensory impairment.

Motor Skills Disorder

315.4 Developmental Coordination Disorder

Developmental Coordination Disorder is essentially equivalent in the motor sphere of development to the Learning Disorders. It is characterized by clumsiness and a delay in the development of motor skills that are sufficiently severe to cause marked impairment. (Refer to DSM-IV, pp. 53–55, for text and criteria.)

Communication Disorders

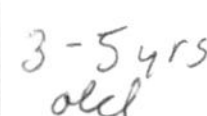

Communication Disorders

315.31	Expressive Language Disorder
315.31	Mixed Receptive-Expressive Language Disorder
315.39	Phonological Disorder
307.0	Stuttering
307.9	Communication Disorder Not Otherwise Specified

Although Communication Disorders are not usually considered mental disorders, they are included in DSM-IV for purposes of differential diagnosis. (Refer to DSM-IV, pp. 55–65, for text and criteria.)

315.31 Expressive Language Disorder

Expressive Language Disorder is characterized by production of verbal or sign language that is significantly impaired compared with the person's receptive language ability and nonverbal intelligence. Like Learning Disorders and Mental Retardation, this disorder requires an evaluation with individually administered standardized measures of language and intelligence.

315.31 Mixed Receptive-Expressive Language Disorder

Mixed Receptive-Expressive Language Disorder is characterized by impairment in receptive language ability (e.g., difficulty understanding words or sentences) in addition to the expressive language problems discussed above.

315.39 Phonological Disorder

Phonological Disorder is characterized by failure to use developmentally appropriate speech sounds that is sufficiently severe to cause marked impairment. There may be sound substitutions, omissions, lisping.

307.0 Stuttering

Stuttering is characterized by developmentally inappropriate disruptions in the fluency and time patterning of speech.

Pervasive Developmental Disorders

Pervasive Developmental Disorders

299.00	Autistic Disorder
299.80	Rett's Disorder
299.10	Childhood Disintegrative Disorder
299.80	Asperger's Disorder
299.80	Pervasive Developmental Disorder Not Otherwise Specified

Pervasive Developmental Disorders are characterized by the early onset of very severe impairments in social interaction and communication and the presence of inflexible or extremely restricted behaviors. The most characteristic and best studied of these disorders is Autistic Disorder. The others are much less well established and have been introduced into DSM-IV to provide greater specificity. Mental Retardation is commonly associated with Pervasive Developmental Disorder, and, when present, it should be coded on Axis II. When Pervasive Developmental Disorder is associated with chromosomal abnormalities, congenital infections, or structural abnormalities of the central nervous system, the Pervasive Developmental Disorder should be coded on Axis I and the associated general medical condition should be coded on Axis III.

299.00 Autistic Disorder

Many children display oddities in behavior and difficulties in social interaction. Only the most severe manifestations qualify for the diagnosis of Autistic Disorder. Those who have some of the features but who do not present with the full syndrome may be diagnosed with Asperger's Disorder or Pervasive Developmental Disorder Not Otherwise Specified. The DSM-IV literature review found that the DSM-III-R criteria set for Autistic Disorder defined a much broader group of individuals as having Autistic Disorder than did DSM-III, ICD-10, and clinician's judgment. The DSM-IV data reanalysis and field trial established a more narrowly defined criteria set that was more in line with these other definitions of Autistic Disorder.

Although the criteria set for Autistic Disorder appears complicated, it boils down to a requirement that there be considerable and characteristic impairment in three specific areas of functioning (social interaction, communication, range of interests and behavior) with an onset before age 3 years. The specific manifestations of this disorder depend on the age of the individual.

DSM-IV diagnostic criteria for 299.00 Autistic Disorder

A. A total of six (or more) items from (1), (2), and (3), with at least two from (1), and one each from (2) and (3):
   (1) qualitative impairment in social interaction, as manifested by at least two of the following:
      (a) marked impairment in the use of multiple nonverbal behaviors such as eye-to-eye gaze, facial expression, body postures, and gestures to regulate social interaction
      (b) failure to develop peer relationships appropriate to developmental level
      (c) a lack of spontaneous seeking to share enjoyment, interests, or achievements with other people (e.g., by a lack of showing, bringing, or pointing out objects of interest)
      (d) lack of social or emotional reciprocity
   (2) qualitative impairments in communication as manifested by at least one of the following:

(continued)

DSM-IV diagnostic criteria for 299.00 Autistic Disorder *(continued)*

(a) delay in, or total lack of, the development of spoken language (not accompanied by an attempt to compensate through alternative modes of communication such as gesture or mime)
(b) in individuals with adequate speech, marked impairment in the ability to initiate or sustain a conversation with others
(c) stereotyped and repetitive use of language or idiosyncratic language
(d) lack of varied, spontaneous make-believe play or social imitative play appropriate to developmental level

(3) restricted repetitive and stereotyped patterns of behavior, interests, and activities, as manifested by at least one of the following:
(a) encompassing preoccupation with one or more stereotyped and restricted patterns of interest that is abnormal either in intensity or focus
(b) apparently inflexible adherence to specific, nonfunctional routines or rituals
(c) stereotyped and repetitive motor mannerisms (e.g., hand or finger flapping or twisting, or complex whole-body movements)
(d) persistent preoccupation with parts of objects

B. Delays or abnormal functioning in at least one of the following areas, with onset prior to age 3 years: (1) social interaction, (2) language as used in social communication, or (3) symbolic or imaginative play.

C. The disturbance is not better accounted for by Rett's Disorder or Childhood Disintegrative Disorder.

Criterion A1. The impairment in social interaction differs with developmental age. Younger children may have virtually no interest in social interactions, whereas older children may interact but in a mechanical or markedly inappropriate way.

Criterion A2. In individuals who do develop speech, it is stereotyped, repetitive, and markedly abnormal with respect to pitch, intonation, rate, rhythm, or stress. There is an inability to comprehend abstract concepts or get jokes. There is an impaired capacity to appreciate the nuances of the social use of language such as implied meaning or indirect requests.

Criterion A3. Individuals with Autistic Disorder have a remarkably low tolerance for change and insist that things be done repetitively in exactly the same way. There may be a narrow and intense focus on particular topics (e.g., train schedules), skills (e.g., memorizing phone numbers), or activities (e.g., switching a light on and off) to the exclusion of everything else.

Criterion B. DSM-III-R eliminated the DSM-III requirement for an onset of symptoms before age 3 years, resulting in a more heterogeneous and inclusive definition. Although not mentioned explicitly in the criteria set, there is almost no period of normal development in the typical case of Autistic Disorder. In the majority of cases (around 75%), the condition is apparent shortly after birth and certainly in the first year of life. Most other cases develop in the second year of life, although it is possible that the age at onset in these children was earlier than that reported retrospectively by the parents.

CRITERION C. DSM-IV has established the following hierarchy for Pervasive Developmental Disorders. Because their definitions are the most specific, Rett's Disorder and Childhood Disintegrative Disorder take precedence over Autistic Disorder. However, Autistic Disorder is diagnosed instead of Asperger's Disorder when criteria are met for both.

299.80 Rett's Disorder

Rett's Disorder has been reported only in girls and is characterized by marked regressions in development (e.g., deceleration in head growth, loss of purposeful hand movements, and restricted interest in social environment) that occur following a period of at least 5 months of normal development after birth.

299.10 Childhood Disintegrative Disorder

Childhood Disintegrative Disorder, which is apparently rare, resembles Autistic Disorder in its symptom profile but differs in that it requires a period of at least 2 years of normal development followed by a loss of previously acquired skills.

299.80 Asperger's Disorder

The diagnosis of Asperger's Disorder has been introduced into DSM-IV to identify a potentially interesting subgroup of patients who have the marked impairments in social interaction and the restricted repetitive and stereotyped behaviors characteristic of Autistic Disorder but who do not have delays in language development. The inclusion of Asperger's Disorder in DSM-IV was controversial. There was considerable concern that it has not been sufficiently well studied, lacks clear definitional boundaries, and probably defines a heterogeneous group of patients. A major reason tilting the balance toward adding Asperger's Disorder was the desire to enhance compatibility with ICD-10, which includes this category.

DSM-IV text for 299.80 Pervasive Developmental Disorder Not Otherwise Specified (including Atypical Autism)

This category should be used when there is a severe and pervasive impairment in the development of reciprocal social interaction or verbal and nonverbal communication skills, or when stereotyped behavior, interests, and activities are present, but the criteria are not met for a specific Pervasive Developmental Disorder, Schizophrenia, Schizotypal Personality Disorder, or Avoidant Personality Disorder. For example, this category includes "atypical autism"—presentations that do not meet the criteria for Autistic Disorder because of late age at onset, atypical symptomatology, or subthreshold symptomatology, or all of these.

Attention-Deficit and Disruptive Behavior Disorders

Attention-Deficit and Disruptive Behavior Disorders

314.xx	Attention-Deficit/Hyperactivity Disorder
314.01	Combined Type
314.00	Predominantly Inattentive Type
314.01	Predominantly Hyperactive-Impulsive Type
314.9	Attention-Deficit/Hyperactivity Disorder Not Otherwise Specified
312.8	Conduct Disorder
313.81	Oppositional Defiant Disorder
312.9	Disruptive Behavior Disorder Not Otherwise Specified

Attention-Deficit/Hyperactivity Disorder

Attention-Deficit/Hyperactivity Disorder has been the subject of considerable controversy and has a long and interesting history. There has not been a wide consensus concerning the boundary between this disorder and age-appropriate distractibility or overactivity. On one hand, some clinicians worry that setting an excessively low threshold will result in an artificially high prevalence, with the children who have a false-positive diagnosis receiving unnecessary and potentially harmful treatments (e.g., stimulants) and stigmatization. In contrast, others worry that setting an excessively high threshold will result in missed cases, undertreatment, and the inappropriate labeling of the children as lazy, "spacey," having "behavior problems," or having low intelligence.

There has also been a difference of opinion concerning whether the definition of this category should focus on inattention or hyperactivity. DSM-II introduced the category of Hyperkinetic Reaction of Childhood (or Adolescence) with an obvious focus on hyperactivity. DSM-III shifted the emphasis of this category toward the symptoms of inattention by replacing the DSM-II definition with Attention-Deficit Disorder With or Without Hyperactivity. In DSM-III-R, Attention-Deficit Disorder Without Hyperactivity was downgraded into a kind of residual category (the only one in the manual without a criteria set). ICD-10 continues to emphasize hyperactivity, including an overarching category for Hyperkinetic Disorders. The DSM-IV literature review, data reanalysis, and field trial results suggested that it is best to define a single Attention-Deficit/Hyperactivity Disorder with subtypes (Combined Type, Predominantly Inattentive Type, Predominantly Hyperactive-Impulsive Type) to indicate that variable degrees of inattention and hyperactivity-impulsivity occur in the presentation of patients with this disorder.

The particular behaviors that typify inattention, hyperactivity, and impulsivity are very much influenced by the patient's age and developmental level. The presentation may evolve from one subtype to another. For example, when the child becomes an adult, hyperactivity may be less prominent so that the Combined Type no longer applies. Furthermore, it is important in assessing the criteria for this disorder to consider the behavior in the context of what constitutes the range of appropriate and inappropriate behaviors for the individual's developmental stage. This disorder occurs much more frequently in males.

DSM-IV diagnostic criteria for Attention-Deficit/ Hyperactivity Disorder

A. Either (1) or (2):

(1) six (or more) of the following symptoms of **inattention** have persisted for at least 6 months to a degree that is maladaptive and inconsistent with developmental level:

Inattention

(a) often fails to give close attention to details or makes careless mistakes in schoolwork, work, or other activities
(b) often has difficulty sustaining attention in tasks or play activities
(c) often does not seem to listen when spoken to directly
(d) often does not follow through on instructions and fails to finish schoolwork, chores, or duties in the workplace (not due to oppositional behavior or failure to understand instructions)
(e) often has difficulty organizing tasks and activities
(f) often avoids, dislikes, or is reluctant to engage in tasks that require sustained mental effort (such as schoolwork or homework)
(g) often loses things necessary for tasks or activities (e.g., toys, school assignments, pencils, books, or tools)
(h) is often easily distracted by extraneous stimuli
(i) is often forgetful in daily activities

(2) six (or more) of the following symptoms of **hyperactivity-impulsivity** have persisted for at least 6 months to a degree that is maladaptive and inconsistent with developmental level:

Hyperactivity

(a) often fidgets with hands or feet or squirms in seat
(b) often leaves seat in classroom or in other situations in which remaining seated is expected
(c) often runs about or climbs excessively in situations in which it is inappropriate (in adolescents or adults, may be limited to subjective feelings of restlessness)
(d) often has difficulty playing or engaging in leisure activities quietly
(e) is often "on the go" or often acts as if "driven by a motor"
(f) often talks excessively

Impulsivity

(g) often blurts out answers before questions have been completed
(h) often has difficulty awaiting turn
(i) often interrupts or intrudes on others (e.g., butts into conversations or games)

B. Some hyperactive-impulsive or inattentive symptoms that caused impairment were present before age 7 years.

(continued)

DSM-IV diagnostic criteria for Attention-Deficit/ Hyperactivity Disorder *(continued)*

C. Some impairment from the symptoms is present in two or more settings (e.g., at school [or work] and at home).

D. There must be clear evidence of clinically significant impairment in social, academic, or occupational functioning.

E. The symptoms do not occur exclusively during the course of a Pervasive Developmental Disorder, Schizophrenia, or other Psychotic Disorder and are not better accounted for by another mental disorder (e.g., Mood Disorder, Anxiety Disorder, Dissociative Disorder, or a Personality Disorder).

Code based on type:

314.01 Attention-Deficit/Hyperactivity Disorder, Combined Type: if both Criteria A1 and A2 are met for the past 6 months

314.00 Attention-Deficit/Hyperactivity Disorder, Predominantly Inattentive Type: if Criterion A1 is met but Criterion A2 is not met for the past 6 months

314.01 Attention-Deficit/Hyperactivity Disorder, Predominantly Hyperactive-Impulsive Type: if Criterion A2 is met but Criterion A1 is not met for the past 6 months

Coding note: For individuals (especially adolescents and adults) who currently have symptoms that no longer meet full criteria, "In Partial Remission" should be specified.

Criterion A1. The requirement that the inattention persist for 6 months and be maladaptive is intended to reduce the incidence of false-positive diagnoses by setting a fairly high threshold that distinguishes clinically significant inattention from developmentally normal distractibility. It is also important to determine that the behaviors described in the criteria set result from inattention rather than other possible causes (e.g., oppositional behavior, depression, learning disorders, failure to understand the nature of the task). This clinical judgment may be difficult because individuals with Attention-Deficit/Hyperactivity Disorder often become secondarily oppositional in response to their feeling frustrated with the poor performance that results from their inability to concentrate on tasks. In adolescents and adults, the inattention is often manifested by frequent shifting of topics in conversation, not listening to what others are saying, and not paying attention to details.

Criterion A2. Many young children may appear to be excessively active, especially to their harried parents. The diagnosis of Attention-Deficit/Hyperactivity Disorder should be made only when the hyperactivity is clearly excessive compared with the activity of children at the same developmental level or when it persists to an age beyond what would be expected. Adolescents and adults often have less extreme manifestations of hyperactivity but may have difficulty containing themselves or participating in sedentary activities. Impulsivity is characterized by difficulty in restraining behavior. The individual tends to respond too quickly, without regard to social appropriateness and to the consequences of the action. This impulsivity may lead to accident proneness and excessive risk taking.

CRITERION B. Attention-Deficit/Hyperactivity Disorder has been placed in this section of DSM-IV because it is usually first diagnosed in childhood. However, symptoms of hyperactivity and inattention may persist into adulthood, although by then the full criteria are usually no longer met. In adolescence and adults, it is important to distinguish this disorder from other causes of inattention or hyperactivity. The most difficult differential diagnosis is with Bipolar Disorder. The requirement that some symptoms be evident by age 7 years is most helpful with this important differential diagnosis because the onset of Bipolar Disorder (and other disorders in the differential) is almost never before age 7.

CRITERIA C AND D. These criteria serve to reduce the risk of false-positive diagnoses. Criterion C ensures that the behavior is not simply a context-specific problem. For example, if the symptoms occur at home but not at school, they may be related to conflicts with parents or siblings rather than representing a more generalized problem with inattention or impulsivity. However, this requirement that symptoms occur in a variety of contexts must be balanced against the observation that the severity of the symptoms often varies depending on the situation. Typically, symptoms are worse in unstructured settings and when the individual is understimulated. In contrast, in tightly structured settings (e.g., in the clinician's office) the symptoms may be much less apparent. Therefore, gathering information from teachers, parents, and other informants is often essential.

312.8 Conduct Disorder

There is some controversy about whether the behavioral pattern defined as Conduct Disorder constitutes a mental disorder or is better conceptualized as a legal, moral, or social-systems problem. Although the DSM-IV definition of mental disorder is sufficiently broad to include Conduct Disorder, others would argue that the behaviors in question result more from a lack of personal responsibility, which should not be considered (and perhaps excused as) a mental disorder. Moreover, it is not clear whether it is appropriate to apply these criteria to individuals who have grown up in neighborhoods in which criminal activity is endemic. This difficult judgment hinges on determining the degree to which the pattern of behavior is seen as a dysfunction within the individual as opposed to a moral failing or a societal problem.

Especially as defined in DSM-III-R (which emphasized aggressive behaviors), Conduct Disorder is diagnosed much more commonly in boys than in girls. Concerns have been raised and partially addressed in DSM-IV that the overwhelming preponderance of boys might in part reflect a gender bias in the criteria set that emphasized the aggressive behaviors characteristic of boys and underemphasized the nonconfrontational behaviors (e.g., lying, truancy, running away, substance use, and prostitution) more characteristic of girls with the disorder.

A final vexing issue in the diagnosis of Conduct Disorder is its relationship to substance use. Does it make sense to give an additional diagnosis of Conduct Disorder if the individual engages in antisocial behavior only while intoxicated or as a means of obtaining drugs? Because of the difficulty in determining the etiology in the seeming chicken-and-egg relationship between antisocial behavior and substance use, the DSM-IV convention is to allow both diagnoses to be made.

DSM-IV diagnostic criteria for 312.8 Conduct Disorder

A. A repetitive and persistent pattern of behavior in which the basic rights of others or major age-appropriate societal norms or rules are violated, as manifested by the presence of three (or more) of the following criteria in the past 12 months, with at least one criterion present in the past 6 months:

Aggression to people and animals

(1) often bullies, threatens, or intimidates others
(2) often initiates physical fights
(3) has used a weapon that can cause serious physical harm to others (e.g., a bat, brick, broken bottle, knife, gun)
(4) has been physically cruel to people
(5) has been physically cruel to animals
(6) has stolen while confronting a victim (e.g., mugging, purse snatching, extortion, armed robbery)
(7) has forced someone into sexual activity

Destruction of property

(8) has deliberately engaged in fire setting with the intention of causing serious damage
(9) has deliberately destroyed others' property (other than by fire setting)

Deceitfulness or theft

(10) has broken into someone else's house, building, or car
(11) often lies to obtain goods or favors or to avoid obligations (i.e., "cons" others)
(12) has stolen items of nontrivial value without confronting a victim and without breaking and entering (e.g., shoplifting, forgery)

Serious violations of rules

(13) often stays out at night despite parental prohibitions, beginning before age 13 years
(14) has run away from home overnight at least twice while living in parental or parental surrogate home (or once without returning for a lengthy period)
(15) is often truant from school, beginning before age 13 years

B. The disturbance in behavior causes clinically significant impairment in social, academic, or occupational functioning.

C. If the individual is age 18 years or older, criteria are not met for Antisocial Personality Disorder.

Specify type based on age at onset:

Childhood-Onset Type: onset of at least one criterion characteristic of Conduct Disorder prior to age 10 years

Adolescent-Onset Type: absence of any criteria characteristic of Conduct Disorder prior to age 10 years

Specify severity:

Mild: few if any conduct problems in excess of those required to make the diagnosis **and** conduct problems cause only minor harm to others

Moderate: number of conduct problems and effect on others intermediate between "mild" and "severe"

Severe: many conduct problems in excess of those required to make the diagnosis **or** conduct problems cause considerable harm to others

CRITERION A. Occasional problems with conduct are a part of normal childhood. The diagnosis of Conduct Disorder is reserved only for those individuals who have an established pattern of antisocial behavior. This criterion includes several elements to help distinguish between isolated conduct problems and Conduct Disorder. It requires that the defining behaviors occur in a cluster over a 12-month period and be repetitive and persistent. The lengthy list of behaviors has been organized into four thematic groups to make them easier to remember and to use in clinical settings.

CRITERION B. Although Conduct Disorder in childhood or adolescence can be the precursor of Antisocial Personality Disorder in adulthood, only about one-third of those with Conduct Disorder go on to manifest Antisocial Personality Disorder. Because Conduct Disorder and Antisocial Personality Disorder are on a developmental continuum, DSM-IV provides the convention that a diagnosis of Antisocial Personality Disorder cannot be given to an individual younger than 18 years of age, and a diagnosis of Conduct Disorder should be used for those over age 18 years only when the criteria are not met for Antisocial Personality Disorder.

SUBTYPES. The DSM-IV literature review indicated that the best predictor of poor long-term outcome (e.g., later violent behavior, development of Antisocial Personality Disorder) is the onset of Conduct Disorder symptoms before the individual reaches 10 years of age. Those with Childhood-Onset Type are prototypically male, physically aggressive toward others, and have problematic relationships with peers. In contrast, those with Adolescent-Onset Type are less predominantly male, are less aggressive, are more likely to have engaged in group (as opposed to solitary) antisocial behaviors, and are more likely to grow out of the disorder.

313.81 Oppositional Defiant Disorder

In DSM-III, this category was called Oppositional Disorder and described a fairly mild condition characterized by disobedient, negativistic, and provocative opposition to authority figures. The diagnosis was specifically excluded when there were violations of major age-appropriate societal norms. DSM-III-R modified the criteria sets and required a somewhat higher threshold of severity.

The DSM-IV literature review suggested that Oppositional Defiant Disorder might be considered a mild variant of Conduct Disorder. Not infrequently, individuals who have Conduct Disorder have a history of previous Oppositional Defiant Disorder, which may have been a developmental prelude. Moreover, some of the items included in the Conduct Disorder criteria set (lying, bullying, physical fighting) are also found to cluster with oppositional behaviors, suggesting that Oppositional Defiant Disorder and Conduct Disorder may embody different stages or levels on a continuum. In fact, it was proposed that there be a single disruptive behavior disorder with three levels of severity, the mildest of which would have been equivalent to Oppositional Defiant Disorder. Nonetheless, DSM-IV has maintained a separate category for Oppositional Defiant Disorder. This was because the evidence was not yet compelling and because many children with Oppositional Defiant Disorder do not go on to develop Conduct Disorder.

DSM-IV diagnostic criteria for 313.81 Oppositional Defiant Disorder

A. A pattern of negativistic, hostile, and defiant behavior lasting at least 6 months, during which four (or more) of the following are present:
   (1) often loses temper
   (2) often argues with adults
   (3) often actively defies or refuses to comply with adults' requests or rules
   (4) often deliberately annoys people
   (5) often blames others for his or her mistakes or misbehavior
   (6) is often touchy or easily annoyed by others
   (7) is often angry and resentful
   (8) is often spiteful or vindictive

   Note: Consider a criterion met only if the behavior occurs more frequently than is typically observed in individuals of comparable age and developmental level.

B. The disturbance in behavior causes clinically significant impairment in social, academic, or occupational functioning.

C. The behaviors do not occur exclusively during the course of a Psychotic or Mood Disorder.

D. Criteria are not met for Conduct Disorder, and, if the individual is age 18 years or older, criteria are not met for Antisocial Personality Disorder.

CRITERIA A AND B. Each of the defining behaviors can and often does occur from time to time in perfectly well-adapted children. Oppositional behaviors are particularly frequent as part of the normal separation and individuation process that must occur in toddlers and adolescents. For a behavior to count toward the diagnosis, it must be persistent and occur much more frequently than is typical for an individual's developmental level. Candidates for this diagnosis are often brought to clinical attention by their parents after a period of problems in the parent-child relationship (e.g., frequent arguments). It is often a difficult clinical judgment whether to diagnose Oppositional Defiant Disorder in the child or a Relational Problem in the family unit, or both, particularly because the informants may have their own ax to grind.

Feeding and Eating Disorders of Infancy or Early Childhood

Feeding and Eating Disorders of Infancy or Early Childhood

307.52 Pica
307.53 Rumination Disorder
307.59 Feeding Disorder of Infancy or Early Childhood

307.52 Pica

Pica refers to eating nonnutritive substances such as dirt and paint. Even normal children under age 2 years may eat strange things. This diagnosis should be considered only when the behavior is severe, persistent, and inappropriate for the individual's developmental age. Furthermore, Pica should not be diagnosed when eating a nonnutritive substance is part of an accepted cultural practice (e.g., clay or dirt eating in many parts of the world) or is a feature of another disorder (e.g., as a result of a delusion). Associated with MR or Pervasive Disorders

307.53 Rumination Disorder

Rumination Disorder describes repeated regurgitation and rechewing of food with a duration of at least a month. For this disorder to be diagnosed, the behavior must be preceded by a period of normal digestive functioning and must not be due to the direct effects of a general medical condition. Although most commonly seen in infants, Rumination Disorder can present in older children with Mental Retardation. Serious general medical complications (malnutrition, weight loss) can result. Associated with inconsistent parenting (Gen med eval 1st)

307.59 Feeding Disorder of Infancy or Early Childhood

Feeding Disorder of Infancy or Early Childhood is one of the few new categories in DSM-IV. It has been introduced to describe what has been generally termed *failure to thrive* or, less frequently, *psychosocial dwarfism.* Infants with this disorder fail to eat adequately and have a significant weight loss or failure to gain weight. This condition may result from a mismatch between a difficult-to-feed child and a frustrated and/or inexperienced caregiver. This condition can result in serious complications, especially in infants. Frequently, the child gains weight when fed by another person (e.g., in the hospital). The diagnosis should not be made when a gastrointestinal condition (e.g., esophageal reflux) accounts for the feeding disturbance.

Tic Disorders

Tic Disorders

307.23	Tourette's Disorder
307.22	Chronic Motor or Vocal Tic Disorder
307.21	Transient Tic Disorder
307.20	Tic Disorder Not Otherwise Specified

The four disorders in this section (Tourette's Disorder, Chronic Motor or Vocal Tic Disorder, Transient Tic Disorder, and Tic Disorder Not Otherwise Specified) are all characterized by the presence of clinically significant tics and differ only with respect to duration and type of tics. The inclusion of four Tic Disorder categories is another example of the "splitter's" approach that informs DSM-IV. Alternatively, a single Tic Disorder could have been included with specifiers to indicate the particularities of the presentation, such as types of tics and duration.

307.23 Tourette's Disorder

DSM-IV diagnostic criteria for 307.23 Tourette's Disorder

A. Both multiple motor and one or more vocal tics have been present at some time during the illness, although not necessarily concurrently. (A *tic* is a sudden, rapid, recurrent, nonrhythmic, stereotyped motor movement or vocalization.)

B. The tics occur many times a day (usually in bouts) nearly every day or intermittently throughout a period of more than 1 year, and during this period there was never a tic-free period of more than 3 consecutive months.

C. The disturbance causes marked distress or significant impairment in social, occupational, or other important areas of functioning.

D. The onset is before age 18 years.

E. The disturbance is not due to the direct physiological effects of a substance (e.g., stimulants) or a general medical condition (e.g., Huntington's disease or postviral encephalitis).

Criterion A. DSM-IV defines a tic as "a sudden, rapid, recurrent, nonrhythmic, stereotyped motor movement or vocalization. It is experienced as irresistible, but can be suppressed for varying lengths of time." Motor tics can be simple (e.g., blinking, grimacing, shrugging) or complex (e.g., grooming behaviors, jumping). Vocal tics can also be simple (e.g., coughing, throat clearing, grunting, barking) or complex (e.g., echolalia, obscene words out of context). The type, location, frequency, and severity of the tics often vary over time.

Criterion B. This 12 months' duration requirement distinguishes Tourette's Disorder from Transient Tic Disorder (see next page).

307.22 Chronic Motor or Vocal Tic Disorder

Chronic Motor or Vocal Tic Disorder resembles (and may be closely related to) Tourette's Disorder but has either motor tics or vocal tics, not both.

307.21 Transient Tic Disorder

Transient Tic Disorder resembles Tourette's Disorder and Chronic Motor or Vocal Tic Disorder in symptom presentation, but its duration is between 1 and 12 months.

Elimination Disorders

Elimination Disorders

—.—	Encopresis
787.6	With Constipation and Overflow Incontinence
307.7	Without Constipation and Overflow Incontinence
307.6	Enuresis (Not Due to a General Medical Condition)

Encopresis

Encopresis consists of repeated defecation into clothing or inappropriate locations that occurs beyond the developmentally expected age. The episodes of defecation must be recurrent and occur at least once a month for 3 months. A major issue in this diagnosis is the age at which failure to be toilet trained should be considered pathological. Clinical judgment is necessary, particularly in children with developmental delays. The DSM-IV convention requires a mental age of at least 4 years before the diagnosis becomes appropriate. The most common presentation is an involuntary overflow fecal incontinence associated with constipation, in which case the DSM-IV diagnostic code is 787.6; otherwise, the code is 307.7. Less often, the encopresis is intentional; when it is intentional, it is usually associated with oppositional behavior.

(Effort to gain power) 1st Born males Occasionaly sexual abuse

307.6 Enuresis (Not Due to a General Medical Condition)

Enuresis consists of repeated urination into clothing or inappropriate locations such as bed. As with Encopresis, clinical judgment is necessary concerning the required frequency of accidents and the age beyond which bed-wetting is inappropriate. The suggested frequency threshold in DSM-IV is at least twice a week for 3 months, and the suggested minimum age is 5 years. Enuresis most typically occurs only during nighttime sleep (Nocturnal subtype), but it can also occur while awake (Diurnal subtype), particularly in individuals who are embarrassed about asking to use the bathroom.

Other Disorders of Infancy, Childhood, or Adolescence

Other Disorders of Infancy, Childhood, or Adolescence

309.21	Separation Anxiety Disorder
313.23	Selective Mutism
313.89	Reactive Attachment Disorder of Infancy or Early Childhood
307.3	Stereotypic Movement Disorder
313.9	Disorder of Infancy, Childhood, or Adolescence Not Otherwise Specified

309.21 Separation Anxiety Disorder

Separation Anxiety Disorder is included in this section of DSM-IV because only rarely is it appropriate to make this diagnosis in adults. Of particular interest is the observation that many adults with an Anxiety Disorder have a history of Separation Anxiety Disorder, which may have been a precursor.

DSM-IV diagnostic criteria for 309.21 Separation Anxiety Disorder

A. Developmentally inappropriate and excessive anxiety concerning separation from home or from those to whom the individual is attached, as evidenced by three (or more) of the following:
   (1) recurrent excessive distress when separation from home or major attachment figures occurs or is anticipated
   (2) persistent and excessive worry about losing, or about possible harm befalling, major attachment figures
   (3) persistent and excessive worry that an untoward event will lead to separation from a major attachment figure (e.g., getting lost or being kidnapped)
   (4) persistent reluctance or refusal to go to school or elsewhere because of fear of separation
   (5) persistently and excessively fearful or reluctant to be alone or without major attachment figures at home or without significant adults in other settings
   (6) persistent reluctance or refusal to go to sleep without being near a major attachment figure or to sleep away from home

(continued)

DSM-IV diagnostic criteria for 309.21 Separation Anxiety Disorder *(continued)*

(7) repeated nightmares involving the theme of separation
(8) repeated complaints of physical symptoms (such as headaches, stomachaches, nausea, or vomiting) when separation from major attachment figures occurs or is anticipated

B. The duration of the disturbance is at least 4 weeks.

C. The onset is before age 18 years.

D. The disturbance causes clinically significant distress or impairment in social, academic (occupational), or other important areas of functioning.

E. The disturbance does not occur exclusively during the course of a Pervasive Developmental Disorder, Schizophrenia, or other Psychotic Disorder and, in adolescents and adults, is not better accounted for by Panic Disorder With Agoraphobia.

Specify if:
Early Onset: if onset occurs before age 6 years

CRITERIA A, B, AND D. Separation anxiety is a normal part of mammalian life. It is especially prominent during developmental phases (e.g., toddler, adolescent) that require separation and individuation from caregivers. This disorder should be diagnosed only when concerns about separation are severe, persistent, impairing, and in excess of what would be considered normal for the individual's developmental level and culture.

CRITERIA C AND E. The onset is often in the preschool years and represents an inability to negotiate the developmental requirements for separation that occur at this time. Occasionally, the onset is in middle childhood and often represents a regression that occurs after a stressful event (e.g., death of a relative or pet, moving to a new community). An onset after early adolescence is unusual and suggests the presence of another disorder (e.g., Panic Disorder With Agoraphobia, Specific Phobia, Social Phobia, Mood Disorder).

313.23 Selective Mutism

Children with Selective Mutism do not speak in certain situations (typically in school) where speech is expected and necessary, but they speak without hesitation in other situations (e.g., with family members). This disorder must be distinguished from normal shyness and other reasons for reluctance to speak such as unfamiliarity with the language. Because children are frequently quiet when entering an unfamiliar classroom, this diagnosis should not be given when the lack of speech occurs only during the first month of school. Moreover, brief periods of selective silence lasting less than a month do not qualify an individual for this diagnosis. This diagnosis was called Elective Mutism in DSM-III-R, which incorrectly implied that the lack of speech was necessarily oppositional in nature rather than related to anxiety, as is often the case.

313.89 Reactive Attachment Disorder of Infancy or Early Childhood

Reactive Attachment Disorder of Infancy or Early Childhood is characterized by either of two forms of inappropriate social relatedness. In the Inhibited Type, the child has difficulty initiating or engaging in social attachments. In the Disinhibited Type, the opposite occurs and the child develops indiscriminate and superficial attachments. The diagnosis requires evidence that the attachment problem is the result of neglect or other forms of grossly pathological care. The onset must be before age 5 years.

307.3 Stereotypic Movement Disorder

Stereotypic Movement Disorder is characterized by "motor behavior that is repetitive, often seemingly driven, and nonfunctional. . . . The stereotypic movements may include hand waving, rocking, playing with hands, fiddling with fingers, twirling objects, head banging, self-biting, picking at skin or bodily orifices, or hitting various parts of one's own body" (DSM-IV, pp. 118–119). Many of the behaviors included in Stereotypic Movement Disorder may result in clinically significant self-injury, which can be indicated by the specifier With Self-Injurious Behavior. Stereotypies are not infrequent in Mental Retardation and should be diagnosed separately only when they are severe enough to be a focus of treatment. Because stereotypies are part of the criteria set for Pervasive Developmental Disorders, an additional diagnosis of Stereotypic Movement Disorder is not made.

The Last Word

The advantage of having a separate section in DSM-IV titled "Disorders Usually First Diagnosed in Infancy, Childhood, or Adolescence" is that it is convenient for those mental health professionals who primarily diagnose and treat children. However, there is a downside to this arrangement. Child specialists tend to pay too little attention to the disorders in the rest of the book, which often have their onset during childhood (e.g., Major Depressive Disorder). At the same time, clinicians who see only adults tend to forgot about this section altogether; thus, they may miss disorders from this section that persist into adulthood (e.g., Attention-Deficit/Hyperactivity Disorder).

CHAPTER 24

Other Conditions That May Be a Focus of Clinical Attention

In Chapter 2, we provide a fairly detailed discussion of some of the issues involved in attempting to define what is and what is not a mental disorder. That discussion pertains to this chapter and to the corresponding section of DSM-IV because the conditions described below are included precisely because they are of clinical importance as a focus of diagnosis and treatment but are not considered to be mental disorders. There are several possible relationships between the conditions described below and the DSM-IV mental disorders. In some cases, the individual does not have a mental disorder as defined in DSM-IV and seeks evaluation and treatment only for one of the problems indicated in this chapter. In other cases, the person has an additional DSM-IV mental disorder that is unrelated to the indicated condition. In still other cases, one of the indicated conditions is related to a mental disorder, but the condition is sufficiently severe or important in its own right to warrant independent clinical attention. For example, when a Parent-Child Relational Problem is sufficiently severe, it may indicated in addition to the mother's Major Depressive Disorder.

The following conditions are all coded on Axis I, except for Borderline Intellectual Functioning, which is coded on Axis II.

Psychological Factors Affecting Medical Condition

The condition known as Psychological Factors Affecting Medical Condition has a long and interesting history. DSM-I and DSM-II contained a detailed section describing 10 psychophysiological disorders (psychosomatic disorders), each involving a different organ system (e.g., skin, cardiovascular, gastrointestinal). The definition in DSM-II stated that "this group of disorders is characterized by physical symptoms that are caused by emotional factors and involve a single organ system, usually under autonomic nervous system innervation" (DSM-II, p. 46).

DSM-III replaced this section with a single category called Psychological Factors Affecting Physical Condition, and the relationship between the psychological factors and the physical symptoms was reconceptualized. The reason for this change was a reaction against what was regarded as a "unicausational concept about disease etiology" (DSM-III, p. 382), namely, that psychological factors in some simple way "cause" physical symptoms rather than a biopsychosocial model involving an interaction among psychological factors and physical symptoms. In the multiaxial system introduced by DSM-III, the presence of psychological factors could be noted on Axis I by using this diagnosis, with the physical condition coded on Axis III. Unfortunately, in practice this category was rarely used—probably because of the limited information conveyed by the DSM-III and DSM-III-R definitions and terminology.

The DSM-IV definition provides more specific descriptions of the ways in which the psychological factors may affect the medical condition, as well as allowing the clinician to specify the type of factors involved. In DSM-IV, Psychological Factors Affecting Medical Condition is not considered to be a mental disorder and therefore is included in this section of DSM-IV.

Because psychological factors are fairly ubiquitous in patients with medical conditions, this category could be overused unless it is reserved for those situations in which the psychological factors have a clinically significant impact on the medical condition or increase the risk of complications or a poor outcome. This category is often confused with other DSM-IV categories that involve both psychological factors and symptoms of a medical condition. Mental Disorders Due to a General Medical Condition also involve a causal relationship between symptoms of a mental disorder and symptoms of a medical condition, but the relationship is reversed (i.e., the medical condition is judged to be the cause of the psychological or behavioral symptoms). Patients with Somatoform Disorders present with symptoms suggesting a medical condition that are often related to psychological factors, but Somatoform Disorders differ from this category in that there is no general medical condition that adequately accounts for the physical symptoms.

DSM-IV criteria for 316 . . . *[Specified Psychological Factor]* Affecting . . . *[Indicate the General Medical Condition]*

A. A general medical condition (coded on Axis III) is present.

B. Psychological factors adversely affect the general medical condition in one of the following ways:

(continued)

DSM-IV criteria for 316 . . . [Specified Psychological Factor] Affecting . . . *[Indicate the General Medical Condition] (continued)*

(1) the factors have influenced the course of the general medical condition as shown by a close temporal association between the psychological factors and the development or exacerbation of, or delayed recovery from, the general medical condition
(2) the factors interfere with the treatment of the general medical condition
(3) the factors constitute additional health risks for the individual
(4) stress-related physiological responses precipitate or exacerbate symptoms of the general medical condition

Choose name based on the nature of the psychological factors (if more than one factor is present, indicate the most prominent):

Mental Disorder Affecting . . . *[Indicate the General Medical Condition]* (e.g., an Axis I disorder such as Major Depressive Disorder delaying recovery from a myocardial infarction)

Psychological Symptoms Affecting . . . *[Indicate the General Medical Condition]* (e.g., depressive symptoms delaying recovery from surgery; anxiety exacerbating asthma)

Personality Traits or Coping Style Affecting . . . *[Indicate the General Medical Condition]* (e.g., pathological denial of the need for surgery in a patient with cancer; hostile, pressured behavior contributing to cardiovascular disease)

Maladaptive Health Behaviors Affecting . . . *[Indicate the General Medical Condition]* (e.g., overeating; lack of exercise; unsafe sex)

Stress-Related Physiological Response Affecting . . . *[Indicate the General Medical Condition]* (e.g., stress-related exacerbations of ulcer, hypertension, arrhythmia, or tension headache)

Other or Unspecified Psychological Factors Affecting . . . *[Indicate the General Medical Condition]* (e.g., interpersonal, cultural, or religious factors)

Medication-Induced Movement Disorders

The medications used in the treatment of mental disorders sometimes result in clinically significant and unfortunate side effects. Particularly common are the movement disorders related to the use of neuroleptic and other psychotropic medications. Medication-Induced Movement Disorders were not included in prior editions of DSM because they are not mental disorders. They are now included in this DSM-IV section because they are clinically important and there is evidence that they are underrecognized and undertreated in clinical practice. Medication-Induced Movement Disorders are associated with noncompliance, serious morbidity (e.g., Tardive Dyskinesia), and even mortality (e.g., Neuroleptic Malignant Syndrome).

It is also important to distinguish between the symptoms caused by Medication-Induced Movement Disorders and similar symptoms that are part of the presentations of many Axis I disorders (e.g., Anxiety Disorder versus Neuroleptic-Induced Acute Akathisia, Catatonia versus Neuroleptic Malignant Syndrome). The movement disorders are included in this section of DSM-IV with diagnostic codes and brief glossary descriptions; much more extensive text descriptions and criteria sets are provided in DSM-IV Appendix B.

DSM-IV text for 332.1 Neuroleptic-Induced Parkinsonism

Parkinsonian tremor, muscular rigidity, or akinesia developing within a few weeks of starting or raising the dose of a neuroleptic medication (or after reducing a medication used to treat extrapyramidal symptoms).

DSM-IV text for 333.92 Neuroleptic Malignant Syndrome

Severe muscle rigidity, elevated temperature, and other related findings (e.g., diaphoresis, dysphagia, incontinence, changes in level of consciousness ranging from confusion to coma, mutism, elevated or labile blood pressure, elevated creatine phosphokinase [CPK]) developing in association with the use of neuroleptic medication.

DSM-IV text for 333.7 Neuroleptic-Induced Acute Dystonia

Abnormal positioning or spasm of the muscles of the head, neck, limbs, or trunk developing within a few days of starting or raising the dose of a neuroleptic medication (or after reducing a medication used to treat extrapyramidal symptoms).

DSM-IV text for 333.99 Neuroleptic-Induced Acute Akathisia

Subjective complaints of restlessness accompanied by observed movements (e.g., fidgety movements of the legs, rocking from foot to foot, pacing, or inability to sit or stand still) developing within a few weeks of starting or raising the dose of a neuroleptic medication (or after reducing a medication used to treat extrapyramidal symptoms).

DSM-IV text for 333.82 Neuroleptic-Induced Tardive Dyskinesia

Involuntary choreiform, athetoid, or rhythmic movements (lasting at least a few weeks) of the tongue, jaw, or extremities developing in association with the use of neuroleptic medication for at least a few months (may be for a shorter period of time in elderly persons).

DSM-IV text for 333.1 Medication-Induced Postural Tremor

Fine tremor occurring during attempts to maintain a posture that develops in association with the use of medication (e.g., lithium, antidepressants, valproate).

DSM-IV text for 333.90 Medication-Induced Movement Disorder Not Otherwise Specified

This category is for Medication-Induced Movement Disorders not classified by any of the specific disorders listed above. Examples include 1) parkinsonism, acute akathisia, acute dystonia, or dyskinetic movement that is associated with a medication other than a neuroleptic; 2) a presentation that resembles neuroleptic malignant syndrome that is associated with a medication other than a neuroleptic; or 3) tardive dystonia.

Other Medication-Induced Disorder

995.2 Adverse Effects of Medication Not Otherwise Specified

The medications used to treat mental disorders do a great deal of good but often have side effects that are distressing, may reduce compliance, and may be confused with the symptoms of the conditions they are meant to be treating. The category of Adverse Effects of Medication Not Otherwise Specified allows clinicians to code side effects of medication other than movement symptoms when these adverse effects become a main focus of clinical attention. Examples include severe hypotension, cardiac arrhythmias, and priapism.

Relational Problems

One of the major criticisms of DSM-III was that it was of little use to clinicians engaged in family and couples therapy. Because the DSM system is a classification of mental disorders that occur in individuals, it does not provide guidance for the classification of problems that are conceptualized as belonging to the family system rather than to any one individual member. To facilitate the use of DSM-IV in family settings, the "Relational Problems" section has been reorganized and expanded. There were also extensive literature reviews, which will appear in the *DSM-IV Sourcebook,* to determine the feasibility of developing research criteria sets for each of the conditions. However, it was concluded that providing such criteria sets would be premature at this time. More research is needed on the items, thresholds, methods of assessment, and implications of possible criteria sets for relational problems.

DSM-IV text for V61.9 Relational Problem Related to a Mental Disorder or General Medical Condition

This category should be used when the focus of clinical attention is a pattern of impaired interaction that is associated with a mental disorder or a general medical condition in a family member.

DSM-IV text for V61.20 Parent-Child Relational Problem

This category should be used when the focus of clinical attention is a pattern of interaction between parent and child (e.g., impaired communication, overprotection, inadequate discipline) that is associated with clinically significant impairment in individual or family functioning or the development of clinically significant symptoms in parent or child.

DSM-IV text for V61.1 Partner Relational Problem

This category should be used when the focus of clinical attention is a pattern of interaction between spouses or partners characterized by negative communication (e.g., criticisms), distorted communication (e.g., unrealistic expectations), or non-communication (e.g., withdrawal) that is associated with clinically significant impairment in individual or family functioning or the development of symptoms in one or both partners.

DSM-IV text for V61.8 Sibling Relational Problem

This category should be used when the focus of clinical attention is a pattern of interaction among siblings that is associated with clinically significant impairment in individual or family functioning or the development of symptoms in one or more of the siblings.

DSM-IV text for V62.81 Relational Problem Not Otherwise Specified

This category should be used when the focus of clinical attention is on relational problems that are not classifiable by any of the specific problems listed above (e.g., difficulties with co-workers).

Problems Related to Abuse or Neglect

Before DSM-IV, no category was available to indicate that the focus of clinical attention was physical or sexual abuse or child neglect. These problems are included in DSM-IV because of their public health importance and because they often come to the attention of mental health professionals. Although we were hoping to include research criteria sets, a review of the literature, to be published in the *DSM-IV Sourcebook,* showed that there is no consensus on how best to define the boundary of these conditions. The issue of setting boundaries has important forensic implications. Setting the boundary too high might discourage early case finding, and setting the boundary too low might lead to false accusations. It was concluded that providing such criteria sets would be premature at this time.

This category is unusual in that two different diagnostic codes are given based on the focus of clinical attention. If this problem is being addressed in the context of the family or relational system, the V code is used. If the focus is exclusively on the victim, the 995 code is specified instead.

DSM-IV text for V61.21 Physical Abuse of Child

This category should be used when the focus of clinical attention is physical abuse of a child.

Coding note: *Specify* **995.5** *if focus of clinical attention is on the victim.*

DSM-IV text for V61.21 Sexual Abuse of Child

This category should be used when the focus of clinical attention is sexual abuse of a child.

Coding note: *Specify* **995.5** *if focus of clinical attention is on the victim.*

DSM-IV text for V61.21 Neglect of Child

This category should be used when the focus of clinical attention is child neglect.

Coding note: *Specify* **995.5** *if focus of clinical attention is on the victim.*

DSM-IV text for V61.1 Physical Abuse of Adult

This category should be used when the focus of clinical attention is physical abuse of an adult (e.g., spouse beating, abuse of elderly parent).

Coding note: *Specify* **995.81** *if focus of clinical attention is on the victim.*

DSM-IV text for V61.1 Sexual Abuse of Adult

This category should be used when the focus of clinical attention is sexual abuse of an adult (e.g., sexual coercion, rape).

Coding note: *Specify* **995.81** *if focus of clinical attention is on the victim.*

Additional Conditions That May Be a Focus of Clinical Attention

The following problems are also included in this section of DSM-IV. By definition, these are not considered mental disorders but may be the subject of evaluation and treatment conducted by a mental health practitioner.

DSM-IV text for V15.81 Noncompliance With Treatment

This category can be used when the focus of clinical attention is noncompliance with an important aspect of the treatment for a mental disorder or a general medical condition. The reasons for noncompliance may include discomfort resulting from treatment (e.g., medication side effects), expense of treatment, decisions based on personal value judgments or religious or cultural beliefs about the advantages and disadvantages of the proposed treatment, maladaptive personality traits or coping styles (e.g., denial of illness), or the presence of a mental disorder (e.g., Schizophrenia, Avoidant Personality Disorder). This category should be used only when the problem is sufficiently severe to warrant independent clinical attention.

DSM-IV text for V65.2 Malingering

The essential feature of Malingering is the intentional production of false or grossly exaggerated physical or psychological symptoms, motivated by external incentives such as avoiding military duty, avoiding work, obtaining financial compensation, evading criminal prosecution, or obtaining drugs. Under some circumstances, Malingering may represent adaptive behavior—for example, feigning illness while a captive of the enemy during wartime.

Malingering should be strongly suspected if any combination of the following is noted:

1. Medicolegal context of presentation (e.g., the person is referred by an attorney to the clinician for examination)
2. Marked discrepancy between the person's claimed stress or disability and the objective findings
3. Lack of cooperation during the diagnostic evaluation and in complying with the prescribed treatment regimen
4. The presence of Antisocial Personality Disorder

Malingering differs from Factitious Disorder in that the motivation for the symptom production in Malingering is an external incentive, whereas in Factitious Disorder external incentives are absent. Evidence of an intrapsychic need to maintain the sick role suggests Factitious Disorder. Malingering is differentiated from Conversion Disorder and other Somatoform Disorders by the intentional production of symptoms and by the obvious, external incentives associated with it. In Malingering (in contrast to Conversion Disorder), symptom relief is not often obtained by suggestion or hypnosis.

DSM-IV text for V71.01 Adult Antisocial Behavior

This category can be used when the focus of clinical attention is adult antisocial behavior that is not due to a mental disorder (e.g., Conduct Disorder, Antisocial Personality Disorder, or an Impulse-Control Disorder). Examples include the behavior of some professional thieves, racketeers, or dealers in illegal substances.

DSM-IV text for V71.02 Child or Adolescent Antisocial Behavior

This category can be used when the focus of clinical attention is antisocial behavior in a child or adolescent that is not due to a mental disorder (e.g., Conduct Disorder or an Impulse-Control Disorder). Examples include isolated antisocial acts of children or adolescents (not a pattern of antisocial behavior).

DSM-IV text for V62.89 Borderline Intellectual Functioning

This category can be used when the focus of clinical attention is associated with borderline intellectual functioning, that is, an IQ in the 71–84 range. Differential diagnosis between Borderline Intellectual Functioning and Mental Retardation (an IQ of 70 or below) is especially difficult when the coexistence of certain mental disorders (e.g., Schizophrenia) is involved.

Coding note: *This is coded on Axis II.*

DSM-IV text for 780.9 Age-Related Cognitive Decline

This category can be used when the focus of clinical attention is an objectively identified decline in cognitive functioning consequent to the aging process that is within normal limits given the person's age. Individuals with this condition may report problems remembering names or appointments or may experience difficulty in solving complex problems. This category should be considered only after it has been determined that the cognitive impairment is not attributable to a specific mental disorder or neurological condition.

Note: See Chapter 8 for further discussion.

DSM-IV text for V62.82 Bereavement

This category can be used when the focus of clinical attention is a reaction to the death of a loved one [this issue is discused in Chapter 12 of the *Guidebook]*. As part of their reaction to the loss, some grieving individuals present with symptoms characteristic of a Major Depressive Episode (e.g., feelings of sadness and associated symptoms such as insomnia, poor appetite, and weight loss). The bereaved individual typically regards the depressed mood as "normal," although the person may seek professional help for relief of associated symptoms such as insomnia or anorexia. The

(continued)

DSM-IV text for V62.82 Bereavement *(continued)*

duration and expression of "normal" bereavement vary considerably among different cultural groups. The diagnosis of Major Depressive Disorder is generally not given unless the symptoms are still present 2 months after the loss. However, the presence of certain symptoms that are not characteristic of a "normal" grief reaction may be helpful in differentiating bereavement from a Major Depressive Episode. These include 1) guilt about things other than actions taken or not taken by the survivor at the time of the death; 2) thoughts of death other than the survivor feeling that he or she would be better off dead or should have died with the deceased person; 3) morbid preoccupation with worthlessness; 4) marked psychomotor retardation; 5) prolonged and marked functional impairment; and 6) hallucinatory experiences other than thinking that he or she hears the voice of, or transiently sees the image of, the deceased person.

DSM-IV text for V62.3 Academic Problem

This category can be used when the focus of clinical attention is an academic problem that is not due to a mental disorder or, if due to a mental disorder, is sufficiently severe to warrant independent clinical attention. An example is a pattern of failing grades or of significant underachievement in a person with adequate intellectual capacity in the absence of a Learning or Communication Disorder or any other mental disorder that would account for the problem.

DSM-IV text for V62.2 Occupational Problem

This category can be used when the focus of clinical attention is an occupational problem that is not due to a mental disorder or, if it is due to a mental disorder, is sufficiently severe to warrant independent clinical attention. Examples include job dissatisfaction and uncertainty about career choices.

DSM-IV text for 313.82 Identity Problem

This category can be used when the focus of clinical attention is uncertainty about multiple issues relating to identity such as long-term goals, career choice, friendship patterns, sexual orientation and behavior, moral values, and group loyalties.

DSM-IV text for V62.89 Religious or Spiritual Problem

This category can be used when the focus of clinical attention is a religious or spiritual problem. Examples include distressing experiences that involve loss or questioning of faith, problems associated with conversion to a new faith, or questioning of spiritual values that may not necessarily be related to an organized church or religious institution.

DSM-IV text for V62.4 Acculturation Problem

This category can be used when the focus of clinical attention is a problem involving adjustment to a different culture (e.g., following migration).

DSM-IV text for V62.89 Phase of Life Problem

This category can be used when the focus of clinical attention is a problem associated with a particular developmental phase or some other life circumstance that is not due to a mental disorder or, if it is due to a mental disorder, is sufficiently severe to warrant independent clinical attention. Examples include problems associated with entering school, leaving parental control, starting a new career, and changes involved in marriage, divorce, and retirement.

The Last Word

Not every important problem that clinicians treat can or should be considered a mental disorder. We are often asked what implications these categories have for reimbursement. The answer is a moving target. Very often, these codes tend to result in reimbursement denials, which should not reduce their important role in clinical communication.

SECTION IV

Not Ready for Prime Time

CHAPTER 25

Some Future Contenders

People often ask us to speculate on the future of psychiatric diagnosis. The most exciting developments in psychiatric diagnosis will emerge from the increasing understanding of pathogenesis afforded by the powerful new tools available to researchers. Gradually, diagnosis by diagnosis, we will move beyond the current emphasis on surface description so that the classification will be increasingly informed by factors related to underlying etiology.

Another, perhaps more immediate direction of advancement will capitalize on the same methods of descriptive diagnosis used in DSM-IV and its predecessors. Indeed, during the preparation of DSM-IV, we received more than 100 suggestions for new diagnostic categories. The passion to create categories seems to be deeply ingrained in human nature and has inspired the efforts of many researchers and clinicians. From the researchers' standpoint, there is a concern that if a category is not added to the system, it will not receive sufficient research attention or funding. From the clinicians' perspective, the desire to include a new category reflects a dissatisfaction with the existing clinical coverage of the system and an unwillingness to settle for one of the Not Otherwise Specified categories to identify the patients who would otherwise be included under the new diagnosis. Clinicians and researchers are also worried that the lack of a specific diagnostic category results in false-negative diagnoses because descriptions included in a Not Otherwise Specified section are less likely to influence diagnostic assessment than a separate code and criteria set would.

At its initial deliberations, the Task Force decided that new diagnoses would be included only when they were supported by a substantial body of research rather than including them as a stimulus to such research. In part, this decision reflected the concern that the number of new diagnoses included in each revision of DSM had increased at a rate that was threatening to make the system entirely too cumbersome. Furthermore, it has been observed that it is far easier to add a new diagnosis than to remove one once it has been included. Because of this very high threshold for change in DSM-IV, only a handful of new diagnoses were included as official categories in DSM-IV.

An appendix for proposed diagnostic categories needing further study was first introduced in DSM-III-R. It contained only three categories—Late Luteal Phase Dysphoric Disorder, Self-Defeating Personality Disorder, and Sadistic Personality Disorder. The idea of this appendix was to provide an opportunity for establishing standardized criteria sets that might stimulate the research that would indicate whether the diagnoses should be included as official categories in later revisions of the classification system.

DSM-IV includes 26 such research criteria sets in a much expanded Appendix B. Each of these categories was considered to be sufficiently promising to be chosen for inclusion in the appendix. However, for a variety of reasons they were not yet ready for inclusion as official categories in DSM-IV:

1. There were insufficient data on optimal criteria and set points, reliability, validity, and impact on prevalence.
2. There were concerns about the implications of possible false-positive diagnoses (e.g., encouraging inappropriate use of medication, forensic misuse, stigmatization).
3. The condition might be of insufficient clinical significance to be considered a mental disorder, and its inclusion would trivialize the entire system.

The disorders listed in Appendix B may ultimately be included in DSM-V or may disappear from the face of the earth. Only the research will tell. In the meantime, they may stimulate research and enrich current clinical practice, but they must be used with caution and clinical judgment. For the most part, these criteria sets were developed during the DSM-IV preparation process and require a great deal more study before they are engraved in stone. This research endeavor will be enhanced if the diagnostic assessments used in the investigations include a wider array of items and thresholds than are included in the criteria sets.

Postconcussional Disorder

The proposed category of postconcussional disorder is intended to cover individuals not currently covered under Dementia Due to Head Trauma, Amnestic Disorder Due to Head Trauma, or Personality Change Due to Head Trauma. In DSM-IV, such presentations are designated Cognitive Disorder Not Otherwise Specified. Postconcussional disorder has a long history of inclusion in the *International Classification of Diseases* and has also been described in an extensive clinical literature. Unfortunately, there has been little systematic research on this condition. The problem with not including this diagnosis in the official nomenclature is that it describes a well-recognized and frequently encountered condition. The problems with including it are the lack of a wide consensus in the field about how the condition should best be defined and the possibility of misuse in forensic and disability settings.

DSM-IV research criteria for postconcussional disorder

A. A history of head trauma that has caused significant cerebral concussion.

Note: The manifestations of concussion include loss of consciousness, posttraumatic amnesia, and, less commonly, posttraumatic onset of seizures. The specific method of defining this criterion needs to be established by further research.

B. Evidence from neuropsychological testing or quantified cognitive assessment of difficulty in attention (concentrating, shifting focus of attention, performing simultaneous cognitive tasks) or memory (learning or recalling information).

C. Three (or more) of the following occur shortly after the trauma and last at least 3 months:
(1) becoming fatigued easily
(2) disordered sleep
(3) headache
(4) vertigo or dizziness
(5) irritability or aggression on little or no provocation
(6) anxiety, depression, or affective lability
(7) changes in personality (e.g., social or sexual inappropriateness)
(8) apathy or lack of spontaneity

D. The symptoms in Criteria B and C have their onset following head trauma or else represent a substantial worsening of preexisting symptoms.

E. The disturbance causes significant impairment in social or occupational functioning and represents a significant decline from a previous level of functioning. In school-age children, the impairment may be manifested by a significant worsening in school or academic performance dating from the trauma.

F. The symptoms do not meet criteria for Dementia Due to Head Trauma and are not better accounted for by another mental disorder (e.g., Amnestic Disorder Due to Head Trauma, Personality Change Due to Head Trauma).

Mild Neurocognitive Disorder

The proposed category of mild neurocognitive disorder is included in *International Statistical Classification of Diseases and Related Health Problems,* 10th Revision (ICD-10). It covers individuals with a cognitive impairment that is below the threshold set in Dementia and Amnestic Disorder Due to a General Medical Condition. In DSM-IV, this type of presentation would be designated as Cognitive Disorder Not Otherwise Specified.

A major reason why this category has been proposed is the increased incidence of human immunodeficiency virus (HIV)-related cognitive disturbances that are below the threshold for Dementia and Amnestic Disorder Due to a General Medical Condition but are nonetheless clinically significant. It was not included as an official category in DSM-IV because there has been relatively little study of the proposed research criteria set. It remains unclear how reliably this disorder can be diagnosed and what its boundaries are with dementia and with the clinically insignificant cognitive impairments that so frequently accompany general medical conditions.

DSM-IV research criteria for mild neurocognitive disorder

A. The presence of two (or more) of the following impairments in cognitive functioning, lasting most of the time for a period of at least 2 weeks (as reported by the individual or a reliable informant):
   (1) memory impairment as identified by a reduced ability to learn or recall information
   (2) disturbance in executive functioning (i.e., planning, organizing, sequencing, abstracting)
   (3) disturbance in attention or speed of information processing
   (4) impairment in perceptual-motor abilities
   (5) impairment in language (e.g., comprehension, word finding)

B. There is objective evidence from physical examination or laboratory findings (including neuroimaging techniques) of a neurological or general medical condition that is judged to be etiologically related to the cognitive disturbance.

C. There is evidence from neuropsychological testing or quantified cognitive assessment of an abnormality or decline in performance.

D. The cognitive deficits cause marked distress or impairment in social, occupational, or other important areas of functioning and represent a decline from a previous level of functioning.

E. The cognitive disturbance does not meet criteria for a delirium, a dementia, or an amnestic disorder and is not better accounted for by another mental disorder (e.g., a Substance-Related Disorder, Major Depressive Disorder).

Caffeine Withdrawal

In DSM-IV, caffeine withdrawal is considered to be an example of a Caffeine-Related Disorder Not Otherwise Specified. There is absolutely no doubt that caffeine withdrawal occurs, probably in varying degrees, and affects millions of people every day. The real question is whether it has sufficient clinical significance to be considered a mental disorder.

DSM-IV research criteria for caffeine withdrawal

A. Prolonged daily use of caffeine.

B. Abrupt cessation of caffeine use, or reduction in the amount of caffeine used, closely followed by headache and one (or more) of the following symptoms:
   (1) marked fatigue or drowsiness
   (2) marked anxiety or depression
   (3) nausea or vomiting

C. The symptoms in Criterion B cause clinically significant distress or impairment in social, occupational, or other important areas of functioning.

D. The symptoms are not due to the direct physiological effects of a general medical condition (e.g., migraine, viral illness) and are not better accounted for by another mental disorder.

Alternative Dimensional Descriptors for Schizophrenia

Alternative dimensional descriptors for Schizophrenia refer to a three-factor dimensional model for recording the severity of psychotic, disorganized, and negative symptoms. This model could be used rather than, or in addition to, the categorical Schizophrenia subtypes (Paranoid, Catatonic, Disorganized, Undifferentiated, Residual) included in DSM-IV. The user is instructed to indicate the severity of each dimension independently. This proposal represents one of DSM-IV's initial forays into the use of dimensional methods for describing psychopathology. It seems likely that dimensional systems will be increasingly important in psychiatric classification, particularly for Schizophrenia and the Personality Disorders.

DSM-IV alternative dimensional descriptors for Schizophrenia

Specify: absent, mild, moderate, severe for each dimension. The prominence of these dimensions may be specified for either (or both) the current episode (i.e., previous 6 months) or the lifetime course of the disorder.

psychotic (hallucinations/delusions) dimension: describes the degree to which hallucinations or delusions have been present

disorganized dimension: describes the degree to which disorganized speech, disorganized behavior, or inappropriate affect have been present

negative (deficit) dimension: describes the degree to which negative symptoms (i.e., affective flattening, alogia, avolition) have been present. **Note:** Do not include symptoms that appear to be secondary to depression, medication side effects, or hallucinations or delusions.

Postpsychotic Depressive Disorder of Schizophrenia

The essential feature of postpsychotic depressive disorder of Schizophrenia is a "Major Depressive Episode that is superimposed on, and occurs only during, the residual phase of Schizophrenia" (DSM-IV, p. 711). This disorder is not meant to include depressive presentations that occur while there are active-phase symptoms. The concept of postpsychotic depressive disorder is very important, particularly because individuals with Schizophrenia have a high rate of suicide and suicide attempts, and such events often occur during depressive episodes associated with this disorder.

In DSM-IV, this presentation would be diagnosed as Depressive Disorder Not Otherwise Specified. A diagnosis of Major Depressive Disorder would not apply because this diagnosis is not compatible with a concurrent diagnosis of Schizophrenia. The major concern with this proposed category is that it may be very difficult to differentiate depressive symptoms from neuroleptic side effects and from negative symptoms (e.g., avolition). There is also a concern about its possible impact on treatment. Including this category would undoubtedly result in increased attention to depressive symptoms in Schizophrenia and in their treatment with antidepressants. Because of the concern that antidepressants might exacerbate psychotic symptoms, this risk would have to be balanced against any improvement in depressive symptoms. Evidence is not available about the risk-to-benefit ratio of such antidepressant use.

DSM-IV research criteria for postpsychotic depressive disorder of Schizophrenia

A. Criteria are met for a Major Depressive Episode.

Note: The Major Depressive Episode must include Criterion A1: depressed mood. Do not include symptoms that are better accounted for as medication side effects or negative symptoms of Schizophrenia.

B. The Major Depressive Episode is superimposed on and occurs only during the residual phase of Schizophrenia.

C. The Major Depressive Episode is not due to the direct physiological effects of a substance or a general medical condition.

Simple Deteriorative Disorder (Simple Schizophrenia)

The proposed category of simple deteriorative disorder has a long and not altogether happy history (e.g., its alleged use as a tool in political repression in the former Soviet Union). It describes individuals who have the negative symptoms and deteriorating course often characteristic of Schizophrenia but who have not had any psychotic episodes. This category has been proposed because this presentation is encountered in clinical practice and currently can be diagnosed only as Unspecified Mental Disorder. The great disadvantage of this suggested category is that its definition is nonspecific and sufficiently broad as to invite confusion with other sources of deteriorating functioning such as Substance Use, Mental Retardation, chronic Mood Disorders, and Schizophrenia.

DSM-IV research criteria for simple deteriorative disorder (simple Schizophrenia)

A. Progressive development over a period of at least a year of all of the following:
   (1) marked decline in occupational or academic functioning
   (2) gradual appearance and deepening of negative symptoms such as affective flattening, alogia, and avolition
   (3) poor interpersonal rapport, social isolation, or social withdrawal

B. Criterion A for Schizophrenia has never been met.

C. The symptoms are not better accounted for by Schizotypal or Schizoid Personality Disorder, a Psychotic Disorder, a Mood Disorder, an Anxiety Disorder, a dementia, or Mental Retardation and are not due to the direct physiological effects of a substance or a general medical condition.

Premenstrual Dysphoric Disorder

Premenstrual dysphoric disorder is discussed in further detail in Chapter 26, "'Hot' Controversies."

DSM-IV research criteria for premenstrual dysphoric disorder

A. In most menstrual cycles during the past year, five (or more) of the following symptoms were present for most of the time during the last week of the luteal phase, began to remit within a few days after the onset of the follicular phase, and were absent in the week postmenses, with at least one of the symptoms being either (1), (2), (3), or (4):
   (1) markedly depressed mood, feelings of hopelessness, or self-deprecating thoughts
   (2) marked anxiety, tension, feelings of being "keyed up," or "on edge"
   (3) marked affective lability (e.g., feeling suddenly sad or tearful or increased sensitivity to rejection)
   (4) persistent and marked anger or irritability or increased interpersonal conflicts

(continued)

DSM-IV research criteria for premenstrual dysphoric disorder *(continued)*

(5) decreased interest in usual activities (e.g., work, school, friends, hobbies)
(6) subjective sense of difficulty in concentrating
(7) lethargy, easy fatigability, or marked lack of energy
(8) marked change in appetite, overeating, or specific food cravings
(9) hypersomnia or insomnia
(10) a subjective sense of being overwhelmed or out of control
(11) other physical symptoms, such as breast tenderness or swelling, headaches, joint or muscle pain, a sensation of "bloating," weight gain

Note: In menstruating females, the luteal phase corresponds to the period between ovulation and the onset of menses, and the follicular phase begins with menses. In nonmenstruating females (e.g., those who have had a hysterectomy), the timing of luteal and follicular phases may require measurement of circulating reproductive hormones.

B. The disturbance markedly interferes with work or school or with usual social activities and relationships with others (e.g., avoidance of social activities, decreased productivity and efficiency at work or school).

C. The disturbance is not merely an exacerbation of the symptoms of another disorder, such as Major Depressive Disorder, Panic Disorder, Dysthymic Disorder, or a Personality Disorder (although it may be superimposed on any of these disorders).

D. Criteria A, B, and C must be confirmed by prospective daily ratings during at least two consecutive symptomatic cycles. (The diagnosis may be made provisionally prior to this confirmation.)

Minor Depressive Disorder, Recurrent Brief Depressive Disorder, Mixed Anxiety-Depressive Disorder

The severity and duration thresholds for the Mood and Anxiety Disorders established in DSM-III and DSM-III-R were necessarily fairly arbitrary and not based on any very strong evidence. It is not surprising, therefore, that a number of studies, particularly those performed in primary care and community settings, report that many patients who fall short of the DSM thresholds for the specific Mood and Anxiety Disorders nonetheless exhibit clinically significant impairment, as measured by functional disability and health care utilization. In fact, three different types of subthreshold presentations have been identified:

1. Minor depressive disorder, which is subthreshold to Major Depressive Disorder in symptom severity
2. Brief recurrent depressive disorder, which is subthreshold to Major Depressive Disorder in duration
3. Mixed anxiety-depressive disorder for presentations characterized by a mix of mood and anxiety symptoms that do not meet criteria for any specific disorder

Supporters of these proposed categories were concerned that their absence from the nomenclature leads to many false-negative diagnoses, particularly in outpatient and primary care settings. These false-negatives may result in incomplete diagnosis and treatment.

The suggestion to include a broader definition of Anxiety and Mood Disorders is appealing, particularly because there is no reason to believe that the current arbitrary thresholds have cut nature at its most appropriate joint. There are also a number of reasons to be cautious. Because there are few data concerning the treatment implications of these proposed categories, we do not know how the risk of false-negatives balances against the risk of false-positives if the diagnoses were available. Although potential patients may be missing valuable treatment because these diagnoses are not included, their inclusion might result in much unnecessary and possibly harmful treatment.

It also seems likely that these proposed categories are at least as prevalent as the official DSM-IV Mood and Anxiety Disorders. Undoubtedly, their inclusion in the nomenclature and in algorithms used to generate diagnoses with semistructured interviews would greatly increase the overall prevalence of Mood and Anxiety Disorders and in turn of all mental disorders. There is no inherent problem with high prevalences of disorders (witness the high rates of hypertension and obesity in our population) as long as it is clear that the threshold established is useful in predicting prognosis or guiding treatment. The concern with adding these proposed categories is that we might create a whole cohort of new patients without sufficient evidence that diagnosis and consequent treatment would promote more good than harm.

DSM-IV research criteria for minor depressive disorder

A. A mood disturbance, defined as follows:
   (1) at least two (but less than five) of the following symptoms have been present during the same 2-week period and represent a change from previous functioning; at least one of the symptoms is either (a) or (b):
      (a) depressed mood most of the day, nearly every day, as indicated by either subjective report (e.g., feels sad or empty) or observation made by others (e.g., appears tearful).
      Note: In children and adolescents, can be irritable mood.
      (b) markedly diminished interest or pleasure in all, or almost all, activities most of the day, nearly every day (as indicated by either subjective account or observation made by others)
      (c) significant weight loss when not dieting or weight gain (e.g., a change of more than 5% of body weight in a month), or decrease or increase in appetite nearly every day. **Note:** In children, consider failure to make expected weight gains.
      (d) insomnia or hypersomnia nearly every day
      (e) psychomotor agitation or retardation nearly every day (observable by others, not merely subjective feelings of restlessness or being slowed down)

(continued)

DSM-IV research criteria for minor depressive disorder *(continued)*

(f) fatigue or loss of energy nearly every day
(g) feelings of worthlessness or excessive or inappropriate guilt (which may be delusional) nearly every day (not merely self-reproach or guilt about being sick)
(h) diminished ability to think or concentrate, or indecisiveness, nearly every day (either by subjective account or as observed by others)
(i) recurrent thoughts of death (not just fear of dying), recurrent suicidal ideation without a specific plan, or a suicide attempt or a specific plan for committing suicide

(2) the symptoms cause clinically significant distress or impairment in social, occupational, or other important areas of functioning
(3) the symptoms are not due to the direct physiological effects of a substance (e.g., a drug of abuse, a medication) or a general medical condition (e.g., hypothyroidism)
(4) the symptoms are not better accounted for by Bereavement (i.e., a normal reaction to the death of a loved one)

B. There has never been a Major Depressive Episode, and criteria are not met for Dysthymic Disorder.

C. There has never been a Manic Episode, a Mixed Episode, or a Hypomanic Episode, and criteria are not met for Cyclothymic Disorder. **Note:** This exclusion does not apply if all of the manic-, mixed-, or hypomanic-like episodes are substance or treatment induced.

D. The mood disturbance does not occur exclusively during Schizophrenia, Schizophreniform Disorder, Schizoaffective Disorder, Delusional Disorder, or Psychotic Disorder Not Otherwise Specified.

DSM-IV research criteria for recurrent brief depressive disorder

A. Criteria, except for duration, are met for a Major Depressive Episode.

B. The depressive periods in Criterion A last at least 2 days but less than 2 weeks.

C. The depressive periods occur at least once a month for 12 consecutive months and are not associated with the menstrual cycle.

D. The periods of depressed mood cause clinically significant distress or impairment in social, occupational, or other important areas of functioning.

E. The symptoms are not due to the direct physiological effects of a substance (e.g., a drug of abuse, a medication) or a general medical condition (e.g., hypothyroidism).

(continued)

DSM-IV research criteria for recurrent brief depressive disorder *(continued)*

F. There has never been a Major Depressive Episode, and criteria are not met for Dysthymic Disorder.

G. There has never been a Manic Episode, a Mixed Episode, or a Hypomanic Episode, and criteria are not met for Cyclothymic Disorder. **Note:** This exclusion does not apply if all of the manic-, mixed-, or hypomanic-like episodes are substance or treatment induced.

H. The mood disturbance does not occur exclusively during Schizophrenia, Schizophreniform Disorder, Schizoaffective Disorder, Delusional Disorder, or Psychotic Disorder Not Otherwise Specified.

DSM-IV research criteria for mixed anxiety-depressive disorder

A. Persistent or recurrent dysphoric mood lasting at least 1 month.

B. The dysphoric mood is accompanied by at least 1 month of four (or more) of the following symptoms:
   (1) difficulty concentrating or mind going blank
   (2) sleep disturbance (difficulty falling or staying asleep, or restless unsatisfying sleep)
   (3) fatigue or low energy
   (4) irritability
   (5) worry
   (6) being easily moved to tears
   (7) hypervigilance
   (8) anticipating the worst
   (9) hopelessness (pervasive pessimism about the future)
   (10) low self-esteem or feelings of worthlessness

C. The symptoms cause clinically significant distress or impairment in social, occupational, or other important areas of functioning.

D. The symptoms are not due to the direct physiological effects of a substance (e.g., a drug of abuse, a medication) or a general medical condition.

E. All of the following:
   (1) criteria have never been met for Major Depressive Disorder, Dysthymic Disorder, Panic Disorder, or Generalized Anxiety Disorder
   (2) criteria are not currently met for any other Anxiety or Mood Disorder (including an Anxiety or Mood Disorder, In Partial Remission)
   (3) the symptoms are not better accounted for by any other mental disorder

Factitious Disorder By Proxy

Factitious disorder by proxy is known colloquially as "Munchausen syndrome by proxy." It is a variant of Factitious Disorder and is diagnosed in DSM-IV as Factitious Disorder Not Otherwise Specified. Most commonly, the diagnosis refers to a parent who produces symptoms in a child. One concern with adding the category was that it might be misused in forensic determinations as a way of avoiding responsibility for the child abuse that is often part of the syndrome.

DSM-IV research criteria for factitious disorder by proxy

A. Intentional production or feigning of physical or psychological signs or symptoms in another person who is under the individual's care.

B. The motivation for the perpetrator's behavior is to assume the sick role by proxy.

C. External incentives for the behavior (such as economic gain) are absent.

D. The behavior is not better accounted for by another mental disorder.

Dissociative Trance Disorder

The proposed category of dissociative trance disorder has been included in ICD-10 and is diagnosed in DSM-IV as Dissociative Disorder Not Otherwise Specified. It is intended to describe abnormal trance states and is especially likely to occur in cultures in which trance states are an everyday part of life.

DSM-IV research criteria for dissociative trance disorder

A. Either (1) or (2):
   (1) trance, i.e., temporary marked alteration in the state of consciousness or loss of customary sense of personal identity without replacement by an alternate identity, associated with at least one of the following:
      (a) narrowing of awareness of immediate surroundings, or unusually narrow and selective focusing on environmental stimuli
      (b) stereotyped behaviors or movements that are experienced as being beyond one's control
   (2) possession trance, a single or episodic alteration in the state of consciousness characterized by the replacement of customary sense of personal

(continued)

DSM-IV research criteria for dissociative trance disorder *(continued)*

identity by a new identity. This is attributed to the influence of a spirit, power, deity, or other person, as evidenced by one (or more) of the following:

(a) stereotyped and culturally determined behaviors or movements that are experienced as being controlled by the possessing agent
(b) full or partial amnesia for the event

B. The trance or possession trance state is not accepted as a normal part of a collective cultural or religious practice.

C. The trance or possession trance state causes clinically significant distress or impairment in social, occupational, or other important areas of functioning.

D. The trance or possession trance state does not occur exclusively during the course of a Psychotic Disorder (including Mood Disorder With Psychotic Features and Brief Psychotic Disorder) or Dissociative Identity Disorder and is not due to the direct physiological effects of a substance or a general medical condition.

Binge-Eating Disorder

The proposed category of binge-eating disorder is akin to Bulimia Nervosa but without the inappropriate compensatory mechanisms (e.g., purging, fasting, excessive exercise) used to counteract the effects of binge eating. It would be diagnosed in DSM-IV as Eating Disorder Not Otherwise Specified. Not surprisingly, this pattern of eating in which the binges are not counterbalanced by measures that eliminate calories is most common in obese individuals.

DSM-IV research criteria for binge-eating disorder

A. Recurrent episodes of binge eating. An episode of binge eating is characterized by both of the following:

(1) eating, in a discrete period of time (e.g., within any 2-hour period), an amount of food that is definitely larger than most people would eat in a similar period of time under similar circumstances
(2) a sense of lack of control over eating during the episode (e.g., a feeling that one cannot stop eating or control what or how much one is eating)

B. The binge-eating episodes are associated with three (or more) of the following:

(1) eating much more rapidly than normal
(2) eating until feeling uncomfortably full
(3) eating large amounts of food when not feeling physically hungry
(4) eating alone because of being embarrassed by how much one is eating
(5) feeling disgusted with oneself, depressed, or very guilty after overeating

(continued)

DSM-IV research criteria for binge-eating disorder *(continued)*

C. Marked distress regarding binge eating is present.

D. The binge eating occurs, on average, at least 2 days a week for 6 months.

Note: The method of determining frequency differs from that used for Bulimia Nervosa; future research should address whether the preferred method of setting a frequency threshold is counting the number of days on which binges occur or counting the number of episodes of binge eating.

E. The binge eating is not associated with the regular use of inappropriate compensatory behaviors (e.g., purging, fasting, excessive exercise) and does not occur exclusively during the course of Anorexia Nervosa or Bulimia Nervosa.

Depressive Personality Disorder

The suggestion for including the diagnosis of depressive personality disorder reflects an ongoing controversy concerning the appropriate boundary between spectrum Personality Disorders and Axis I disorders. Depressive personality disorder would be related to Mood Disorders as Schizotypal Personality Disorder is related to Schizophrenia and Avoidant Personality Disorder is related to Anxiety Disorders. In DSM-IV, this proposed category is included as an example of Personality Disorder Not Otherwise Specified. The major question regarding this category is whether it stands separately from Dysthymic Disorder. Although the DSM-IV field trial suggested that Dysthymic Disorder and depressive personality disorder might be distinguished, more studies are necessary to further elucidate their relationship. Therefore, one should also consider the diagnosis of Dysthymic Disorder, Early Onset.

DSM-IV research criteria for depressive personality disorder

A. A pervasive pattern of depressive cognitions and behaviors beginning by early adulthood and present in a variety of contexts, as indicated by five (or more) of the following:

(1) usual mood is dominated by dejection, gloominess, cheerlessness, joylessness, unhappiness
(2) self-concept centers around beliefs of inadequacy, worthlessness, and low self-esteem
(3) is critical, blaming, and derogatory toward self
(4) is brooding and given to worry
(5) is negativistic, critical, and judgmental toward others
(6) is pessimistic
(7) is prone to feeling guilty or remorseful

B. Does not occur exclusively during Major Depressive Episodes and is not better accounted for by Dysthymic Disorder.

Passive-Aggressive Personality (Negativistic Personality Disorder)

Passive-aggressive personality disorder was an official category in DSM-III-R and has been demoted to this section. Its lack of support as a separate diagnosis reflects concerns that 1) such behaviors more often represent a reaction to an oppressive environment rather than a feature inherent in the individual, 2) it was so narrowly defined that it represented more the habitual use of a particular coping style rather than a full-fledged Personality Disorder, and 3) it was rarely diagnosed in the absence of other Personality Disorders. The criteria set included here has been modified to include additional items meant to broaden the construct toward a negativistic personality disorder.

DSM-IV research criteria for passive-aggressive personality disorder

A. A pervasive pattern of negativistic attitudes and passive resistance to demands for adequate performance, beginning by early adulthood and present in a variety of contexts, as indicated by four (or more) of the following:

(1) passively resists fulfilling routine social and occupational tasks
(2) complains of being misunderstood and unappreciated by others
(3) is sullen and argumentative
(4) unreasonably criticizes and scorns authority
(5) expresses envy and resentment toward those apparently more fortunate
(6) voices exaggerated and persistent complaints of personal misfortune
(7) alternates between hostile defiance and contrition

B. Does not occur exclusively during Major Depressive Episodes and is not better accounted for by Dysthymic Disorder.

Medication-Induced Movement Disorders

The Medication-Induced Movement Disorders are included in the section titled "Other Conditions That May Be a Focus of Clinical Attention" but without text or criteria sets (see DSM-IV, pp. 678–680). The following proposed research criteria sets were developed for DSM-IV.

DSM-IV research criteria for 332.1 Neuroleptic-Induced Parkinsonism

A. One (or more) of the following signs or symptoms has developed in association with the use of neuroleptic medication:
   (1) parkinsonian tremor (i.e., a coarse, rhythmic, resting tremor with a frequency between 3 and 6 cycles per second, affecting the limbs, head, mouth, or tongue)
   (2) parkinsonian muscular rigidity (i.e., cogwheel rigidity or continuous "lead-pipe" rigidity)
   (3) akinesia (i.e., a decrease in spontaneous facial expressions, gestures, speech, or body movements)

B. The symptoms in Criterion A developed within a few weeks of starting or raising the dose of a neuroleptic medication, or of reducing a medication used to treat (or prevent) acute extrapyramidal symptoms (e.g., anticholinergic agents).

C. The symptoms in Criterion A are not better accounted for by a mental disorder (e.g., catatonic or negative symptoms in Schizophrenia, psychomotor retardation in a Major Depressive Episode). Evidence that the symptoms are better accounted for by a mental disorder might include the following: the symptoms precede the exposure to neuroleptic medication or are not compatible with the pattern of pharmacological intervention (e.g., no improvement after lowering the neuroleptic dose or administering anticholinergic medication).

D. The symptoms in Criterion A are not due to a nonneuroleptic substance or to a neurological or other general medical condition (e.g., Parkinson's disease, Wilson's disease). Evidence that the symptoms are due to a general medical condition might include the following: the symptoms precede exposure to neuroleptic medication, unexplained focal neurological signs are present, or the symptoms progress despite a stable medication regimen.

DSM-IV research criteria for 333.92 Neuroleptic Malignant Syndrome

A. The development of severe muscle rigidity and elevated temperature associated with the use of neuroleptic medication.

B. Two (or more) of the following:
   (1) diaphoresis
   (2) dysphagia
   (3) tremor
   (4) incontinence
   (5) changes in level of consciousness ranging from confusion to coma
   (6) mutism
   (7) tachycardia
   (8) elevated or labile blood pressure
   (9) leucocytosis
   (10) laboratory evidence of muscle injury (e.g., elevated CPK)

C. The symptoms in Criteria A and B are not due to another substance (e.g., phencyclidine) or a neurological or other general medical condition (e.g., viral encephalitis).

D. The symptoms in Criteria A and B are not better accounted for by a mental disorder (e.g., Mood Disorder With Catatonic Features).

DSM-IV research criteria for 333.7 Neuroleptic-Induced Acute Dystonia

A. One (or more) of the following signs or symptoms has developed in association with the use of neuroleptic medication:
   (1) abnormal positioning of the head and neck in relation to the body (e.g., retrocollis, torticollis)
   (2) spasms of the jaw muscles (trismus, gaping, grimacing)
   (3) impaired swallowing (dysphagia), speaking, or breathing (laryngeal-pharyngeal spasm, dysphonia)
   (4) thickened or slurred speech due to hypertonic or enlarged tongue (dysarthria, macroglossia)
   (5) tongue protrusion or tongue dysfunction
   (6) eyes deviated up, down, or sideward (oculogyric crisis)
   (7) abnormal positioning of the distal limbs or trunk

B. The signs or symptoms in Criterion A developed within 7 days of starting or rapidly raising the dose of neuroleptic medication, or of reducing a medication used to treat (or prevent) acute extrapyramidal symptoms (e.g., anticholinergic agents).

C. The symptoms in Criterion A are not better accounted for by a mental disorder (e.g., catatonic symptoms in Schizophrenia). Evidence that the symptoms are better accounted for by a mental disorder might include the following: the symptoms precede the exposure to neuroleptic medication or are not compatible with the pattern of pharmacological intervention (e.g., no improvement after neuroleptic lowering or anticholinergic administration).

D. The symptoms in Criterion A are not due to a nonneuroleptic substance or to a neurological or other general medical condition. Evidence that the symptoms are due to a general medical condition might include the following: the symptoms precede the exposure to the neuroleptic medication, unexplained focal neurological signs are present, or the symptoms progress in the absence of change in medication.

DSM-IV research criteria for 333.99 Neuroleptic-Induced Acute Akathisia

A. The development of subjective complaints of restlessness after exposure to a neuroleptic medication.

B. At least one of the following is observed:
   (1) fidgety movements or swinging of the legs
   (2) rocking from foot to foot while standing
   (3) pacing to relieve restlessness
   (4) inability to sit or stand still for at least several minutes

C. The onset of the symptoms in Criteria A and B occurs within 4 weeks of initiating or increasing the dose of the neuroleptic, or of reducing medication used to treat (or prevent) acute extrapyramidal symptoms (e.g., anticholinergic agents).

(continued)

DSM-IV research criteria for 333.99 Neuroleptic-Induced Acute Akathisia *(continued)*

D. The symptoms in Criterion A are not better accounted for by a mental disorder (e.g., Schizophrenia, Substance Withdrawal, agitation from a Major Depressive or Manic Episode, hyperactivity in Attention-Deficit/ Hyperactivity Disorder). Evidence that symptoms may be better accounted for by a mental disorder might include the following: the onset of symptoms preceding the exposure to the neuroleptics, the absence of increasing restlessness with increasing neuroleptic doses, and the absence of relief with pharmacological interventions (e.g., no improvement after decreasing the neuroleptic dose or treatment with medication intended to treat the akathisia).

E. The symptoms in Criterion A are not due to a nonneuroleptic substance or to a neurological or other general medical condition. Evidence that symptoms are due to a general medical condition might include the onset of the symptoms preceding the exposure to neuroleptics or the progression of symptoms in the absence of a change in medication.

DSM-IV research criteria for 333.82 Neuroleptic-Induced Tardive Dyskinesia

A. Involuntary movements of the tongue, jaw, trunk, or extremities have developed in association with the use of neuroleptic medication.

B. The involuntary movements are present over a period of at least 4 weeks and occur in any of the following patterns:
   (1) choreiform movements (i.e., rapid, jerky, nonrepetitive)
   (2) athetoid movements (i.e., slow, sinuous, continual)
   (3) rhythmic movements (i.e., stereotypies)

C. The signs or symptoms in Criteria A and B develop during exposure to a neuroleptic medication or within 4 weeks of withdrawal from an oral (or within 8 weeks of withdrawal from a depot) neuroleptic medication.

D. There has been exposure to neuroleptic medication for at least 3 months (1 month if age 60 years or older).

E. The symptoms are not due to a neurological or general medical condition (e.g., Huntington's disease, Sydenham's chorea, spontaneous dyskinesia, hyperthyroidism, Wilson's disease), ill-fitting dentures, or exposure to other medications that cause acute reversible dyskinesia (e.g., L-dopa, bromocriptine). Evidence that the symptoms are due to one of these etiologies might include the following: the symptoms precede the exposure to the neuroleptic medication or unexplained focal neurological signs are present.

F. The symptoms are not better accounted for by a neuroleptic-induced acute movement disorder (e.g., Neuroleptic-Induced Acute Dystonia, Neuroleptic-Induced Acute Akathisia).

DSM-IV research criteria for 333.1 Medication-Induced Postural Tremor

A. A fine postural tremor that has developed in association with the use of a medication (e.g., lithium, antidepressant medication, valproic acid).

B. The tremor (i.e., a regular, rhythmic oscillation of the limbs, head, mouth, or tongue) has a frequency between 8 and 12 cycles per second.

C. The symptoms are not due to a preexisting nonpharmacologically induced tremor. Evidence that the symptoms are due to a preexisting tremor might include the following: the tremor was present prior to the introduction of the medication, the tremor does not correlate with serum levels of the medication, and the tremor persists after discontinuation of the medication.

D. The symptoms are not better accounted for by Neuroleptic-Induced Parkinsonism.

CHAPTER 26

"Hot" Controversies

For the most part, the preparation of DSM-IV was remarkably free of controversy. The adoption of the three-stage method of empirical review replaced passionate argument with the deliberative poring over and interpretation of piles of tables and figures. Literally hundreds of questions were settled with consensus decisions that may not have pleased everyone but were generally regarded as fair and consistent with the data.

The "hot" controversies presented in this chapter did not occur among the Task Force and the Work Group members but rather were played out in a larger arena. For the most part, scientific issues were settled without much controversy. The controversial issues touched on value questions that went far beyond the diagnostic system and could not be answered with empirical data currently available. It is of some interest that all of the hot controversies surrounding DSM-III, DSM-III-R, and now DSM-IV have been in some way related to sexual orientation or gender. It appears that attempts to categorize human behavior related to such sensitive topics are inherently fraught with the potential to arouse widespread interest and disagreement.

In this chapter, we present our perspective on the decision-making process about how best to handle two controversial categories included in DSM-III-R Appendix A: late luteal phase dysphoric disorder and self-defeating personality disorder. The fate of these categories became at least temporarily the focus of extensive media coverage. It is unfortunate, but perhaps not surprising, that the issues involved in these controversies were presented in an often distorted fashion seemingly intended to highlight acrimony rather than to offer a balanced perspective of the pros and cons. Although we are mindful that our own views may be biased by our close participation in these discussions, it may nonetheless be useful to provide an insider's view of the process and substance of these controversies.

Premenstrual Dysphoric Disorder

In DSM-III-R, this proposed category (then called Late Luteal Phase Dysphoric Disorder) was included in Appendix A, "Proposed Diagnostic Categories Needing Further Study," and as an example under Unspecified Mental Disorder (Nonpsychotic). The suggestion that this category be included in DSM-III-R had created a firestorm of concern that it would result in the wholesale stigmatization of women. On the other hand, proponents maintained that late luteal phase dysphoric disorder is a clinically significant condition supported by a research and clinical literature and that its omission might lead to underdiagnosis, misdiagnosis, and failure to give appropriate treatment. Proponents also argued that the potential for stigmatization cuts both ways—not including this diagnosis might lead to women with these problems being ignored or blamed as temperamental.

As we planned the development of DSM-IV, it was clear that this proposed category was likely to arouse concerns similar to those voiced in the DSM-III-R process. A Work Group was formed with 5 members, 1 consultant, and 36 advisers to deal with this one specific question. The composition of the Work Group was balanced to include those with serious concerns about the possible misuse of the diagnosis, those whose clinical and research experiences suggested its utility, and those with an interest in the area but who were as yet undecided. The group was charged with the responsibility for making a recommendation that would be based on the widest possible empirical review and elicitation of opinion from the field. The options to be considered were whether late luteal phase dysphoric disorder should 1) continue to appear in the appendix of DSM-IV, 2) be included in the main body of the manual, 3) be included in the section titled "Other Clinically Significant Conditions That May Be a Focus of Clinical Attention," 4) be considered a nonpsychiatric genitourinary condition, or 5) be omitted altogether.

The decision-making process began with a remarkably detailed review of the literature, which went through many revisions in response to comments from the various Work Group members, their advisers, and other interested parties. The literature review, which included over 500 articles on late luteal phase dysphoric disorder and premenstrual syndrome, had several purposes:

1. To determine the performance characteristics of the defining items included in DSM-III-R, as well as other suggested items
2. To determine the utility and validity of the condition by studying its course, relationship to other psychiatric disorders, biological test results, and treatment response
3. To determine the condition's likely prevalence in community and clinical samples and its possible relationship to the far more common and far less severe premenstrual syndrome
4. To consider the social, forensic, and occupational implications of including the condition as a disorder in DSM-IV

Although there was considerable disagreement on how best to interpret the extensive data that were collected in the literature review, there was widespread consensus that the review was performed in a comprehensive manner and provided a fair presentation of the issues. Everyone agreed that there were a number of methodological problems in this literature (e.g., unclear definitions, small sample sizes, lack of control groups, lack of prospective daily ratings, possibly biased sample selection, failure to delineate the timing and duration of symptoms, failure to collect adequate hormonal samples). The Work Group members did disagree, however, concerning the degree to which the methodological problems were disabling and whether an especially compelling body of evidence should be required to justify the inclusion of this proposed disorder, given the potential for misuse of the diagnosis.

The major findings of the literature review were that

1. The criteria listed in DSM-III-R Appendix A had acceptable reliability and other performance characteristics.
2. A relatively circumscribed group of women (3%–5%) suffer from severe and clinically significant dysphoria related to the premenstrual period.
3. The condition co-occurs with a number of other mental disorders but also occurs independently.
4. There is suggestive evidence about specific relationships to biological test results and treatment response, but the power of these relationships was interpreted variably by Work Group members and advisers.

To supplement the information gained from the published literature, the Work Group also conducted a reanalysis of previously collected data from over 900 subjects from five different sites. The results of these reanalyses supported the clinical utility of the criteria set for late luteal phase dysphoric disorder but suggested an emphasis on the dysphoric nature of the symptoms to indicate that the disturbance is most closely related to Mood Disorder.

Although this Work Group labored long, hard, and collegially to reach a consensus (and almost succeeded), ultimately they were unable to do so. A majority of the Work Group favored the following recommendations:

1. Changing the name from late luteal phase dysphoric disorder to premenstrual dysphoric disorder; late luteal phase dysphoric disorder was a misleading name because the symptoms may not be related to the endocrinological changes of the late luteal phase
2. Retaining the proposed criteria set, with some modifications, in DSM-IV Appendix B, "Criteria Sets and Axes Provided for Further Study"
3. Noting premenstrual dysphoric disorder as an example under Depressive Disorder Not Otherwise Specified

A complete consensus within the Work Group could not be achieved. The next step in the decision-making process was taken by the DSM-IV Task Force, which considered the Work Group's deliberations, literature review, data reanalyses, and input from advisers. The Task Force recommended that the opinion of the Work Group's majority be accepted.

More so than the considerations involved in any other section of DSM-IV, the considerations of this Work Group were scrutinized by those in the profession and the public who had developed strong opinions on what the ultimate outcome of the deliberations should be. Those who had led the efforts against this proposed diagnosis during the DSM-III-R discussions were very vocal in trying to influence the DSM-IV deliberative and empirical review process. They embarked on a concerted and well-orchestrated media effort to shape public opinion and to exert pressure on the Work Group and Task Force.

Premenstrual dysphoric disorder became a focus of attention in the major national newsweeklies and newspapers and a topic of discussion on daytime television and radio talk shows. Many of these media presentations were informative and well balanced, serving the useful purpose of calling public attention to the condition and helping some individuals identify themselves as having it.

Unfortunately, however, some of the media coverage was poorly informed and misleading. The most egregious distortion was carried in headlines that DSM-IV was planning to label the 60% of women with some premenstrual discomfort as having a mental disorder. In fact, the data that were emerging from the literature reviews (which were well known by the critics who were speaking out against the proposal) suggested that only 3%–5% of women have conditions that would satisfy the premenstrual dysphoric disorder criteria. That is because the criteria set for premenstrual dysphoric disorder establishes a high symptom threshold and requires both severe impairment and prospective monthly ratings. We did our best to present a balanced view of the pros and cons of the issue and to correct the most misleading statements.

Although public controversy swirled around premenstrual dysphoric disorder, it was our impression that this controversy had little or no influence on the deliberations of the Work Group and Task Force, which remained thoughtful and close to the issues. Like most questions in DSM-IV, there is no clear right or wrong answer as to the diagnostic status of premenstrual dysphoric disorder. The pros of including the diagnosis as an official category were improved case finding, more specific treatment planning, reduced stigma for the individual woman with this problem who might otherwise be dismissed as temperamental or complaining, and encouragement of research. The cons of including the diagnosis were questions concerning the depth, methodological rigor, and pertinence of the supporting research evidence and the concern that the diagnosis might serve to stigmatize women more generally.

Plausible arguments were made for the different options of including premenstrual dysphoric disorder as an official category, keeping it in an appendix, or eliminating it altogether. The conservative final decision of keeping it in an appendix has the great advantage of encouraging additional research without prejudging the question. Indeed, the most desirable result of the DSM-III-R decision to create an appendix to include this condition has been the wealth of valuable research stimulated by it. All in all, the Work Group and Task Force debates on this issue were informative and responsible and resulted in a reasonable resolution. The public debate probably generated more heat than light, but it also may have been educational.

Self-Defeating Personality Disorder

Self-defeating personality disorder was included in Appendix A of DSM-III-R, also amid considerable public controversy. The major arguments against including this category were concerns that it, in effect, blamed the victim for "inviting" abuse and would pathologize traits that society inculcates are desirable in women (e.g., altruism, self-sacrifice). In considering whether to continue to include self-defeating personality disorder in DSM-IV Appendix B, the conceptual and empirical foundation for this proposed disorder was thoroughly studied by the DSM-IV Personality Disorders Work Group and by the DSM-IV Task Force.

The literature review for self-defeating personality disorder indicated that this newly proposed diagnosis had received very little research attention since its inclusion in DSM-III-R Appendix A. Indeed, very few investigations of self-defeating personality disorder involved the clinical evaluation of real patients. Most of the few available studies consisted of surveys of clinicians' opinions or diagnosis of written case examples. The Work Group was also concerned about the utility of adding yet another Personality Disorder diagnosis.

The clinical studies suggested that self-defeating personality disorder would overlap a great deal with depression and with the other Personality Disorders included in DSM-IV. The overlap with other Personality Disorders is particularly problematic because most clinicians and researchers believe that there are already too many Personality Disorders, creating a system that is cumbersome to use in clinical and research practice and that usually results in multiple diagnoses of Personality Disorders.

The original impetus for the suggestion to include this disorder was an attempt to capture the behaviors described by Freud under the concept of *moral masochism.* It is widely accepted, even by some of those who were very opposed to the inclusion of self-defeating personality disorder in DSM-IV, that some individuals manage to repeatedly pull defeat from the jaws of victory and seem to do so because of internalized psychological conflicts.

However useful the concept of masochism remains in the practice of psychotherapy, there are serious structural problems that prevent its simple translation from a psychodynamic construct into an operational criteria set defining a specific personality disorder. The research criteria set for self-defeating personality disorder included in Appendix A of DSM-III-R was an attempt to operationalize the psychodynamic construct that unconscious forces may lead to a masochistic pattern of interpersonal relationships and behaviors.

The analytic literature has attributed this masochistic pattern to a variety of unconscious motivations, including self-punishment consequent to superego pathology, an external reenactment of introjected early sadomasochistic relationships, self-directed aggression as a defense against sadism, and pathological narcissism. In the psychotherapy situation, the evaluation of these unconscious motivations usually requires a careful and prolonged assessment of the patient's transferential attitudes and behaviors in the treatment relationship. This judgment depends on a good deal of psychodynamic expertise and inference and usually can be confirmed only by the patient's masochistic treatment behavior, not just by the evaluation of problems presented in the diagnostic interview.

The self-defeating personality disorder criteria represented an attempt to draft a set of behavioral and interpersonal criteria that would capture the surface manifestations of the presumed unconscious motivation for masochistic behavior. However, this task turned out to be inherently impossible. One cannot convert this particular psychodynamic construct inferring unconscious masochistic motivation into a behavioral (and less inferential) criteria set that is not confounded by the individual's interactions with the environment.

This effort did not fail because of any deficiencies in the specific self-defeating personality disorder criteria that were selected. It was not simply a matter of studying and improving the existing criteria set. The basic issue is that much self-defeating behavior occurs for reasons other than the specific unconscious masochistic motivations meant to be at the heart of self-defeating personality disorder. It is usually impossible within the context of a general psychiatric evaluation to determine whether the individual's pattern of self-defeating behavior is an expression of unconscious motivation that would play out over and over again regardless of the environment in which the individual exists or whether the self-defeating pattern of behavior is an understandable and perhaps adaptive result of the need to survive in a harsh and punishing environment.

In addition, many mental disorders are characterized by behaviors and symptoms that are self-defeating in their effect but not masochistic in their unconscious motivations. That is particularly true for chronic depression, but it is also true for many other psychiatric disorders. The concept of self-defeating personality disorder is inherently confounded with self-defeating behaviors that are secondary consequences of other mental disorders. There were also no studies to document that the diagnosis described a behavior pattern that was not already adequately represented by an existing Axis I or Axis II diagnosis. Although self-defeating behaviors are encountered commonly enough in clinical practice, it is not clear that the self-defeating personality disorder diagnosis is specific in capturing the central or predominant pathology in most of these cases.

Another major concern about the proposed self-defeating personality disorder diagnosis was that it might be used to blame victims of spouse abuse for their own victimization. The proposed criteria set did attempt to deal with this issue by providing an exclusion criterion stating that the diagnosis would not apply when the self-defeating behavior occurred exclusively in response to or in anticipation of being physically, sexually, or psychologically abused. However, many of the instruments that were developed to assess self-defeating personality disorder failed to consider this exclusion criterion, and many victims are reluctant to acknowledge the presence of actual abuse. The research on self-defeating personality disorder often failed to consider the occurrence and influence of victimization on the diagnosis, and the research on victimization has failed to assess adequately the role and influence of self-defeating personality traits.

Although there undoubtedly are individuals with self-defeating personality patterns, the utility and validity of the construct as a psychiatric diagnosis have not yet been established. The Personality Disorders Work Group concluded that providing the diagnosis in an appendix to DSM-IV would provide it with credibility and recognition that it did not yet warrant. As a culmination of its review process, the Personality Disorders Work Group recommended that self-defeating personality disorder not be included in the main body or Appendix B of DSM-IV. A diagnosis that has the potential for misuse should be held to an especially high standard of validation before it is given any official credibility. Nevertheless, the concept of self-defeating unconscious motivations is sometimes useful in understanding or treating individuals encountered in clinical practice.

The Last Word

Most DSM-IV decisions were made after a comprehensive review of the empirical data. With this method as a framework for decision making, there was surprisingly little controversy in the discussions of the DSM-IV Work Groups and Task Force. The issues described in this chapter became relatively hot controversies precisely because they touched on larger value questions that did not lend themselves to answers that could be based exclusively on an interpretation of the empirical data.

SECTION V

Study Guides

CHAPTER 27

The Capsule Summary

What Everyone Should Know About DSM-IV

Perhaps the best way to close this *guidebook* is with a capsule summary to refresh your memory about the wide range of disorders included in DSM-IV.

Disorders Usually First Diagnosed in Infancy, Childhood or Adolescence

This section contains disorders that are most often first diagnosed in childhood, although treatment for these disorders may not be sought until the individual has reached adulthood. It must be remarked that the disorders in the other sections in the manual may be and often are applicable to children.

The childhood disorders are grouped into several subsections. Mental Retardation, Learning Disorders (Reading Disorder, Mathematics Disorder, Disorder of Written Expression), and Motor Skills Disorder (Developmental Coordination Disorder) are characterized by a prominent disturbance in the acquisition of cognitive, language, or motor skills. Communication Disorders (Expressive Language Disorder, Mixed Receptive-Expressive Language Disorder, Phonological Disorder, Stuttering) involve an impairment in written or vocal communication. Pervasive Developmental Disorders (Autistic Disorder, Rett's Disorder, Childhood Disintegrative Disorder, and Asperger's Disorder) are characterized by serious impairments in social interaction and verbal and nonverbal skills development.

Attention-Deficit and Disruptive Behavior Disorders (Attention-Deficit/Hyperactivity Disorder, Conduct Disorder, and Oppositional Defiant Disorder) are typified by impulsive, inattentive, or disruptive behavior. The Tic Disorders (Tourette's Disorder, Chronic Motor or Vocal Tic Disorder, and Transient Tic Disorder) are characterized by sudden, involuntary movements or vocalizations. The Elimination Disorders (Encopresis and Enuresis) involve repeated passage of feces or voiding of urine in inappropriate places (e.g., clothing or bed) in children above the ages of 4 and 5 years, respectively. Other Disorders of Infancy, Childhood, or Adolescence include Separation Anxiety Disorder (anxiety concerning separation from home or loved ones), Selective Mutism (consistent failure to speak in specific situations), Reactive Attachment Disorder of Infancy or Early Childhood (markedly disturbed social relatedness), and Stereotypic Movement Disorder (repetitive, nonfunctional motor behavior).

Delirium, Dementia, Amnestic, and Other Cognitive Disorders

The primary feature of delirium, dementia, amnestic, and other cognitive disorders is a change or deficit in memory or cognition. Three patterns of cognitive deficits are distinguished. Delirium is characterized by a disturbance in consciousness (i.e., reduced clarity of awareness of the environment) and a change in cognition that develops rapidly and tends to fluctuate during the day. Dementia is characterized by multiple cognitive deficits (one of which must be impairment in memory) that are usually chronic and tend to get progressively worse over time. Amnestic disorders are distinguished by memory impairment (which is manifest by the inability to learn new information or recall information previously learned) occurring in the absence of other significant cognitive deficits. Unlike most disorders in DSM-IV, the etiology of the delirium, dementia, or amnestic disorder must be specified—for example, whether it is substance induced, due to a general medical condition, or due to multiple etiologies.

Mental Disorders Due to a General Medical Condition Not Elsewhere Classified

These disorders are judged to be caused directly by the physiological consequences of a general medical condition, in contrast to disorders that are judged to be caused by the psychological consequences of a general medical condition (e.g., Adjustment Disorder). To facilitate differential diagnosis, the text and criteria for most of these disorders are located within the diagnostic class with which they share phenomenology. For example, Anxiety Disorder Due to a General Medical Condition is listed within the Anxiety Disorders section of DSM-IV. However, text and criteria for Personality Change Due to a General Medical Condition and Catatonic Disorder Due to a General Medical Condition are included in this section because there are no relevant diagnostic classes with which they share phenomenology. Catatonic Disorder Due to a

General Medical Condition is a new disorder in DSM-IV that is meant to enlarge the differential diagnosis of catatonia (which also includes Mood Disorders, Neuroleptic-Induced Movement Disorders, and Schizophrenia).

Substance-Related Disorders

Substances are defined in DSM-IV as drugs of abuse, medications, and toxins. The Substance-Related Disorders are divided into the Substance Use Disorders (Dependence and Abuse) and Substance-Induced Disorders (Intoxication, Withdrawal, Delirium, Dementia, Amnestic Disorder, Psychotic Disorder, Mood Disorder, Anxiety Disorder, Sexual Dysfunction, and Sleep Disorder). Because most forms of psychopathology can be and often are caused by substances, the Substance-Induced Disorders are an important part of the differential diagnosis for virtually every condition in DSM-IV. The DSM-IV conception of Substance Dependence is broad, characterized by some combination of physiological dependence (tolerance or withdrawal) and psychological dependence (compulsive use). Substance Abuse is characterized by serious adverse consequences of substance use occurring in individuals who have never had Substance Dependence.

Schizophrenia and Other Psychotic Disorders

Schizophrenia is a disorder with a minimum of 6 months' duration and is characterized by an active psychotic phase with two or more of the following symptoms present for at least 1 month: delusions, hallucinations, disorganized speech, grossly disorganized behavior, and negative symptoms. Schizophreniform Disorder has a similar symptomatic picture but a duration of 1–6 months. Schizoaffective Disorder straddles the boundary between Schizophrenia and Mood Disorders with symptom features characteristic of both. Delusional Disorder consists of persistent, nonbizarre delusions in the absence of other significant psychotic symptoms. Brief Psychotic Disorder covers those episodes of psychotic symptoms that last for at least a day but no more than 1 month. Shared Psychotic Disorder is the ungainly DSM-IV term for the more poetically named folie à deux.

Mood Disorders

The primary Mood Disorders are divided into *unipolar* and *bipolar* disorders. The unipolar Depressive Disorders include Major Depressive Disorder (one or more episodes of severely depressed mood or loss of interest occurring for at least 2 weeks) and Dysthymic Disorder (depressed mood more days than not for at least 2 years). Bipolar Disorders are distinguished by the presence of one or more Manic, Mixed, or Hypomanic Episodes. A Manic Episode is characterized by a period of persistent elevated or irritable mood accompanied by symptoms such as decreased need for sleep and increased self-esteem. A Hypomanic Episode is phenomenologically identical to a Manic Episode but is not severe enough to cause marked impairment. There are two types of Bipolar Disorder: Bipolar I Disorder is characterized by Manic or Mixed Episodes and Major Depressive Episodes, and Bipolar II Disorder is characterized by Hypomanic Episodes and Major Depressive Episodes. Additionally, Cyclothymic Disorder is characterized by periods of hypomania and depressive symptoms (not at the severity level of a Major Depressive Episode) alternating over a period of at least 2 years.

Anxiety Disorders

The Anxiety Disorders consist of a varied group of clinical presentations that share anxiety as an important feature. Panic Disorder consists of recurrent unexpected Panic Attacks. Panic Disorder can occur with and without Agoraphobia. A much rarer condition, Agoraphobia Without History of Panic Disorder, is characterized by avoidance of situations in which an incapacitating or embarrassing symptom may develop. Specific Phobia is characterized by fear or avoidance behavior cued by a specific situation or stimulus. The hallmark of Social Phobia is avoidance of social situations for fear of being embarrassed. Obsessive-Compulsive Disorder is defined by the presence of obsessions or compulsions that cause marked distress, are time consuming, or significantly impair the individual's normal functioning. Two disorders in this section involve reactions to extremely traumatic, life-threatening events. Posttraumatic Stress Disorder involves the persistent reexperiencing of a traumatic event, avoidance of stimuli associated with the event, and symptoms of increased arousal lasting at least 1 month. Acute Stress Disorder involves similar features lasting less than 4 weeks. Generalized Anxiety Disorder is defined by excessive worry about a number of events or activities, accompanied by restlessness, fatigue, or other physical symptoms.

Somatoform Disorders

Somatoform Disorders are characterized by preoccupation with illness or by the presence of physical symptoms that cannot be fully accounted for by a general medical condition. Unlike Factitious Disorder and Malingering (see below), the symptoms in Somatoform Disorders are not intentionally feigned. Somatization Disorder involves a history of multiple physical complaints over a period of several years. Undifferentiated Somatoform Disorder is a residual category for presentations that involve fewer symptoms. Conversion Disorder is distinguished by pseudoneurological symptoms affecting voluntary motor or sensory function. Pain Disorder is characterized by pain occurring in association with psychological factors. Hypochondriasis is the fear of, or the idea that one has, a serious physical illness. Body Dysmorphic Disorder is a preoccupation with an imagined defect in appearance.

Factitious Disorder

The essential feature of Factitious Disorder is the intentional feigning of physical or psychological symptoms to assume the sick role. In contrast to Malingering, external motivations for such behavior (such as economic gain) are absent.

Dissociative Disorders

The essential feature of Dissociative Disorders is a disturbance in the integrative functions of identity, memory, and consciousness. Dissociative Amnesia involves inability to remember important personal information. Dissociative Fugue involves sudden, unexpected travel away from home with the inability to recall one's past. Dissociative Identity Disorder (previously referred to as Multiple Personality Disorder) is distinguished by the presence of two or more personality states and the inability of the individual to recall important personal information. Symptoms of Depersonalization Disorder include the feeling that one is detached from one's own mental processes.

Sexual and Gender Identity Disorders

The Sexual and Gender Identity Disorders are subdivided into three sections. Sexual Dysfunctions are characterized by a reduction in, or absence of, sexual desire; a disturbance in arousal or orgasm; or pain occurring before, during, or after sexual intercourse. Paraphilias involve recurrent sexual urges and fantasies involving inappropriate objects, individuals, or situations, which cause marked distress or impairment in functioning. Gender Identity Disorder is marked by strong and persistent cross-gender identification and discomfort with one's own sex or a sense of inappropriateness in the gender role of that sex.

Eating Disorders

The Eating Disorders include Anorexia Nervosa and Bulimia Nervosa. Anorexia Nervosa is characterized by refusal to maintain body weight, intense fear of gaining weight, and amenorrhea. In Bulimia Nervosa, there is recurrent binge eating that is compensated for by inappropriate behavior such as use of laxatives, vomiting, fasting, or excessive exercise.

Sleep Disorders

Sleep Disorders are grouped based on etiology: Primary Sleep Disorders (the Dyssomnias and the Parasomnias), Sleep Disorders Related to Another Mental Disorder, and Other Sleep Disorders (Sleep Disorder Due to a General Medical Condition and Substance-Induced Sleep Disorder). The Dyssomnias are disorders of sleep or wakefulness. These include Primary Insomnia (difficulty initiating or maintaining sleep), Primary Hypersomnia (excessive sleepiness), Narcolepsy (irresistible sleep attacks), Breathing-Related Sleep Disorder (a sleep disruption judged to be related to a sleep-related breathing disorder, e.g., sleep apnea), and Circadian Rhythm Sleep Disorder (recurrent sleep disruption due to shift work or recurrent travel across time zones). The Parasomnias consist of abnormal behavior or physiological events occurring during sleep or the sleep-wake transition. These include Nightmare Disorder, Sleep Terror Disorder (without recall of the contents of the dream), and Sleepwalking Disorder.

Impulse-Control Disorders Not Elsewhere Classified

Impulse-Control Disorders Not Elsewhere Classified are distinguished by the failure to control an impulse to perform an act harmful to oneself or another person. Intermittent Explosive Disorder involves episodes of aggressive impulses that result in assaultive acts or destruction of property, that are grossly out of proportion to any psychosocial stressors, and that are not better accounted for by another mental disorder (e.g., Antisocial Personality Disorder). Other disorders of impulse control include Kleptomania (theft of objects not needed for personal use or for their monetary value), Pyromania (fire setting), Pathological Gambling, and Trichotillomania (pulling out one's hair resulting in noticeable hair loss).

Adjustment Disorder

Adjustment Disorder is a residual category for stress-related maladaptive disturbances that do not meet the criteria for another mental disorder. Normal reactions to stressful life events (e.g., death of a loved one) are not included here unless symptoms persist or are in excess of what would be expected.

Personality Disorders

Personality Disorders are distinguished by enduring, maladaptive, and inflexible patterns of perceiving, relating to, or thinking about one's environment or oneself. The maladaptive patterns cause an impairment in functioning or cause distress to the individual. The Personality Disorders are subdivided into three clusters. Cluster A (odd-eccentric cluster) contains Paranoid Personality Disorder, Schizoid Personality Disorder, and Schizotypal Personality Disorder, which are distinguished by suspicious or odd behavior. Cluster B (dramatic-emotional cluster) includes Antisocial Personality Disorder, Borderline Personality Disorder, Histrionic Personality Disorder, and Narcissistic Personality Disorder. Cluster C (anxious-fearful cluster) includes Avoidant Personality Disorder, Dependent Personality Disorder, and Obsessive-Compulsive Personality Disorder.

Other Conditions That May Be a Focus of Clinical Attention

In addition to the 16 major diagnostic classes, DSM-IV contains a section that describes conditions that may be a focus of clinical attention but that are not themselves mental disorders.

CHAPTER 28

Quiz Yourself

100 Questions Toward DSM-IV Mastery

In this chapter, we provide a quiz to test your knowledge of DSM-IV. The correct answer is provided after each question.

1. The best way to differentiate Delirium from Dementia is
   a. Memory loss
   b. Disorientation
   c. Inability to maintain attention
   d. Psychotic symptoms

   Correct answer: *C.* The characteristic symptom of Delirium is disturbance in consciousness. In Dementia, there are memory impairment and other cognitive deficits, but the ability to maintain attention is preserved except in the latest stages of the illness. Dementia and delirium often occur together.

2. All of the following are true statements about dementia ***except***
   a. It is always irreversible
   b. There is a significant decline from previous cognitive functioning
   c. It must include memory impairment
   d. It is always due to a general medical condition or a substance

   Correct answer: *A.* The DSM-IV definition of Dementia describes a pattern of cognitive deficits that may be progressive, static, or remitting. It is often, but not always, irreversible, and the prognosis depends on the underlying etiology.

3. Dementia of the Alzheimer's Type is frequently accompanied by
   a. Delirium
   b. Psychotic symptoms
   c. Mood symptoms
   d. All of the above

   Correct answer: ***D.*** Also look for behavioral disturbances.

4. Which of the following statements are true about amnestic disorder?
   a. It almost always causes minimal impairment
   b. There are characteristic deficits in executive functioning
   c. It is often associated with prolonged alcohol use and nutritional deficiency
   d. The memory loss is more commonly retrograde than anterograde

   Correct answer: ***C.*** The memory loss is usually anterograde and may be associated with severe impairment. A memory deficit combined with a deficit in executive functioning would indicate dementia. Alcohol-Induced Persisting Amnestic Disorder has been called Korsakoff's syndrome and is related to thiamine deficiency.

5. Types of Personality Change Due to a General Medical Condition include
   a. Labile
   b. Paranoid
   c. Aggressive
   d. All of the above

   Correct answer: ***D.*** Two other types of Personality Change Due to a General Medical Condition are the Apathetic Type and the Disinhibited Type. The presentation in personality change does not have to conform to the symptomatic pictures of the Axis II Personality Disorders. Personality Change Due to a General Medical Condition is coded on Axis I.

6. The term *substance* in DSM-IV includes which of the following?
   a. Drugs of abuse
   b. Medications
   c. Toxins
   d. All of the above

   Correct answer: ***D.*** Psychopathology due to medications is often missed in clinical practice.

7. The definition of Substance Dependence in DSM-IV requires which of the following?
   a. Tolerance
   b. Withdrawal
   c. Persistent desire to cut down use
   d. None of the above

   Correct answer: ***D.*** Although tolerance, withdrawal, and persistent desire to curtail use are typically part of the clinical picture of Dependence, no one of these is required for the diagnosis. The DSM-IV algorithm requires that at least three of the Dependence items be present during a 12-month period.

8. The definition of Substance Abuse in DSM-IV requires which of the following?
   a. Tolerance
   b. Withdrawal
   c. Adverse consequences
   d. Compulsive use

   Correct answer: ***C.*** In fact, a diagnosis of Substance Abuse for a particular substance cannot be made if the person currently has, or has ever had, a history of Substance Dependence for that same class of substance.

9. One goes from Substance Dependence in Early Remission to Substance Dependence in Sustained Remission when the full criteria for Dependence have not been met for at least
   a. 1 month
   b. 3 months
   c. 6 months
   d. 12 months

   Correct answer: ***D.*** This duration of remission predicts a lower likelihood of relapse.

10. Drug blood levels can be helpful in which of the following situations?
    a. Confirming tolerance
    b. Distinguishing intoxication from withdrawal
    c. Establishing recent drug use
    d. All of the above

    Correct answer: ***D.*** Blood levels are often helpful because users of drugs are not always the most reliable historians.

11. The route of administration that results in the ***least*** rapid entry of the substance into the bloodstream is
    a. Smoking
    b. Snorting
    c. Intravenous use
    d. Oral administration

    Correct answer: ***D.*** The routes of administration with rapid entry into the bloodstream are more likely to promote Dependence.

12. Substance-Induced Psychotic Disorder is distinguished from Substance Intoxication With Perceptual Disturbances by
    a. Lack of reality testing regarding the perceptual experiences
    b. The content of the perceptual experiences
    c. The sensory modality of the perceptual experiences
    d. The frequency and intensity of the perceptual experiences

    Correct answer: ***A.*** Perceptual disturbances are a common and an expected aspect of the use of a number of substances. They are not considered to be evidence of psychosis as long as the individual maintains reality testing and appreciates that the perceptual experiences are related to substance use.

13. The class of substances most similar to alcohol is
    a. Amphetamines
    b. Sedatives
    c. Opioids
    d. Cannabis

    Correct answer: *B.* The criteria sets for Intoxication and Withdrawal are identical for alcohol and the sedatives, hypnotics, or anxiolytics, and these classes of substances have cross-tolerance to one another.

14. The class of substances most similar to cocaine is
    a. Phencyclidine
    b. Hallucinogens
    c. Caffeine
    d. Amphetamines

    Correct answer: *D.* The criteria sets for Intoxication and Withdrawal for cocaine and amphetamines are also the same. Caffeine is a stimulant but with very different characteristics.

15. The class of substances most similar to hallucinogens is
    a. Amphetamines
    b. Cocaine
    c. Phencyclidine
    d. Inhalants

    Correct answer: *C.* Even though it is considered a separate class of substance in DSM-IV, phencyclidine is a form of hallucinogen.

16. Which of the following drug classes do ***not*** have a clear-cut withdrawal syndrome?
    a. Cannabis
    b. Inhalants
    c. Hallucinogens
    d. All of the above

    Correct answer: *D.* Although these substances may sometimes cause withdrawal symptoms, these are not of sufficient clinical significance to warrant a separate criteria set for Withdrawal in DSM-IV.

17. The drug which has the highest ratio of use to Dependence is
    a. Alcohol
    b. Nicotine
    c. Cocaine
    d. Opioids

    Correct answer: *B.* More than 90% of nicotine users develop Dependence, which belies the notion that nicotine is not an addictive substance.

18. Which class of drugs is associated with Withdrawal Delirium?
    a. Alcohol
    b. Sedatives, hypnotics, or anxiolytics
    c. Both
    d. Neither

Correct answer: ***C.*** Significant morbidity and mortality are associated with untreated Withdrawal Delirium. Also look for the presence of an associated general medical condition (e.g., head trauma, which commonly predisposes to the development of Withdrawal Delirium).

19. Which of the following does ***not*** differentiate between Schizophrenia and Delusional Disorder?
    a. The presence of nonbizarre delusions
    b. The presence of auditory hallucinations lasting at least 1 month
    c. The presence of disorganized speech lasting at least 1 month
    d. General deterioration in functioning

    Correct answer: ***A.*** Although a diagnosis of Delusional Disorder is not compatible with bizarre delusions, a diagnosis of Schizophrenia can be characterized by nonbizarre delusions as long as they are also accompanied by other psychotic symptoms. A diagnosis of Delusional Disorder is not consistent with the simultaneous presence of prominent auditory hallucinations, disorganized speech, or general deterioration in functioning.

20. The duration of Brief Psychotic Disorder is
    a. Less than a day
    b. More than a day but less than 1 month
    c. Less than 3 months
    d. Less than 6 months

    Correct answer: ***B.*** This disorder covers all brief psychotic episodes except those that are better accounted for by a Mood Disorder or are due to substance use or a general medical condition.

21. The duration of Schizophreniform Disorder is
    a. More than a day but less than 1 month
    b. More than 1 month but less than 3 months
    c. More than 1 month but less than 6 months
    d. More than 3 months

    Correct answer: ***C.*** Schizophreniform Disorder is a briefer, better prognosis version of Schizophrenia. If the duration of psychotic symptoms is less than a month, the diagnosis would be Brief Psychotic Disorder.

22. The duration of Schizophrenia is
    a. 1 month or more
    b. 3 months or more
    c. 6 months or more
    d. 2 years or more

    Correct answer: ***C.*** Studies showed that a duration of more than 6 months is the best predictor of a poorer prognosis.

23. The duration of Delusional Disorder is
    a. More than 1 day but less than 1 month
    b. 1 month or more
    c. 3 months or more
    d. 6 months or more

    Correct answer: ***B.*** Delusional episodes lasting less than 1 month would be diagnosed as Brief Psychotic Disorder.

24. Which of the following is not considered to be a negative symptom of Schizophrenia?
    a. Avolition
    b. Alogia
    c. Disorganized speech
    d. Affective flattening

Correct answer: ***C.*** Factor-analytic studies of schizophrenic symptoms find three factors: a psychotic factor, a disorganized factor, and a negative factor. Disorganized speech correlates with the disorganized factor.

25. Which of the following is not required for the diagnosis of Schizophrenia?
    a. A total duration of 6 months
    b. Marked decline in functioning
    c. The presence of prodromal or residual symptoms
    d. 1 month of active-phase symptoms

Correct answer: ***C.*** Although typical of Schizophrenia, prodromal or residual symptoms are not required. Some individuals with Schizophrenia do not receive or respond to treatment and remain chronically in the active phase.

26. Negative symptoms of Schizophrenia must be distinguished from
    a. Medication side effects
    b. Depression
    c. Lack of environmental stimulation
    d. All of the above

Correct answer: ***D.*** In addition, negative symptoms must also be differentiated from behavior that is the consequence of positive symptoms (e.g., the patient does not move because of a command hallucination telling him or her not to, rather than because of avolition).

27. The differential diagnosis of Catatonia includes
    a. Schizophrenia
    b. Mood Disorder
    c. Neurological conditions
    d. All of the above

Correct answer: ***D.*** Also don't forget that certain medications and drugs of abuse can cause a catatonic syndrome.

28. Which of the following distinguishes Schizoaffective Disorder from Mood Disorder With Psychotic Features?
    a. The content of the delusions
    b. The occurrence of delusions or hallucinations for at least 2 weeks in the absence of prominent mood symptoms
    c. The relative severity of the mood symptoms and the psychotic symptoms
    d. None of the above

Correct answer: ***B.*** Regardless of their content or severity, psychotic symptoms are considered to be part of a mood episode unless they precede the mood symptoms or persist after the mood symptoms have resolved.

29. All of the following are true about Shared Psychotic Disorder ***except***
    a. The psychotic symptoms usually resolve when the patient is removed from under the influence of the inducer
    b. The content of the delusions is the same for the inducer and the patient
    c. The content of the delusions must be bizarre
    d. There is a very close relationship between the inducer and the patient

    Correct answer: *C.* Although the delusions may be bizarre in content, this is not a requirement; typically, they are persecutory rather than bizarre.

30. Which of the following were reasons for increasing the duration of the active-phase symptoms of Schizophrenia from 1 week to 1 month?
    a. To increase compatibility with the ICD-10 definition of Schizophrenia
    b. To reduce false-positive diagnoses in first-break patients
    c. To sharpen the differential diagnosis with Substance-Induced Psychotic Disorder
    d. All of the above

    Correct answer: *D.* The change in minimum duration from 1 week to 1 month has no effect on the diagnosis of chronic patients but is important in the differential diagnosis of first-break patients.

31. The Psychotic Disorder that is diagnosed with the poorest reliability is
    a. Schizophrenia
    b. Delusional Disorder
    c. Mood Disorder With Psychotic Features
    d. Schizoaffective Disorder

    Correct answer: *D.* Boundary conditions are inherently difficult to diagnosis reliably. The reliability of Schizoaffective Disorder is particularly problematic because it requires extremely difficult judgments about the relationship of the psychotic and mood symptoms.

32. Which of the following is ***not*** required in the diagnosis of Bipolar I Disorder?
    a. A Manic Episode
    b. Significant impairment or hospitalization
    c. Absence of a general medical condition or substance etiology
    d. A Major Depressive Episode

    Correct answer: *D.* Approximately 5%–10% of Bipolar I patients have had only Manic Episodes, at least thus far in their course.

33. Which of the following is ***not*** compatible with a diagnosis of Major Depressive Disorder?
    a. A Manic Episode
    b. A Mixed Episode
    c. A Hypomanic Episode
    d. All of the above

    Correct answer: *D.* The occurrence of any one of these episodes at any point in the course changes the diagnosis from Major Depressive Disorder to Bipolar I Disorder or Bipolar II Disorder.

34. A person is fired from his or her job and develops 2 weeks of depressed mood, insomnia, loss of appetite, difficulty concentrating, and fatigue. The best diagnosis is
    a. 309.0 Adjustment Disorder With Depressed Mood
    b. 296.21 Major Depressive Disorder
    c. V62.2 Occupational Problem
    d. V62.82 Bereavement

    Correct answer: *B.* Once the criteria are met for a Major Depressive Disorder, it is diagnosed regardless of whether it may have occurred in response to a stressor. The only exception is when the stressor is the loss of a loved one, in which case Bereavement should be considered.

35. Which of the following symptoms must be present in all cases of Major Depressive Disorder?
    a. Loss of interest
    b. Insomnia
    c. Depressed mood
    d. None of the above

    Correct answer: *D.* No single symptom is required for the diagnosis of a Major Depressive Episode. Any five of nine symptoms are required for at least 2 weeks, as long as at least one of the symptoms is either depressed mood or loss of interest.

36. Which of the following is ***not*** compatible with a diagnosis of Dysthymic Disorder?
    a. Alcohol Dependence
    b. Major Depressive Disorder
    c. A Hypomanic Episode
    d. Panic Disorder

    Correct answer: *C.* There is a great deal of comorbidity between Dysthymic Disorder and other disorders. Dysthymic Disorder is within the unipolar spectrum. The presence of a Hypomanic Episode would move the diagnosis into the bipolar spectrum.

37. A patient develops a first Manic Episode while on fluoxetine. This is diagnosed as
    a. Fluoxetine-Induced Mood Disorder, With Manic Features
    b. Bipolar I Disorder
    c. Manic Episode
    d. Schizoaffective Disorder, Bipolar Type

    Correct answer: *A.* The degree to which a treatment-induced Manic Episode indicates that the patient has a Bipolar Disorder remains controversial. DSM-IV takes a conservative stance on the question and does not assume that such episodes necessarily indicate a Bipolar Disorder.

38. After the death of his spouse, Mr. A. develops 2 weeks of depressed mood, insomnia, loss of appetite, difficulty concentrating, and fatigue. The best diagnosis is
    a. 309.0 Adjustment Disorder With Depressed Mood
    b. 296.21 Major Depressive Disorder
    c. V61.1 Partner Relational Problem
    d. V62.82 Bereavement

Correct answer: ***D.*** If the full criteria for a Major Depressive Episode are met 2 months after the loss of a loved one, a diagnosis of Major Depressive Disorder should be considered.

39. Which of the following would be the most likely evolution of a mood episode?
    a. A Manic Episode to a Mixed Episode to a Major Depressive Episode
    b. A Major Depressive Episode to a Mixed Episode to a Manic Episode
    c. A Mixed Episode to a Manic Episode to a Major Depressive Episode
    d. A Mixed Episode to a Major Depressive Episode to a Manic Episode

    Correct answer: ***A.*** This is a common pattern of response of a Manic Episode to treatment. Patients are at highest risk for suicide during the Mixed Episodes.

40. All of the following are part of the definition of a Hypomanic Episode ***except***
    a. There must be clinically significant impairment or distress
    b. The same symptom list as a Manic Episode
    c. There must be an unequivocal change in functioning
    d. The change must be observable to others

    Correct answer: ***A.*** Some people function even better when they are having a Hypomanic Episode than when they are not. Because a Hypomanic Episode is by itself not considered to be a mental disorder, clinically significant impairment or distress is not required.

41. Which of the following is ***not*** required for a diagnosis of Bipolar II Disorder?
    a. A history of at least one Hypomanic Episode
    b. A history of at least one Manic Episode
    c. A history of at least one Major Depressive Episode
    d. There must be clinically significant impairment or distress

    Correct answer: ***B.*** The presence of a Manic Episode makes the diagnosis Bipolar I Disorder rather than Bipolar II Disorder.

42. Which mood specifier has features that are most opposite to those of the specifier With Atypical Features?
    a. With Postpartum Onset
    b. With Seasonal Pattern
    c. With Melancholic Features
    d. With Rapid Cycling

    Correct answer: ***C.*** With Atypical Features and With Melancholic Features are opposite in terms of mood reactivity, hypersomia versus insomnia, and overeating versus anorexia; they may also differ in their response to medication.

43. The following specifiers apply to the most recent mood episode ***except***
    a. With Atypical Features
    b. With Melancholic Features
    c. With Postpartum Onset
    d. With Rapid Cycling

    Correct answer: ***D.*** The Rapid Cycling specifier applies instead to the pattern of mood episodes. This is also true for the Longitudinal Course and Seasonal Pattern specifiers.

44. Which of the following is a requirement for the diagnosis of Panic Disorder?
    a. Unexpected Panic Attacks
    b. Situationally bound Panic Attacks
    c. Situationally predisposed Panic Attacks
    d. All of the above

    Correct answer: ***A.*** Although these other types of Panic Attacks can occur in Panic Disorder, they are not required.

45. The subtype of Specific Phobia with the latest age at onset is
    a. Animal Type
    b. Situational Type
    c. Blood-Injection-Injury Type
    d. Natural Environment Type

    Correct answer: ***B.*** This subtype is closest to Agoraphobia in onset and in other ways as well.

46. Which of the following would ***not*** qualify as a compulsion?
    a. Brooding anxiously that *GOD* is *DOG* spelled backward
    b. Hand washing
    c. Checking 50 times to see whether the door is unlocked
    d. Thinking *1-2-3-4-5-6-7-8-9-10* 10 times to banish a blasphemous thought

    Correct answer: ***A.*** Choice A is an obsession. Choice D is a cognitive compulsion.

47. Which of the following would ***not*** qualify as an extreme stressor in Posttraumatic Stress Disorder?
    a. Being in combat
    b. Being fired from work
    c. Being a victim of rape
    d. None of the above

    Correct answer: ***B.*** The stressor in Posttraumatic Stress Disorder is restricted to a life-threatening event.

48. The symptom duration that distinguishes Posttraumatic Stress Disorder from Acute Stress Disorder is
    a. 2 days
    b. 2 weeks
    c. 1 month
    d. 3 months

    Correct answer: ***C.*** Acute Stress Disorder covers the responses that occur in the immediate aftermath of an extreme stressor. It was added to DSM-IV because it predicts a vulnerability to the later development of Posttraumatic Stress Disorder.

49. Which of the following situations are commonly avoided in Agoraphobia?
    a. Being alone
    b. Being outside one's home
    c. Being in a crowd
    d. All of the above

    Correct answer: ***D.*** Other commonly avoided situations include standing in line, being on a bridge, and traveling in a bus, train, or automobile.

50. The Anxiety Disorder diagnosis with the poorest reliability is
    a. Specific Phobia
    b. Posttraumatic Stress Disorder
    c. Generalized Anxiety Disorder
    d. Panic Disorder

    Correct answer: ***C.*** This poor reliability is probably related to the difficulties in finding clear boundaries between Generalized Anxiety Disorder and normality and between Generalized Anxiety Disorder and Mood, Somatoform, and other Anxiety Disorders.

51. Which DSM-III-R childhood disorder has been subsumed by Social Phobia in DSM-IV?
    a. Overanxious Disorder of Childhood
    b. Identity Disorder
    c. Separation Anxiety Disorder
    d. Avoidant Disorder of Childhood

    Correct answer: ***D.*** Similarly, the DSM-III-R category Overanxious Disorder of Childhood was subsumed by the DSM-IV category Generalized Anxiety Disorder.

52. Which of the following are known to induce anxiety?
    a. Caffeine Intoxication
    b. Cocaine Intoxication
    c. Alcohol Withdrawal
    d. All of the above

    Correct answer: ***D.*** Substance Use should always be ruled out in the differential diagnosis of an Anxiety Disorder.

53. Which of the following general medical conditions are known to induce anxiety?
    a. Pheochromocytoma
    b. Hyperthyroidism
    c. Hypoglycemia
    d. All of the above

    Correct answer: ***D.*** General medical conditions should always be ruled out in the differential diagnosis of an Anxiety Disorder.

54. Which of the following unexplained general medical symptoms would ***not*** count toward a diagnosis of Somatization Disorder?
    a. Back pain
    b. Diarrhea
    c. Irregular menses
    d. Shortness of breath

    Correct answer: ***D.*** The pattern of symptoms that defines DSM-IV Somatization Disorder is four pain symptoms, two gastrointestinal symptoms, one sexual symptom, and one pseudoneurological symptom. Shortness of breath is a more characteristic symptom of a Panic Attack.

55. Which of the following unexplained general medical symptoms would ***not*** qualify for a diagnosis of Conversion Disorder?
    a. Blindness
    b. Paralysis
    c. Seizures
    d. Pseudocyesis

    Correct answer: ***D.*** Pseudocyesis (false pregnancy) is not a symptom that affects the "voluntary motor or sensory function," as is required in the definition of Conversion Disorder. Instead, pseudocyesis would be diagnosed as Somatoform Disorder Not Otherwise Specified.

56. Which of the following is most characteristic of Hypochondriasis?
    a. The belief that one has a serious physical illness
    b. The fear that one might contract a physical illness
    c. The belief that one has a defect in physical appearance
    d. The delusional conviction that one has a serious physical illness

    Correct answer: ***A.*** Choice B would be Specific Phobia; choice C would be Body Dysmorphic Disorder; and choice D would be Delusional Disorder, Somatic Type.

57. Which of the following ***cannot*** be diagnosed at the same time as Somatization Disorder?
    a. Pain Disorder Associated With Psychological Factors
    b. Conversion Disorder
    c. Undifferentiated Somatoform Disorder
    d. All of the above

    Correct answer: ***D.*** The definition of Somatization Disorder includes all of these other less pervasive disorders.

58. The motivation behind feigning the symptoms in Factitious Disorder is
    a. To obtain financial compensation
    b. To obtain drugs
    c. To assume the sick role
    d. To avoid military service

    Correct answer: ***C.*** The motivation for Malingering differs from that for Factitious Disorder in that Malingering is done for understandable external incentives.

59. Before making a diagnosis of Depersonalization Disorder, one should rule out
    a. Panic Disorder
    b. Posttraumatic Stress Disorder
    c. Schizophrenia
    d. All of the above

    Correct answer: ***D.*** The symptom of depersonalization occurs commonly in normal people as part of Substance Intoxication and as a result of certain general medical conditions (e.g., seizures). Depersonalization is a common symptom, but Depersonalization Disorder is an uncommon diagnosis.

60. Which of the following is ***not*** characteristic of memory loss in Dissociative Amnesia?
    a. The lost memories can sometimes be recovered through hypnosis
    b. The lost memories are of a traumatic nature
    c. The lost memories are accompanied by other cognitive deficits
    d. The ability to lay down new memories is preserved

    Correct answer: ***C.*** The presence of other cognitive deficits suggests that the memory impairment is part of delirium, dementia, or amnestic disorder.

61. Those who believe that Dissociative Identity Disorder has recently been overdiagnosed attribute this overdiagnosis to
    a. Therapist zeal
    b. Patient suggestibility
    c. Media attention
    d. All of the above

    Correct answer: ***D.*** Because of these concerns, one should exercise caution before making a diagnosis of Dissociative Identity Disorder and should first consider whether the psychopathology is not better accounted for by some other more specific disorder.

62. Which of the following phases of the sexual response cycle does ***not*** have a DSM-IV Sexual Dysfunction associated with it?
    a. Desire
    b. Excitement
    c. Orgasm
    d. Resolution

    Correct answer: ***D.*** Note that Sexual Dysfunction occurring during one phase of the cycle often leads to dysfunction in other phases (e.g., erectile dysfunction can lead to hypoactive sexual desire and vice versa).

63. Which of the following is evidence that erectile dysfunction is ***not*** due to a general medical condition?
    a. Erections are present during masturbation
    b. Erections occur during rapid-eye-movement sleep
    c. Erections occur with some partners and not others
    d. All of the above

    Correct answer: ***D.*** Asking these questions provides a simple way of ruling out erectile dysfunction due to a general medical condition or to substance use without having to resort to elaborate laboratory procedures.

64. Which of the following Paraphilias are least likely to involve a nonconsenting person?
    a. Transvestic Fetishism
    b. Voyeurism
    c. Pedophilia
    d. Frotteurism

    Correct answer: ***A.*** Transvestic Fetishism consists of sexual gratification from cross-dressing and does not require the participation of another person.

65. Which of the following is ***not*** evidence for a Gender Identity Disorder?
    a. Expressed desire for a sex-change operation
    b. Stated desire to be the other sex
    c. Persistent cross-dressing (not for sexual stimulation)
    d. Expressed desire for the cultural advantages of being the other sex

    Correct answer: ***D.*** To qualify for a diagnosis of Gender Identity Disorder, the individual must also experience distress or impairment.

66. Which of the following is ***not*** a required feature of Anorexia Nervosa?
    a. Self-induced vomiting
    b. Low body weight
    c. Refusal to maintain normal body weight
    d. Intense fear of getting fat

    Correct answer: ***A.*** Although self-induced vomiting is a common enough method for maintaining abnormally low body weight in Anorexia Nervosa and is the basis for subtyping (Binge-Eating/Purging Type), it is not required for the diagnosis. The other methods of maintaining inadequate body weight include fasting and excessive exercise (Restricting Type).

67. Which of the following is an example of an inappropriate compensatory behavior in Bulimia Nervosa?
    a. Self-induced vomiting
    b. Excessive exercise
    c. Misuse of diuretics
    d. All of the above

    Correct answer: ***D.*** Other inappropriate mechanisms include fasting; misuse of laxatives or enemas; and for diabetic patients, not taking enough insulin.

68. All of the following statements about Nightmare Disorder are correct ***except***
    a. On awakening the person rapidly becomes oriented
    b. Nightmares are most likely to occur during the first third of the major sleep period
    c. Nightmare Disorder is a Parasomnia
    d. The content of the nightmare usually involves threats to survival, security, or self-esteem

    Correct answer: ***B.*** Sleep terrors and sleepwalking are more likely to occur during the first third of the major sleep period. Nightmares, which occur during rapid-eye-movement sleep, are more likely during the second half of the night.

69. All of the following statements about Narcolepsy are true ***except***
    a. Narcolepsy should be considered in the differential diagnosis for Hypersomnia
    b. The person usually feels refreshed after a sleep attack
    c. Episodes of sudden loss of muscle tone may be present
    d. It is usually related to overuse of hypnotic medications

    Correct answer: ***D.*** Narcolepsy is not considered to be a mental disorder, and it is included in DSM-IV only for purposes of differential diagnosis with the other Sleep Disorders.

70. All of the following statements about Intermittent Explosive Disorder are correct ***except***
   a. There may be abnormalities on electroencephalography
   b. The degree of aggressiveness is grossly out of proportion to any precipitating stressor
   c. Other causes of aggressive episodes must first be ruled out
   d. An isolated aggressive act is sufficient for the diagnosis if it is serious enough

   Correct answer: *D.* As its name implies, Intermittent Explosive Disorder requires several discrete episodes. Although aggressive behavior due to a definite general medical condition would be diagnosed as Personality Change Due to a General Medical Condition, nonspecific findings (such as electroencephalographic changes) are still consistent with the diagnosis of Intermittent Explosive Disorder.

71. The upper limit for the duration of Adjustment Disorder is
   a. 1 month
   b. 3 months
   c. 6 months
   d. None of the above

   Correct answer: *D.* There is no upper limit on the duration of Adjustment Disorder if the stressor is chronic or has long-standing consequences. However, the disturbance must remit within 6 months of the termination of the stressor or its consequences for it to qualify for a diagnosis of Adjustment Disorder.

72. All of the following characterize Personality Disorders ***except***
   a. They are inflexible
   b. They are not influenced by Axis I conditions
   c. They have an onset by adolescence or early adulthood
   d. They are pervasive across a broad range of situations

   Correct answer: *B.* Personality Disorders interact with Axis I conditions in complicated ways. Axis I conditions may mimic or worsen Personality Disorders, and Personality Disorders can exacerbate or complicate the treatment of Axis I disorders.

73. Which of the following must be present for a diagnosis of Antisocial Personality Disorder?
   a. Some evidence of Conduct Disorder before age 15
   b. Impulsivity
   c. Irresponsibility
   d. Lack of remorse

   Correct answer: *A.* It is true that choices B, C, and D are included in the criteria set for Antisocial Personality Disorder; however, because only four of seven items are required, no one of these criteria is required. In contrast, there must be evidence of Conduct Disorder before age 15 years.

74. Which of the following Personality Disorders is most closely related to Social Phobia, Generalized Type?
   a. Dependent Personality Disorder
   b. Obsessive-Compulsive Personality Disorder
   c. Avoidant Personality Disorder
   d. Schizoid Personality Disorder

Correct answer: *C.* In fact, in some studies, these two diagnoses overlap almost completely. They may represent two different ways of looking at the same disorder.

75. Which of the following Personality Disorders is most closely related to Schizophrenia?
    a. Schizoid Personality Disorder
    b. Schizotypal Personality Disorder
    c. Paranoid Personality Disorder
    d. Borderline Personality Disorder

    Correct answer: *B.* Genetic studies confirm that Schizotypal Personality Disorder is in the Schizophrenia spectrum. The same is probably true of Paranoid Personality Disorder. The evidence is less clear, one way or another, for Schizoid Personality Disorder. Finally, it is clear that Borderline Personality Disorder is not in the Schizophrenia spectrum.

76. Which of the following Personality Disorders is associated with a rate of completed suicide of between 5% and 10%?
    a. Antisocial Personality Disorder
    b. Borderline Personality Disorder
    c. Both
    d. Neither

    Correct answer: *C.* These are the only two Personality Disorders that predict successful suicide. They may further enhance the risk of suicide in those individuals who also have Substance-Related Disorders and Mood Disorders.

77. The Personality Disorder with the highest ratio of males to females is
    a. Avoidant Personality Disorder
    b. Antisocial Personality Disorder
    c. Obsessive-Compulsive Personality Disorder
    d. Schizotypal Personality Disorder

    Correct answer: *B.* The high ratio also reflects the fact that the preponderance of individuals with Conduct Disorder are male.

78. Which of the following are diagnosed much more commonly in women than in men?
    a. Dependent Personality Disorder
    b. Histrionic Personality Disorder
    c. Borderline Personality Disorder
    d. All of the above

    Correct answer: *D.* There are those who believe that at least some of the female preponderance may be explained by gender bias in the wording of the criteria sets, bias in the assessment of these disorders, and/or the fact that most studies are conducted in clinical settings.

79. The only Personality Disorder that ***cannot*** be diagnosed in young adolescents is
    a. Borderline Personality Disorder
    b. Schizoid Personality Disorder
    c. Antisocial Personality Disorder
    d. Obsessive-Compulsive Personality Disorder

Correct answer: ***C.*** Antisocial behaviors in young adolescents are diagnosed as Conduct Disorder. Antisocial Personality Disorder cannot be diagnosed in individuals under 18 years of age. Although DSM-IV allows diagnosis of the other Personality Disorders in individuals under 18 years of age, it recommends caution because persisting personality features must be distinguished from more self-limited developmental manifestations.

80. Which of the following are required before a diagnosis of Mental Retardation can be made?
    a. Measurement of IQ on an individually administered IQ test
    b. An evaluation of the level of adaptive functioning
    c. A consideration of the age at onset of the intellectual deficits
    d. All of the above

Correct answer: ***D.*** Some people mistakenly assume that Mental Retardation can be assessed by using group-administered tests or by measuring IQ alone. Mental Retardation can be diagnosed by using individually administered IQ tests, and the low IQ must cause problems in adaptive functioning. If IQ becomes reduced after age 18, a diagnosis of Dementia should be considered.

81. Which of the following are characteristic of Autistic Disorder?
    a. Qualitative impairment in social interaction
    b. Qualitative impairment in communication
    c. Stereotyped pattern of behavior
    d. All of the above

Correct answer: ***D.*** Autistic Disorder also requires an onset before age 3 years, and most children show some evidence of disturbance within their first year.

82. Which of the following Pervasive Developmental Disorders have the best prognosis?
    a. Autistic Disorder
    b. Rett's Disorder
    c. Asperger's Disorder
    d. Childhood Disintegrative Disorder

Correct answer: ***C.*** Asperger's Disorder is characterized by qualitative impairment in social interaction and stereotyped pattern of behavior (choices A and C in question 81), occurring in the absence of a delay in language development.

83. All of the following are helpful in differentiating between a Pervasive Developmental Disorder and Schizophrenia ***except***
    a. The presence of delusions
    b. The presence of hallucinations
    c. Age at onset
    d. The presence of social awkwardness

Correct answer: ***D.*** To give an additional diagnosis of Schizophrenia to someone previously diagnosed with Pervasive Developmental Disorder, there must be the additional presence of prominent delusions or hallucinations. The typical age at onset for Pervasive Developmental Disorder is soon after birth. For Schizophrenia, it is adolescence or early adulthood.

84. The best way to differentiate Attention-Deficit/Hyperactivity Disorder from Bipolar Disorder is
    a. Distractibility
    b. Age at onset
    c. Irritable mood
    d. Increased activity level

    Correct answer: ***B.*** The behavioral patterns of the two disorders can look very similar. However, some of the symptoms of Attention-Deficit/Hyperactivity Disorder must be present before age 7 years. In contrast, the onset of Bipolar Disorder is rarely this early.

85. Which of the following statements about Attention-Deficit/Hyperactivity Disorder is ***not*** true?
    a. The onset must be before age 7
    b. There must be symptoms of both inattention and hyperactivity/impulsivity
    c. The symptoms must be present in two or more different situations
    d. The symptoms must cause clinically significant impairment or distress

    Correct answer: ***B.*** Although most individuals with Attention-Deficit/Hyperactivity Disorder have the Combined Subtype, there are some who are predominantly inattentive and others who are predominantly hyperactive. The criteria covered in choices C and D serve to ensure clinical significance and to reduce false-positive diagnoses.

86. Compared with the Adolescent-Onset Type, the Childhood-Onset Type of Conduct Disorder is more likely to be associated with
    a. The later evolution into Antisocial Personality Disorder
    b. Physical aggressiveness
    c. Male sex
    d. Less disturbed peer relationships

    Correct answer: ***D.*** This subtyping of Conduct Disorder may be useful in distinguishing those whose disorder is more the result of intrinsic factors from those whose behavior is more related to peer influences.

87. What percentage of individuals with Conduct Disorder go on to have Antisocial Personality Disorder?
    a. 10%
    b. 30%
    c. 60%
    d. 90%

    Correct answer: ***B.*** Although Conduct Disorder is the best predictor of adult antisocial behavior, it is reassuring that the majority of children and adolescents with Conduct Disorder will grow out of it.

88. Which of the following is ***not*** characteristic of Feeding Disorder of Infancy and Early Childhood?
    a. Persistent failure to eat adequately
    b. Significant failure to gain weight
    c. Improvement when fed by a more experienced caregiver
    d. Weight loss due to a diagnosed gastrointestinal condition

    Correct answer: ***D.*** Weight loss related to a diagnosed gastrointestinal condition does not warrant a mental disorder diagnosis.

89. Which of the following is ***not*** a requirement for a diagnosis of Tourette's Disorder?
    a. Vocal tics
    b. Motor tics
    c. Duration at least 12 months
    d. Age at onset over 18

    Correct answer: ***D.*** Although the onset of Tourette's Disorder may be as early as age 2 years, it usually is during early childhood or adolescence.

90. Which one of the following statements about enuresis is ***not*** true?
    a. It must occur at least 2 times a week for at least 3 consecutive months
    b. The individual's chronological age must be at least 5 years (or equivalent developmental level)
    c. It is defined as intentional or involuntary voiding of urine into bed or clothes
    d. The diurnal subtype is more common in girls

    Correct answer: ***A.*** Ha! This is a trick question—the only one we've included in this test. It is meant to illustrate a point near and dear to our hearts, namely, the importance of using clinical judgment in applying the guidelines provided in the criteria sets. Although choice A does indicate the specified frequency in the criteria set, the criteria also allow the diagnosis to be made when the bed-wetting occurs less frequently if it otherwise causes clinically significant distress or impairment.

91. All of the following are characteristic of Separation Anxiety Disorder ***except***
    a. Worry about possible harm befalling major attachment figures
    b. Nightmares involving themes of separation
    c. Worry about school performance
    d. Complaints about physical symptoms

    Correct answer: ***C.*** Worry about school performance is not a requirement for Separation Anxiety Disorder and is more likely to be part of Generalized Anxiety Disorder.

92. Selective Mutism should ***not*** be diagnosed
    a. During the first month of school
    b. If the duration is less than 1 month
    c. If the child is unfamiliar with the required language
    d. All of the above

    Correct answer: ***D.*** Choices A and C describe situations in which the silence is due to reasons that would not warrant diagnosis of a mental disorder. Choice B describes transient periods of silence that are without clinical significance.

93. Compared to adult presentations, childhood presentations of Major Depressive Disorder are likely to be characterized by
    a. Somatic complaints
    b. Psychomotor retardation
    c. Hypersomnia
    d. Delusions

    Correct answer: ***A.*** Children are also less likely to have the cognitive symptoms of depression.

94. The diagnosis of Psychological Factor Affecting Medical Condition applies to all of the following situations ***except***
    a. Stress-related peptic ulcer
    b. Overeating affecting diabetes
    c. Pathological denial affecting treatment of ovarian cancer
    d. Depression in response to a diagnosis of cancer

Correct answer: ***D.*** The condition described in choice D would be diagnosed as Adjustment Disorder or a Major Depressive Episode, depending on the severity. In contrast to Psychological Factors Affecting a Medical Condition, the direction of causality in choice D is a medical condition causing a psychological response.

95. All of the following DSM-IV Medication-Induced Movement Disorders are most frequently caused by neuroleptics ***except***
    a. Drug-induced parkinsonism
    b. Drug-induced acute akathisia
    c. Drug-induced acute dystonia
    d. Drug-induced postural tremor

Correct answer: ***D.*** The most common cause of postural tremor is lithium.

96. Which of the following is ***not*** true about Relational Problems in DSM-IV?
    a. They are not included at all in DSM-IV
    b. They can be coded on Axis I if they are a focus of clinical attention
    c. They can be listed on Axis IV if they have an impact on a mental disorder
    d. Relational functioning can be rated on an optional axis

Correct answer: ***A.*** Relational Problems are included in the DSM-IV section titled "Other Conditions That May Be a Focus of Attention," are listed as examples of environmental and psychosocial problems on the Axis IV checklist, and contribute to ratings on an optional axis, the Global Assessment of Relational Functioning (GARF) Scale.

97. A patient has made a recent suicide attempt. The highest possible Global Assessment of Functioning score is
    a. 20
    b. 30
    c. 40
    d. 50

Correct answer: ***A.*** The Global Assessment of Functioning rating is dragged down by whichever is lowest: the severity of the patient's symptoms or the level of social or occupational impairment. Even if the level of social or occupational functioning is much higher, the 11–20 range is appropriate because it includes the symptom "some danger of hurting self or others."

98. All of the following statements about Axis II are true ***except***
    a. Personality Disorders are coded on Axis II
    b. Mental Retardation is coded on Axis II
    c. Personality features can be listed on Axis II
    d. Axis II conditions are fundamentally different from Axis I disorders

Correct answer: ***D.*** The distinction between Axis I and Axis II has been useful in providing a more rounded view of the patient but does not imply that there are inherent differences in pathogenesis or treatment response.

99. A diagnosis of Not Otherwise Specified would apply to all of the following presentations ***except***
    a. A subthreshold condition that is in response to a stressor
    b. A subthreshold condition unrelated to a stressor
    c. A condition included in DSM-IV Appendix B (Criteria Sets and Axes Provided for Further Study)
    d. Insufficient information to make a more specific diagnosis

    Correct answer: *A.* The diagnosis in this case would be Adjustment Disorder.

100. The course specifier In Full Remission is preferable to considering the individual "recovered" (and without any diagnosis) in which of the following situations?
    a. No remaining symptoms of Bipolar Disorder but on maintenance lithium
    b. Abstinent but attending Alcoholics Anonymous
    c. No remaining symptoms of Major Depressive Disorder but on maintenance psychotherapy
    d. All of the above

    Correct answer: *D.* The specifier In Full Remission applies if it is still clinically relevant to note the former presence of the disorder (e.g., if continuing therapy is required). If the former presence of the disorder is no longer clinically relevant, the clinician can either list no diagnosis or use the specifier Prior History (e.g., to note the presence of risk factors).

CHAPTER 29

Afterword

Psychiatric classification provides a system of communication that bridges the gap between research and clinical practice and facilitates our improved understanding of the causes and treatment of mental disorders. The evolving editions of the *Diagnostic and Statistical Manual of Mental Disorders* have become increasingly precise, reliable, and grounded in empirical evidence. The major limitation of the current system is that it remains on a descriptive level. Fortunately, we are at the brink of a scientific revolution. The increasingly sophisticated tools of psychiatric research provide great promise that major advances in psychiatric diagnosis will soon be made.

As more knowledge is gained, future classification systems will be based on a much deeper understanding of what causes psychiatric illness. Looking ahead, we can expect the following:

1. Certain psychiatric disorders (e.g., Schizophrenia, Bipolar Disorder) will soon be subclassified not just on the basis of descriptive typing but rather on the basis of differences in etiology or pathogenesis.
2. Dimensional models will increasingly inform clinical practice and research and will likely be integrated into parts of DSM-V (e.g., Schizophrenia subtyping, Personality Disorders).
3. More precise guidelines will be provided for determining whether a clinical presentation is substance induced or due to a general medical condition.
4. Our knowledge of how psychosocial and cultural factors affect the diagnosis and treatment of mental disorders will be advanced.

There has been an unfortunate tendency, especially in the popular press, to label DSM-IV as the "bible" of psychiatry. Although DSM-IV is extremely useful, we should not be too wedded to the current diagnostic system. Bibles are meant to embody an absolute truth that transcends the generations. In contrast, DSM-IV represents a way of organizing psychiatric knowledge circa 1994. The manual was prepared with the full hope and expectation that it contains the tools for generating the new knowledge that will render it obsolete. In the meantime, we hope that DSM-IV will play a useful role in clinical practice, in aiding future research efforts, and in strengthening the linkage between the two. We have learned a great deal in preparing DSM-IV and this *DSM-IV Guidebook* and hope that you find them to be instructive tools.

Bibliography

First MB: Trends in psychiatric classification: DSM-III-R to DSM-IV. Psychiatria Hungarica 7:539–546, 1992

First MB: Computer-assisted assessment of DSM-III-R diagnoses. Psychiatric Annals 24:25–29, 1994

First MB, Gladis MM: Diagnosis and differential diagnosis of psychiatric and substance use disorders, in Dual Diagnosis: Evaluation, Treatment, Training and Proqram Development. Edited by Solomon J, Zimberg S, Shollar E. New York, Plenum, 1993, pp 23–38

First MB, Williams JBW, Spitzer RL: DTREE: the electronic DSM-III-R (computer software, User's Guide, Case Workbook). Washington, DC, American Psychiatric Press, and Toronto, Canada, Multi-Health Systems, 1989

First MB, Spitzer RL, Williams JBW: Exclusionary principles and the comorbidity of psychiatric diagnoses: a historical review and implications for the future, in Comorbidity of Anxiety and Depression. Edited by Masser J, Cloninger R. Washington, DC, American Psychiatric Press, 1990, pp 86–104

First MB, Gibbon M, Williams JBW, et al: Mini-SCID: computer-administered DSM-III-R screener based on the Structured Clinical Interview for DSM-III-R (computer software, User's Guide). Washington, DC, American Psychiatric Press, and Toronto, Canada, Multi-Health Systems, 1990

First MB, Gibbon M, Williams JBW, et al: AUTOSCID-II: computer-administered version of the SCID-II for DSM-III-R personality disorders (computer software, User's Guide). Washington, DC, American Psychiatric Press, and Toronto, Canada, Multi-Health Systems, 1991

First MB, Frances A, Widiger TA, et al: DSM-IV and behavioral assessment. Behavioral Assessment 14:307–321, 1992

First MB, Opler LA, Hamilton RM, et al: Evaluation in an inpatient setting of DTREE, a computer-assisted diagnostic assessment procedure. Compr Psychiatry 34:171–175, 1993

Forman LM, Jones C, Frances A: The multiaxial system in psychiatric treatment, in Treatments of Psychiatric Disorders, 2nd Edition. Edited by Gabbard GA. Washington, DC, American Psychiatric Press, 1995

Frances A: Differential diagnosis: a review of the Diagnostic and Statistical Manual of Mental Disorders–IV study, in Epidemiology, Diagnosis and Treatment of Panic Disorders. Edited by Lapierre YD. Princeton, NJ, Excerpta Medica, 1991, pp 8–15

Frances A: Further reflections on the DSM-IV process and method (letter). Harvard Review Psychiatry 1:128, 1993

Frances A: Foreword, in Philosophical Perspectives on Psychiatric Diagnostic Classification. Edited by Sadler JZ, Wiggins OP, Schwartz MA. Baltimore, MD, Johns Hopkins University Press, 1994, pp VII–IX

Frances A: Foreword, in Premenstrual Dysphoria. Edited by Gold JH, Severino SK. Washington, DC, American Psychiatric Press, 1994, pp XIII–XIV

Frances A, Hall W: Work in progress on the DSM-IV mood disorders, in Diagnosis of Depression. Edited by Feighner J. New York, Wiley, 1991, pp 49–64

Frances A, Pincus H, Widiger T, et al: DSM-IV: work in progress. Am J Psychiatry 147:1439–1448, 1990

Frances A, Pincus H, Widiger T, et al: An introduction to DSM-IV. Hosp Community Psychiatry 41:493–494, 1990

Frances A, First M, Widiger T, et al: An A–Z glossary of DSM-IV conundrums. J Abnorm Psychol 100:407–412, 1991

Frances A, Davis W, Kline M: The DSM-IV field trials: moving towards an empirically derived classification. European Psychiatry 6:307–314, 1991

Frances A, First M, Pincus H, et al: DSM-IV Options Book. Washington, DC, American Psychiatric Press, 1991

Frances A, Widiger T, First M, et al: DSM-IV: Toward a more empirical diagnostic system. Canadian Psychology 32:174–176, 1991

Frances A, Hall W, First M, et al: Issues and proposals for changes in mood disorders in DSM-IV. J Clin Psychiatry 1:5–9, 1991

Frances A, Liebowitz MR, Widiger T, et al: Moving towards the DSM-IV classification of anxiety disorders, in Panic and Related Disorders: Current Knowledge and Perspectives. Edited by Sacchetti E, Cassano GB. Lugano, Italy, Giardini Editori, 1992, pp 58–70

Frances A, Miele GM, Widiger TA, et al: The classification of panic disorders: from Freud to DSM-IV. J Psychiatr Res 27 (suppl 1):3–10, 1993

Frances A, Widiger T, Fyer MR: The influence of classification methods on comorbidity, in Comorbidity of Mood and Anxiety Disorders. Edited by Maser JD, Cloninger CR. Washington, DC, American Psychiatric Press, 1990, pp 41–59

Frances A, McKinney K, Hall W, et al: DSM-IV and primary care, in Cultural and Psychiatric Diagnosis: A World Perspective. Edited by Honda Y, Kastrup M, Mezzich J. New York, Springer-Verlag, 1994, pp 263–266

Frances A, Mack AH, First MB, et al: DSM-IV meets philosophy. J Med Philos 19:207–218, 1994

Frances A, Mack AH, First MB, et al: DSM-IV and psychiatric epidemiology, in Textbook of Psychiatric Epidemiology. Edited by Tohen M. New York, Wiley (in press)

Frances A, Mack AH, Ross R, et al: The DSM-IV classification and psychopharmacology, in Psychopharmacology: The Fourth Generation of Progress. Edited by Bloom FE, Kupfer DJ. New York, Raven (in press)

Frances A, Mack A, First M, et al: DSM-IV: issues in development. Psychiatric Annals (in press)

Frances A, Shimada M, First M, et al: Nosological perspectives on culture and diagnosis, in Culture and Psychiatric Diaqnosis. Edited by Mezzich J, Kleinman A, Fabrega H, et al. Washington, DC, American Psychiatric Press (in press)

Koenig HG, Frances A: Diagnosis and treatment of chronic depression, in The Encyclopedia of Aging, Vol 2. Edited by Maddox GL. New York, Springer (in press)

Lopez-Ibor JJ, Frances A, Jones C: Dysthymic disorder: a comparison of DSM-IV and ICD-10 and issues in differential diagnosis. Acta Psychiatr Scand 89 (suppl 383):12–18, 1994

Mack AH, Forman L, Brown R, et al: A brief history of psychiatric classification: from the ancients to DSM-IV. Psychiatr Clin North Am 17:515–523, 1994

Miele G, Tilly S, First M, et al: The definition of dependence and behavioural addictions. British Journal of Addiction 85:1421–1423, 1990

Pincus HA, Frances A, Wakefield-Davis W, et al: DSM-IV and new diagnostic categories: holding the line on proliferation. Am J Psychiatry 149:112–117, 1992

Pincus HA, Vettorello N, First MB, et al: Classifying mental disorders: Diagnostic and Statistical Manual of Mental Disorders, in Review of General Psychiatry, 4th Edition. Edited by Goldman HH. Norwalk, CT, Appleton & Lange (in press)

Ross R, Frances A, Widiger TA: Gender issues in DSM-IV, in American Psychiatric Press Press Review of Psychiatry, Vol 14. Edited by Oldham JM, Riba MB. Washington, DC, American Psychiatric Press, 1995

Spitzer RL, Williams JBW, First MB, et al: A proposal for DSM-IV: solving the "organic/non-organic problem" (editorial). Journal of Neuropsychiatry 1:1, 1989

Spitzer RL, First MB, Williams JBW, et al: Now is-the time to retire the term "organic mental disorders." Am J Psychiatry 149:240–244, 1992

Spitzer RL, Williams JBW, Gibbon M, et al: The Structured Clinical Interview for DSM-III-R (SCID); I: history, rationale, and description. Arch Gen Psychiatry 49:625–629, 1992

Widiger TA, Frances AJ: Toward a dimensional model for the personality disorders, in Personality Disorders and the Five-Factor Model of Personality. Edited by Costa PT, Widiger TA. Washington, DC, American Psychological Association, 1994, pp 19–39

Widiger T, Frances A, Pincus H, et al: DSM-IV literature reviews: rationale, process, limitations. Journal of Psychopathology and Behavioral Assessment 12:189–202, 1990

Widiger T, Frances A, Pincus H, et al: Toward an empirical classification for DSM-IV. J Abnorm Psychol 100:280–288, 1991

Williams JBW, Gibbon M, First MB, et al: The Structured Clinical Interview for DSM-III-R (SCID); II: multi-site test-retest reliability. Arch Gen Psychiatry 49:630–636, 1992

Index

*Page numbers printed in **boldface** type refer to tables or figures.*